Time Out Chicago

2010

Eating
& Drinking

EDITION 3

timeoutchicago.com

Gonna BYOB? *Think Sam's!*

Pair your fave BYOB eats with these tips from Sam's

Asian
Asian cooking can be as salty as tears.
Bring light Whites like **SPANISH ALBARIÑO** or **ARGENTINE TORRONTES**.

Seafood
Be adventurous & go Red, but light-styled and with zesty acidity.
Snag a **LOIRE CHINON** or a **BEAUJOLAIS**. Chill it a bit.

Indian
Paint Indian's many colors, flavors & aromas against a laid-back, crisp White.
Go for **PORTUGUESE VINHO VERDE**.

Italian
See Red. **TUSCAN CHIANTI. SICILIAN NERO D'AVOLO.**
PIEDMONTESE NEBBIOLO. Just Red.

Pizza
Chicago style? **CHICAGO BEER.** New York Style? **CHICAGO BEER.**

Sushi
Nothing's groovier with raw fish and rice than **AUSTRIAN GRÜNER VELTLINER**
or **AMERICAN SAUVIGNON BLANC**.

Simone's

Time Out Chicago

Chicago

Time Out Chicago Eating & Drinking 2010
Editor Heather Shouse
Copy Editors Rebecca Maughan (chief), Karen D'Souza, Kay Riley, Michelle Stevens
Art Director Stephanie Gladney
Designer Erik Romstad
Photo Editor Erica Gannett
Editorial Interns Eve Fuller, Ali Jarvis, John Moss, Margaret Rhodes
Guides Sales and Marketing Director Lisa Levinson

Time Out Chicago

Editorial
Editor-in-Chief/General Manager Frank Sennett
Executive Editor Amy Carr
Eat Out/Drink Up David Tamarkin (Editor), Julia Kramer (Writer), Heather Shouse (Senior Correspondent)

Art
Art Director Stephanie Gladney
Associate Art Director Mike Novak
Designer Vince Cerasani
Associate Photo Editors Nicole Radja, Martha Williams

Production
Production Manager Cheryl Magiera
Associate Production Manager Nooreen Furquan
Image Specialist Jamie Ramsay

Online
Digital Production Director Amanda Meffert
Web Editor John Dugan
Associate Online Producer Jessica Johnson

Information Technology
Technology Manager Kim R. Russell
Systems Coordinator David Gibson

Advertising
Publisher David Garland
Advertising Director Vicki Pelling
Senior Account Managers Trevor Mikus, David Wilson
Account Managers January Overton, Mari Taisch, Erik Uppenberg-Croone
Online Account Manager Aidan Enright
Advertising and Marketing Coordinator Ariana Bennett

Marketing
Marketing Director Julie Sprich-Hammer
Marketing Manager, Events, Promotions and Publicity Tuck Shepard
Integrated Marketing Designer Erin Delahanty

Consumer Marketing/Circulation
Group Consumer Marketing Director Niki Lathroum
Consumer Marketing Manager Peter Chiu
Partnership Manager Kate Lowery
Assistant Consumer Marketing Manager Angela Sundstrom
Consumer Marketing Coordinator Leah Johnston
Assistant Retail Marketing Manager Josh Stringer

Finance
Accounting Manager Kelly Rizo
Senior Accountant Yang Guo
Staff Accountant April Apodaca
Credit Analyst Marla Tarantino

Administration
Human Resources Manager Andy Katzman
Office Coordinator Carly Mulliken

President Alison Tocci
Group Publisher Marisa Fariña
Chief Financial Officer Daniel P. Reilly
Editorial Director Elizabeth Barr
Digital Business Manager Marci Weisler

Published by Time Out Chicago Partners, L.L.L.P.
Chairman Tony Elliott
Executive Committee William Louis-Dreyfus, Joe Mansueto, Kevin S. Moore

Printed and bound in the USA
Brown Printing Company, Woodstock, IL
ISBN 978-0-9793984-7-6

On the cover Photograph by Chris Litwin; hand model, Brenda Burns/Stewart Talent. Urbanbelly Ramen at Urban Belly, 3053 N California Ave.

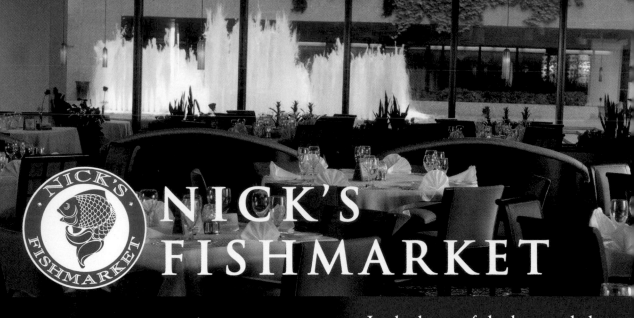

Amp Rock Lounge

Contents

Introduction

Getting back to the basics, Chicago's most talented chefs and restaurateurs push through lean times.

GO FISH Homey serviceware and simple preparations are among the keys to the Publican's success.

It could be said that Chicago chefs took a collective sigh in 2009. As the economy ground to a halt, chefs took their cue to slow down a bit, simplifying plates and presentations, elevating farm-to-table consciousness and reconnecting with Old World traditions, from butchering whole animals in-house and preparing labor-intensive charcuterie to amassing beer lists packed with gems from centuries-old breweries.

Of the new restaurants to emerge on the scene under this M.O., few excelled quite like **the Publican**, the readers' choice for *Time Out Chicago*'s annual Eat Out Awards Best New Restaurant. As the third project from the team behind **Blackbird** and **Avec**, the Publican cemented Paul Kahan and crew's national rep as a force to be reckoned with (and they're not done yet: Their Wicker Park tacos-and-beer joint should be open by the time you read this).

Keeping the Publican company are fellow newcomers **the Bristol** and **Mado**. Chalkboard menus, long wooden communal tables and a rotating selection of offal-based dishes seemed to multiply around town after the success of these two spots—**the Grocery** opened as a carbon copy of Mado (aesthetically, anyway, plus the wallet-friendly BYOB policy), while **Duchamp** managed to switch things up a bit by sticking their communal tables outside on the patio and **Urban Belly** stood out for its pan-Asian format and stellar execution. And just as these creative menus rotate with the seasons, the Lula Café crew's **Nightwood** upped the ante by rotating theirs (or at least parts of it) every day of the week.

Save for the BYOBs, each of these hits can credit some of their success to expertly curated craft beer lists and carefully concocted cocktails, making them drinking destinations, too. On the flipside, 2009 saw a surplus of bars stepping it up a notch from the typical poppers-and-wings bar-food formula. Of these, **Rootstock** was the best at the formula, delivering delicious small plates alongside an unbeatable selection of beer and wine from small producers, and doing it in a casual setting as suitable for jeans as for a Saturday night out. For more lounges with elevated takes on pub grub, look toward the opposite end of the swank spectrum and you'll find **ROOF, Terrace at Trump** and **C-View**—hotspot hotel rooftop patios, where the view and the eye candy should impress as much as, or maybe more than, the food.

Looking at the plenitude of new hotels popping up around town (and with them, hotel restaurants like **Pelago, cibo matto, State & Lake, C-House, Elate, Balsan** and **Ria**), it's tough to tell 2009 was hit by a recession. But the economy claimed plenty of respectable restaurants in the last year, including Aigre Doux, Mantou Noodle Bar, Century Public House, Rustik, Powerhouse, Brasserie Ruhlmann, DeLaCosta, copperblue, Le Lan and Blue Water Grill. What's more, celebrity chefs rumored to join the local scene turned out to be no-shows, Govind Armstrong and Joel Robuchon included. But finally, after a lull in openings that could surely be tied to the economy, a spike of exciting arrivals (**Gemini Bistro, Purple Pig, XOCO, Mercadito**) signaled what stalwart restaurants already know: Even during the toughest times, Chicagoans won't abandon going out to eat and drink…they'll just seek out the best from the rest.—*Heather Shouse, Eating & Drinking Guide Editor*

simple inspiration, every day

guided by market-fresh inspiration, chef michael mcdonald's contemporary american cuisine celebrates daily life. a stylish west loop restaurant, one sixtyblue captures the essence of leisurely dining at the american table.

MENUS, CHEF BIO, IMAGES AND MORE AVAILABLE ONLINE AT ONESIXTYBLUE.COM.

one sixty**blue**

1400 west randolph st. • chicago, il • 312.850.0303 • www.onesixtyblue.com

The lowdown

How to use this guide

Restaurants are divided alphabetically by cuisine or type of establishment (Chinese, Kosher, Steakhouses). Our largest cuisine (Classic American) is divided into two price categories, based on the average cost of an entrée: $15 and under, $16 and over. Bars and Lounges are organized by neighborhoods (several have been grouped by geography, i.e., Lakeview/Roscoe Village/Wrigleyville or Bridgeport/Chinatown). Starting on page 173, you'll find subject indexes (brunch, BYOB, outdoor seating) as well as alphabetical and neighborhood indexes.

★ **Critics' picks**
A red star next to a restaurant's name means we think it's very good for its cuisine or category, and especially worth checking out.

▽ **Vegetarian-friendly**

☉ **Cheap eats**
This symbol denotes places where the average cost of a main course (or equivalent) is $10 or less. You'll find nearly 400 restaurants with this icon in the guide.

▼ **Gay/lesbian-friendly**

♨ **Fireplace**

❋ **Outdoor seating**

(**Restaurants serving after 10pm; bars serving after 2am Sun–Fri, 3am Sat**

B **Brunch served**

BYOB **Bring your own beer/wine**

✗ **Bars serving food**

Nightwood

Before you set out
Although information was updated right up until this book went to press, some restaurants' hours, chefs and menus may have changed. Please call the restaurant or check timeoutchicago.com for the latest details.

Addresses
All cross streets are conveniently listed.

Business hours
We include the days that the restaurant is open and the meals it serves (i.e., breakfast, lunch, dinner). Note that the kitchen may stop taking orders for food earlier than its closing time, and hours may change during the summer or for holidays.

Cash only
We've noted establishments that only take cash; otherwise, all major credit cards are accepted.

Pricing information
Not everyone orders appetizers, drinks and desserts at each meal, so we've listed the average price of each restaurant's main courses. At

timeoutchicago.com
To stay current with all the new places opening throughout the year, be sure to read the Eat Out section in the weekly *Time Out Chicago* magazine, or visit timeoutchicago.com. Complete reviews from both the magazine and the *Eating & Drinking* guide can be found online by many criteria (such as name, neighborhood, cuisine or bar type).

places that don't serve meals à la carte, we give an equivalent (e.g., pizza, baked good or typical nigiri at sushi spots).

Additional locations
Sister restaurants and branches are listed at the end of reviews.

Transportation
We list the nearest El stop or bus line for each restaurant. For places in the suburbs, Metra train or Pace bus information is listed where appropriate. At press time, certain El stations (such as Washington on the Red Line or Paulina on the Brown Line) were being repaired or under construction. Double-check your route at transitchicago.com.

2009 Eat Out Awards
Time Out Chicago magazine bestows awards annually on restaurants and bars of particular note. The awards include both Critics' Picks and Readers' Choices. We highlight the entries of each winning restaurant or bar by noting their awards in red.

This is how we do it
The establishments that appear in this guide are chosen by *TOC*'s food critics. We visit each one anonymously and pay for our own meals and drinks in order to best evaluate the experience any diner might have when visiting the restaurant or bar.

Our advertisers
The *Time Out Chicago Eating & Drinking* guide, like the weekly *TOC* magazine, accepts advertising. We would like to stress that our advertisers receive no special favors and have no influence over our editorial content. No establishment has been included and/or given a favorable review because its owners have advertised in the magazine, online or in this guide. An advertiser may receive a bad review or no review at all.

The top chefs in the country have one thing in common. Their address.

Restaurants

porchetta di testa.
beef tartare. pickle
eggplant agnolotti, s
pappardelle. octopus
halibut, borlotti, fren
charred quail, arugula
cheese board, gooseb

les freres - c
big ed's-cow.s
bleu affinee - c

Brewed *for* food.

Matilda

Belgian Style Ale

Too new to review

Don't miss these noteworthy newcomers.

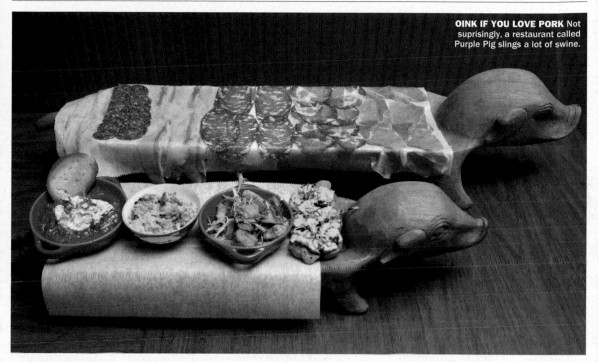

OINK IF YOU LOVE PORK Not suprisingly, a restaurant called Purple Pig slings a lot of swine.

Balsan and **Ria** Chef Jason McLeod is at the stove of both of these restaurants in the Elysian Hotel. Balsan is cheaper, more casual and serves all day; Ria is the flashy dinner-only spot. Both come with desserts by HotChocolate's Mindy Segal. *11 E Walton St between State and Rush Sts (312-646-1300). El: Red to Chicago. Bus: 36, 66, 143, 144, 145, 146, 147, 148, 151. Breakfast (Balsan), lunch (Balsan), dinner.*

▼ **Belly Shack** After the success of their downscale noodle bar Urban Belly, Bill Kim and his wife Yvonne Cadiz-Kim set their sights on this space beneath the El tracks (formerly Vella Café) for a casual Asian-Latino catery. *1912 N Western Ave between Cortland and Homer Sts (773-489-7777). El: Blue to Western. Bus: 49, X49, 56, 74.*

▼ **Floriole** This Frenchy, organic-y bakery can barely keep the crowds at bay at Green City Market. We don't expect the crowds to be any better when it starts slinging its *canelés* at a storefront in Lincoln Park. *Location TBD.*

Gemini Bistro After pulling the plug on a massive, three-year project in River North, Jason Paskewitz decided to downsize. This American bistro is smaller, cheaper and more casual than what Paskewitz was aiming for, but the food— steak frites, mussels, pork belly with quail eggs and duck confit nachos—remains true to his personality. *2075 N Lincoln Ave between Armitage and Dickens Aves (773-525-2522). El: Brown, Purple (rush hrs) to Armitage. Bus: 11, 73, 74. Dinner. Average main course: $18.*

B **Hearty** The Hearty Boys (Steve McDonagh and Dan Smith) are entering the restaurant game again, and their take on comfort food is sharper than ever. Expect rabbit corn dogs, bacon-studded meatloaf and classic, three-layer cakes. *3819 N Broadway between Grace St and Sheridan Rd (773-244-9866). El: Red to Sheridan. Bus: 22, 36, 80, 151. Brunch (Sun), dinner (Wed–Sun). Average main course: $20.*

La Farine West Town will get another artisan baker when Rida Shahin expands his client base from restaurants (HotChocolate, West Town Tavern) to include the general public. *1461 W Chicago Ave between Bishop and Armour Sts (312-850-4019). El: Blue to Chicago. Bus: 9, 66.*

Mercadito After conquering Manhattan, Patricio Sandoval is bringing his tacos-and-tequila concept to Chicago, where he's planting a lounge-bar-restaurant in the former La Pomme Rouge space. *108 W Kinzie St between Clark and LaSalle Sts (312-245-9555). El: Brown, Purple (rush hrs) to Merchandise Mart. Bus: 11, 125, 156.*

Nella Pizzeria Napoletana Co-owners Scott Harris (Mia Francesca) and Nella and Frank Grassano (Nella was formerly the pizza maker at Spacca Napoli) imported not just the materials for their pizza oven from Italy—but the craftsmen to build it, too. *2423 N Clark St between Fullerton Ave and Arlington Pl. El: Brown, Purple (rush hrs), Red to Fullerton. Bus: 22, 36, 74.*

Pelago Chef Mauro Mafrici has been known in New York for years, thanks to his now-shuttered Soho restaurant, Lo Scalco. Now he's taken control of the restaurant in the Rafaello Hotel, where he's doing Italian takes on seafood for dinner, as well as Italian breakfast and lunch. *201 E Delaware Pl between Seneca St and DeWitt Pl (312-943-5000). El: Red to Chicago. Bus: 10, 143, 144, 145, 146, 147, 151. Breakfast, lunch, dinner. Average main course: $25.*

Revolution Brewing Handlebar co-owner Josh Deth will soon be brewing and pouring his own at this Logan Square brewpub. *2323 N Milwaukee Ave between Belden and Medill Aves. El: Blue to California. Bus: 52, 56, 74.*

Purple Pig It's in the name of swine that Heaven on Seven's Jimmy Bannos, Bannos's son Jimmy Jr., and Mia Francesca's Scott Harris came together to open a wine-heavy Mediterranean spot on the Mag Mile. *500 N Michigan Ave between Illinois St and Grand Ave. El: Red to Grand. Bus: 3, 65, 145, 146, 147, 151, 157.*

Revolution Brewing Handlebar co-owner Josh Deth will soon be brewing and pouring his own at this Logan Square brewpub. *2323 N Milwaukee Ave between Belden and Medill Aves. El: Blue to California. Bus: 52, 56, 74.*

Rustico Grill Even after an expansion that doubled its size, Mixteco Grill still can't hold all the people trying to get into it. So chef Raul Arreola opened this Logan Square outpost, where he's serving Mixteco favorites in a hipstery space—this time with margaritas. *2515 N California Ave between Altgeld St and Logan Blvd (773-235-0002). El: Blue to California. Bus: 52, 56, 74. Average main course: $17.*

XOCO Rick Bayless has dedicated his street-food shack next door to Frontera Grill and Topolobampo to Mexican mainstays such as *tortas, caldos* and *churros.* But there's one thing the restaurant's chefs are doing that nobody else in the city can touch: making chocolate from raw cocoa beans. *449 N Clark St at Illinois St. El: Brown, Purple (rush hrs) to Merchandise Mart; Red to Grand. Bus: 22, 29, 36, 65. Breakfast, lunch, dinner (closed Sun).*

African

HOOK, LINE AND SINKER Crispy tilapia is one of many delicious draws at Café Senegal.

▼ **Abyssinia Restaurant** This addition to Broadway's Ethiopian strip is often overlooked, maybe because in comparison to the tomes found at the nearby competition, the menu seems small at just under a dozen options (plus five more if you get there early enough for breakfast). The Abyssinia special, a pureed stew of beans, onions, garlic and peppers, is the best of the vegetarian dishes—it has layers of flavors that betray its pedestrian looks. But the earthy yellow peas, spicy lentils and juicy lamb are nothing to sneeze at. And because there's not much else to order, there's no excuse not to order it all. *5842 N Broadway between Ardmore and Rosedale Aves (773-271-7133). El: Red to Thorndale. Bus: 36, 147. Breakfast, lunch, dinner. Average main course: $10.*

★ ▼ **Addis Abeba** The shuttered Wrigleyville Ethiopian stalwart has reopened in Evanston, where an NU crowd uses *injera* bread to sop up traditional entrées. Combo plates offer the best deal, allowing you to try as many as four entrées, like *yeater kik wot* (yellow split peas with garlic, cloves and cinnamon), *yesiga wot* (a spicy beef stew) and *azifa* (cold lentils with tomatoes and jalapeño). Go with someone you want to cozy up with, since food is served on a *mesob*—a single, large platter symbolizing intimacy and loyalty. *1322 Chicago Ave, Evanston (847-328-5411). El: Purple to Dempster. Bus: 201, 205. Lunch, dinner. Average main course: $13.*

African Harambee Sisay Abebe (formerly of Edgewater's Ethiopian Diamond) is behind this pan-African spot where, together with chef-partner Martha Yimer, he serves food "from Casa Blanca to Cape Town; the land of Sheba to the Ashanti Kingdom." That translates to beef dredged in seasoned pea flour, catfish in turmeric-spiked tahini sauce and lamb in dried-fruit curry. And the *jollof* rice—beef, chicken, or lamb sautéed with onion, thyme, garlic and green peppers—is thoroughly spiced (though, unlike many of these dishes, not at all spicy). *7537 N Clark St between Birchwood Ave and Howard St (773-764-2200). El: Purple, Red, Yellow to Howard. Bus: 22, 97, 147, 151, 201, 205, Pace 215, Pace 290. Lunch, dinner. Average main course: $13.*

☺ BYOB **B and Q Afro Root Cuisine** The meaty menu is pretty idiot-proof at this no-frills Nigerian restaurant; you simply point to one of the color pictures. Carnivores won't be disappointed with the tender-to-the-bone beef and chicken or the wintertime pepper soup with goat. Hard-core vegetarians can construct a meal out of entrée sides like black-eyed peas with white rice and überspicy chile sauce, *dodo* (fried plantains) and soft yam porridge. Regardless of whether you go with meat or veg, bring oodles of ice-cold beer to fight off the searing heat. *4701 N Kenmore Ave between Leland and Lawrence Aves (773-878-7489). El: Red to Lawrence. Bus: 22, 36, 81. Lunch, dinner. Average main course: $10.*

★ ☺ **Blue Nile Restaurant** This unassuming strip-mall gem is breathing new life into the Ethiopian food scene. There are many dishes we're tempted to pile onto the *injera*, from the *kifto* (buttery yet fiery ground beef) to the *lega tibs* (garlicky, oniony but slightly tough lamb). No matter what, the *yekuanta firfir* is a must—the chunks of flavorful charred jerk beef mixed with *berbere* sauce is so delicious it should keep this place from going extinct. *6118 N Ravenswood Ave between Norwood St and Hood Ave (773-465-6710). Bus: 22, 84, 155. Lunch, dinner. Average main course: $9.*

☺ BYOB **Café Senegal** Don't pay too much attention to the menus here; there's little that ink on paper can do to convey the depth of flavor brimming in this food. The word *nem* doesn't hint that the eggroll-like appetizer is stuffed with a savory, peppery blend of shrimp and chicken, and the words *beef patty* don't come close to describing the homey comfort these housemade pies hide. *Debbé* doesn't sum up how tender the lamb is or how piquant its tomato-and-pepper sauce is. And while *firire* is described as "fried fish," that description says nothing about how crispy the tilapia's skin is—or about the flakiness of the flesh underneath it. *2131 W Howard St between Ridge and Hoyne Aves (773-465-5643). El: Red to Howard. Bus: 97. Breakfast, lunch, dinner. Average main course: $8.*

★ ▼ ☀ **Demera Ethiopian** The long waits for food at this Ethiopian spot in Uptown can be frustrating, especially when you see how good the dishes around you look. But keep your cool: Once you get your hands on the flaky, lentil-filled *sambusas*, the *kik alitcha* (mild yellow split peas transformed into a silky ginger-and-garlic–riddled puree) and the cool *kitfo*

(Ethiopian steak tartare), you'll understand why everybody in the restaurant seems so unfazed. *4801 N Broadway at Lawrence Ave (773-334-8787). El: Red to Lawrence. Bus: 36, 81, 151. Lunch, dinner. Average main course: $12.*

★ ▼ ☺ BYOB **Ethiopian Diamond**
This Ethiopian choice stands out for consistency and punchy flavors. The ground beef in the sambusa is livened with peppers, and vegetables shine in the entrées, starring two types of split peas: the rich yet tame *alitcha* and the spicy *wat*, both stewed to melt-in-your-mouth perfection and served with *injera* bread. Fat and bones abound, but don't let that stop you from gnawing on the *kay wat*, beef cubes simmered in the "diamond sauce," a gingery, cumin-laced red sauce with a nice chile kick. *6120 N Broadway between Glenlake and Hood Aves (773-338-6100). El: Red to Granville. Bus: 36, 147, 151. Lunch, dinner. Average main course: $9.50.*

★ ☺ **Icosium Kafé** See Mediterranean for review.

▼ ☺ **Iyanze** African restaurants are well known for their leisurely pace, but here the mother-and-son team behind Bolat go the exact opposite route: Customers place their orders at a counter, get in line at a buffet and watch as their food goes from steam table to plate in a matter of minutes. Technically, that makes this stuff fast food, but the flavors are clearly the result of slow cooking. Goat meat has seemingly endless layers of hot and mild peppers; peanut soup has that nut's savory edge but also a peppery bite; and jerk chicken is cloaked in a sauce redolent with cardamom and cloves. *4623 N Broadway between Wilson and Leland Aves (773-944-1417). El: Red to Wilson. Bus: 36, 78, 145. Mon–Sat 7am–9pm; Sun 11am–7pm. Average main course: $5.*

▼ ☺ BYOB **Lalibela** This Ethiopian restaurant might have a small menu, but it's mighty. What's usually a pages-long tome of various stews is here whittled down to a handful of options, making it easy to try everything. Don't skip the *shuro*, a delectable chickpea dish with a complex, gradual heat; the *yemisir azifah*, a cold lentil dish with a great piquant tang, and the "Lalibela special tibs," sumptuous bites of sautéed lamb. Of course, if you focus on those dishes, you won't need the menu at all. *5633 N Ashland Ave at Olive Ave (773-944-0585). El: Red to Bryn Mawr. Bus: 22, 50. Lunch, dinner (closed Mon). Average main course: $10.*

BYOB **Le Conakry** It takes some time to fall for this French-African spot—luckily, you'll have plenty of time while you wait for your meal. A platter of delicate meat patties and sweet, ripe plantains can take so long to arrive that you'll be ready to eat your place mat. But it doesn't matter how long it takes for the earthy, spinachish cassava-leaf stew or the sweet-and-just-barely-spicy fish with onion sauce to arrive. Because when they do, you'll find flavors so complex that they demanded savoring—and soon you'll be the one who's taking it slow. *2049 W Howard St between Seeley and Hoyne Aves (773-262-6955). El: Red to Howard. Bus: 97. Lunch, dinner. Average main course: $9.*

★ ▼ ✳ ◖ **Ras Dashen Ethiopian Restaurant** Spinach sambusas—hot, crispy dumplings—are a fine way to start your meal at this Ethiopian hot spot. When you get to the main courses, be brave and try the fiery *zilzil*

BYOB Tip: *African*

Wine: *Beaujolais or pinot noir*

To keep from clashing with or intensifying the meat-and-heat flavors of African classics, you need plenty of fruit and low alcohol—two qualities both these varietals have.

Beer: *Stout or ginger beer*

Lagers are the most common beer in Africa, but we love the way creamy, low-alcohol stouts complement the earthy sweetness in African food, just as ginger beer mimics the food's flavors.

Buy it at Foremost Liquors (*1040 W Argyle St, 773-989-0808*) then **bring it** to B and Q Afro Root Cuisine (p.14).

Buy it at In Fine Spirits (*5418 N Clark St, 773-334-9463*) then **bring it** to Lalibela (this page).

Buy it at Taste Food & Wine (*1506 W Jarvis Ave, 773-262-6955*) then **bring it** to Le Conakry (this page).

tibs, beef strips sautéed with peppers in *berbere* sauce, an Ethiopian specialty made with red peppers and cumin. Or go for the *doro alicha*, a fragrant, tender, milder chicken dish. This stuff is likely to induce a food coma, so snag a table with big, cushy chairs. *5846 N Broadway between Ardmore and Rosedale Aves (773-506-9601). El: Red to Thorndale. Bus: 36, 84, 147. Lunch, dinner. Average main course: $13.*

B BYOB **Sikia** This may be a venue in which Washburne Culinary Institute students hone their skills, but it doesn't look, feel or taste like a student project. Just as the slick dining room is accented with African touches, so too is the menu: A nuanced African ambrosia salad has mango, red onion and yams; black-eyed-pea fritters arrive with a fiery red pepper sauce; and cornmeal pie has sticky, addictive caramel notes. There's plenty for those not interested in African food, too, like a juicy (if mild) jerk chicken. *740 W 63rd St at Halsted St (773-602-5200). El: Green to Halsted. Bus: 8, 63. Brunch (Sun), dinner (Thu–Sat). Average main course: $12.*

☺ BYOB **Yassa** The Senegalese chef at this eatery uses slow methods of cooking mingled with the wild flavor of West African spices to make Old World, yet innovative, dishes. Signature entrees include *mafe*, a thick stew of lamb with ground peanuts and habanero peppers, and the succulent chicken *yassa*, grilled chicken that's marinated in mustard powder, vinegar and lemon juice. But we'd move mountains for the *dakhine*, seared lamb shank with onions, tomato paste and peanut butter. *716 E 79th St between Evans and Langley Aves (773-488-5599). El: Red to 79th St. Bus: 3, 4, 79. Lunch, dinner. Average main course: $10.*

FAMILY MATTERS Madieye Gueye, his wife Awa (pictured, left), and daughter Soda welcome you to Yassa.

Bakeries/Cafés

★ ▽ ☀ **B** **Angel Food Bakery**
Regressing back to childhood is a very good thing when you're doing it at this lively, lime-green café. Pastry chef Stephanie Samuels makes the kind of desserts you used to find in your lunch box: Ding Dongs, Thin Mints and superb cream-filled cupcakes. She provides pre-dessert nourishment with seasonal soups, grilled chicken club sandwiches with Russian dressing, and a breakfast and Sunday brunch menu that includes powdered sugar–dusted squares of French toast with marmalade syrup and salmon cakes with tangy lemon aioli. *1636 W Montrose Ave at Paulina St (773-728-1512). Bus: 22, 50, 78. Tue–Fri 7am–5pm; Sat 8am–5pm; Sun 9am–2pm. Brunch (Sun). Average main course: $8.*

▽ ☺ ☀ **Beverly Bakery & Cafe** You know you're in a neighborhood favorite when a cop stopping in for his "usual" knows the name of the stroller-pushing mom who's come to pick up her sister's birthday cake. The couple running this sparse but cheerful daytime-only spot take it all in stride—they may have only opened in 2004 but their Beverly roots go back plenty. That would explain the careful local sourcing: Sage-rich breakfast sausage, thick applewood-smoked bacon and Fratelli coffee are all produced in the Chicago area. *10528 S Western Ave between 105th and 106th Sts (773-238-5580). Bus: 49A, 103, Pace 349. Tue–Fri 6am–2pm; Sat–Sun 8am–2pm; (closed Mon). Average baked good: $2.*

★ ☺ **Bittersweet Pastry Shop** Stop by midday for chef Judy Contino's acclaimed pastries and desserts, and chances are you'll pull up a chair in the tiny, charming bakery café for lunch. You won't go wrong with any of the handful of rotating daily menu options such as carrot jalapeño soup, spinach salad with blue cheese and lemon vinaigrette, and roasted eggplant–and–goat cheese sandwiches—perfect light fare before you dive into that beautiful meringue tart or the delicious ice cream scooped out into chocolate-lined Chinese takeout containers (try the intense chocolate almond). *1114 W Belmont Ave between Clifton and Seminary Aves (773-929-1100). El: Brown, Purple (rush hrs), Red to Belmont. Bus: 22, 77. Tue–Fri 7am–7pm; Sat 8am–7pm; Sun 8am–6pm. Average sandwich: $9.*

▽ **Bleeding Heart Bakery** Pastry chef Michelle Garcia runs this punky, organic, vegan-friendly bakery in Roscoe Village. Here, she's doing all the bars and cookies that she did in her previous space on Chicago Avenue, as well as egg, cheese and bacon tea cakes (for those who don't subsist purely on sugar). Don't miss the Elvis cake (chocolate cake with peanut butter and bacon)—available through special order—or the cupcake menu, which varies every month. *1955 W Belmont Ave between Damen and Wolcott Aves (773-327-6934). Bus: 50, 77. 7am–7pm. Average pastry: $3.25.*

Blue Sky Bakery & Café By employing homeless and otherwise at-risk youth, this nonprofit café doubles as a social venture. But we've had their cookies, granola and sandwiches and think they perform a much-needed service of their own. Skip the sugar and grab a cheddar-herb scone for lunch—the

friendly staffers are sweet enough. *4749 N Albany Ave between Leland and Lawrence Aves (773-710-7346). El: Brown to Kedzie. Bus: 81, 93. Tue–Fri 7am–2pm; Sat 8am–3pm; Sun 9am–3pm. Average baked good: $2.*

★ ☺ **B** **Bombon Café** This bright, roomy space offers ample seating to indulge a rich chorizo *torta* piled with Oaxacan cheese and avocado and a mixed greens *provinciana* salad with *pepitas* and roasted corn. Don't forget co-owner and chef Laura Cid-Perea's signature pastries: Sampling from several varieties of her incredible *tres leches* cake is the perfect way to end a meal. *36 S Ashland Ave at Ogden Ave (312-733-8717). El: Blue to Medical Center. Bus: 9, X9, 20, X20, 126. Mon–Sat 7am–7pm, Sun 8am–4pm. Average sandwich: $7.*

☺ **Brown Sugar Bakery** Past the red door of this South Shore spot's new location, Stephanie Hart turns out a number of "down-home delights" that smack of her bakery's eponymous ingredient. Peach cobbler, pineapple upside down cake, and sweet potato pie, as well as by-the-slice or whole cakes such as caramel, German chocolate and red velvet are just a sample of Hart's cavity-causing creations. *328 E 75th St between Calumet and Prairie Aves (773-224-6262). El: Red to 79th. Bus: 3, 75. Mon–Sat 10am–8pm. Average baked good: $3.*

★ ☀ **Café Colao** See Puerto Rican for review.

★ ▽ ☀ **B** **Café Selmarie** You might have stopped into this Lincoln Square bakery for a croissant to go and missed the dining room hidden in back. The first-come, first-served policy means you'll have a half-hour wait for brunch, but a cup of coffee and slice of coffee cake will tide you over. For the main event, don't miss the corned-beef hash: The smoky-salty beef and potatoes are flecked with herbs and topped with two perfectly poached eggs. Lunch and dinner during the week focus on comfort foods, including a yummy, grown-up mac and cheese with leeks. *4729 N Lincoln Ave between Leland and Lawrence Aves (773-989-5595). El: Brown to Western. Bus: 11, 49, X49, 81. Mon 11am–3pm (lunch); Tue–Thu 8am–9pm; Fri, Sat 8am–10pm; Sun 9am–9pm. Brunch (Sat, Sun). Average main course: $13.*

★ ▽ ☺ ☀ **The Coffee Studio** *2009 Eat Out Award, Critics' Pick: Proof That Evolution Exists (a coffee shop with sleek, modern design)* Andersonville is nuts about this coffee shop, which offers a colorful variety of organic, sustainable menu items. The recently added quiche selection, featuring a hearty wild mushroom pie, is definitely a draw, as are the handful of can't-believe-it's-vegan desserts. But the smooth, expertly pulled shots of espresso, and smart, midcentury modern design make this the sexiest coffee shop on the block. *5628 N Clark St at Olive Ave (773-271-7881). El: Red to Bryn Mawr. Bus: 22, 84. 6:30am–9pm. Average coffee drink: $3.*

▽ ☺ ☀ **B** **de.li.cious café** It's a coffee shop with vegan tendencies, but de.li.cious doesn't have that kumbaya vibe. Instead, it appears to be just another coffee shop. The vegan breakfast

sandwich (tofu fried "egg" and vegan sausage) is a respectable (and filling) attempt; the vegan muffins do a better job of standing in for the real thing. But at the end of the day, it's not the food you'll come here for: It's the Chemex coffee, brewed so smooth and silky it's well worth the eight-minute wait to get it. *3827 N Lincoln Ave at Berenice Ave (773-477-9840). El: Brown to Irving Park. Bus: 11, 50, 80, X80. Mon–Fri 6:30am–7pm; Sat 8am–7:30pm; Sun 9am–5pm. Average baked good: $2.50.*

▽ ☺ **B** **Demitasse** A blend of cozy bohemian hangout and hoppin' breakfast haunt, this spot's sun-splashed walls inspire all-day coffee sipping while leafing through the menu. Try the tasty frittatas (basically open-face omelettes) and the French toast, a gooey mayhem of brioche slices stuffed with sweet cream, covered with fresh strawberries and bananas, and smothered in raspberry sauce. Lunch lightens the ingredient load, with perfectly crisp panini (the pesto caprese features homegrown tomatoes and freshly picked basil) and made-from-scratch tuna sandwiches. *1066 W Taylor St between Carpenter and Aberdeen Sts (312-226-7666). El: Blue to Racine. Bus: 7, 12, 60. Tue–Fri 6:30am–3pm; Sat, Sun 7:30am–2:30pm (closed Mon). Brunch (Sat, Sun). Average main course: $8.*

☺ **Flourish Bakery Café** Midwesterners who pine for old-fashioned salads, sandwiches and baked goods like Mom used to make will find a good selection (macaroni, pea and pearl-onion salad, anyone?) at this sunny Edgewater bakery/café. We like the more modern panini—especially the caprese with prosciutto—as well as the rotating assortment of fresh-baked breads, including multigrain and hearty deli rye. The Metropolis coffee—a special blend brewed exclusively for the bakery—may not be as retro as a packet of Ma's Sanka, but we like it that way. *1138 W Bryn Mawr Ave between Winthrop Ave and Broadway (773-271-2253). El: Red to Bryn Mawr. Bus: 22, 36, 50, 84, 151. Mon–Sat 7:30am–9pm; Sun 8am–6pm. Average baked good: $2.50.*

☺ **Fritz Pastry** Former Blue Water Grill pastry chef Nathaniel Meads is behind this Lakeview pastry shop, and he's managed to convince hungry wanderers that there is indeed a reason to look beyond the shop's dreary tinted windows. Incredibly friendly counter help makes up for the rather dark atmosphere, and solid coffee cakes and streusel-topped fruit tarts make nice latte companions. Chocolate proves the best of six macaron varieties, while filled croissants outshine their classic sibling. *1408 W Diversey Pkwy at Southport Ave (773-857-2989). El: Brown, Purple (rush hrs) to Diversey. Bus: 9, 11, 76. 7am–7pm daily. Average baked good: $2.*

☺ **Istria Café** With a mantra like "corporate coffee tastes funny," the boys behind Hyde Park's Istria better be prepared to resist expansion. That may be difficult: People are bound to respond to roasted-to-order coffee, fresh panini and the dozen varieties of housemade gelato. They're the antithesis to Starbucks now, but with a second location at the Hyde Park Art Center, better get it while it's still indie. *1520 E 57th St at Lake Park Ave (773-955-2556). Bus: 6, 15, 28,*

UNO, DOS, TRES Laura Cid-Perea's legendary *tres leches* have earned Bombon Café legions of fans.

Side dish

THINKING OF DRINKING Sip and surf day or night at the Map Room.

Surfing the Wi-Fi wave

Get off the couch and log on to café culture.

Cruising the Web from your apartment is all well and good, but there's something about getting out of the house, grabbing a cup of coffee and taking advantage of a shop's Wi-Fi that makes the process much more enjoyable.

At most places, lots of hidden nooks mean covert hookups and missed connections. The beehive of private spots at **Sip** (1223 W Grand Ave, 312-492-7686) serves a different function: Group meetings take place in a corner stuffed with comfy couches, solo workers slip on headphones and hide out in the shady inner courtyard, and folks generally seem to hold court all day at any table in the house.

Sip's soothing seafoam-green walls and bright, airy rooms sometimes seem just too…happy. Buena Park's **Dollop Coffee Co** (4181 N Clarendon Ave, 773-755-1955) has the worn-in feel of a place you've been going to forever. Both the big perks (a back room with plenty of space to camp out) and the small ones (Metropolis coffee and Hoosier Mama pies) set Dollop apart from the pack.

Surfing the Web for a job? Marking up the classifieds can get you only so far: For professional help, grab a copy of *How'd You Score That Gig?: A Guide to the Coolest Jobs and How to Get Them* off the shelf at **The Book Cellar** (4736–38 N Lincoln Ave, 773-293-2665), an independent bookshop in Lincoln Square. There's free wireless, and even though there's only a handful of tables to choose from, it shouldn't be a problem to snag one for the afternoon—along with a cup of Julius Meinl java or a glass of wine (if it's that kind of day).

Fitting right in with Old Town's quaint-village feel is **La Sera** (1143 N Wells St, 312-274-0442), a warm and inviting café filled with dark wood and creamy leather banquettes. Sink in and log on, and if you need fuel for your surfing, balance out the healthy wraps with a crème brûleé finale.

If you're the kind of person who likes to surf the Net with a beer in hand, there are few better spots for this than **the Map Room** (p.149). Bucktown's traveler-themed tavern opens at—get this—6:30am with one of the best deals in town: a buck for a cup of Intelligentsia coffee, and two bucks for up to four cups. Plus, Bennison's Bakery delivers croissants and other pastries every morning. So grab a seat at the bar or claim a table in the back and down as much java as you can until the clock strikes 11am: You'll need all that caffeine once you start working your way through the massive beer selection.

But let's say you can't afford to guzzle craft beers all day, and maybe you're not interested in gulping coffee. Free Wi-Fi should mean free: No purchase necessary. And that's where the **Chicago Cultural Center** (78 E Washington St, 312-744-6630) comes in. The former public library is home to exhibits, public concerts and, best of all, complimentary, no-strings-attached wireless. The coffee and snacks at the first-floor Randolph Café aren't so hot, so BYO thermos and settle in for the long haul. Trust us, you won't be the only one in the room taking advantage of the peace, quiet and, of course, free Wi-Fi.—*Julia Kramer*

X28, 55, X55. Mon–Fri 6:30am–8:30pm; Sat 7am–8:30pm; Sun 8:30am–8:30pm. Average sandwich: $5. ● Other location: 5020 S Cornell Ave (773-324-9660).

✱ (**Julius Meinl Café** The problem: A café as lovely and sunny as this—and with coffee this good—inspires lingering. But lingering requires cup upon cup of caffeine, and that could become hazardous. This European export has a solution for all that, though: a full menu of food, most of it the unlikeliest coffeehouse food you've come across. Roasted lamb is served with golden, toothsome spaetzle, and braised pork arrives with soft dumplings. At the end of the meal, a slice of impeccable opera cake is a necessity. And with it, yet another cup of coffee. *4363 N Lincoln Ave at Montrose Ave (773-868-1876). El: Brown to Montrose. Bus: 11, 49, 78. Mon–Thurs 6am–10pm; Fri 6am–midnight; Sat 7am–midnight; Sun 7am–10pm. Average main course: $10.*

▼ ✱ B **Little Branch Café** Sitting on one of the tree-stump stools at this sleek coffeehouse doesn't really make for an outdoorsy experience—the room is too influenced by midcentury-modern design to conjure the outdoors. But it is a lovely experience nonetheless, thanks to oversized mugs filled with lavender-scented chai lattes and hot turkey Reubens on crisp marble rye. A bar area means nighttime stops for a different kind of fuel, making Little Branch an all-day affair. *1251 S Prairie Ave between Roosevelt Rd and 13th St (312-360-0101). El: Green, Orange, Red to Roosevelt. Bus: 3, 12, 29, 62, 146. Mon, Tues 7am–4pm; Wed–Fri 7am–10pm; Sat 8am–10pm; Sun 8am–8pm. Average main course: $7.*

★ ▼ ☺ **Lovely: A Bake Shop** Brooke Dailey and Gina Howie, two friends who met at the French Pastry School, are behind this homey bakery filled with vintage tables and knickknacks. And though we hate to state the expected, we have to admit it: This place is pretty damn lovely. From cakey, star-shaped muffins to flaky *pain au chocolat*, the pastries are just as sweet and delicious as they should be. And their brownies? Tinged with crème fraîche and dark chocolate, they are some of the most serious and decadent we've ever had the pleasure of savoring. *1130 N Milwaukee Ave between Thomas St and Haddon Ave (773-572-4766). El: Blue to Division. Bus: 9, 56, 70. Mon–Fri 7am–7pm; Sat 9am–6pm; Sun 9am–4pm. Average baked good: $3.*

✱ **Lutz Continental Café & Pastry Shop** See German for review.

★ ▼ ☺ ✱ B **Milk & Honey** This sunny joint helps kick-start the day with baked goods and specialty coffees, but it's the basic sandwiches gussied up with impeccable ingredients that get us in the afternoon. Our favorites: the BLT made with extra-thick bacon and the juicy, rosemary-and-thyme–encrusted roast beef. The weekend crowd can be a bitch, so be prepared to either fight your way to the front of the line or just head home with a bag of the cafe's signature granola. *1920 W Division St between Wolcott and Winchester Aves (773-395-9434). El: Blue to Division. Bus: 9, 50, 70. Mon–Fri 7am–4pm; Sat 8am–5pm; Sun 8am–4pm. Average sandwich: $7.*

▼ **Molly's Cupcakes** Owner John Nicolaides named this cute cupcake shop after his favorite grade-school teacher, who baked cupcakes for students' birthdays. In our two favorites of the half-dozen cupcakes, bits of bright carrot mesh with cream-cheese buttercream, and tangy dollops of lemon curd cut a rich vanilla cake. Reenact your own grade-school days by having a cupcake at the swing-style chairs flanking the counter. *2536 N Clark St between Wrightwood Ave and Deming Pl (773-883-7220). El: Red, Brown, Purple (rush hrs) to Fullerton. Bus: 22, 36, 151. Mon noon–10pm; Tue–Thu 8am–10pm; Fri, Sat 8am–midnight; Sun 8am–10pm. Average cupcake: $3.*

★ **More Cupcakes** No cupcake has ever tasted quite like the BLT concoction at this sleek (and tiny) Gold Coast cupcakery: Sweet cake is filled with salty pieces of bacon, smeared with a completely savory ranch "icing" and topped with fresh slices of tomato. It's jarring at first, but it works so well that it's perhaps the most convincing proof that cupcakes can swing both ways. Showcased in a glass display, the rotating selection of cupcakes (including classics like red velvet and chocolate for the more conservative cupcake connoisseur) look like works of art—because they are. *1 E Delaware Pl at State St (312-951-0001). El: Red to Chicago. Bus: 22, 36, 146. Mon–Fri 8am–8pm; Sat 9am–8pm; Sun 10am–6pm. Average cupcake: $3.50.*

◉ **Old Fashioned Donuts** We could take a cue from the cops who stalk this bare-bones doughnut shop and go for a couple of the poofy glazed beauties in the case. Or we could make like the locals and snatch up chocolate-slathered cake doughnuts as if there was a blackout coming. But really, anytime we make it to this South Side institution, we're too busy honing in on the apple fritters—unparalleled rounds, as big as your head, with cinnamon-spilted peaks and valleys dotted with gooey apple hunks. If you can find one better in the city limits, we're buying. *11248 S Michigan Ave between 112th Pl and 113th St (773-995-7420). Bus: 34, 103, 106, 119. Mon–Sat 6am–6pm. Average baked good: $2.*

★ ◉ **Pasticceria Natalina** On weekends, start with the savory items (available only on Saturdays and Sundays)—you won't regret digging into treats such as the fiercely herbal mint-and-pea *fazzoletti*. But the focus of this Sicilian bakeshop is desserts including the *sfogliatelle* cookie (delicate layers of pastry encase orange-kissed ricotta); ricotta-filled cannoli; and the *barca di crema*, a square of puff pastry filled with cream and topped with amarena cherries that are so intoxicatingly delicious you'll swear they've been soaking in liqueur. Beware that the shop closes early if the day's supply runs dry. *5406 N Clark St between Balmoral and Catalpa Aves (773-989-0662). Bus: 22, 92. Wed–Sun noon–8pm (closed Mon, Tue; occasionally open late). Average pastry: $3.50.*

★ ◉ **Southport Grocery and Café** Go ahead and believe the hype about the cupcake: It's moist, it's substantial but not heavy, and the thick, sugary icing hides deep flavors of chocolate and vanilla. If you're going to pick up a dozen, you may as well stick around for breakfast or lunch. A bright start is the sweet and savory French toast with rosemary-roasted ham. Later, try the albacore tuna melt with local butterkase cheese and green olive aioli. Eat up, but save room for one of those cupcakes. *3552 N Southport Ave between Eddy and Addison Sts (773-665-0100). El: Brown to Southport. Bus: 9, X9, 152, 154. Mon–Fri 7am–4pm; Sat 8am–5pm; Sun 8am–4pm. Average main course: $8.*

★ ▽ ◉ BYOB **Swim Café** Karen Gerod elevates lunch at her West Town café, and you may never want to make your own sandwich again. Using Red Hen breads and the freshest and most seasonal ingredients, she comes up with different concoctions every day (expect

WANT SOME MORE? The Gold Coast's More Cupcakes gives modern spins to a classic sweet.

creations such as turkey piled with cucumber, red onion, avocado, Swiss and a yogurt dressing). The former caterer and wedding-cake maker also bakes scones and cookies daily and serves her own organic ice cream. (BYOB Tue–Fri, after 6pm) *1357 W Chicago Ave between Ada and Noble Sts (312-492-8600). El: Blue to Chicago. Bus: 9, 56, 66. Mon, Sat, Sun 6am–6pm Tue–Fri 6am–10pm. Average main course: $7.*

▽ ◉ ✳ B **35th Street Café** The owners may hail from a corporate restaurant background, but 35th Street Café strives to be a neighborhood jewel. Benches and tables fill the wooden floored main and overflow rooms while large windows invite people to watch patrons and vice versa. All edibles are made in-house and offer a little something for everyone: an extensive breakfast menu (including a low-carb omelette and crepes) for families and early birds, various espresso drinks for those jonesing a caffeine fix, and fresh soups and sandwiches/ wraps for lunchers. The lattes and daily-made chili should dominate the winter months but the outdoor seating should reign in warmer weather. *1735 W 35th St at Hermitage Ave (773-523-3500). El: Orange to 35th/Archer. Bus: 9, 35, 50. Mon–Fri 6am–8pm; Sat 7am–6pm; Sun 7am–4pm. Average sandwich: $6.*

★ ◉ **Twisted Baker** There's nothing twisted or off-kilter about this second-story Old Town bakeshop. In fact, the tarts (banana cream, apple pie) and cupcakes (red velvet, carrot cake) are pure, straightforward old-fashioned goodness. It's the cookies, though, like rustic cornmeal rounds with a hint of lime and buttery shortbread, that are instant classics. *1543 N Wells St between Schiller St and North Ave (312-932-1128). El: Brown, Purple (rush hrs) to Sedgwick. Bus: 11, 72. Mon–Fri 10am–10pm; Sat, Sun 9am–9pm. Average baked good: $2.*

★ ◉ **Ventrella's Caffé** When we dream about leaving it all behind for *la dolce vita* in Italy, this is the kind of neighborhood café we picture whiling away the hours in: vintage furnishings, a great selection of Italian newspapers and magazines, and a well-chosen assortment of pastries, panini and gelati. We'd start the day with strong Lavazza coffee and a croissant, hang around till lunchtime for a grilled prosciutto, provolone and green-apple panino, then spend the rest of the day making our way through the rich, creamy gelato flavors (starting with pistachio). *Magnifico. 4947 N Damen Ave between Argyle and Ainslie Sts (773-506-0708). El: Brown to Damen. Bus: 50, 81, 92, 145. Mon–Fri 10am–8pm; Sat 10am–7pm; Sun 10am–5pm. Average gelato: $3.50.*

Chinese

HOT STUFF Namesake peppercorns bring the heat in Lao Sze Chuan's *ma po tofu.*

Ben Pao The torchbearers for authentic indie eateries are recommending a LEYE Chinese spot? Well, yes, but with caveats. As opposed to the pan-Asian Big Bowl, the theme here is regional Chinese, with renditions of Mongolian, Cantonese, Shanghai and Szechuan dishes. The menu is massive, so sip on the citrus vodka–spiked, frozen ginger ale while perusing. Best bets include crispy cubes of sesame-coated tofu drizzled with garlic sauce; salty-sweet star anise–braised pork with scallion pancakes for wrapping; and shrimp with wheat noodles and mushrooms in a spicy chile sauce. *52 W Illinois St at Dearborn St (312-222-1888). El: Red to Grand. Bus: 22, 36, 65. Lunch (Mon–Fri), dinner. Average main course: $10.*

Chi Café With neon-orange and bright-blue graphics and booths featuring built-in drawers for storing napkins and cutlery, this casual Chinatown spot seems inspired by the Austin Powers school of interior design. The chow spans the Asian map—Hong Kong veggies, Szechuan heat, Singapore noodles and Malaysian satay. If you look carefully, you'll spot less-common items like duck kidney and ox tongue. With this broad range, everyone is likely to find something to like, making this a good place for groups to share. *2160-A S Archer Ave between Wentworth and Princeton Aves (312-842-9993). El: Red to Cermak/Chinatown. Bus: 18, 21, 62. Breakfast, lunch, dinner. Average main course: $6.*

BYOB Double Li Amiable owner Mr. Li used to guide diners through specials written on the wall in Chinese only, but now those

have made it onto the English-language menu, adding to the many fantastic Szechuan options available for those looking to get out of a fried-rice rut. Both the fish with cabbage in chile oil and the mapo tofu pack plenty of earthy spice via a fistful of Szechuan peppercorns. To balance the heat, order the sugar-cured housemade bacon wok-tossed with snow peas, leeks and hefty slices of ginger. And if softshell or blue crabs are on offer, get them. *228 W Cermak Rd between Wentworth and Archer Aves (312-842-7818). El: Red to Cermak/Chinatown. Bus: 18, 24, 29. Lunch, dinner. Average main course: $9.*

BYOB Ed's Potsticker House We wish the Chinese diners that flock here would share their secrets to sidestepping land mines on the menu—we've found many bummers, but the winners have us hooked. The potstickers are among our favorite (ask for house chile oil to stir into the dipping sauce). Sweet-and-sour fans order the crispy sticks of eggplant glazed in garlic sauce, and the sautéed lamb with cumin and sesame seeds, whole red chiles, onions and jalapeños is a bit fatty but flavorful. *3139 S Halsted St between 32nd and 31st Sts (312-326-6898). El: Orange to Halsted. Bus: 8, 35, 44. Lunch, dinner. Average main course: $7.*

BYOB Friendship Chinese Restaurant After his father passed away, Alan Yuen renovated his family's chop suey house (even installing beautiful hardwood floors himself) and set about turning out solid Canto-American classics. Sesame beef and honey-walnut shrimp are joined by creations like

stir-fried seafood in a shredded potato "bird's nest," pan-seared salmon with lemongrass curry, and boneless Peking duck with Grand Marnier sauce. Don't want to go out? Take advantage of the brisk delivery service. *2830 N Milwaukee Ave between Diversey and Dawson Aves (773-227-0970). El: Blue to Logan Square. Bus: 56, 76, 82. Lunch (Mon–Sat), dinner. Average main course: $12.*

Furama For some, Sundays are for church. For others, it's dim sum time. This spot offers one of the largest selections in town and proves the most consistent overall. People pack into the giant banquet space to settle in for the barrage of carts that wheel by brimming with a dozen different dumplings (shrimp-peanut, chive and pork stand out); fluffy buns (barbecue pork and pan-fried veggie-pork are awesome); and various fried and steamed morsels of hangover-absorbing snacks. Don't miss the taro puff, ribs, potstickers and sweet egg custard tarts. *4936 N Broadway between Ainslie and Argyle Sts (773-271-1161). El: Red to Argyle. Bus: 22, 36, 92, 151. Breakfast, lunch, dinner. Average main course: $7.*

Happy Chef When in Chinatown, it's often hard to distinguish between the good, the bad and the General Tsao's chicken. But if you're at this popular pick, you should do okay. Start with crispy shrimp dumplings (the menu says they're pan-fried, but they look dropped-in-a-vat to us) and follow them with the pork chop in a sweet, aromatic barbecue sauce and crispy shrimp coated in a salty, spicy mix that stars the revered Szechuan peppercorn. *2164 S Archer*

Ave between Wentworth and Princeton Aves (312-808-3689). El: Red to Cermak/Chinatown. Bus: 18, 21, 62. Breakfast, lunch, dinner. Average main course: $9.

★ ◔ **BYOB Hon Kee** Those ducks hanging in the window? Yeah, you're going to want to order one—you'll want to experience the interplay of the crispy skin, the soft fat and the rich, gamey meat. You'll also want the spiced, hot shrimp encased in an addictively crisp and salty coating; the sweet roasted pork with scrambled egg over rice; and the fresh dumplings, so thin you can see the pink shrimp and cabbage hiding within. *1064 W Argyle St between Kenmore and Winthrop Aves (773-878-6650). El: Red to Argyle. Bus: 36, 81, 151. Lunch, dinner (closed Tue). Average main course: $6.*

◔ **Joy Yee's Noodles** See Pan Asian for review.

★ ◔ **Katy's Dumpling House** You city dwellers might ask, Why drive to the 'burbs for Chinese when we've got Chinatown? But we swear that you won't find noodles this fresh in the city. Start with the dumplings—ethereal pockets of noodle skin encasing scallion-flecked pork—and move on to a heaping bowl of beef noodle soup. In this Chinese version of pho, the ginger, garlic, chilies, pickles and unbeatable long, soft noodles make this house signature stand out. *665 N Cass Ave, Westmont (630-323-9393). Lunch, dinner (closed Wed). Average main course: $6.*

BYOB Lao Beijing Tony Hu of Lao Sze Chuan must be looking to become the mayor of Chinatown—he's opened this spot specializing in the food of Beijing as well as another just down the strip mall focusing on Shanghai cuisine (see Lao Shanghai). Here, a traditional three-course Peking duck meal is served, as well as dozens of types of dumplings. *2138 S Archer Ave, Chinatown Square (312-881-0168). El: Red to Cermak/Chinatown. Bus: 21, 62. Lunch, dinner. Average main course: $13.*

▽ ◔ **BYOB Lao Shanghai** Maybe our American palates just aren't set up to fall in love with Shanghai cuisine, the namesake food that anchors the menu at this small restaurant (Lao Sze Chuan's sibling). However, when a Shanghainese friend explored the menu, she declared these eats the real deal. For a tasting of classics, order the dry bean curd salad, the smoked fish, the cold shell-on shrimp in sweet soy, the authentically slimy stir-fried yellow eel, sautéed *gi cai* greens with bamboo and the weather-appropriate casserole of salted pork. *2163 S China Pl, Chinatown Square (312-808-0830). El: Red to Cermak/Chinatown. Bus: 18, 21, 62. Average main course: $10.*

★ ◔ ◖ **Lao Sze Chuan** This place is the best spot for Szechuan cuisine in town, evident by the nightly lines of heat-seekers out the door. It uses plenty of Szechuan pepper, dried chilies, garlic and ginger to create flavors that are incredibly addictive. Our favorites are Chengdu dumplings, crispy Chinese eggplant with ground pork, twice-cooked pork, *ma po tofu*, Szechuan prawns and "chef's special" dry chili chicken. Trust us or choose at random—you won't be disappointed. *2172 S Archer Ave between Wentworth and Princeton Aves (312-326-5040). El: Red to Cermak/Chinatown. Bus: 18, 21, 62. Lunch, dinner. Average main course: $10.*

◔ **Lee Wing Wah** Every table here is brimming with the pan-fried "salt and spice" shrimp, giant shell-on beauties with a thin layer of crispy crunch. (Ask for chile oil for dipping.) Go family-style and feed four with the shrimp, a heaping bowl of curry-laced Singapore noodles, a plate of garlicky Chinese spinach and a roasted duck with tangy hoisin sauce for dipping. Fresh-fruit smoothies make for the perfect ending. *2147 S China Square (312-808-1628). El: Red to Cermak/Chinatown. Bus: 18, 21, 62. Lunch, dinner. Average main course: $10.*

◔ **Mandarin Kitchen** At this Shanghai-style Chinese restaurant, the *xiao long bao*, or soup dumplings, is a magical creation of hot soup broth and pork or crab encased in dough. The restaurant also offers Beijing specialties like cumin-coated grilled lamb skewers, and the classic Chinese hot pot, which has been somewhat successful in luring diners seeking the wonders of the fonduelike, do-it-yourself meal. Whether it's the soup dumplings that tempt you—or the chewy homemade noodles in spicy sesame oil—you'll wonder how you've gone without for so long. *2143 S Archer Ave between Wentworth Ave and Cermak Rd (312-328-0228). El: Red to Cermak/Chinatown. Bus: 18, 21, 62 (24 hrs). Lunch, dinner. Average main course: $10.*

▽ ✳ ◖ **Opera** Yes, it's pricier than Chinatown, but this is Chinese food on steroids—food that goes hand in hand with owner Jerry Kleiner's trademark over-the-top decor. Mongolian beef with broccoli is a safe bet; while the sea scallops paired with a crispy pork belly and hoisin demi sauce is a nice play on surf-and-turf. Peking duck comes in three forms: The crispy-skinned breast gets moo shu pancakes, leg and thigh are roasted to juicy perfection and extra bits are stir-fried with shiitake, oyster sauce and chow fun noodles. *1301 S Wabash Ave at 13th St (312-461-0161). El: Green, Orange, Red to Roosevelt. Bus: 1, 3, X3, 4, X4, 12. Lunch (Mon–Fri), dinner. Average main course: $20.*

P.F. Chang's China Bistro Far more Michigan Avenue than Cermak Road, this double-decker restaurant lures hungry bag-toting shoppers and tourists with contemporary, simplified (some would say bastardized) versions of what one would find in Chinatown in a sleek, modern setting. A nod to the low-carb craze, the lettuce wraps, available with chicken and vegetarian fillings, are a popular item. Standards like wonton soup, lo mein and moo shu pork are also on offer. *530 N Wabash Ave at Grand Ave*

(312-828-9977). El: Red to Grand. Bus: 29, 36, 65. Lunch, dinner. Average main course: $12.

▽ ◔ ✳ **Papajin** See Pan Asian for review.

◔ **Phoenix Restaurant** Nine-to-fivers will have to skip work to avoid the crowds at this dim sum stalwart, but it's worth it to bypass the weekend frenzy. What's the fuss? Hangover cures in the form of fried or steamed dough stuffed with savory, sometimes spicy pork and more pork. The classic *bao* are proper pillowy buns and crêpes are characteristically silky wraps for shrimp, beef or greens—try the pan-fried version of both for a bit of crispness. Save room for interesting options like tender baby octopus with a vaguely curry flavor and crispy eggplant stuffed with steamed squid. *2131 S Archer Ave, suite 2, between Wentworth Ave and Cermak Rd (312-328-0848). El: Red to Cermak/Chinatown. Bus: 18, 21, 24, 62. Breakfast, lunch, dinner (dim-sum menu served until 3pm). Average main course: $12.*

◔ **Saint's Alp Teahouse** Hailing from Hong Kong (where there are 40 locations), Saint's Alp probably doesn't raise an eyebrow among anybody back in the homeland. Here in the States, however, this fast-food teahouse is a novelty. The teas here are great (we particularly liked the creamy and full-flavored sesame-milk variety), but the food lacks excitement. But at least there's a view. Sucking down a bowl of vermicelli noodles while taking in the sights of bustling Chinatown is this spot's strong suit. *2131 S Archer Ave between Wentworth Ave and Cermak Rd (312-842-1886). El: Red to Cermak/Chinatown. Bus: 18, 21, 62. Lunch, dinner. Average small plate: $3.50.*

★ ✳ **Shanghai Terrace** Normally we don't condone paying through the nose for Chinese food when Chinatown options abound, but this gorgeous fourth floor terrace, brimming with fresh flowers and offering a view of the historic Water Tower, is hard to beat. And the elevated takes on five-spiced duck, wok-fried kung pao chicken in a ginger sauce and wok-baked lobster mostly surpass expectations. *The Peninsula Chicago, 108 E Superior St between Michigan Ave and Rush St (312-573-6744). El: Red to Chicago. Bus: 3, X4, 10, 26, 29, 66, 143, 144, 145, 146, 147, 148, 151, 157. Lunch, dinner (closed Sun). Average main course: $20.*

▽ ✳ **B BYOB Shine** See Pan Asian for review.

BASKETS OF PLENTY Shui Wah lures loyalists with its dim sum and then some.

DUCK DUCK BREW Bring your own beer (a lambic if you can find one) to Sun Wah.

★ ◷ **Shui Wah** Check off your dim sum order on the provided paper and soon you'll be stuffed with all the classics, from Chiu Chow–style (meaning, hailing from Hong Kong and its surrounding region) dumplings to memorable salt-and-pepper squid. Come 3pm, the dim-sum menu is replaced by dinner offerings; best bets include clams in slightly spicy black-bean sauce, salty egg tofu with four types of 'shrooms, green beans with dried fish slivers and minced pork, and Japanese-ish eggplant with beef. *2162 S Archer Ave between Wentworth and Princeton Aves (312-225-8811). El: Red to Cermak/Chinatown. Bus: 18, 21, 62. Breakfast (dim sum 8am–3pm), lunch, dinner. Average main course: $9.*

◷ BYOB **Silver Seafood** Seafood's the name of the game at this modest Chinese staple, so start off right with crispy salt-and-pepper calamari dotted with crunchy onion and jalapeño bits, or opt for the land portion of the menu with crispy chicken—a half or whole bird with golden, crackly skin and fresh lemon and spiced salt to add simple zing. The huge menu spans from kung pao chicken and pineapple fried rice to shark-fin soup and stir-fried abalone with sea cucumbers. *4829 N Broadway between Lawrence Ave and Gunnison St (773-784-0668). El: Red to Lawrence. Bus: 22, 36, 81, 92, 148, 151. Lunch, dinner. Average main course: $10.*

★ ◷ **Spring World** If the gloopy, corn-starch-heavy dishes of traditional Cantonese restaurants around town aren't doing it for you, try this place. Try the hand-shredded chicken with spicy sesame vinaigrette dotted with peanuts, garlic, sesame seeds and scallion slivers or the crispy whole tilapia topped with tangy garlic-ginger-chili paste. Other favorites include spicy baby chicken with ginger, cold noodles in sesame-chili-vinegar sauce and crispy scallion cake, perfect for dipping in the chili sesame oil on the table. *2109-A S China Pl, Chinatown Square (312-326-9966). El: Red to Cermak/Chinatown. Bus: 18, 21, 62. Lunch, dinner. Average main course: $10.*

★ ◷ BYOB **Sun Wah Bar-B-Q Restaurant** This no-frills joint tempts passersby with lacquer-skinned roast ducks hanging by their necks in the steamed-up window. The menu is expansive but inexpensive: The Pei Par BBQ duck and the Hong-Kong-style barbecued pig are sublime in their simplicity, savory and slick with fat. Chinese broccoli arrives jade-green and crisp, and the beef chow fun comes out charred and tasting of the properly smoking wok. Even the egg rolls are notable, dotted with bits of roasted pork. Our advice? Order lots and eat the leftovers at home. *1132–34 W Argyle St between Broadway St and Winthrop Ave (773-769-1254). El: Red to Argyle. Bus: 22, 36, 81, 92, 151. Breakfast, lunch, dinner (closed Thu). Average main course: $6.*

★ ◷ ☾ BYOB **Three Happiness Restaurant** The first thing to know before heading for this Chinatown gem is that it's not the giant Three Happiness on the corner of Wentworth Avenue, and we stress this because the difference is monumental. Ignore the far-from-spotless decor (or lack thereof) and skip the so-so appetizers in favor of black pepper beef with rice noodles (ordered "crispy"), stir-fried Dungeness crab in chili-seafood XO sauce, crispy salt-and-pepper shrimp and Cantonese-style crispy-skin chicken. *209 W Cermak Rd between Wentworth and Archer Aves (312-842-1964). El: Red to Cermak/Chinatown. Bus: 18, 21, 62. Breakfast, lunch, dinner. Average main course: $8.*

Classic American

▼ ✳ **B Atwood Café** Chef Heather Terhune's food draws mobs of tourists and local ladies seeking nourishment after a particularly grueling shopping session at Macy's. For them, her seasonal menu of updated American classics is perfect—sophisticated and unintimidating. Case in point: a recent spring menu that offered thyme-and-mace–roasted duck breast with pea tendrils and crispy potato cakes; rock shrimp pappardelle with garlic cream, spring peas and basil pesto; and a warm strawberry-rhubarb and almond tart with vanilla-bean ice cream. *1 W Washington St at State St (312-368-1900). El: Blue, Red to Washington. Bus: 56, 60, 124, 157. Breakfast (Mon–Sat), brunch (Sun), lunch (Mon–Sat), dinner. Average main course: $23.*

▼ **Chalkboard** This upscale comfort-food spot boasts a soothing room, a fairly priced wine list and a handful of specialties from chef Gilbert Langlois. Ever-changing entrées are a bit hit-or-miss, but the fish and beef are typically highlights of the menu. Exciting seasonal dishes may include seared scallops with sugar-cured Kalamata olives, vanilla-bean "mayo," pumpkin oil, sage and roasted walnuts; and braised short ribs with celery-root puree, roasted chestnuts, pickled fennel and chocolate. *4343 N Lincoln Ave between Cullom and Montrose Aves (773-477-7144). El: Brown to Western. Bus: 11, 49, X49, 50, 78. Dinner (closed Tue). Average main course: $20.*

★ **Cordis Bros Supper Club** Dan and Mike Cordis set out to create a modern-day supper club, and quite frankly, they failed—their restaurant feels so authentically homey, old-school and nourishing that there are few modern things about it. But this is a good thing: It means you get a complimentary relish tray to start your meal (though the hummus on it would be the exception to the aforementioned authenticity); a buttery crab cocktail and a well-dressed Caesar salad as appetizers; and a hefty slice of lasagna, redolent of nutmeg, for an entrée. *1625 W Irving Park Rd at Marshfield Ave (773-935-1000). El: Brown to Irving Park. Bus: 9, X9, 80, X80. Dinner (closed Mon) Average main course: $20*

▼ ✳ **B Deleece** We can't blame you if you're still heading to Deleece every Sunday for brunch—the breakfast pasta (spaghetti with tomatoes, goat cheese and eggs), cheddar-and-Nueske-bacon frittata and cinnamon-orange French toast are hard to leave behind. But you also might consider staying for dinner: Chef Josh Hansen has added several delicious dishes to the menu, including a braised lamb flatbread, a sage-cured chicken with rosemary stuffing, and beer-braised short ribs with Irish cheddar gratin. And if you still have an appetite the next weekend, *then* you can go to brunch. *4004 N Southport Ave between Irving Park Rd and Cuyler Ave (773-325-1710). El: Brown to Irving Park; Red to Sheridan. Bus: 9, 22, 80, X80. Brunch (Sat, Sun), lunch (Tue–Fri), dinner. Average main course: $16.*

▼ ✳ **B Dine** This retro hotel restaurant promises to bring you back to the 1940s, which is a lot less sexy when you see meat loaf and wedges of iceberg lettuce on the menu. But all is not lost: A bit of modernity sneaks into the wonderfully juicy pork chop, and good roasted chicken. Desserts like red-velvet cake, strawberry shortcake and lemon meringue pie won't send you to the '40s, either, but they will give you flashbacks to childhood. *733 W Madison Ave at Halsted St (312-602-2100). Bus: 8, 20, 126. Breakfast, brunch (Sun), lunch, dinner. Average main course: $20.*

✳ **B Four Farthings** This family-owned neighborhood pub does beer, wine and food better than most in their category. The beer selection—around 15 on tap and 13 in bottles—is surpassed only by the wine list—100 are available by the bottle and 12 by the glass. Those looking to dine can take a seat on the patio in the warmer months and pick from a lengthy menu featuring Gorgonzola ravioli with Parmesan cream sauce, black olives and tomatoes; blackened flank steak and mushroom salad; and a small selection of poultry and chops. *2060 N Cleveland Ave at Lincoln Ave (773-935-2060). El: Brown, Purple (rush hrs) to Armitage. Bus: 11, 22, 36, 73. Brunch (Sun), lunch, dinner. Average main course: $20.*

B Gale Street Inn From the second you take your seat and a manager asks, "Howyadoin'?" in her thick Chicago accent, you know this place is about as classically Chicago as they come. And judging by how crowded it is, it may be one of the main culprits behind the city's obesity problem: Enormous entrées like tender baked ribs and juicy barbecue chicken come with bread, salad and big, hearty sides like the twice-baked, cheesy gratin potatoes. *Real* Chicagoans, however, should have no trouble cleaning their plates. *4914 N Milwaukee Ave*

TURN ON THE BRIGHT Chalkboard chef Gilbert Langlois creates food as colorful as the surroundings.

between Gale St and Higgins Ave (773-725-1300). El: Blue to Jefferson Park. Bus: 56, 56A, 81, 85, 85A. Brunch (Sun), lunch (Tue–Fri), dinner. Average main course: $22.

▼ **Geja's Café** This dimly lit fondue spot is a reliably romantic date destination. The four-course Prince Geja Combination, while pricey, allows couples a chance get cozy while experimenting with various dips. A salad starter is followed by the cheese fondue appetizer with bread, grapes and apples. Then, beef tenderloin, chicken breast, lobster tail, jumbo shrimp and sea scallops are brought out to be cooked in the tableside hot oil pot. Be sure to save room for the flaming chocolate fondue dessert. 340 W Armitage Ave between Orleans and Sedgwick Sts (773-281-9101). Bus: 11, 22, 36, 73, 151, 156. Dinner. Average fondue dinner: $50.

❋ ☾ **Hub 51** R.J. and Jerrod Melman, sons of Lettuce Entertain You Enterprises impresario Rich Melman, are behind this midscale River North catchall that offers a menu that ranges from open-faced BLTs to halibut tacos. The crowd is as varied as the eats—tourists, ladies who lunch and working stiffs rub elbows—and everyone seems content with the large portions and boisterous scene. Braised pork tacos with housemade tortillas are a surprise hit, and plump maki do the trick if sushi cravings hit. 51 W Hubbard St at Dearborn St (312-828-0051). El: Red to Grand. Bus: 22, 29, 36, 65. Lunch (Mon–Sat), dinner. Average main course: $20.

▼ B **Jack's on Halsted** Awash in underwater blue-green hues and pulsing with ambient techno (lest we forget we're in Boystown), this spot is a neighborhood draw for older gay couples and even older Lakeview lifers. While the solid menu offers few surprises, what Jack's does, it does well: a grilled calamari starter with spicy tomato-pesto that's as simple as it is delicious; and a four-inch-high ice-cream turtle pie that's a gut-busting ender. 3201 N Halsted St at Belmont Ave (773-244-9191). El: Red, Brown, Purple (rush hrs) to Belmont. Bus: 8, 22, 77. Brunch (Sun), dinner. Average main course: $19.

L. Woods Tap & Pine Lodge We were briefly fooled into thinking that this old-school-looking lodge truly was old-school. But once we got past the exterior and saw Niman Ranch ribs on the menu, it became obvious it was a Lettuce Entertain You spot. Still, it's gotten some parts of a Wisconsin lodge experience right (for one thing, bacon cheeseburgers are listed as "light dinners"). The tomato soup is creamy and sweet, and crusted whitefish is flaky and buttery. Stick around for dessert—the creamy ice cream and sundaes are some of the best outside of the Dairy State. 7110 N Lincoln Ave, Lincolnwood (847-677-3350). Bus: Pace 290. Lunch (Mon–Sat), dinner. Average main course: $20.

Lawry's the Prime Rib Old-school doesn't begin to describe this Chicago landmark. Though not the original (which opened in 1938 in Beverly Hills), the Lawry empire's second notch has stood its downtown ground since 1974. When we need a break from the fancy cheeses and foams, we head here for comforting nostalgia. Order the Lawry cut medium-rare, use the crispy Yorkshire pudding to sop up the mahogany gravy, go for the lobster tail add-on, finish with a dense, simply delicious slice of chocolate cake and savor every last minute in our favorite time warp. 100 E Ontario St at Rush St (312-787-5000). El: Red to Grand. Bus: 29, 65, 145, 146, 147,

151. Lunch (Mon–Sat), dinner. Average main course: $30.

♨ ☾ B **Mike Ditka's** Decades ago, Da Coach helped the Bears shuffle to a Super Bowl win, but currently the only bowls Iron Mike is associated with are the piping-hot "souper bowls" of corn chowder and crab bisque coming out of his restaurant's kitchen. Predictably, the memorabilia-rich decor and the menu reference Ditka's former sports glories: "Kickoffs" include fried calamari, chicken wings and crab cakes, and the half-pound Fridge Burger is appropriately, if gratuitously, large. Tremont Hotel, 100 E Chestnut St at Rush St (312-587-8989). El: Red to Chicago. Bus: 3, X4, 10, 26, 66, 125, 143, 144, 145, 146, 147, 151. Breakfast, brunch (Sun), lunch, dinner. Average main course: $20.

▼ ❋ ☾ B **Moreland** This Rogers Park restaurant/concert venue/bar could have creepy ventriloquists "entertaining" diners and a menu composed solely of Hot Pockets, and it would still bring in business—there aren't many restaurants in the immediate area. Yet it overachieves with favorites such as the Creole-spiced crab cakes and breaded and fried mac-and-cheese wedges with a chipotle-cumin dipping sauce—and nods to area hippies with the vegan Moroccan veggie tagine and vegan burger. 1218 W Morse Ave between Glenwood Ave and Sheridan Rd (773-764-8900). El: Red to Morse. Bus: 147. Brunch (Sun), dinner. Average main course: $17.

Park 52 Jerry Kleiner has brought midscale swank and classic American eats to Hyde Park's Harper Court, making for a nice night out for locals who desperately need more options. If spinach artichoke dip and iceberg wedge salad don't excite you, try chef Rachel Everett's juicy New York strip or pan-seared halibut flavored with a smoked tomato vinaigrette and a side of mashed potatoes with a sweet maple vanilla rum butter. Good thing the banquettes are comfy—after a meal like this, you'll need 'em. 5201 S Harper Ct at 52nd St (773-241-5200). Bus: 6, 15, 28, 55. Metra: Electric Main to 51st–53rd St. Lunch, dinner. Average main course: $23.

❋ **Park Grill** Overlooking the Millennium Park has its pros and cons: Watching flailing ice skaters or sun-worshipping tourists is transfixing, but with food this good, you want to focus on your meal. Seasonal offerings might include whisper-thin beef carpaccio sprinkled with Parmesan and juicy capers or jumbo lump crab cake with yellow-curry sauce. We can think of no better last meal than the Kobe burger: melted Gorgonzola topping thick-as-your fist beef between buttery brioche. Skip the defib—strap on some skates or stroll the park to get your heart pumping again. 11 N Michigan Ave at Madison St (312-521-7275). El: Brown, Green, Orange, Pink, Purple (rush hrs) to Madison; Red, Blue to Monroe. Bus: 3, 4, X4, 14, 26, 145, 147, 148, 151. Lunch, dinner. Average main course: $19.

★ B **Prairie Grass Café** If you ever ate Sarah Stegner's food during her much-lauded tenure as chef of the Dining Room at the Ritz-Carlton, you understand how happy we are that we don't have to sell a kidney to eat her cooking anymore. We'll even endure the drive to the 'burbs to dig into garlicky, vinegary skirt steak topped with sautéed 'shrooms; her housemade lamb sausage with sweet fennel and warm goat cheese; and her mom's (no kidding) seasonal pie selection. Incredible food we can

eat while wearing jeans—perfect. 601 Skokie Blvd, Northbrook (847-205-4433). Brunch (Sat, Sun), lunch (Mon–Fri), dinner. Average main course: $17.

❋ B **RL** A restaurant in a preppy clothing store on the corner of Michigan and Chicago Avenues; could anything be more precious? The short answer is no. But while you will undoubtedly be entertained watching fur-clad women whisking in and sitting down for two bites of a Waldorf salad, there are a few other things worth experiencing here. The Dover sole, for instance, is prepared tableside with so much pomp you'll think you're eating with the Queen of England. Us? We'll take one of the expertly shaken sidecars and the burger, which, surprisingly, is pretty damn good. 115 E Chicago Ave between Michigan Ave and Rush St (312-475-1100). El: Red to Chicago. Bus: 3, X4, 10, 26, 36, 66, 143, 144, 145, 146, 147, 151. Brunch (Sun), lunch, dinner. Average main course: $25.

★ ▼ ❋ B **Sola** It always feels like a warm, sunny day when we eat chef Carol Wallack's Hawaiian-influenced food. Dishes such as a pan-seared pork trio with a port and red curry jus, lemongrass-crusted mahi mahi with coconut-jasmine rice and ginger-glazed grilled salmon with edamame puree beg to be eaten outside on the restaurant's patio, but in winter, you'll do just as well by taking a few bites, closing your eyes and dreaming of brighter days. 3868 N Lincoln Ave at Byron St (773-327-3868). El: Brown to Irving Park. Bus: 11, 50, 80, X80. Brunch (Sat, Sun), lunch (Thu, Fri), dinner. Average main course: $25.

State & Lake Since you'll barely be able to see the menu in the pitch-black of the Wit Hotel's first-floor, all-day restaurant, let us make some recommendations. Small plates are the best bet—and, thanks to their uncharacteristically generous size, the best deal. Juicy, marinated tomatoes delicately offset breaded-and-fried slices of mozzarella; a trio of roasted bones—not your average hotel food—yields luscious marrow; and juicy shrimp glazed in Louisiana-style BBQ sauce deftly balance heat and sweet. Bigger plates and desserts can feel like placeholders, so those you'll have to order blindly. 201 N State St (312-239-9400). El: Brown, Green, Orange, Pink, Purple (rush hrs) to State. Breakfast, lunch, dinner. Average main course: $24.

★ ♨ B **TABLE fifty-two** Chef Art Smith (you know, Oprah's former chef?) is behind this spot, which may be small, but the menu is full of big-flavored, butter-laden Southern-inspired foods. Squash-onion casserole, three-cheese mac, chile-crusted pork chops with pickled peaches and buttermilk-fried chicken are some of the rib-sticking offerings. And much like O, Smith leads a feel-good operation—he often walks around the dining room checking on each and every guest. 52 W Elm St between Clark and Dearborn Sts (312-573-4000). El: Red to Clark/Division. Bus: 22, 36, 70. Brunch (Sun), lunch, dinner (closed Mon). Average main course: $25.

♨ **Tavern at the Park** Chef John Hogan of Keefer's Restaurant caters to the tourist clientele of Millennium Park with updated standards such as a barbecue-chicken sandwich (completed with a cherry-cola barbecue sauce), double-cut pork chops, chicken potpie, housemade shredded onion straws and shoestring fries served with white-truffle aioli. After dinner, play tourist yourself and walk it all off with a stroll around the park.

CURTAIN CALL Theatrical decor combines with comforting cuisine at Park 52.

130 E Randolph St between Beaubien Ct and Stetson Ave (312-552-0070). El: Brown, Green, Orange, Pink, Purple (rush hrs) to Randolph. Lunch (Mon–Fri), dinner (closed Sun). Average main course: $20.

▽ ✳ ◖ Ⓑ **Tavern on Rush** Full of worn brown-leather couches and dark, polished wood, this room exudes an Ivy League kind of pomp. Yet when there's a football game on, it quickly becomes about as dignified as a locker room. Artichoke dip and pizzas appease the fans, but the real finds are old-school staples, such as juicy, mushroom-topped London broil. Those football fans may come in handy if you order the chocolate cake for dessert—you'll need at least a few of them to help you finish it. *1031 N Rush St at Bellevue Pl (312-664-9600). El: Red to Clark/Division. Bus: 22, 36, 66, 70. Breakfast, lunch, dinner. Average main course: $30.*

✳ **Twin Anchors** Nothing's changed much in the 77 years since this Old Town rib institution first started packing in the crowds, and that's okay with us. Once in a while, we'll still cram our way into the old tavern to wait among the masses for the falling-off-the-bone, baked-then-grilled baby backs with a side of the "zesty" (really tangy) sauce. Add a side of the pork-flecked baked beans and an Old Style, and it's a perfect Chicago meal. *1655 N Sedgwick St between Concord Pl and Eugenie St (312-266-1616). El: Brown, Purple (rush hrs) to Sedgwick. Bus: 72, 156. Lunch (Sat, Sun), dinner. Average main course: $20.*

✳ **Weber Grill** We're not going to pretend this place isn't tourist hell. But if you can deal with the waits and the T.G.I. Friday's vibe, you'll be rewarded with surprisingly delicious grill fare. Steak skewers—plated atop an enormous heap of addictive fried onions—are sweet and succulent. Golden "beer can chicken" get its intense flavor from loads of garlic and an herbal spice rub. And thick Black Angus burgers drip with juices. All of which prompts one question: Why are we letting tourists have this place? *539 N State St at Grand Ave (312-467-9696). El: Red to Grand. Bus: 22, 36, 65. Breakfast, lunch, dinner. Average main course: $19.*

★ ✳ **West Town Tavern** We wish every neighborhood had a cozy spot like this—unfussy food, fun wines, and jeans and suits mingling sans attitude. Chef-owner Susan Goss and her husband, Drew, not only are pillars in the local food community, but they also keep us coming back weekly for different nightly specials, like the killer buttermilk biscuit–and–fried chicken platter. Other nights, the staple menu—antipasto plate, skillet-roasted mussels and bourbon pecan pie—is supplemented by seasonal specials. *1329 W Chicago Ave at Throop St (312-666-6175). El: Blue to Chicago. Bus: 9, 56, 66. Dinner (closed Sun). Average main course: $18.*

Wildfire The only thing that's wild about this place is how popular it is—even on a sleepy Tuesday, you'll need a reservation. Other than that, though, the menu will be familiar (think upscale T.G.I. Friday's). Steaks seem to be a favorite among regulars, but we found that the seafood fared better: Meaty swordfish "London Broil" is topped with juicy roasted tomatoes and sweet roasted red onion, and crab-crusted shrimp are the epitome of guilty pleasures. *159 W Erie St between LaSalle and Wells Sts (312-787-9000). El: Blue, Brown, Orange, Pink, Purple (rush hrs) to LaSalle. Bus: 1, 7, 22, 24, X28, 125, 151. Dinner. Average main course: $20.*

SEARED SUCKERS Plump scallops and a nice glass of wine await theWit Hotel guests at State & Lake.

Looking for sustenance in the wee hours? "The Slinger" at Diner Grill (p.29) only makes sense at 4am, when breakfast, lunch and dinner are rolled into one via two cheeseburgers on hashbrowns topped with over-easy eggs and doused with chili. Nookies Tree (p.35) follows suit with its "Hangover Helper," a chili-coated mess of hashbrowns and poached eggs. Dessert after midnight? Take a cue from the cops and grab doughnuts from Huck Finn (p.33). More health conscious? Pick Me Up Café (p.37) is open 24 hours on weekends, with a Haight-Ashbury vibe and vegetarian options galore.

⊙ Al's Italian Beef

Unwrap your Italian beef sandwich (you ordered peppers on it, right?) and spread out the paper like a tablecloth. Grab your sandwich with both hands and hold it in front of you, keeping your elbows on the table. To take a bite, lean toward the sandwich; do *not*, under any circumstances, move the sandwich toward you. Doing so will only lead to juices spilled onto your clothes—and if you're simultaneously working on a messy side of cheese fries (which you should be), you don't need the added risk. *169 W Ontario St between Wells St and LaSalle Blvd (312-943-3222). El: Brown, Purple (rush hrs) to Chicago; Red to Grand. Bus: 22, 125, 156. Lunch, dinner. Average main course: $5.*

⊙ Aloha Eats

There's enough starch and Spam in this casual little Hawaiian café to keep you set through a weeklong power outage, but don't wait for one to dive into the Big Island classics. Best bets include the curry-chicken *katsu* (crispy, *panko*-breaded, boneless chicken with subtly spicy curry gravy) and the kalua pork (perfectly tender pulled pork tossed with stewed cabbage). The "seafood-BBQ" platter comes with crunchy fish and shrimp, plus sweet, sticky, grilled short ribs; chicken; or beef. *2534 N Clark St between Deming and St. James Pl (773-935-6828). El: Brown, Purple (rush hrs), Red to Fullerton. Bus: 11, 22, 36. Lunch, dinner. Average main course: $7.*

Bananas Foster

John Winslow (formerly general manager at Blue Plate Catering) is behind this all-day café, which serves a little bit of everything, including egg sandwiches for breakfast, panini for lunch and an eclectic lineup of dishes ranging from gnocchi to bouillabaisse for dinner. Lines snake out the door and onto the sidewalk during brunch hours, but we think the real treasures here are the dinner dishes, like the crispy fish-and-chips and the hearty shepherd's pie—not the least bit because many of them hover around $10. *1147 W Granville Ave at Broadway (773-262-9855). El: Red to Granville. Bus: 36, 151. Breakfast, lunch, dinner. Average main course: $10.*

⊙ Billy Goat Tavern

The stories are true—this subterranean tavern is still the best spot to get a made to order "cheezborger" with a side of shtick. Sam Sianis, nephew of Billy Sianis, the Greek immigrant who founded the legendary haunt in 1934, still hollers out orders from behind the U-shaped counter. Avoid weekends unless the atmosphere you're in search of includes fannypacks and camera flashes. Weekday lunch still offers a glimpse of hungry reporters, cops and downtown characters bellied up to bar in true Mike Royko fashion. Just remember: no fries, cheeps; no Pepsi, Coke. *430 N Lower Michigan Ave at Kinzie St (312-222-1525). El: Red to*

Grand. *Bus: 3, 145, 146, 147, 151, 157. Lunch, dinner. Average main course: $6.*

▼ ✴ BYOB Birchwood Kitchen

The Pastoral vets behind this cozy BYOB know the secret to making a great sandwich: sourcing. That's why they let a brunch plate of smoked salmon take its cues from creamy Zingerman's goat cheese, and why Mint Creek Farms lamb gets sliced onto a baguette then dipped in a sweet jus. Start tacking on tempting sides like a salad of delicate green lentils mingling with crunchy bacon, and the tab adds up a little too quickly ($8.50 for a small slice of quiche gave us sticker shock). Not that it keeps us at bay, or even from picking up breakfast for the next day: buttery scones and granola bars from Evanston's Sugar & Spice are worth the dough. *2211 W North Ave between Leavitt St and Bell Ave (773-276-2100). El: Blue to Damen, Bus: 49, 50, 72. Mon–Fri 10:30am–8pm; Sat–Sun 9am–5pm. Average sandwich: $8.*

▼ ⊙ B BYOB Bite

Could the sibling restaurant to the Empty Bottle turn out good food? Surprisingly, yes, but with caveats. We've been underwhelmed by regular menu mainstays, but after repeated visits, we figured out that the specials board is where it's at. It changes frequently, but recurring hits include crunchy fried chicken and adobo chicken cooked in coconut milk, plated with fried spinach and sweet-potato fries. Season comes into play with rotating specials like chilled cucumber soup and watermelon lemonade. *1039 N Western Ave at Cortez St (773-395-2483). Bus: 49, X49, 70. Breakfast, brunch (Sat, Sun), lunch, dinner. Average main course: $9.*

★ ⊙ Bombacigno's J and C Inn

Since 1972 she (that'd be Claudette, the C in the name) has worked the register while he (J is for Joe) has churned out house specialties like Italian Beef Pizziola, a big, wet mess of an Italian beef with mozzarella and tomato sauce that's so flavorful it reminds us why this sandwich became famous in the first place. The signature cold pasta—angel hair tossed with romano, basil, garlic and olive oil—is a side we can't pass up. *558 W Van Buren St between Clinton and Jefferson Sts (312-663-4114). El: Blue to Clinton. Bus: 56, 125. Lunch (closed Sat, Sun). Average main course: $7.*

⊙ Bongo Room

First it opened as Room 12, but the wise owners behind this brunch-lunch spot decided to reopen as Bongo Room to remind people of their affiliation with the Wicker Park brunch icon. A diverse clientele of South Loop locals mingle over the same menu of lemon ricotta–and–toasted coconut blueberry pancakes and creamy rock shrimp–and–avocado breakfast burritos. Only they get to do it in a cheery, sunlight-filled room where a table can be scored within a comparatively quick ten to twenty minutes. *1152 S Wabash Ave between 11th St and Roosevelt Rd (312-291-0100). El: Red, Green, Orange to Roosevelt. Bus: 12, 29, 62. Breakfast, lunch. Average main course: $8.*

▼ ⊙ The Brown Sack

Locals cram in to this West Logan Square sandwich-and-shake shack and eat everything in sight. That means that not everything on the chalkboard menu will be in stock, but if you're lucky you'll snag a bowl of thick, housemade spicy corn chowder. Sandwiches (such as the Reuben, filled with thick slices of beef and mercifully light on Thousand Island dressing) and hand-dipped shakes are the stars of the show, but it wasn't until we tried the superb sweet-potato pie that we truly understood

what all the fuss was about. *3706 W Armitage Ave between Lawndale and Ridgeway Aves (773-661-0675). Bus: 53, 73, 82. Lunch, dinner (closed Mon). Average sandwich: $6.*

B BYOB Caffé Florian

After years of housing U. of C. students and their professors, the booths in this cavernous, brick-walled café are pretty worn. So are the menus, and the mugs, and the tables, etc. That's half the point of coming here—to sit ceremoniously, drink coffee and make your own mark on the place. The other half is for the deep-dish pizza or, during the weekends, the brunch: Spinach-and-feta–stuffed "Florian" omelettes and crisp waffles slathered in soft butter, both of which you'll be tempted to devour quickly, so drag out your stay with a slice of pie from the dessert case. *1450 E 57th St between Blackstone and Harper Aves (773-752-4100). Bus: 6, 15, 28, X28, 55, X55. Brunch (Sat, Sun), lunch (Mon–Fri), dinner. Average main course: $8.*

⊙ Charcoal Delights

For all of you without a grill, here's hope: The fare here is grilled over charcoal, and the results are akin to what you'd get on your patio. Actually, let us amend that: The dogs here have a crackly skin (we like the Chow dog, topped with a cheddar sauce) and the burgers, though thin, sport char marks and big piles of fresh toppings. So it doesn't taste like what *you'd* grill—it could very well taste better. *3139 W Foster Ave between Troy St and Kedzie Ave (773-583-0056). Bus: 82, 92, 93. Breakfast, lunch, dinner. Average main course: $5.*

⊙ Charmer's Cafe

Owner Dan Sullivan, whose great-grandfather built the space in 1915, recently merged his cafe with his adjacent sandwich haven Dagel & Beli. His infatuation with spoonerisms (the transposition of the initial consonants of two words) inspired this sandwich shop's moniker, and also led to some interesting names for its steamed bagel sandwiches, such as Fart Smella (roast beef and blue cheese on an onion bagel) and Royola Lubin (corned beef, sauerkraut and Swiss on a rye bagel). *1500 W Jarvis Ave at Fargo Aves (773-743-2233). El: Red to Jarvis. Bus: 22, 147, 151. Breakfast, lunch, dinner. Average sandwich: $6.*

★ ▼ ✴ B Chicago Diner

See Vegetarian for review.

⊙ Choo-Choo

When it opened in 1951, Choo-Choo was a pioneer of "fast food," serving its Choo-Choo burgers, Dairy Cars and Train Cupcakes via model train. The barely changed diner has gone on to become a local favorite for kids and adults alike, though it hasn't quite kept up with fellow Des Plaines burger joint McDonald's. Of course, with only one Choo-Choo and hordes of kiddies vying to eat a burger fresh off the gravy train, the management asks that you limit your visit to 30 minutes—they don't call it fast food for nothing. *600 Lee St at Miner St, Des Plaines (847-391-9815). Mon–Wed 10:30am–3pm; Thu, Fri 10:30am–8pm. Average main course: $10.*

⊙ Club 81 Too

If you're a small-town kid at heart, head far south to Hegewisch. This place is packed with local families on Wednesdays and Fridays for the house specialties: fried chicken and walleye pike. Aside from the simple, thin-crusted, greaseless chicken and the hefty portions of crispy fish, you'll get pickled beets, cottage cheese, fries, slaw and raw green onion—all for around ten bucks. "Down-home" doesn't do the scene justice; the brother-and-sister team that runs the place hands out Hot Wheels to kids who finish their meal. *13157 S Ave M between 131st and 132nd Sts (773-646-4292). Bus: 30, Pace 355, Pace 358, Pace 364. Lunch, dinner (Wed, Fri). Average main course: $11.*

◔ **Cobblestones Bar & Grill** For many Sox fans, this bare-bones, wood-paneled room is the best place to catch the game. A couple of beers and a few home runs are all these guys need to nourish them. You, on the other hand, need a muffaletta (an enormous sandwich stuffed with salami, cappicola and provolone, topped with a tapenade) or the "CB&G" sandwich, which piles on succulent roast beef soaking in its own juices. Hoping for something fancier? What are you, a Cubs fan? *514 W Pershing Rd between Normal and Parnell Aves (773-624-3630). Bus: 39, 44. Lunch (Mon–Fri), dinner (Tue–Fri), open on weekends during Sox games. Average main course: $8.50.*

★ ▼ ✳ **Coopers—A Neighborhood Eatery** Even though former Joffrey Ballet dancer Sam Franke took over this neighborhood joint a year ago, the goal of original owners Craig Fass and Mandy Franklin to have a pub with good grub and an ever-expanding beer list remains. Thankfully nobody told him that dishes like the rich and creamy duck confit mac-and-cheese, and the pulled pork panini topped with creamy coleslaw go way beyond the call of duty of normal pub grub. If we're lucky, nobody ever will. *1232 W Belmont Ave between Racine and Lakewood Aves (773-929-2667). El: Brown, Purple (rush hrs), Red to Belmont. Bus: 9, 11, 77. Dinner. Average main course: $11.*

★ ◔ **The Depot American Diner** Everything on the Depot's menu is simple and excellently seasoned: Golden breakfast potatoes get a sprinkling of paprika, big bowls of chili have enough bite to wake your taste buds up (but not burn them off) and the juicy pieces of turkey on the open-faced sandwich are covered in thick, peppery gravy—so much that you may have trouble finding the bread underneath it all. Housemade desserts tempt from behind the counter; sadly, they look better than they taste, so stick with coffee. *5840 W Roosevelt Rd between Mayfield and Monitor Aves (773-261-8422). El: Blue to Austin (Forest Park). Bus: 12, 91, Pace 305, Pace 315. Breakfast, lunch, dinner. Average main course: $8.*

◔ (**Diner Grill** There are no seats here—just stools. There's barely a menu, either. The burgers are thin little things; but stacked up two or three on a bun, they're exactly what you come to diners for: food that's hot, greasy, cheesy and cheap. Of course, you may be here for breakfast, in which case the bacon is extra-crispy and the pancakes are substantial enough to get you through the day. (But if, like most people here, you're eating them in the middle of the night, that's beside the point.) *1635 W Irving Park Rd at Paulina St (773-248-2030). El: Brown to Irving Park. Bus: 9, X9, 80, X80. Open 24 hours. Average main course: $6.*

Drew's Eatery Although Andrew Baker has made a commitment to serving only organics at this charming parkside café, he hasn't lost his appetite for junk food: The limited menu essentially consists of nitrate-free hot dogs (topped with the savory housemade chili, if that's your thing), plump spinach-and-feta chicken sausages and potato chips. Like the Trader's Point ice cream that goes into the sundaes and ice-cream sandwiches here, it's all

Morning glory

We sampled through the city's best breakfasts to find our favorites—with no brunch spots allowed.

BEST WAFFLES: The waffle at **Tweet** (p.38) is damn fine: hiding an airy, fluffy middle and tanned like an Alaskan in Hawaii. Crispy as all get out, the waffle at **Tempo** (*6 E Chestnut St, 312-943-4373*) needs nothing more than a slather of soft butter and a schmear of this Greek diner's housemade marmalade. But put these two in a cage match with the malted specimen at **Lou Mitchell's** (p.33) and they don't stand a chance.

BEST EGGS: If you're an omelette fan, try the textbook examples at **Southport Grocery** (p.19) or **Lula Cafe** (p.43), whose offerings change every other week or so but are always perfectly prepared. For that coveted over-medium egg, your best bets are **Orange** (p.35) and **Nookies Tree** (p.35), but because getting the perfect over-medium is reliant upon landing the right line cook, we can't guarantee that our experiences can be replicated every visit. And for nice, soft scrambled curds of egg, lightly salted and sans browned bits, our hat gets tipped to **Feed** (p.31).

BEST POTATOES: Forget hash browns—our love affair is with breakfast potatoes, a.k.a. home fries. Our favorites are **Army & Lou's** (p.115), where the crispy-edged hunks are specked with onion bits and seasoned perfectly with paprika, garlic powder and salt, and the brown-edged, soft-middled, fresh-red-pepper-and-onion-dotted breakfast potatoes at **m. henry** (p.34).

BEST PANCAKES: The thin, crêpelike Swedish pancakes at **Tre Kronor** (p.111) are so spongy and light, they practically dissolve in your mouth, while tart lingonberries provide the perfect foil for the slight sweetness. For the Heavenly Hots at **Ina's** (p.33), breakfast queen Ina Pinkney adds a ton of sour cream to the batter, making for a pancake so incredibly moist and flavorful you won't need syrup.

BEST SAUSAGE: We all know the best pork products come from the hotspot dinner destinations where they make their own bacon and sausage for their weekend brunch, but for the best value breakfast links, we found nice sage flavor and a blistered exterior with good snap at **Beverly Bakery** (p.16). For old-school pucks of perfectly crispy, red-pepper-flecked and slightly greasy (in a good way), it's tough to beat the patties at **Edna's** (p.116), sourced from Parker House Sausage Company in Bronzeville. Note to gluttons: They're even better tucked into Edna's famous biscuits and topped with cheesy scrambled eggs.

BEST BACON: While the cooks at **Sweet Maple Cafe** (*1339 W Taylor St, 312-243-8908*) won't release the recipe for their fantastic bacon, we're guessing there's a dry rub and some cast iron involved. You'll find similar kick in the Nueske black peppercorn bacon at **Uncommon Ground** (p.48). But for a sweet and salty combo that's impossible to beat, go for the cinnamon-glazed bacon at **Lucky Platter** (p.34).

BEST FRENCH TOAST: Milk & Honey (p.18) nails perfection with its classic French toast: It's crisp from a proper griddling, crunchy from toasted sliced almonds, and sweetened—but only slightly—with a dusting of powdered sugar. Likewise, the French toast at **Victory's Banner** (p.130) is crisply griddled, custardlike on the inside, satisfying, substantial and practically an advertisement for the versatility of a slice of bread.

satisfying and good—if not necessarily good for you. *2207 W Montrose Ave between Lincoln and Bell Aves (773-463-7397). El: Brown to Western. Bus: 11, 49, 78. Tue–Thu 11am–8pm; Fri–Sat 11am–9pm; Sun 11am–8pm. Average main course: $5.*

⊙ ✳ ◖ B Dunlay's on the Square
When Sunday morning finds you cranky and in desperate need of coffee (read: hungover), the wait for a table at nearby Lula can seem like cruel punishment. That's when this handy standby comes in. The grace and sophistication of Lula's food might be missing, but the thick and hearty oatmeal pancakes become surprisingly dreamy with a slathering of maple butter; the salmon (smoked in-house) is thick, meaty and smoky-sweet; and the Irish breakfast pairs delicious sausage with a pint of Guinness. The best part: There's no wait—at least not yet. *3137 W Logan Blvd at Milwaukee Ave (773-227-2400). El: Blue to Logan Square. Bus: 56, 74. Brunch (Sat, Sun), dinner. Average main course: $11.*

⊙ Ed Debevic's
The wise-cracking wait staff is as much a part of the gimmick as the memorabilia and music dating from the 1950s to 1970s at this Disney-esque diner, which is a particularly fun visit for families but not necessarily anyone else. The food's almost an afterthought, but you can't go wrong with classic burger, french fries and gravy, and kitschy-cool desserts like the world's smallest ice cream sundae (basically a shot glass–sized portion). *640 N Wells St between Erie and Ontario Sts (312-664-1707). El: Red to Grand. Bus: 22, 65, 156. Breakfast (Sat–Sun), lunch, dinner. Average main course: $9.*

⊙ Epic Burger
2009 Eat Out Awards, Readers' Choice: Best Loop Lunch By now you may have heard all about how this burger joint sports Slow Food principles (beef and chicken are all natural, hand-cut fries are cooked in trans fat–free vegetable oil), but is the food any good? Pretty good. Burgers are hand-formed to almost an inch thick and cooked to a nice pinky medium. Opt for aged cheddar, bacon and egg toppings, and be sure to add on the earthy, skin-on fries. Shakes are decent, but our favorite sipper is the Lemon Squeeze, a blend of fro-yo, strawberries and lemonade. *517 S State St between Congress Pkwy and Harrison St (312-913-1373). El: Red to Harrison. Bus: 2, 6, 10, 29, 32, 62, 146. Lunch, dinner. Average burger: $6.*

⊙ Evanston Chicken Shack
Regulars at this roadside dive know to call in their orders ahead of time so they don't have to drool for 20-plus minutes waiting for their fresh-from-the-fryer, juicy birds. You'll find a few tables next to the pop machines, but this is mostly a takeout joint that caters to a steady stream of NU students and fried-chicken fanatics who go bonkers for the slightly peppery, battered chicken dinners, complete with fries, cole slaw and bread for sopping the grease. *1925 N Ridge Ave, Evanston (847-328-9360). El: Purple to Central. Lunch, dinner (closed Sun). Average main course: $7.*

✳ B Fat Cat
Though the sign outside gets the '40s-ish feeling just right, keep your zoot suit at home: Inside, Rihanna is singing and martinis are made with pomegranate juice. Skip the appetizers and head for the braised pork belly Cuban sandwich, the rich meat mingling with vinegary pickles to great success. Or try the argyle burger topped with julienned carrots, red peppers, ginger, *sambal*, a chile pepper and salt mixture, and hoisin sauce so spicy and

complicated it's hard to stop eating. *4840 N Broadway at Gunnison St (773-506-3100). El: Red to Lawrence. Bus: 22, 36, 81, 151. Brunch (Sat, Sun), dinner. Average main course: $10.*

★ ⊙ Feed
There's a fine line between kitsch and authenticity, and this homely chicken shack sits right in the middle. Because despite the crowds of gay Moby-lookalikes, Starter-jacket-clad teenagers and yuppie moms sneaking in cigarettes after devouring whole birds, this place still looks and feels the way we imagine a rural Kentucky chicken shack does. And that's a good thing, since it means juicy rotisserie chickens flanked by tortillas, salsa, sides like sweet corn pudding, plus banana pudding and a rotating roster of freshly made fruit pies. *2803 W Chicago Ave at California Ave (773-489-4600). Bus: 52, 65, 66. Breakfast, lunch, dinner (closed Sun). Average main course: $7.*

★ ⊙ First Slice Pie Café
You might expect to walk into Lillstreet Art Center and be assaulted by paint fumes. But with First Slice Café inside, you'll instead inhale the aroma of fresh-baked pie (red wine and poached pear, and standbys like apple). First Slice donates part of its profits to help feed the hungry, and uses local ingredients so you won't feel like you're sacrificing anything. In fact, we'd return for the chicken–and–blue cheese sandwich no matter who was benefiting from our tab. *In the Lillstreet Art Center, 4401 N Ravenswood Ave at Montrose Ave (773-506-7380). Bus: 50, 78, 145. Lunch, dinner (closed Sun). Average main course: $6.*

⊙ ✳ ◖ Fish Keg
See Seafood for review.

⊙ Five Guys Burgers & Fries
The hand-formed burgers and fresh-cut fries at this wildly popular Virginia-based chain are good enough to counter the painful combo of office-bright lighting, stark white-and-red decor and kitschy sacks of potatoes scattered about. Burgers are juicy, double-patty affairs that can be ordered with all manner of gratis toppings (grilled 'shrooms and onions, A-1 sauce, even jalapeños). Perfectly crispy fries come piping hot in their own paper bag, regular or Cajun-style (just a sprinkling of Old Bay). *2140 N Clybourn Ave between Wayne and Southport Aves (773-327-5953). Bus: 9, X9, 74. Lunch, dinner. Average main course: $5.* ● *Other locations: 1115 Lake St, Oak Park (708-358-0856), 6500 N Sheridan Rd (773-262-9810), 2368 N Clark St (773-883-8930).*

▽ B Flo
Folk-art collectors Renee and Rodney Carswell's funky, casual dining room is an all-day draw for those looking for an interesting meal for a reasonable price. The brunch and breakfast menu standouts include New Mexico–influenced tongue-scorchers like green-chile enchiladas and *huevos rancheros*—perfect when balanced with fresh-fruit smoothies and strong coffee. At dinner, local and often organic produce appear as salads and sides for comforting classics like fish tacos, chorizo meat loaf and roasted chicken *mole*. *1434 W Chicago Ave between Greenview Ave and Bishop St (312-243-0477). El: Blue to Chicago. Bus: 9, X9, 66. Breakfast (Tue–Fri), brunch (Sat, Sun), lunch (Tue–Fri), dinner (Tue–Sat). Average main course: $13.*

▽ ⊙ B Flying Saucer
Don't be fooled by the 1950s greasy spoon atmosphere. That's just retro decor; this Humboldt Park diner focuses on local ingredients and healthy options. Hormone-free meat is the name of the game here,

so eat your breakfast sausage without guilt. And breakfast is served until 3pm, so you don't even have to get up early. Order up the sweet potato and tofu hash or the Flying Tofu Bowl. The menu can change depending on what's in season, but there are always a number of solid standard egg dishes and Mexican-inspired options. *1123 N California Ave between Thomas St and Haddon Ave (773-342-9076). Bus: 49, X49, 52, 70. Breakfast, brunch (Sat, Sun), lunch. Average main course: $9.*

BYOB Gaudi Coffee and Grill
We could tell you about Veronica and Betty Romo, the two sweet sisters who make this simple BYOB café feel warm and welcoming. Or we could recommend something from the array of tapas—we'd go with juicy dates wrapped in crispy bacon rather than the boring potatoes in marinara sauce. But we need all our energy to focus on the Gaudi Fest burger: a hunk of juicy, perfectly medium-rare, nicely seasoned ground beef, smothered in a housemade barbecue sauce, piled with thick cuts of bacon, charred onions and a mound of shredded cheddar. Because, really, that's all you need to know about. *624 N Ashland Ave between Ontario and Erie Sts (312-733-9528). El: Green, Pink to Ashland. Bus: 9, X9, 65. Breakfast, lunch, dinner. Average main course: $9.*

⊙ Gene & Jude's Red Hot Stand
Do not ask for ketchup when you order one of the legendary slender, snappy hot dogs that come topped with a fistful of fries at this SRO institution that's been serving 'em up since 1951. The surly types behind the counter don't go for sissy stuff like that. Claim your place at the end of the perpetually long line and entertain yourself by watching potatoes being cut and fried into perfect greasy strips while you wait. Once it's your turn, order your dog with everything, then count your blessings for the wax paper–wrapped bliss that lies before you. *2720 N River Rd, River Grove (708-452-7634). Lunch, dinner. Single dog and fries: $1.80.*

▽ ⊙ B Glonn'o Diner
More than 30 varieties of cereal with free second and third helpings. Blackboard fresh-catch tilapia specials. Huge salads (no iceberg lettuce here). Red Hot pancakes. (Yep, that's pancakes with Red Hots cinnamon candies baked inside.) Any place with that varied a menu is going to have some hits and misses. Needing a steak knife to eat our stuffed bell pepper makes that dish a miss. But the salads, grilled sandwiches and enormous omelettes are all made with fresh veggies, and there's no greasy-spoon feel. Plus, there's never anything wrong with a big bowl of Cocoa Puffs. *1820 W Montrose Ave at Honore St (773-506-1720). Bus: 50, 78, 145. Breakfast, brunch, lunch, dinner. Average main course: $8.*

◖ Goose Island Brew Pub
If everything on John Manion's new menu at Goose Island were as good as his pork sliders, Hopleaf would go out of business, Kuma's might, too. And note to fish-taco purveyors in the city: The tortillas piled with perfectly crisp tilapia, cool cabbage and a spicy chipotle mayo pose a threat. Not everything is perfect (mussels and crostini are average), but with offerings like the "Ham Burger," a beef patty slathered with pork rillettes, topped with country ham and finished with a fried egg, Goose Island may soon become a dining destination with a good beer list instead of a drinking destination that serves food. *1800 N Clybourn Ave at Willow St (312-915-0071). El: Brown, Purple (rush hrs) to Armitage. Bus: 8, 72, 73. Lunch, dinner. Average main course: $10.* ● *Other location: 3535 N Clark St (773-832-9040).*

FEED STORE The country-kitsch look works for Feed, Humboldt's best bet for bird.

⊙ **Grandaddy's Subs** Mistletoe hangs over the counter year-round, but the only encouragement you'll need to kiss the cooks at this brick and timber sub shop is a bite of their sandwiches. Though provolone takes the place of traditional Cheez Whiz, the peppery, paper-thin beef mixed with grilled onion and ribbons of green pepper makes this version one of the best local examples of the venerable regional classic. Lean corned beef or roast turkey BLT piled high on rye are great no-fuss lunch treats for smaller appetites. *2343 W Taylor St between Claremont and Western Ave (312-243-4200). Bus: 12, 38, 49. Lunch. Average main course: $6.*

⊙ ✳ **Grant's Wonderburger Grill** If you've been looking for oil paintings of Chicago athletes, this one-stop diner is the place for you. The diner was established in 1954, and everything here—from the clothes-pinned order slips above the grill to the Hamilton Beach milkshake machines—is a throwback. Malts are wet cement–thick, and freshly ground beef patties are topped with sweet caramelized onions on pillowy white buns and arrive with a nest of crispy "curly-q" fries. *11045 S Kedzie Ave between 110th and 111th Sts (773-238-7200). Bus: 52A, 112. Lunch, dinner (closed Sun). Average main course: $4.*

⊙ ✳ **Hackney's on Harms** Want to escape to a simpler life this weekend? Head to this 60-something-year-old hideaway. Before it was a restaurant, it was a family's farmhouse with a porch where friends would stop in for cold beer and corned-beef sandwiches. Pan-fried burgers on house-baked black rye came along

soon after (as did a full-fledged business), and are still the spot's signature. Friday night's lake perch fish fry is also a hit. A couple of crispy filets slathered in tartar sauce and a tall glass of *weiss* beer on the tree-shaded porch and we're happy. *1241 Harms Rd, Glenview (847-724-5577). Lunch, dinner. Average main course: $9.*

▼ ✳ ☾ B **Halsted's Bar & Grill** The owners of X/O have left their creative small plates and inventive wine list behind and replaced it all with a more generic concept: Standard American food in a casual atmosphere. A few of the fried foods—the jalapeño poppers especially—are nice accompaniments to a cold beer, and the chicken sandwiches are perfectly solid (but, being chicken sandwiches, not much more). Those who really miss X/O may still be able to find some comfort here come summer, however: Sitting in the back patio on a warm night is lovely enough to take your mind off anything. *3441 N Halsted St between Newport and Cornelia Aves (773-348-9696). El: Red to Addison. Bus: 8. Dinner (closed Tue). Average main course: $9.*

⊙ ☾ **Hamburger Mary's** Could anything be more fabulous than a gay hamburger chain? Not if you're into fried food and burgers so over-the-top that they border on obnoxious. Sandwiches here are less about the meat and more about the toppings: "Buffy (the Hamburger Slayer)" packs in big flavors of red wine and aioli; the "Barbra-Q Bacon Cheeseburger" has so much on it (onion rings, barbecue sauce, bacon) it can hardly be held. If big burgers aren't your thing, head straight for the fried Twinkies; they're universally appealing, no matter what team you

bat for. *5400 N Clark St at Balmoral Ave (773-784-6969). El: Red to Berwyn. Bus: 22, 50, 92. Lunch, dinner. Average main course: $10.*

▼ ✳ B **Harmony Grill** If you're into comfort food, huge portions and supporting local farmers, this casual folk art–filled dining room is for you. Seasonal specials sure to please meat-eaters might include a grilled grass-fed sirloin with wild mushroom-leek ragout. But vegetarians get plenty of love, too, with dishes like chipotle hummus, smoked tofu-veggie chili, and killer mac and cheese. Brunch favorites include kid-friendly peanut butter and jelly pancakes. If you're finishing up with a show at the adjacent Schubas, prepare to hear the music from a food coma. *3159 N Southport Ave at Belmont Ave (773-525-2508). El: Brown to Southport. Bus: 9 (24 hrs), X9 11, 77. Brunch, lunch, dinner. Average main course: $12.*

★ ⊙ **Harold's Chicken Shack #24** For years, outposts of this empire have multiplied like rabbits, making it tough to go five blocks without bumping into another shack turning out the best fried chicken around. Why highlight this one? We believe it's the best. Order the four- or six-wing plate, ask for it "fried hard" (extra crispy) with pepper (lemon-pepper if you want zing) and get both mild and hot sauce on the side for dipping. (It's a few cents more for sauce on the side, but do it unless you want your chicken drenched.) *407 E 75th St between Vernon Ave and King Dr (773-488-9533). El: Red to 79th. Bus: 75. Lunch, dinner. Average main course: $5. ● Other locations include 1361 N Milwaukee Ave (773-252-2424).*

Hashbrowns The smooth service and easy-going atmosphere here are thanks to the Italian family who runs the joint. The Ruffolos have extended the most important meal of the day to cater to late-risers, serving their hangover-helpers until 3pm. Whether it's dressed-up omelettes or straight-up bacon and eggs, all breakfasts come with the namesake hash browns. But our vote goes to the "killer" hash browns, a massive attack of potatoes topped with cheese, onions, sour cream and cornflakes that's baked to bubbly perfection. *731 W Maxwell St between Union Ave and Halsted St (312-226-8000). El: Blue to UIC/Halsted. Bus: 8, 12, 168. Breakfast, lunch. Average main course: $6.*

Heartland Café Heartland is as much a playground for twenty- and thirtysomethings as it is a restaurant. Local music acts ranging from folk to rockabilly to jazz flock to its stage as frequently as the local art on the walls changes. Top billing, however, belongs to the menu. To the delight of vegans, vegetarians and the cholesterol conscious, organic whole wheat breads, salad plates, seitan dishes and black bean burgers are offered, but red meat–seekers won't be disappointed when the turkey alternatives to bacon and ham arrive plated next to their generously sized omelettes. *7000 N Glenwood Ave at Lunt Ave (773-465-8005). El: Red to Morse. Bus: 22, 147, 96, 155. Breakfast, lunch, dinner. Average main course: $12.*

Hop Haus If you can stomach the bro-tastic Houlihan's-esque décor (stained-glass lamps over booths, flat-screens at every turn, and sports-related photos that range from Anna Kournikova eating a banana to a female Packers fan donning a cheese bra), your next bite will reward you with capable pub grub. Wings and pizza are passable, but burgers and beer are the real draw. The beer list is lengthy and varied, and burgers arrive well-seasoned, juicy, creatively topped and on hands-down delicious pretzel buns. A trio of mini ostrich, boar and lamb burgers is both interesting and well executed—it's likely to be favored by adventurous drunks eating up the joint's 4am closing time Wednesday through Saturday. *7545 N Clark St between Birchwood Ave and Howard St (773-262-3783). El: Purple (rush hrs), Red to Howard. Bus: 22, 147, 151. Brunch (Sat–Sun), lunch (Fri–Sun), dinner. Average main course: $10.*

★ ▼ **Hot Doug's** Doug Sohn's homage to encased meat is packed with suits, students and blue-collar lunch breakers. They'll stand together in longer-than-ever lines and put up with limited hours to get classic Chicago dogs and brats served with Doug's untouchable flair for flavor. There are veggie dogs for vegetarians, bagel dogs for kids, specialties like cranberry-and-cognac chicken sausage for high-brow hot-doggers and, of course, the famous fries cooked in duck fat (available only on Fridays and Saturdays). *3324 N California Ave between Henderson and Roscoe (773-279-9550). Bus: 52, 77, 152. Lunch (closed Sun). Average dog: $2.50.*

Huck Finn Restaurant This minichain (there are three scattered throughout the South Side) operates on the theory that there are three major food groups: ice cream, doughnuts and everything else. That means the savory food may be perfectly solid—tuna melts are stuffed so full they could feed three; burgers are charred on the outside and juicy within—but the real focus is what comes next. For most people, that means a doughnut topped with housemade ice cream. But for our money, a hot apple fritter does the job better. *3414 S Archer Ave at Damen Ave (773-247-5515). El: Orange to 35th/Archer. Bus: 35, 50, 62. 24 hours. Average main course: $10.*

Huey's Hotdogs It's hard not to like a mustard- and ketchup-hued hot dog joint with its own foosball table and a menu of artery cloggers named for the owner's family members. Try Kali's Killer chili cheese dog or Pokey's grilled Polish with all the trimmings and a free side of fries to boot. The menu also offers burgers, sandwiches, veggie dogs and some salads, but why bother? A dog and one of Huey's thick "rockstar" milkshakes are the best to load up on nitrates and saturated fat. *1507 W Balmoral Ave at Clark St (773-293-4800). El: Red to Berwyn. Bus: 22, 92, 147. Lunch, dinner. Average main course: $7.*

★ **Ina's** Judging from the long lines on the weekends, people seem willing to wait forever for the Scrapple (a crispy, slightly spicy polentalike dish flanked by eggs and chorizo) and Heavenly Hots (sour cream pancakes with fruit compote) on the breakfast menu. But that same comfort-food theme can be found at dinner as well, when Ina cooks her famous fried chicken (made with trans-fat–free soy oil that allegedly lowers cholesterol) and serves breakfast all day on the weekends. *1235 W Randolph St between Racine Ave and Elizabeth St (312-226-8227). El: Green, Pink to Ashland. Bus: 20. Breakfast, lunch (Mon–Sat), dinner (Tue–Sat). Average main course: $9.*

Jeri's Grill There is a bevy of 24-hour greasy-spoon diners in this city, but none of them offer anything as curious as Jeri's "jailhouse special," a plate of fried bologna, eggs, hash browns and toast. Kind of makes you wonder what Jeri was up to before the grill, doesn't it? Get there before 2pm for the biscuits and gravy; the rest of the cheap eats are served all day and include fries and patty melts. *4357 N Western Ave between Pensacola and Montrose Aves (773-604-8775). Bus: 49, X49, 78. Open 24 hours. Average main course: $6.*

Jerry's Sandwiches If this design-your-own-sandwich bar—with its selection of eight breads, 28 fillings and 25 sauces—doesn't make you slip into a coma of indecision, then, we're sorry, but you're probably one of the most boring people on Earth. A list of suggestions is on hand to help indecisive lunchers, but with 100 selections, all of them as tempting as the Diego R. (steak, avocado, cilantro, cheddar, chipotle chutney and adobo sauce), it doesn't really help. So when you're here, grab a menu to study from at home. *1045 W Madison St between Carpenter and Aberdeen Sts (312-563-1008). Bus: 8, 20. Lunch, dinner (Mon–Fri). Average main course: $9. ● Other location: 1938 W Division St (773-235-1006).*

▼ **Joey's Brickhouse** Dinners here start when your server hands you the Long Island iced tea list—15 ways to get really wasted, really fast. The menu is accordingly full of the kind of simple, filling food you want to eat when you're drunk. We liked the tomato soup with "grilled cheese croutons" (actually an entire sandwich), but we'll never forgive our server for suggesting the dreadful lemon-pepper chicken. The meatball casserole and s'mores were more successful: hearty, tasty dishes that only a snob wouldn't love. *1258 W Belmont Ave between Racine and Lakewood Aves (773-296-1300). El: Brown, Purple (rush hrs), Red to Belmont. Bus: 9, 11, 77. Brunch (Sat, Sun), dinner. Average main course: $15.*

▼ **John's Place Roscoe Village** The Roscoe Village spin-off of the wildly popular Lincoln Park original, John's Place

dishes up a similar polyglot mix of comfort-food basics: hummus and veggies, carne asada with chipotle mashed potatoes, chicken pot pie. If only it did it better. A Roscoe Burger was overcooked and topped with desiccated bacon jerky, while an entrée of teriyaki salmon was oddly bland under its sweet soy glaze. Still, desserts like a gooey toffee blondie and warm, solicitous servers go a long way. *2132 W Roscoe St at Hamilton Ave (773-244-6430). El: Brown to Addison. Bus: 49, X49, 152. Brunch (Sat, Sun), lunch (Tue–Sun), dinner (Tue–Sun). Average main course: $12. ● Other location: 1200 W Webster Ave (773-525-6670).*

Ken's Diner and Grill See Kosher for review.

Kitsch'n on Roscoe Packaging timeless diner fare in the kitsch of the seventies helps this candy-colored eatery draw large crowds. Rays of retro sunshine pour from the flower power interior. The menu playfully follows (leisure) suit with items like "Green Eggs and Ham" (spinach pesto, scallions, smoked ham, Texas toast and hashed browns) and "Not Your Mom's Meatloaf," served with rosemary-garlic mashed potatoes. *2005 W Roscoe St between Damen and Seeley Aves (773-248-7372). Bus: 11, 50, 77, 152. Breakfast (Mon–Sat), brunch (Sun), lunch, dinner (Tue–Sat). Average main course: $7. ● Other location: 600 W Chicago Ave (312-644-1500).*

Kroll's South Loop Cheeseheads reserve most of their enthusiasm for pigskins, but they can muster some excitement over curds once in a while, too. At this offshoot of a Green Bay staple, you can do both: Flat screens show football and other sports, and the kitchen puts out authentic Dairyland fare. Butter burgers—topped with ketchup, pickles, raw white onions and, of course, a buttered, grilled bun—are cutely wrapped up in butcher paper. Otherwise, thin-crusted pizzas and chewy, golden fried curds make good beer accompaniments. *1736 S Michigan Ave at 18th St (312-235-1400). Bus: 3, X3, 4, X4, 29, 62. Lunch, dinner. Average main course: $13.*

★ ▼ **Kuma's Corner** *2009 Eat Out Award, Readers' Choice: Best Burger* The servers here sport more ink than a Bic factory, and the metal is cranked up so loud you can't hear yourself talking, but therein lies the charm. Squeeze through the ass-to-elbows crowds and up to the long bar, where you might be in for a lengthy wait. What's the draw? Well, the Slayer burger, for one—a pile of fries topped with a half-pound burger, chili, cherry peppers, andouille, onions and Jack cheese, on a pretzel bun. That, and the extensive menu of highbrow brews (which most certainly does not include pedestrian beers like Bud or Miller). *2900 W Belmont Ave at Francisco Ave (773-604-8769). El: Blue to Belmont. Bus: 52, 77. Lunch, dinner. Average main course: $13.*

★ **Lou Mitchell's Restaurant** Thinking of spending your Sunday morning at this classic Chicago diner? Better check the weather: The line snakes out the door and onto Lou Mitchell Way well into the afternoon. Customers are treated to fresh, sugar-dusted doughnut holes (and, if you're a woman, Milk Duds) while they wait, but the real feast starts when you sit down. Stacks of "meltaway" pancakes are perfectly browned, omelettes come in hot skillets (try the sweet, rich apple-and-cheese variety) and juicy, gooey patty melts seem too big to finish. *565 W Jackson Blvd between*

I'M STUFFED Hannah's Bretzel fills their signature pretzel roll to the brim

$15 and under **Classic American**

The 'wich is back

Fast, easy, and cheap, sandwiches are the ultimate bargain eats. These are the best thing since sliced bread.

"Seasoning pork belly" banh mi @ Nhu Lan Bakery (p.131) Not only do owner Lee Tran and his crew bake their own crusty loaves of French-style bread, but they make each element of our favorite "seasoning pork belly" banh mi (No. 5), from the braised pork belly to the black pepper–spiked pâté. Jalapeño, cilantro and quick-pickled carrots, cucumber and daikon complete the package.

Will Special @ Riviera Italian Foods (p.80) The hot sopressata, spicy cappicola, fresh mozzarella and giardinera that get piled onto the torpedo roll at this Italian carryout deli are all housemade, and are joined by imported prosciutto di Parma and salami. We've never met Will in the flesh, but here's an official shout out.

Buttermilk Fried Chicken Club @ Lux Bar (p.34) We know, we know—we didn't think the rosemary-scented fried chicken at Lux Bar could get any better, either. But topped with tomato, lettuce and bacon and stuck between slices of white bread, when you get ahold of this sandwich there's no doubt that you're eating one of the greatest combinations known to man.

Serrano ham and Manchego cheese @ Hannah's Bretzel (233 N. Michigan Ave, 312-621 1111) Any day now this local minichain is going to start popping up all over the country. Until then, we'll continue noshing on its Spanish ham-and-cheese sandwich, crowned with crunchy fennel and slathered with spiced fig chutney, and bragging to all our out-of-town friends about how you can only get it here.

Cemita de Milanesa @ Taqueria Puebla (p.100) Our favorite of the pig plates at this father-and-son–run shrine to pork is this traditional Mexican sandwich, which dresses up a crispy, breaded, pounded-thin pork tenderloin with a schmear of smoky smashed chipotles in adobo sauce, fresh avocado, Oaxacan string cheese and *papalo*, a pungent cousin of cilantro.

Banana-nutella panino @ Ventrella's Caffé (p.19) You won't find this sweet treat listed on the menu board, but the panino's special-request status certainly doesn't hurt its popularity. With plenty of banana slices and creamy nutella, spread between two perfectly toasted slices of bread and then lightly dusted with powdered sugar, this creation deserves more than a special space on the menu, it should get a star on the sidewalk.

Pepito @ Irazú (p.93) It's easy to see Irazú's pepito sandwich as Costa Rica's answer to the Philly cheesesteak. The gooey mess—a combo of rib-eye steak, sautéed onions, Muenster cheese and pinto beans on a toasted loaf of French bread—hits all the right grease buttons, just like Philadelphia's famous export. So what does it have that the Philly doesn't? A side of cinnamon-rich horchata to wash it down.

Shawarma @ The Nile (p.104) Not all shawarma is the same—it just looks that way. As proof, head to this 63rd Street dive, have them pile the infinitely flavorful an incredibly juicy shawarma into a pita, and then tell us it tastes anything like the stuff you're used to.

Jefferson and Clinton Sts (312-939-3111). El: Blue to Clinton. Bus: 7, 60, 124, 125, 126, 156. Breakfast, lunch. Average main course: $9.

▽ **The Lucky Platter** There's always a wait for a table at the Lucky Platter. All three square meals are favorites with both locals and NU students, who crowd into the small booths and tables. Peruse the extensive collection of art on the walls while you wait, and once you're seated, try the veggie-potato hash at breakfast, the jambalaya at lunch and Tandoori chicken at dinner. The sides are fantastic: Mashed potatoes and gravy, sweet-potato fries and gratis corn bread are all equally tasty. *514 Main St, Evanston (847-869-4064). El: Purple to Main. Bus: 200, 201, 205. Breakfast, lunch, dinner. Average main course: $11.*

⊕ **Lumes Pancake House** Warning: most people leave Lumes so stuffed with pancakes that they're ready to take a nap. The basic buttermilk pancakes (which come with almost everything on the menu, including the veggie-packed, Nerf football–size omelettes) are fluffy, and blintzes are thin and filled with sweet cheese. But it's worth forgoing all that and waiting 30 minutes for the German-style "Dutch Baby," a bowl-shaped pancake with crisp edges and a warm, soft middle. Finishing it will definitely make you want to crawl back into bed. *11601 S Western Ave at 116th St (773-233-2323). Bus: 49A, 111, 119, Pace 349. Breakfast, lunch. Average main course: $7.*

⊕ **Lunch Rolls** Soup specials like a velvety Moroccan-spiced lentil are among a few reminders of this Loop lunch spot's former life as Spa Cafe. Most of the nine sandwiches are tasty (brisket and whitefish are smoked in-house, and delicious because of it), but with minimal veggie toppings, many wind up as little more than meat and bread. Banana-bread pudding is a memorable closer, but judging by the sparse crowds, nine-to-fivers aren't looking to follow lunch with a nap. *112 W Monroe St between Clark and LaSalle Sts (312-551-0000). El: Blue, Red to Monroe. Lunch (Mon–Fri). Average sandwich: $6.*

★ ⏾ ✳ ☾ **Lux Bar** When this Gibsons offshoot calls itself "Lux," it means it in an old-school way. Both the food and space seem to be imported from a simpler era, with dishes like luscious filet mignon "sliders" and impossibly crispy, impeccably juicy fried chicken presented without fanfare. Sometimes the straightforward approach can backfire (like with the bland turkey burger) but for the most part this spot's a gem. Especially for those who appreciate well-made cocktails and solid food. *18 E Bellevue Pl at Rush St (312-642-3400). El: Red to Clark/Division. Bus: 22, 36, 70. Breakfast, lunch, dinner. Average main course: $15.*

★ ▽ ⊕ ✳ **B BYOB m. henry** At this adorable, sunny, daytime-only café, health food is tasty enough to eat. The owners are committed to organics and offer meat-free options, but they're okay with a little cheese, butter and sugar every now and then. Case in point: thick, dense blueberry pancakes and a heaping breakfast sandwich of fried egg, gorgonzola, applewood-smoked bacon and fresh thyme. If that's too good and gooey for you health nuts, there's always the Vegan Epiphany, an organic tofu scramble that just may live up to its name. *5707 N Clark St between Hollywood and Edgewater Aves (773-561-1600). El: Red to Bryn Mawr. Bus: 22, 50, 84, 147. Breakfast, brunch (Sat, Sun), lunch (closed Mon). Average main course: $8.*

Mac's ✳ B If you tried to explain to the posthipsters at this Division Street staple that the menu is more carefully thought out than it is at most bars around town, you'd be greeted with little more than a puff of cigarette smoke in your face. Luckily, the kitchen musters more enthusiasm about their hearty, no-frills comfort food. Opt for a round of beers and a platter of cheesy, jalapeño-spiked nachos; an impressive slice of onion-studded meatloaf; and salty, hand-cut fries. *1801 W Division St at Wood St (773-782-4400). El: Blue to Division. Bus: 9, 50, 56, 70. Brunch (Sat, Sun), lunch (Mon–Fri), dinner. Average main course: $11.*

Man-Jo-Vin's ☺ Though you wouldn't know it from the shiny interior, this diner has been slinging burgers in Roscoe Village since 1953. After a renovation, its new incarnation actually feels more beach shack than diner—the doors prop open to create a breezy feel, and the limited seating means most people take their food to go. But the menu—cheeseburgers topped with sweet grilled onions, Chicago-style dogs (all-beef franks heavy on the celery salt) and a full lineup of shakes and sundaes—is diner all the way. *3224 N Damen Ave between Melrose St and Belmont Ave (773-935-0727). Bus: 50, 77. Lunch, dinner (Tue–Fri). Average main course: $6.*

★ Manny's Coffee Shop & Deli See Delis for review.

▼ ☺ The Meatloaf Bakery Like a sci-fi flick or fantasy novel, the Meatloaf Bakery requires a certain suspension of disbelief. In this alternate universe, pastry cases beckon with massive "cakes" of ground meats draped in delicately piped mashed-potato "frosting." "A Wing and a Prayer" cupcakes—juicy ground chicken oozing mild blue cheese—should qualify as a ritual, and no dinner party could be complete without a dozen bite-sized "Loafitos Del Fuego": olive-flecked pastry shells encasing chorizo. But the "Burger" loaf's greasy beef patty opens the bad-meatloaf-memory floodgates of American lore, and not even dainty puff pastry can convince us that salmon should meet its end in a fishy meatloaf. These hunks of meat are far superior hot, so prepare to spend 20 minutes waiting. *2464 N Clark St between Arlington and Deming Pls (773-698-6667). El: Brown, Purple (rush hrs), Red to Fullerton. Bus: 8, 11, 22, 36, 74. Tue–Sat 11am–8pm; Sun noon–5pm. Average main course: $9.*

☺ ✳ B BYOB Medici Bring a Sharpie and an appetite for burgers and pan pizza when you hit this University of Chicago hangout. Patrons have left poetry and political rants on the Med's booths since it opened in 1963. Among the surprisingly good takes on typical student fare are specialty burgers and shakes, as well as great late-night salads. Go for the simple but classic Ensalada Kimba—blue cheese, apples and pecans over crisp romaine. The restaurant also serves freshly baked pastries from its sister bakery next door. *1327 E 57th St between Kenwood and Kimbark Aves (773-667-7394). El: Red to 55th. Bus: 2, 6, 15, 28. Brunch (Sat, Sun), lunch, dinner. Average main course: $7.*

☺ Meli Mornings at Meli appear to be the epitome of a picture-perfect breakfast: Fresh juices are made to order; omelettes are fluffy and made from Phil's "cage free" eggs; "Meli toast," the signature French toast, is drizzled with honey; and (slightly thin) marmalades are made in-house. It's not revolutionary food, but it's

solid, and so long as you skip the disappointing soups and sandwiches served during lunch, you may just have yourself a new place to call second home. *301 S Halsted St at Jackson Blvd (312-454-0748). El: Blue to UIC/Halsted. Bus: 7, 8, 60, 126. Breakfast, lunch. Average main course: $8.*

☺ Metro Klub See Kosher for review.

★ ▼ ☺ ✳ B Milk & Honey See Bakeries/Cafés for review.

☺ Moon's Sandwich Shop If you're going down Western Avenue and happen to blink, you'll miss this lunchtime spot that resembles an abandoned shack. If you do muster up the courage to saunter through the front door, you'll feel like you've stepped into a Mississippi short-order grill. The assembly line of cooks whips up mile-high, shaved-to-order corned beef sandwiches, moist meatloaf between soft white bread (Tue, Thu, Sat, Sun only), and breakfast hangover cures like buttery flapjacks, bowls of grits and griddled ham with fried eggs. *16 S Western Ave between Madison and Monroe Sts (312-226-5094). El: Blue to Western (Forest Park). Bus: 20, 49, X49. Breakfast, lunch. Average main course: $7.*

☺ Mr. Beef You're here for one thing: the Italian beef sandwich. Get it as "wet" and "hot" as you can (that is, ask for extra gravy and an extra spoonful of the crunchy giardiniera). The thin strips of beef are tender and flavorful enough as it is, but the sandwich doesn't really sing until it's got a little kick of spice. Alternatively, you could order the combo, which seasons your beef sandwich with a crackly skinned Italian sausage. But come on—you couldn't possibly hate yourself that much, could you? *666 N Orleans St between Erie and Huron Sts (312-337-8500). El: Brown, Purple (rush hrs) to Chicago, Red to Chicago. Bus: 65, 66, 156. Lunch, dinner (closed Sun). Average main course: $6.*

☺ Murphy's Red Hots You can't walk a dozen blocks in this town without bumping into a Chicago-style hot dog, so what's so special about this one? We think it's owner Jim Murphy, who takes a lot of pride in greeting regulars and walking new customers through their orders—this man clearly loves his job. Polish sausages and Italian beef are on offer, but we keep it sweet and simple with a red hot, grilled and dragged through the garden, with a side of hand-cut, skin-on fries, dropped in bubbling oil only when you order them to ensure freshness. *1211 W Belmont Ave between Lakewood and Racine Aves (773-935-2882). El: Red, Brown, Purple (rush hrs) to Belmont. Bus: 22, 77. Lunch, dinner. Average main course: $4.*

☺ ▼ ⟨ Nookies Tree We'll admit it: We've never really considered trying the food here when we were sober enough to taste it. No. 3 in the local "chain" of diners has always been a 3am favorite of Boystown barhoppers, so we were pleasantly surprised to find that in the light of day, this place can cook. Fruit filled pancakes and French toast are hits, as are the frittatas (try the combo of bacon, mushroom, Gouda cheese and caramelized onions). It's a great way to start the day—or end the night. *3334 N Halsted St at Buckingham Pl (773-248-9888). El: Brown, Purple (rush hrs), Red to Belmont. Bus: 8, 22, 77. Breakfast, brunch, lunch, dinner (24 hrs Fri, Sat). Average main course: $7.*

☺ B BYOB Orange This sunny, popular brunch spot earned its rep with "frushi" (fruit and coconut milk–laced rice) and pancake flights. Brunch is still served daily until 3pm, pastries are baked on-site and the signature juice machines are in place at the bar. Sweet fiends should fall in love with the coconut-infused French toast kebab, while those looking for a savory day-starter could opt for "omelet #6," fluffy eggs stuffed with garlicky asparagus and mushrooms topped with toasted almonds and a drizzle of balsamic. *3231 N Clark St between Belmont Ave and School St (773-549-4400). El: Brown, Purple (rush hrs), Red to Belmont. Bus: 22. Breakfast, brunch, lunch. Average main course: $9. ● Other locations: 2011 W Roscoe St (773-248-0999); 75 W Harrison St (312-447-1000).*

☺ The Original Pancake House The subterranean outpost of this Portland, Oreg.–based chain (so much for it being "original") typically has less of a wait than its Gold Coast sibling. This is a good thing because watching people partake in that enormous apple pancake—a mountain of caramelized cinnamon apples—can be torture. It's foolish not to at least try the perfect buttermilk pancakes when you're here, even if you're more in the mood for the fluffy salami scramble; luckily almost everything comes with a short stack. *2020 N Lincoln Park West between Clark St and Dickens Ave (773-929-8130). Bus: 11, 22, 73, 151. Breakfast, lunch. Average main course: $7.*

☺ Paradise Pup If you don't mind waiting 15 minutes for what would otherwise be called "fast food," then a cheddar charburger served on a challah roll (or Bavarian rye at no extra charge) and three-layer fries smothered in Merkt's cheddar spread, sour cream and bacon bits is as close to heaven as you can get in Des Plaines. Resist gluttony and stay away from the double, as the meat-to-bun ratio equates with a wad of wet paper towels sandwiched between two dainty cotton balls, leaving you with a mess euphemistically called "burger salad." The chocolate malt is divine, and the patio seating is paradise on a summer afternoon. Interested? Get in line. *1724 S River Rd, Des Plaines (847-699-8590). Average main course: $5.*

☺ Patty Burger Started by CEO Gregg Majewski—a man who was instrumental in the Jimmy John's sandwich chain—this local burger shack hopes to bring its Black Angus burgers, soft brioche buns and thick chocolate-peanut-butter shakes to all corners of the country. Maybe that accounts for the streamlined menu—burgers, fries, shakes, and breakfast egg sandwiches are the only items on offer. But the things they are cooking they're cooking well: Burgers are thick and juicy, piled with fresh toppings and flanked by tasty (if McDonald's-ish) fries. *72 E Adams St between Wabash and Michigan Aves (312-987-0900). El: Brown, Green, Orange, Pink, Purple (rush hrs) to Adams. Breakfast (Mon–Fri), lunch (Mon–Sat), dinner (Mon–Fri) (closed Sun). Average main course: $4.*

☺ Pauline's The portions are as big as the personality of this breakfast-and-lunch institution that's packed with tchotchkes and mismatched chairs. Blueberry-studded pancakes the size of dinner plates are dense with fruit; and giant chunks of flaky salmon, white and green asparagus, and goat cheese stuff a five-egg omelette served with crispy potatoes. Of the sandwiches, the turkey Reuben stands out, thick with 1/3 pound of turkey, kraut and

gooey cheese, with double-battered fries and housemade soup on the side. The only thing scaled back here? The prices. *1754 W Balmoral Ave between Paulina and Ravenswood Aves (773-561-8573). El: Red to Berwyn. Bus: 22, 50, 92. Breakfast, lunch. Average main course: $7.*

▼ ☺ (**Pick Me Up Café** Open 24-hours on the weekends, Pick Me Up Café is a veggie organic alternative to late night grease, with vintage hodgepodge décor and a Haight-Ashbury vibe. Standout moo-free items include the falafel wrap, the vegan chili, macaroni and cheese and the tummy-warming French toast. *3408 N Clark St between Newport Ave and Roscoe Street (773-248-6613). El: Brown, Purple (rush hrs), Red to Belmont; Red to Addison. Bus: 22, 152. Breakfast, lunch, dinner. Average main course: $8.*

☺ **R.J. Grunts** The man behind TRU and Everest started his Lettuce Entertain You empire with this shabby joint? Opened in 1971—with, we're assuming, much of the same look it has today—this tightly packed hamburger shack is where to get the thick, juicy "Gruntburger," topped with addictive fried onions and blue-cheese dressing; sloppy buffalo wings; and spoonable milkshakes with thick whipped cream. *2056 N Lincoln Park West between Clark St and Dickens Ave (773-929-5363). El: Brown, Purple (rush hrs) to Armitage. Bus: 11, 22, 36, 73. Lunch, dinner. Average main course: $8.*

☺ **Ramova Grill** For a heaping helping of Bridgeport from days gone by, this Edward Hopper–esque joint offers reliable renditions of the BLT and freshly griddled hamburgers, all served with a steaming side of sleeves-up, workingman's reality. The chili recipe is allegedly a "family secret," but we suspect that family is the Hormel clan; slightly soupy bowls of red are quirkily priced at "$3.25 or $3.50 without beans." *3510 S Halsted St between 35th St and 35th Pl (773-847-9058). El: Red to Sox/35th. Bus: 8, 35. Breakfast, lunch, dinner. Average main course: $8.*

☺ ☀ (B **Silver Cloud Bar and Grill** Busy sipping on the ridiculous-but-tasty tropical-teaser cocktails and gazing at all the pretty passersby on Damen Avenue from one of the 20 sidewalk tables, it never dawned on us to try this joint's burgers. Good thing we did, because they're the best on the block. The half-pound of Black Angus beef is cooked perfectly medium-rare and served on a buttered and grilled bun, which is key. We're torn between the blue cheese and the brie with caramelized onions. *1700 N Damen Ave at Wabansia Ave (773-489-6212). El: Blue to Damen. Bus: 50, 56, 72. Brunch (Sat, Sun), lunch, dinner. Average main course: $10.*

☀ (**The Silver Palm** If you've been in a train's dining car recently, you know the menu ranges from Doritos to Ruffles and most of the clientele is passed out with cans of Bud Light at their feet. Thankfully, this dining car is nothing like that. The menu includes gems like light, crispy calamari and a club sandwich with sliced duck breast and prosciutto. Wrap up your visit with a caramelly apple pie or a perfectly made classic cocktail from the attached bar, Matchbox. *768 N Milwaukee Ave at Ogden Ave (312-666-9322). El: Blue to Chicago. Bus: 56, 66. Dinner (closed Mon). Average main course: $11.*

▼ ☺ (BYOB **Skewerz** One of the Moonshine owners partnered with a chef from Hawaii for this all-day kebab shop that offers quick sticks of Caribbean-tinged eats like lemongrass

GO WITH THE FLO Catching up over coffee is easier during Flo's mellow weekday breakfast than its packed weekend brunch.

tuna and passion-fruit salmon. Best bets are the artichoke app, yucca fries with banana ketchup, grilled shrimp and sweet potato fritters. Late-night hours enable the surrounding bar crowds, but the BYOB status makes it a good spot for lunch or dinner before the bar hopping begins. *1560 N Damen Ave at North and Milwaukee Aves (773-276-9805). El: Blue to Damen. Bus: 50, 56, 72. Lunch, dinner. Average main course: $9.*

▼ ☺ **Soupbox** You can take Emergen-C, pop Tylenol and swig DayQuil all you want, but you're never going to get over that cold without some chicken-noodle soup. Luckily, with three locations, you're likely to find Soupbox's freshly made soup somewhere nearby. This one also features made-to-order salads for everyday eating, but when you get sick, go for one of the 12 daily soups on offer. We like the delicious (but slightly thin) vegetarian chili and hearty Southwestern bean. *50 E Chicago Ave between Wabash Ave and Rush St (312-951-5900). El: Red to Chicago. Bus: 3, 4, X4, 10, 26, 66, 125, 143, 144, 145, 146, 147, 151. Lunch, dinner. Average bowl of soup: $5.50. ● Other locations: 500 W Madison St (312-993-1019); 2943 N Broadway (773-938-9800).*

☺ **Spicy Pickle** You heard it here first: This place is poised to become the next Chipotle. Just like the burrito chain, the sandwich shop hails from Denver and operates on a higher plane of the quick-service industry. The main draw is the list of condiments that can be piled on sandwiches: basil mayo, banana peppers and kalamata olives just for starters. The suggested combos—a turkey sandwich with chipotle mayo, corn relish and avocado; a thin pizza with artichokes, olives, feta and oregano—lean toward bold flavors. But with a build-your-own option, the possibilities are endless. *2312 N Lincoln Ave between Belden and Fullerton Aves (773-935-1398). El: Brown, Purple (rush hrs), Red to Fullerton. Bus: 8, 11, 74. Lunch, dinner. Average main course: $6.*

The Spread We know it doesn't look much different from every other sports bar. But trust us, if you venture to eat the Spread's food, you'll find better-than-pub-grub fare. The Bookee Sandwich, for instance, is an instant classic: kosher salami, caramelized onions and Merkt cheddar stuffed into a pretzel roll. Ditto for the Race Horse slider, topped with pepper jack, horseradish and fried onions. And if it's a salad you want, try the "Field," blue cheese tossed in a balsamic vinaigrette over spinach. (We said the

food was *good, not revolutionary.*) *2476 Lincoln Ave between Montana and Altgeld Sts (773-857-5074). El: Brown, Purple (rush hrs), Red to Fullerton. Bus: 8, 11, 74. Lunch (Sat, Sun), dinner. Average main course: $10.*

☺ BYOB **Stages** If we told you that Bridgeport's best diner was connected to a gas station, would you believe us? If you didn't, you'd miss out on housemade, chunky French onion soup; table-flamed saganaki with a hot golden crust; enormous Greek salads; and a juicy baked chicken doused with lemon and dried herbs that's worth the 45-minute wait to prepare it. Is the Friday fried fish special any good? Hardly—it's the one dish we could do without. But hey, it's this or a gas station hot dog. *657 W 31st St between Lowe and Union Aves (312-225-0396). El: Red to Sox/35th. Bus: 24, 35, 44. Breakfast, lunch, dinner. Average main course: $7.*

☺ B **Stanley's Kitchen & Tap** This Southern-style comfort food isn't the best in town, but it still has enough cream, grease and sugar to keep you happy. Especially when you're hanging out at a comfy bar with a beer and a basket full of corn bread, hush puppies and apple butter. You could also take a seat in the dining room and clog your arteries with the fat, drive-in burger and creamy chicken shortcake. Don't leave your liver out—there's a list of more than 70 domestic whiskeys. *1970 N Lincoln Ave at Armitage (312-642-0007). Bus: 11, 22, 36, 72, 73. Brunch (Sat, Sun), lunch, dinner. Average main course: $8. ● Other location: 324 S Racine Ave (312-433-0007).*

☺ ☀ **Sunrise Café** Seemingly untouched by neighborhood change, this cozy, attitude-free diner is all about breakfast. Ukrainian Village locals stumble in for fluffy omelettes with golden hash browns or the house special, Smokey Mountain eggs: an artery-busting plate of biscuits topped with sausage gravy, eggs and bacon. But it's not all hearty, starchy fare. The neighborhood's Mexican influences are reflected in plates of chorizo and eggs with a zippy green tomatillo salsa, as well as savory chilaquiles. *2012 W Chicago Ave between Damen and Hoyne Aves (773-276-8290). Bus: 49, 50, 66. Breakfast, lunch (closed Tue). Average main course: $7.*

★ ☺ **Superdawg Drive-In** Despite a renovation in 1999, this hot dog drive-in is still as old-fashioned as ever, with uniformed servers bringing your order directly to your car window. Apparently scared of copycats, the owners have trademarked almost every dish, the main draw being the "Superdawg," an all-beef frank so plump it's hard to remove it from its cartoon-covered box. *6363 N Milwaukee Ave at Devon Ave (773-763-0660). Bus: 56A, 91. Lunch, dinner. Average main course: $5.*

▼ ⊙ **Tiztal Café** A breakfast joint that focuses almost solely on omelettes, waffles and fruit might sound like a place with a limiting menu. But it turns out those fluffy omelettes are stuffed with all kinds of fillings, from a lively ranchero sauce to spicy chorizo. The fruit takes on three forms: a cocktail sprinkled with salt, chile powder and lemon; fresh juice; and satisfying smoothies. And the crisp waffles, while good enough on their own, can be topped with pecans and fruit. So good luck deciding among the three. *4631 N Clark St between Wilson and Leland Aves (773-271-4631). El: Red to Lawrence. Bus: 9, 22, 81. Breakfast, lunch. Average main course: $8.*

⊙ B **Toast** Brave enough to fight the crowds at this adorable brunch spot? Bring a snack. A hostess may give you a cup of coffee while you wait, but you won't be eating anything until you sit down. But as legions of fans have found, the cobb salad sandwiches (chicken, avocado and blue cheese on toasted challah), hearty buckwheat-blueberry pancakes and decadent French toasts (an "orgy" puts the chocolate, strawberry and mascarpone–stuffed varieties all on one plate) are well worth the wait. *2046 N Damen Ave at Dickens Ave (773-772-5600). El: Blue to Western. Bus: 49, 50, 73. Breakfast, brunch, lunch. Average main course: $9. ● Other location: 746 W Webster Ave (773-935-5600).*

⊙ ✳ ☾ **Toon's Bar & Grill** When we're in the mood for bar food, this laid-back neighborhood favorite is among the first spots to come to mind. The TV-packed room might hint at average pub grub but excellent eats and unique touches (housemade pineapple-infused vodka, for one) elevate the experience. Try the juicy burger (order it medium-rare, topped with cheddar and sub onion rings) and the Memphis combo, a duo of crunchy fried redfish and massive, meaty spare ribs with good smoke and tender meat. *3857 N Southport Ave between Grace and Byron Sts (773-935-1919). El: Brown to Irving Park. Bus: 9, 22, 80, X80. Lunch, dinner. Average main course: $8.*

Top Notch Beefburger The Beverly neighborhood has a relaxed small-town-in-1965 feel, and one of the contributing reasons is this dose of Americana, both old enough and friendly enough to be your grandmother. The namesake burger is old-school minimalist, served with the simplest toppings—grilled onions and ketchup-mustard-pickle on a feather-light bun. Just as good are the fresh-cut fries, cooked in beef tallow, and as long as you're dining out if it's 1965, finish up with a thick chocolate shake. *2116 W 95th St between Hamilton and Hoyne Sts (773-445-7218). Bus: 9, 49A, 95W, Pace 349, Pace 381. Breakfast, lunch and dinner (closed Sun). Average main course: $7.*

★ ▼ ✳ B **Tweet** Michelle Fire's theory for her restaurant is "good food for nice people." Her popular brunch is constantly evolving; standouts include "Bib im Bop," a play on *bibimbap*, the Korean casserole of rice, veggies and egg; organic corn *arepas* topped with organic eggs

and avocado; and biscuits and gravy made with Amish sausages from Michigan and Indiana. As dedicated to art as she is to organic ingredients, Fire features brunch dishes made from recipes from artists, whose work covers the walls. *5020 N Sheridan Rd between Carmen and Argyle Sts (773-728-5576). El: Red to Argyle. Bus: 81, 92, 151. Breakfast, brunch (Sat, Sun), lunch (closed Tue). Average main course: $15.*

★ ⊙ B **Twisted Spoke** When you begin brunch by showing your ID at the door, you know you're in the right place for a Bloody Mary. Spicy and sweet, garnished with salami and completed with a beer back, it's practically a meal in itself. Don't let that distract you from the food, however. Breakfast tacos are a good way to spice up your egg intake. And the Spoke's signature "fatboy" burgers are thick, juicy and perfectly tender. Take it down with a pile of those fantastic fries and you'll be living proof that you are what you eat. *501 N Ogden Ave at Grand Ave (312-666-1500). El: Blue to Grand. Bus: 8, 9, 65. Brunch (Sat, Sun), lunch, dinner. Average main course: $9.*

⊙ **Valois** Quick thinking is the key to success at this classic cafeteria: Once the line reaches the counter, you have only a few seconds to place your order, pick a side, order a drink and pay. For breakfast, we like the generous stack of French toast with a side of poached eggs. For lunch, it's the baked chicken, so sumptuous that the meat falls off the bone. There's always the question of whether to eat the sweet, cakey biscuits with your meal or save them for dessert; either way, make your choice the first time around. Otherwise, it's back to the line. *1518 E 53rd St between Lake Park and Harper Aves (773-667-0647). Bus: 6, 28, 55, X55, 171. Metra: Electric Main to 55th-56th-57th. Breakfast, lunch, dinner. Average main course: $7.*

⊙ **Walker Bros. Original Pancake House** Of the six locations of this homegrown pancake chain, this is the original. Settling on one kind of 'cake is tough, so go with a group and graze. The apple pancake is killer, with apple chunks, cinnamon and sugar baked together until the edges caramelize. Plump blueberries burst out of fluffy hotcakes that arrive with warm blueberry sauce alongside. Swedish-style pancakes have perfect lacy edges and a topping of lingonberries; couple them with smoky sausage patties for a perfect breakfast, and don't forget to down a glass of freshly squeezed OJ. *153 Green Bay Rd, Wilmette (847-251-6000). Bus: 201, Pace 213. Breakfast, lunch, dinner. Average main course: $8.*

▼ **Wally & Agador's Gourmet Café** This campy deli creates food that's just as over-the-top as the Broadway tunes it plays. The "Marilyn Monroe" sandwich boasts luscious slathers of duck pâté, chicken-liver mousse and Brie; the "Wham Sammich" pairs delectable lamb with goat cheese and eggplant; and the Valrhona chocolate soufflé is topped with a creamy housemade truffle—for no reason, really. Just because. It's lovely food, but at the end of the day it's akin to Garland's pouty "Over The Rainbow" shtick: best taken in small doses. *3310 N Halsted St between Aldine Ave and Buckingham Pl (773-325-9664). El: Red, Brown, Purple (rush hrs) to Belmont. Bus: 8, 22, 77. Sun, Tue–Thu 11am–8pm; Fri 11am–9pm; Sat 11am–10pm. Average sandwich: $9.*

⊙ **West Egg Café** Don't lose your appetite just looking at the long lines that plague breakfast joints—brisk service ensures

that the wait will never be too long, and full thermoses of coffee set on your table promise that you'll always have a full cup. Java is crucial when navigating this sunny café's lengthy menu: The pages are packed with options like sweet, plate-size pancakes, thin feta frittatas and classic diner sandwiches like BLTs (or BLTEs, which add an egg to the mix). *620 N Fairbanks Ct at Ontario St (312-280-8366). El: Red to Grand. Bus: 3, 10, 26, 66, 125, 143, 144, 145, 146, 147, 148, 151, 157. Breakfast, lunch. Average main course: $7.*

⊙ **Wiener and Still Champion** This Evanston stalwart has been going strong for more than 30 years on the reputation of its "dipping dog"—otherwise known as a corn dog. The secret is that the batter is only lightly sweet, and it actually tastes like corn instead of fake flavorings. But then, everything here is done the way it should be: Chicago dogs exhibit their proper snap, thin burgers are served on fresh, fluffy rolls; and the fries—well, we know this is a hot-dog joint, but the fries are so perfectly crisp that they steal the show. *802 Dempster St, Evanston (847-869-0100). El: Purple to Dempster. Bus: 201 Central/Sherman, 205. Lunch, dinner (Mon–Sat). Average main course: $5.*

▼ ⊙ ✳ ☾ **The Wieners Circle** The sassy hot-dog girls behind the counter at this classic roadside shack have had enough of drunk yuppies' crap. Enough so that they've developed their own brand of smack-talking that's now synonymous with a late-night dog run here. Get your Chicago red hot with the traditional fixings—mustard, onion, neon-green relish, pickle spear, tomato, celery salt and sport peppers—an order of thick-cut fries and a big, fat lemonade. If meat's not your thing, don't worry—they've got veggie burgers on hand, too. *2622 N Clark St between Wrightwood Ave and Drummond Pl (773-477-7444). El: Brown, Purple (rush hrs) to Diversey. Bus: 22, 36, 76. Lunch, dinner. Average hot dog: $2.50.*

⊙ **Wolfy's** In the pantheon of Chicago hot-dog stands, Wolfy's deserves a seat on the dais. The room is sparkling clean and the staff is sweet—think of it as the anti–Wieners Circle. Though it offers a lot more, take a cue from the iconic signage that features an impaled hot dog on a sparkling fork and stick to the sausages. The Vienna Beef chargrilled polish is near-perfect, but it's Wolfy's hot dog, one of the best in the city, that will make even the most jaded hot-dog eater smile. *2734 W Peterson Ave at Fairfield Ave (773-743-0207). Bus: 11, 84, 93. Lunch, dinner. Average main course: $3.50.*

⊙ BYOB **Yolk** No matter the schizophrenic nature of Chicago's ever-fluctuating weather, things will always remain bright and sunny in this blue-and-yellow, breakfast-and-lunch–only spot. Enormous omelettes like the California—stuffed with avocado, tomato and green onion—are good standbys, but don't discount the quirkier fare: "Bacon waffles" add bits of bacon to waffle batter for surprisingly tasty results. For lunch, the patty melt is a greasy, cheesy, delicious mess—exactly what it should be. Unfortunately, the same can't be said about the lackluster housemade pecan and cinnamon rolls. *1120 S Michigan Ave between 11th St and Roosevelt Rd (312-789-9655). El: Green, Orange, Red to Roosevelt. Bus: 1, 3, 4, 12. Breakfast, lunch. Average main course: $9. ● Other location: 747 N Wells 312-787-2277.*

Contemporary American

SMALL PLATES, BIG AMBITION
At the Bristol, shareable dishes like this crispy chicken thigh rotate often.

★ **Alinea** In 2008, *Gourmet* magazine anointed Alinea the No. 1 restaurant in the country. What's all the fuss? Chef/mastermind Grant Achatz serves food the likes of which you've never seen. Sit back and enjoy the show, a well-orchestrated ride that plays with textures, temperatures and notions of "normal" cuisine, while somehow remaining grounded in season, flavor and flawless execution. Past menu stunners have included squab with peppercorn custard, sorrel and strawberries and cocoa-coated watermelon with cubed Kobe beef. But you never know what dish will steal the show when you're in the audience. *1723 N Halsted St between North Ave and Willow St (312-867-0110). El: Red to North/Clybourn. Bus: 8, 72. Dinner (Wed–Sun). Average degustation: $145.*

▽ **Avenues** Replacing culinary wizard Graham Elliot Bowles is no small feat, which is why Avenues chose Curtis Duffy to do so. With stints at Alinea, Trio annd Charlie Trotter's under his belt, Duffy's progressive cuisine is both spontaneous and organic. The formal dining room glows golden with a view of the Mag Mile below—a perfect setting to splurge, sit back and let the sumptuous experience unfold. *Peninsula Hotel, 108 E Superior St between Rush St and Michigan Ave (312-573-6754). El: Red to Chicago. Bus: 3, X3, 4, X4, 10, 26, 125, 144, 145, 146, 147, 151. Dinner (Tue–Sat). Average degustation: $70.*

❲ **Between Boutique Café and Lounge** It's hard to keep up with the back-of-the-house changes at this sultry lounge: First, Chef Radhika "Rad" Desai took her *Top Chef* fame and hit the pavement. Then, after a brief and promising stint at the helm, her former sous

chef Noah Sandoval peaced out, too. Now "chef-consultant" Jose Victorio has introduced a menu of contemporary American food with Peruvian and Asian twists such as tilapia ceviche dotted with Andean corn kernels and ahi tuna–topped flatbread with wasabi aioli. *1324 N Milwaukee Ave between Paulina St and Hermitage Ave (773-292-0585). El: Blue to Division. Bus: 9, X9, 56, 72. Dinner. Average main course: $10.*

▽ **BIN 36** This swank institution in the House of Blues complex gives wine top billing. Choose from 50 wines by the glass to pair with a menu of rich American bistro-style dishes. Though the seasonal menu changes often, you can expect dishes such as peppercorn-crusted blue marlin; smoky beef short ribs; unbelievably fluffy hand-formed gnocchi; and sweet pickled blueberries with Bourbon whiskey waffles for dessert. The subtle flavors back the wine up like the Pharmacists back up Ted Leo, a band you might just catch onstage only steps away. *339 N Dearborn St between Kinzie St and Wacker Dr (312-755-9463). El: Red to Grand. Bus: 29, 36, 62. Breakfast, lunch, dinner. Average main course: $22.*

★ ▽ ✷ ❲ **B bin wine café** The focus at this cozy storefront by the folks behind BIN 36 is wine—36 are offered by the glass—and chef John Caputo's global cuisine. The dinner menu is full of delicious seasonal plates, such as winter's slow-roasted pork ribs with blood-orange barbecue sauce and summer's seared Montana ruby red trout with sweet corn salsa and a watercress salad. But it's the brunch that's really making us fat. With must-trys like chocolate-chip pancakes, housemade granola, and chicken hash, you'll probably be too full to eat dinner.

1559 N Milwaukee Ave between Honore St and North Ave (773-486-2233). El: Blue to Damen. Bus: 50, 56, 72. Brunch (Sat, Sun), dinner. Average small plate: $10.

★ ▽ ✷ **Blackbird** Paul Kahan's James Beard Award–winning, minimalist chic restaurant is as popular as ever, with chef Mike Sheerin (from NYC's WD-50) feeding the too-cool-for-school crowd and pastry chef Tim Dahl (formerly of Naha) indulging their sweet tooth. You'll find evidence of the duo's handiwork at this creative, contemporary stunner in dishes like crispy veal sweetbreads and cool Meyer-lemon mousse flanked by nibs of dehydrated olive, fennel and grapefruit bits. Lunch prix fixes for around twenty bucks make the experience easier on the wallet. *619 W Randolph St between Jefferson and Desplaines Sts (312-715-0708). El: Green, Pink to Clinton. Bus: 8, 56, 125. Lunch (Mon–Fri), dinner (Mon–Sat) (closed Sun). Average main course: $33.*

Bluprint Power lunch just isn't what it used to be: It's cheaper. Prices on this contemporary cuisine in the Merch Mart have come down with the market. Make a stylish Loop lunch out of a beet and blossom salad and a corned beef sandwich with avocado and salt-and-vinegar chips. Dinner is equally satisfying; the kitchen here knows its fish, and seasonal seafood offerings are bright ones. Look for dishes like grilled baby octopus with white beans, tangerine and olive oil and striped bass dressed with sunchokes, cipollini onions and salsa verde. *222 Merchandise Mart Plaza, suite 135 (312-410-9800). El: Brown, Purple (rush hrs) to Merchandise Mart. Bus: 65, 125, 156. Lunch, dinner (Mon–Fri). Average main course: $14.*

INSIDE TRACK
BLOODY GOOD

Ah, the Bloody Mary. This spicy trickster masquerades as a liquid vitamin, its salty perfection and hangover-curing abilities offering a reason to get up on Sunday mornings. But where to find the best? The version at Dunlays On Clark (p.41) brims with olives, soppressata and lime, with a shot of Guinness alongside for creamy contrast. The Road Rash Mary at Twisted Spoke (p.157) is dubbed "a sandwich in a glass," filling you up with a fiery salami, onion and double pepperoncini garnish. Handlebar (p.149) goes vegan via splashes of "The Wizard," an anchovy-less Worcestershire, while ordering your Mary "Snazzy" at Silver Cloud (p.37) yields a spicy concoction skewered with a tri-color pepper, grilled shrimp and artichoke. With a "shorty" pour of seasonal beer on the side, it's the hair of the dog that bit you…plus another dose of dog.

★ ✳ **BOKA** Giuseppe Tentori—a Trotter's alum with a gentle, sophisticated touch—works magic with seasonal dishes at this Lincoln Park hot spot. The menu changes often, but past hits have included smoked trout with potato terrine, dill sauce, pickled red cauliflower and smoked roe and an Angus strip loin with grilled elephant garlic and spinach flan. Dessert fans can indulge in pastry chef Elizabeth Dahl's creations like semolina pudding cake with plums, golden tomatoes and mascarpone ice cream. *1729 N Halsted St between North Ave and Willow St (312-337-6070). El: Red to North/Clybourn. Bus: 8, 72. Dinner. Average main course: $24.*

★ ☺ **B Bongo Room** Hungover rock stars, early-rising soccer moms and everybody in between seem to flock to this bright, cheery spot for fancy morning cocktails and a bite or two. Among the run-of-the-mill numbers on the menu are some dishes worth the often-very-long wait. The chocolate tower French toast—no doubt the menu's pièce de résistance—is a creamy, luxurious pile of chocolate bread smothered in what is essentially melted banana crème brûlée. It's definitely more dessert than breakfast, but sweet tooths won't complain. *1470 N Milwaukee Ave between Evergreen Ave and Honore St (773-489-0690). El: Blue to Damen. Bus: 50, 56, 72. Breakfast (Mon–Fri), brunch (Sat, Sun), lunch (Mon–Fri). Average main course: $10. ●Other location: 1152 S Wabash Ave (312-291-0100).*

★ ✳ **BYOB Bonsoiree** This former prepared foods shop is now a full-fledged restaurant that's carved out a niche with its reservation-only Saturday night "underground" dinners and tasting menu–only format (four courses for $55, seven for $85, 13 for $150). Value comes via the spot's BYOB status, and dishes that put season at the forefront but are also consistently creative. The menu changes according to the chef's whim: Think rhubarb with tea-smoked baby octopus, stinging nettles in a mussel-studded miso broth and fiddleheads with spring lamb leg. Take advantage of the back patio on warm nights. *2728 W Armitage Ave at Fairfield Ave (773-486-7511). El: Blue to California. Bus: 52, 73. Dinner (closed Mon). Average tasting menu: $85.*

★ ▼ **B The Bristol** The waits on weekends are an indicator of this Bucktown spot's continual buzz, and a few bites of Chris Pandel's New American food is all it takes to join the ranks of fans. We're smitten with signatures like the salad of heirloom apples and Manchego; the grilled sardines with chickpea fries; the thick, juicy burger; and the devastatingly delicious egg-and-ricotta-filled raviolo. Now that he's nailed dinner, Pandel is taking brunch to the next level with dishes like skirt steak and eggs in béarnaise sauce and a skillet loaded with tender duck, greens and fingerlings, as well as a selection of brunch cocktails like a bacon-infused Manhattan. *2152 N Damen Ave between Shakespeare and Webster Aves (773-862-5555). El: Blue to Western. Bus: 50, 73, 74. Brunch (Sun), dinner. Average main course: $16.*

★ ▼ ✳ **B BYOB Browntrout** Sean Sanders's homey, green-minded North Center restaurant may not look like much of a destination, nor does his menu read like a list of must-haves. But don't be fooled: The food, while on the simpler side, is rife with flavors both big and nuanced. Juicy chicken thighs get paired with rich polenta, beautifully seared walleye gets a lively dressing of salsa verde, and the Browntrout fish trio is comprised of some of the silkiest cured fish in the city. Some dishes fall flat, but for the most part, eating simply just got a lot more exciting. *4111 N Lincoln Ave at Belle Plaine Ave (773-472-4111). El: Brown to Irving Park. Bus: 11, 50, 80. Brunch (Sun), lunch, dinner (closed Tue). Average main course: $20.*

B C-House New York chef Marcus Samuelsson enters the Chicago market with this seafood spot on the ground floor of the Affinia Hotel, but we're pretty convinced the Scandinavian chef is little more than the name attached to the project. Chef de cuisine Seth Siegel-Gardner has the tough task of creating a dining destination. As it is, we'd recommend seeking it out primarily for cocktails on the rooftop patio C-View, for pastry chef Toni Roberts's seasonal classics, and a handful of plates like pork belly with greens and a poached duck egg. The latter may veer far from the seafood platform, but it's the stuff this kitchen does best. *166 E Superior St at St. Clair St (312-523-0923). El: Red to Chicago. Bus: 3, X3, 4, X4, 10, 26, 143, 144, 145, 146, 147, 151. Breakfast, brunch (Sat, Sun), lunch, dinner. Average main course: $30.*

BYOB Café 103 This small, simple and slightly upscale BYOB by the owners of Beverly's Pantry is proving that creative and contemporary food isn't just happening on the North Side. The menu is kept to about a dozen items to focus on freshness and seasonality. In summer, for instance, heirloom tomatoes pop up everywhere: paired with crispy walleye and English peas; in a mixed green salad with goat cheese, black grapes and walnuts; and in a summer squash trio entrée. *1909 W 103rd St between Walden Pkwy and Longwood Dr (773-238-5115). Bus: 9, 103, 112. Metra: Rock Island to 103rd St. Lunch (Wed–Sat), dinner (Wed–Sun). Average main course: $22.*

★ ▼ **Charlie Trotter's** Trotter remains one of the best chefs in the country, proving nightly that not only did he train the younger talent in town, but he can still school them. À la carte doesn't exist here, so go full throttle with the impeccable, contemporary eight-course tasting menu and tack on wine pairings; this team hits them out of the park. Trotter changes the menu every other week or so, but his salutations to a season may include Millbrook Farm venison loin with coriander, preserved pearl onions and hedgehog mushrooms, plus roasted Muscovy duck with bitter melon and duck consommé. *816 W Armitage Ave between Halsted and Dayton Sts*

LAWN AND GARDEN
Duchamp's communal patio tables show where the action is in summer.

(773-248-6228). El: Brown, Purple (rush hrs) to Armitage. Bus: 8, 73. Dinner (Tue–Sat). Average degustation: $140.

▼ **Crofton on Wells** We hope Suzy Crofton likes the clean, contemporary look of her restaurant, because as owner, manager, sommelier and chef, she spends a lot of time here. Her seasonal American cooking has inspired a couple of dishes that regulars won't let her take off the menu, like the jumbo lump crabmeat crab cake and the smoked-apple chutney–topped Gunthorp Farms pork belly. The service is one of the most attentive in the city. *535 N Wells St between Grand Ave and Ohio St (312-755-1790). El: Red to Grand. Bus: 65, 125. Dinner (closed Sun). Average main course: $28.*

★ (**The Drawing Room at Le Passage** Now that Le Passage's adjacent dining room is relevant again, chef Nick Lacasse intends to keep it that way. He might be cooking for patrons with clubbing on their minds, but he's keeping them well fed with seasonal dishes like a springy pasta tossed with morels, ramps and chèvre or wintery braised short ribs with citrus zest. Mixologist Charles Joly adjusts his "culinary cocktail" menu accordingly, ensuring that everything on your table is as *au courant* as the Gold Coast regulars. *937 N Rush St between Walton Pl and Oak St (312-255-0022). El: Red to Chicago. Bus: 10, 36, 143, 144, 145, 146, 147, 151. Dinner (Tue–Sat). Average small plate: $12.*

✴ ▣ **Duchamp** A joint venture between the guys behind Lumen and chef Michael Taus, Duchamp has all the elements of a great restaurant: a modern but cozy room, an incomparable patio in the warmer months and a established chef putting out French and American classics. The problem is that the food only lives up to its potential half the time. For every great dish (impossibly tender braised pork shoulder; sweet, spicy and crispy chicken wings) there is a lackluster one (pasty gnocchi; underseasoned fish and chips). Thankfully, the rest of the experience tends to outweigh even the most disappointing bites. *2118 N Damen Ave at Charleston St (773-235-6434). El: Blue to Western. Bus: 49, 50, 73. Dinner. Average main course: $17.*

✴ **Dunlay's On Clark** Lincoln Park outdoor café/bars are a dime a dozen. But we'd gladly plunk down more than ten cents to hang at this comfy, friendly American neighborhood bistro. Standouts include pork tenderloin and trout, prepared simply but solidly, often updated with seasonal sides. And, yes, what you've heard is true: There's a $8 chocolate chip cookie on the menu (made in a cast iron skillet) and, yes, it is worth every penny. *2600 N Clark Ave at Wrightwood Ave (773-883-6000). El: Brown, Purple (rush hrs) to Diversey. Bus: 22, 36, 76. Brunch (Sat–Sun), lunch (Tue–Sun), dinner. Average main course: $11.*

Eve Stellar cocktails get things off to a good start at this sophisticated sibling of Lincoln Square's Tallulah (we love the smoky whiskey-like notes of the fig-infused vodka). But be forewarned that when it comes to the food, chef Troy Graves's menu is hit or miss. Skip the sweetbreads and the prawns, both of which strangely pair up hot and cold elements, but if they're still around, try the juicy lobster sausage with chanterelles, the ricotta dumplings with expertly cooked lamb chops and the tenderloin with housemade sauerkraut. And if all else fails, order another cocktail. *840 N Wabash Ave at Chestnut St (312-266-3383). El: Red to Chicago. Bus: 36, 66. Lunch (Mon–Sat), dinner (Mon–Sun). Average main course: $27.*

Side dish

EDIBLE ART Free bottle of wine to whoever can guess just what's on this plate at Schwa.

Choose your own adventure

To ensure a successful evening, we've selected the right spot for a range of occasions—but you can take the credit.

The restaurant bound to make Grandma happy is quite different from the bar that gets you lucky (let's hope), so allow us to suggest the perfect places to take your…

…gadget-obsessed little brother
Your kid brother lives in the 'burbs with Mom. He spends his days playing *World of Warcraft* and hardly gets out unless it's to American Science & Surplus to buy new industrial-grade magnets for the shoes he's patenting. And he just turned 21, so there's no better place to take him than **Simone's** (p.172). Amid the collection of repurposed vintage bowling lanes, old pinball decks, high-school chem lab tables and church pews, he'll be more than visually satisfied, especially with *Young Frankenstein* on repeat and no-frills pub-grub. And if you're not drowning in nostalgia by now, the Pop Rocks–rimmed "Double Bubble" cocktail will definitely do the trick.

…blind date
After a few flirtatious e-mails via Chemistry.com, you arrange to meet her at **Francesca's Forno** (p.76). Tell her to bring a single rose like in *You've Got Mail*. You like what you see, and after a slightly awkward hug, you peruse the expansive Italian menu. Extremely attentive service usually annoys, but in this case it's a welcome distraction from the conversation you may (or may not) be having, and thank God for the floor-to-ceiling windows and fantastic people-watching in Wicker Park. Rendezvous took a nasty turn? Never fear. Francesca's prime corner location boasts exits on each side, so you effortlessly excuse yourself (duty calls!) and discretely sneak away.

…superhip older sister
She's an art dealer by day, self-proclaimed food critic by night. Pick up a nice tempranillo and take her to **Schwa** (p.47), where food is art and vice versa in the überminimalist space. Chef Michael Carlson himself greets you at the door and escorts you inside: There are no waiters here. Go for the nine-course onslaught and watch as the cooks parade each one to the table, armed with a detailed synopsis for every sculpted oeuvre. If you weren't lucky enough to get a reservation, the city-slick space and eclectic pan-Asian cuisine at nearby **rodan** (p.107) will impress perhaps *almost* as well.

…mistress
So you have a secret lover. Nowadays, who doesn't? You want to enjoy the same things that non-clandestine folk do but are afraid of exposing yourself. Play it safe and take her to the **Violet Hour** (p.151). With no advertising or signs, the Violet Hour transports you to a place filled with secrecy and seduction behind curtains of velvet. The 19th-century Georgian design increases Violet Hour's otherworldliness, and high-backed chairs transform the room into intimate pockets perfectly conducive to slipping bacony deviled eggs into one another's mouths.

…beer-loving cousin
Your cousin brews his own in the basement. He expertly discriminates between wheat and rye. Take him to **Hopleaf** (p.60). With more than 200 beers, mostly hailing from Belgium but also plenty of local stuff, this Old World tavern is just the place for a beer geek. Cuz will feel right at home with his Metropolitan Flywheel and a big pile of mussels and frites.—*Ali Jarvis*

Marion Street
EST. 2004
CHEESE MARKET

We're a Cheese Shop – We offer the finest artisan and farmstead cheeses and charcuterie, an extensive selection of domestic craft beer, handmade gourmet chocolates, unique wines and a great choice of gourmet foods. Stop in to create the ultimate "foodie" gift basket for any occasion!

We're a Bistro – Under the direction of Chef Leonard Hollander, we combine the freshest ingredients from local farms and food artisans to create a contemporary approach to American cuisine. The menu changes seasonally and is created with sustainability in mind and the desire to help support local food systems. We provide an exceptional dining experience for our guests. Join us for lunch, dinner or weekend brunch.

We're a Wine Bar – A great place to relax and savor a glass of wine or craft beer, enjoy a cheese and charcuterie flight, and listen to jazz and other live music every weekend. Bring some friends and come check us out!

Marion Street Cheese Market is located just steps off the Green Line and Metra stops in downtown Oak Park.

marion street cheese market
cheese shop + bistro + wine bar

100 S. Marion Street, Oak Park, IL
www.marionstreetcheesemarket.com • 708.725.7200

☆ ✲ (Feast Who knew Gold Coast residents would be so excited about fish sticks and burgers? But, oh, how they are: They've wasted no time crowding the bar at this new location of Bucktown's pubby stalwart. The wine list is still as on par as it was when the joint was Cru, so there are good bottles to be had. Only now you can pair them with comfort-food like crispy calamari; thin, charred pizzas topped with prosciutto; and butternut squash ravioli. *25 E Delaware St at Wabash Ave (312-337-4001). El: Red to Chicago. Bus: 36, 143, 144, 145, 146, 147, 151. Breakfast, lunch, dinner. Average main course: $16.* ● Other location: *1616 N Damen Ave (773-772-7100).*

▽ ✲ Firefly Rumor has it that if you aren't gay, male and cute, the service you get at this Boystown stalwart will be less than kind. We'd like to squash that rumor right now because these waiters are nice to *everyone*—gay, straight and in-between. If you can brush off the attitude, you can make a nice meal out of the decadent Parmesan deviled eggs (oddly but pleasantly served warm) or the ribeye steak sandwich with blue cheese fondue on *ciabatta* bread. *3335 N Halsted St between Buckingham Pl and Roscoe St (773-525-2505). El: Brown, Purple (rush hrs), Red to Belmont. Bus: 8, 22, 77. Dinner (closed Tue). Average main course: $18.*

★ ✲ graham elliot Just how much you'll love Graham Elliot Bowles's dressed-down solo project depends on your tolerance for quirky. Want Whoppers with your peanut butter brownie and Nilla wafers on peach cobbler? You'll be happy here. Still, even doubters should be silenced when it really works, as with the massive bison skirt steak with baked beans, coleslaw, a rootbeer-based barbecue sauce and onion rings. Purists can stick to solid seasonal creations such as cucumber gazpacho with lump crab and radish slivers, and expect frequent menu changes to keep things interesting. *217 W Huron St between Wells and Franklin Sts (312-624-9975). El: Brown, Purple (rush hrs) to Chicago. Bus: 66, 156. Dinner (closed Sun). Average main course: $32.*

★ ▽ B Green Zebra See Vegetarian for review.

BYOB The Grocery The people at this rustic West Loop café have a lot of ideas for their tiny restaurant. Some of them, like ridiculously flavorful chicken thighs with gorgonzola polenta, are quite good. But for every successful comfort food dish pulled off (spicy lamb, lobster-enhanced brandade), there's a "creative" dish (potato chip–coated skate wing, tempura-fried sushi) that falls flat. This can create for a wildly fluctuating experience, but if you steer clear of the stabs at wackiness you should be okay. *804 W Washington Blvd between Halsted and Green Sts (312-850-9291). Bus: 8, 9, 20. Dinner (closed Sun). Average main course: $12.*

★ ▽ B BYOB HB Home Bistro Let's go over this one more time, because it's still a little confusing: The Hearty Boys used to own this restaurant, but no more—now they're running their own place in a studiolike complex around the corner. Their longtime chef Joncarl Lachman has taken over this spot, and he puts out great, seasonal American food. The ever-changing menu might include a creamy mushroom soup with lavender and thyme; Amsterdam-style mushrooms in a beer broth; or spiced lamb pie alongside almond-garlic mashed potatoes. *3404 N Halsted St between Roscoe St and Newport Ave (773-661-0299). El: Brown, Purple (rush hrs),*

Red to Belmont. Bus: 8, 22, 77, 135, 145. Dinner (Wed–Sun). Average main course: $17.

★ ▽ B HotChocolate Don't let the name fool you—it's not just desserts here; the seasonal, savory menu is just as tempting. Chef de cuisine Mark Steuer and pastry chef Mindy Segal are both sticklers for season, so expect an everchanging assortment of dishes, from cold weather classics like brined, bone-in pork chop with sautéed spaetzle to springy pan-seared trout with citrus, radishes and fennel. Segal shines with finales like banana brioche bread pudding and brunch standouts such as duck confit and apple butter croissants. *1747 N Damen Ave at Willow St (773-489-1747). El: Blue to Damen. Bus: 50, 56, 72, 73. Brunch (Sat, Sun), lunch (Wed–Fri), dinner (closed Mon). Average main course: $20.*

★ ▽ B BYOB Jam On the heels of the success of Chickpea, Jerry Suqi opened this charming breakfast-and-lunch-only spot. This time, however, it's not his mom in the kitchen but chef (and co-owner) Jeffrey Mauro, a Charlie Trotter's alum, who puts out dishes such as egg sandwiches with pork cheeks and lamb crepes with Asian pear. Even breakfast tropes here (like omelettes or steak-and-eggs) exhibit a degree of care that usually gets lost in mounds of poached eggs. Breakfast amuse-bouches (such as a mini raspberry muffin drizzled with honey) get things off to the right start. *937 N Damen Ave between Walton St and Augusta Blvd (773-489-0302). Bus: 50, 66, 70. Breakfast, lunch (closed Tue). Average main course: $9. Cash only.*

▽ ✲ B Karyn's Cooked See Vegetarian for review.

★ L2O See Seafood for review.

▽ Landmark Scene reigns supreme at this venture from Rob Katz and Kevin Boehm, owners of the steps-away BOKA. Settle into a comfy bar booth and start with one of the stellar cocktails while perusing the seasonal menu. In the summer, expect dishes like wood-grilled trout served with berries, pea shoots and shallots poached in Riesling; and a confit of Swan Creek spring lamb with nettle pudding and morels. Whatever's in season for the main, save room for Elizabeth Dahl's delicious desserts. *1633 N Halsted St between North Ave and Willow St (312-587-1600). El: Red to North/Clybourn. Bus: 8, 72. Dinner (closed Mon, Sun). Average main course: $20.*

✲ (Little Bucharest Bistro When André Christopher, former chef of the Grocery Bistro, landed at this 30-year-old, historically Romanian restaurant, his fans were hoping for a repeat of his sausage-stuffed chicken thighs and chocolate panini. The chicken thighs they'll find, but most of the menu is dedicated to traditional Eastern European fare. The schnitzel is done perfectly, but the bland eggplant spread and DiGiorno-quality flatbreads fall fast and flat. But there is an accordion player who roams the dining room, so at least someone in the place is making music. *3661 N Elston Ave (773-604-8500). Bus: 82, 152. Dinner. Average main course: $15.*

The Lobby Everything's fabulous at the Peninsula, and the opulent and aptly-named lobby restaurant is no different than the rest of the chi-chi hotel. Stop in for afternoon tea and enjoy background harp or violin music whilst

you sip with your pinkies properly pointed. For heartier appetites, there are well-executed seasonal dishes like Thai basil chicken served over jasmine rice and roasted monkfish with spicy blue crab pot au feu. On Friday and Saturday evenings, they break out Chocolate the Pen, a decadent chocolate-themed dessert buffet. *Peninsula Hotel, 108 E Superior St between Michigan Ave and Rush St (312-573-6760). El: 2, 3, X4, 10, 26, 66, 143, 144, 145, 146, 147, 151, 157. Breakfast, lunch, dinner. Average main course: $30.*

Lockwood The Palmer House Hilton's recent $150 million makeover included the addition of this restaurant, a contemporary dining room entrusted to chef Phillip Foss. European dishes get a modern American makeover, resulting in items like lobster beignets topped with shaved pears and "faux gras" with peppered quince, leek marmalade and sherry caramel. To check out the hotel's new look without dropping the dough for dinner, stop in for a cocktail in the lobby bar and nosh on small bites like the charcuterie plate or Kobe sliders. *17 E Monroe St between State St and Wabash Ave (312-917-3404). El: Blue, Red to Monroe. Breakfast, lunch, dinner. Average main course: $32.*

★ ▽ ✲ B Lula Cafe This funky restaurant has one of our favorite seasonally driven menus. For a sunny brunch or breakfast, vie for a seat at a small table indoors or on the sidewalk cafe, where planters spill over with the same herbs you'll find in your eggs Florentine or red-pepper strata. Local organic eggs and sausage pair perfectly with the black sambal Bloody Mary or blackberry Bellini. At night, try creative specials that range from artichoke-and-Meyer-lemon soup with a dollop of caviar and bits of roasted squab breast to striped marlin with pickled ramps. *2537 N Kedzie Blvd between Linden Pl and Logan Blvd (773-489-9554). El: Blue to Logan Square. Bus: 56, 74. Breakfast, brunch (Sat, Sun), lunch, dinner (closed Tue). Average main course: $15.*

★ B BYOB Mado The combination of exemplary ingredients and minimalist preparation is at the heart of every dish at this simple BYOB, and this turns out to be an excellent way to cook. It allows sunchokes, dressed with lemon and parsley, to show off their crunchy earthiness, housemade charcuterie to exhibit its lingering richness, and flaky shortbreads to simply melt in your mouth with no distractions. The food is so naked that it can't hide even the smallest flaws. Luckily, those flaws are few and far between. *1647 N Milwaukee Ave between Caton St and Concord Pl (773-342-2340). El: Blue to Damen. Bus: 50, 56, 72. Brunch (Sun), dinner (closed Mon). Average main course: $18.*

★ ▽ ❂ Mana Food Bar See Vegetarian for review.

✲ Marion Street Cheese Market Obviously, cheese is the focus at this deli/café/retail store, and the menu of small plates offers it in a myriad of forms: on thin, charred pizzas; in a funky, gratinlike potato raclette; and straight-up in themed flights (such as a "Midwest" flight of local cheeses). But the best vehicle by far is the cheese puffs, which are crisp and light on the outside but give way to a completely molten interior. All that cheese can get a little greasy, but believe it or not, fried green tomatoes and olive-oil-laden olive plates qualify as palate cleansers here. *100 S Marion Street, Oak Park (708-725-7200). El: Green to Harlem. Bus: Pace 307. Breakfast (Sat, Sun), lunch (Tue–Sun), dinner (Tue–Sat). Average small plate: $9.*

COVET THY NEIGHBOR'S BITE
Communal dining at the Grocery
brings strangers elbow to elbow.

NOW YOU SEE IT, NOW YOU DON'T
It's best not to get attached to any dish
in this photo; Nightwood changes its
menu daily.

MarketHouse We realize you're not likely to rush over to the DoubleTree for dinner (deep-pocketed remodeling or not) without the promise of deliciousness, so consider this an endorsement. Executive chef Scott Walton and chef de cuisine Thomas Rice are putting out flavorful, smart, well-executed comfort classics, slightly updated with seasonal flair. Think pastrami-cured salmon; a salad of apples, beets, arugula and blue cheese; and simple endings of berry-topped panna cotta or apple crumble—all simple, but simply good. *300 E Ohio St at Fairbanks Ct (312-224-2200). El: Red to Grand. Bus: 2, 3, 66, 157. Breakfast, lunch, dinner. Average main course: $26.*

★ ▼ **May Street Market** Chef-owner Alex Cheswick has turned his Grand Avenue restaurant into a contemporary food–lover's destination. Regulars tend to fall back on signature favorites (such as the Maytag blue cheese–cake appetizer), but we like to stop by for the bar menu, which showcases Cheswick's talent with gourmet burgers and tasty pommes frites. A three-course prix-fixe menu for the penny pinchers is offered every night. *1132 W Grand Ave at May St (312-421-5547). El: Blue to Grand. Bus: 8, 9, X9, 65. Dinner (closed Sun). Average main course: $21.*

★ ▼ **mk** Michael Kornick's initials still emblazon the exterior of this River North stalwart, but chef Erick Williams executes the day-to-day, drawing in newbies and satisfying loyalists with elegant and seasonal contemporary American cuisine. The spacious and tasteful room (think rich architect's home) is comfortable enough to settle in for Williams's tasting menu, where he's been known to show off the market's larder via confit artichokes and spring garlic puree alongside Peking duck breast or by pureeing roasted sunchokes into a deceptively simple soup. *868 N Franklin St at Chestnut St (312-482-9179). El: Brown, Purple (rush hrs) to Chicago. Bus: 66, 156. Dinner. Average main course: $38.*

Moto The buzz on chef Homaro Cantu has reached fever pitch: He's working with the government to "end world hunger" with edible paper and cooking with military-issued lasers. But what's going on in the mad scientist's restaurant? More of the same, and always something new. It's anybody's guess what the night's tasting menu holds, but past trickery included a play on Vietnamese egg-drop soup in which frozen egg- and microgreen-pellets were dropped tableside into steaming soup, and triple-seared beef was paired with "caramelaserized wine." And yes, a laser was involved in a wine pairing. *945 W Fulton Mkt between Sangamon and Morgan Sts (312-491-0058). El: Blue to Grand. Bus: 8, 65. Dinner (Tue–Sat). Average degustation: $115.*

★ ✳ **Naha** Chef Carrie Nahabedian delivers an upscale experience minus the pomp, courtesy of a snazzy room, great service and a seasonal menu that reads like a who's who in regional, sustainable foods. The menu changes weekly, so expect anything from seasonal veggies—French wild asparagus, spring peas and sugar-snap peas—accompanying a wild Yukon River Alaskan salmon to slow-roasted salmon with morels, sugar snap peas and cipollini onions. *500 N Clark St at Illinois St (312-321-6242). El: Red to Grand. Bus: 22, 65. Lunch (Mon–Fri), dinner (Mon–Sat). Average main course: $33.*

★ ▼ **Nightwood** The most consistently successful dishes at this modern, understated Pilsen restaurant from the Lula Cafe crew share two traits: First, that fresh-from-the-garden

---

Side dish

ON TOP OF THE WORLD The view is so good at ROOF, who needs food and drinks?

Room with a view

There's a lot more to look at in this town than the bottom of your glass.

Spend enough nights in your neighborhood dive bar and suddenly skyline views become relegated to tourists. Which is a shame, since looking at the city from above is enough to make any jaded longtime resident short of breath. Splurge for a special occasion at one of these rooftop spots for a reminder of the city's stunning architecture, the beauty of that seemingly never-ending lake and a cocktail in a crowd that's just happy to be in your town.

C-View (p.162)
This swanky rooftop offshoot of chef Marcus Samuelsson's seafood-focused restaurant in the Affinia Hotel serves delicious, creative cocktails like the lavender gin fizz and housemade pineapple sangria. They're drinks worth sipping at any restaurant, but add in the outdoor lounge and the warm, modern interior and you have an irresistible combination.

NoMI (p.47)
Get a table next to the huge, angular windows that wrap around the perimeter of this sleek space and you'll feel as though you're pressed against the skyline. You're only seven floors up, but you'll feel even higher, giddy on chef Ryan LaRoche's expertly cooked meats and three dining areas (including an open-air garden) as stunning as the food itself.

Cityscape (p.157)
Sure, you may be sitting in a Holiday Inn bar munching on passable food and sipping cocktails with cheesy names. But with your chair turned toward the breathtaking, 15-stories-high view, you'll forget where exactly you are other than

on top of a sparkling Chicago. Besides, those cocktails like the green tea–based Zentini? They're actually pretty tasty.

ROOF (p.169)
Even the most bare-bones setup would feel luxurious 27 floors in the sky. But ROOF's popularity isn't based on height alone. The space is a stylish, lush indoor-outdoor lounge where those lucky enough to get a table hang out on modern furniture surrounding fire pits, enjoying handcrafted cocktails and a solid menu of Mediterranean small plates. The view from atop theWit Hotel is a nice one, but the people-watching here is what really makes fighting the crowds worth your while.

Whiskey Sky (p.165)
This enclosed rooftop hotel bar is small enough without the tourists jamming it up, but one glance out the panoramic window and you'll suddenly feel as if you've got a lot more space. The expansive view sweeps across Lake Michigan and a glittering Navy Pier, making a window-side seat and one of the bar's well-crafted cocktails all you need to feel serene.

Terrace at Trump (p.162)
This patio lounge is smack-dab in the middle of some of the city's finest architecture, a sight equally impressive to locals and tourists alike. And while the price for drinks here is equal to the cost of a decent takeout dinner, they're not the point. The point is that you couldn't be on a more sophisticated patio. So give in to the posh surroundings and the fact that you just dropped 20 bucks for a glass of wine.
—*Sarah Grainer*

liveliness that's garnered Lula its cultish status. (See, e.g., a "stone soup" filled with bright lima beans or a squash salad accented with crunchy purslane.) Second, a distinctive wood-grilled flavor that gives an intoxicating aroma to a juicy half-chicken and earthy cheeseburger. The sweet side of the menu hits all the right notes (think light and simple blueberry cake), but the dining room is so cozy you might just linger with a liquid ending. *2119 S Halsted St between 21st St and Cermak Rd (312-526-3385). Bus: 8, 21, 62. Dinner Tue–Sat. Average main course: $20.*

★ ❋ B **NoMI** The view of Michigan Avenue from the seventh floor of the Park Hyatt Chicago is impressive, but what's going on inside this French-and-Asian restaurant impresses even more. Chef Christophe David takes where his food comes from very seriously. His menu changes each season, but there are always creative options, like morels served with Virginia ham or veal paired with polenta and chanterelle mushrooms. End on a high note with pastry chef Frederic Moreau's fantastic, slightly molecular versions of crème brulée and mille-feuille. *800 N Michigan Ave between Chicago Ave and Pearson St (312-239-4030). El: Red to Chicago. Bus: 3, 10, 26, 66, 125, 143, 144, 145, 146, 147, 151. Breakfast, brunch (Sat, Sun), lunch (Mon–Fri), dinner. Average main course: $42.*

★ ▽ ♨ B **North Pond** Okay, so technically you're not eating outside, but when you're only a few feet from a pond in the middle of Lincoln Park, you are as close to nature as it gets in the city. Even more so when you sample chef Bruce Sherman's latest elevated contemporary menu that's concocted with as much locally grown organic food as he can get his hands on. Sherman's ever-changing offerings have included English peas with minted goat cheese gnocchi, pickled watermelon radish and crab with a ramp soup, and maple-kissed crêpes with royal trumpet mushrooms. *2610 N Cannon Dr between Fullerton Pkwy and Lake Shore Dr (773-477-5845). Bus: 76, 151, 156. Brunch (Sun), lunch (Tue–Fri), dinner (Tue–Sun). Average main course: $30.*

★ ▽ ♨ B **one sixtyblue** If you noticed something different about the food at this West Loop favorite, you must be a regular. The change is that Martial Noguier has moved on to Sofitel, and chef Michael McDonald has taken the reins. McDonald shows occasional glimpses of greatness, including pillow-soft leek gnocchi, house-cured salmon and a fantastic pork chop teeming with salty-sweet juices and plates with housemade 'kraut and crispy-edged spaetzle. Don't skip dessert—Stephanie Prida knows balance and season, and creations like candied buddha hand citrus with cheesecake custard and lemon sherbet proves it. *1400 W Randolph St between Ada St and Ogden Ave (312-850-0303). El: Green, Pink to Ashland. Bus: 9, 20, 65. Dinner (closed Sun). Average main course: $25.*

♨ **Otom** While its name literally mirrors Moto—chef Homaro Cantu's hyper-modern science lab of a restaurant—Otom's menu doesn't exactly reflect the extraterrestrial creations or sky-high prices of its adjacent sibling. This place is more casual and laid-back, and the magic here is in chef Thomas Elliott Bowman's rehashing of low-brow, classic dishes. So there is mac and cheese on the menu, but it is *andouille sausage with anise* mac and cheese. You won't get the full Moto experience, but you don't pay the full prices, either. *951 W Fulton Mkt between Sangamon and Morgan Sts (312-491-5804). El: Green, Pink to Clinton. Bus: 8, 20. Dinner. Average main course: $18.*

▽ ⊙ B BYOB **Over Easy Café** Ravenswood locals can wave good-bye to Toast, Orange and all those other funky brunch spots in town. Because, thanks to Jon Cignarale—himself a veteran of m. henry and Uncommon Ground—they have their own. Dishes like oversize pancakes stuffed with blackberries and topped with orange butter, eggs served "sassy" (atop chorizo hash) and spicy vegan chilaquiles (who knew tofu could be greasy?) are carried through this bright, cheery dining room by the tray-full during the busy weekend brunch. *4943 N Damen Ave between Ainslie and Argyle Sts (773-506-2605). El: Brown to Damen. Bus: 50, 81, 92. Breakfast, brunch (Sun), lunch (closed Mon). Average main course: $10.*

★ ❋ B **Perennial** Chef Ryan Poli is squarely at the helm of the latest venture from BOKA's Kevin Boehm and Rob Katz—and the results are impressive. It's tough to decide which is better, the black truffle gnocchi with tender squash and deliciously bitter chard or the rectangle of vanilla-scented crispy-skinned veal breast—get 'em both. Just don't be disappointed if they're not around by the time you're reading this—Poli likes to mix things up to keep up with the well-heeled regulars that have become fixtures in the place. *1800 N Lincoln Ave at Clark St (312-981-7070). Bus: 11, 22, 36, 72, 73. Brunch (Sat, Sun), dinner. Average main course: $22.*

★ ❋ **Province** See Latin American for review.

★ ❋ B **The Publican** See Gastropub for review.

★ ♨ ❋ **Quince** The most storied dining room in the Chicago area changed names years ago (when restaurateur Henry Adaniya left, he took the name "Trio" with him). But the room that gave Chicago Shawn McClain and Grant Achatz still puts out great food. Contemporary American is the gist of what's served, but new chef Andy Motto interjects French and East Asian elements into the mix as well. *1625 Hinman Ave, Evanston (847-570-8400). El: Purple to Davis. Bus: 93, 201, Pace 206. Dinner (Tue–Sun). Average main course: $20.*

❋ **Rhapsody** With its built-in clientele of symphony fans, this place could get away with subpar food and rushed "preshow" meal deals. Luckily, it doesn't, so you don't have to be down with Mahler to be down with its seasonal menu. Appetizers, like the orange-infused Peking-duck gnocchi and cured yellowfin tuna in the spring, make choosing what to eat here difficult; entrées like oven-roasted spring rack of lamb with caramelized artichokes don't help matters. And as if giving the Loop a decent place to dine weren't sweet enough, the roasted hazelnut–and–pineapple cake is. *65 E Adams St between Wabash and Michigan Aves (312-786-9911). El: Brown, Green, Orange, Pink, Purple (rush hrs) to Adams. Lunch, dinner. Average main course: $22.*

▽ **Ritz-Carlton Café** The Ritz's The Dining Room ended its era (although banquets and private affairs may still be held there), so chef Mark Payne has shifted his focus to the Café. Winners abound: Roasted Vidalia onion soup is sweet from caramelized onions and rich from beef shank braised in the broth, and there's a fantastic ricotta gnocchi tossed in tomato-basil cream sauce. Ingredients are top notch and execution is nearly flawless, but it's the Ritz-style high prices that keep us from making the Café a regular spot. *160 E Pearson St between Michigan Ave and Mies van der Rohe Way (312-573-5223). El: Red to Chicago. Bus: 3, 4, X4, 10, 26, 125, 143, 144, 145, 146, 147, 151. Breakfast, lunch, dinner. Average degustation: $75.*

❋ ☾ B **Rockit Bar & Grill** Most of the guys who go to this sporty, sceney homage to stainless steel don't seem to care what the food tastes like—it's more of a tits and beer thing for them. But if they'd pay attention, they'd find that most of the menu is much better than the chewy, cardboardish pizzas. As counter-intuitive as it may seem, the antibar food is where the gems are, like the mildly spicy braised lamb lettuce wraps and the perfectly golden roasted chicken. *22 W Hubbard St between State and Dearborn Sts (312-645-6000). El: Red to Grand. Bus: 29, 36, 65. Brunch (Sun), lunch, dinner. Average main course: $17. ● Other location: 3700 N Clark St (773-645-4400).*

★ ▽ BYOB **Schwa** Fewer than 30 diners can fit in this tiny restaurant and all of them must have made reservations weeks in advance. But as a 2006 *Food & Wine* best new chef, chef-owner Michael Carlson has a right to call the shots. Let him. You'll be treated to intriguing creations like pine-flavored peckytoe crabs with marinated royal king mushrooms or sumptuous venison with a white chocolate foam. The menu changes often, but whatever Carlson has up his sleeve, you're certain to have a meal like nowhere else in town. *1466 N Ashland Ave at Le Moyne St (773-252-1466). El: Blue to Division. Bus: 9, 50, 70. Dinner (closed Sun, Mon). Average degustation: $75.*

♨ B **Seasons Restaurant** Far above the hustle and bustle of Michigan Avenue lies the serene tranquility and decadence that is Seasons. Chef Kevin Hickey's creative dishes might include garden pea and coconut bisque with Vietnamese mint prosciutto dumplings, and roast Colorado lamb served with feta gnocchi and kalamata olive jus. It's the stuff power lunches and dinners are made of, but Seasons makes an effort to be family-friendly, too, with children's and tween menus (think fruit kebabs and design-your-own tacos) for proper little ladies and gents. *Four Seasons Hotel, 120 E Delaware Pl between Michigan Ave and Rush St (312-649-2349). El: Red to Chicago. Bus: 10, 143, 144, 145, 146, 147, 151. Breakfast (Mon–Sat), brunch (Sun), lunch, dinner (Tue–Sat). Average main course: $27.*

★ ▽ ❋ **Sepia** The newbie sheen having worn off of this acclaimed West Looper, Sepia has taken on the qualities of a stalwart: a classic place serving standouts like rabbit over buttery biscuits and crispy-skinned trout with smoky bacon—not to mention working a cocktail and wine program that sets the bar for Chicago. No time for dinner? Opt for the lounge, a gingery Sepia Mule cocktail and the sweet-salty-smoky flatbread of fresh peaches, creamy blue cheese and bacon. *123 N Jefferson St between Washington Blvd and Randolph St (312-441-1920). El: Green, Pink to Clinton. Bus: 8, 56, 125. Lunch (Mon–Fri), dinner. Average main course: $26.*

▽ **Shikago** See Pan Asian for review.

B **Sixteen** The stately dining room on the 16th floor of the Trump Tower is indeed impressive, but the close-up view of architectural gems like the Wrigley Building and Tribune Tower and the supremely polished, doting staff come with a price. Chef Frank Brunacci's

ONE BONE ABOUT IT Chef Ryan Poli rethinks classics (like this reconstructed chicken drumstick) at Perennial.

menus ranging from a $95 three-course with sarsaparilla quail and Moroccan lamb three ways to a $145 nine-course "Chef's collection" featuring frog legs and pan-seared foie with bay scallops. Of course, you can always rewind time and add on Tramonto's caviar staircase for an upcharge. *676 N St. Clair St at Huron St (312-202-0001). El: Red to Chicago. Bus: 3, 66, 151, 157. Dinner (closed Sun). Average three-course prix fixe: $95.*

▼ ♨ ℂ **Uncommon Ground** For its second location, Uncommon Ground went with a perfect space, a room that is so warm and log-cabin chic that, unfortunately, the food can't compete. So if you're going to make a point to visit (and you should, because once here you'll never want to leave), go with the basics: Salads, meatloaf, their justifiably famous brunch (the Uncommon Breakfast Melt is brilliant). That way, your focus will remain on the real attraction of the place: the room. *1401 W Devon Ave at Glenwood Ave (773-465-9801). El: Red to Loyola. Bus: 36, 147, 151, 155. Breakfast, lunch, dinner. Average main course: $17.* ● *Other location: 3800 N Clark St (773-929-3680).*

✳ **Viand** See Mediterranean for review.

★ ▼ **Vie** Rent a car, con a friend into driving or take the Metra—do whatever it takes to get to this classy, comfortable restaurant. Chef Paul Virant's (a 2007 *Food & Wine* best new chef) penchant for old-school canning makes for a jam-packed pantry in winter, but other times of the year, he pairs local produce with farm-fresh cheeses and meats. The menu changes often, but the flavors are consistently sublime, with dishes such as halibut treated with cranberry beans, herb mayo and pickled asparagus, and butter cake topped with Traders Point frozen yogurt, cinnamon and poached plums. *4471 Lawn Ave, Western Springs (708-246-2082). Metra: Burlington/Santa Fe to Western Springs. Dinner (closed Sun). Average main course: $29.*

◎ **Volo** Owner Jon Young of Kitsch'n on Roscoe and Kitsch'n River North has teamed up with chef Stephen Dunne (also his partner at Paramount Room) to create one cozy small-plates wine bar. Dunne's best dishes are the rich ones—intense duck confit with haricots vert and lentils, seared diver scallops topped with caviar and crispy leeks, and roasted veal marrow bones with toast—but specials like peekytoe-crab salad with preserved lemon and avocado suit us just fine, too. The eclectic wine list is well thought out with plenty of food-friendly flights available. *2008 W Roscoe St between Damen and Seeley Aves (773-348-4600). Bus: 50, 77, 152. Dinner (closed Sun). Average small plate: $8.*

✳ **Wave, W Chicago Lakeshore** See Mediterranean for review.

▼ **Zealous** After more than 15 years in business, Michael Taus's baby remains as innovative as ever. His creative menu, offset by the minimalist décor, showcases seasonal ingredients in new ways. Look for vegetarian-friendly dishes packed with signatures such as truffled sweet potato risotto, Asian crab cakes with mango-basil emulsion and macadamia nut–crusted grouper with rock shrimp–taro root hash. Don't forget to pair your meal with one of the 750 wines from the breathtaking wine cellar. *419 W Superior St between Sedgwick and Kingsbury Sts (312-475-9112). Bus: 66. Dinner (Tue–Sat). Average main course: $30.*

artistically presented food includes dishes like fresh pasta and escargots in cream sauce with truffles and lamb loin cooked sous vide and plated with trumpet mushrooms, salsify and harissa. For those looking to impress a client or a date with a fine-dining experience, this spot is for you. *401 N Wabash Ave at Kinzie St (312-588-8030). El: Red to Grand. Bus: 29, 36, 65. Breakfast, brunch (Sun), lunch (Mon–Fri), dinner. Average main course: $42.*

★ ▼ ✳ **B** **Sola** See Classic American $16 and up for review.

★ ▼ **Spring** Chef Shawn McClain may be more well known for his contemporary steak spot Custom House or his veg-head haven Green Zebra, but this upscale dining room is really where his solo career in the city took root. Here, he combines Asian elements and locally sourced ingredients to subtle results. A few signatures dot the menu, but the seasonal specials are the strength. Possibilities include yellowfin tuna tartare with avocado foam; spring garlic-potato soup; and Meyer-lemon mousse chiffon cake with grapefruit parfait. *2039 W North Ave between Damen and Hoyne Aves (773-395-7100). El: Blue to Damen. Bus: 50, 56, 72. Dinner. Closed for dinner on Mon, but the bar is open 6–midnight. Average main course: $25.*

State & Lake See Classic American $16 and Up for review.

✳ **B** **Tallulah** Chef Troy Graves (of the defunct Meritage) dresses up comfort classics

at this upscale Lincoln Square spot that sports three white-on-white and simple dining rooms. Opt for a table toward the back for more intimacy, and start with the delicious pork belly over housemade kimchi. Mussels in herbaceous coconut milk broth and squash-gorgonzola ravioli are other stellar starters, as is the grilled asparagus topped with a poached egg salad (available seasonally). In fact, you might be happiest making an all-app meal, as entrées and desserts somewhat pale in comparison. *4539 N Lincoln Ave between Sunnyside and Wilson Aves (773-942-7585). El: Brown to Western. Bus: 11, 49, X49, 78, 81. Brunch (Sun), dinner (Tue–Sun). Average main course: $21.*

▼ ◎ ✳ **B** **BYOB** **Treat** The small menu at this friendly BYOB is heavy on sandwiches, and the few entrées on offer—pan-seared salmon, mild chicken *tikka masala*—don't stand out for their creativity. But the kitchen has a way of sneaking surprising flavors into otherwise standard fare. Case in point: spicy, creamy and endlessly flavorful *harissa aioli* that covers an otherwise predictable pile of hot, crispy calamari. The Indian touch carries over to brunch, where buttermilk pancakes are topped with chai syrup, and tamarind chutneys come alongside chickpea pancakes. *1616 N Kedzie Ave between North and Wabansia Aves (773-772-1201). Bus: 52, 72, 82. Brunch (Sat, Sun), dinner. Average main course: $10.*

▼ **TRU** Almost ten years after opening, chef-partners Rick Tramonto and Gale Gand are busy tending to other projects while exec chef Tim Graham and pastry chef Meg Galus keep TRU relevant. They do it with splurge-worthy

Cuban

✳ B Café 28 Cuban food goes upscale at this pleasant spot, with touches like saffron cream and garlic polenta. It's all executed with competence, but with a little less oomph than the menu descriptions suggest. Pork chops arrive tender with plenty of honey flavor, but only a trace of the advertised jalapeño. The *ropa vieja*, flanked by sugary plantains, is juicy and fork-tender, but you can't help feeling as if you could order it at your local Cuban dive for half the price. *1800 W Irving Park Rd at Ravenswood Ave (773-528-2883). El: Brown to Irving Park. Bus: 9, 11, 50, 80. Brunch (Sat, Sun), lunch (Tue–Fri), dinner. Average main course: $16.*

▼ ✳ Café Bolero Part Cuban, part Spanish, we find the line gets blurred and our criticism wanes the more sangria we drink—follow suit and you'll leave happy. If you're into deep-fried, try the combo platter of crispy, meat-stuffed potato croquettes with plantains and a moist tamale. We also like the curiously pickle-less (but nonetheless delicious) Cuban sandwich and spicy shrimp creole. If you're looking to venture into the Spanish offerings, the vegetarian paella isn't bad. *2252 N Western Ave between Lyndale St and Belden Ave (773-227-9000). El: Blue to Western. Bus: 49, 74. Lunch, dinner. Average main course: $12.*

★ ◑ Cafécito You don't have to claim a bunk at the adjacent Hostel International to get your hands on one of this café's ridiculously good Cuban sandwiches. The Cubano's crusty bread is toasted just right, its roast pork juicy, its pickles thick, and its mustard and gooey cheese plentiful. And once it's devoured, only a potent *cortadito* will keep you from calling the café's comfy couch home for the day. *26 E Congress Pkwy (312-922-2233). Breakfast, lunch, dinner (closes 6pm Sat, Sun). Average sandwich: $5.*

◑ Café con Leche Breakfast choices run heavy at this tiny gem, with *huevos* (eggs) mentioned no less than 15 times on the menu. Get your daily quota in tortas, sandwiches or burritos that head south of the border with a twist. Cuban sandwiches and Mexican *molletes* (vegetarian pizzas) keep company with American favorites like Philly cheesesteaks and burgers. *2714 N Milwaukee Ave between Spaulding and Sawyer Aves (773-289-4274). El: Blue to Logan Square. Bus: 56, 74, 76, 82. Breakfast, lunch, dinner. Average main course: $5.*

✳ Café Cubano Skip the overwhelming menu here and ask the server what's looking good. You might get steered toward meaty oxtails, which are doused with rich stock-based sauce perfect for sopping up with crusty Cuban bread slathered in oregano-butter. Couple this dish with the boiled yuca—dense tubers splashed with garlic—and start with ham croquettes, which are crunchy on the outside, creamy within, and offset by a slightly spiced tomato sauce. *7426 W North Ave, Elmwood Park (708-456-6100). Bus: 90, Pace 307, Pace 318. Lunch, dinner. Average main course: $12.*

EL FRESCO The owners of 90 Miles Cuban Café take a break over one of their toasted sandwiches.

◈ Café Laguardia The cocktails veer toward the fruity side at this Bucktown favorite, but the Cuban food is right on target. Fried pork chops (*cerdo frito*) yellow rice and pigeon peas, spicy "volcano shrimp," caramelized plantains and Cuban flan feel right at home in the lively dining room. Live salsa bands on Tuesday nights and Brazilian bands on Wednesday nights make up for the sometimes slow-paced service. *2111 W Armitage Ave between Hoyne Ave and Leavitt St (773-862-5996). El: Blue to Western. Bus: 50, 56, 73. Lunch, dinner. Average main course: $13.*

◑ Cafeteria Marianao This Cuban lunch counter is no-frills, and that's just fine with the regulars who line up every morning for their eye-opening *cafe cortado* or their belly-filling toasted sandwiches. The big draw seems to be the steak sandwich, piled with thin slices of juice-dripping beef topped with griddled onions and toasted on the hot press. It's standing room only, and can get rather chaotic here, so head for the parking lot if you want to wolf lunch in peace. *2246 N Milwaukee Ave at Prindiville St (773-278-4533). El: Blue to California. Bus: 52, 56, 74. Breakfast, lunch, dinner (closed Sun). Average main course: $5.*

★ ◑ El Cubanito It seems counterintuitive, but trust us: You're going to want to eat a sandwich as your entrée here and then get a second sandwich for dessert. Start with one of the *cubanos*—the crusty bread grilled to a flaky crunch, the pork and ham complemented by a healthy slathering of mustard—or the *ropa vieja* sandwich, stuffed with so much succulent beef it's hard to keep the juices contained. But don't miss the *pan con timba*—warm bread, mild slices of Swiss and a sweet center of guava. *2555 N Pulaski Ave between Altgeld St and Wrightwood Ave (773-235-2555). Bus: 53, 76. Breakfast, lunch. Average sandwich: $4. ● Other location: 5306 W Fullerton (773-237-1577)*

★ ◑ El Rinconcito Cubano Yellowed photos of sunny Cuban beaches line the walls of this tiny storefront, a casual meeting place for the local Cuban community. The standout is the *ropa vieja*, a soft pile of garlicky, tomatoey shredded beef that releases juice and flavor with every chew. Traditionalists will love the authentic *bacalao* (salt cod), the fried pork chops and the *boliche* (slow-cooked eye-of-round offered only on Thursdays). Show up early—you may see some older Cuban men inside, but if it's after 8:30pm they won't let you in. *3238 W Fullerton Ave between Sawyer and Spaulding Aves (773-489-4440). El: Blue to Logan Square. Bus: 74, 77. Lunch, dinner. Average main course: $8.50.*

◑ Habana Libre Aromas of garlic assault you at the door, and they don't stop there. *Tostones* (crispy plantains) and the fried yuca come with a garlic sauce so strong you'll feel it in your pores the next day. Yet garlic's not the only thing on offer here. *Papas rellenas* crack open to reveal silky potato, the fragile crust of the *empanada de carne* is buttery and flaky, and creamy pork *croquetas* outshine their fish and chicken counterparts. But seriously, watch out for that garlic—or else you'll have to cancel your romantic rendezvous. *1440 W Chicago Ave at Bishop St (312-243-3303). El: Blue to Chicago. Bus: 9, X9, 66. Lunch, dinner. Average main course: $8.*

(Cuban)

Smackdown: Cuban sandwiches

After sampling our weight in the king of toasted sandwiches, we've narrowed down the best.

We could debate forever the history of the Cuban sandwich (some say it's truly a Cuban invention; others say it first popped up at Cuban-run lunch counters in Florida). Regardless, let's go over a few key points. (1) It should consist of sliced ham, roasted pork, mustard, pickles and a Swiss-type white cheese on "Cuban" bread that is softer and wider than a baguette. (2) Cuban sandwiches should be toasted on a sandwich press known as a *plancha*. (3) Cubanos average five bucks, are ordered over a counter and should be eaten while standing—all the more reason they are among the world's greatest inventions. Now, let's begin, starting at the bottom and working our way to the best…

6 **Cafeteria Marianao** (p.49)
The granddaddy of the area's Cuban lunch counters ascribes to the no-muss, no-fuss theory, meaning this sandwich is the thinnest, most minimal version around. The roasted pork is well salted but not delicious enough to eat on its own, however that's not our biggest gripe: Only the tiniest sliver of pickle was found, and not even a whisper of mustard was used.

5 **La Unica** (see this page)
Mayo haters beware: This place loves the stuff. It's slathered on the bread and even between the slices of ham. That sin aside, this sandwich has a hefty dose of pickles, incredibly gooey cheese and juicy, tender roasted pork.

4 **90 Miles Cuban Cafe** (see this page)
Uhm, wheat bread? A tofu Cubano? Is the griddle guy practicing Bikram yoga?

What the hell is going on here? Actually, the disarmingly friendly owners of this newcomer are just looking to accommodate those seeking healthier options. But of course, we went straight for the cheese-and-pork-packed original—the thickest of any Cubano we tried. The roasted pork is nicely caramelized and sandwiched between two helpings of ham, with plenty of cheese and lengthwise strips of pickles sliced thicker than most. Good value but almost too much to manage.

3 **Con Sabor Cubano** *(1833 W Wilson Ave, 773-769-6859)*
Deli slices are swapped out for fantastic thickly sliced country-style ham, and salty, cured *jamón serrano* popped up out of nowhere, confusing but ultimately wooing us. But the roasted pork killed the mood, with its slightly dry, somewhat stringy texture. Fix that and you have one hell of a sandwich.

2 **Habana Libre** (p.49)
Incredibly tender, marinated, slow-roasted pork is piled onto garlic bread between slices of sugar-and-salt-cured country-style ham with pickle, Swiss cheese and mustard for an elevated take on the Cuban. The only thing that detracts is the undertoasted, poofy bread slathered with garlic butter.

1 **Cafecito** (pictured above; p.49)
Textbook and delicious, the key to this sandwich's success is the citrus-garlic-marinated, cumin-rubbed *lechon asado* and the perfect toasting (whoever is operating the *plancha* deserves a raise).—*Heather Shouse*

★ ☻ **La Unica** Wind through the aisles of this "food mart" to the rear corner and you'll find a dozen tables, a friendly counterman and a wall lined with brightly colored signs touting house specialties. (Grab an English menu from the counter if your Spanish is weak.) The Cuban sandwich is among the best in town; pork-filled tamales, crunchy *bacalao* (salt cod), the roasted pork dinner with yellow rice, and garlicky green and caramelized sweet plantains are all must-haves, too. Top off the meal with a perfectly rich and slightly sweet *café con leche. 1515 W Devon Ave between Bosworth and Greenview Aves (773-274-7788). El: Red to Loyola. Bus: 22, 36, 151, 155. Breakfast, lunch, dinner. Average main course: $6.*

▼ ☾ **90 Miles Cuban Café** If you're looking for a morning pick-me-up, don't miss this cigar-box-sized Cuban carryout spot. Potent *café con leche* and *cortaditos* are the perfect pair with guava and cream cheese pastries, best enjoyed at one of the counter stools while waiting on a lunch order for later. Best bets include the meaty Cuban sandwich or the Guajrito, essentially a Puerto Rican jibarito that piles marinated nickle-thin steak, grilled onions and cheese onto crispy green plantains. *3101 N Clybourn Ave at Barry Ave (773-248-2822). Bus: 49, 50, 77. Breakfast, lunch, dinner. Average main course: $9.* ● *Other location: 2540 W Armitage (773-227-2822).*

▼ **BYOB Sabor a Cuba** The Cuban vibe is alive in this pleasantly bright and tidy dining room, complete with high-backed wooden chairs and rustic cast-iron barstools. Entry-level Cuban dishes include snapper *a la criolla* with an intense garlicky red sauce and *lechon asado* (roasted pork), served with rice, black beans and sweet platanos maduros. Tropical fruit *batidas* (milkshakes), Latin sodas (like Malta and Champ's Cola) and soulful desserts like the caramel flan to end things on a sweet note. *1833 W Wilson Ave between Wolcott and Ravenswood Aves (773-769-6859). El: Brown to Damen. Bus: 50, 81, 145, 148. Lunch, dinner (closed Mon). Average main course: $9.*

BYOB Señor Pan The food tastes more of a grandma's kitchen than a marketing department, regardless of the chain-like look of this Cuban café. The Cuban sandwich is built on a hearty foundation of moist and flavorful roasted pork, and other classics like *ropa vieja* (shredded beef in a tomatoey sauce) and *media noche* (ham, pork and cheese on sweet bread) are also solid renditions. Soul-warming black beans are a particular standout among the sides, and for an exotic touch, try a shake in tropical fruit flavors like mamey and guanabana. *4612 W Fullerton Ave at Kenton Ave (773-227-1020). El: Blue to California. Bus: 54, X54, 74. Breakfast, lunch, dinner. Average main course: $6.*

☻ **Tropi Cuba** This bare-bones grocery store on the edge of Logan Square has a secret. Crammed in the back behind rows of provisions is a bar-stool-only Cuban dive pumping out tasty pressed Cuban sandwiches (served with paper-thin, hand-cut french fries) and wickedly strong Cuban coffee, all at bargain prices. For an even cheaper alternative, go for the dollar hotbox items up front; the *papa rellena* (a huge, crispy potato ball packed with ground beef) is a great snack on the go. *3000 W Lyndale St at Sacramento Ave (773-252-0230). El: Blue to California. Bus: 52, 56, 73, 74. Breakfast, lunch, dinner. Average main course: $5.*

Delis

THE RYE HAS IT Buttery pastrami on soft rye bread is among Ada's Deli's signatures.

○ **Ada's Deli** If the mark of a good Jewish deli is the schmaltz, Ada's is in good shape: Circles of oil glimmer on top of the matzo-ball soup, and the peppery hot pastrami is rich with soft fat. And it gets even better: Latkes, appropriately greasy yet crisp, can be substituted for rye in the pastrami sandwich (a worthy option if your health can handle it). Plus, it has decent bagels for schmearing thick layers of cream cheese. The only area that's not so schmaltzy? The service, which, in a rejection of true deli culture, is downright sweet. *10 S Wabash Ave between Madison and Monroe Sts (312-372-7696). El: Blue, Red to Monroe; Brown, Green, Orange, Pink, Purple (rush hrs) to Madison. Breakfast, lunch, dinner. Average main course: $9.*

○ **Ashkenaz Deli** For deli fiends for whom the Chicago–versus–New York debate never ceases, here's hope: a Chicago deli with a New York touch. The pastrami at this tiny place (which reigned in the '70s on Morse Avenue) is top notch, and even diehard Chicagoans find it hard to resist this place's pastrami, lox, herring, corned beef and gefilte fish. Like all good delis, Ashkenaz puts its efforts into its food, not its decor, so do as a New Yorker would do: Deal with it. *12 E Cedar St between State St and Lake Shore Dr (312-944-5006). El: Red to Clark/Division. Bus: 22, 36, 70. Breakfast, lunch, dinner. Average sandwich: $7.*

○ **Augustino's Rock & Roll Deli** When just walking down Wells Street has left your wallet looking slim, stop into Augustino's for a hot meal that won't break the bank. Try the Supreme meatball sub, Augie's "to die for" blue cheese steak sandwich or homemade lasagna. The three-restaurant chain has been serving up pizzas, pastas and subs to Chicago for over 25 years. *233 S Wacker Dr, Sears Tower (312-258-1840). El: Red to North/Clybourn. Bus: 22, 36, 72. Breakfast, lunch, dinner. Average main course: $8. ● Other locations: 246 S Schmale Rd, Carol Stream (630-665-5585), 300 W North Ave, West Chicago (630-293-8602).*

★ ○ **The Bagel** The Bagel never closes…it just moves locations. In its current spot (the third since 1950) the deli has managed to bring a little Jewish curmudgeonliness to Boystown. So, when you're at the counter ordering your potato knish, or sitting in one of the booths dipping a fluffy roll into the magnificent, housemade chicken soup, expect to have a brusque comment or two thrown your way. After all, the Bagel hasn't survived all these years by being *nice*. *3107 N Broadway between Barry Ave and Briar Pl (773-477-0300). El: Brown, Purple (rush hrs), Red to Belmont. Bus: 36, 77, 145, 146, 151. Breakfast, lunch, dinner. Average main course: $9.*

○ **Bari Foods** See Italian/Pizza for review.

○ **Bryn Mawr Deli** First of all, there's the Bryn Mawr Combo, overstuffed with roast beef, corned beef, turkey, ham, provolone and crunchy red onion. True, it's the kind of sandwich you can get at a million delis around town. So why come to this one? Because instead of brisk and annoyed service, the family that runs this operation is exceedingly friendly. If that weren't enough, they also make mean Middle Eastern specialties, like hand-rolled stuffed grape leaves and a thick and bold hummus. *1101 Bryn Mawr Ave at Winthrop Ave (773-271-4880). El: Red to Bryn Mawr. Bus: 36, 84, 151. Breakfast, lunch, dinner. Average main course: $5.*

★ ▽ ○ **Cipollina** This Italian-leaning deli from the folks behind stellar sandwich shop Milk & Honey offer cured meats, cheeses and antipasti by the pound, making it a perfect post-work or pre-picnic stop. For snacking instead of shopping, order up one of the dozen panini and sandwich creations, the best of which is the *porchetta*, tender roast pork dressed with ricotta salata, arugula, walnut pistou and truffle oil. The frittata panini and Intelligentsia coffee make for a good breakfast; Italian sodas and Black Dog gelato are stellar refreshers. *1543 N Damen Ave between Pierce and North Aves (773-227-6300). El: Blue to Damen. Bus: 50, 56, 72. Mon–Sat 8am–7pm; Sun 8am–4pm. Average sandwich: $7.*

○ **Deli Boutique** Jana Buchtova knows that Chicagoans are well-traveled, and with her European-style deli, she reminds them of where they've been. She's likely to succeed: Her breads are imported, par-baked, from Europe, and she's using them on her panini, including one that layers prosciutto, fresh mozzarella and an olive tapenade. She also has a whole line of imported meats and cheeses, and serves Italian coffee drinks using Lavazza beans. *2318 N Clark St between Belden Ave and Fullerton Pkwy (773-880-9820). El: Red to Fullerton. Bus: 22, 36, 74. 8am–8pm. Average main course: $7.*

Eleven City Diner Owner Brad Rubin scoured the country to research this Jewish deli/diner. His pastrami is tender, fatty and full of flavor; the milkshakes are thick and oversized; matzo balls are enormous; and the brisket is good enough that any grandmother, Jewish or not, would want to claim it. Does it hold a candle to other Jewish spots in the country? It's hard to say. But Rubin definitely holds his own as the charming/obnoxious host, giving this place enough character to become a fixture in its own right. *1112 S Wabash Ave between 11th St and Roosevelt Rd (312-212-1112). El: Green, Orange, Red to Roosevelt. Bus: 1, 3, X3, 4, X4, 12. Breakfast, lunch, dinner. Average main course: $8.*

★ **Eppy's Deli** "Larry the Jew" is at the helm of this slick garden-level operation, which has all the chutzpah of a New York Jewish deli but none of the grittiness. Ordering a sandwich on the marbled rye is your best bet, and whether you go with thinly sliced turkey or celery-flecked tuna salad, the goods are piled on thick and high. Sides like tangy potato salad and an assortment of mustards will keep you happy, but it's the heart-stopping grilled Reuben that will keep you coming back. *224 E Ontario St between St. Clair St and Fairbanks Ct (312-943-7797). El: Red to Grand. Bus: 2, 3, X3, 66, 145, 146, 147, 151, 157. Breakfast, lunch, dinner. Average sandwich: $7. ● Other location: 160 N Franklin St (312-345-7771).*

✳ **Finkel's** Don't be misled by the location: Finkel's has nothing to do with Kendall College (even though it's on the first floor of the cooking school's building). And don't be fooled by the name, either—this Finkel's has nothing to do

with the legendary Finkl's that used to be in the Loop. Nevertheless, it's doing its best to hold up the classic deli traditions. The food is hit and miss: The pastrami is warm and nicely fatty, but the egg salad needs salt. On the other hand, the authentic, sweet-and-salty deli service is something it's gotten just right. *926 N North Branch St at Halsted St (312-335-0050). Bus: 8, 66, 70. Breakfast, lunch (closed Sun). Average sandwich: $5.*

JB's Deli This counter—like every good Jewish deli—is manned by workers who are gruff, efficient and impatient. The food is equally no-frills: Thinly sliced corned beef is piled on high; lox platters include red onion, cream cheese and tomato, but lettuce stands in for capers (which are available for an extra charge per request); housemade blintzes are small pockets of delicious creaminess served on paper plates. *5501 N Clark St at Catalpa Ave (773-728-0600). El: Red to Bryn Mawr. Bus: 22, 36, 50. Breakfast, lunch, dinner. Average main course: $10.*

★ **Manny's Coffee Shop & Deli** Chicago's most quintessential restaurant is not a steakhouse or a laboratory-like kitchen putting out cutting-edge cuisine. It's a cafeteria. Decide what you want before you get in line at this 66-year-old institution. You'll pass plates of Jell-O and chicken salad, but this line moves too quickly to decide on the spot. Our advice? Grab one of the oversized corned beef or pastrami sandwiches, a potato pancake on the side and a packet of Tums for dessert. *1141 S Jefferson St at Grenshaw St (312-939-2855). El: Blue to Clinton. Bus: 8, 12. Breakfast, lunch, dinner (closed Sun). Average main course: $10.*

★ ▼ ✳ **My Pie/Li'l Guys** A good deli and a good pizza place—does a neighborhood need anything else? By serving deep-dish with a rich crust and chunky, slightly spicy sauce, owner Rich Aronson is continuing a family tradition (his father opened the first My Pie in 1971). The deli, on the other hand, was his idea—and a good one. Juicy house-cured corned beef, fresh-fruit smoothies and fudgy brownies you *wish* your mom could bake are three reasons why he may have another tradition on his hands. *2010 N Damen Ave at McLean Ave (773-394-6900). El: Blue to Western. Bus: 50, 73. Lunch, dinner. Average pie: $15.*

Original Frances' Deli Boasting enough root beer flavors for every day of the week, Frances' knows how to indulge its Lincoln Park customers. The simple menu and gigantic portions have kept this Lincoln Park staple in business for more than 70 years. Try a triple-decker corned beef with hot pastrami ($9.95), but skip the fries and go for the potato pancake side. Hopefully, there is still room for chicken matzo ball soup and a gigantic chocolate-chip cookie for dessert. *2552 N Clark St between Deming Pl and Wrightwood Ave (773-248-4580). Bus: 22, 36. Breakfast, lunch, dinner. Average main course: $10.*

★ **Perry's** The closest thing Chicago has to the "soup Nazi," Perry's is a lunchtime institution with a fiercely enforced no-cell-phones policy. The wait is rewarded with deli classics like matzo ball soup (though, unfortunately, it's only served up on Mondays); egg salad sandwiches; hot, juicy pastrami; and "Perry's Favorite"—corned beef, Jack cheese, coleslaw and Russian dressing piled high on fresh rye. It's also one of the few places in the area to get a chocolate malt, and a tasty one at that. *174 N Franklin St at Couch Pl (312-372-7557). El: Blue, Brown, Green, Orange, Pink, Purple (rush hrs) to Clark/Lake. Lunch (closed Sat, Sun). Average sandwich: $7. ● Other location: 719 W Maxwell St (312-243-1633).*

Steve's Deli So maybe the carrots in the chicken soup here are undercooked, and maybe the broth itself is weak. Doesn't matter. People will order the soup for the good matzo balls, because a good matzo ball in Chicago is hard to find. And good sablefish? Good lox? Happily, these elusive goods are also found at Steve's. No, the bagel you put the fish on isn't great. And this isn't a corned-beef place, either—the beef is leaner than the economy. But all of this can be forgiven. Because what would a Jewish deli be without something to kvetch about? *354 W Hubbard St at N Orleans St (312-467-6868). El: Brown, Purple (rush hrs) to Merchandise Mart. Bus: 11, 65, 125. Breakfast, lunch, dinner. Average sandwich: $8.75.*

★ ✳ **Zaleski & Horvath Market Cafe** A couple of Hyde Park veterans (the former owners of Istria Café) and a sandwich maker from the suburbs (the owner of the now-defunct Shane's Deli in Wheaton) have joined forces to open a casual but high-quality grocery store and sandwich shop. The shelves are stocked with gourmet groceries, but the crowds tend to gather at the deli counter for quince paste and Spanish jamon sandwiches and panini with farmstead cheese and ham pressed between pretzel bread. Oatmeal-chocolate-chip cookies are a hot item, too; still, with only four tables, the most coveted thing in the place is a seat. *1126 E 47th St between Woodlawn and Greenwood Aves (773-538-7372). Bus: 2, 15, 47. 7am–7pm. Average main course: $7.*

TRIO GRAND Steve's Deli puts out a spread of classics from latkes to lox.

Eastern European

I'M A PEPPER, TOO Comforting dishes like sauteed chicken with peppers are typical plates at Restaurant Bulgaria.

Avant Garde We didn't stick around very late, but given all the chrome, sexy lighting and bared midriffs we saw, we're pretty sure this place turns into the city's consummate Bulgarian nightclub. (That would also explain the 2am closing time.) During lunch and dinner hours, however, it's a surprisingly good restaurant. The menu is full of small plates like herbaceous sausages, dill-flecked yogurt-cucumber salads, fried zucchini and feta-packed *burek*—all of which taste good even without a cocktail in hand. *5241 N Harlem Ave between Foster and Farragut Ave (773-594-9742). El: Blue to Harlem. Bus: 64, 90. Lunch, dinner. Average main course: $8.*

Chaihanna In the mood for Uzbek food? No idea what that is? Start with palate-perker uppers pickled herring, watermelon or cabbage. Then eggplant salad, rich with bittersweet chunks, sparkles with cilantro and is excellent plopped atop *lepeshki*, the round bread of Uzbekistan. Move on to luscious lamb meat over roasted long beans and zucchini. Finish with the *chak-chak*, a block of fried noodles heavy with honey that's something of an Uzbek take on the Rice Krispies treat. *19 E Dundee Rd, Buffalo Grove (847-215-5044). Lunch, dinner (closed Mon). Average main course: $9.*

★ **Deta's Pita** If you're lucky, the older lady with the Midas touch who cooks here will bake some of her breads from scratch while you're there (it takes about 30 minutes). Order one meat-and-potato and one spinach-and-cheese, and soon she'll flip a hot pan over a paper plate, coaxing out a round of steaming, fragrant bread

that resembles a stuffed Danish. She calls it pita—we think it's more like *burek*—but the buttery, flaky pastries are so luscious we don't really care what they're called. *7555 N Ridge Blvd between Birchwood Ave and Howard St (773-973-1505). Bus: 49D, 97, 201, Pace 215. Breakfast, lunch, dinner. Average main course: $6.*

Duke's Eatery and Deli Behind Duke's nondescript façade, you'll discover what seems to be the wild fantasy of some hunting enthusiast/interior designer. In a room of dark wood, heraldry and portraits of medieval nobility, diners enjoy hearty sausages, sauces and pickles favored in Baltic states. The "fried bread hill" is a perfect drinking buddy: a bready Lincoln Log–like construction coated with garlicky cheese. For an entrée, try the smoked pork served with sauerkraut and potatoes on the side. *6312 S Harlem Ave, Summit (708-594-5622). Bus: 62H, 62W, Pace 307. Lunch, dinner. Average main course: $10.*

▼ **B BYOB The Epicurean Hungarian** The staff here serves up a generous menu of down-home Eastern European entrées with simple ingredients in pleasing combinations. Sour cherry soup is a sweet and satisfying starter. The lamb shank "Transylvanian style" is subtly seasoned and served with nutty egg "barley" pasta, while a cut of filet mignon gets sweet pepper, peas and sliced liver. Goulashes, schnitzels and other fresh foods are served at reasonable prices and with palpable bonhomie. *4431 W Roosevelt Rd, Hillside (708-449-1000). Brunch (Sun), lunch (Wed–Sun), dinner (Wed–Sun). Average main course: $16.*

★ **Healthy Food** As delicious as the heavy Lithuanian food at this diner is, its name is about as far from the truth as possible. Focus on Lithuanian specialties like *kugelis*, a pan-fried square of potato pudding that's rich with the flavors of bacon and onions, and sweet, crêpelike pancakes called *blynai*, topped with fruit (order them unfilled rather than stuffed with the dry and spongy cheese). Pork lovers will flip for the fresh bacon buns, served on weekends only, which are exactly what they sound like. *3236 S Halsted St between 32nd and 33rd Sts (312-326-2724). Bus: 8, 35, 39, 44. Breakfast, lunch, dinner (closed Mon). Average main course: $9.*

Nelly's Saloon On weekends (when there's live music) or when there's a soccer game on, you'll find handsome Romanian imports chowing down on the earthy cuisine of the motherland: platters of *mititei* (grilled sausages); fried kraut with bits of bacon fat; heaping bowls of polenta with feta; and pan-fried chicken wings. Any other time, it's likely to be just you and namesake owner Nelly, the queen of amaretto stone sours. *3256 N Elston Ave between Belmont Ave and Henderson St (773-588-4494). El: Blue to Belmont. Bus: 52, 77, 82. Lunch, dinner (closed Mon). Average main course: $10.*

★ **Old L'Viv** If there's one thing here you definitely don't want to make a choice between, it's the soups. Before digging into this Ukrainian restaurant's buffet, you'll have to decide between the silky and gorgeous borscht, the chicken soup sprinkled with fresh dill, or cabbage soup that's tart with housemade sauerkraut. Can't call it? Go

TAKE FLIGHT Start the night with a trio of infused vodkas at Russian Tea Time.

Baba Marta, a holiday that commemorates spring. Your money is better spent on comfort fare like *shopsko gyoveche*, a baked casserole of feta, egg and hot peppers, or *katin meze*, a goulashlike plate of roasted meat and sautéed onions slathered in tomato sauce. *4724 W Lawrence Ave between Edens Expwy and Kilpatrick Ave (773-282-0300). Bus: 54A, 81, 92. Lunch, dinner. Average main course: $12.*

BYOB Restaurant Sarajevo There are salads and fried calamari and sliced chicken breast on this menu, but if you're ordering the right things, you're actually only hitting three foods: bread, three housemade varieties of which arrive at the beginning of the meal; cheese, whether in the form of the Bulgarian feta or in the mild (but highly addictive) three-cheese spread that comes with the bread; and meat, from succulent housemade sausages like the luscious *cevapcici* to thinly sliced veal. Welcome to the Bosnian diet. *2701 W Lawrence Ave at Washtenaw Ave (773-275-5310). El: Brown to Western. Bus: 11, 49, 81. Breakfast, lunch, dinner. Average main course: $11.*

★ **Russian Tea Time** A classy choice for the symphony set and couples looking to indulge, this institution proves excess is best. Slide into a cozy booth and start the assault with classic borscht, sour cream-slathered dumplings and caviar blini. Follow up with creamy beef Stroganoff or oniony, nutmeg-laced, ground beef–stuffed cabbage rolls. Finish up with hot farmer's-cheese blintzes or Klara's apricot-and-plum strudel, a family recipe. Be sure to order a flight of house-infused vodkas (horseradish, ginger, black currant tea, coriander and more). *77 E Adams St between Michigan and Wabash Aves (312-360-0000). El: Brown, Green, Orange, Pink, Purple (rush hrs) to Adams; Red, Blue to Jackson. Bus: 3, 4, X4, 6, 7, 14, 26, X28, 145, 147, 148, 151. Lunch, dinner. Average main course: $20.*

🕐 **Sak's Ukrainian Village** Past the dark bar (where regulars pour tall bottles of beer into frosted glasses) lies a dining room heavily decorated with oil paintings and plastic flowers. Remember, you're not here for burgers and steaks, so stick to the Ukrainian side of the menu. Dense stuffed cabbage is topped with a thick mushroom gravy, and potato pancakes are thin and crispy. But it's all just a vehicle to get to dessert: powdered sugar–dusted blintzes with browned and crispy exteriors that give way to sweet, decadent cheese. *2301 W Chicago Ave at Oakley Blvd (773-278-4445). Bus: 49, X49, 50, 66. Lunch, dinner (Mon). Average main course: $10.*

★ ▼ 🕐 ☀ **BYOB Shokolad** Anyone who fears Ukrainian Village is losing its ethnicity can take solace in this bakery and café. Well-heeled women chat over coffee and cake, a handful of sugar-rushing kids scrape the bottom of their fruit parfaits, and neighborhood elders, including men of the cloth, tuck into particularly good bowls of borscht, all to the tune of Ukrainian chatter. The younger of the mother-daughter team behind the classy, casual spot is right to recommend her mom's baked goods (the airy, sour cream–layered napolean cake goes fast for a reason), but the savory crêpes, buttery panini and delicious soups are worth a visit on their own. *2524 W Chicago Ave at Maplewood Ave (773-276-6402). Bus: 49, X49, 66. Breakfast, lunch, dinner (Fri, Sat). Average main course: $7.*

🕐 **Staropolska** See Polish for review.

TAKE THE CAKE Traditional Ukrainian sweets are the specialty at Shokolad.

crazy and order all three. You're going to gorge yourself on the oniony potato pancakes, tender *schnitzel* and rich, creamy blintzes anyway…so why not get a head start? *2228 W Chicago Ave between Leavitt St and Oakley Blvd (773-772-7250). Bus: 49, 66. Lunch, dinner (closed Mon). Buffet: $9.*

☾ **Restaurant Bulgaria** This squat brick citadel is a community gathering spot where Bulgarian dance troupes come for midweek practice while gruff-looking expats throw down Stella Artois for $2.50 each Monday through Friday. Grandmothers stop in to peddle *martenitzas*, red and white bracelets to celebrate

French

RAISING THE STEAK (FRITES)
Le Bouchon executes bistro
classics as well as your favorite
Parisian spot.

★ ☀ B **Bistro Campagne** With a name that translates as "countryside bistro," this restaurant is so warm and inviting we could stay all night. Ingredients are organic across the board and meld into French bistro classics with unforgettable flavors. There isn't a bad thing on the menu, but if we had to limit ourselves, we'd go with onion soup, mussels steamed in Belgian ale, roasted chicken and pan-seared flatiron steak flanked by amazing frites. Oh, and all of the day's ice creams. *4518 N Lincoln Ave between Sunnyside and Wilson Aves (773-271-6100). El: Brown to Western. Bus: 11, 49, X49, 78, 81. Brunch (Sun), dinner. Average main course: $22.*

☀ B **Bistrot Margot** The only way this bistro could get more French is if Gérard Depardieu were tap dancing on a table. Until then, Francophiles will have to make do with a menu of French onion soup brimming with soft, sweet onions; smoked salmon; and the seasonal coq au vin, a straight-from-the-oven crock of roasted lemon garlic chicken. Lest anybody think the French too serious, the dining room features photos of the chef-owner's young daughter, Margot, posing as a painter, dancer and, of course, a chef. *1437–39 N Wells St between Schiller St and Burton Pl (312-587-3660). El: Brown, Purple (rush hrs) to Sedgwick. Bus: 72. Brunch (Sat, Sun), lunch (Mon–Fri), dinner. Average main course: $18.*

☀ B **Bistro 110** Weary shoppers have long escaped the Mag Mile for respite in a glass of *vin* and a heaping bowl of steamed mussels at this solid bistro. Hanging hats, comfy banquettes, brass accents and a lengthy bar add to the Frenchie flair. The menu sticks to standards, of which the roasted chicken, steak frites and crème brûlée scratch that Right Bank itch. A sidewalk patio offers prime people-watching in warm weather, as well as a nice place to enjoy weekend brunch. *110 E Pearson St between Michigan Ave and Rush St (312-266-3110). El: Red to Chicago. Bus: 10, 66, 125, 143, 144, 145, 146, 147, 151. Brunch (Sun), lunch (Mon–Sat), dinner. Average main course: $27.*

B **Bistrot Zinc** Amid tony Gold Coast restaurants is this surprisingly authentic Paris-style bistro, complete with the day's paper dangling from wooden rods, silver-plated egg stands beckoning hungry drinkers to the zinc-topped bar and a menu that delivers all the classics in reliable fashion. Wine-steamed mussels and butter-drenched escargots sate shellfish-lovers, while onion soup's beefy broth and gobs of Gruyère satisfy comfort-food cravings. Steak frites is fine, but thin. Opt instead for the peppercorn-crusted New York strip, if you're craving red meat. *1131 N State St between Cedar and Elm Sts (312-337-1131). El: Red to Clark/Division. Bus: 22, 36, 70. Brunch (Sat, Sun), lunch (Mon–Fri), dinner. Average main course: $20.*

☀ **Brasserie Jo** Chef Jean Joho is best known for the jacket-required dining style of Everest, but this brasserie is casual both in design and spirit. The menu of simple Alsatian food matches: The classic salad lyonnaise, rife with chewy *lardons*, is a solid starter, but it can't compete with the crispy, onion-filled *tarte flambé*. The chicken in the creamy riesling coq au vin arrives with a delectable pile of doughy, salty *knejtla*. Somebody get the chef a cocktail—he should relax like this more often. *59 W Hubbard St between Dearborn and Clark Sts (312-595-0800). El: Red to Grand. Bus: 22, 36, 65, 156. Dinner. Average main course: $20.*

☀ **The Brasserie's Market** What's better than eating at Old Town Brasserie? Eating there cheaper. That's the benefit (if not the idea behind) the Brasserie's Market, a closet-size take-away shop squeezed next to the Brasserie's lobby. Taking the (seasonal) silky artichoke-garlic soup, herb-stuffed roasted chicken, sprightly beet salad and chewy chocolate-chip cookies to go is always an option. But taking it into the restaurant's sunny dining room and reaping benefits like silverware and water service is an experience that gets you much more for your money. *1209 N Wells St at Division St (312-943-3000). El: Red to Clark/Division. Bus: 22, 36, 70, 156. Breakfast, lunch, dinner. Average main course: $10.*

▼ ☀ **Café Bernard** This Lincoln Park stalwart may have shot itself in the foot by opening Red Rooster, the more casual dining room in the back of the building—on a recent Saturday night, Bernard was barely half full. Have people forgotten about the classic fare this spot has been dishing out since 1973? If they have, they should get their

INSIDE TRACK
VIVA PARIS!

Anyone who's been lucky enough to visit the undeniably romantic city of Paris has likely looked to relive the experience after returning to their own city, stumbling upon that quintessential neighborhood bistro for the perfect steak frites. For the best spots to replicate Parisian nights in Chicago, Le Bouchon (p.58) is tough to beat, but Bistrot Margot (p.55) isn't far behind. Both Kiki's Bistro (this page) and Bistro Campagne (p.55) have the cozy theme perfected, while Bistrot Zinc (p.55) nails the details, from tiny-tile floors to wooden newspaper rods to red-trimmed windows that fling open for fresh air.

hands on the housemade duck pâté, plump scallops drizzled with balsamic, and peppery filet mignon flanked by soft, creamy potatoes. It's a meal they won't soon forget again. *2100 N Halsted St at Dickens Ave (773-871-2100). El: Brown, Purple (rush hrs) to Armitage. Bus: 8, 73, 74. Dinner. Average main course: $20.*

★ ✳ B **Café des Architectes** *2009 Eat Out Award, Critics' Pick: Best Revival Act (getting Martial Noguier to revive Sofitel's restaurant)* Martial Noguier could have slowed down now that he's got a cushy hotel job at the Sofitel. Instead, he's putting out some of the best French food in town. His dishes—delicate hamachi carpaccio, beef tenderloin with a green garlic puree—brim with intricate flavors and textural details, all of which get wrapped up into one exciting, singular package. Desserts from pastry chef Suzanne Imaz (who worked with Noguier at one sixtyblue) follow suit. Maybe this team was always this good, but one thing is for certain: In the new Gold Coast digs, many more people will get to experience it. *20 E Chestnut St at Wabash Ave (312-324-4063). El: Red to Chicago. Bus: 36, 66, 143, 144, 145, 146, 147, 148, 151. Breakfast, brunch (Sat, Sun), lunch, dinner. Average main course: $29.*

▼ **Café Matou** The ever-changing menu of rich French flavors at this Wicker Park staple includes venison "scallops" in a Syrah sauce and a grilled pork chop in lemon-sage cream sauce—dishes that are simple, hearty and, at the end of the day, just delicious enough to get the job done. A three-course prix-fixe menu—offered Sunday through Thursday evenings for only $24—changes as often as the regular menu, but recent offerings have included grilled asparagus with chive vinaigrette and sautéed Pacific rockfish in Chardonnay-thyme cream sauce. *1846 N Milwaukee Ave between Bloomingdale Ave and Moffat St (773-384-8911). El: Blue to Western. Bus: 49, X49, 56, 73. Dinner (closed Mon). Average main course: $21.*

▼ ✳ **Chez Joël** Little Italy is not just about red-sauce joints. Another option is this quaint spot, where the walls are the color of buttercream and the pâté is just as smooth. The mushroom quiche is thick with earthy 'shrooms and crunchy bread crumbs, and the steak frites comes with a particularly herbal maître d'butter and habit-forming shoestring fries. This place might just be that dependable little spot you've been looking for when the wait at Le Bouchon is insane. *1119 W Taylor St at May St (312-226-6479). El: Blue to Racine. Bus: 7, 12, 60. Lunch (Tue–Fri), dinner (closed Mon). Average main course: $20.*

▼ ☺ BYOB **Couture Crêpe Café** The monochromatic color scheme and the

Lichtenstein-ish paintings may not have legs for the long haul, but in the meantime, this is the mod antidote to the Franco-cheesiness of stalwart La Creperie. Its thinner sweet crêpes are superior to its puffy savory counterparts, so for the main event, go with the chicken and avocado panini with fresh basil and garlic dressing. Finish with the eponymous sweet, specifically the French pear crêpe topped with a red wine reduction. *2568 N Clark St between Deming and Wrightwood Aves (773-857-2638). El: Brown, Purple (rush hrs), Red to Fullerton. Bus: 8, 11, 22, 36, 74. Breakfast, lunch and dinner. Average main course: $9.*

▼ ☺ BYOB **Crêpe Bistro** This Loop creperie—with its stainless-steel pendant lamps and black lacquer tables—skews more *Sex In the City* than Saint Germain Boulevard. But look past the ladies nursing cups of java and slinging gossip and you'll find one of Chicago's better creperies. The spongy griddle-caramelized things are cooked to order, with fillings that'll whisk you from Russia (salmon roe and sour cream) to France (*coq au vin*). During your voyage, stop for the Katmandhu, curried chicken drizzled with spicy-sweet chutney. *186 N Wells St between Lake and Couch Sts (312-269-0300). El: Blue, Brown, Green, Orange, Pink, Purple (rush hrs) to Clark/Lake. Tues–Thurs 11am–8pm, Fri–Sat 11am–10pm. Average crêpe: $7.*

☺ **Crêpes Café** Those who crave the stuff of San Francisco crêpe stands can find a suitable substitute until their next Bay trip at this cheerful Loop café. The $7–$12 price point may seem stiff for a little French pancake, but savories (mushroom, beef Stroganoff) come with salads and desserts are a la mode. Plus, while the namesake crêpes may be thicker than the lacy-edged ideal, they're jam-packed with fillings, the best of which include a seafood-studded *frutti di mare* option. *410 S Clark St between Van Buren St and Congress Pkwy (312-341-1313). El: Blue, Brown, Orange, Pink, Purple (rush hrs) to LaSalle. Lunch (Mon–Fri). Average main course: $10.*

★ ✳ **Cyrano's Bistrot & Wine Bar** Via vintage movie posters, Cyrano de Bergerac's long, obtrusive nose pokes its way into every corner of this charming bistro—just as the town of Bergerac's cuisine fills every part of the menu. Chef Didier Durand has built a loyal following for his southwestern French fare, like crisp-skinned rotisserie duck with orange sauce, succulent skirt steak with a hot pile of frites and the most adorable cheese plate known to man–and he's revered for the crème brûlée. *546 N Wells St between Grand Ave and Ohio St (312-467-0546). El: Brown, Purple (rush hrs) to Merchandise Mart; Red to Grand. Bus: 65. Dinner (closed Sun). Average main course: $20.*

✳ **Cyrano's Café and Wine Bar on the Riverwalk** We won't blame you if you arrive at this outdoor café and doubt its ability to put out quality French entrées. The kitchen is in a shack, after all, and the whole operation looks perilously makeshift. But if you avoid the hot dishes (a disappointing—rubbery, even—slice of quiche almost confirmed those initial doubts) and focus on chef Didier Durand's renowned pâtés instead, a shift can occur. With a view of the river and skyline, a glass of rosé in hand and a table crowded with jars of duck rillettes and baskets of bread, you'll go from dubious to devoted. *233 E Riverwalk South between Michigan Ave and Columbus Dr (312-616-1400). El: Brown, Green, Orange, Pink, Purple to State; Red to Lake. Lunch, dinner. Average main course: $12.*

▼ BYOB **Dorado** See Mexican for review.

✳ B **Duchamp** See Contemporary American for review.

▼ **Everest** For years, Everest has lived up to its name, becoming the pinnacle of high-end French dining in the Windy City. Atop the Chicago Stock Exchange, it is still the height of elegance, with views of the rooftops that made the city famous. Chef Jean Joho's seasonal menu—though often-changing—features carefully executed French specialties like boneless rabbit with horseradish, frogs legs and black cod. But the real surprise is the sense of elegance you feel just from having dined at this level. *440 S LaSalle St at Van Buren St (312-663-8920). El: Brown, Orange, Pink, Purple (rush hrs) to LaSalle. Dinner (closed Sun, Mon). Average degustation: $110.*

★ ✳ **Gabriel's** For more than a decade chef-owner Gabriel Viti has been the culinary darling of the North Shore. His eponymous restaurant is the flagship of his restaurant empire, and it is easy to see why. The white tablecloths are offset by the mahogany interior, and the service and food are equally elegant. Expect seasonal French and Italian cuisine, a large selection of pasta and an impressive wine list. *310 Green Bay Rd, Highwood (847-433-0031). Metra: Union Pacific N to Highwood. Dinner (closed Sun, Mon). Average main course: $28.*

✳ **Kiki's Bistro** A good French bistro never gets old—even as it ages. This charming standby still packs in customers, sending them off happier and fatter than they were when they arrived. The seasonal menu may include irresistibles like *navarin d'agneau printanier* (lamb stew) and the seasonal oven-roasted pork tenderloin with apple-Calvados sauce. Kiki's proves getting older doesn't mean losing your touch. *900 N Franklin St at Locust St (312-335-5454). El: Brown, Purple (rush hrs) to Chicago. Bus: 36, 66. Lunch (Mon–Fri), dinner (closed Sun). Average main course: $20.*

Koda Bistro The Beverly neighborhood breaks out of its friendly tavern mode with this upscale French bistro that is more contemporary chic than country chic. The owners, Patrick and Janice Daley, may be green, but chef Aaron Browning earned his Franco stripes in the revered local kitchens of Le Vichyssoise and Everest. Here, his menu gives classic French dishes a dose of seasonal and contemporary flair, such as skate with a caper and brown butter sauce. *10352 S Western Ave between 103rd and 104th Sts (773-445-5632). Bus: 49A, 103, Pace 349. Lunch (Mon–Fri), dinner. Average main course: $20.*

☺ ✳ **La Crêperie** With its dim bar, faded posters of Paris and battered leather banquette, it's no wonder this mainstay is a draw for local bohemians who seem content to sit for hours eating, drinking and typing on their laptops. The atmosphere is so comfortable that it almost overshadows the food. Almost. Once you try the trio of pâtés, the simple steak flanked by crispy frites or any of the namesake crêpes, you'll understand how it's weathered more than three decades. *2845 N Clark St between Diversey Pkwy and Surf St (773-528-9050). El: Brown, Purple (rush hrs) to Diversey. Bus: 8, 22, 76. Lunch, dinner (closed Mon). Average main course: $9.*

La Petite Folie A midlife career change prompted chef Mary Mastricola to open this

SITTIN' PRETTY Chef Martial Noguier gives an artistic spin to classics like roasted lamb chops at Café des Architectes.

LADY IN WAITING Mary Beth Liccioni holds court in her Les Nomades dining room.

almost-hidden, slightly upscale spot eight years ago. The French wine list offers affordable choices and the trusty menu gets updated with seasonal additions every month or so. Early-fall eats include boneless rabbit filled with truffled hazelnut mousse, monkfish paella with jumbo shrimp and trout Grenobloise, and there's a three-course prix fixe (offered 5–6:30pm), while younger couples from the neighborhood take the last reservations for a solid night out. *1504 E 55th St, in the Hyde Park Shopping Center between 55th Pl and Harper Ave (773-493-1394). Bus: X28 SB, 55, X55. Metra: Electric Line to 55-56-57th St. Lunch (Tue–Fri), dinner (Sat, Sun) (closed Mon). Average main course: $21.*

La Sardine Devotees of Wicker Park's Le Bouchon might tell you otherwise, but the bistro essentials at this sibling spot are just as tasty as those at the homebase. The setting is much more open and airy than at Bouchon, but the rest of the package is pretty much the same: plump mussels drenched in creamy white-wine broth, onion soup that tests even serious cheese-lovers' thresholds, juicy grilled hanger steak with bordelaise and simple bouillabaisse jam-packed with seafood. The wine list is half price Mondays, and there's a $25 three-course meal Tuesdays. *111 N Carpenter St between Washington Blvd and Randolph St (312-421-2800). Bus: 8, 9, 19, 20. Lunch (Mon–Fri), dinner (closed Sun). Average main course: $18.*

▼ ✳ B **La Tache** This Andersonville eatery is the place to go if you're looking for classic French bistro with a little something different. The menu boasts ever-changing seasonal specials such as the horseradish-crusted halibut or the *kurobuta* pork chop with peach custard and savory bread pudding—but it's hard to go wrong with classics such as the steak frites or the choice of four burgers with a selection of four sauces or compound butters. *1475 W Balmoral Ave between Clark St and Glenwood Ave (773-334-7168). El: Red to Berwyn. Bus: 22, 36, 92. Brunch (Sun), dinner. Average main course: $18.*

★ **Le Bouchon** Yes, it's small and crowded, and you'll have to wait at the bar for a bit even with a reservation. But it's the closest thing Chicago has to that adorable little bistro in Paris. Regulars have their never-fail favorites: the flaky, caramelly onion tart; the robust onion soup with a gluttonous amount of Gruyère; the butter-topped

steak flanked by perfectly crisp frites; the hard-to-find seared veal kidneys with mustard sauce; the feeds-two duck à l'orange; and the simple profiteroles. Only snootier waiters could make for a more French experience. *1958 N Damen Ave between Homer St and Armitage Ave (773-862-6600). El: Blue to Damen. Bus: 50, 73. Lunch, dinner (closed Sun). Average main course: $17.*

Le Petit Paris Even those who know the local food scene may not have heard of Le Petit Paris. Too bad for them…it just means you are more likely to get a seat at this excellent French bistro. The seasonally changing menu is full of French classics, like the mushroom-laden beef bourguignonne, luscious veal "Marengo," and half-price bottles of wine on Thursdays never disappoint. *260 E Chestnut St between DeWitt Pl and Lake Shore Dr (312-787-8260). El: Red to Chicago. Bus: 10, 125, 157. Dinner. Average main course: $20.*

♨ **Les Nomades** It's no longer a private club, but after more than 30 years in business, this is still the most regal restaurant in town. Owner Mary Beth Liccioni keeps the grounds (a townhouse built in 1895) decked out like something out of *Dynasty*: lush fabrics, ornate carpeting, giant arrangements of flowers. But chef Chris Nugent's ever-changing French-American menu keeps the food current (if still pretty rich). Guys, take note: This remains a good place to propose (or beg forgiveness). But make sure you're wearing a jacket—you wouldn't want to get scolded in front of your date, would you? *222 E Ontario St between Fairbanks Ct and St. Clair St (312-649-9010). El: Red to Grand. Bus: 10, 145, 147. Dinner (closed Sun–Mon). Average main course: $28.*

✳ **Marché** You'd think that in Randolph Row's ever-evolving restaurant climate the block's old-timer either would have become obsolete or changed with the times. It's done neither. The decor still looks like a drag queen catfight; the Frenchie bistro menu remains relatively intact; and the crowd fills every single jewel-toned seat in the house, especially on weekends. The onion soup, spit-roasted chicken, steak frites and unbeatable apple tarte Tatin with housemade ice cream continue to satisfy, even with flaming makis across the street. *833 W Randolph St at Halsted St (312-226-8399). El: Green, Pink to Clinton. Bus: 8, 20. Lunch (Mon–Fri), dinner. Average main course: $25.*

★ B **Mexique** See Mexican for review.

★ **Michael** Chef Michael Lachowicz made a name for himself at other local and beloved French eateries. He made such a name, in fact, that he christened this venture after himself. Though he's not reinventing the wheel here, the man can cook. Delectable classics abound: gooey cheese puffs, smoked salmon-topped potato pancake, an impossibly tender filet–and–short rib duo, and a rich hot chocolate–and–soufflé combo. Lachowicz proves that no matter whose name is on the room, the draw is what's on the plate. *64 Green Bay Rd, Winnetka (847-441-3100). Metra: Union Pacific North to Hubbard Woods. Lunch (Fri), dinner. Average main course: $34.*

✳ **Mon Ami Gabi** They say practice makes perfect, and the pitch-perfect bistro dishes here show years of rehearsal. The Epcot Center feel of some other Lettuce Entertain You restaurants is missing. Instead, you get a cozy and bustling bistro serving everything from steamed mussels in a white ale broth to a bananas Foster crêpe. Nightly *plats du jour* like duck à l'orange and steak tartare are as consistently delicious as menu stalwarts such as seared skate wing in lemony caper butter and the awesome steak frites. *2300 N Lincoln Park West at Belden Ave (773-348-8886). El: Brown, Purple (rush hrs), Red to Fullerton. Bus: 22, 36, 134, 143, 151, 156. Dinner. Average main course: $19.*

★ ✳ B **NoMI** See Contemporary American for review.

❰ **Old Town Brasserie** Chef Christian Phernetton has taken over for Andrew Motto at this tony brasserie, and though the room is still as classic as ever, the food has been updated. The restaurant offers a ravioli *du jour* and pork cured in *sake*. There are some less-exciting dishes here, too—a sleepy salmon with quinoa, for instance. But ignore those and you'll get a contemporary, exciting experience that, based on the room, you'd never have expected. *1209 N Wells St at Division St (312-943-3000). El: Red to Clark/Division. Bus: 22, 36, 70, 156. Brunch (Sun only), dinner. Average main course: $26.*

★ ✳ **Pierrot Gourmet** In the morning, these communal dining tables are packed with folks fueling up on cappuccinos and buttery croissants. In the evening, however, you're likely to have the place to yourself. Which is curious, because we love the simple, French fare: flambé and crunchy Alsatian tarts resembling thin-crust pizzas. The pride of Pierrot is the pastry, and we like to take them one step further by dipping them in the Valrhona chocolate fondue. Be warned of the unusual early close time: 7 every night. *108 E Superior St at Rush St (312-573-6749). El: Red to Chicago. Bus: 3, 66, 145, 146, 147, 151. Breakfast, lunch, dinner. Average main course: $13.*

✳ **Red Rooster** This tiny, cozy bistro has a side-street entrance that is tough to spot. Keep your eyes peeled because there's nothing like warming up with hearty French provincial food—such as tender beef bourguignonne on a bed of egg noodles or duck confit ladled with berry sauce—when it's extremity-numbing cold outside. Heck, we'll cozy up to the meaty snails in bubbling garlic butter and shockingly inexpensive wine list—many bottles are $29 or less—even in milder temps. *2100 N Halsted St at Dickens Ave (773-929-7660). El: Brown, Purple (rush hrs) to Armitage. Bus: 8, 73, 74. Dinner. Average main course: $16.*

Gastropubs

A THOUSAND POINTS OF LIGHT
Glowing globes illuminate the beer-friendly grub at the Publican.

✳ **Black Duck** The stretch of Halsted Street that lays claim to this classy tavern is packed with upscale eateries. More gastropub than sports bar, this spot keeps the scene grounded. Grab one of the tables that surround the beautiful, dark-wood bar and start with a Black Duck martini and plate of scallops wrapped in salty bacon. Move on to the New York strip seasoned simply with salt, pepper and rosemary. It's not Alinea, BOKA or Landmark. But then again, it's not supposed to be. *1800 N Halsted St at Willow St (312-664-1801). El: Red to North/Clybourn. Bus: 8, 72. Dinner. Average main course: $14.*

▽ Θ ♦ **The Bluebird** This beer-focused tavern didn't intend to be such a food destination, but the eats here are taking center stage. Tempting small plates such as braised rabbit over a saffron risotto, *serrano* and Manchego flatbreads are tough to choose from, so don't—spend the evening grazing while sampling through the vast beer list. Don't know good suds from duds? The staff is pretty well-versed, and even when they're slammed on weekend nights, they tend to field questions or offer up suggestions. *1749 N Damen Ave at Willow St (773-486-2473). El: Blue to Damen. Bus: 50, 56, 72. Dinner. Average small plate: $10.*

Θ ✳ **Celtic Crown Public House**
The marquee outside announces daily specials to the neighborhood. Time your visit based on the signage and you may find yourself with a bill for $1 burgers or 25-cent wings. Even at full price, Celtic Crown is still worth a visit for better-than-average bar food. As you'd expect at an Irish pub, the corned-beef sandwich is satisfying, as is the baked barbecue-rib plate (note to true 'cue fans: The meat is baked, not smoked). The atmosphere is loud, but the waitstaff never overlooks the diners for drinkers. *4301 N Western Ave at Cullom Ave (773-588-1110). El: Brown to Western. Bus: 49, X49, 78. Lunch, dinner. Average main course: $6.*

Θ ✳ **Cullen's Bar and Grill** With the waitresses brandishing brogues along with the shepherd's pie and Guinness pints, you know this Lakeview Irish pub is the real deal. Besides potpies, fish and chips and other Emerald Isle imports, everyone from neighborhood families to tipsy Cubs fans stops in for the above-par bar grub. You can't go wrong with the char-grilled skirt-steak sandwich, turkey-and-corned-beef Reubens, and Bass Ale–battered onion rings the size of your head. *3741 N Southport Ave between Addison St and Irving Park Rd (773-975-0600). El: Brown to Southport. Bus: 9, 22, 152. Lunch, dinner. Average main course: $10.*

♦ ✳ **Duke of Perth** You'll never know how relaxing Celtic music can be until you spend an afternoon at this Scottish ale house. Listen closely as you hang out on the serene outdoor patio, eating fish and chips (it's all-you-can-eat on Wednesdays and Fridays) and drinking from one of the best Scotch whiskey lists in the city—soon you'll be humming along. *2913 N Clark St between Surf St and Oakdale Ave (773-477-1741). El: Brown, Purple (rush hrs) to Diversey. Bus: 8, 22, 76. Lunch (Tue–Sun), dinner. Average main course: $10.*

✳ ☾ **English** With high-top tables and a long bar, it's clear this Britishish spot is putting its pounds on the pub scene. Drinks include a traditional Pimm's Cup and an Earl Grey–mint martini, while classic fish-and-chips and a turkey burger topped with mushrooms and goat cheese are among the food choices. The Newcastle-battered cod is crispy, fat and flaky, and the DIY meatball sandwich comes with a comforting mushroom gravy. Attention to detail fails with the music, though; Starship's "We Built This City" wrecks the Brit-pub vibe. *444 N LaSalle St at Hubbard St (312-222-6200). El: Brown, Purple (rush hrs) to Merchandise Mart. Bus: 65, 125, 156. Lunch, dinner. Average main course: $12.*

★ ✳ **The Gage** Owner Billy Lawless and chef Dirk Flanigan have a hit on their hands with this downtown gastropub. The whiskey

Side dish

New to brew?

Use this beer 101 primer so you're not coming up empty when it's pint time at beer bars and gastropubs.

PALE ALE
These low-alcohol beers are usually light gold with a fruity aroma but decent hop content, meaning they have good bitterness (the more hops, the more bitterness to help balance the sweetness of the malts). The hops are more aggressive in American pale ales, while the malts stand out more in British pale ales.
Our favorites: Goose Island Honkers Ale, Three Floyds Alpha King

INDIA PALE ALE (IPA)
In the 1700s, this bitter ale was brewed in England and exported to British troops in India. Its bitterness comes from the extra dose of hops that acted as a preservative for the voyage. That brewing style remains the same today, although American versions are more flavorful; Brits still like theirs bitter.
Our favorites: Dogfish Head 90 Minute IPA, New Holland Mad Hatter

WHEAT
These yellow beers are refreshing, and light to medium in body. Whether American or German (German wheat beers are labeled *weisse* or *hefeweizen*; the latter means it's unfiltered so it's cloudy and yeastier), expect banana and clove flavors. Belgian witbier is tinged with coriander and orange.
Our favorites: Schneider Weisse, Top Heavy Hefeweizen

PORTER
Originally a British creation, these dark brown, malty beers can give off flavors ranging from espresso to the smokiness you'd associate with beef jerky. These flavors are achieved by type of malt; the malts' toastiness varies according to how long they've been roasted.
Our favorites: Great Lakes Edmund Fitzgerald, Flag Porter

STOUT
Nearly black with a creamy, tan head, these beers (essentially strong porters) get their color and flavor from heavily roasted malts. The Irish and English versions tend to be drier and a bit lighter in body (but still dark in color).
Our favorites: De Dolle Special Extra Export Stout, North Coast Old No. 38

PILSNER
This Czech style takes its name from the city of Pilsen. The translucent beers are usually straw to golden in color, and have a spicy floralness in flavor and smell. German pilsners tend to have more hop bitterness; ditto for American pils, but with more malty sweetness.
Our favorites: Pinkus Ur Pils Organic Pilsner, Victory's Prima Pils

DORTMUNDER/EXPORT
This pale lager is a clean, balanced beer with a biscuity taste and good carbonation. Originally, dortmunder was brewed in two strengths: the lighter lagerbier and a stronger export. The former fell out of favor and disappeared; the latter got its name because it was intended to be exported.
Our favorites: Two Brothers Dog Days, Great Lakes Dortmunder Gold

BOCK
The Germans came up with this potent, belly-warming style in medieval days to survive rough winters. The caramelly, malty beers range in color from amber to chocolate. Doppelbock means "doublebock" and is even stronger, but eisbock is the strongest of all bocks.
Our favorites: Einbecker Ur-Bock, Aventinus Eisbock.—*Heather Shouse*

list is lengthy, beer options reach beyond the basics and wines are accompanied by clever, straightforward descriptions. Flanigan's food is rich and aggressively flavorful, from the perfect-for-snacking Scotch egg to the Gage burger, served a juicy medium-rare and dripping with melted onion marmalade and gobs of stinky Midwestern Camembert. *24 S Michigan Ave between Monroe and Madison Sts (312-372-4243). El: Brown, Green, Orange, Pink, Purple (rush hrs) to Madison. Lunch, dinner. Average main course: $24.*

★ ▽ ♦ ✳ ☾ **Hopleaf** *2009 Eat Out Award, Readers' Choice: Best Beer Bar* Thought this was just a bar to belly up to with a Belgian brew in hand? One bite from the seasonal menu and you'll know there's much more. Carnivores can exercise their organic options with the likes of roasted spring chicken with oven-roasted artichokes, spring onions and mashed potatoes; and CB&J, a grilled sandwich of housemade cashew butter, fig jam and Morbier cheese on sourdough bread. The wait can be a brutal, but somehow we keep coming back for the abuse. *5148 N Clark St between Winona St and Foster Ave (773-334-9851). El: Red to Berwyn. Bus: 22, 92. Dinner. Average main course: $18.*

★ ♦ ✳ B **Mrs. Murphy and Sons** Soda bread? Black-and-white pudding? Not so much. This Irish bistro serves food you'd find in modern-day Dublin, which means Guinness isn't just on the epic beer list, but also in a rich onion–and–white cheddar soup. You'll also find it in the beef stew, along with chunks of parsnips and carrots. Other creative takes include orange-marmalade glazed lamb with goat cheese, dried cherries and pistachios served on a bed of arugula. Not hungry? Stop by for a great Irish whiskey at the gorgeous bar. *3905 N Lincoln Ave between Byron St and Larchmont Ave (773-248-3905). Bus: 11, 50, 80, 152. Brunch (Sat, Sun), dinner (closed Mon). Average main course: $18.*

★ B **Paramount Room** Determined to intertwine the eating and drinking experience, chef Stephen Dunne focuses on elevated bar food at this West Town spot. Some of his food (fried pickle spears, a Wagyu burger) act merely as sponges for the impressive beer list. But the duck confit is sublime, the fish-and-chips crisp and flavorful, and the crab salad light and inspired. The ultimate beer and food pairing, though, comes at dessert, with the addictive Black & Tan Float, a root-beer float made with Guinness ice cream. *415 N Milwaukee Ave between Kinzie and Hubbard Sts (312-829-6300). El: Blue to Grand. Bus: 8, 56, 65. Brunch (Sat, Sun), lunch, dinner. Average main course: $17.*

★ ✳ B **The Publican** *2009 Eat Out Award, Readers' Choice: Best New Restaurant* Diners come to this megaproject from Paul Kahan and crew for three things: to sample the massive list of brews while basking in the golden-hued, beer hall–like space; to sample impeccable charcuterie and amazing oysters from chef Brian Huston's dinner menu; or to begin their Sundays with arguably the best brunch in town. We oscillate, but currently we're in the latter camp, and once you taste the housemade ricotta, the fig-pistachio scone, the wood-fired eggs with harissa and the thick slabs of "Publican bacon" (not the strips that come with the omelette but the top-shelf stuff), you will be too. *837 W Fulton Market at Green St (312-733-9555). El: Green, Pink to Clinton. Bus: 8, 65. Brunch (Sun), dinner. Average shared plate: $19.*

German

Chicago Brauhaus Lincoln Square may have lost many of the Germans who settled there over the first half of the 20th century, but this bastion of oompah fun, baron-sized beers and heaping platters of carb-tastic classics remains. The lederhosen-clad Brauhaus Trio performs nightly, packing the raucous dining hall with duos who ditch their *rouladen* to jump up and dance *zwiefacher*-style (think polka with quick turns). *4732 N Lincoln Ave between Leland and Lawrence Aves (773-784-4444). El: Brown to Western. Bus: 11, 49, X49, 81. Lunch, dinner (closed Tue). Average main course: $14.*

Dinkel's Baking in the Lakeview neighborhood since 1922, this popular German bakery reliably turns out cinnamon-raisin stollen, German chocolate and butter cookies and its signature "sip'n whisky cake," a moist bundt cake made with sour mash whiskey. The real draw, though, is the strudel, which comes in several varieties such as praline-pecan, cherry-cheese and poppy seed. *3329 N Lincoln Ave between School and Roscoe Sts (773-281-7300). El: Brown to Addison. Bus: 9, 11, 77. Mon–Fri 6am–7pm; Sat 6am–5pm; Sun 9am–3pm. Average baked good: $1.*

Edelweiss It may look as if the owners forgot to take down the holiday glitz, but the strands of white lights and greenery are up year-round, adding to the festive feel of the cozy space. Meat and potatoes fill the menu, with the best bet being the combo platter of smoked pork chop, roasted pork loin, bratwurst, *rouladen*, griddled potatoes and spaetzle. The thin, flavorful veal cuts with perfect, crispy breading are great with your pick of nearly two dozen German beers. *7650 W Irving Park Rd, Norridge (708-452-6040). Bus: 80, Pace 326. Lunch, dinner. Average main course: $10.*

★ ✳ **Glunz Bavarian Haus** The cute, German-accented waitresses are happy to make ale and lager recommendations in between doling out soft pretzels with mustard and platters of sausages, cheese, pickles and olives. Stick-to-your-ribs entrées include sauerbraten, tender, red wine–braised beef served with cheesy spaetzle dotted with marjoram and onions. Before you roll out the door, have a bite or two of the housemade *sacher torte* or apple strudel. *4128 N Lincoln Ave at Warner Ave (773-472-0965). El: Brown to Irving Park. Bus: 11, 80. Lunch, dinner. Average main course: $16.*

★ ✳ ☾ **Laschet's Inn** If you were to wander in off the street, you might think this gem is little more than a charming German pub. It is, and it has been since '71, but since '91 it's also been one of the best spots in town for *rouladen*, thin beef rolled with bacon, onions and pickles. The German comfort food staple is served with tasty brown gravy, sweet braised cabbage and perfect, fluffy spaetzle dumplings. Try other authentic offerings like *hackepeter* (rich, fresh steak tartare on rye with capers and onions) and the Wiener schnitzel (pounded-thin veal breaded and fried crispy). The gratis fruit schnapps is a perfect ending to the meal. *2119 W Irving Park Rd between Hoyne and Hamilton Aves (773-478-7915). El: Brown to Irving Park. Bus: 11, 50, 80. Lunch, dinner. Average main course: $14.*

PROST WITH THE MOST Schnitzel and steins (plus the old men who love them) lend an authentic vibe to Laschet's Inn.

✳ **Lutz Continental Café & Pastry Shop** Old school in the best sense of the phrase, Lutz has rows of glass cases filled with sweets the likes of which you haven't seen since Grandma was out cutting a rug. It's hard to go wrong with these German goodies, but we love anything Lutz makes with marzipan, as well as the coffee cakes and traditional pastries. Delicate cookies are sold by the pound, and cakes are available for special order. *2458 W Montrose Ave between Campbell St and Western Ave. El: Brown to Western. Bus: 49, 78. Pastry shop: Sun–Thu 7am–7pm; Fri, Sat 7am–8pm. Café: 11am–4pm. Average main course: $11.*

Mirabell The cozy side room and larger dinner-hall are the kind of authentic setups you usually associate with tourist brochures. But there's nothing contrived about the food; a carnivore's delight, the menu features tremendous sauerbraten, an outstanding sausage sampler and some of the best goulash in the English-speaking world. Mirabell may be best known for its bar—featuring a staggering array of heady German beers—but the restaurant shouldn't be overlooked. *3454 W Addison St between Bernard St and St. Louis Ave (773-463-1962). El: Blue to Addison. Bus: 82, 152. Lunch, dinner (closed Sun). Average main course: $12.*

✳ **Resi's Bierstube** From the shingled roof to the oompah music, this North Side fave is the place to get your Teutonic eat on. Many trundle in for the extensive collection of German beer (and who doesn't want to hoist a stein of Weihenstephaner?), but the food is *sehr gut*, too. The butter-soft smoked Thuringer sausage has a great mellow taste, while the Sheboygan brat makes a delicious mess with mustard and a heaping pile of sauerkraut. Try the hearty *rahmschnitzel*, a breaded pork loin swimming in mushroom gravy. *2034 W Irving Park Rd between Seeley and Hoyne Aves (773-472-1749). El: Brown to Irving Park. Bus: 11, 50, 80. Dinner. Average main course: $11.*

17 West at the Berghoff After supposedly closing, the 100-year-old Berghoff reopened about a week after shuttering. It's now dubbed "17 West," but not a thing about the place has changed. Well, technically the legendary space is now owned by the Berghoff's daughter, who's added a few modern dishes, but the carving station still serves sandwiches, the bar still pours Berghoff beer and root beer, and the kitchen still slings Wiener schnitzel, sauerbraten and the like. *17 W Adams St between State and Dearborn Sts (312-427-3170). El: Blue, Red to Monroe. Bus: 1, 2, 6, 7, 10, 22, 24, X28, 36, 62, 126, 151. Lunch, dinner (closed Sun). Average main course: $4.50.*

INSIDE TRACK
TOTALLY TEUTONIC

When Germans miss the comforts of their homeland, they don't put on plastic hats and start swaying with glass boots of lager like we're led to believe. If you really want to blend in with the expats at local German haunts, indulge in authentic classics like tender oxtail, hearty goulash, and slow-simmered sauerbraten at Mirabell (see this page). Follow suit at Glunz Bavarian Haus (see this page) and pair fig-infused Kleiner Feigling vodka or fruity-sweet Mosel riesling with salty bratwurst or rich rouladen. And to digest all of that stick-to-your-ribs cuisine, end your meal at Laschet's Inn (see this page) as Germans do, with the herbal bitter Underberg.

Greek

▼ ◊ ✻ **Athena** The massive outdoor patio with a close-up view of the city skyline is the main draw of this Greektown spot in the warmer months, but there are reasons to dine inside, too. The restaurant's signature dish—lamb and artichokes in lemon sauce—is tender and nicely tangy, and other menu standbys, such as creamy *taramasalata* (fish roe spread), charbroiled octopus and well-seasoned gyros, are up to neighborhood standards. Opt for the dreamy *galaktibouriko*, lemon custard in honey-coated phyllo dough, for dessert. *212 S Halsted St at Adams St (312-655-0000). Bus: 8, 20. Lunch, dinner. Average main course: $14.*

✻ ◖ **Barba Yianni** Consider this Lincoln Square stalwart "Greektown North"—it's got the same tangy *taramasalata*, creamy egg-lemon soup and the same moussaka as the rest of them. It's what this place has that the others *don't*—namely its signature lemon-and-oregano rubbed chicken and its selection of *zimarika* (cheesy Greek-style pastas)—that makes it worth venturing out of Greektown for. That, and the fact that it's not nearly as crowded, which means shorter waits, fewer people and—most important—less flaming *saganaki*. *4761 N Lincoln Ave between Giddings St and Lawrence Ave (773-878-6400). El: Brown to Western. Bus: 11, 49, 81. Lunch, dinner. Average main course: $14.*

★ ▼ **Costa's** All Greektown restaurants are not created equal, and when it comes to *taramasalata, tzatziki* and *htipiti* (a spicy feta spread), this elegant stalwart rises above the rest. From there you can go one of many routes: two thick, juicy (but unadorned) lamb chops; the "Shrimp Costas," big, garlicky crustaceans piled atop angel-hair pasta; or the meaty gyros. No matter which route you take, make the simple, cinnamony, housemade rice pudding your final stop. And to expand your global wine knowledge, ask the server for some details on the handful of Greek picks from the list, all an exceptional value. *340 S Halsted St at Van Buren St (312-263-9700). El: Blue to UIC/Halsted. Bus: 7, 8, 126. Lunch, dinner. Average main course: $20.*

★ ▼ ◷ **Cross Rhodes** To say that you get more than you pay for at this dinerish

---

**INSIDE TRACK
OVAH OPAH**

If you've had it up to here with flaming saganaki and even cheesier Greektown theatrics, venture out to spots that offer unique twists and updated takes on Greek standbys. The hip crowd at 9 Muses (this page) nibbles Mediterranean panini and feta-stuffed peppers, while Mythos Greek Taverna (this page) serves artisanal olive bread alongside a tart three-cheese spread. At Wicker Park's Taxim (p.63), season dictates much of the contemporary Greek menu, as chef Jan Rickerl stuffs ramps inside flaky phyllo puffs come spring and leans on citrus and braised meats during colder weather.

Greek joint is an obscene understatement. It's not just that the portions are huge (the $8 gyros platter is piled about 10 inches high)—it's that the food is well-spiced and fresh. In other words, it's a refreshing change from most Greek spots. And refreshing for vegetarians, too, with its veggie versions of rich moussaka and *pastitsio*. Not so refreshing: the $11 bottles of wine, where you absolutely *do* get what you pay for, if not less. *913 Chicago Ave, Evanston (847-475-4475). El: Purple to Main. Bus: 201, 205. Lunch (Mon–Sat), dinner. Average main course: $8.*

▼ ✻ **Greek Islands** Half the joy of eating at this Greektown stalwart is seeing how many times you can get your server to say "*Opa!*" The other half comes in the form of the savory *saganaki* and the *keftedakia*—small, luscious meatballs simmered in tomato sauce. The sea bass lacks punch, so choose the rich and flaky spinach-cheese pie or the fantastic *loukanika* sausage instead. Honey-laden desserts are solid across the board, so order with confidence. But for maximum "*Opa!*" make sure you finish with a cup of the potent coffee. *200 S Halsted St at Adams St (312-782-9855). El: Blue to UIC/Halsted. Bus: 8, 126. Lunch, dinner. Average main course: $14.*

★ BYOB **Mythos Greek Taverna** A casual but classy oasis of ocean-blue hues, the dining room is constantly manned by the smooth-talking, personality half of the Greek-American sister duo who owns the restaurant. The other sibling spends her nights in the kitchen, turning out cheesy fried zucchini patties, a deliciously juicy sausage brightened with distinctive orange zest and the lightly charred octopus as an occasional special. Entrées can be a tad lackluster, but the baked béchamel-topped, shepherd's pie–ish *pastitsio* is comforting on a cold evening. *2030 W Montrose Ave at Seeley Ave (773-334-2000). El: Brown to Montrose. Bus: 11, 50, 78. Dinner (Tues–Sun). Average main course: $16.*

★ ◷ ✻ ◖ **9 Muses** Do the young Greeks who pack this trendy, clubby restaurant know something you don't? Yes. And they probably want to keep this place to themselves. But we have to crash on nights when we want Greek munchies like the Florina peppers (two roasted red peppers stuffed with creamy feta), *loukanika* (a pork-lamb sausage), "toasts" (essentially panini) and huge gyro platters. If you can stop yourself from talking by shoveling in the food, nobody will know you don't belong. *315 S Halsted St between Jackson Blvd and Van Buren St (312-902-9922). El: Blue to UIC/Halsted. Bus: 7, 8, 60, 126. Lunch, dinner. Average main course: $10.*

★ ▼ ✻ **Papaspiros** Schlep to the 'burbs for a Greek meal when Greektown's a stone's throw away? You will once you taste this cozy eatery's crispy fries doused in lamb gravy and feta (ask nicely for this unlisted treasure); tender, falling-off-the-bone lamb; earthy, monk-made wines like *Agioritikos*;

---

and addictive *fasolia gigantes* (lima beans in a heavy tomato sauce). Spiro and Sofia Papageorge, the enchanting owners, treat every patron like long-lost family. *733 Lake St, Oak Park (708-358-1700). El: Green to Oak Park. Bus: Pace 309, Pace 311, Pace 313, N20. Lunch, dinner. Average main course: $15.*

◖ **Parthenon** The waiters at this Greektown staple have lit so many plates of *saganaki* that their spirited cries of "Opa!" have dwindled to bored, tired whimpers. And who can blame them? Parthenon claims to have invented the flaming cheese, so it's supposedly been doing this shtick longer than anyone. As far as saganaki goes, it's pretty good. So is the garlicky gyro meat (another dish the restaurant claims to have invented, having the first patent on a rotating cone rotisserie). But the less-ordered suckling pig is where this kitchen really shows off its experience. *314 S Halsted St between Jackson Blvd and Van Buren St (312-726-2407). El: Blue to UIC/Halsted. Bus: 7, 8, 20, 60, 126. Lunch, dinner. Average main course: $14.*

▼ ✻ **Pegasus** The name of this joint makes you think the food here will be so good you'll sprout wings and fly. That didn't *quite* happen when we dug in to the *loukanika* (hearty Greek sausage) or the tangy *taramasalata*, but it got the meal off to a good start. The entrées we could take or leave, so go right from apps to dessert. Brought in from sister restaurant Artopolis Bakery, sweets include the delicious *milopita* (flaky apple pie spiked with cinnamon and honey). *130 S Halsted St between Adams and Monroe Sts (312-226-3377). El: Blue to UIC/Halsted. Bus: 8, 20. Lunch, dinner. Average main course: $15.*

▼ ◖ **Roditys** You'll find the usual staples at this Greektown mainstay, from spreads like *tzatziki* and *taramasalata* to gyros platters and moussaka. There are twists here and there (you can order the requisite flaming *saganaki* studded with shrimp), but not much will surprise you. To us, the biggest draw is the service. From the host with a genuine smile who sat our party to the fatherly waiter who made wonderful wine suggestions and nudged us to finish the food on our plates, we felt like we were in caring hands throughout our entire meal—a refreshing change from the snippy service we've received at other restaurants on this strip. *222 S Halsted St between Adams St and Jackson Blvd (312-454-0800). El: Blue to UIC/Halsted. Bus: 8, 20, 126. Lunch, dinner. Average main course: $12.*

★ ◊ ✻ **Santorini** If Greektown makes you feel as if you're drowning in a sea of bad food and obnoxious tourists, here's your life jacket. The Kontos family serves food that is impeccably fresh, importing organic olive oil and oregano from the family farm in Sparta. Look for starters like sprightly spanakopita to hit your palate with fresh herb flavor. Like most of the seafood, the whole red snapper needs nothing more than a squeeze of lemon to show off its delicate flesh and subtle flavor.

GO GREEK At Taxim, standard classics are eshewed in favor of dishes like ramp-filled puff pastry with goat feta.

You may jump a little every time a ball of flaming *saganaki* cheese erupts at nearly every table, but if your nerves can handle it, your taste buds will thank you. *800 W Adams St at Halsted St (312-829 8820). El: Blue to UIC/Halsted. Bus: 8, 126. Lunch, dinner. Average main course: $17.*

★ ▼ ☀ ☾ **Taxim** The cozy, cushy, Byzantine-style dining room of Wicker Park's dim new Greek den is all owner David Schneider, but he gets help from former Scylla chef Jan Rickerl on the simple (and often simply delicious) seasonal Mediterranean food.

Minimal ingredients are needed for spit-roasted duck glazed in pomegranate molasses or a whole loup de mar with crackly-crisp skin aside dandelion salad, but solid execution yields maximum flavors. Nice prices and a share-everything platform means more dough for sampling through the superb Greek wine list. *1558 N Milwaukee Ave between Honore St and North Ave (773-252-1558). El: Blue to Damen. Bus: 50, 56, 72. Breakfast and lunch (daily), dinner (Wed–Mon). Average main course: $22.*

★ ☾ **Venus Greek-Cypriot Cuisine**
Just on the cusp of Greektown's eating mecca

lies this sprawling spot known for cuisine that's from the Mediterranean island of Cyprus. The owners have taken the traditional, rustic village food and added a luscious, upscale touch. Try the *halloumi* (a milder version of *saganaki*) and the incredibly tender six-hour slow-baked lamb, served tableside in foil. Everything is made to order, so enjoy the wait with a bottle from the Greek wine list. Your *pastitsio tsoukas*, long noodles layered with ground beef and covered in a crispy béchamel topping, will be worth it. *820 W Jackson Blvd between Halsted and Green Sts (312-714-1001). El: Blue to UIC/Halsted. Bus: 8, 126. Lunch (Sun), dinner. Average main course: $17.*

Ice Cream/Sweets

TRIPLE THREAT Creamy, cool custard steals the show at Scooter's.

⊙ **Annette's Homemade Italian Ice** Bellying up to the sidewalk window is the easy part. Deciding on a cool treat from the lengthy menu—therein lies the rub. While soft-serve frozen yogurt, ice-cream sundaes and milkshakes are available, it's the more than 20 flavors of homemade Italian ice on offer that are the real draw. From strawberry and peach to passion fruit and coconut-banana, you can beat the heat here with virtually any fruit under the sun. *2011 N Bissell St at Armitage Ave (773-868-9000). El: Brown, Purple (rush hrs) to Armitage. Bus: 8, 73. Noon–11pm daily. Average cup: $3.*

⊙ ☀ **Bellezza Gelato Café** While many places offering "housemade gelati" start with factory-made mixes, here they serve fresh, high-quality gelati and sorbetti from scratch. Try the Venetian berry *carnivale*, double dutch chocolate or pistachio. The Turkish-coffee gelato is an eye-opener and goes well with slightly sweet "nazooks," walnut-cinnamon pastries based on co-owner Tim Ashorian's Assyrian family recipe. For another jolt, try the *affogato*, a shot of espresso over gelato. *3637 N Harlem Ave between Addison St and Waveland Ave (773-545-1239). Bus: 90, 152. Tues– Sat 1–9pm; Sun 4–8pm (closed Mon). Average cup: $3.25.*

⊙ ☾ **Berry Chill** *2009 Eat Out Awards, Readers' Choice: Best New Frozen Yogurt* With the arrival of this Pinkberry-esque yogurt shop, the coasts' frozen-yogurt trend officially descended on Chicago. The 'yo's texture here is about as good as can be, balancing between

light and creamy. Their original flavor has a hint of citrus, bumping up the yogurt's natural tartness to a tongue-tingling, lemonlike taste. Be sure and sample the many other flavors as they make monthly appearances, such as strawberry banana or pina colada. *635 N State St between Ontario and Erie Sts (312-266-2445). El: Red to Grand. Bus: 22, 36, 65. Sun–Thu 8am–midnight; Fri, Sat 8am–4am. Average cup: $5.* ● *Other locations: 500 W Madison (312-993-9644), 135 N. LaSalle (312-533-2145).*

⊙ ★ **Bobtail Ice Cream Company** What would a soda fountain be without an outdoor spot from which to watch the world go by? Late-night hours (till 11pm weekdays, midnight weekends) mean you can get a postdinner jolt from the caffeinated "cream express" milkshake (vanilla and espresso). Or grab a scoop of the Lakeview Barhopper (chocolate ice cream with Jack Daniel's) to get a jump on the night's festivities. *2951 N Broadway at Wellington Ave (773-880-7372). El: Brown, Purple (rush hrs) to Wellington. Bus: 22, 36, 76, 156. Mon–Thu 10am–11pm; Fri, Sat 11am–midnight; Sun 11am–11pm. Average ice-cream cone: $3.50.* ● *Other location: 3425 N Southport Ave (773-248-6104). Kiosk at Buckingham Fountain.*

⊙ ▽ ☀ **Caffe Gelato** You'll feel as though you stepped into a Sicilian gelato bar at this little spot, where everything from the chocolate and nuts to the furniture and gelato machines is imported from Italy. All flavors are made in fresh batches daily, including rich,

creamy hazelnut, pistachio and *bacio* (a chocolate and hazelnut blend named for Baci candies). Seasonal fruit gelati and sorbets also fill the menu, as do a couple panini and expertly made Illy coffee drinks. *2034 W Division St between Damen and Hoyne Aves (773-227-7333). El: Blue to Division. Bus: 50, 76 Division. Mon–Thu 10am–10pm; Fri, Sat 10am–11pm; Sun 10am–10pm. Average cup: $4.25.*

⊙ **Capannari Ice Cream** A general store and post office in the late 19th century, Capannari's building currently houses this ice creamery and parlor, which offers more than 20 standard flavors of ice cream, with hard-to-find flavors such as Irish cream, ginger and pineapple rotating in and out of the freezers throughout the year. It also shakes things up with seasonal flavors like sweet potato pie, eggnog and blue cheese with pear compote. *10 S Pine St, Mount Prospect (847-392-2277). Metra: Union Pacific Northwest to Mount Prospect. Sun–Thu noon–10pm; Fri, Sat noon–10:30pm. Average ice-cream cone: $3.*

⊙ **Dairy Star** Line up with the crowds on the rainbow sprinkle–coated blacktop outside this ice-cream shack to get a soft-serve cone dipped in chocolate or cherry coating. Grab a bench for watching a great cross-section of city types—blue-collar workers stealing a quick break, large Orthodox Jewish families indulging in certified kosher creamy goodness and high schoolers on first dates. Try the Buddy parfait, made with vanilla ice cream, hot fudge and peanuts. *3472 W Devon Ave at St Louis*

Ave (847-679-3472). Bus: 11, 96, Pace 210. Noon–11pm. Average ice-cream cone: $3.

◷ ★ **Flamingo's** Owner Guadalupe Lopez uses 14 percent cream from the local Elgin Dairy and a wild imagination to create 130 flavors of her amazing ice cream. Adding as little sugar as possible, she captures the essence of each flavor—even Parmesan cheese or sweet corn bread. Don't miss the jalapeño, tequila, mamey, avocado and roasted coconut options. Lopez also makes popsicles that she sells in the store. 6733 W Cermak Rd, Berwyn (708-749-4287). Bus: 21, X21, 25, Pace 304, Pace 311, Pace 322. Noon–10pm daily. Average ice-cream cone: $2. ● Other location: 2635 W 51st St (773-434-3917).

◷ ✻ **Freddy's Pizzeria** This haven for true Italian gelato serves up astonishingly creamy scoops that surge with flavor. Owner Giuseppe "Joe" Quercia—who emigrated from Naples, Italy, in 1968—makes the rotating nine flavors with 14 percent milk and no eggs. It's tough to go wrong with any flavor, but we're addicted to the frutti di bosco (vanilla with wildberries), the nicciola (hazelnut) and the refreshing limoncello ice. 1600 S 61st Ave, Cicero (708-863-9289). Bus: Pace 304, Pace 305, Pace 315. 10am–7pm (closed Sun). Average ice-cream cone: $2.50.

◷ ▽ **George's Ice Cream & Sweets** Sweet Occasions fans can stop their mourning: The new ice-cream slinger in this space is practically identical—only upgraded. The walls are decked out in grays and dark blues, and the savory menu now includes hot panini, crêpes and waffles. Most important, the ice cream is the same (Chocolate Shoppe from Madison, Wisconsin). The scoops are now offered in over-the-top sundaes, but save the cash and the sugar overload—this ice cream holds up well enough on its own. 5306 N Clark St between Summerdale and Berwyn Aves (773-271-7600). El: Red to Berwyn. Bus: 22, 50, 92. Sun–Thu 11am–11pm; Fri–Sat 11am–midnight. Average ice-cream cone: $3.20.

◷ **Gertie's Ice Cream/Lindy's Chili** Gertie's has been serving ice cream from its original location at 55th and California since 1901. Lindy's launched its biz in 1924, and its famed chili supposedly is still made from the original recipe, but when the time comes for a tasty treat, we go for the refreshing ice cream. Superrich milkshakes and malts are perfect for sipping while reading framed newspaper clippings from Gertie's golden oldie days. 7600 S Pulaski Rd at 76th St (773-582-2510). Bus: 53A, 79. 11am–9pm. Average ice-cream cone: $3.

◷ ✻ **Gina's Italian Ice** Right about where Oak Park meets Berwyn, you'll find Gina Tremonte scooping out Italian ice to her legion of loyal families in the summertime. She uses fresh fruit in most of the dozen flavors, with lemon, watermelon and cantaloupe as the top three sellers. Supertart lemon ice fans won't be disappointed here, and fans of campy horror can stroll two doors down to Horrorbles to pick up a Svengoolie rubber chicken or a signed Basil Gogos book. 6737 W Roosevelt Rd, Berwyn (708-484-0944). El: Blue to Oak Park. Bus: Pace 305, Pace 311. 1–10pm daily. Average cup: $2.75.

◷ **Hartigan's Ice Cream Shoppe** The Hartigans took a sizable risk when, in 1996, they decided to transform their Baskin-Robbins franchise store into a family owned-and-operated

NICE STACK Request extra napkins with the namesake creation at Original Rainbow Cone.

ice-cream shop. It seems the gamble has paid off, though. The store now carries more than 50 flavors from Wisconsin-based ice creamery Cedar Crest, and everyone from Northwestern students to stroller-pushing moms and dads can be seen coming in for a double-dip cone and cup of joe. 2909 Central St, Evanston (847-491-1232). 11am–11pm daily. Average ice-cream cone: $3.50.

◷ **Icebox** There are three locations of this decade-old, homegrown carry-out spot, but this is the original. Once the cold days are behind us, the store transforms from Soupbox (where a dozen soups are on offer) into Icebox and starts scooping out 20 flavors of "icyfruit." Mango and chocolate are among our favorites, and we love digging into the watermelon and coming up with chunks of fruit, proof that this place favors the real deal over fruit syrups. 2943 N Broadway between Oakdale and Wellington Aves (773-935-9800). Bus: 36, 22, 156. 11am–10pm daily. Average cup: $2.25. ● Other locations: 50 E Chicago Ave (312-951-5900); 500 W Madison St (312-993-1019).

◷ **Istria Café** See Bakeries/Cafés for review.

◷ **Margie's Candies** It's nostalgia that draws people out in droves to this kitschy diner/ice-cream parlor. Fancy silver trays, paper doilies and saucers filled with chocolate and caramel sauces bring back fond memories for many who've made this place a tradition since it opened in 1921. Equally as reminiscent of the good old days are the display shelves, which are crowded with memorabilia from the Beatles, who just had to have some Margie's ice cream after they played Comiskey. 1960 N Western Ave at Armitage Ave (773-384-1035). El: Blue to Western. Bus: 49, 56, 73. 9am–midnight. Average ice-cream cone: $3. ● Other location: 1813 W Montrose Ave (773-348-0400).

◷ ❨ **Mario's Italian Lemonade** This no-frills seasonal stand has been churning out Italian lemonade since 1954. Though it serves random items such as snowball cupcakes, you're really there for the namesake goods: delicately shaved ice with pieces of lemon rinds and flecks of zest that taste like the real thing, so not too tart or overly sweet. Flavors get fancy—like chocolate or piña colada—but for our money, stick to the fruits (cantaloupe, for example, comes with melon chunks). 1068 W Taylor St between Carpenter and Aberdeen Sts (no phone). El: Blue

MAGIC MOUNTAIN Don't try to finish Margie's massive "Royal George" alone.

The big scoop

No matter what your preference for ice cream is, we've found the best cold stuff around.

BEST GELATO Freddy's Pizzeria (p.65) The nocciola here would do any Italian mama proud—exceptionally creamy and smooth, not sugary, with a fully charged flavor of toasted hazelnuts (real bits of nuts in there, too), and a soft, thick and luscious texture. Judging from the exuberant crowd, there's no doubt owner Joe Quercia has a tried-and-true recipe. After all, he's been perfecting it for 40 years.

BEST ITALIAN ICE Johnnie's Beef (7500 W North Ave, Elmwood Park, 708-452-6000)
Assuming you can be heard over the din of beef-language (you know, the calls of "beef hot, well-dipped," and "beef mild, dry"), order a "small ice." The seasoned team behind the counter of this old-school carryout spot won't hand over a cup of frozen water; they know you're talking about lemon Italian ice. Fans of smack-you-in-the-face tartness or sugar-fiends looking for a fix might initially be underwhelmed. But eat it slowly, and soon the ice's balance and consistency will win you over. Better make that a "large ice."

BEST CLASSIC ICE CREAM Capannari Ice Cream (p.64)
It's not just the quaint charm of this ice-cream company's suburban storefront that won it such a fervent fan base. Housed in a former general store built in 1882, the gorgeous ice-cream parlor casts a spell on Mount Prospect residents, especially during the summer, when they all seem to walk in a daze toward the light (maybe it's the films projected on the outside wall of the store during Summer Movie Nights). But this

place has more going for it than good looks: The chocolate ice cream (made in small batches, like all the flavors) is thick, sweet and rich, with a consistency that borders on gelato—even when eaten outside of the shop's cozy confines, it's capable of lulling you into a state of bliss.

BEST FROZEN YOGURT Red Mango (p.67) and **Berry Chill** (p. 64)
This one's debatable. We say Red Mango, but our readers chose Berry Chill as the best fro-yo in the most recent *Time Out Chicago* Eat Out Awards. Maybe it's the fact that the place sports more flat-screen televisions than a Rush Street sports bar, an army of spacey plastic resin chairs and tables and a touch-screen ordering system. Or maybe the secret to its success is the distinctive tang of its yogurt, a deeply tart spoonful that makes you squinch up your face like Renée Zellweger.

BEST OVER-THE-TOP CONCOCTION
Only those with a serious case of the munchies could take down the "Royal George a la George" at **Margie's Candies** (p.65). The massive creation includes 25 scoops of ice cream drowned in hot fudge and caramel and served in a punch bowl bigger than your head. No biggie, you say? Upgrade to Margie's "World's Largest Sundae," a half-gallon of your favorite ice cream topped with fudge, whipped cream, caramel and bananas. (We can't verify if its title is official, but it has to be close.)
—*Eve Fuller and Michael Nagrant*

to UIC/Halsted. Bus: 7, 8, 12, 60. 11am–midnight (open May–Sept). Average cup: $3.

⊙ **Massa** Smack-dab in this North Avenue strip dominated by Italian-American eateries you'll find this casual café. Pizza, *panzerotti*, sandwiches and salads are on offer, but we stop by for a scoop of gelato. At least two dozen flavors are on offer daily (a combo of mainstays and rotating options) and each is made in-house from a base that's imported from Italy. Flavors like hazelnut and pistachio are solid picks, but branch out and you may find a delicious new favorite. *7434 W North Ave, Elmwood Park (708-583-1111). Sun–Thu 11am–10:30pm; Fri, Sat 11am–midnight. Average cup: $3.50.*

⊙ ★ ✳ **Miko's Italian Ice** The quaint Bucktown take-out window has set up this second shop west of the original in Logan Square. Passersby will find it hard to resist the refreshing watermelon, the fresh strawberry (with seeds and pulp galore) and the sweet, creamy mango. The banana with chocolate chips and coconut is a more acquired taste, but it's one that, luckily, more people now have the opportunity to try. *2236 N Sacramento Ave between Lyndale St and Belden Ave (773-645-9664). El: Blue to California. Bus: 56, 76, 82. Mon–Fri 2pm–10pm; Sat, Sun noon–10pm. Average cup: $3.* ● *Other location: 1846 N Damen Ave (773-645-9664).*

⊙ ✳ **Original Rainbow Cone** For 82 years, the awning-covered picnic tables of this Far South Side ice-cream shop have been packed with locals feeding their sweet tooth. Their signature five-flavor Rainbow Cone features slices of chocolate, strawberry, Palmer House (vanilla with cherries and walnuts), pistachio and orange sherbet stacked one on top of the other for an unbeatable combination of flavors. *9233 S Western Ave between 91st St and 92nd Pl (773-238-7075). Bus: 49A, X49, 95W. Mon–Wed noon–9:30pm; Thurs–Sun noon–10pm. Average ice-cream cone: $3.75.*

⊙ ❨ **The Original Taurus Flavors** There's nothing particularly astrological about this place; it's quite grounded, actually. The salt-of-the-earth regulars have a lot of pride in the greasy hoagies and steak sandwiches, but they still manage to give love to (and save room for) the ice cream. Around a dozen flavors, including cookies and cream, butter pecan and New York cherry, are served in the cup, cone or blended into a thick milkshake. *8534 S Stony Island Ave at 85th Pl (773-374-1872). Bus: 28, 87. Sun–Thurs 10am–3am; Fri–Sat 10am–5am. Average ice-cream cup: $2.45.* ● *Other location: 3832 W 147th St (708-371-4230).*

⊙ ✳ **Papa Smiles** Love old-fashioned ice-cream parlors but desire cleanliness and flavor missing at other joints? Head to this charming throwback run by "Papa" Ron Kozak. The quaint decor—a soda fountain, jukebox and walls plastered with historical photos of the 'hood—hearkens back to a simpler time. Order scoops of Homer's and Hershey's ice cream (especially pistachio), deliciously greasy chili dogs and housemade taffy apples. *6955 W Archer Ave between Newland and Sayre Aves (773-788-0388). Bus: 62, 62H, Pace 307. Noon–9pm daily. Average ice-cream cone: $3.*

⊙ ★ **Petersen's** These folks have been making their rich, fatty ice cream since 1910, and they haven't survived all this time on summer business alone. Since the restaurant portion of

Petersen's closed, the savories are no longer available. But that's okay—it was always merely a preamble to the hot-fudge sundaes (two mounds of luscious vanilla flanked by a pitcher of the viscous sauce), the tall root-beer floats and the infinitely creamy milkshakes. *1100 Chicago Ave, Oak Park (708-386-6131). El: Green to Harlem/ Lake. Bus: Pace 305, Pace 307, Pace 309, Pace 313, Pace 318. 11am–10pm. Average ice-cream cone: $3.50.*

◉ ▽ **Piccolo** Pastry chef Jessie Oloroso is behind the Black Dog label gelato creations at this casual counter-service gelato/panini spot. Play the odds and sample to find your own favorite; signatures include whiskey gelato with Jim Beam, Mexican hot chocolate and goat cheese cashew caramel. For sustenance before the main attraction, try Piccolo's standout panini, including giardiniera-topped spicy *capocollo* and the house-cured *bresaola* with pickled onion. *859 N Damen Ave at Rice St (773-772-3355). Bus: 50, 66. Lunch, dinner. Average main course: $7.*

◉ ★ **Red Mango** The Korean fro-yo chain (which opened its first store in 2002 and claims to have been the inspiration for its rival Pinkberry) picked Evanston as their Chicagoland testing ground, then opened in Naperville right after, and is finally in the city proper. What's all the fuss? It's wonderful stuff, with a true yogurt tang and clean, refreshing sweetness. And best of all: the texture, which is smooth as silk, but not scary-slick like DQ soft-serve. *809 Davis St, Evanston (847-866-0998). El: Purple to Davis. Bus: 93, 205, Pace 208, Pace 213, Pace 215. Sun–Thu 11am–10pm; Fri, Sat 11am–11pm. Average frozen yogurt: $3.50.* ● *Other location: 2806 N Clark St (773-296-6304).*

◉ ★ ✳ **Sarah's Pastries and Candies** Sarah Levy re-opened her popular candy store/bakery at 70 East Oak Street, where there's more room for her crunchy clusters of chocolate and nuts and her decadent baked goods like chocolate-raspberry brioche. Her expanded menu includes pressed sandwiches, such as a grilled prosciutto with truffle oil, and a fabulous gelato selection. We'd scream at her for making our bodies decidedly not swimsuit-ready, but, alas, when we're here, our mouths are always full *70 E Oak St between Rush St and Michigan Ave (312-664-6223). El: Red to Chicago. Bus: 36, 66, 143, 144, 145, 146, 147, 148, 151. Mon–Sat 8am–6pm; Sun 10am–6pm. Average bag of candy: $6.*

▽ ◉ ✳ ◖ **Scoops** Aromas of fresh waffles pervade the air of this Bridgeport parlor, evidence of the signature, housemade waffle cones. Dipped in chocolate and adorned with various brightly colored candies, these deep cones are indulgent carriers for both types of chocolate ice cream on offer (though our preference is for the darker variety). Should the ice cream be too rich, you're in luck: Like all good Italians, these guys focus on espresso, the perfect antidote to your forthcoming sugar crash. *608 W 31st St between Wallace St and Lowe Ave (312-842-3300). El: Orange to Halsted. Bus: 8, 35, 62. 11am–midnight daily. Average ice-cream cone: $3.*

◉ ★ **Scooter's Frozen Custard** Walk into Scooter's, and disregard the hot dogs, Italian ice and anything else that doesn't contain the words *frozen* and *custard*. Order a Boston shake, and quiver in awe as the towering milkshake topped with hot fudge and whipped cream is handed over. As you taste how dense, thick, buttery and rich the custard is, you'll soon be on your way to a full

stomach and an ice-cream headache. And it'll be worth it. *1658 W Belmont Ave at Paulina St (773-244-6415). El: Brown to Paulina. Bus: 9, 11, 77. Mon–Fri 2–10pm; Sat 1–10pm; Sun 1–9pm. Average cup: $3.*

◉ ◖ **Starfruit** Like the unflavored kefir drink put out by owner Lifeway Foods, this stuff is sour. Not citrusy tart like Berry Chill's stuff, but the type of sour that leads most people to choose flavored yogurt over plain. Problem is, the flavor of the day we sampled had a strangely fakey peach flavor and overly grainy texture, while the plain just didn't stack up to the yogurt it's made from. *1745 W Division St between Wood St and Hermitage Ave (773-328-2900). El: Blue to Division. Bus: 8, 50, 70. 8am–10pm daily. Average cup: $5.* ● *Other location: 2142 N Halsted (773-868-4900).*

◉ **Tom and Wendee's Homemade Italian Ice** With all-natural, nonfat ices, this corner Italian ice spot is nice to our waistlines. We appreciate the classic lemon ice for its full flavor and bit of lemon rind sprinkled throughout, as well as the chocolate ices, which are made with cocoa and packed with rich chocolate flavor. You'd swear something like the "chocolate toffee crunch" is bad for you—and let's be honest, the sugar in it probably is—but we'll continue to eat it in ignorant bliss. *1136 W Armitage Ave at Clifton Ave (773-327-2885). El: Brown, Purple (rush*

hrs) to Armitage. Bus: 8, 73. Noon–10pm daily. Average cup: $3.75.

◉ **Treats** Treats prides itself on offering servings of ice cream with only one gram of fat, which is good because you're probably going to want to eat a lot of it. Along with chocolate and vanilla, four featured flavors are on offer daily (call for specials). If you're lucky, you can try caramel fudge éclair, banana or chocolate marshmallow. The "mess" option lets you create your own creation by choosing two toppings from the selection of syrups, fruit, nuts and candies. *2224 N Clark St between Webster Ave and Grant Pl (773-472-6666). Bus: 22, 36, 73. Mon–Thu 11am–10pm; Fri–Sat 11am–midnight. Average ice-cream cone: $4.*

◉ **Windy City Sweets** Although there is a large selection of novelty gift items and homemade candies here (truffles, chocolate-covered pretzels and fudge), the nightly post-dinner rush is mainly for the ice cream. Standouts among the store's more than 30 flavors include blueberry cheesecake and green tea. Employees are generous with the scoops, which they plop down onto everything from small, plain cake cones to hulking chocolate- and candy-dipped sugar cones. *3308 N Broadway at Aldine Ave (773-477-6100). El: Brown, Purple (rush hrs), Red to Belmont. Bus: 8, 22, 36, 77. 11am–11:15pm daily. Average ice-cream cone: $3.50.*

Indian/Pakistani

ROLL ONE UP The potato-filled *dosa* pancake has legions of fans at Udupi Palace.

▼ ● BYOB **Arya Bhavan** Vegetarians and vegans hit pay dirt with this meat-free spot. During the week, they go for popular South Indian dishes like *dosas* (thin, crispy rice-lentil crêpes filled with potatoes and onions) and *uttapam* (thicker like pancakes, with onions dropped into the batter). On the weekends (Friday through Sunday), the main attraction is the buffet—a massive spread of about a dozen North Indian dishes. *2508 W Devon Ave between Campbell and Maplewood Aves (773-274-5800). Bus: 49B, 155. Lunch, dinner (buffet Fri–Sun). Average main course: $9.*

● BYOB **Bhabi's Kitchen** The owner-waiter is Mr. Syed (who goes by Bobby), the cook is his lovely wife and the name Bhabi means "sister-in-law." Well, at least the food's not confusing. You might just rub elbows with some of the area's top chefs digging into delicious vegetable samosas, nearly two dozen unique breads and flavorful entrées like pureed rapini, baby eggplant and butter chicken in spicy tomato-cream sauce. Be warned: The spice level is definitely not Americanized. *6352 N Oakley Blvd between Devon and Rosemont Aves (773-764-7007). Bus: 49B, 155. Lunch (Wed–Mon), dinner. Average main course: $8.*

★ ● ☾ **Chopal Kabab & Steak** You'll often find members of the local Indo-Pak community sitting on the ornate and brightly colored furniture, discussing what appear to be important matters, but we know they're chatting about how incredible the food is: lentils rife with roasted garlic; lemon-kissed rapini; fiery chunks of chile chicken; and delicious, tender goat chops. Quell the heat with the amazing Chopal lassi, and refrain from bringing wine or beer out of respect for the devout Muslim staff and diners. *2242 W Devon Ave between Bell and Oakley Aves (773-338-4080). Bus: 49B, 155. Lunch, dinner. Average main course: $7.*

▼ **Gaylord India Restaurant** The subterranean dining room is large, the staff outnumbers the patrons, and the "mulligatawny" soup is chicken broth while the tomato smacks of Campbell's. But there's no overlooking the amazing lunch buffet. Start by smothering samosas in *raita*, chutneys, chickpeas and crunchy *sev*, then move on to flavorful lentils, spiced cabbage and chicken in buttery *makhani* sauce. Save room for rose-scented and sweet *ras malai*. *100 E Walton Pl between Rush St and Michigan Ave (312-664-1700). El: Red to Chicago. Bus: 10, 66, 145, 146, 147, 151. Lunch, dinner. Average main course: $14.*

★ ● **Ghareeb Nawaz** The large crowd at the counter of this bare-bones Indo-Pak spot seems chaotic, but the diners are really just waiting for their postmeal chai. So push your way through and order a bowl of delicious dal, loaded with bay leaves and chile peppers. Ask for the chile chicken and spoon the greasy, delicious, fiery red chunks onto the dense *paratha*. No matter what you order, you'll get your money's worth; most things here only cost about four bucks. *2032 W Devon Ave at Seeley Ave (773-761-5300). Bus: 49B, 155. Breakfast, lunch, dinner. Average main course: $4.*

▼ BYOB **Hema's Kitchen** Hema Potla moved her restaurant after almost a decade of making Oakley Avenue a destination for Devon diners. The new spot is spacious, with chandeliers, tiny bouquets and the always-smiling namesake floating around the room. The new kitchen turns out additions like nan and kebabs. Old favorites include fiery lentils with spinach, eggplant with lamb, and tender chicken in "Hariyali," a gravy of cilantro, curry leaves, peppers, yogurt, ginger and garlic. *2439 W Devon Ave between Artesian and Campbell Aves (773-338-1627). Bus: 49B, 155. Lunch, dinner. Average main course: $11.*

● ☾ **Hyderabad House** With no veggie options on the menu, the cabbies, locals and neighboring auto-shop clientele have no choice but to load up on piquant bowls of soft mutton in silky gravy and heaping plates of steaming lamb *biryani*. Be prepared to make multiple lightning-quick beelines for the water cooler if you choose the chicken *paratha*—its tasty but potent fire level can be a bit much for beginners. Cool off with a tasty bowl of homemade *kheer* (rice pudding). *2225 W Devon Ave between Bell Ave and Leavitt St (773-381-1230). Bus: 49B, 93, 155. Lunch, dinner. Average main course: $8.*

▼ **India House** The dinner prices reflect this spot's downtown address and swank decor, so we like to take advantage of the daily lunch buffet ($14.95 Thurs–Sun; $13.95 Mon–Wed) that's one of the best in town. The hot line usually includes creamy chicken tikka masala, cardamom-flavored lamb rogan josh, spicy coconut-flecked fish Goa curry. Tender, smoky chicken vindaloo and fresh nan come straight from the kitchen rather than sitting on the buffet. *59 W Grand Ave between Dearborn and Clark Sts (312-645-9500). El:*

Red to Grand. Bus: 22, 36, 65. Lunch, dinner. Average main course: $15.

▼ **Indian Garden** This Devon Avenue spot is great for your spice-phobic parents (the personable service always meets requests for various heat levels) while still managing to get good grub and throw back an Indian beer or two. Go for the vegetarian *thali*, a combo platter of mashed, roasted eggplant; creamy spinach; simmered black lentils; rice and nan. Meat-eaters should try the *murg methi chaman*, a fenugreek chicken dish bursting with fresh herb flavor. *2546 W Devon Ave between Maplewood Ave and Rockwell St (773-338-2929). Bus: 49B, 93, 155. Lunch, dinner (Sat, Sun). Average main course: $13.* ● *Other location: 247 E Ontario St (312-280-4910).*

★ ▼ ☺ **Khan B.B.Q.** The spicy, marinated, chargrilled chicken chunks (*boti*), the juicy sausage-shaped ground-beef patties (*seekh kebab*), and veggie dishes like creamy spinach with potato chunks (*aloo palak*) are all as great (and cheap) as they were at the old Khan. Service is slower at this larger space, but the trade-off is that the air isn't *quite* as thick with the charcoal smoke that ultimately destroyed the previous location. *2401 W Devon Ave at Western Ave (773-274-8600). Bus: 49B, 155. Lunch, dinner. Average main course: $6.50.*

▼ **BYOB Little India** Being that this restaurant is from the owners of Zam Zam sweet shop, it's funny that sweets play just a small role here. Instead, the huge menu focuses on savory Indian staples. You can get through the menu piece by piece if you wish (start with the spicy, fist-sized samosas). But if you want to try everything before 2020, hit the juicy tandoori chicken, tender *seekh kebab* (beef) and spicy Bihari kebabs all at once with the mixed grill. *1109 W Bryn Mawr Ave between Winthrop Ave and Broadway (773-728-7012). El: Red to Bryn Mawr. Bus: 36, 84, 136. Lunch, dinner. Average main course: $15.*

★ ▼ ✳ **Marigold** This Uptown spot is a haven for those seeking upscale Indian eats. The room is dateworthy; the wine list is pairing friendly. And many of the contemporary dishes—like the duck-leg confit with blistered green beans, seared peppercorn-crusted thick yogurt with orange-coriander–dressed greens, and expertly grilled *kalonji* chicken with almond and raisin–studded rice *pulao*—are worth the extra dough you'll spend eating here rather than on Devon. *4832 N Broadway between Lawrence Ave and Gunnison St (773-293-4653). El: Red to Lawrence. Bus: 22, 36, 81. Dinner (closed Mon). Average main course: $16.*

▼ B **Raj Darbar** Normally we wouldn't shell out more cash than we would on Devon's reasonably priced restaurant row, but the perk here is delivery. Fried-food fans love the mix platter, packed with samosas, potato patties, crispy prawns and Indian-style onion rings. Try the yellow lentil, roasted eggplant or okra, and if you're a carnivore, go for the raisin-and-cashew-studded chicken *shahi korma*. Since the heat levels cater to the Anglo neighborhood, request "spicy" if you're looking for scorchers. *2660 N Halsted St between Wrightwood and Schubert Aves (773-348-1010). El: Brown, Purple (rush hrs) to Diversey. Bus: 8, 74, 76. Brunch (Sun), dinner. Average main course: $11.*

☺ **Sabri Nehari** Be warned that the namesake dish, *nehari*, a spicy Pakistani pot

---

BYOB Tip: *Indian*

Wine: *Chardonnay or pinot gris*

To continue the lusciousness of all the butter and cream going on in Indian food, a buttery chardonnay is ideal. But to cut through the fat and spice, a bright, sweet pinot gris is key.

Beer: *Witbiers or pilsners*

Belgian-style wheats are low in alcohol, so they won't intensify the heat of Indian food, plus there's good sweetness and carbonation. Though more crisp, pilsners pull it off just the same.

Buy it at Foremost Liquors *(6015 N Lincoln Ave, 773-338-1188)* then **bring it** to Uru Swati (p. 70).

Buy it at In Fine Spirits *(5418 N Clark St, 773-334-9463)* then **bring it** to Little India (see this page).

HEAT RELIEF Bring along ice-cold pilsner to wash down vegetarian Indian classics at Uru Swati.

roast, will induce craving so strong you'll consider relocating to Devon. First-timers should know that the half-inch oil slick atop the gingery gravy is supposed to be there; it's ghee (clarified butter) and should be stirred in before ladling the comfort food onto fluffy rice. For a complete meal, order the Frontier Chicken and use garlicky nan to sop up the cumin- and chile-laced yellow dal. *2502 W Devon Ave at Campbell Ave (773-743-6200). Bus: 49B, 155. Lunch, dinner. Average main course: $10.*

▼ ◷ **Sukhadia Sweets & Snacks**
Indian sweets are an acquired taste, and this is a great shop to acquire some. Make a meal out of the *chaat*—fried snacks like *pani puri* (hollow puffs for scooping up masala-spiced chickpeas) and spicy chutney-drizzled *bhel puri*. Save room for technicolor desserts like doughnuty *gulab jamun* with *ras malai* (cream-soaked paneer) and baklava-like treats layered with pistachios. *2559 W Devon Ave at Rockwell St (773-338-5400). Bus: 49B, 93, 155. Breakfast, lunch, dinner. Average snack: $3.* ● *Other location: 1016 Golf Rd, Hoffman Estates (847-490-4400).*

▼ ◷ **Tiffin** The meat-loving sibling of Udupi Palace, this spot is one of the classier restaurants on the block, so entrées are about a buck more than elsewhere. Try the crispy vegetable *pakoras*, massive rounds of bubbly nan, a fiery *bhindi masala* (okra sautéed with onions and tomatoes) and a chicken tikka masala dripping in spicy sauce upon request. Indian beer is tempting, but nothing's going to tame the fire in your mouth like a creamy mango lassi. *2536 W Devon Ave between Maplewood and Rockwell Aves (773-338-2143).*

Bus: 49B, 93, 155. Lunch, dinner. Average main course: $9.

★ ▼ ◷ BYOB **Udupi Palace** Carnivores seem to think that without meat on their plates they'd starve. But this 100% vegetarian South Indian spot puts an end to that theory with its famous *dosai*—a gigantic cumin-, potato- and onion-filled rice and lentil crêpe that comes in a dozen varieties. Other good bets include vegetable *pullav* (a cardamom, clove and cinnamon-laced rice dish) and the "Madras-style" okra curry that regulars swear by. *2543 W Devon Ave at Maplewood Ave (773-338-2152). Bus: 49B, 155. Lunch, dinner. Average main course: $11.* ● *Other location: 730 Schaumburg Rd, Schaumburg (847-884-9510).*

★ ▼ ◷ BYOB **Uru-Swati** Ask for the *TOC* translated menu here, and voila: you'll find descriptions of the overwhelming options. Potatoes with mustard seed and cumin are perfect for the crispy, two-foot long paper *dosa*; order it "masala" and get a smear of tangy chutney. Try the Swati samosa chaat, a smashed potato pocket drenched in silky yogurt, tamarind chutney and subtly spicy "salsa." Not sure? Order anything and you're bound to get fresh, flavorful, meat-free eats for a good price. *2629 W Devon Ave at Talman Ave (773-262-5280). Bus: 49B, 155. Lunch, dinner (closed Tue). Average main course: $6.*

◷ ♦ ☾ **Usmania** Formerly a dingy dive that served up some great Indo-Pak food, Usmania now resides across the street in a swankier spot. Luckily, the food is the same. The menu yields well-executed versions of

Pakistani standards like *nehari* and kebabs, and the rice *biryanis* are great, particularly the one made with mutton. The warm staff earnestly tries to live up to its claim of being "the finest family restaurant in Chicago," and it's not far off. *2244 W Devon between Bell and Oakley Aves (773-262-1900). Bus: 49B, 155. Lunch, dinner. Average main course: $8.*

★ ▼ ✳ **Veerasway** This modern spot does a nice job updating the fiery cuisine with snazzy street snacks (try the fried banana peppers stuffed with lentils and paneer) and cocktails (the cardamom-packed "Bengali Tiger" is delicious). Heat-seekers should request extra fire with classics like chicken tikka masala and lamb rogan josh, while those looking for something new will find it with tamarind-date glazed chicken or grilled shrimp cachoombar salad with spicy tomato chutney. *844 W Randolph St between Green and Peoria Sts (312-491-0844). El: Green, Pink to Clinton. Bus: 8, 20. Lunch (Friday only), dinner. Average main course: $15.*

▼ ✳ **Vermilion** This female owner-and-chef team (both of Indian descent) isn't doing Devon; they're elevating Indian cuisine for the swank set that wouldn't venture north of Belmont Avenue. The seasonal dishes boast a Latin American flair and are more interesting and flavorful than straight-up Indian. Try the chile glazed eggplant, the gobi Portuguese and the tandoori steak with fried plantain chips and fresh *pico de gallo*. *10 W Hubbard St between State and Dearborn Sts (312-527-4060). El: Red to Grand. Bus: 22, 29, 36, 65. Lunch (Mon–Fri), dinner. Average main course: $30.*

SOMETHING OLD, SOMETHING NEW
Veerasway serves traditional chicken tikka alongside contemporary cocktails like the Bengali Tiger.

Italian/Pizza

GET INKED Terragusto's housemade pasta gains color from squid ink and its flavor from fresh, plump shrimp.

★ ✳ **A Mano** The BIN 36 team is behind this trattoria downstairs from its popular wine bar, and they've added plenty of incentives to stop by. Lunch offers a pressed panini or wood-fired pizza for $12. (Other lunch items include the oven-roasted tuna, olive and lemon burger on *ciabatta* with a side of polenta frites and the grilled veggie panini). After work, bar plates like bruschetta go for five bucks, and in nice weather, the patio is the perfect spot to sample the excellent gelato. *335 N Dearborn St between Kinzie St and Wacker Dr (312-629-3500). El: Red to Grand; Brown, Purple (rush hrs) to Merchandise Mart. Bus: 22, 36. Lunch (Mon–Fri), dinner. Average main course: $22.*

★ ▼ ✳ **A Tavola** This tiny Ukrainian Village dining room is tight on tables and menu items—there are about a dozen of each—but what it lacks in size makes up for with charm. The simple Italian fare has no bells or whistles, but most dishes don't need any. A duo of meaty mushrooms is dressed only with balsamic and thyme, and the roasted chicken gets by on its golden, crispy skin alone. *2148 W Chicago Ave between Hoyne Ave and Leavitt St (773-276-7567). Bus: 49, 50, 66. Dinner (closed Sun). Average main course: $23.*

▼ ✳ **B BYOB Adesso** There's a lot to love about this casual Italian Boystown eatery: It's BYOB; it's bustling without being a clubby mob scene; the design is sleek but comfortable; and the simple Italian dishes are much-needed in this Italian-bereft 'hood. Dishes to try include the *pollo al mattone*, a Tuscan herb–rubbed half chicken; *salmon arrosto*, pan-seared salmon with a saffron risotto; and the comforting baked eggplant *melanzane alla parmigiana*. *3332 N Broadway at Buckingham Pl (773-868-1516). El: Brown, Purple (rush hrs), Red to Belmont. Bus: 36, 77, 145, 146, 152. Brunch (Sat, Sun), lunch, dinner. Average main course: $14. ● Other location: 401 E Ontario St (312-587-7117).*

◉ ⟨ **Al's #1 Italian Beef** Though it was franchised at the turn of the millennium, this location of Al's is the oldest (having opened in 1938), and the only direct descendant of the original (a wooden stand at Laflin and Harrison). These days, you'll find Italian beefs all over town, but there's something special about eating one at this surviving piece of Little Italy. A six-inch bun piled with tender, thinly sliced beef is only better as a "combo" (topped with char-grilled sausage), "dipped" in beef jus and finished with hot giardiniera. Skin-on fries smothered with cheese are required eating for a meal lingering locals would be proud of. *1079 W Taylor St between Carpenter and Aberdeen Sts (312-226-4017). El: Blue to Racine. Bus: 7, 12, 60. Lunch, dinner. Average main course: $5.*

▼ **Anna Maria Pasteria** This Italian stalwart has retained all of the charm it had when it made Wrigleyville home: The exposed brick, rustic, frescoed walls and flickering candlelight could warm even the residents of the cemetery across the street. The menu features traditional pasta and meat dishes that, while not earth-shattering, are satisfying. All your marsalas, piccatas and parmigianas are represented, but don't miss the lemony grilled calamari starter or the *rigatoni al pomodoro secco*, with its fat mushrooms and just-heavy-enough Gorgonzola sauce. *4400 N Clark St at Montrose Ave (773-506-2662). Bus: 22, 78, 145, 148. Dinner (closed Mon). Average main course: $15.*

★ ▼ ✳ **Anteprima** What's not to like about this Andersonville trattoria? It's cute, it's bustling, service is helpful, and the food

borders between good and great. Year-round don't-miss items include the tender, lemon-kissed grilled octopus; the salumi plate; and the value-packed antipasti platter. Like any good trattoria, Anteprima rotates much of the menu according to season, but housemade pastas prove as perfect with rabbit *ragù* in cold weather as they do with bright fava beans and ricotta in spring. In warm weather, seek out the secluded back patio. *5316 N Clark St between Berwyn and Summerdale Aves (773-506-9990). Bus: 22, 92. Dinner. Average main course: $19.*

▼ ✳ BYOB **Antica Pizzeria** Simple is not a word that's used casually at Antica: The dining room is so nondescript you'll hardly remember being in it, and the only thing rare about the food is how honest it is. The Margherita may not pass muster with Neapolitan snobs—the crust is just millimeters too thick and a little too dry. But anybody who can get past those details will be rewarded with a crisp crust and a piquant sauce, praiseworthy not because it's complicated, but specifically because it isn't. *5663 N Clark St between Olive and Hollywood Aves (773-944-1492). El: Red to Bryn Mawr. Bus: 22, 50. Dinner. Average pizza: $13.*

▼ **Apart Pizza** Designer pizza's all the rage right now, but we've still been longing for a simple, no-frills Neapolitan pie—the kind that's cut into perfect triangular slices, not kiddy-size squares. Salvation has come by way of this immaculate Lincoln Square storefront, where the industrial-size mixer is a cue that this place takes its thin crust seriously. Add a perfect sauce-to-topping ratio, a smattering of fresh salads and housemade dressing options, and the result is the perfect little takeout pizza joint. Bonus: Delivery's free. *2205 W Montrose Ave at Lincoln Ave (773-588-1550). El: Brown to Western. Bus: 11, 49, 78. Lunch (Wed–Sun), dinner. Average pizza: $13.*

★ ▼ BYOB **The Art of Pizza** Don't get us wrong; we love the fresh toppings, including meaty chunks of mild sausage and fresh vegetables that are crisp and crunchy when you bite into them. But it's really the sauce—full of fresh tomato flavor, speckled with oregano, basil and the faintest hint of red pepper—that's made this pizzeria a Chicago institution. Both the deep dish and the (not very thin) thin-crust lack the flakiness of other local pies, but they resist sogginess after a night in the fridge, making them the breakfast of champions. *3033 N Ashland Ave at Nelson St (773-327-5600). El: Brown to Paulina. Bus: 9, X9, 11, 77. Lunch, dinner. Average pie: $14.*

◉ **Bari Foods** If you're anywhere near the West Loop, you *have* to stop at this Italian grocery. Work your way through the tiny aisles with jam-packed shelves offering imported pastas, olive oils and biscotti galore and head for the deli counter in back. It's there that you'll find one of the best Italian subs in town: a crusty sub loaf (baked next door at D'Amato's) brimming with cappicola, genoa salami, mortadella, provolone, oregano, tomato and housemade giardiniera. Grab a San Pellegrino and a pint of Ciao Bella gelato and you've got one of the tastiest lunches in town for less than a ten-spot. Plus, you can stock your pantry while you're grabbing lunch *1120 W Grand Ave between Aberdeen and May Sts (312-666-0730). Bus: 65. Lunch. Average sandwich: $5.*

BYOB Tip: *Italian/Pizza*

Wine: *Dolcetto d'Alba or Trebbiano*

Red sauces don't need more acidity, they need full fruit, something you'll find in a dark red like Dolcetto d'Alba. If you're looking for a white to match with seafood, pretty Trebbiano is it.

Beer: *Belgian-style pale ale or tripel*

Belgian pale ales have good roasted malt flavor and a bit of bitterness to counter red-sauced pastas or pizza, while tripels deliver herbal hoppiness for pesto, rosemary chicken and the like.

Buy it at In Fine Spirits (5418 N Clark St, 773-506-9463) then **bring it** to Great Lake (p.77).

Buy it at West Lakeview Liquors (2156 W Addison St, 773-525-1916) then **bring it** to Terragusto on Addison (p.81).

Buy it at Kafka Wine Co (3325 N Halsted St, 773-975-9463) then **bring it** to Adesso (p.71).

▼ ✳ ◉ **Bice Ristorante** You don't hear much about this big, bilevel restaurant in Streeterville. But there's something to be said about an Italian spot that's outlasted countless restaurants in the nearly two decades it's been open (and even if it's part of a chain, at least it's a chain that was born in Italy). We think its secret is keeping things simple: The warm and inviting dining room and curvaceous bar entice diners, and the food doesn't disappoint. There's the impeccably fresh buffalo mozzarella; hearty bowls of cheesy, housemade gnocchi; and a wine list that—like everything else—is nothing if not dependable. *158 E Ontario St between Michigan Ave and St. Clair St (312-664-1474). El: Red to Grand. Bus: 3, 10, 26, 125, 143, 144, 145, 146, 147, 148, 151. Lunch, dinner. Average main course: $20.*

◉ **Bionda To-Go Café** Joe Farina added this counter-service lunch spot to his expanding network of Italian eateries, and for our money, it's the star of the family. Pastas and salads join signatures like Joe Mama's Meatball Bomber sandwich, which is our pick for best of the lot thanks to bright, zesty tomato sauce and the massive meat-to-bread ratio of the meatballs. Eggplant parm is nearly as good an option for those looking to eat relatively healthy, and the Italian beef with both sweet and mild giardiniera is the best within a Turano-roll toss of the tiny carryout space. *400 S Financial Pl at Van Buren St (312-435-0400). El: Brown, Orange, Pink, Purple (rush hrs) to LaSalle/Van Buren. Lunch. Average main course: $8.*

▼ **Bricks** Should thick-crust theorists and thin-crust connoisseurs ever stop their quarreling, this is where they'll come together. Because here, the bubbly crust fits somewhere between those two camps. Whether piled with feta and spinach (like the garlicky Popeye) or housemade meatballs and mozz, the simultaneously crispy and fluffy crust never buckles. Nor does it get in the way, so both sides should be satiated. And if they're not, the beer list (including Fat Tire and the entire Anchor Brewing lineup) can be tapped to calm things down. *1909 N Lincoln Ave at Wisconsin St (312-255-0851). Bus: 11, 22, 36. Dinner. Average pizza: $15.*

▼ **Bruna's Ristorante** This old-school favorite opened its doors in the Heart of Italy neighborhood in 1933, which almost explains the faded travel posters and weary saloon decor. But the kitchen is far from tired, going beyond typical pastas and parmigianas to specialize in rustic dishes from Siena. Tucked between the chicken Vesuvio and the stuffed

shells are a rich ravioli filled with porcini mushrooms and a spirited rendition of penne alla puttanesca. Stop at the bar for a digestif with the locals on your way out. *2424 S Oakley Ave between 24th Pl and 24th St (773-254-5550). El: Pink to Western. Bus: 21, 49, X49, 60. Lunch, dinner. Average main course: $18.*

★ ▼ **Burt's Place** Before opening this antique- and jazz-filled pizza joint, Burt Katz owned Inferno, Gullivers and Pequod's, concocting his signature, crunchy, nearly-burnt crust. Toppings are across-the-board fresh, with tricolor peppers, portobello, quarter-sized Italian sausage patties and tangy sauce all adding up to one hell of a pie. Katz and his wife Sharon are a two-person team (save for a guy who helps out on the floor on Saturday nights) and will likely welcome you like family once you become a regular. *8541 N Ferris Ave, Morton Grove (847-965-7997). Metra: Milwaukee N to Morton Grove. Lunch (Wed–Fri), dinner (closed Mon, Tue). Average pizza: $16.*

◉ BYOB **Café Luigi Pizza** The only way this old-school slice shop could get more New York is if Woody Allen was rolling the dough, Sarah Jessica Parker was tending the sauce and Michael Bloomberg was working the register. Big, foldable slices are thin and can be piled with spinach, artichokes, ricotta and fresh tomato—though real New Yorkers know that plain is the way to go. Housemade sausage and pepperoni-stuffed "New York rolls" and thick Sicilian slices round out the menu, and the BYOB status keeps things cheap. *2548 N Clark St at Deming Pl (773-404-0200). El: Brown, Purple (rush hrs) to Diversey. Bus: 8, 22, 36, 76. Lunch, dinner. Average main course: $4.*

★ ▼ **Café Spiaggia** If you want to dine at Spiaggia but just can't foot the bill, your solution is this adjacent sibling café. The ingredients come from the same kitchen, so they're just as impeccable, and the attention to regional Italian tradition is just as detailed. The room is more casual, prices are lower and service is less formal, making it a perfect lunch escape from Mag Mile shopping. Save room for incredible pastas, like gnocchi pillows in perfect wild-boar *ragù* or strands of *perciatelle* tossed with *guanciale*, Calabrian peppers, garlic, onion and fresh basil. And leaving without sampling Spiaggia's legendary gelato would be a crime. *980 N Michigan Ave between Oak St and Walton Pl (312-280-2750). El: Red to Clark/Division. Bus: 143, 144, 145, 146, 147, 151. Lunch, dinner. Average main course: $17.*

WHAT A LUSH Surrounded by greenery, Anteprima's back patio is an ideal urban escape.

Secret gardens

Some patios are front-and-center scenes, but we prefer these hidden respites for under-the-radar escapes.

True, the mural of a unibrowed Kahlo at **La Cocina de Frida** (p.98) can be a little discomfiting at first. But once you settle beneath the fruit trees in the pastel-colored confines of the patio, you can't help but relax. Order the *pollo mole* and a fresh margarita so good it'll put hair on your chest (or between your eyebrows).

You overheated while backpacking in Rome and jumped into the Trevi Fountain. During summer, relive that Italian experience by escaping to the pastoral yard at **Anteprima** (p.73). House-grown vegetables and herbs enhance the rustic, seasonal fare. So do glasses of crisp prosecco. But if even the wine doesn't cool you down, there's a bubbling fountain near the ivy-covered coach house. You know what to do.

Even the most tireless twinks need a break from Boystown's party scene. The garden at **Arco de Cuchilleros** (p.119) gets the job done with towering trees, sparkling lights and soft Spanish music. Indulge in tortilla Española or cod loins sautéed in olive oil, white wine, garlic and cayenne. Wash it down with a pitcher of potent sangria before heading back out into the madness.

Fish oil, beef liver and egg yolks offer tons of vitamin D. Luckily for vegans, so does sunlight, which they can get plenty of on the back patio at Lakeview's meatless mecca **Chicago Diner** (p.129). Order a black-bean burger and a seasonal beer and chill in the outdoor space, which owner Mickey Hornick is considering enclosing.

If there's a place where eating a juicy (read: messy) blue-cheese burger can be romantic, it's **Jury's** (p.139). As the sunlight fades, the hanging lights take over, casting a warm yet dim glow over you and your lover. Everybody looks good in this light—even with beef juice running down their chin.

Make it a pub crawl by hitting both **Ten Cat** (p.144) and nearby **Long Room** (p.142), where dozens of imported and domestic craft brews will keep you sated on patios teeming with flowers, ivy, prairie grass and other flora. But don't think about the garbage-lined alleys just over the wall.

The patio at **Enoteca Roma** (p.76) doesn't feel so much like Rome as it does the Italian countryside—wisteria, geranium, impatiens and bountiful trees surround you while you dig into insalata caprese, bruschetta and salmon. It's enough to start you daydreaming about moving to Italy and becoming a gardener, or at least hiring one.

You have to work, but if you can snag a "working from home" day, take it at West Town coffee shop **Sip** (*1223 W Grand Ave, 312-492-7686*). There, you can do all your e-mailing on the sun-drenched patio (thanks to the free Wi-Fi) and down mug after mug of Intelligentsia. Take a break to watch birds peck at the handcrafted feeders or play a round of Scrabble or Monopoly. And if you need another day of fresh air? Call in sick and say you got swine flu.
—*Ari Bendersky*

▼ B **BYOB Caffé Florian** See Classic American $15 and under for review.

▼ ✳ **Caffe Gelato** See Ice Cream and Sweets for review.

☺ **Calo Ristorante** Tucked between the Swedish stalwarts and shiny new bistros and sushi houses in Andersonville is this red-sauce Italian spot, which has been serving up can't-go-wrong classics to the locals since 1963. The menu's solidly old-school dishes include crisp chicken *parmigiana* and shells stuffed to the hilt with fresh ricotta. Feeling fancy? Try the fluffy gnocchi filled with Gorgonzola and served under a blanket of tomato cream sauce. *5343 N Clark St between Summerdale and Balmoral Aves (773-271-7725). Bus: 22, 50, 92. Lunch, dinner. Average main course: $13.*

▼ ✳ **Campagnola** This Evanston spot is run by chef Vince DiBattista and focuses on sophisticated Italian food made with organic ingredients, including a simple pappardelle bolognese that gets a boost from its delicate veal, pork and pancetta *ragù*. Though limited, the mostly Italian wine list offers some exciting choices, especially the dark, velvety Liveli *negro amaro*. *815 Chicago Ave, Evanston (847-475-6100). El: Purple to Main. Bus: 205. Dinner (closed Mon). Average main course: $22.*

▼ **BYOB Caro Mio** The deep-red walls and friendly service make this charming Ravenswood spot as warm as the food. And because it's BYOB, it's hard to beat the value. Bring a bottle of Sangiovese to match with the soft grilled polenta topped with the chunky house ragù. The housemade tricolored rotolo is our favorite of the pastas, stuffed with ricotta and spinach, then baked to hot perfection. Specials like chicken parmigiana baked in a cream-based red sauce are winners—as are most of the dishes on the menu. *1827 W Wilson Ave between Ravenswood and Wolcott Aves (773-275-5000). El: Brown to Damen. Bus: 50, 145. Lunch (Mon–Fri), dinner. Average main course: $15.*

▼ ❨ **Cibo Matto** Todd Stein has a lot of good ideas for theWit's high-end dining spot, some of which result in really great dishes. His rich roasted chicken livers, for instance, are paired with polenta and mushrooms to a deliciously earthy effect. But he's often heavy handed with ingredients, overshadowing what could be complex flavor combinations (chicken with pancetta) with one big, clunky taste (a big slathering of honey). Luckily he's a master of pasta, and his *corzetti* topped with sweet corn and thick *bucatini* with bacon is enough to make this place a destination. For at least one course, anyway. *201 N State St, theWit Hotel second floor (312-239-9500). El: Brown, Green, Orange, Pink, Purple (rush hrs) to State/Lake; Red to Lake. Dinner. Average main course: $30.*

▼ **Cipollina** See Delis for review.

▼ ✳ ❨ B **Club Lucky** The nearby condo dwellers with kids in tow may be a different crowd than the Polish regulars who frequented the joint post-Prohibition, but the owners have gone out of their way to restore the original cocktail-culture look of the '50s. The place is always packed, thanks to a dependable, old-school, family-style Italian menu with standouts like grilled calamari, chicken Vesuvio, and escarole with sausage and beans. But if you're kidphobic, go late for the lounge vibe of Sinatra standards and signature martinis. *1824 W*

Italian/Pizza

ANTI UP Imported salumi, glazed cipollini onions and shelled fava beans make up Francesca Forno's antipasti plate.

INSIDE TRACK
ITALIAN STALLION

The midcentury construction of the Eisenhower Expressway and the UIC campus displaced most of the Italians in Chicago's Little Italy, but the neighborhood still soldiers on, relying on the National Italian American Sports Hall of Fame (1431 W Taylor St, 312-226-5566) and a handful of remaining restaurants to help it live up to its name. For a quick tour of greatest hits, have an Italian beef at Al's (p.71), stop for an intermezzo cup of Italian ice at Mario's (p.65), then settle into an upstairs table at RoSal's (p.80), where the solid red-sauced pastas and platters of crispy calamari are as hefty as the regulars.

Wabansia Ave at Honore St (773-227-2300). El: Blue to Damen. Bus: 50, 56, 72. Lunch (Mon–Fri), brunch (Sun), dinner. Average main course: $16.

★ ▼ **Coal Fire** The East Coast–style pizzas are immensely impressive, with slightly charred bubbles here and there and crisp edges that give way to a salty, yeasty chew. We're fans of the sweet-heat combo on the Fiorentino, a marriage of red peppers and hot salami. The housemade sauce incorporates canned tomatoes, but they're high quality and taste fresh and bright. Fans of ricotta could skip red pies and go with either the white pizza or the pesto (salty black olives combine with the fresh ricotta for perfect balance). *1321 W Grand Ave between Elizabeth and Ada Sts (312-226-2625). El: Blue to Chicago. Bus: 9, X9, 65. Dinner (closed Mon). Average pizza: $13.*

★ ▼ **Coco Pazzo** The soft focaccia and fruity olive oil delivered to your table at this popular Gold Coast mainstay are good indicators of what's to come. Start with some antipasti—on your way in, you probably passed a table stocked with the wonderful chunks of Parmesan, white beans slick with olive oil and herbs, and thin slices of tender prosciutto. The garganelli pasta dish is doused in lamb *ragù*; and housemade gelati are decadent endings. *300 W Hubbard St at Franklin St (312-836-0900). El: Brown, Purple (rush hrs only) to Merchandise Mart. Bus: 65, 125. Lunch (Mon–Fri), dinner. Average main course: $17.* ● *Other location: Coco Pazzo Café, 636 N St. Clair St (312-664-2777).*

★ ▼ ✳ ☾ **Crust** The motto of Crust, Michael Altenberg's certified-organic pizzeria, is "Eat Real." Eat simple and good is more like it, as that's the general take on straightforward salads composed of impeccably fresh vegetables; tender pulled pork topped with crunchy slaw on soft housemade brioche; and the pizza (appearing on the menu as "flatbreads"), which has a bubbly, half-inch–thick crust that is slightly, pleasantly chewy. When it is topped with béchamel, caramelized onion, bacon and caraway seeds—like the "Flammkuchen" is—it can be very good indeed. *2056 W Division St at Hoyne Ave (773-235-5511). El: Blue to Division. Bus: 50, 70. Brunch (Sat, Sun), lunch, dinner. Average main course: $12.*

▼ ◎ ☾ **Da'Nali's** See Kosher for review.

Dave's Italian Kitchen In lots of ways, eating here is like going to your Italian grandmother's house for Sunday dinner. It's loud, a little dysfunctional and the decor is pretty worn, but all that fades into the background at your first taste of housemade red sauce. Neighborhood families allow Dave's to be the Grandma they never had, crowding the basement-level eatery for mega portions of mostaccioli, eggplant Parmesan and half-moon calzones. Wine snobs dine here, too, to see what new bottles oenophile Dave is serving up from his ambitious global collection. *1635 Chicago Ave, Evanston (847-864-6000). El: Purple to Davis. Bus: 201. Dinner. Average main course: $12.*

◎ **Enoteca Piattini** This trusty Italian spot lures locals into its sunny dining room with its extensive wine list and keeps them there with its solid menu. Tender meatballs simmering in marinara seem the perfect mate for a medium-bodied Italian red, while entrées like saltimbocca Siciliana—chicken topped with savory prosciutto and fontina—seem made for a lemony glass of white. End dinner on a sweet note with the housemade tiramisu. *934 W Webster Ave at Bissell St (773-935-8466). El: Brown, Purple (rush hrs), Red to Fullerton. Bus: 8, 73, 74. Dinner (closed Mon). Average main course: $14.*

▼ ◎ ✳ **Enoteca Roma** The family behind Letizia's Natural Bakery brings you one of the best back patios in the Ukie Village/Wicker Park area. Cop a seat among the greenery and dive into the wine list; it's playful, varied (i.e., not limited to Italians) and built for food. The bruschetta varieties—topped with toothsome ingredients like Brie and honey, cannellini beans and black-olive puree—are the favorite sons of the extensive menu, but don't overlook the Roman-style pizzas and Letizia's soft, salty focaccia with spicy mustard. *2146 W Division St between Hoyne Ave and Leavitt St (773-342-1011). El: Blue to Division. Bus: 49, X49, 50, 70. Dinner. Average main course: $8.*

★ ▼ ✳ **Follia** Owners Bruno and Melissa Abate decorated their high-style Italian restaurant with a wall of simulated grass and mannequins dressed in flashy couture, but the diverse crowd comes for the food, not the fashion. We love the crispy, paper-thin pizzas from a wood-burning oven (try the napoletana, topped with oregano and anchovies) and the pastas (a simple but spectacular risotto bolognese was a recent special). Entrées are hit-or-miss, but the personable servers make reliable recommendations. *953 W Fulton St at Morgan St (312-243-2888). El: Blue to Grand. Bus: 8, 65. Dinner. Average main course: $20.*

◎ ⓑ **Francesca's Forno** This Wicker Park outpost of the Francesca's chain packs in the hungry and hip for small plates of simple Italian fare for dinner, but it seems few people know it also serves brunch. The steak sandwich goes above standard with herb butter on roasted onion bread, plus a handful of pecorino and truffle oil–laced fries. And while we're not sure why it's called "panettone" French toast, since the Italian bread isn't used, it's a good dish nonetheless, topped with sweet mascarpone cream, fresh berries and aged balsamic vinegar. *1576 N Milwaukee Ave at North Ave (773-770-0184). El: Blue to Damen. Bus: 50, 56, 72. Brunch (Sat, Sun), lunch (Mon–Fri), dinner. Average small plate: $8.*

▼ **Frankie's Scaloppine** The mall location and the LEYE association might bring out the skeptic in hard-core foodies, but we have to admit the food at this affordable Italian spot is good enough to justify a casual dinner after shopping on the Mag Mile. Sardinian-style pizzas featuring red onion, fennel or garlic get things off to a good start. Pastas are standard and typically substantial, but you'd do better to save room for the pepper-smothered, crispy-skinned brick chicken or the tender veal *limone*. Servers have the robotic spiel down, but if chef "Frankie" is working the room, you'll glean some genuine hospitality. *900 N Michigan Ave, fifth floor, between Delaware Pl and Walton Pl (312-266-2500). El: Red to Clark/Division. Bus: 143, 144, 145, 146, 147, 151. Lunch (Mon–Sat), dinner. Average main course: $14.*

▼ ✳ **Frasca Pizzeria and Wine Bar** With wood-fired pizza spots recently surpassing the number of deep-dish options in town, it seems like thin-crust pizza has replaced sushi as Chicago's trendiest cuisine. The swankiest of the bunch is Frasca, with arches reminiscent of a Tuscan wine cellar, sexy red leather banquettes and wallpaper of bare branches climbing up the curved walls. The cavernous space is packed to conversation-inhibiting capacity with twentysomethings chomping on chewy thin-crust pizzas—we like the fennel sausage, onion and mozz Capone—and tossing back reasonably priced wines. *3358 N Paulina St between School and Roscoe Sts (773-248-5222). El: Brown to Paulina. Bus: 9, 11, 77, 152. Brunch (Sat, Sun), dinner. Average main course: $16.*

▼ ✳ **Fresco** A better name for this place might be Alfresco, because the wine garden in back—with its walls covered with murals depicting provincial Italian life—is the restaurant's most sought-after asset in the summer. Sitting here, it's nearly impossible not to take advantage of the restaurant's white wine list (or its considerably un-Italian pitchers of sangria) while noshing on tender grilled calamari with feta and roasted red peppers, or light, crispy artichoke fritters. *1202 W Grand Ave between Racine and Ogden Aves (312-733-6378). El: Blue to Grand. Bus: 8, 9, X9, 65. Lunch, dinner. Average main course: $12.*

★ ✳ **Gabriel's** See French for review.

▼ ✳ **Gino's East** This Chicago-style pizza institution is no longer at its original Superior Street location (where it debuted in '66), but tourists still flock in droves, so skip weekends. The famous deep-dish has a cornmeal crust that's void of the butter glaze others give the pan, so it's not greasy (but also not very flavorful). Luckily, the punch comes from the sauce, which is tangy and ripe. Try half spinach–half sausage (let it sit for a minute when it arrives to avoid a runny mess), and wash it down with a refreshing Goose Island 312. *633 N Wells St at Ontario St (312-943-1124). El: Brown, Purple (rush hrs) to Chicago. Bus: 65, 125. Lunch, dinner. Average pizza: $20.*

▼ **Gio** After 12 years of expressing his Spanish side at Tapas Barcelona, Spanish-Italian owner Giovanni Garelli decided to channel his mother's Italian heritage by opening Gio in 2003. Service is friendly, and the long bar is comfy for grabbing a quick bite. But we tend to linger, starting with antipasti of fennel salad and wood-roasted peppers, moving on to the fettuccine with rich porcini sauce or mezzaluna stuffed with lobster and ricotta, and wrapping up with the veal *limone* or *cioppino* seafood stew. *1631 Chicago Ave, Evanston (847-869-3900). El: Purple to Davis. Bus: 201, 205. Metra: Union Pacific North Line to Evanston-Davis. Lunch (Mon–Fri), dinner. Average main course: $15.*

▼ ✴ B Gioco Chef Danny Sweiss excels at hearty, unfussy pastas like the penne with prosciutto, spring peas and mushrooms in Parmesan cream sauce. Seasonal produce shows up in several salads; we like the combination of baby arugula, fresh pears, candied hazelnuts, pancetta and shaved ricotta tossed in a creamy Italian vinaigrette. The kitchen typically nails classics like the ridiculously huge 40-ounce porterhouse. Go ahead and try to finish it; there's no need to save room for the skippable desserts. *1312 S Wabash Ave at 13th St (312-939-3870). El: Green, Orange, Red to Roosevelt. Bus: 12, 29, 62. Brunch (Sun), lunch (Mon–Fri), dinner. Average main course: $28.*

☉ Golden Crust Italian Pizzeria Sometimes you don't want artisanal ingredients manipulated by globe-trotting chefs. Sometimes you want the stuff of your childhood memories—actual comfort food—not nuevo comfort food. This is where you go when you want those absurdly large portions of lasagna, pizza and other Italian classics, topped with almost too much Parmesan and red sauce. You'll dine in a dated booth, on paper place mats emblazoned with a map of Italy. Take leftovers home for lunch tomorrow, and go back to low carbs the day after. *4620 N Kedzie Ave between Wilson and Eastwood Aves (773-539-5860). El: Brown to Kedzie. Bus: 78, 81, 82. Lunch (Sat, Sun), dinner. Average main course: $8.*

★ BYOB Great Lake Warning: Everything at this new high-design pizzeria is tiny. The space fits one communal table and a shelf of carefully selected sundries, while the menu consists of only four pizzas (and no, a create-your-own option isn't one of them). Perhaps most important, the pizza oven is also small, allowing for only one pizza to be cooked at a time. Could it be worth the wait? Thanks to the puffy, chewy crust; the house-pulled mozzarella; layers of fresh, earthy mushrooms; and an obsessive eye for detail, the answer, if your mouth isn't already watering, is yes. *1477 W Balmoral Ave between Clark St and Glenwood Ave (773-334-9270). El: Red to Berwyn. Bus: 22, 36, 92. Lunch (Fri–Sat), dinner (Wed–Sat). Average pizza: $18.*

▼ ✴ B Gruppo di Amici Owners Lori Alderete and Phaedra Divras lure East Rogers Parkers desperate for higher-end options. Their wood-fired hearth that cooks their Roman-style pizzas was custom-made in Italy, for chrissakes—and their dedication pays off with a devoted clientele who pack the house for the capricciosa pie (a delicious heap of hard-boiled egg, prosciutto, olives, artichokes and mushrooms on a chewy crust), simple margherita and tangy *funghi e formaggi* (goat cheese, mushroom, EVOO). *1508 W Jarvis Ave at Greenview Ave (773-508-5565). El: Red to Jarvis. Bus: 22, 147, 151. Dinner (closed Mon). Average main course: $13.*

✴ Harry Caray's The legendary Cubs announcer may be gone, but his spirit lives on at his popular namesake eatery. These days Caray's widow, Dutchie, greets patrons who continue to crowd the place during Cubs games as well as the off-season for gargantuan steaks (23-ounce porterhouse, anyone?) and classic Italian dishes like chicken Vesuvio, sausage and peppers and veal picatta. The walls are awash in memorabilia that will keep sports fans entertained for ages. *33 W Kinzie St between State and Dearborn Sts (312-828-0966). El: Red to Grand. Bus: 22, 36, 65. Lunch, dinner. Average main course: $20.*

BYOB I Monelli Trattoria Pizzeria The owner of Pizza Metro and a former pie-slinger for Pizza D.O.C. combined wits on what they do best at this corner spot. It's clear after one bite of the rectangular pizzas that it's Metro that's driving the style—Roman in shape and structure, the pies are thin (but not cracker-thin), crunchy (but not dry) and topped with tasty combos like al dente eggplant and zucchini or a perfect balance of salty, tart and rich with diced ham, fresh mushrooms, artichoke and black olives. *5019 N Western Ave at Winnemac Ave (773-561-8499). El: Brown to Western. Bus: 11, 49, X49, 81. Lunch, dinner (closed Tue). Average pizza: $15.*

♨ ✴ Il Mulino New York Years of fending off the Zagat-clutching crowds at their flagship Greenwich Village spot gave the brothers behind this New York classic the confidence to expand, which is exactly what they've done: to Tokyo, Las Vegas and now, the Gold Coast's Biggs Mansion. Every meal here starts with complimentary antipasto, fried zucchini and garlic bread sticks, followed by entrées such as saltimbocca (veal sautéed with sage and prosciutto) and spaghettini bolognese—with a healthy slice of New York attitude on the side. *1150 N Dearborn St between Elm and Division Sts (312-440-8888). El: Red to Clark/Division. Bus: 36, 70, 151, 156. Lunch (Mon–Fri), dinner. Average main course: $35.*

▼ ✴ Il Vicinato Loosely translated, *vicinato* is Italian for neighborhood, and though this corner tavern may not be in yours, it's worth a trip to eat good in the Heart of Italy. Expect big plates of traditional fare, including *bianco nero* ("white black"), a wide bowl of tasty mussels and clams in garlicky broth, and pillow-y potato

gnocchi made in-house and topped with a meaty *ragù*. For dessert, share a dark chocolate ice-cream *tartufo* the size of Tony Soprano's fist. *2435 S Western Ave at 24th Pl (773-927-5444). El: Pink to Western. Bus: 21, 49, X49. Lunch (Mon–Fri), dinner (Mon–Sat) (closed Sun). Average main course: $16.*

★ ▼ ✱ **La Bocca della Verita** The simple rooms at this Roman-style trattoria are matched by an authentically simple menu. We love the *caprese* (the mozz is so good we order it even when tomatoes aren't in season) and the tart green apple and celery salad dressed only with olive oil, fresh lemon and shavings of delicious Parmesan. Couple these starters with the warm, crusty bread and follow up with the *guanciale*-dotted spaghetti alla carbonara and the sage-, shallot- and duck breast–filled ravioli in tomato cream, and you can skip main courses altogether. *4618 N Lincoln Ave between Wilson and Eastwood Aves (773-784-6222). El: Brown to Western. Bus: 11, 49, X49, 81. Lunch, dinner. Average main course: $12.*

▼ B **La Donna** The pasta menu at this Andersonville staple allows you to choose a housemade pasta and pair it with a sauce of your choice. While you may feel qualified to make such a choice, some of the delicious sauces, like the carbonara, don't work with every pasta. Play it safe and order from the entrée menu, where combos are already paired for you. There, *misto di pesce* (grilled seafood) gets the calamari, octopus and shrimp cooked perfectly, and tender (if fatty) osso buco comes with a delicious side of saffron cavatelli. *5146 N Clark St between Winona St and Foster Ave (773-561-9400). El: Red to Berwyn. Bus: 22, 36, 92. Brunch (Sun), lunch, dinner. Average main course: $17.*

▼ ✱ **La Madia** La Madia's menu is slightly bigger for dinner than it is for lunch. Still, we think the food is better for midday dining. What's fine for lunch (pizza fondue, for example) doesn't always pass muster for dinner. The pizzas can sometimes transition (a taleggio-and-grape pizza came out of the wood-burning oven with a thin, crisp crust), then again, sometimes they can't (a spinach-and-speck pie was too soft and overly bready). Luckily there's always the Wisconsin "electric" butter cookies, which are sumptuous, crumbly and delightful any time of day. In fact, take a few home and you might find they make a good breakfast. *59 W Grand Ave between Dearborn and Clark Sts (312-329-0400). El: Red to Grand. Bus: 22, 36, 65. Lunch, dinner. Average pizza: $13.*

▼ ♨ **La Scarola** It's okay to splash a little red sauce on the butcher-paper-topped tables in this raucous storefront. Old friends and big families admire the autographed celebrity photos and shots of the owner's family faced to the frescoed walls. Smiling waiters squeeze between tables juggling huge plates of eggplant parmigiana and bottles of decent Italian red. Order any of the appropriately garlicky pastas and a plate of escarole and beans for the table; the leftovers will warm up just fine tomorrow. *721 W Grand Ave between Union Ave and Halsted St (312-243-1740). El: Blue to Grand. Bus: 8, 56, 65. Lunch (Mon–Fri), dinner. Average main course: $17.*

▼ **La Trattoria de Merlo** The team behind the Merlo mini empire has added a third to the family, this one decidedly downscale with mismatched plates, wooden tables topped with rustic runners and a menu of trattoria staples, many hailing from the family's hometown of

Bologna. Tender, chilled rabbit meat on crostini and yellow fin house-cured in EVOO are a good start, and housemade pastas are simple yet tasty (after a request for the salt shaker). The accolades belong to the braised chicken legs in a forest's worth of 'shrooms and the tremendous desserts, including a rice pudding cake studded with candied citrus and Amaretti cookies. *1967 N Halsted St between Willow St and Armitage Ave (312-951-8200). El: Brown, Purple (rush hrs) to Armitage. Bus: 8, 73. Dinner. Average main course: $16.*

☺ ✱ **Lou Malnati's Pizzeria** There are two kinds of Chicagoans. No, not North Siders and South Siders. We're talking Giordano's people and Lou Malnati's people. Lou Malnati's deep-dish is the pinnacle of cheesy Chicago-style goodness. Everything else on the menu—including pastas and salads—is passable, but not worth passing on the 'za. Get the butter crust. And don't worry when you develop a Lou Malnati's addiction: They Fed-Ex pizza anywhere in the country. *439 N Wells St at Hubbard St (312-828-9800). El: Brown, Purple (rush hrs) to Merchandise Mart. Bus: 65, 125. Lunch, dinner. Average pizza: $13.*

☺ **Mangia Fresca** Being just steps from the Orange Line has given this tiny takeout joint an instant following—so much of a following, actually, that the few tables in the place are consistently packed with people shoveling hot eggplant Parmesan into their mouths while they watch the local news. The cheesy arancini are one of the restaurant's best bets; the panini, stuffed with fresh mozzarella and thin prosciutto, are a close second. And though this may not be the best red-sauce food you've ever had, the cannolis are filled to order, making for an ending that's pretty hard to argue with. *2556 S Archer Ave at Poplar Ave (312-225-7100). El: Orange to Halsted. Bus: 8, 44, 62. Breakfast (Mon–Sat), lunch (Mon–Sat), dinner (Mon–Fri). Average main course: $7.*

☺ **New York Slices** East Coast–style pizza joints are more common nowadays, but the majority are sad imitators of the real deal. Not this Highland Park spot. It's as though the Edens led us straight to Brooklyn, from the bubbly crusted pies made with a perfect sauce-to-cheese ratio to the slick-haired customers folding their slices and watching the oil drip onto their paper plates. You'll find calzones and garlic knots, too, and—pinch us, it's like we're dreaming—cups of Mario's Italian Ices with wooden spoons and cakelike black-and-white cookies. *1843 Second St, Highland Park (847-432-6979). Lunch, dinner. Average slice: $3.50.*

★ ▼ ✱ **Osteria Via Stato** The masterminds behind TRU have done it again, but this time think Italian share plates for a nice price. Servers will steer you toward the "Italian dinner party," but anything can be ordered à la carte. For the fixed price, seasonal tastes arrive in waves and you choose only your entrée. Marinated olives in herbed oil with warm focaccia are followed by antipasti like veal meatballs. Hearty pastas rotate, but may include a tasty bolognese pappardelle. Skip the wine list and try the creative "Just Bring Me Wine" pairings. *620 N State St at Ontario St (312-642-8450). El: Red to Grand. Bus: 22, 36, 65. Lunch (Sat, Sun), dinner. Average main course: $18.*

▼ ✱ **Pane Caldo** The authentic Northern Italian eats at this tony Gold Coast mainstay are luscious enough to make you forget their inflated price tags. But if you can swing it, go all the way, dahling. The menu changes often, but

on any given week, you could start by ordering a bottle of Barolo and buttery risotto sprinkled with slices of black truffles. Follow up with organic chicken stuffed with spinach, mozzarella and wild mushrooms. Dessert shifts gears by heading for France, with bombes as dolled up as most of the patrons. *72 E Walton St between Ernst Ct and Michigan Ave (312-649-0055). El: Red to Chicago. Bus: 36, 66, 143, 144, 145, 146, 147, 148, 151. Lunch, dinner. Average main course: $30.*

▼ ◖ **Pequod's Pizza** Exposed brick and plasma-screen TVs have taken the place of worn pool tables and dart boards after a fire forced a redesign of this neighborhood dive. But while the digs may be snazzier, the signature pan pizza—in all its glory with a ring of caramelized cheese around the crust—remains the same. Skip flavorless fried-vegetable appetizers, salads and sandwiches and save your appetite for ginormous slices of a sausage pie, dotted with perfectly spiced, Ping Pong ball–size pieces of seasoned ground pork. *2207 N Clybourn Ave at Webster Ave (773-327-1512). Bus: 9, X9, 74. Lunch, dinner. Average pizza: $13.*

✱ **Petterino's** It's 6pm, we're going to an 8pm play and we're in the middle of an assholes-to-elbows crowd at this theater-district restaurant. Wait for a table? Hell, no—we'll sit at the bright, window-filled bar, where we can order from the full menu and ask the busy bartenders to keep the sidecars coming. The New York strip steak au poivre is ridiculously tender and, even better, topped with caramelized onions. With service this fast, we have time to linger over the baked-in-house desserts and still catch the show. *150 N Dearborn St at Randolph St (312-422-0150). El: Red to Lake; Blue, Brown, Green, Orange, Purple (rush hrs), Pink to Clark/Lake. Bus: 22, 156. Lunch (Mon–Fri), dinner. Average main course: $19.*

▼ ◖ **Phil's Pizza** From Vito and Nick's in Ashburn to Pat's Pizza in Lincoln Park, it seems every neighborhood has its favored thin-crust pie. And for 48 years, Bridgeport's preference has been for Phil's. Unfortunately, in 2008, it closed its original wood-paneled spot on Halsted, leaving those years of hard-earned personality behind for a boring dining room a few blocks away. Luckily, the owners took their old-school Blodgett ovens with them, and the crispy exterior crust, chewy interior crust and hunks of fennel-flecked sausage honor the tasty tradition of the original. *1102 W 35th St between Aberdeen St and Racine Ave (773-523-0947). El: Orange to Ashland. Bus: 8, 9, 35. Dinner. Average main course: $12.*

▼ **Piccolo** See Ice Cream and Sweets for review.

★ ▼ ✱ **Piccolo Sogno** *2009 Eat Out Award, Critics' Pick: The Urban Oasis Award (best patio)* Two Coco Pazzo vets—chef Tony Priolo and wine guru Ciro Longobardo—have taken over the former Thyme/Timo space, capitalizing on the massive back patio space by creating one of the lushest urban retreats we've yet to find. We had the best luck with the starters and pizzas, which are perfect for passing among a big group. Order up a few bottles from the solid all-Italian wine list, and dig in to crispy calamari, fontina-stuffed squash blossoms, fresh pasta ribbons in veal *ragù* and a bubbly Margherita pizza. Velvety gelato in flavors like pistachio and hazelnut are a suitably simple ending. *464 N Halsted St at Grand Ave (312-421-0077). El: Blue to Grand. Bus: 8, 56, 65. Dinner. Average main course: $18.*

▼ (**Pie Hole** Like almost everything Twisted Spoke's owners (the Einhorn brothers) do, this tiny pizza joint has unexpected details of excellence that betray its machismo, carefree atmosphere. Fresh garlic and pristine basil (free for the asking), bacon, French olives and more all add up to some pretty delicious pizza. The red pesto pie has two standout features: the meaty and brilliantly spiced sausage and the chewy crust. *737 W Roscoe St between Halsted St and Elaine Pl (773-525-8888). El: Brown, Purple (rush hrs), Red to Belmont. Bus: 8, 36, 152. Dinner. Average pizza: $17.*

★ ▼ **Piece** Two things keep this place from going the route of sports-bar-beer-bong culture: excellent house brews and expertly executed pizzas. The crispy pies hold a lot of weight, so after you choose your pizza style—red, white or New Haven–style "plain" (red sauce, no mozzarella)—start piling on the toppings. (If you're really going New Haven–style, try one with clams and bacon.) Wash it down with a pitcher of the crisp Golden Arm, and you'll never disparagingly say "pizza and beer joint" again. *1927 W North Ave between Wolcott and Winchester Aves (773-772-4422). El: Blue to Damen. Bus: 50, 56, 72. Lunch, dinner. Average pizza: $13.50.*

◷ **Pizza Art Café** This candlelit room and wood-burning oven with two dozen types of pie—between Chicago-style bar pizza and the relatively spare Neapolitan varieties—has made us fans of the Pugliese pizza with onion and pecorino cheese. There's also strong representation from Italy's Dalmatian coast neighbors; some Bosnian specialties show up on a "secret" menu. Our favorite of the lot is the must-have house-cured smoked beef: dense, chewy, salty and, like most great works of art, complex. *4658 N Rockwell St between Eastwood and Leland Aves (773-539-0645). El: Brown to Rockwell. Bus: 49, X49, 81. Dinner (Tue–Sun). Average main course: $10.*

▼ ✳ (**Pizzeria Due** This crowd-pleasing sister to the original Uno's pizza institution features a cozy, below-street-level dining room/bar that reeks of that "old Chicago" feel, complete with black-and-white tiled floor, historical photos, and plenty of Ditka and Butkus memorabilia. Knife-and-fork, deep-dish pizza is its sole *raison d'être*, with a rich crust that gets crisp from its time in a traditional black-iron pan. We prefer the bright-green fresh spinach and broccoli over the bland sausage. Tourists love it, but, secretly, jaded locals do, too. *619 N Wabash Ave between Ohio and Ontario Sts (312-943-2400). El: Red to Grand. Bus: 29, 36, 65. Lunch, dinner. Average main course: $15.*

◷ ✳ **Pizzeria Uno** Drawn by tales of this pizzeria originating Chicago deep-dish, tourists and new transplants often flock here for their first Windy City meal. Around lunchtime, a crowd can be found in the lobby ordering their pizza while waiting for one of eighteen tables. Each pizza takes at least 45 minutes to cook, but it's worth the wait when your steaming pan with cheese-heavy slices arrives. If you've got a larger party or just can't stand the wait, head down the street to Pizzeria Due (619 N Wabash Ave), Uno's more spacious sister. *29 E Ohio St at Wabash Ave (312-321-1000). El: Red to Grand. Bus: 29, 36, 65. Lunch, dinner. Average main course: $7.*

▼ ✳ **Pizzeria via Stato** Hope you like salad. The pizza at this newly reconceptualized,

former lounge adjacent to Osteria via Stato is as thin as paper. And while that provides an excellent crispy base for the bright San Marzano tomatoes in the Margherita and the earthy combination of pancetta, fingerlings and smoked mozzarella on the sauceless potato pie, it's hard to get full off this stuff. So you'll need the arugula salad studded with sweet dates, and probably the Caesar salad, too. And while you're at it, may as well throw in the indulgent spinach-and-pecorino *fonduta*. *620 N State St at Ontario St (312-642-8450). El: Red to Grand. Bus: 22, 36, 65. Lunch (Mon–Sat), dinner. Average pizza: $12.*

▼ ◷ ✳ **Pompei on Taylor** The thin-versus-thick debate means nothing at the original Pompei, which has been making traditional thin, square, Italian bakery–style pizza since 1909. Pompei has fancier digs and a gussied-up menu this century, luring healthy types from the nearby medical centers for crisp salads with addictive housemade dressings. Scoot through the long cafeteria lines with the diehards who come in for slices of sausage, hand-cut pastas with gargantuan meatballs, and classic pepper-and-egg sandwiches. *1531 W Taylor St at Ashland Ave (312-421-5179). El: Pink to Polk. Bus: 9, 12. Lunch, dinner. Average main course: $8.*

◷ ✳ **Quartino** The Gibsons folks go rustic Italian with this cavernous dining room decked out with reclaimed wood and subway tiles, vintage mirrors and mismatched chairs. To ensure authenticity on the plate, they've enlisted chef John Coletta, who doesn't disappoint with housemade *salumi* like beef bresaola, spicy soppressata and duck prosciutto served with housemade giardiniera and *mostarda*. The pizza is among the better thin-crust versions in town. Living up to the name, the affordable, half-Italian, half-global wine list is offered in quarter, half and full liters. *626 N State St at Ontario St (312-698-5000). El: Red to Grand. Bus: 22, 36, 65, 156. Lunch, dinner. Average small plate: $5.*

★ ◷ **Riccardo Trattoria** One of the best Italian restaurants in town isn't tucked away on some corner in Little Italy. Surprisingly, it's smack-dab in vanilla Lincoln Park. Chef Riccardo Michi's family founded the Bice restaurant empire in Milan, so he knows a thing or two about regional Italian food. Don't miss the orecchiette with wild-boar sausage, garlicky rapini and pecorino cheese or the rack of lamb. Become a regular and the Italian waiters might cap off your meal with a slice of ricotta cheesecake. *2119 N Clark St between Dickens and Webster Aves (773-549-0038). El: Brown, Purple (rush hrs), Red to Fullerton. Bus: 22, 74. Dinner. Average main course: $20.*

★ ◷ **Riviera Italian Foods** At this family-owned Italian grocery, there is a lunchtime ordering procedure. Choose a crusty roll from the bread bin and get in line at the deli counter. Hand your roll to the man behind the counter and choose from generous quantities of prosciutto, fresh mozzarella and ridiculously good *soppressata*. Many of the items are made or cured in-house, including the mozz, the soppressata and the *capocollo*. Before you check out, take some time to scan the aisles for imported pastas, olives, tomatoes and sweets. *3220 N Harlem Ave between Belmont Ave and School Sts (773-637-4252). Bus: 77, 90. Average main course: $5.*

▼ **RoSal's** Typically, we'd tell the server to save the speech, but here, it's somehow

still charming when the bubbly girl "from da neighborhood" explains how the namesake owners Roseanne and Salvatore came to open their Little Italy spot. Cozy cuteness aside, the food's among the best on the Taylor Street strip. Start with the lightly charred but tender grilled calamari; get a pasta course of big, fat garlicky shrimp tossed with shells and broccoli; and go for the veal saltimbocca with a side of spinach for the main event. *1154 W Taylor St between May St and Racine Ave (312-243-2357). El: Blue to Racine. Bus: 7, 12, 60. Dinner (closed Sun). Average main course: $18.*

▼ ✳ **Rose Angelis** Lincoln Park locals seem to head to this adorable Italian eatery at least once a week, so there's always a wait, especially for the garden tables. The cozy-cute surroundings inspire foodies to let the spotty menu slide, but we enjoy the *mezzalune al burro*, a subtle yet hearty preparation of ricotta-and-spinach–stuffed pasta in brown butter; *raviolini alla Maria*, salmon-filled ravioli in a creamy pesto sauce; thin, whole-wheat pizzas; and manicotti preparations that change weekly. *1314 W Wrightwood Ave between Lakewood and Wayne Aves (773-296-0081). El: Brown, Purple (rush hrs), Red to Fullerton. Bus: 11, 74, 76. Lunch (Tue–Fri), dinner (closed Mon). Average main course: $14.*

▼ **Sabatino's** A dark and cozy date-friendly ambience, seasoned servers and old-school Italian dishes—what's not to like about this place? Couples should snag a booth, the perfect spot for sipping a well-priced bottle of Chianti and kicking the night off with the signature cheesy garlic bread. Shrimp de jonghe is fresh, ricotta-filled manicotti and gnocchi in meat sauce won't disappoint, and the extrathick New York strip is seasoned only with salt and pepper before hitting the grill for a spot-on medium-rare. *4441 W Irving Park Rd between Kenneth and Kilbourn Aves (773-283-8331). El: Blue to Irving Park. Bus: 53, 54A, X54, 80, X80. Lunch, dinner. Average main course: $14.*

★ ▼ BYOB **Sapore di Napoli** This member of the legion of Chicago's Neapolitan pizza joints is good enough to become your favorite neighborhood spot. The *quattro stagioni* piles big cuts of high-quality prosciutto, fat artichokes, mushrooms and olives onto bubbly crust, and the *verdure*, with its heaps of asparagus, peppers, eggplant and zucchini, nearly takes care of your daily veggie requirements in one bite. Follow your pie with *gelati* as smooth and creamy as any we've had in European *gelaterias*. *1406 W Belmont Ave at Southport Ave (773-935-1212). El: Brown to Southport. Bus: 9, X9, 77. Lunch (Sat, Sun), dinner (closed Mon). Average pizza: $12.*

▼ ✳ **Scoozi!** It's not the hot spot it was when it put River North on the map in the early '80s, but this cavernous Italian mainstay still keeps the crowds coming. The flatbread pizzas are a good bet, especially the Yellow Tomato *Bianca* with housemade mozzarella and aged provolone. The wine list is as big as the dinner menu, with more than 30 by-the-glass options. Expect a huge family crowd on Sundays, when kids 12 and under get to don chef gear and make their own pizzas at no charge from 5–6:30pm. *410 W Huron St between Sedgwick St and Hudson Ave (312-943-5900). El: Brown, Purple (rush hrs) to Chicago. Bus: 66. Dinner. Average main course: $20.*

★ ▼ ✳ **Spacca Napoli** *2009 Eat Out Award, Readers' Choice: Best Thin-Crust Pizza*

UPPER CRUST The classic Margherita pizza at Spacca Napoli is the way to go.

This place is serious about Neapolitan pizza: A custom-built, oak-stoked oven kicks out bubbling beauties with perfectly charred peaks and valleys in less than two minutes. The hand-formed crust is paper-thin at the center, thicker toward the edges and the unmistakable chew of a true Neapolitan pie. Aside from the simple marinara or Margherita (which can also be had with fresh buffalo mozz that's flown in each Thursday), toppings run the gamut from fennel-flecked sausage to bitter rapini to prosciutto ribbons. Add a humble Italian wine-and-beer list, after-dinner options such as espresso and limoncello, and you've got a great night out. *1769 W Sunnyside Ave between Hermitage and Ravenswood Aves (773-878-2420). El: Brown to Damen. Bus: 50, 78, 145. Lunch (Wed–Sun), dinner (Tue–Sun). Average pizza: $12.*

★ ▼ **Spiaggia** Want to skip rent this month and have the best Italian fine-dining experience in town? Splurge here. Chef Tony Mantuano marries imported Italian foodstuffs with top-notch American ingredients and a deep understanding of cuisine from the north end of "the boot." Wood-roasted filet mignon with marrow and herb crust is served with hen of the woods mushrooms, roasted red pearl onions and purple potato puree. Pastas like gnocchi (served with ricotta and black truffle sauce) are made fresh every day. Toss in a two-dozen–choice cheese cave and perfect service, and you've got a night that's worth dodging the landlord. *980 N Michigan Ave between Oak St and Walton Pl (312-280-2750). El: Red to Clark/Division. Bus: 143, 144, 145, 146, 147, 151. Dinner. Average main course: $37.*

▼ ◐ **Tel Aviv Kosher Pizza** See Kosher for review.

★ ▼ BYOB **Terragusto on Addison** Theo Gilbert has a master plan for his customers: They're going to sit down and eat a four-course Italian meal made with local, organic, sustainable ingredients. And they're going to like it. And you *will* like the food: *Ripiene* (filled pasta) are delicate and delectable; pan-fried polenta is a luscious base for bitter rapini and sweet onions, and roasted chicken is plump and juicy inside, salty and crispy on the outside. But do you really need four courses? No. Save yourself the stomachache—and the cash—and settle for three. *1851 W Addison St between Lincoln and Wolcott Aves (773-248-2777). El: Brown to Addison. Bus: 11, 50, 152. Dinner (closed Mon). Average main course: $16.*

Terragusto on Armitage The sibling location of Theo Gilbert's Italian spot is almost identical to the original, with two exceptions: This one has a wine list and a lot less seating. That latter point could become a problem when people start realizing that this place serves addictive antipasto (rich, crispy-edged polenta) and pastas (pasta neri, black with briny cuttlefish ink; buttery "pope's hats" stuffed with sweet squash). As at the original, the menu here changes seasonally, but is reliably tasty year-round. *340 W Armitage Ave between Orleans and Sedgwick Sts (773-281-7200). Bus: 11, 22, 36, 73, 151, 156. Dinner. Average main course: $16.*

▼ ✳ B **312 Chicago** Luca Corazzina has taken over the reins at this Italian stalwart now that chef Dean Zanella has moved on. While the changes have been minimal on paper, a recent visit yielded an unremarkable dinner, revealing that the real draws now are the cocktails and the desserts. At the bar, expect seasonal fruity concoctions like refreshing cucumber puree in a Tom Collins and muddled navel oranges that transport a mint julep from the South to southern Italy. Pastry chef Kimberly Schwenke also keeps season in mind by topping crumbly pistachio shortcake with ripe strawberries and a delicious ricotta-stawberry jam gelato and gives a blueberry-coconut crostata a scoop of coconut gelato. *Hotel Allegro, 136 N LaSalle St at Randolph St (312-696-2420). El: Brown, Pink, Orange, Purple (rush hrs) to Washington/Wells. Bus: 14, 20, X20, 56, 60, 124, 157. Brunch (Sun), lunch (Tue–Fri), dinner. Average main course: $20.*

▼ ✳ **Tocco** Bruno Abate, the dapper proprietor of Fulton Market's Follia, is at it again. This time, he's brought his game to Wicker Park with a dining room that could be an Alessi showroom, an affordable wine list and a menu of housemade pastas and wood-fired pizzas that tops out at 20 bucks. While we can't recommend blowing much on main courses, we *are* partial to the pizzas, with consistently delicious thin crusts and toppings like silky prosciutto and fresh mozz. *1266 N Milwaukee Ave between Division and Paulina Sts (773-687-8895). El: Blue to Division. Bus: 9, 56, 70. Dinner (closed Mon). Average main course: $18.*

★ ▼ ✳ **Trattoria D.O.C.** This bright space houses a wood-fired oven that churns out 29 varieties of the original location's signature thin-crust, uncut 12-inch pizzas. Don't miss the *spaghetti alle vongole e bottarga*, a perfectly seasoned plate of pasta and clams with a nice crunch from dried roe. If you're trying to limit your carbs, the mahi mahi with garlicky capers

NO SPOON NEEDED Scoop up every last drop of Piccolo Sogno's seafood soup with rustic wood-grilled bread.

and olives won't seem like a sacrifice at all. *706 Main St, Evanston (847-475-1111). El: Purple to Main. Bus: 200, 201, 205. Lunch, dinner. Average main course: $14.*

★ ▼ ✳ **Trattoria Demi** This unassuming Italian spot is proof that you shouldn't judge a restaurant by its dining room. The generic tables and chairs—usually filled with Northwestern students and young families—do nothing to hint at the sophisticated food that comes out of the kitchen. Creamy asparagus soup gets a crunchy disk of pancetta and a swirl of tangy balsamic; luscious lamb shank is pulled from the bone and stuffed into mezzaluna; and an organic chicken is cooked to juicy, crispy-skinned perfection. *1571 Sherman Ave, Evanston (847-332-2330). El: Purple to Davis. Bus: 93, 201, 205. Lunch, dinner. Average main course: $15.*

▼ **Trattoria No. 10** This basement dining room remains somewhat of a secret after-work spot. Guys tuck their ties into their shirts so they can dig into the signature ravioli, such as delicious butternut and acorn squash, with abandon. The seasonal sweet-potato gnocchi, fragrant with orange rind, comes in a brown-butter sauce, and the veal scaloppine is drizzled with a delectable porcini-sage-veal reduction. Take a cue from the businessmen and protect your clothes: You'll want every last drop to land in your mouth. *10 N Dearborn St between Madison St and Calhoun Pl (312-984-1718). El: Brown, Green, Pink, Purple (rush hrs), Orange to Madison; Blue, Red to Washington. Bus: 14, 20, X20, 124, 157. Lunch (Mon–Fri), dinner (Mon–Sat) (closed Sun). Average main course: $23.*

▼ ✳ ☾ **Trattoria Trullo** Chef-owner Giovanni DeNigris brought his Pugliese dishes with him when he relocated his Evanston trattoria to Lincoln Square. Portions are hefty: Prosciutto with melon arrived with half a shaved pig on the plate. Pasta dishes include inspired turns, like ziti with fava-bean puree and chicory-tomato stew, and *cavatelli crudaiola*, housemade corkscrews with tomato pulp, basil, arugula and ricotta. The lunchtime café menu is loaded with Italian comfort food, while a deli area sells imported olive oils, dry pastas and cured meats. *4767 N Lincoln Ave between Leland and Lawrence Aves (773-506-0093). El: Brown to Western. Bus: 11, 49, X49, 81. Lunch, dinner. Average main course: $15.*

▼ ✳ **Tufano's Vernon Park Tap** This old-school Italian joint is holding strong in its ever-changing 'hood. The chalkboard menu rarely changes, and regulars never even glance at it before ordering the house specialty: lemon chicken Vesuvio. Flavored by a fistful of garlic, the roasted, citrus-spritzed chicken is among the best around. After a couple of bites, you'll get caught up in the tradition of the place, enough to overlook iceberg salads, standard pastas and carafes of jug wine. *1073 W Vernon Park Pl between Carpenter and Aberdeen Sts (312-733-3393). El: Blue to Racine. Bus: 7, 12, 60. Lunch (Tue–Fri), dinner (Tue–Sun). Average main course: $14.*

▼ **Union Pizzeria** Sure, there's pizza at this design-minded pizzeria, and it isn't half bad: The bottom crust is impressively crispy, while the crust around the perimeter is puffy. But compared to the small plates that come before it (silky kale braised in white wine; herbaceous veal-pork-ricotta meatballs; calamari with a spicy white wine tomato sauce), and the desserts that come after (a polenta pound cake topped with sweet peaches; a rich chocolate panna cotta), the pizza will probably make the smallest impression. That's not a bad thing—it's just not a pizzeria thing. *1245 Chicago Ave, Evanston (847-475-2400). El: Purple to Dempster. Dinner. Average pizza: $12.*

★ ▼ ♨ ✳ **Va Pensiero** In addition to the extensive, all-Italian wine list, this quiet restaurant on the first floor of the Margarita European Inn also offers a list of well-executed, appetite-inducing apertivos. And there's even food to go with it—dishes like stalks of spring asparagus paired with a nutty Parmesan and lively tomato *fonduta*; housemade ravioli stuffed with a sweet-and-savory combination of caramelized onions, pancetta and spring peas; and juicy slices of lamb lined with flavorful char marks from the grill. *1566 Oak Ave, Evanston (847-475-7779). El: Purple to Davis. Bus: 93, 201, 205, Pace 213. Dinner. Average main course: $28.*

✳ **Via Carducci La Sorella** Sister to the popular Carducci in Lincoln Park, this spot seems a tad out of place amid the other trendier-than-thou eateries on Division. But crowds still pour in and dig into red-sauce favorites. Some dishes miss, like paper-thin eggplant overloaded with goat cheese and marinara and a caprese salad made with some not-so-summery–looking tomatoes. But others are right on the mark: Linguini *frutti di mar* has a garlicky bite and is studded with plump shrimp, clams, mussels and calamari; meatballs and thin-crust pizza would do any *nonni* proud. *1928 W Division St between Wolcott and Damen Aves (773-252-2244). El: Blue to Division. Bus: 50, 56, 70. Lunch, dinner. Average main course: $13.*

✳ **Viaggio Ristorante & Lounge** If Viaggio were like other restaurants of its kind—Italian-American joints where the red sauce has no nuance—there would be no reason to order classics like the Sunday gravy or meatballs. But this West Loop joint is different precisely because it takes care with dishes that so many other people simply slap together. Here, the meatballs are juicy, the veal is perfectly pan-fried and the gravy is immensely hearty. So even though you've had these dishes countless times before, it feels like the first time. *1330 W Madison St between Ada and Loomis Sts (312-829-3333). Bus: 9, 19, 20. Lunch (Mon–Fri), dinner (closed Sun). Average main course: $28.*

◗ **Vito and Nick's** Serving pizza to the Southwest Side since 1949, Vito and Nick's is the king of thin-crust pizza done Chicago-style. With Old Style on tap and the Bears on TV, surly waitresses shuffle bubbling-hot pies to a full room of revelers. The crispy but pliant crust, tangy sauce and top-quality sausage separate this pizza from other Chicago thin crusts. The wait times for pie can run a little long on weekends, so order your drinks by the pitcher, and enjoy a true Chicago scene. *8433 S Pulaski Rd at 84th Pl (773-735-2050). Bus: 53A, 87. Lunch, dinner. Average main course: $10.*

Vivere The best of the three restaurants that make up the multi-level Italian Village, Vivere boasts a menu as contemporary as its decor. That's quite a feat when your dining room looks like an Italian baroque version of Alice's Wonderland. The menu is a balance of classics and interesting twists to housemade pastas, fragrant seafood stews and grilled game. Oenophiles will geek out over the wine tome. *71 W Monroe St between Clark and Dearborn Sts (312-332-7005). El: Blue, Red to Monroe. Lunch (Mon–Fri), dinner (Mon–Sat) (closed Sun). Average main course: $20.*

Jamaican

★ ☺ **Café Trinidad** The Caribbean rhythms bouncing out of the speakers are as happy as the family who runs this Chatham gem: three generations, with Grandma in the kitchen, the daughter taking orders and the little ones busing tables just about as tall as they are. Try the rich curry goat; crispy whole red snapper splashed with oniony curry sauce; the roti wrap, a giant, paper-thin, crêpelike bread that's filled with curried potato, chickpeas and fantastic jerk chicken; and oxtails that, while a bit difficult to maneuver, are flavorful and much less salty than most versions. Don't miss the housemade ginger beer and sorrell, a tangy, magenta, hibiscuslike refresher. *557 E 75th St between Rhodes and St. Lawrence Aves (773-846-8081). Bus: 3, X3, 4, X4, 75. Lunch, dinner (closed Mon). Average main course: $9.*

☺ B **Calypso Café** The food at this Caribbean spot is a lot like the Tommy Bahama–ish decor: It's not exactly authentic, but it'll pass in a pinch. Jerk chicken wings are absolutely enormous and have an equally big, spicy flavor. Shrimp and conch fritters are crispy and golden brown on the outside, and fluffy in the middle. Plantain-encrusted tilapia is curiously bland, but the juicy *ropa vieja* sandwich on soft, house-baked bread makes up for it. *5211 S Harper Ave between 52nd Pl and 52nd St (773-955-0229). Bus: 2, 15, X28. Brunch (Sun), lunch, dinner. Average main course: $10.*

☺ **Daddy-O's Jerk Pit** You'll meet Daddy-O right away, as each regular who walks through the door hollers out nearly the same carryout order: "Half jerk, dark, Daddy." He'll scoot to the window-box smoker near the front door, slide back a pane and pull out a jerk spiced chicken, plop it on a plate, carry it to the back, and pack it up with plantains, beans and rice. Add on an order of the curry goat or braised oxtails and he may just toss in a cup of the gumbo and a wink. *7518 S Cottage Grove Ave between 75th and 76th Sts (773-651-7355). Bus: 3, X3, 4, X4, 75. Lunch (Tue–Sun), dinner (Tue–Sat) (closed Mon). Average main course: $9.*

☺ **Good To Go** Whether you're grabbing a meal to go or sitting down to eat at the counter of this bright storefront, expect your food to be served in a Styrofoam container with plastic forks. That's fine by us, because the dinners—such as the tender and gamey curried goat—are so generous you'll want to take part of it home. The specialty of the house is excellent jerk chicken (sweet, hot and saucy) and juice concoctions made from fresh fruits and veggies, but the caramel cake is hot on the trail to becoming a signature standout. *1947 W Howard St between Damen and Winchester Aves (773-381-7777). El: Red, Purple (rush hrs), Yellow to Howard. Bus: 22, 97, Pace 215. Lunch, dinner. Average main course: $7.*

★ ✳ **Ja' Grill** *Irie* is not what we'd call Lincoln Park…until now. The meaty catfish at this Jamaican joint tucked into a shopping strip is heightened with the warm spiciness of the jerk rub (the jerk chicken flavors are even more pronounced, the result of a two-day marinade).

ISLAND TIME Red snapper with curry vegetables and plantains has won over the neighborhood at Café Trinidad.

Meat pies are small but pack a spicy punch, and the oxtail meat is full-flavored (even though the sauce isn't). Reggae pulses throughout the dining room, encouraging you to stay and try a *bomba*, a passion-fruit sorbet in a white chocolate shell. *1008 W Armitage Ave between Sheffield and Kenmore Aves (773-929-5375). El: Brown, Purple (rush hrs) to Armitage. Bus: 8, 73. Lunch, dinner. Average main course: $14.*

✳ **Jamaica Jamaica** The blended fruit cocktails at this sultry Caribbean joint make surprisingly apt counterparts to the spicy food, though they won't completely take the heat off dishes like the housemade meat patties. Nor will it dull the aromatic curry chicken or the fall-apart jerk chicken, whose warming allspice and Scotch bonnets cause a sweat. Coconut shrimp in creamy broth is a subtler option; ditto for lusciously fatty oxtail. Caramel cake won't hurt a bit, either. *1512 Sherman Ave, Evanston (847-328-1000). El: Purple to Davis. Bus: 205; Pace 208, 250. Lunch, dinner. Average main course: $13.*

★ ☺ B BYOB **Jamaica Jerk** The Chicago-Evanston border is a gold mine of Jamaican cuisine. Among the tried-and-true, we like this tranquil ocean-blue dining room. Conch fritters are juicy and flavorful; *channa cakes* (fried chickpea patties) are greaseless with fragrant curry notes; and the saltfish—salty, slightly funky pieces of dried fish hiding tiny morsels of bacon and peppers—is a must-try for the adventurous. Jerk chicken is deliciously seasoned and juicy, but far from spicy, so speak up if you'd like more heat. Don't skip dessert—coconut carrot cake and Grape Nuts ice cream are knockouts. *1631 W Howard St between Paulina St and Marshfield Ave (773-764-1546). El: Red, Purple, Yellow to Howard. Bus: 22, 97, 147, 151, Pace 215, Pace 290. Brunch (Sun), lunch, dinner (closed Mon). Average main course: $10.*

☺ **Jamaican Jerk Chicken** Smoky jerk chicken is the main reason to stop in, but don't skip the rest of the menu at this Jamaican favorite. Braised oxtails are meaty, thickly coated with a savory-sweet sauce that melts into the bean-studded rice, and come with braised cabbage and a couple of greaseless plantains. With a few drops of jerk sauce, the moist, spice-rubbed catfish becomes a fiery addiction. Grab a ginger beer and banana pudding to round out the order. *8216 S Kedzie Ave between 82nd and 83rd Sts (773-434-2408). Bus: 52A, 79. Lunch, dinner. Average main course: $8.*

★ **Life Line Tropical Island & Juice** After success with two Life Line restaurants on the South Side, the owners created this little counter-service spot in West Rogers Park. Thatched roofs adorn the custom-built wooden bar and two TVs fill the space with the sounds of Jamaica's MTV. Accordingly with island time, it takes a half hour for whole red snapper, but you'll be rewarded with a massive beauty—crispy-skinned and smothered in an allspice-dotted medley of peppers and onions. Jerk chicken emits great smokiness, while oxtails are supple mounds of cinnamon-laced beef that, admittedly, take some gnawing to get around the bits of gristle, but yield bites so good you won't mind the work. *7217 N Damen Ave (773-262-4818). El: Red to Jarvis. Bus: 22, 49B, Pace 290. Lunch, dinner. Average main course: $11.*

★ ☺ ☾ **Tropic Island Jerk Chicken** The Chatham residents who mill about inside this smoke-scented Jamaican carryout spot are all waiting on the same thing: the best jerk chicken around. Members of the Grant family work in tandem, taking orders for rich, allspice-laced oxtails and jerk-rubbed chickens out of foggy smokers before packaging them along with sides of cinnamon-candied yams and buttery braised greens. Order an extra side of the lappable jerk sauce to dip your chicken in, but be prepared to either make do with one of only two rickety tables or eat in your car. *419 E 79th St between King Dr and Vernon Ave (773-224-7766). El: Red to 79th. Bus: 3, X3, 29, 79. Lunch, dinner. Average main course: $7.*

Japanese

SITTING PRETTY Toshiko shows *tatami* manners at her 30-year-old restaurant Sakura.

▽ ✳ ◖ **Agami** It looks as if someone took decorating tips from the Mad Hatter and color cues from a Life Savers roll in here. Somehow, the decor, along with equally wild takes on maki, works. In addition to eye-crossingly delicious nigiri, try the Ocean Drive, a refreshing roll of tuna, yellowtail, avocado, green peppers, spicy mayo and cilantro wrapped in cod sheet. Also excellent is the Dragon Festival, an amalgam of flavors and textures like soft-shell crab, cucumber, avocado, eel and *tobiko*. *4712 N Broadway at Leland Ave (773-506-1854). El: Red to Lawrence. Bus: 22, 36, 78, 81. Dinner. Average nigiri: $3.*

♨ ✳ ◖ **Ai** Chef Toyoji Hemmi considers himself an artist—at Tsuki, he built a reputation for himself as an arbiter of "creative" sushi joints, and this one is no different. His hamachi carpaccio topped with ceviche, cilantro citrus *obha* sauce and wasabi filet mignon served with Japanese sweet potato are masterpieces. But like most artists, his stuff isn't for everybody—particularly the perplexing maki rolls, one of which includes pine nuts in a spicy tuna roll to disappointing effect. *358 W Ontario St between Orleans and Kingsbury Sts (312-335-9888). El: Brown, Purple (rush hrs) to Chicago. Bus: 65, 125. Lunch (Mon–Fri), dinner. Average nigiri: $3.50.*

▽ **Bluefin** Locals return to this sexy, dimly lit space for the fresh, generous cuts of fish and the inventive maki (don't miss the perfectly crunchy Hot Night), most of which stop just short of ridiculous (with exception of the Shiroyama, a goopy, mayo-soaked mess topped with baked scallops). Chef's specials change monthly, but we're praying the creamy Brazilian lobster sashimi will

stick around forever—it's so sweet and smooth you won't mind that there's only ice cream for dessert. *1952 W North Ave at Milwaukee Ave (773-394-7373). El: Blue to Damen. Bus: 50, 56, 72. Lunch, dinner. Average nigiri: $3.*

★ ▽ ♨ ✳ ◖ **Bob San** Think sidewalk spots along Division are divey hangs for local hipsters? This high-quality sushi star debunks that theory. We've always had good luck asking servers what's freshest, and we're not ashamed to admit they've got us hooked on their nontraditional rolls, like the House Crunch. Added bonus: When the weather warms up, the outdoor seating is a refuge from the ubiquitous sushi-bar house music. *1805 W Division St between Wood and Honore Sts (773-235-8888). El: Blue to Division. Bus: 9, 70. Dinner. Average nigiri: $2.50.*

▽ ✳ BYOB **Café Blossom** With only a smattering of tables and stools, this tucked-away sushi house is ideal for folks who like their fish with a dose of intimate, family-run personality. Begin with *ika sansa*, a wildly flavorful marinated squid, and the *tatiki* salad of mixed greens topped with flame-seared tuna. The bright and fresh maki rolls come with whimsical names like Granny Smith, Smoky Bear, and our favorite, Winter Blossom (salmon, yellowtail and Japanese mint muddled with black tobiko). *608 W Barry Ave at Broadway (773-935-5284). El: Brown, Purple (rush hrs), Red to Belmont. Bus: 8, 22, 36, 77, 156. Dinner (closed Sun). Average nigiri: $2.*

▽ BYOB **Café Furaibo** This family-run spot excels at maki and traditional Japanese

dishes. Vegetarians are well fed with a teriyaki-sauced grilled tofu steak and steamed spinach in bonito soy sauce, while the best-of-the-rest includes broiled salmon collar, *panko*-encrusted shrimp with *katsu* sauce and pan-fried pork dumplings. The textural contrast and flavor combo of yellowtail, gourd, *masago,* mayo, asparagus and tempura crumbs in the Caribbean Secret maki will make you a regular at this little gem. *2907 N Lincoln Ave between George St and Wellington Ave (773-472-7017). Bus: 11, 76, 77. Lunch (Mon–Fri), dinner. Average maki: $7.*

★ ▽ **Chiyo** The fish is supremely fresh at this sushi and hot pot restaurant, but don't stop there: The more social options are the *shabu-shabu* or *sukiyaki*. Both are self-cooked, one-pot meals of either sirloin or Wagyu beef and a heaping array of tofu and veggies. But while the meat is simmered in seaweed broth for *shabu-shabu,* it's seared in melted pork fat for *sukiyaki* before a sugary mirin-soy broth is added. (We prefer the more savory *shabu-shabu* to the supersweet *sukiyaki*.) *3800 W Lawrence Ave at Hamlin Ave (773-267-1555). El: Brown to Kimball. Bus: 53, 81, 82. Dinner (closed Mon). Average main course: $15.*

★ ▽ ◖ BYOB **Coast** This place knows how to exploit sushi's sex appeal while maintaining a low-key vibe. Curvaceous morsels of tuna, yellowtail, salmon and more are served in a sultry dining room full of slick minimalist furniture and tableware. The focus is great-quality raw fish, but a few liberties are taken, and with success. Ceviche maki pairs lime-marinated scallop with mango, cilantro and jalapeño, and salmon gets stuffed in a spring roll, fried and served with green curry dipping sauce. *2045 N Damen Ave between McLean and Dickens Aves (773-235-5775). El: Blue to Western. Bus: 50, 73. Dinner. Average nigiri: $2.50.* ● *Other location: South Coast, 1700 S Michigan Ave (312 662-1700).*

Ginza Japanese Restaurant
Don't be turned off by the Depression-era Tokyo Hotel that houses Ginza Japanese Restaurant, and don't bother with inconsistent sushi. Instead, focus on the unique kitchen dishes like the *natto*, fermented soybean with a bittersweet punch, or *yamakake*, a bowl of liquefied mountain yam with raw tuna (good with *natto*). Juicy deep-fried oysters dusted with *panko* are excellent; grilled yellowfin neck is tender with fatty meat; and servers couldn't be sweeter. *19 E Ohio St between State St and Wabash Ave (312-222-0600). El: Red to Grand. Bus: 29, 36, 125. Lunch (Mon–Fri), dinner (Mon–Sat). Average nigiri: $5.*

▽ BYOB Grand Katachi
In a neighborhood with sparse options for Japanese, this place suits raw-fish lovers just fine. There's a good assortment of nice slabs of nigiri and signature rolls, including Ocean Drive maki (spicy yellowtail, jalapeño, cilantro, cucumber and mango with tuna) and Red Line maki (spicy shrimp with snapper). Vegetarians are happy with creative maki additions like spinach and sweet potato, plus a small menu of rice and noodle dishes. *4747 N Damen Ave at Lawrence Ave (773 271 1641). El: Brown to Western Bus: 49, 50, 81. Dinner. Average nigiri: $2.*

▽ BYOB Green Tea
Sometimes you want a good piece of sushi without the black-clad servers, hip house beats, triple-digit bill and lighting so dim you can't tell your *toro* from your *tako*. This tiny, no-frills sushi café offers just that, slicing up fresh, meaty cuts of all the standards, including tasty salmon, fatty tuna, mackerel and yellowtail. Try the housemade pickles and the soy-sesame-ginger marinated, grilled baby octopus. If you're into Americanized, the Chicago Spicy Crazy is the one to try. *2206 N Clark St between Webster Ave and Grant Pl (773-883-8812). El: Brown, Purple (rush hrs), Red to Fullerton. Bus: 22, 74. Lunch (Tue–Sat), dinner (Tue–Sun) (closed Monday). Average nigiri: $2.*

▽ ✳ Hachi's Kitchen
Chef Jim Bee's loyal followers are not limited to catching his cuisine only at Lincoln Park's legendary Sai Café, thanks to this sister spot in Logan Square. The decor is sophisticated but not sceney, the *sake* and wine lists are packed with ideal sushi partners, and creative starters and maki steal the show from the thick, glossy cuts of expected fish varieties. Try the crunchy-creamy tuna *masako*, the citrus and sesame oil–kissed chilled octopus, and the slick miso-glazed black cod. *2521 N California Ave between Allgeld St and Logan Blvd (773-276-8080). El: Blue to California. Bus: 52, 56, 74. Dinner. Average nigiri: $2.50.* ● *Other location: Sai Café, 2010 N Sheffield Ave (773-472-8080).*

▽ BYOB Hama Matsu
This spot claims to be a Korean/Japanese restaurant, but the specialty is sushi, and it's done well. The house roll takes a kitchen-sink approach, combining asparagus, smoked salmon, unagi, crabmeat, avocado, green onion and teriyaki sauce into one bloated, delicious bite. The Low Carb Maki's lettuce, zucchini, avocado and crab is bland (no shock there), but the dragon roll (unagi, avocado, shrimp tempura) is crunchy, sweet and artfully plated. *5143 N Clark St at Winona St (773-506-2978).*

El: Red to Berwyn. Bus: 22, 92. Lunch (Sat–Sun), dinner. Average nigiri: $2.50.

✳ Inari Sushi
Move beyond the crowd (glittery bebe tops and deep tans) to the real deal: creative and tasty food at good prices. Though the sushi is generous and fresh, the real gems are originals such as pistachio crusted Atlantic salmon and the *togarashi*-dusted crispy calamari with addictive honey-wasabi sauce. The Godzilla will more than satisfy die-hard maki fans, with shrimp tempura, cream cheese, avocado, scallions, topped with tempura crunch, unagi sauce, black tobiko and spicy-wasabi mayo. *7428 W North Ave, Elmwood Park (708-583-2300). Bus: 72, 90, Pace 307, Pace 318. Lunch, dinner. Average nigiri: $6.50.*

▽ ✳ ☾ BYOB Izumi Sushi Bar and Restaurant
The volume of the doont-doont-doont beats at this overlooked spot on Randolph Row is tolerable enough that we can focus on our friends and our food. The best of the latter includes thick squares of sashimi (fresh salmon, superwhite tuna and yellowtail) and the punch-packing Lion maki roll (yellowtail, tuna, avocado, cilantro and jalapeño rolled tight and drizzled with chile sauce). Wash it all down with the value-priced sake; two people can sip for around $12. *731 W Randolph St at Court Pl (312-207-5299). El: Green, Pink to Clinton. Bus: 8, 20. Lunch (Mon–Fri), dinner. Average nigiri: $3.*

★ ✳ Japonais
Spend a million bucks on building a restaurant in an undeveloped part of town, and you too can have a spot capable of transporting Chicagoans to a distant land. The Ian Schrager–esque space is swank, sexy, vibrant and the kitchen offers incredible cuisine, centering around superb-quality raw fish, presented simply or whacked out into tasty rolls. Must-haves include the Kobe carpaccio, Tokyo drums, *kani nigiri*, *yukke toro* and "Le Quack Japonais." *600 W Chicago Ave at Larrabee St (312-822-9600). El: Brown, Purple (rush hrs) to Chicago. Bus: 8, 66. Lunch (Mon–Fri), dinner. Average main course: $25.*

▽ ✳ ☾ Kamehachi
Long before Chicago's great sushi boom, this Old Town stalwart (opened in '67) taught us how to tell nigiri from sashimi and miso from udon. It's still packing in the crowds: Old-timers relax at the sushi bar, funky types seriously dig the lounge upstairs, and everyone mixes together in their pretty, flower-filled garden patio out back. *1400 N Wells St at Schiller St (312-664-3663). Bus: 11, 72. Lunch, dinner. Average nigiri: $3.* ● *Other locations: 240 E Ontario St (312-587-0600), 320 N Dearborn St (312-744-1900), 311 S Wacker Dr (312-765-8701).*

▽ ✳ Kansaku
Judging by the young, hip crowd packing this sophisticated spot on a Friday night, it's obvious the folks behind Kansaku really know their sushi. We were enamored with the presentation and freshness of dishes like the salmon sashimi with *pico de gallo*, green onion, wasabi mayo and spicy sauce in a taco basket. Rolls are the usual gaudy extravaganzas, but our favorite was a simple twist on a classic: salmon maki topped with toasted garlic. *1514 Sherman Ave, Evanston (847-864-4386). El: Purple to Davis. Bus: 93, 201, 205. Lunch (Mon–Fri), dinner. Average nigiri: $2.25.*

★ Katsu
The best raw fish in town is at this small, unassuming West Rogers Park hideaway. Here you'll find incredibly fresh, melt-in-your-mouth, superpremium yellowtail, bluefin, mackerel and fatty tuna. Beyond the raw, Katsu's crew has skills on the grill, turning out a tasty marinated duck breast and a crispy yellowtail collar (great with a dab of shaved, pickled daikon, a sprinkle of sea salt and a squirt of lemon). *2651 W Peterson Ave between Talman and Washtenaw Aves (773-784-3383). Bus: 49B, 84. Dinner (closed Mon and Tue). Average nigiri: $5.*

▽ ✳ Kaze
Gifted with the hands of a warrior, Chef Macku slays fish instead of dragons at his sophisticated Japanese storefront. Yearly sojourns around the globe for inspiration result in a fusion that dresses up slick cuts of nigiri with seasonal, cooked toppings and includes creations like whitefish tempura wrapped in shrimp and drizzled with a parsley butter. Menus change with the seasons, and Tuesday nights are a steal: Four courses with wine pairings go for $45. *2032 W Roscoe St at Seeley Ave (773-327-4860). El: Brown to Paulina. Bus: 49, 50, 77. Dinner. Average nigiri: $4.50.*

▽ Kohan
Located in the University Village neighborhood, this casual spot's service is warm enough to fool you into believing it's an old favorite. Half of the menu is dedicated to *teppan* (Benihana-style open grill), and the teriyaki-glazed shrimp, but the sushi offerings impress more. Stick with the specials board for interesting and supremely fresh catches like shaved ginger-topped *aji* (horse mackerel), meaty bluefin and rich, grilled yellowfin collar. *730 W Maxwell St between Union Ave and Halsted St (312-421-6254). El: Blue to UIC/Halsted. Bus: 8, 12, 168. Lunch (Mon–Fri), dinner. Average nigiri: $2.25.*

☺ Matsuya
The combination of *cheap* and *sushi* usually sends us running, but the popularity of this Wrigleyville spot leads us to believe otherwise. One bite of the silky salmon confirmed

Side dish

EGGSCELLENT Savory egg custard known as *chawan mushi* is a specialty at Sakura.

Umami dearest

Go beyond swank sushi bars for a taste of honbon (authentic) Japan.

Ask Japanese nationals living in the city what their favorite place to get authentic sushi is, and there's a pretty good chance they'll tell you **Itto Sushi** (*2616 N Halsted St, 773-871-1800*). This Japanese-owned restaurant has been in business for more than 24 years, experience that shows in simple things like the bowl of hot, fluffy rice that comes with *tonkatsu*, a crispy pork cutlet. The specialty of the house is the sushi, naturally, with perfectly warm rice and buttery, fresh fish. Ask the bilingual staff for suggestions about what's in season.

Not a fan of the raw? **Sunshine Café** (p. 88) might not look like much from the outside, but it's one of the few places in the city where you can get homestyle Japanese cooking. Try unpretentious basics like *gyoza* dumplings, *katsudon* (fried, breaded pork cutlet sautéed with egg and onion and served over rice), *koroke* (fried mashed potato croquettes, served with fruity brown sauce) and *kinpira gobo* (julienned burdock root in a sweet-spicy soy-based sauce).

For an interactive group meal, **Chiyo** (p. 84) focuses on table-cooked hot-pot dishes like *shabu-shabu* and *sukiyaki*. Paper-thin slices of Wagyu or Kobe beef are rapidly cooked in a vat of boiling water at your table, then dipped in citrus-based *ponzu* or sesame sauce. The complete dinner arrives with a plate heaping with tofu and vegetables also intended to be cooked in the pot, as well as a small cooked appetizer (*kobachi*), sashimi, pickles and rice (served after you've finished the beef so you don't fill up too fast), and dessert, typically mochi ice cream and *mizu manju* (sweet

red-bean paste encased in clear jelly).

Heading north of the city toward the suburbs (where the majority of Chicagoland's Japanese nationals live and work), **Renga Tei** (p. 87) offers a well-rounded bilingual menu of sushi, *ippin ryori* (small plates) and entrées. The trademark balance of sweet and savory flavors shows up best in the sauce accompanying the beef-wrapped asparagus, while *agedashi* tofu shows off signature textural contrast, the battered and fried tofu crumbling into a rich broth laced with green onions. It's the little things that make the meal here—a shaker of traditional *sansho* (Szechuan pepper) served with unagi *kabayaki* (barbecue eel) and a generous portion of chunky adzuki paste that adorns the bowl of green-tea ice cream.

Japanese TV programs, plus a collection of manga, serve as entertainment at **Sakura** (p. 87), a 30-year-old restaurant that features seven traditional tatami rooms, electronic doors that greet you in Japanese as you enter and the lovely kimono-clad manager, Toshiko. The sushi is excellent and fresh, the tempura is hot and crispy, and *chawan mushi* (savory custard) is a specialty. In addition to a $35 *kaiseki* dinner, hot-pot dishes and a variety of *chazuke* (green tea poured over rice with seasonings), Sakura serves great *nasu dengaku*, fried eggplant topped with sweet miso sauce, and natto maki, sushi topped with viscous, fermented soy beans. Don't be frightened—dive in fork-first and your Japanese culinary immersion will be complete.—*Bianca Jarvis*

that some of the nigiri fares perfectly well on its own. But when it's paired with spicy mayo and cilantro in the "Mexican" roll, or with layers of tempura in the "crunch" roll, you can't tell that it's not the highest quality sushi around. And if you can—well, order their delicious beef teriyaki instead. *3469 N Clark St at Sheffield Ave (773-248-2677). El: Red to Addison. Bus: 22, 152. Lunch (Sat, Sun), dinner. Average nigiri: $2.50.*

★ ▽ ✱ **Meiji** This sophisticated spot dabbles in traditional Japanese dishes like egg-custard soup. On the sushi side, both novices and traditionalists will be happy: Rolls bursting with cream cheese and tempura crunch are balanced by fresh, razor-thin cuts of fatty tuna and fluke, as well as rare seasonal cuts of fatty yellowtail, goldeneye snapper and *shirauo*, slick slivers of white fish—known as ice fish—served in a cucumber cup. Freshly shaved wasabi seals the deal. *623 W Randolph St between Jefferson and Desplaines Sts (312-887-9999). El: Green, Pink to Clinton. Bus: 56, 125. Lunch (Mon–Fri), dinner. Average nigiri: $4.*

★ ▽ ✱ **Mirai Sushi** Signatures like *yukke toro* (fatty tuna tartare with quail egg and housemade soy sauce) and *kani nigiri* (seaweed-filled spicy crab) aren't exclusive to this restaurant, but the funky neighborhood and surrounding postdinner bar choices are. The prices are a bit cheaper than Japonais—with which Mirai shares a head chef—so use the extra cash to attack the specials sheet, which offers fresh flights of tuna and whitefish of varying fattiness. *2020 W Division St between Damen and Hoyne Aves (773-862-8500). El: Blue to Division. Bus: 50, 70. Lunch (Mon–Sat), dinner. Average nigiri: $4.*

〔 **Murasaki** After 22 years as Cafe Shino, this Gold Coast stalwart has transformed into a sake lounge, complete with two dozen varieties of rice wine, a private karaoke room, and a menu of *otsumami*, traditional Japanese small plates (we're fans of the crispy-edged hot-dog bites, plummy baby octopus, spicy salmon hand rolls and tempura-topped sobo noodles). For a primer on sake, ask manager Kerry Tamura, who's happy to steer you in the right direction. *211 E Ontario St between St. Clair St and Fairbanks Ct (312-266-2280). El: Red to Grand. Bus: 2, 3, X3, 66, 145, 146, 147, 151, 157. Dinner Mon–Sat (closed Sundays). Average small plate: $5.*

◑ **Noodles by Takashi** Good ramen is hard to find, especially in the Loop. And while we're grateful for Chef Takashi Yagahashi's return to Chicago (after successful runs in Detroit and Vegas), we have to try hard to shrug off the $8 price tag for a bowl of noodles in broth. Our advice is to go with a friend, split the *shio* ramen (noodles in soy-miso broth, ground pork, baby bok choy, ground ginger and sesame seeds), and supplement with starters like the steamed bun stuffed with glistening braised pork. *Macy's on State Street, 111 N State St, seventh floor, at Washington St (312-781-2955). El: Blue, Red to Washington; Brown, Green, Orange, Pink, Purple (rush hrs) to Randolph. Bus: 3, 4, X4, 14, 20, 26, 60, 145, 147, 148, 151. Lunch (Mon–Sat). Average main course: $8.*

▽ 〔 **BYOB** **Oh Fusion** This spot is slick and sophisticated with dim lighting, black wood booths and…fusion cuisine. Traditional standbys are joined by their Chinese, Indian and Thai cohorts like Mongolian beef and kung pao chicken, a rainbow of curries and all the regular suffixes for pad (–thai, –see ew, –kea mao). In terms of sushi, the *donburi* set (fresh cuts of fish on sushi rice) and *yakisoba* are solid and inspired choices. *3911 N Sheridan Rd between Byron and Dakin Sts (773-880-5340). El: Red to Sheridan. Bus: 36, 80, X80, 145, 151. Lunch, dinner. Average main course: $10.*

▼ **Osaka** The sushi here isn't going to change your life, but we love this carryout spot as an easy Loop lunch option. Zippy chefs concoct daily specials like eel rainbow rolls on the fly, while the refrigerated case is stocked with just-made combos (Cali, Philly and spicy tuna is a good one). But our favorite thing about the place is the "wall of fruit": It's the sign that true fresh-fruit smoothies are being made instead of drinks with that grainy, premade powder, tapioca-drink crap. *400 S Michigan Ave at Van Buren St (312-566-0118). El: Brown, Green, Orange, Pink, Purple (rush hrs) to Adams; Red, Blue to Jackson. Bus: 1, 3, 4, X4, 6, 7, 14, 26, X28, 126, 145. Lunch, dinner (closed Sun). Average nigiri: $1.75.* ● *Other location: 1311 W Taylor St (312-829-0288).*

▼ ✳ **Oysy Sushi** Sashimi is the way to go at this popular South Loop spot—big, thick cuts of fresh, cool standards are dependable and tasty, and richer indulgences like fatty tuna and sea urchin are equally good and almost always available. Interestingly, the cooked menu is offered as small plates, making it easy to try a handful of unique dishes like roasted chicken-stuffed lotus root in crispy tempura batter and baked sesame-crusted scallops with wasabi mayo. *50 E Grand Ave between Wabash Ave and Rush St (312-670-6750). El: Red to Grand. Bus: 29, 36, 65. Lunch, dinner. Average nigiri: $2.* ● *Other location: 888 S Michigan Ave (312-922-1127).*

(**Ra Sushi** In true Gold Coast fashion, this sushi spot does little in moderation; the menu is a massive collection of creations like pineapple cheese wontons and bulging maki. Abandon ideas of simplicity and just enjoy over-the-top signatures like crispy "RAckin' shrimp," garlic mango lobster spring rolls, and the spicy albacore "Pacific" roll finished with red-beet tempura and sautéed cashews and pine nuts. Skip super-sweet desserts in favor of delicious sake sangria. *1139 N State St at Elm St (312-274-0011). El: Red to Clark/Division. Bus: 22, 36, 70, 151. Lunch, dinner. Average nigiri: $5.* ● *Other locations: Glenview, 2601 Aviator Ln (847-510-1100); Lombard, 310 Yorktown Center (630-627-6800).*

▼ **Renga-Tei** Near the strip mall that's home to the popular Mexican joint Wholly Frijoles is this tasty, affordable Japanese joint, where waitresses dole out dishes faster than lightning. Start with crispy flounder triangles wrapped in seaweed with Japanese mint and a touch of plum paste, and the French maki, an addictive roll of shrimp tempura, red-leaf lettuce, rice and mayo. The seven-piece "Sushi B" platter is a steal considering the chefs cut sushi twice the size we're accustomed to. *3956 W Touhy Ave, Lincolnwood (847-675-5177). Bus: 11 Kedzie, Pace 290. Lunch (Mon, Wed–Fri), dinner (closed Tue). Average maki: $5.*

★ ✳ **Restaurant Takashi** With this restaurant, Vetted chef Takashi Yagihashi has created a veritable Zen den showcasing food that deftly combines his Japanese heritage with French training and American ingredients. Subtle flavors balance delicate and beautiful presentation, and Yagihashi's frequent use of local seasonal produce means sunny summer rolls with shrimp, smoked salmon, caviar and a caper–golden raisin dressing; likewise, winter ushers in a shrimp roll or pork belly

with steamed bun. *1952 N Damen Ave between Homer St and Armitage Ave (773-772-6170). El: Blue to Western. Bus: 50, 73. Dinner (closed Mon). Average main course: $22.*

▼ ✳ **Rise** This spot is often packed with chic "too-cool-for-school" SoPo types, and there are a few head-scratchers on the maki menu (a "fire roll" made with salmon, jalapeño and melted provolone). But the chef's creativity works with dishes like the Mexican maki filled with yellowtail, avocado, cilantro, jalapeño and a squeeze of fresh lime juice. Non–sushi eaters have plenty of good options, including gingery beef tenderloin and crispy crêpe–wrapped duck breast. *3401 N Southport Ave at Roscoe St (773-525-3535). El: Brown to Southport. Bus: 9, X9, 77. Dinner. Average nigiri: $3.*

BYOB Rollapalooza From the spider roll to the rainbow roll to the tuna hand-roll, the maki at this stylish new sushi joint is consistently enjoyable, but the buzzword here is definitely "big." The rolls are so enormous that you'll only need one or two to fill you up, and fitting the pieces into your mouth can be messy and embarrassing. Then again, if you can swallow the name of this place, you can probably swallow anything. *3344 N Halsted St between Buckingham Pl and Roscoe St (773-281-6400). El: Brown, Purple (rush hrs), Red to Belmont. Bus: 8, 22, 77. Dinner (closed Mon). Average maki: $10.*

▼ ✳ (**Sai Café** For two decades, this traditional Japanese spot has offered more of a steakhouse atmosphere—with low lights, jazz tunes and TVs at the bar—and keeps the focus on food with thick, meaty cuts of sashimi and perfect, warm rice for contrast. Try some not-so-common choices like sea urchin and escolar, a firm, oily fish with full flavor. Aside from sushi, try the *kani su*, a salad of cucumbers and meaty pieces of crab in tangy vinegar dressing. *2010 N Sheffield Ave between Armitage and Dickens Ave (773-472-8080). El: Brown, Purple (rush hrs) to Armitage. Bus: 8, 73. Dinner. Average nigiri: $2.50.* ● *Other location: Hachi's Kitchen, 2521 N California Ave (773-276-8080).*

▼ ♨ **Sakuma** Sakuma offers eight small courses to give you a chance to sample the breadth of Japanese cooking in a single meal. If your idea of Japanese food involves mango salsa, cream cheese and tempura crunch, then these delicate soups, pristine sashimi and ethereal tempura will quietly readjust your taste buds. Not that the food isn't exciting—a first course of wasabi-spiked lobster salad, sweet soy black beans and deep-fried shrimp balls will pique your interest for what's to come. *43 S Sutton Rd, Streamwood (630-483-0289). Lunch, dinner. Average tasting menu: $40.*

▼ **Sakura** It's worth the trip to the 'burbs just for a chance to dine in this 30-year-old restaurant's authentic Japanese-style tatami rooms. But the fresh sushi and extensive udon menu may convince you to invest in a monthly Metra pass. The children's platter—tempura, a jumbo sushi roll, chicken teriyaki, gyoza, fruit and soup for $9.99—is a refreshing alternative for chicken nugget-weary parents. Reserve tatami rooms in advance for no additional charge. *105 S Main St, Mount Prospect (847-577-0444). Metra: Union Pacific Northwest to Mount Prospect. Lunch (Tue–Fri), dinner (Tue–Sun). Average main course: $13.*

▼ ✳ **BYOB Sashimi Sashimi** This fish is so nice that they named it twice. Counter service might scare purists off, but you'll be pleasantly surprised when you pick up your tray of artfully presented maki (go for the spicy Mexican roll of hamachi, cilantro and jalapeños, and the tropical roll filled with shrimp tempura, eel, cucumber, avocado and mango puree). Lunchtime maki meal deals are a big hit with Northwestern students, as are the sweet and colorful bubble teas. *640 Church St, Evanston (847-475-7274). El: Purple to Davis. Bus: 201. Lunch, dinner. Average maki: $3.*

▼ **BYOB Shiso** Don't let its tiny size and proximity to Mediocrity Row fool you—this BYOB sushi newcomer offers up plenty of creative gems. Munch on crispy salt-and-pepper calamari and silky spinach (*goma ae*) appetizers while perusing the massive maki list. Or just

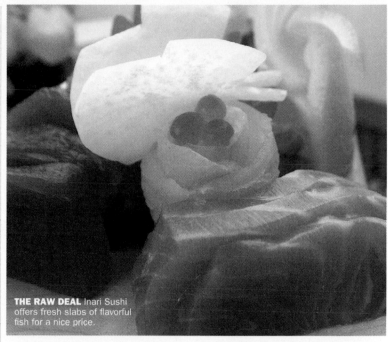

THE RAW DEAL Inari Sushi offers fresh slabs of flavorful fish for a nice price.

SAKE TO ME Sushi Mike gets creative behind the bar at Tanoshii.

take our advice and go for the Volcano. Tiny tobiko and smelt roe add briny pop, tempura lends crunch, spicy mayo brings the heat, and cool hamachi and escolar smooth out the edges. *449 W North Ave between Cleveland and Hudson Aves (312-649-1234). El: Brown, Purple (rush hrs) to Sedgwick. Bus: 11, 22, 72. Lunch, dinner. Average maki: $7.*

◉ **BYOB Sunshine Café** You know a place is authentic when Japanese old-timers shuffle through the door like they're simply coming home. We've become best friends with the thicker-than-usual miso soup and the lightly fried potato croquettes. We also love the giant shrimp tempura, the flavorful *goma ae* and the sweet unagi (eel) rice bowl. But what this home-style cafeteria is known for is piping hot udon with thick noodles edging out bits of meat and fresh-chopped vegetables. *5449 N Clark St between Rascher and Catalpa Aves (773-334-6214). El: Red to Berwyn. Bus: 22, 84, 92, 151. Dinner (closed Mon). Average main course: $9.*

▼ ✳ **Sushi Naniwa** The older sibling to the trendy Ukie Village Bob San, this old-school sushi house hasn't changed much during its 10 years. Straight-up sushi (luscious salmon, slick mackerel and bass with *ponzu* are standouts) and classics like Japanese pickles and boiled-spinach apps hold their ground, while dragon and rainbow rolls are about as crazy as it gets. *607 N Wells St between Ohio and Ontario Sts (312-255-8555). El: Red to Grand. Bus: 65, 125, 156. Lunch (Mon–Fri), dinner. Average nigiri: $2.25.*

▼ **BYOB Sushi Para II** The crowds clamor here for all-you-can-eat sushi for $17.99 a person. Salmon, yellowtail and tuna *nigiri* are fine, but if your sushi standards are anywhere near snobby, go with maki and drink plenty of whatever wine you brought. The avocado and tempura–packed Palatine and Volcano rolls are good bets, but be sure to finish what you order. You'll be charged extra for anything left on your plate, and that includes nigiri rice. *2256 N Clark St between Grant Pl and Belden Ave (773-477-3219). Bus: 11, 22. Lunch, dinner. All you can eat: $17.*

✳ **BYOB Sushi Pink** Sushi Pink, with its reasonably priced sashimi and imaginative maki, threatens to tinker with tradition the West Loop sushi market cornered by Sushi Wabi and Starfish. Creamy chunks of lobster over spicy salmon and avocado topped with masago is purely religious in the Holy roll, while the Bloody Mary maki spikes raw tuna

with Korean red pepper paste. The Wild Animal maki featuring roast steak, duck and pork with a touch of scallion will sate the most voracious carnivore. *909 W Washington Blvd between Peoria and Sangamon Sts (312-226-1666). Bus: 8, 9, 20. Lunch, dinner. Average nigiri: $3.50.*

SushiSamba Rio See Pan Asian for review.

★ ▼ ◖ **Sushi Wabi** Countering this joint's black-clad servers, Sade remix–loving DJ and throngs of clubgoers are incredibly fresh sushi and creatively cooked dishes. Flash-cooked, citrus-tinged shrimp tops green tea–soba noodles; spicy, vinegar-tossed slaw is topped with tempura soft-shell crab drizzled with wasabi honey; grilled salmon gets earthy plum sauce and *mizuna* greens; and crunchy, gooey maki like the Ecuador, Godzilla and Tarantula overload our senses and stand in for dessert. *842 W Randolph St between Green and Peoria Sts (312-563-1224). El: Green, Pink to Clinton. Bus: 8, 20. Lunch (Mon–Fri), dinner. Average nigiri: $6.*

▼ **BYOB Sushi X** The projection of Japanime onto a beaded curtain is a clue that this is a relation of the maki-only spot on Chicago Avenue. Déjà vu continues throughout the meal: "Neo" and "Mega" rolls will satisfy those looking for over-the-top concoctions (combining bacon, hamachi, pineapple and avocado isn't our thing but maybe it's yours). The nigiri are large and fresh, but pricey. Stick with simple rolls and the delicious seaweed salad, and enjoy the show. *543 W Diversey Pkwy between Clark St and Hampden Ct (773-248-1808). El: Brown, Purple (rush hrs) to Diversey. Bus: 22, 36, 76. Lunch (Sat–Sun), dinner. Average maki: $7.* ● *Other location: 1136 W Chicago Ave (312-491-9232).*

▼ ✳ **Tank Sushi** This Lincoln Square hot spot serves up consistently fresh fish and perfectly seasoned rice. Their salmon and white tuna rival the best places in town, though sometimes at prices to match. Seasonal small plates, like refreshing sesame-watermelon salad, can be as good as the sushi. Come late night, the techno turns, but guests who can't handle the din can book a tatami room, which seats up to eight. Half-price lunchtime maki may just be the best deal in town. *4514 N Lincoln Ave between Sunnyside and Wilson Aves (773-769-2600). El: Brown to Western. Bus: 11, 49, X49, 78, 81. Lunch, dinner. Average nigiri: $3.*

▼ ◖ **BYOB Tanoshii** Look for the loyal following of Mike-heads: sushi foodies who've followed chef "Sushi Mike" from Hama Matsu and San Soo Gap San to his new post at this small, casual sushi bar. If you try the cooked items, you're likely not to go back. If you order your own sushi, you're likely to offer up a "So what." But if you make like the regulars and put yourself in Sushi Mike's hands (name your price, and he creates a combo), you might just become a believer. *5547 N Clark St between Gregory St and Bryn Mawr Ave (773-878-6886). El: Red to Bryn Mawr. Bus: 22, 50, 84, 147. Dinner. Average nigiri: $3.*

Torishin In biz for more than 30 years, Torishin serves *izakaya*-style "drinking foods" favored by Japanese salarymen though perhaps less familiar to *gaijin*. Try the *buta ponzu*, sliced pork served on ice with vinegar sauce that offers unique textures and temperatures. Seafood standouts include *maguro shiso age*, marinated tuna wrapped in shiso leaf and fried tempura, and *ika-maruyaki*, flavorful grilled squid topped with ginger. *1584 S Busse Rd, Mount Prospect (847-437-4590). Lunch, dinner. Average main course: $8.*

▼ **BYOB Toro** This place had us at the premeal hand towels: aspirinlike tablets that grow into towelettes when servers pour hot water over them. But this pint-size spot offers more than just gimmicks. Sushi man Mitch takes pride in serving oversize nigiri (that's how he was taught, and he's not changing) and creative rolls (we love the Crazy Horse combo of tuna, salmon, yellowtail and avocado topped with tobiko). Non–sushi eaters can opt for traditional Japanese dishes or house specials. *2546 N Clark St at Deming Pl (773-348-4877). El: Red, Brown, Purple (rush hrs) to Fullerton. Bus: 22, 36, 151. Lunch (Fri–Sun), dinner (Tue–Sun). Average nigiri: $5.*

▼ **Triad** Luckily, these slick, contemporary digs are more than just a pretty face. The *kaki* shooter—oysters, scallion, quail eggs and a lemon-soy sauce—is a tangy tongue teaser. Try the "dynamite"—shellfish and mushrooms baked with spicy mayonnaise. For entrées, the Asian-spiced lamb chop is a solid choice, or you can go the raw route with the luscious sushi. The flat-screen TV in the lounge and a private room for parties add to the draw. *1933 S Indiana Ave at Cullerton St (312-225-8833). El: Red to Cermak/Chinatown. Bus: 1, 3, 4, 62. Dinner. Average nigiri: $2.50.*

Tsuki The sultry, candlelit dining room features modern tableware and an eccentric Japanese menu. Chef Hemmi drops sweet clusters of crab atop greens, oranges and avocados for a tasty starter. The pricey nigiri and sashimi deliver, with clean flavors and meaty cuts. The smoky-sweet duck nigiri is delicious. But skip the spicy tuna sampler— toppings like pine nuts, caviar and avocado add interest but little flavor. *1441 W Fullerton Ave between Janssen and Greenview Aves (773-883-8722). Bus: 9, 74. Dinner. Average nigiri: $3.50.*

★ ✳ **Wakamono** This cool-conscious place focuses on small plates of dishes such as fresh tofu sprinkled with chile oil and peanuts, and prosciutto topped with *ponzu* sauce, crunchy toasted shallots and charred asparagus are a brilliant, unexpected combination of flavors. And the always-fresh sushi is simply impeccable. Yet the biggest surprise is the service: Unlike across the street at überstylized sister restaurant Ping Pong, the servers here actually smile. *3317 N Broadway between Aldine Ave and Buckingham Pl (773-296-6800). El: Brown, Purple (rush hrs), Red to Belmont. Bus: 36, 77, 152. Dinner. Average small plate: $5.*

Korean

★ ▼ ⟨ Chicago Kalbi Korean Restaurant Cooking at home may be a bore, but an indoor Korean barbecue is an adventure. Your server sets white-hot charcoal on your well-ventilated table and then brings out marinated raw meats such as *kalbi* (short ribs) or Kobe beef for you to grill. Included are about a dozen salty, spicy side dishes known as *banchan.* If you don't feel like cooking, *dolsot bibimbap* served in a stone casserole is one of the tastier traditional rice bowls in town. *3752 W Lawrence Ave between Ridgeway and Hamlin Aves (773-604-8183). El: Brown to Kimball. Bus: 53, 81. Dinner (Wed–Mon). Average main course: $13.*

⊙ Cho Sun Ok The intoxicating aromas of soy sauce, sugar, rice vinegar and garlic tell you this place is good before you walk in the door. Talk the server into letting you cook your own sliced beef (as is customary at Korean-barbecue restaurants) because the salty-sweet marinated meats we cooked tableside were more tender than the kitchen's version. Of the giant wave of little side dishes that accompany the barbecue, don't pass up the moist fish cake, perfect with a bottle of Korean beer. *4200 N Lincoln Ave at Berteau Ave (773-549-5555). El: Brown to Irving Park. Bus: 11, 50, 78, 80, X80. Lunch, dinner. Average main course: $10.*

★ ▼ ⊙ BYOB Crisp The chicken is fresh, of good quality and comes slathered in three different sauces: a sticky barbecue, a hot sauce–laced Buffalo and a sesame-soy glaze dubbed "Seoul Sassy." There's also a decent *bibimbap* (best ordered with "marinated" vegetables, beef, an egg and brown rice) and Korean-style burritos whose fresh vegetables benefit from a liberal slather of sweetish hot sauce, but the chicken is the thing. *2940 N Broadway between Oakdale and Wellington Aves (877-693-8653). El: Brown, Purple (rush hrs) to Diversey. Bus: 22, 36, 76. Lunch, dinner (closed Monday). Average main course: $9.*

★ ▼ ⟨ Hae Woon Dae Korean barbecue joints distinguish themselves by the quality of their meat, marinades and side dishes (*banchan*). This mainstay nails all three. Strips of tender beef (*kalbi*) get a garlic-soy-sesame oil marinade, while slices of pork (*bulgogi*) are saturated with a similar, but spicier, mixture. While your meat sizzles, sample your way through banchan such as pickled turnips, kimchi, eggy potato salad and tofu skin with green chile and a big bottle of Korean beer (OB or Hite). *6240 N California Ave between Granville and Rosemont Aves (773-764-8018). Bus: 84, 93, 155. Lunch (Sat, Sun), dinner. Average main course: $12.*

▼ Jin Ju When we tell you that this Korean spot is slick, sexy and seductive, we're referring to the servers, the space and, of course, the food. There's no tabletop grilling here, but the kitchen does it better than you could. Opt for the delicious *o jinga bokum*, strips of squid imparted with the heat and flavor of chiles, or the *kalbi*, grilled slices of beef short rib that are sweet, salty and every bit as tasty as the vinegar-soaked daikon underneath. *5203 N Clark St between Foster and Farragut Aves (773-334-6377). El: Red to Berwyn. Bus: 22,*

STAKEOUT THIS TAKEOUT Little Brother's boxes up flavorful Korean eats for on-the-go gourmands.

36, 92. Dinner (closed Mon). Average main course: $13.

★ Kangnam The *dolsot bibimbap* here has garnered a cult following over the years. The steaming classic of egg, beef, veggies and rice *is* delicious, but don't ignore the other treats on hand. The *bulgogi*, grilled on your table over a bowl of hot coals, is sweet and garlicky and accompanied by paper-thin slices of vinegar-soaked daikon, a spicy yet cooling cucumber kimchi and an impossibly flavorful soup with tender cubes of tofu. *4849 N Kedzie Ave between Lawrence Ave and Ainslie St (773-539-2524). Bus: 81, 82, 93. Lunch, dinner. Average main course: $13.*

⟨ Korean Seoulfood Café You'll notice the prices for basic Korean classics such as deep-fried *mandoo* dumplings and rice cake in red-pepper sauce (*duk boki*) are a bit steeper than you'd find up around "K Town," but in the virtual Korean-food desert of the West Loop, we take what we can get. The best value might be the $8.99 lunch buffet, and *bibimbap* is a house special, but take a cue from the handful of post-work Korean-Americans pairing their beer with spicy beef broth kimchi casseroles. *560 W Van Buren St at Clinton St (312-427-4293). El: Blue to Clinton. Bus: 7, 38, 60, 125, 126, 157. Lunch, dinner. Average main course: $13.*

▼ ⊙ Little Brother's It *looks* like fast food, but this Korean joint cooks everything to order, so the food actually takes a few minutes

to arrive. And when it does, it's impressive: Both the BBQ steak and the marinated chicken are lean and tender, the coleslaw sports enticing whispers of wasabi, and the cucumber salad is a refreshing foil to the crisp tofu. In short, it tastes like there's a real chef in the kitchen—and what fast food spot can claim that? *818 W Fullerton Ave between Halsted St and Chalmer Pl (773-661-6482). El: Red to Fullerton. Bus: 8, 11, 74. Lunch, dinner (closed Sun). Average main course: $7.*

New Dowon This isn't a place for Korean barbecue. Not that the *bulgogi* isn't any good—it is, but take it from us and stick with the stews, such as a spicy tofu and seafood with silky tofu, hard-boiled eggs, baby squid and an irresistible, throat-tickling spice. Supplement it with a seafood pancake (as thick and crusty as deep-dish pizza) and the exceptional *banchan*, little bowls of sweet seaweed, pickles and seasoned mung beans that will have you grazing long after your entrée is gone. *5695 N Lincoln Ave at Fairfield Ave (773-878-5888). Bus: 49B, 84. Lunch, dinner. Average main course: $12.*

⟨ San Soo Gap San You'll leave here with the essence of ash wafting from your clothes, but that's no reason to stay away from the charcoal-fueled Korean barbecue. The *wang kalbi* and *dai ji kalbi* are marinated, not saturated, in their respective sauces, which gives the high-quality meats a chance to speak for themselves. Don't want to smell like a campfire? Try the *bibim naeng Myun*, a big bowl of cold buckwheat noodles and beef topped with a spicy

Side dish

HIP TO SIP *Soju* cocktails and drinking snacks like *duk boki* draw those in the know to Nara Lounge.

Seoul mates

Explore Chicago's Korean culture the best way we know of—through your stomach.

Karaoke bars and swank lounges catering to the Korean community might seem daunting to the uninitiated, but the regulars are quite welcoming if you just dive right in for *soju,* a distilled liquor similar to vodka, and *anju,* small plates of Korean classics intended to be eaten while drinking. Use this anju glossary and guide to the best spots to blend in.

COMMON ANJU (AHN-joo)
Duk boki (duck bo-KEY) Plump, gnocchilike rice cakes in sweet and spicy red pepper sauce.
Samgyupsal (SOM-gyup-sahl) Grilled pork belly slices with miso paste, salt, pepper and sesame oil for dipping.
Dubu kimchi (DOO-boo kim-CHEE) Fermented cabbage mixed with sliced pork in a spicy chile paste surrounded by slices of boiled tofu.
Tonkatsu (TONG-kah-tzu) Breaded and fried pork cutlet cut into strips and topped with tonkatsu sauce (a sweet, tart combo of Worcestershire, soy, ketchup and spices).
Odeng (OH-dang) Soup of soy-flavored broth with cooked fish cake and chile powder–spiked soy sauce on the side, used for fish cake dipping.
Yang nyam tongdak (YAHNG nyum TONG-dahk) Fried chicken wings brushed with sweet and spicy sauce.
Dry plate Grilled dried squid, grilled cuttlefish and marinated dried squid with *gochujang* (GO-choo-jahng; fermented hot sauce) and mayo for dipping.

TOP KOREAN EATING AND DRINKING SPOTS

Nara Lounge (*623 W Randolph St, 312-887-9999*) In the cozy space, Korean-Americans show up around midnight, refill soju glasses often and counter the buzz with a never-ending stream of anju.
Yeowoosai (*6248 N California Ave, 773-465-7660*) Its name translates to "Let's talk about love at this place," but instead of couples, expect fresh-faced Koreans sipping soju cocktails and singing along to projected music videos.
Dancen (*5114 N Lincoln Ave, 773-878-2400*) This dark pocket of a bar lures drinkers with pitchers of melon and yogurt soju cocktails and tasty skewers of garlic and gingko nuts that come fresh off the grill built into the tiny bar.
Hourglass (*3658 W Lawrence Ave, 773-478-4050*) Named for a classic Korean TV drama, this stalwart draws an eclectic crowd that seeks out its famous fried chicken and its trippy, rustic rainforest/military bunker look.
Orange (*5639 N Lincoln Ave, 773-275-5040*) Grab a seat at an aquamarine booth and sample through the $6 "tapas" menu of anju classics.
Lincoln Karaoke (*5526 N Lincoln Ave, 773-895-2299*) There are plenty of English songs to choose from, but this is still a real-deal *noraebang* ("song room"). Choose from rooms of various sizes that sport plasma TVs, disco lighting, wireless mikes and customer-service buttons so you don't have to stop your Stevie Nicks impersonation to request more soju.
Goo-Tee Karaoke Restaurant (*6248 N California Ave, 773-274-1166*). Situated in a strip mall next to barbecue spot Hae Woon Dae and Yeowoosai (see "Similar spots"), this joint is usually the last stop of the night for most Korean songbirds, which might explain the slurred singing and incessant giggling coming out of the half-dozen rooms.—*Heather Shouse*

and flavorful chili sauce. *5247 N Western Ave between Farragut and Berwyn Ave (773-334-1589). Bus: 11, 49 X49, 49B, 92. 24 hrs. Average main course: $15.*

⊙ **Seoul Corea** The sign outside reads Cafe Corea and the menu says Korean Bistro. Confusing, but this tiny one-room, two-person show manages to turn out Korean fare that rivals bigger operations. Get your fix of capsaicin in every dish—from the beef, egg, and vegetable combination of *bibimbap* to the *haemool suntofu,* a tofu and seafood stew. Don't skip the quirky drinks such as *shik hye,* a sugary rice broth, and *soo jeong gwa,* a cinnamon punch. *1603 E 55th St between Cornell Ave and Hyde Park Blvd (773-288-1795). El: Red to Garfield. Bus: 6, 28, 55, X55, 171. Lunch (Mon–Fri), dinner (closed Sun). Average main course: $10.*

★ BYOB **Solga** The aroma of grilled short ribs emanated so strongly from this unsuspecting spot that we abandoned our previous plans and swerved into the parking lot. From the first bite of seafood pancake, we knew it was a good move. Enormous bowls of slippery noodles were a bland waste of time, but the *kalbi* barbecue's soft layers of fat melted on our tongues, and the tasty *banchan* (fish cakes loaded with flavorful kimchi spice) had us hooked. *5828 N Lincoln Ave between Francisco Ave and Richmond St (773-728-0802). Bus: 11, 84, 93. Lunch, dinner. Average main course: $14.*

▼ BYOB **Ssyal Ginseng House** There's an entire bird in this Korean restaurant's signature ginseng-chicken soup, and it sits in a wildly bubbling broth that's subtly enriched with ginseng. In Korea, this stuff is served in the summer, but this is a quintessential winter soup, too—not aggressive in flavor but in comfort. For something a little stronger, try the spicy tofu stew, which proves that when served soft and warm and swimming in chile broth, tofu can be just as comforting as chicken. *4201 W Lawrence Ave at Keeler Ave (773-427-5296). Bus: 53, 81. Lunch, dinner (closed Sun). Average main course: $10.*

⊙ **Susie's Noon Hour Grill** Owner Soon Hee Lee ("Susie") is a one-woman show who takes orders, serves them and buses tables, all the while sneaking gingersnap cookies to her younger patrons. Somehow, she also finds time to helm the wok and flattop, turning out airy *pajun* (Korean pancakes) slathered with a fiery jalapeño sauce, soul-satisfying *bibimbap* and a spicy, sweet Chop Chae—a sautéed mix of vegetables, beef and glass noodles perfumed with ginger and hit with a touch of pancake syrup. *6930 N Glenwood Ave between Farwell and Morse Aves (773-338-9494). El: Red to Morse. Bus: 22, 96, 147, 155. Breakfast, lunch, dinner (Tue–Sat, May–Dec only). Average main course: $6.*

▼ ☾ **Woo Chon** Korean food is all about the barbecue, so imagine our surprise when we realized that the *kalbi* was taking a backseat. At Woo Chon, we'd gladly forgo it for the rich *dolsot bibimbap,* a fantastic version of the classic rice-egg-meat-veggie casserole, the seafood pancake or the *doeji kimchi bokkum,* luscious slices of pork mixed with spicy kimchi. Then there's the best surprise of all: the tofu soup, which gets props not just for its deep layers of flavors, but also for being free. *5744 N California Ave between Ardmore and Lincoln Aves (773-728-8001). Bus: 11, 84, 93. Lunch, dinner. Average main course: $10.*

Kosher

▼ ☺ (**Da'Nali's** Da'Nali's is hidden in an unassuming Skokie strip mall, but that's only the first of its many surprises. This yummy family-friendly pizza place is the only brick-oven, kosher vegetarian restaurant around. It is also one of the only restaurants with a kosher pastry chef. Save room for the great cheesecakes. Like many kosher restaurants, post-Shabbat evening hours are hopping busy, with lots of live music. *4032 Oakton St, Skokie (847-677-2782). Bus: 97. Lunch, dinner (closed sundown Fri–sundown Sat). Average main course: $12.*

☺ **Dairy Star** See Ice Cream and Sweets for review.

☺ (**Ken's Diner and Grill** Ken's Diner and Grill is the Johnny Rockets of kosher eating. Head to this old school soda foundation for fat, messy, tasty burgers and perfectly seasoned fries. Also on the menu are bison burgers, pie and homemade cookies. The shakes, of course, are strictly non-dairy. *3353 Dempster St, Skokie (847-679-2850). Bus: Pace 250. Lunch, dinner (closed sundown Fri–sundown Sat). Average main course: $8.*

☺ **Metro Klub** To get to Metro Klub, you need to walk through the Crowne Plaza Chicago Metro hotel or its Dine restaurant. But if you are looking for a kosher restaurant downtown, it is worth the slight maze, as this is your only option within the 312 area code. This Glatt eatery serves up turkey clubs, skirt steak, salmon and other non-dairy lunch dishes in an atmosphere that's more upscale than most kosher restaurants. *733 W Madison St at Halsted St (312-602-2104). Bus: 8, 20, 126. Lunch (Mon–Thu). Average main course: $15.*

▼ ☺ ✳ **Mizrahi Grill** Rarely do we get to compare the North Shore to Brooklyn, but step into this strip-mall restaurant and you'll swear you're in Crown Heights. Standard items include curry-laden shawarma in fluffy pita, grilled kebabs and thick-cut french fries, but the real kicker is that this place is kosher and observes Shabbat by closing early on Friday and not reopening until Sunday. This explains the frenzy of frum diners, standing in line among enlarged photographs of the Western Wall. *215 Skokie Valley Rd, Highland Park (847-831-1400). Lunch (Sun–Fri), Dinner (Sun–Thu). Average main course: $15.*

☺ **Original Frances' Deli** See Delis for review.

✳ **Shallots Bistro** The waitstaff and diners schmooze like one big happy family at this kosher, clubby French bistro. The melt-in-your-mouth steaks rival many pricier downtown steakhouses (the bordelaise, in a red-wine reduction topped with crispy onions, was our favorite). Standouts include hearty seasonal stews and the special Black Hat dessert, a molten Belgian chocolate cake with sorbet that somehow tastes distinctive in the sea of chocolate lava cakes served all over

THE GREAT DEBATE Whether over the Talmud or the merit of Taboun Grill's shawarma, discussion rages on.

town. *4741 Main St, Skokie (847-677-3463). El: Yellow to Skokie. Bus: 54A, 97, Pace 254, Pace 250. Lunch (Mon–Thu), dinner (Sun–Thu, Sat after sundown; closed Fri). Average main course: $25.*

▼ **Slice of Life/Hy Life Bistro** Slice of Life and Hy Life Bistro are a one-two kosher punch. Slice of Life, the dairy kosher kitchen, serves up a sweet-and-sour mock chicken that is large enough for leftovers the next day. The spinach citrus salad is a non-dairy treat, with a wine vinaigrette instead of the standard bacon dressing that ruins so many spinach salads. Hy Life Bistro has a cozy, intimate vibe and a more substantial menu. Choose from honey Dijon chicken, BBQ skirt steak and more. *4120 W Dempster St, Skokie (847-674-2021). Bus: Pace 215, Pace 250. Breakfast (Sun), lunch, dinner. Average main course: $20.*

☺ B **Steve's Deli** See Delis for review.

▼ ☺ B BYOB **Taboun Grill** This Israeli grill's buttery hunks of certified rib eye, prime skirt steak and aged prime rib put it in the culinary category of Gibsons for the yarmulke set. Families and couples come from as far as Milwaukee for tasty rib eye kebabs, lamb chops, schnitzel and shawarma. Unlike some other kosher eateries, the service here is friendly, regardless of whether you're a regular. BYO certified kosher wine or domestic beer; the latter is inherently kosher. *6339 N California Ave between Devon Ave and Rosemont Ave (773-*

381-2606). Bus: 93, 155. Lunch (Sun–Fri), dinner (after sundown Sat–Thu). Average main course: $9. ● Other location: 8808 Gross Point Rd (847-965-1818).

★ ✶ **Tel Aviv Bakery** You may come in here determined to buy only one thing—a fluffy loaf of challah, for example. But few can resist the magical aromas of cinnamon and chocolate. Almost immediately after entering this kosher bakery the spell takes over and you're ordering bags of rugalach, a dozen black-and-white cookies, and whatever that was that the person in front of you in the perpetually winding line ordered. Carbs be damned, and don't say we didn't warn you. *2944 W Devon Ave between Richmond St and Sacramento Ave (773-764-8877). Bus: 11, 155. Sun–Wed 6am–6pm; Thu 6am–4:30pm (closed Sat). Average baked good: $2.*

▼ ☺ **Tel Aviv Kosher Pizza** Were it not for the name, you'd never know this place was kosher. Okay, maybe the yarmulke-clad Jew running the place will tip you off, or the fact that there's no meat on the menu. Still, the main dishes—pizza (a crispy crust gives the slices a bit of crunch), lasagna (served in its own bubbling dish) and a few Middle Eastern dishes (such as the over-cooked, but still tasty, falafel)—don't taste like they've been made according to ancient dietary laws. Which is exactly the point. *6349 N California Ave between Devon and Rosemont Aves (773-764-3776). Bus: 93, 155. Lunch (Mon–Fri), dinner (Mon–Thu, Sat). Average pizza: $14.*

GRAB A GUIDE

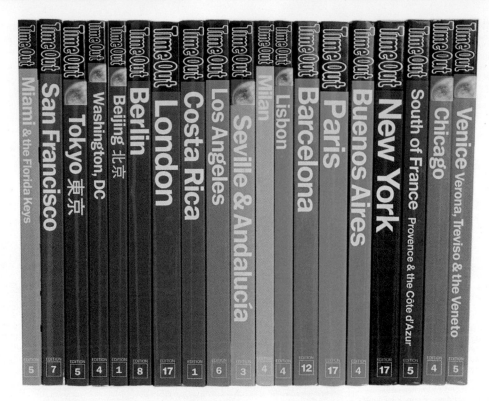

AND GO!

More than 100 destinations, written by local experts

Latin American

★ ✳ ☾ **Carnivale** When a restaurant this size is this busy (it seats 400, but an hour wait is typical), it must be making somebody happy. Jerry Kleiner's colorful—if slightly dated—design *can* make a person smile, and the mojitos and margaritas don't hurt, either. You'll find all sorts of variations on traditional fare, like the grilled skirt steak *arranchera* and mini whitefish tacos. Some of them, like the juicy *ropa vieja*, raise this restaurant's bar, but it's the crowd here that entertains the most. *702 W Fulton St at Union Ave (312-850-5005). Bus: 8, 65. Lunch (Mon–Fri), dinner. Average main course: $24.*

▽ ✳ ☾ B **Coobah** Given the neighborhood and decor, this pan-Latin joint seems akin to Chi-Chi's. But it takes only a promising pair of subtle *lumpia*—Filipino egg rolls stuffed with duck, peppers, red cabbage and onions—to realize that this spot deserves a closer look. Tilapia arrives in blue corn flour and served on a rice-paper tostada; Chicken Negra Modelo is glazed in its namesake beer and flanked by spinach and cheese *chilaquiles*; and the Sandwich Coobah is as solid a Cuban sandwich as any other. *3423 N Southport Ave between Roscoe St and Newport Ave (773-528-2220). El: Brown to Southport. Bus: 9, 22, 152. Brunch (Sat, Sun), lunch (Mon–Fri), dinner. Average main course: $20.*

▽ ✳ ☾ B **Cuatro** This Nuevo Latino hot spot has the looks of a lounge but it isn't all show. Menu standouts like the citrus marinated salmon *ceviche*, crispy flautas stuffed with agave-roasted beef and the beer-braised short rib remain, but it's in the pre-theater prix fixe dinner specials—starting with a fire-roasted corn and potato chowder that gets a kick with Mexican chiles—where chef Edie Jimenez breathes new life into relatively ho-hum dishes. *2030 S Wabash Ave between Cullerton and 21st Sts (312-842-8856). El: Red to Cermak/Chinatown. Bus: 21, 24, 29, 62. Brunch (Sun), dinner. Average main course: $23.*

◷ BYOB **Curio Café** This Latin-tinged menu offers plenty of comforts. In the morning, pair fair-trade coffee with the *plato típico*, a breakfast plate of free-range eggs topped with vibrant red salsa, refried black beans, slices of avocado, salty cheese and impeccable fried plantains. The daily soups and juicy skirt steak—along with rice, guacamole and beans—are the highlights at dinner. A friend of the owners makes all the cakes, including the hulking double-chocolate that's homestyle-good. *3400 N Lawndale Ave between Belmont Ave and Addison St (773-463-2233). El: Blue to Belmont. Bus: 56, 77, 82. Breakfast, lunch, dinner (Fri–Sat). Average main course: $13.*

★ BYOB **El Llano** This small, cheery room is packed with Colombian tchotchkes (as well as a stuffed armadillo hanging on the wall), which gives the place a festive vibe. What are they celebrating? Chicken, and the fact that they turn this blank-slate-of-foods into a dinner that's plump, juicy, golden, perfectly charred and endlessly flavorful. Tender brisket immersed in mild tomato sauce, crisp fried yuca, and a strip steak with fresh and lively chimichurri grace this menu, too. *3941 N*

BRANCH OUT Petrified trees are among the many ways Randy Zweiban brings the outside in at Province.

Lincoln Ave between Larchmont Ave and Irving Park Rd (773-868-1708). El: Brown to Irving Park. Bus: 11, 50, 80, 152. Lunch, dinner. Average main course: $11.

◷ **El Salvador Restaurante** This cozy Brighton Park Salvadorean restaurant is our favorite for *empanadas de leche* (sugary fried plantain pockets stuffed with thick condensed milk), *pupusa chichurrones* (pork-filled cornmeal pancakes) and chunks of deep-fried yuca. The *panes con pavo* is also an interesting find: housemade bread smothered with gravy-laden turkey. The back of the menu is saved for Mexican offerings (just in case you can't find Mexican anywhere else in the city). *4125 S Archer Ave at Francisco Ave (773-579-0405). El: Orange to 35th/Archer. Bus: 35, 62. Lunch, dinner. Average main course: $10.*

◷ B **El Tinajón** With two decades under its belt, it might just be the oldest Guatemalan spot in town. Start off with the bright pink tamarind-and-rum cocktail, and you'll blend right into the cozy room's color scheme. The menu is heavy on seafood, with standouts that include grilled tilapia, grilled shrimp and seafood soup. The *chuchitos* (Guatemalan tamales) are excellent, and the burritos aren't your standard Mexican variation but instead emphasize fresh veggies and black beans. *2054 W Roscoe St at Hoyne Ave (773-525-8455). El: Brown to Paulina. Bus: 50, 77, 152. Lunch, dinner. Average main course: $10.*

✳ BYOB **Gloria's Café** Colombian chef-owner Gloria Santiago and her Puerto Rican husband, Jaime, have put their hearts into this colorful eatery. The space is modest, but the food is complex and filling. The steaming bowl of herb-flecked *sancocho* (hen stew), makes for a great lunch, packed with yuca, plantains and corn. For a dinner for two, go with the brown-skinned rotisserie chicken and the *bandeja paisa* (country plate), an assortment of meats and traditional vegetables and beans. *3300 W Fullerton Ave at Spaulding Ave (773-342-1050). El: Blue to Logan Square. Bus: 56, 74, 82. Lunch, dinner. Average main course: $11.*

▼ ◷ ✳ BYOB **Irazú** Never tried Central American food? This spot is simple, authentic, cheap, supercasual and friendly—just what the doctor ordered. Start with the hearts of palm salad—tangy stalks on a bed of shredded cabbage that's been tossed in a lime vinaigrette, along with radishes, cilantro, cucumber, pickled beets and ripe avocado. Make it a meal by adding a side of white rice, soupy black beans and sweet plantains. Bring a bottle of Malbec to match, and end the meal with an oatmeal shake. *1865 N Milwaukee Ave between Oakley and Western Aves (773-252-5687). El: Blue to Western. Bus: 49, 56, 73. Lunch, dinner (closed Sun). Average main course: $8.*

◷ **La Brasa Roja** If you can walk by this place and not be drawn in by the sight of plump, juicy rotisserie chickens rotating over smoldering coals just on the other side of the window, you're either a vegetarian or devoid of taste buds. Assuming you're neither, get into this Colombian eatery, order the droolworthy chicken, and don't stop there. Try the cheesy corn cakes, meat-filled turnovers, tangy marinated skirt steaks topped with bright green chimichurri, sweet plantains and fresh fruit drinks. *3125 W Montrose Ave at Troy St (773-866-2252). El: Brown to Francisco. Bus: 78, 82. Breakfast, lunch, dinner. Average main course: $10.*

▼ ✳ **La Fonda Latino Grill** Every meal at this solid spot should start with the small, but tasty, beef and spinach-mushroom empanadas with spicy avocado sauce. Red snapper, shrimp, squid, scallops and clams get tossed in the *cazuela de mariscos'* creamy tomato sauce, and the flank steak (*sobrebarriga a la criolla*) is so tender, chewing is almost a formality. Savor it, though, just as you should the delicious margaritas—shaken and poured into martini glasses tableside. *5350 N Broadway between Berwyn and Balmoral Aves (773-271-3935). El: Red to Berwyn. Bus: 36, 92, 147. Lunch, dinner (closed Mon). Average main course: $15.*

◷ ✳ BYOB **La Sierra** Work up an appetite before you arrive at this Ravenswood BYOB; deciding between the Mexican and Ecuadorian specialties is almost impossible, so you'll probably end up choosing both. Make sure to try the Llampingachos, two savory potato pancakes paired with a peanut sauce and a fried egg (mix the runny yolk with the sauce for maximum creaminess); oversize spicy pork *sopes*; and rich and tender goat stew, cooked with beer and laced with the faintest trace of cumin. *1637 W Montrose Ave between Ashland Ave and Paulina St (773-549-5538). El: Brown to Montrose. Bus: 22, 50, 78, 145. Breakfast, lunch, dinner. Average main course: $13.*

★ ✳ BYOB **Las Tablas** The *arepa chorriada* (pseudo-polenta smothered in melted cheese and onion-and-tomato *criolla* sauce) here is dense, greasy and unattractive. But before you know it, you've scraped the plate. And before you can exclaim how enormous the *bandeja paisa* combination is, you've already sliced into the juicy New York strip, torn off a crisp piece of fried pork and broken the fried egg and mixed the yolk with the beans. And by that time, your mouth is too full to get the words out anyway. *2965 N Lincoln Ave between Wellington Ave and George St (773-871-2414). El: Brown, Purple (rush hrs) to Diversey. Bus: 9, 11, 76, 77. Lunch, dinner. Average main course: $16.* ● Other location: 4920 W Irving Park Rd (773-202-0999).

BYOB **Machu Picchu** Even if the dining room of this Peruvian spot wasn't pleasant (which it is), chances are the food would still win you over. Ceviche *mixto*, full of toothsome shrimp, squid and octopus, sports a bright, tangy flavor; shredded chicken is flavored with a delicious mix of lime juice and cilantro; and *pescado a lo macho* smothers crispy fried fish in a delectable tomato sauce. *3856 N Ashland Ave between Grace and Byron Sts (773-472-0471). Bus: 9, 80, 152. Lunch, dinner. Average main course: $10.*

★ ▼ ✳ BYOB **May Street Café** This pan-Latin mecca manages to brighten a dreary, industrial corner. Chef-owner Mario Santiago drops fresh avocados and grilled chicken into a perfectly spicy tortilla soup, pairs juicy mangos and plump shrimp in a quesadilla and gives chicken fajitas a kick with gobs of cinnamon and chipotle. Three little coins of mango flan make for an insanely decadent ending—but it's only truly insane if you forgo it. *1146 W Cermak Rd between May St and Racine Ave (312-421-4442). Bus: 8, 21. Dinner (Tue–Sat). Average main course: $18.*

★ ✳ **Nacional 27** DJs spinning and customers dancing in the dining room may not be for everyone, but if you're into it, you're in for a treat with this pan-Latin restaurant's food. The kitchen puts out locally grown seasonal dishes, which include a chimichurri-crusted filet mignon with three potato-chorizo hash, and a Malbec reduction. If your dinner falls on a Wednesday, try the chef's four-course party menu, which kicks off with a glass of passion-ginger sangria, on the house. *325 W Huron St between Franklin and Orleans Sts (312-664-2727). El: Brown, Purple (rush hrs) to Chicago. Bus: 66. Dinner (closed Sun). Average main course: $19.*

★ ✳ **Province** "Big" is the key word at Randy Zweiban's West Loop spot, a swank take on eco-modern design where powerfully flavorful Latin touches meet elegant, American dishes. Chorizo and smoked onions join barbecued lamb, while rabbit confit is paired with a thick marcona-almond emulsion. When a dish (basic shrimp and grits; fluke ceviche) disappoints, it's not because it's bad, but because it just can't hold up next to the more aggressive food on the table. *161 N Jefferson St between Randolph and Lake St (312-669-9900). El: Green, Pink to Clinton. Bus: 14, 20, 38, 56. Lunch, dinner (closed Sun). Average main course: $17.*

◖ **Pueblito Viejo** Plan for the full experience at this Colombian steakhouse, crammed with an array of artificial flora and fauna and waiters dressed à la Juan Valdez. Once the music starts playing, crowds young and old hit the dance floor, but stay put and take in the action while feasting on *arepas*, fried white-corn pancakes filled with cheese and sausage. Also try one of the Colombian combo plates, which include fried flank steak or pork, plus melt-in-your-mouth plantains and yuca. *5429 N Lincoln Ave at Rascher Ave (773-784-9135). Bus: 11, 49, X49, 49B, 92, 93. Dinner (closed Mon). Average main course: $15.*

◷ **Pupuseria el Salvador** Tucked in a South Side basement enclave is this tiny *pupuseria*, known for made-to-order *pupusas* (corn-meal pancakes stuffed with pork, zucchini, or cheese and frijoles). The three-table room is often full, but grab a stool at the little bar for a bird's-eye view of the lovely bandana-clad *chicas* grilling up Salvadorian sausage and stirring

pots of sweet tamales. *3557 E 106th St between Avenue L and Avenue M (773-374-0490). Bus: 26, 30, 100. Lunch, dinner (closed Tue). Average main course: $4.*

★ ▼ ◷ **Pupusería Las Delicias** *Pupusas*—pancake-like patties made from masa and stuffed with a variety of meats, vegetables and cheeses—are the focus of the menu, but we liked other menu items even better: Soft, sweet corn tamales drizzled with *crema*, crispy Guatemalan tostadas with beans and salsa and a sweet glass of *horchata*, a drink that doubles as dessert. *3300 W Montrose Ave at Spaulding Ave (773-267-5346). El: Brown to Kedzie. Bus: 78, 82, 93. Breakfast, lunch, dinner. Average main course: $7.*

▼ ◷ **Pupuseria los Planes and American Grill** This Mexican/Salvadoran crossbreed specializes in namesake cornmeal pockets packed with decadent *chicharron*, creamy beans or delicate *loroco* flowers. With across-the-board cheapo prices, adding a hen tamale and a meat-stuffed torta won't break the bank, so take a group, add on the standout steak *sope*, and wash it all down with rich *tamarindo*. *7109 N Clark St between Estes and Touhy Aves (773-465-9338). El: Red to Morse. Bus: 22, 96, 147. Lunch, dinner. Average main course: $6.*

★ ◷ BYOB **Pupuseria y Restaurante Cuscatleco** Stuffed and griddled cornmeal patties, a.k.a. *pupusas*, are the main draw of this tidy family-run spot. For our money, the *mixta* of pork rinds, beans and cheese is the winner, which we smother with red and green salsas and crunchy slaw. Supplement the pupusas with a hen tamale and an order of *pasteles de carne*, crispy pinched-shut pockets of oniony beef. And don't leave without trying the plantain fritters filled with *crema salvadoreña* (crème fraîche). *3125 W Lawrence Ave at Troy St (773-539-0977). El: Brown to Kedzie. Bus: 81, 82. Lunch, dinner. Average main course: $5.50.*

◖ **Rumba** Latin fusion is the name of the game at this upscale River North restaurant where Cuban, Puerto Rican and Peruvian influences mingle on the dance floor as well as the kitchen. The glammed-up, mojito-sipping clientele is usually loud and lively. If you're looking for a little more privacy, the six-seat, reservation-only chef's room gives front-row seats to the chef's culinary show. Latin bands and DJs perform on weekends, and complimentary salsa lessons are held Wednesday through Saturday. *351 W Hubbard St at Orleans St (312-222-1226). El: Brown, Purple (rush hrs) to Merchandise Mart. Bus: 125. Dinner (closed Sun, Mon). Average main course: $28.*

◷ BYOB **Super Pollo** Tucked away on one of Logan Square's residential streets, this Latin American spot is a neighborhood gem that deserves a little community support (we're often depressed to find we're the only ones in the dining room). The quiet guy behind the counter is a fantastic cook, evident in his four vibrant housemade salsas that start the meal; the greaseless, flattened *tostones* (request with garlic, or "*con ajo*"); fluffy rice with pigeon peas; and crispy-skinned, juice-packed rotisserie chicken, the namesake and star of the show. All of this for six bucks? Sold. *3640 W Wrightwood Ave between Monticello and Lawndale Aves (773-725-0700). El: Blue to Logan Square. Bus: 53, 56, 74, 76. Breakfast, lunch, dinner. Average main course: $6.*

Mediterranean

★ **Avec** Owner Donnie Madia and chef Koren Grieveson's tiny space looks like a sauna, has communal seating, doesn't take reservations and is loud as hell. But it is always the must-eat spot for foodies in the know. Small plate mainstays like chorizo-stuffed dates and salty brandade are unbeatable. Wood oven–roasted braised pork shoulder with garlic sausage, summer squash, pasta tagliati and basil pesto is another favorite, but the menu changes with the season. You'll like Grieveson's picks, no matter the time of year. *615 W Randolph St between Jefferson and Desplaines Sts (312-377-2002). El: Green, Pink to Clinton. Bus: 56, 125. Dinner. Average small plate: $10.*

☺ **BYOB Catedral Café** This place is decked out with so much Catholic imagery, it looks like a garage sale thrown by the pope. But as long as you don't have an aversion to angels, this Little Village spot won't disappoint. Upscale café grub—thin crêpes stuffed with smoked salmon on fresh greens; a chicken-breast panino with layers of silky mango— is balanced by basic pastas and breakfast fare. Expertly prepared cappuccinos, earnest service, and endorsements from Will Ferrell and Maggie Gyllenhaal (who filmed scenes from *Stranger Than Fiction* here) will make you a believer. *2500 S Christiana Ave at 25th St (773-277-2233). Bus: 52, 60. Breakfast, lunch, dinner. Average main course: $7.*

★ ☺ **Icosium Kafé** This Algerian crêpe place makes the standard French crêperie pale in comparison. You'll find typical butter-and-sugar or banana-and-Nutella combos, but savory crêpes are where Icosium lets its Algerian flag fly. Fillings include mostly organic vegetables, halal meats (including *merguez*, a lamb sausage) and even escargot. Those who are watching their carbs can opt for the same ingredients in salads. Even everyday green tea seems special here, served in a charming teapot with a teacup rimmed in gold with fresh mint leaves on request. *5200 N Clark St at Foster Ave (773-271-5233). El: Red to Berwyn. Bus: 22, 50, 92. Breakfast, lunch, dinner. Average main course: $8.50. ● Other location: 2433 N Clark St (773-404-1300).*

▼ ✳ ☾ **Nia** Nia Asimis—whose family has a long history of food service on Randolph Street— has opened this small-plates spot, where she serves food and drinks from every region of the Mediterranean. It's not a bad idea, but the experience can be fairly erratic: For every good move that Nia's kitchen makes (a trio of Mediterranean sausages, including a tender *loukanika*), there seems to be an equally bad one (piquillo peppers stuffed with chewy braised oxtail). The kitchen seems to do best with lamb, so stick to the juicy lamb-feta meatballs and the braised lamb shoulder, which is so tender it barely requires chewing. *803 W Randolph St at Halsted Ave (312-226-3110). El: Green, Pink to Clinton. Bus: 8, 20. Lunch, dinner. Average small plate: $10.*

▼ ☺ **Pannenkoeken Café** A wet-behind-the-ears mother-daughter team turns out the eponymous Dutch pancakes at this bright and cheery café in Lincoln Square. Slightly thicker than a crêpe and 11 inches in diameter, the *pannenkoeken* come in seven varieties with baked-on toppings like thinly sliced apples with cinnamon, bacon with cheese and a chocolate-banana version topped with Dutch chocolate syrup, cocoa and hazelnuts. *4757 N Western Ave between Leland and Lawrence Aves (773-769 8800). El: Brown to Western. Bus: 11, 49, X49, 81. Breakfast, lunch (closed Tues). Average main course: $8. ● Other location: 2257 W North Ave.*

▼ ✳ **Socca** If you could see the classy, airy space this Mediterranean restaurant takes up, you'd never guess it used to be the infamous pick-up joint Buddies. This incarnation is named for the chickpea crêpe that hails from Provence, a dish always present on the menu. But we like to start with the loaded antipasto board, move on to housemade pastas and end with rich comforts like hanger steak frites. *3301 N Clark St at Aldine (773-248-1155). El: Brown, Purple (rush hrs), Red to Belmont. Bus: 8, 22, 77. Dinner. Average main course: $18.*

☾ **Swirl Wine Bar** Because drinking on an empty stomach is a one-way ticket to drunk-dialing your ex, falling asleep in the bathroom or other drama, we're thankful this wine bar puts just as much focus on the food. The housemade empanada hides earthy mushrooms inside its flaky crust; hefty crab cakes get a golden exterior of panko crumbs; and a pizza topped with caramelized onions and pears goes perfectly with an off-dry riesling. *111 W Hubbard St between Clark St and LaSalle Blvd (312-828-9000). El: Brown, Purple (rush hrs) to Merchandise Mart; Red to Grand. Bus: 22, 36, 62, 65. Dinner (Tue–Sat). Average main course: $10.*

✳ **Viand** Chef Steve Chiappetti focuses on a more upscale experience for diners at this tourist standby. And overall, it works: A carrot-curry-crab soup is a beautiful dish, each ingredient distinct yet in harmony with the others, and "Chiappetti's Lamb" arrived at our table so tender, it could barely be moved from tagine to plate. Still, Chiappetti's whimsical approach to serving—the "junk food cart" of housemade marshmallows and brownies arrives in a mini-shopping cart—keeps the experience from getting too haughty. *155 E Ontario St between Michigan Ave and St. Clair St (312-255-8505). El: Red to Grand. Bus: 65, 146, 147, 151. Breakfast, lunch (Mon–Fri), dinner. Average main course: $18.*

✳ **Wave, W Chicago Lakeshore** Hotel lobbies aren't our dining rooms of choice, but we make an exception for the sultry vibe of this low-lit Mediterranean spot with a lake view from the patio. Many of the small plates are overpriced, so avoid buyer's remorse with standouts like the watermelon salad, which pairs cool cubes of melon with fiery spice-cured beef and creamy feta; and *crudo* (slivers of raw scallops and tuna) packing big, sprightly flavors. Ignore the waiter's hard sell; three small plates or two large feed a group of four just fine. *644 N Lake Shore Dr between Ontario and Erie Sts (312-255-4460). Bus: 134, 135, 136. Breakfast, lunch, dinner. Average small plate: $11.*

IT'S A DATE Avec's famous bacon-wrapped dates can be blamed for that long wait you'll endure.

Mexican

THEY'VE GOT SOL Clementina Flores and Carlos Tello are behind the delicious regional specialties at Sol de Mexico.

★ ▽ ☀ B **Adobo Grill** They call them *las señoras cocineras*—"the cooking ladies"—and every morning they're the first people here. They use their own recipes to make the rich *mole* poblano for the wood-roasted chicken and the handmade tortillas that wrap up light, crispy skate wing. An ex-server named Max supplied many of the colorful paintings on the wall, and the rotating cast of bartenders makes great margaritas (go for the "smoky floater" of mezcal). *2005 W Division St at Damen Ave (773-252-9990). El: Blue to Division. Bus: 50, 70. Brunch (Sat, Sun), lunch (Sat, Sun), dinner. Average main course: $17.* ● *Other locations: 1610 N Wells St (312-266-7999); 356 Yorktown Shopping Center, Lombard (630-627-9990).*

★ BYOB **Birrieria Zaragoza** Thick handmade tortillas, salsas made-to-order in molcajetes, cinnamon-laced coffee. You can get all of that here. Their only purpose, however, is to accompany this restaurant's signature platters of chopped goat meat. As opposed to other birrierias, this goat doesn't touch a consommé until it's plated, when some of the tomato-based broth is spooned over it. At that point, a good dousing of the restaurant's intricate hot sauce, and maybe a squeeze of lime and some onions, is all you need for one of the city's best goat tacos. (Though having a bottle of grapefruit Jarritos on hand doesn't hurt, either.) *4852 S Pulaski Rd between 48th and 49th Sts (773-523-3700). El: Orange to Pulaski. Bus: 47, 53A, 62. Mon, Wed, Thu, Fri 10am–7pm; closed Tue; Sat, Sun 8am–4pm. Average main course: $8.*

★ ☺ B **Bombon Café** See Bakeries/Cafés for review.

▽ ☀ **de cero** This taqueria fancies itself as edgy and upscale. We don't know if battered fish tacos fit the bill, but they make for a delicious guilty pleasure. More refined tacos include the ahi tuna, coupled with a mango salsa and bursting with bright, fresh flavors, and the chorizo, whose kick is tempered by cool *crema*. Fresh corn tamales shine with straight-off-the-cob flavor that goes perfectly with one of the tart hibiscus margaritas. The fresh berries in lime honey (the least fussy dessert on the list) is worth every penny. *814 W Randolph St between Green and Halsted Sts (313 455 8114). El: Green, Pink to Clinton. Bus: 8, 20. Brunch (Sun), lunch (Mon–Fri), dinner. Average main course: $13.*

▽ BYOB **Dorado** The concept here is Mexican-French (chef Luis Perez spent 18 years cooking French food before opening this spot in 2004), but at first glance this menu seems pretty straight-up Mexican. A closer read reveals that the nachos are topped with juicy, smoky morsels of duck and the chiles rellenos are stuffed with plump shrimp and tiny bay scallops. So seek out the fusion and don't look back—until dessert, that is. The *tres leches* doesn't have an ounce of French in it, but it's the right way to end. *2301 W Foster Ave at Oakley Ave (773-561-3780). El: Brown to Western. Bus: 49, X49, 92. Dinner (closed Mon). Average main course: $14.*

▽ ☺ ♨ ☀ ⊂ **El Cid** This Mexican mainstay has an amazing back patio; potent and fruity margaritas; sweet-as-pie servers; and reliably tasty dishes for a nice price. We've sampled our way through the menu to narrow down some favorites: garlicky tilapia tacos; inky black beans with perfect white rice; skirt steak; plantains with crispy edges; and the giant red snapper with crispy coating, smothered in tart tomato-and-olive Veracruz sauce. The potato tacos keep vegetarians happy, as does the ever-present owner, José, who's quick to pour tequila shots for newcomers and old friends. *2645 N Kedzie Ave between Milwaukee and Wrightwood Aves (773-395-0505). El: Blue to Logan Square. Bus: 56, 76. Breakfast, lunch, dinner. Average main course: $9.* ● *Other location: 2115 N Milwaukee Ave (773-252-4747).*

☺ BYOB **El Milagro** This sunny Pilsen café, which is covered in bright purple, yellow and orange paint inside and out, is next door to one of the city's most successful purveyors of corn and flour tortillas. Employees clearly know how to put those tortillas to good use: piling them with tender chicken legs submerged in *mole rojo*, or sumptuous, slow-cooked beef in a rich tomato sauce. Satisfying tamales are available for a more portable meal—but keep in mind that you can't take the sunniness with you. *1927 S Blue Island Ave between 19th and Cullerton Sts (312-433-7620). El: Pink to 18th. Bus: 9, 18, 21, 60. 8am–8pm. Average main course: $4.* ● *Other locations: 3050 W 26th St (773-579-6120); 1434 W Belmont (773-975-2348).*

☺ ⊂ B BYOB **Estrella Negra** This art-riddled BYOB has the disheveled look of a coffee shop, but the small plates coming out of the kitchen reveal that there's something more than espresso here. Warm bowls of *posole* are packed with rich chicken and toothsome hominy; savory chorizo tacos are lightened by their lettuce-cup shells; and chunky guacamole is sprinkled with mango or pomegranate seeds, which help cool the heat from diced jalapeño. There are no pomegranate seeds to save you from the tongue-searing shrimp "*diablo*," however, so if you plan to order that, BYO gallon of milk. *2346 W Fullerton Ave between Oakley and Western Aves (773-227-5993). El: Blue to California. Bus: 49, 74. Brunch, lunch, dinner (closed Mon). Average main course: $12.*

Flaco's Tacos The Hackney's crew opened this Mexican sibling to cater to the Columbia students and sprinkling of office workers in Printers Row. The former should be happy with the low prices and accessible gringo fare like quesadillas and burritos, while the latter can unwind over lunch with a cold *cerveza*. A handful of fillings can be had in tacos, tortas or burritos, and while the chicken and steak were consistently dry, the *al pastor* fared better, nice and juicy with a bit of kick. Specials, like a recent chicken *posole*, help set the place apart from Mexichains. *725 S Dearborn St between Harrison and Polk Sts (312-922-8226). El: Red to Harrison. Bus: 22, 36, 62. Lunch, dinner. Average taco: $2.25.*

▾ B Flo See Classic American $15 and under for review.

★ ✳ Fonda del Mar Angel Hernandez's menu is a nod to traditional Mexican fish houses known as *marisquerias*. He tosses firm chunks of marlin with olives, cilantro and onions for lively ceviche, and serves *callos de hacha zacualtipan*, seared scallops in a pasilla chile sauce, flanked by a "torta chiapaneca" plantain and black bean cake. But land-based dishes like the *conchinita pibil*, a braised pork in achiote paste, sour orange and spices, are worth a sampling as well. *3749 W Fullerton Ave between Ridgeway and Hamlin Aves (773-489-3748). El: Blue to Logan Square. Bus: 53, 74, 82. Metra: Milwaukee North to Healy. Dinner. Average main course: $16.*

✳ Frida's Marlene Benitez's follow-up to Andersonville's La Cocina de Frida has the same ambition as her original spot: classic, homestyle Mexican food, some of it with a minor twist. Funnily enough, this new outpost seems to be doing a better job with the execution. The guac is rich and creamy, the ceviche balanced between sweet and spicy, the chicken immersed in a complex peanut and *guajillo* chile salsa. In fact, anybody who has found themselves disappointed in the Andersonville locale may find checking this one out worth the trip. *3755 N Southport Ave at Grace St (773-935-2330). El: Brown to Southport. Bus: 9, 80, 152. Brunch (Sat, Sun), dinner. Average main course: $14.* ● *Other location (La Cocina de Frida): 5403 N Clark St, 773-271-1907.*

★ ▾ ✳ B Frontera Grill Most chefs behind culinary empires branch to other cities, leaving the original back home to suffer. Rick Bayless kept close to the kitchen and chose to expand in other ways (packaged food line, cookbooks, TV shows). Lucky us. For two decades, this has been the spot for intensely flavorful, impeccably fresh Mexican food. We like the upscale sister Topolobampo, but Frontera offers a vibrant slice of Mexico City, a place to chow down on ceviches, earthy *mole*, wood-grilled steak tucked into housemade tortillas, and of course, insanely good margaritas. *445 N Clark St between Hubbard and Illinois Sts (312-661-1434). El: Brown, Purple (rush hrs) to Merchandise Mart; Red to Grand. Bus: 22, 29, 36, 65. Brunch (Sat), lunch (Tue–Fri), dinner (Tue–Sat). Average main course: $15.*

(Fuego Mexican Grill & Margarita Bar Don't let the massive stature and the slick, chain look of this Logan Square Mexican spot scare you away—there are actually some mighty tasty dishes lurking about, and downright delicious margaritas to wash them down with. Start with the app of crispy corn tortillas filled with braised lamb meat and topped with a mound of fuschia pickled onions, then move on to anything smothered in one of the *mole* sauces (the pillow-soft tamales or the roasted chicken are our favorites). A fried ice cream finale will indulge the kids (or the kid in you). *2047 N Milwaukee Ave between Campbell and Maplewood Aves (773-252-1122). El: Blue to Western. Bus: 49, X49, 56, 73. Lunch (Sat, Sun), dinner. Average main course: $15.*

★ La Casa de Samuel If you haven't explored Little Village, this would be a good starting point. As at all good Mexican joints, the owner's regional heritage shows up in the food, and in this case, the inspiration is the state of Guerrero. This means you can expect a few exotic options, including bull's testicles, rattlesnake, wild boar and alligator. We go with house specialties like fried smelts; thin, cured venison *cecina*; and tender baked goat served with chunky guac, warm housemade tortillas and an addictive, thick, smoky *pasilla* chile sauce. *2834 W Cermak St between California Ave and Marshall Blvd (773-376-7474). El: Pink to California. Bus: 21, 94. Breakfast, lunch, dinner. Average main course: $12.*

★ ▾ La Oaxaqueña With hundreds of Mexican joints to choose from in the city, why do we love this one? Maybe it's because we dream about the *Huatulco torta*, a huge sandwich that layers spicy housemade chorizo, caramelized onions, a slather of pinto beans and fresh avocado atop amazing *cecina*, thin beef that's marinated for two days in lemon, salt

and oregano and then grilled. Or maybe it's the roasted Cornish hen smothered in Oaxacan *mole* or the crispy red snapper hiding under pickled red onions. Maybe there are too many reasons to count. *3382 N Milwaukee Ave between Pulaski and Keeler Aves (773-545-8585). El: Blue to Irving Park. Bus: 53, 56. Breakfast, lunch, dinner. Average main course: $9.* ● *Other location: 6113 W Diversey Ave (773-637-8709).*

◉ Las Islas Marias Las Islas Marias is turning into a Mexican seafood empire. The chef-owners are from Nayarit, Mexico, and just like their many other spots around Chicago (two on South Pulaski alone), this place specializes in *langostinos* and ceviche. Plates heaped with the lobsterlike crustaceans head to almost every table. Coated in a secret garlicky, salty, fiery "seven-spice" mixture, they're known to inspire die-hard fans. This location isn't BYOB, but some are—call ahead. *6635 N Clark St between Wallen and North Shore Aves (773-973-4752). El: Red to Loyola. Bus: 22, 36, 151, 155. Lunch, dinner. Average main course: $10.* ● *Other locations: 4770 W Grand Ave (773-637-8233); 5401 S Pulaski Rd (773-767-0908); 2400 S Pulaski Ave (773-522-1300).*

▾ ✳ B Las Palmas We're dubious of a Mexican joint where the servers push mojitos as their favorite drink. But it made sense when we saw a menu that started somewhere in Mexico and took cues from around the world. Expect rotating specials like crêpes filled with cream cheese and caramel and *camarones teporochos*, shrimp glazed in honey, lime and rum and served with poblano rice and mixed greens. Like the food, the mariachi goes global, singing traditional Mexican ditties only to segue into tunes like "Ruby Tuesday" and "Cecilia." *1835 W North Ave at Honore St (773-289-4991). El: Blue to Damen. Bus: 50, 72. Brunch, lunch (Sat, Sun), dinner. Average main course: $15.*

◉ La Encantada Mexican cuisine in Humboldt Park is as commonplace as fireworks on 4th of July. But beyond taquerias and take-out burrito joints, options are fairly limited, which is why this spot is so welcome. The menu is full of refreshingly different, modern Mexican dishes like plantain-filled enchiladas with *mole* sauce; side salads topped with guava dressing; and *chile en nogada*—a poblano pepper filled with ground beef, fruit and nuts. Not to mention the decor is attractive and the waitstaff is eager to please. *3437 W North Ave between Troy St and Kedzie Ave (773-539-6627). El: Brown to Kedzie. Bus: 82, 92, 93. Breakfast, lunch, dinner. Average main course: $8.*

✳ BYOB Los Moles By now, almost every Mexican-food enthusiast knows how chef Geno Bahena cooks. In fact, Bahena has opened (and closed) so many restaurants in the past four years that many people can probably recite the menu at this joint before they see it. But if this is an unsurprising experience, it is at least unsurprisingly *good*: The ceviche is sharp with lime juice and olives, the steaks are cooked perfectly medium-rare and, of course, there are the *moles*. Each one is distinctive in its layers of sweetness and spice, proving that there are no bad Geno Bahena restaurants. Just predictable ones. *3140 N Lincoln Ave between Barry and Belmont Aves (773-935-9620). El: Brown, Purple (rush hrs), Red to Belmont. Bus: 9, X9, 11, 77. Dinner (closed Tues). Average main course: $15.*

◉ Los Nopales The chef-co-owner here is a former cook at the Palmer House Hilton and Heaven on Seven, so he's capable of elevating typical taqueria fare. Standouts include the *caldo* *de pollo*, a gargantuan serving of Mexican chicken soup served with rice and tortillas (perfect for a chilly night); the ceviche with citrus-spiked tilapia and shrimp; and cactus salad dotted with jicama, avocado and mango-chipotle dressing (perfect for a sweltering night). Expect weekend queues. *4544 N Western Ave between Wilson and Sunnyside Aves (773-334-3149). El: Brown to Western. Bus: 11, 49, X49, 78, 81. Lunch, dinner (closed Mon). Average main course: $12.*

★ ☺ ☀ **Maiz** This is one of our favorites for feeding our need for every type of corn creation under the sun. The banana leaf–steamed tamale is delicious, with a feather-light exterior of smooth masa hiding tender shredded chicken kicked up with green chiles, and the empanadas are the lightest and flakiest in town. The *sopes* (lightly griddled, dense corn patties) can be topped with everything from *pastor* (roasted pork) to *huitlacoche* ('shroomlike corn fungus) to spinach. Skip dessert and finish with a "bull"—a blend of rum, lime juice and beer with a tart tamarind flavor. *1041 N California Ave between Cortez and Thomas Sts (773-276-3149). Bus: 53, 66, 70. Dinner (closed Mon). Average main course: $7.*

★ ⓑ **Mexique** Chef Carlos Gaytan is going for Mexican-French here, but most of his food comes off as upscale versions of the former. This isn't a problem: You'll be too busy eating to notice the lack of French flair in dishes like the perfect lamb chops accompanied with a delicious barbacoa *sope*; beautiful ceviche; and excellent, beer-battered fish tacos. And when the fusion thing works, as it does with the *cochinita rillettes* and the luscious duck confit tacos, it's nothing short of *magnifique*. *1529 W Chicago Ave between Armour St and Ashland Ave (312-850-0288). El: Blue to Chicago. Bus: 9, X9, 66. Brunch (Sat, Sun), lunch, dinner (closed Mon). Average main course: $20.*

★ ⓑ BYOB **Mixteco Grill** The *moles* here steal the show. *Sopes* get a dose of the brooding, smoky *mole rojo*, and mahi-mahi gets treated with a lighter yellow *mole verde*. And while its not a mole, the smooth poblano sauce pooled around perfectly grilled shrimp is so lappable, we almost don't need the seafood. In fact, we don't *need* any of the proteins here. All we need is some sauce, a bowl to put it in, and some handmade tortillas to sop it all up. *1601 W Montrose Ave at Ashland Ave (773-868-1601). El: Brown to Montrose. Bus: 22, 50, 78, 145. Brunch (Sat–Sun), dinner (Tue–Sun). Average main course: $17.*

ⓑ **Mundial–Cocina Mestiza** Since chef-owners Kate and Eusevio Garcia sold their innovative Pilsen restaurant to partner Mario Cota, the menu's stayed just as creative. (Even if, with the revocation of the BYOB policy, it has become more expensive.) New chef Hector Marcial has a knack for adding excitement to dishes like the Ensalada India, with its contrasts of crisp jicama, ripe mango and crunchy tortilla chips, or the El Mozzer, where poached eggs are layered atop zucchini and yellow squash over crumbly corn cakes. Main courses tend to read better than they taste, and service can be slow, but a spongy hibiscus cake nearly makes up for the shortcomings. *1640 W 18th St between Ashland Ave and Paulina St (312-491-9908). El: Pink to 18th. Bus: 9, 18, 168. Brunch (Sat, Sun), lunch, dinner. Average main course: $21.*

BYOB **Real Tenochtitlan** Geno Bahena has done his thing in every corner of the city: in Lincoln Park (Tepatulco), in River North (Chilpancingo), even on the Indiana-Chicago border (Delicioso y Sabroso). But at Real Tenochtitlan he took his food back to Logan Square, where he started with Ixcapuzalco in 2000. True to Bahena's formula,

Smackdown: Steak tacos

A taqueria trek reveals just who's the king of Chicago's most popular Mexican classic.

Whether you call it steak or carne asada, this marinated, grilled meat makes for a succulent taco designed to satisfy even the hungriest of carnivores. But with taquerias adorning almost every block in Chicago, a deconstruction of what's *muy bueno* and what misses the mark is in order. What follows is a sampling of seven of Chicago's steak tacos, all ordered simply, with only chopped white onion and cilantro on soft corn tortillas.

7 Green House Steaks at Maxwell Street Market *(548 W Roosevelt Rd, 312-745-4676)* Tacos reign supreme when it comes to street food. But this vendor, near the Roosevelt Road entrance of the Sunday flea market, doesn't get it quite right. The carne asada is char-grilled before it's ordered, but it's full of gristle and an unwelcome hamburger taste.

6 Las Asadas *(2072 N Western Ave, 773-235-5538)* The menu at this Bucktown taqueria boasts "succulent, mouth-watering steak"—it's not quite all that. The first bite is juicy and peppery but soon leaves you working on a chewy piece of steak wrapped in a lackluster corn tortilla.

5 Carniceria Y Taqueria Tierra Callente *(1400 N Ashland Ave, 773-772-9804)* The vibe at this unsuspecting grocery is just right: Tacos are ordered from behind the counter and served up quick, just as they should be. But the carne asada, albeit savory, is a bit on the stringy side, and the toppings are run-of-the-mill. Not to worry—wash it down with a Jarritos and enjoy the company at the counter.

4 Tio Luis *(3856 S Archer Ave, 773-843-0098)* The carne asada shines at this McKinley Park joint. Napkins are a must for chowing down on the juicy, shredded steak taco, but a warning to the health-conscious: This could be due in part to the fat streaking through the meat.

3 La Pasadita *(1132 N Ashland Ave, 773-384-6537)* With three neighboring storefronts and hungry customers waiting in each one, it seems La Pasadita's winning reputation is well-deserved. As expected, the tacos here don't disappoint: Freshly cut onions and cilantro sit atop slightly pink steak hot off the griddle, all enveloped in moist corn tortillas.

2 Taquería el Asadero *(2213 W Montrose Ave, 773-583-5563)* This Irving Park taqueria is often hailed by taco fiends as Chicago's best steak taco—and it would be, save for the mediocre onions and cilantro toppings.

1 Manolo's at Maxwell Street Market *(548 W Roosevelt Rd, 312-745-4676)* Hidden among the secondhand goods and novelty items at this open-air market lives the taco asada that will steal your heart. Found near the Cabrini and Desplaines Streets intersection, Manolo's serves up delicious charred carne asada straight off the grill in a freshly made corn tortilla, but it's the crisp, piquant onions and cilantro that make this taco the *ganador del gran premio.—Margaret Rhodes*

moles take center stage—a different one is made every day of the week (though we're partial to the *mole blanco*). In addition to his signature moles, expect upscale Mexican entrées like roasted duck breast with *guajillo* chile sauce and ancho chiles stuffed with chorizo. *2451 N Milwaukee Ave between Richmond St and Sacramento Ave (773-227-1050). El: Blue to Logan Square. Bus: 52, 56, 74. Dinner (closed Mon). Average main course: $20.*

★ ✳ B **¡Salpicon!** This swanky Mexican spot is known for perfect margaritas, a *Wine Spectator*–recognized wine tome, and chef Priscila Satkoff's traditional salsas, *queso fundido* and earthy *mole* served with handmade tortillas. These classics are served in a lively, art-splashed dining room that's similar to the contemporary restaurants you'd find in the chef's hometown of Mexico City. Authentic classics from blue-marlin ceviche to lacy *crepas* filled with goat's milk caramel are explained by the warm and friendly staff. *1252 N Wells St between Scott and Goethe Sts (312-988-7811). El: Red to Clark/Division. Bus: 11, 36, 70, 156. Brunch (Sun), dinner. Average main course: $24.*

★ ◷ **Sol de Mexico** Clementina Flores is a *mole* goddess, a woman sent from the heavens to create sauces so rich and complex, you'll want to ingest them with a straw. Formerly the *mole* master at Chilpancingo and Ixcapuzalco, she now combines her *mole* with chef Carlos Tello's food, and magic happens. For each season, *mole*-doused entrées take on new flavors. Keep an eye

out for the *callos de hacha al coco*, a tropical take on sea scallops with a sauce combining coconut, tomatoes and cilantro. *3018 N Cicero Ave between Wellington Ave and Nelson St (773-282-4119). Bus: 54, 77. Lunch, dinner (closed Tue). Average main course: $19.*

◷ **BYOB Taquería Puebla** This primarily Spanish-speaking restaurant specializes in the authentic street food of Puebla, the central Mexico town credited as the birthplace of *mole poblano*. Because Puebla has a large concentration of Lebanese immigrants, you'll find tacos *arabes*, pork tacos with thick, pitalike wrappers. At Taquería Puebla, these chipotle-spiked beauties and their friend the *cemita milanesa* (a breaded pork steak with cheese and avocado on a sesame-studded bun) are among the best of the menu. *3619 W North Ave between Monticello and Central Park Aves (773-772-8435). Bus: 72, 82. Lunch, dinner. Average main course: $6.50.*

★ **Topolobampo** The more sophisticated side of Rick Bayless is no less delicious than his lively Frontera Grill side—it's merely more exquisite. His careful attention to authentic flavors can be seen throughout seasonal menus, like a tempting list in the wintertime that includes slow-cooked duck "*carnitas*" with wild arugula and sunflower shoots, roasted rock hen with fennel stew and toasted almonds, and roasted pork loin with *pasilla* chile-fig sauce and red-chile bread pudding. Three chef's tasting menus are offered from $85; add paired wines for $50. *445 N Clark St between Hubbard and*

Illinois Sts (312-661-1434). El: Brown, Purple (rush hrs) to Merchandise Mart; Red to Grand. Bus: 22, 29, 36, 65, 156. Lunch (Tue–Fri), dinner (Tue–Sat) (closed Sun, Mon). Average main course: $37.

★ ◷ **Xni-Pec** The name (pronounced "shnee pek") refers to the runny nose–inducing, housemade habanero salsa, but everything here is worth a mention. Must-haves include Yucatecan specialties like *tacos de cochinita*, rich pork tacos cut by pickled onions, and *papadzules*, housemade tortillas stuffed with egg and topped with sprightly pumpkin-seed sauce. If the *relleno negro* tacos are available, order as many as you can—the shredded pork-chicken-beef mixture is immersed in a midnight-black sauce with endless flavor. *5135 W 25th St, Cicero (708-652-8680). El: Pink to Cicero. Bus: 54, 54B. Lunch, dinner (closed Mon). Average main course: $9.*

Zocalo There's a lot to choose from on the menu at this cavernous after-work spot. Gone is the small-plates format with which the restaurant opened. In its place is a trio of sprightly ceviches; a duo of tamales, one stuffed with fiery strips of jalapeño; *alambre al pastor* paired with a *guajillo* pineapple glaze; and fish tacos that join grilled tilapia with crunchy pickled onions. *358 W Ontario St between Orleans and Kingsbury Sts (312-302-9977). El: Brown, Purple (rush hrs) to Chicago. Bus: 65, 125. Lunch (Mon–Fri), dinner. Average main course: $17.*

A LITTLE BIT FRUITY De Cero gets fancy by topping ahi tuna tacos with fresh mango and grilled shrimp with watermelon.

Middle Eastern

CHARRED, I'M SURE Grilled-to-order kebobs and herb-packed salads lure legions to Semiramis.

▼ (**A La Turka** This dining room hearkens to times of eating on luxurious floor cushions and sucking on hookahs as if they're Tic Tacs. You can make a meal out of the cold appetizer platter—select any five items such as the *cacik* (homemade yogurt) or a traditional Turkish salad. Or fill up on a classic kebab with sautéed vegetables or the *moussaka* eggplant casserole. Portions are sized for big appetites, so you won't leave hungry, and belly dancers on weekends ensure no matter how lame your date is, you won't be bored. *3134 N Lincoln Ave between Barry and Belmont Aves (773-935-6101). El: Brown to Paulina. Bus: 9, 11, 77. Lunch (Wed–Sun), dinner. Average main course: $15.*

★ ☺ **Afghan Kabob** You could assume that the eggplant dip *bourani badenjan* will be like baba ghanoush, but you'd be wrong: It's more complex, a little sweet (thanks to caramelized onions) and a bit tangy (thanks to yogurt). That's the theme here, where the food tastes better than expected. After trying the *aushak*, beef-stuffed raviolilike pasta, and *kabuli palaw*, a lamb shank cooked with carrots and raisins, you'll get a handle on Afghan cuisine. And you'll wonder why there isn't more of it locally. *4040 W Montrose Ave between Pulaski Rd and Elston Ave (773-427-5041). El: Blue to Montrose. Bus: 53, 78. Lunch, dinner (closed Mon). Average main course: $8.*

▼ ☺ (**Al Amira** One of the newest and most ambitious entrants to the long-established (and rather static) Middle Eastern strip in Albany Park is this Iraqi restaurant, outfitted with a snazzy interior and late-night hours. So far, the menu seems to follow the standard offerings of its neighbors, but everything is prepared as well as anywhere: Falafel were freshly fried and served with garlicky *toum*, and shawarma tasted of good-quality meat and was thankfully moist and tender. Service couldn't have been more welcoming at noon, and by reports it's the same at midnight, making it a civilized alternative to late-night greasy spoons. *3200 W Lawrence Ave at Kedzie Ave (773-267-0333). El: Brown to Kedzie. Bus: 81, 82, 93. Breakfast, lunch, dinner. Average main course: $9.*

▼ (B **Al Bawadi Grill** It may be hard to imagine how you could turn an old Arby's in Bridgeview into a pasha's pleasure den, but that's pretty much what Al Bawadi has done. The over-the-top decor is matched by the superb hand with wood-grilled meats in the kitchen, producing kebabs, chicken and (unusual for a Middle Eastern restaurant) seafood with perfect juiciness and char flavor. Veggie items— psychedelically bright green falafel, tart fattoush salad, smoky baba ghanoush—also pop with a brightness of flavor that they haven't had in a long time, though the tastiest thing of all might have been a freebie: the complimentary garlicky eggplant dip that started the meal. *7216 W 87th St, Bridgeview (708-599-1999). Pace: 385, 386. Breakfast, lunch, dinner. Average main course: $11.*

★ ☺ BYOB **Al Khayameih** It gets overlooked among the many Middle Eastern restaurants that dot Kedzie Avenue, but the exceptionally fresh fare puts this Lebanese spot at the head of its class. Pita bread makes for a soft, warm utensil to scoop up *moutabal*, a spread of eggplant mashed with onions and peppers. *Kibbeh* is made to order and is one of the least greasy and most flavorful versions in the city. Best of all, unlike its popular neighbors, there's never a long wait to get inside. *4748 N Kedzie Ave between Leland and Lawrence Aves (773-583-0999). El: Brown to Kedzie. Bus: 81. Breakfast, lunch, dinner. Average main course: $10.*

▼ ☺ B **Al-Amal Grocery & Bakery** The Southwest Side's Middle Eastern expats know to head for this Bridgeview grocery for its solid meat counter and impressive assortment of locally-baked pitas, some made in-house and others sourced from reputable bakeries nearby. The evidence is found in breads still warm in the package—our favorite are sprinkled with *za'atar*, a zesty mix of sesame seeds and herbs. *7289 W 87th St, Bridgeview (708-237-2625). Pace: 385, 386. 9am–11pm daily. Average baked good: $3.*

▼ ◊ (**Alhambra Palace** This opulent, 24,000-square-foot multiroom space serves a limited menu of kebabs, hummus, lentil soup and a few tagines. Everything is cooked appropriately, but it all needs a bit more salt

BYOB Tip: *Middle Eastern*

Wine: *Sauvignon blanc or cabernet blend*

Sprightly sauvignons heighten the bright flavors in tabouli and herbaceous spinach pies, while dusty cabernet blends (especially those with grenache) hold up to meaty kebabs perfectly.

Beer: *American blond ale or English porter*

For falafel, hummus and citrusy salads, keep the beer just as crisp and clean with an American blond ale. But to play up grilled-meat flavors, match them with English porter's roasted malts.

Buy it at Binny's Beverage Depot (3000 N Clark St, 773-935-9400) then **bring it** to Fattoush (this page).

Buy it at West Lakeview Liquors (2156 W Addison St, 773-525-1916) then **bring it** to Café Orchid (this page).

Buy it at Rogers Park Fine Wine & Spirits (6733 N Clark St, 773-761-1906) then **bring it** to Masouleh (p.103).

or other flavor enhancers. Still, it's worth it to go once, if only to gawk at the amazing tile work, fabrics and weekend belly dancers–who are more than happy to let you get a good look. *1240 W Randolph St between Racine Ave and Elizabeth St (312-666-9555). El: Green, Pink to Ashland. Bus: 20. Lunch, dinner. Average main course: $24.*

▼ **Alma Pita** At this cheerful mom-and-pop decorated with photos of the nearby Uptown Theater, there's a little cognitive dissonance in seeing standard Lebanese items offered side by side with Indian curry specials. But go with the flow and you'll see the charms of washing your falafel down with a housemade blueberry lassi. Vegetarians fare especially well here, as the falafel are fresh and brightly spiced, the dolmas are tart, and there's a meatless special each day (usually a simple stew or curry). Carnivores with light wallets will appreciate chicken kebab sandwiches, and *kifta* are easy to like at such modest prices, too. *4600 N Magnolia Ave, suite F, at Wilson Ave (773-561-2787). El: Red to Wilson. Bus: 22, 145, 148. Lunch, dinner. Average main course: $9.*

▼ ♦ ✳ (**Andies Restaurant** Andersonville's *other* Mediterranean spot (located next door to its competition, Reza's) heavily touts the health benefits of its food. But you're likely to stuff yourself so silly that those benefits will be canceled out. The gluttony starts with complimentary rounds of warm, thick pita and incredible, select daily wine specials. Continue with the aromatic Moroccan chicken buried under toothsome couscous and juicy kebabs (the *kefta* is particularly tender). Don't stop until the last spoonful of Tunisian housemade rice pudding is gone. *5253 N Clark St between Berwyn and Farragut Aves (773-784-8616). Bus: 22, 92. Lunch, dinner. Average main course: $11.* ● *Other location: 1467 W Montrose Ave (773-348-0654).*

◉ (**Baba Pita** Not everything on the menu is always available (our request for spinach pie was met with "How badly do you want it?"). Luckily, everything you *can* get is just as cheap and solid as the next items. Of course, there are standouts: The grilled salmon is satisfying (save for the out-of-place tartar sauce); the kebabs are delicious; and the steak, chicken and *kefta* are all succulent and tender. *1032 W Lake St at Carpenter St (312-243-3439). El: Green, Pink to Clinton. Bus: 9, 20. Lunch, dinner. Average main course: $8.* ● *Other location: 2233 N Lincoln Ave (773-549-7272).*

▼ **Baladi Restaurant** It would be easy to miss Baladi Restaurant, as it is hidden behind a pancake house in a tiny Bridgeview strip mall. But the quality of its Middle Eastern offerings would make that a shame. The classics are tastily prepared (the baba ghanoush is especially good), and the complimentary tea with dried sage might be reason enough to return. But be sure to ask what the Arabic-only specials board has to offer—on one trip we had a grilled whole chicken, accompanied by a tangy red-pepper dipping sauce, that was tender and delicious, setting off mouth-fireworks of spices and crispy charred bits. *7209 W 84th St, Bridgeview (708-233-1025). Pace: 385, 386. Breakfast, lunch, dinner. Average main course: $11.*

★ ▼ ◉ BYOB **Big Buns and Pita (Sahara Kabob)** Don't pay attention to the first half of this restaurant's name, which refers to the expendable portion of the menu devoted to American food. What you want is the *lahim beajin*, a crisp pita topped with fiery ground beef; the *burek*, an eggroll-like shell stuffed with a savory blend of meat and spices; and the simple but delicious lentil soup. Still want big buns? Continue your binge with some shawarma and falafel, and you'll be on your way. *6649 N Clark St between Wallen and North Shore Aves (773-262-2000). El: Red to Loyola. Bus: 22, 36, 151, 155. Lunch, dinner. Average main course: $7.*

▼ (**Byblos** The stage is literally set for this Middle Eastern restaurant to become a vivacious nightclub in the wee hours: Tables are arranged around a small dance floor, and instruments for a full band (drum set, etc.) are on display. Yet the food is no afterthought. Care is obviously taken with the meze, which includes a piquant eggplant salad, herbaceous tabouli and golden cheese *borek*. Entrées like the *chilifried* (a spicy lamb stew) and the grilled quail are slightly less successful. But don't worry: If you don't feel like singing the food's praises, one of the band members soon will. *2639 W Peterson Ave between Talman and Washtenaw Aves (773-989-0500). Bus: 11, 49B, 84. Lunch, dinner. Average main course: $12.*

★ ▼ ✳ BYOB **Café Orchid** The Middle Eastern crowd at this Turkish spot should tip you off that it isn't another watered-down outlet for hummus and pita chips. If you aren't convinced, the menu reveals its authenticity. It's filled with Turkish dishes that are largely unfamiliar in these parts, such as *balik sarma*, grape leaves stuffed with sardines and crisped around the edges for an aggressively flavorful, crispy starter;

cig borek, a savory, deep-fried pastry stuffed with ground lamb; and *manti*, dumpling-like "Turkish ravioli" stuffed with more lamb and topped with a garlic-yogurt sauce. *1746 W Addison St at Hermitage Ave (773-327-3808). Bus: 9, 11, 50, 152. Lunch (Mon–Sat), dinner. Average main course: $11.*

◉ **Cedars Mediterranean Kitchen** Cedars' falafel, hummus, baba ghanoush, lentil soup—pretty much everything that goes with its delicious, warm pita bread—have us hooked. We could fill up on appetizers and salads here, but should you venture into the entrées, be prepared for huge portions and bring friends. The family-style special for parties of four or more gets you ten dishes for dinner ($15.50 per person) and seven for lunch ($12.95). Service can be unpredictable, but the potent house coffee and three kinds of baklava (traditional, pistachio or walnut) will help you to overlook it. *1206 E 53rd St at Woodlawn Ave (773-324-6227). Bus: 2, 6, 15, 28, 55, X55, 171, 172. Lunch, dinner. Average main course: $11.*

▼ ◉ **Chickpea** *2009 Eat Out Award, Readers' Choice: Best New Middle Eastern* Some regulars hit this casual, snazzy little Middle Eastern spot for the hummus and the baba, which is all merely fine. What's special is the *kibbeh*, with its delicate, thin layer of bulgur encasing cinnamon-dusted ground beef and pine nuts. And the lamb pie, packed with sweet onions. And the lamb kebabs, rubbed with salt and ridiculously tender. This is food that has clearly been cared for by chef Amni Suqi (owner Jerry Suqi's mother). In fact, if you find the matriarch on the right night, she'll pull up a chair and explain how much she cares for it herself. *2018 W Chicago Ave between Damen and Hoyne Aves (773-384-9930). Bus: 50, 66, 70. lunch, Dinner. Average main course: $8.*

★ ◉ BYOB **Couscous House** At this Algerian addition to Lawrence Avenue, the falafel cracks open to reveal soft, warm, fluffy middles, and the lamb shank arrives falling apart on a pile of couscous. But we found that the best items weren't even on the menu: Ask for a cup of the magnificent green tea spiked with mint, which provides a delicious interplay of sweet and bitter, and the juicy Cornish hen tagine, spiced with a pinch of paprika. *4624 W Lawrence Ave at Kentucky Ave (773-777-9801). Bus: 53, 54, 81. Lunch (closed Fri), dinner. Average main course: $11.*

▼ BYOB **Cousin's I.V.** See Vegetarian for review.

◉ (BYOB **Dawali** This spot, with its counter setup and self-serve soda fountain, has a slightly McMediterranean feel to it. Thankfully, that ends when the food is brought out. Avoid the pedestrian hummus; instead, dredge your pita through refreshing cucumber yogurt salad or the *galaya*, a simmering skillet of lamb-and-tomato stew. Or skip pita altogether and get your carb fix with a warm lamb pie. Whatever you do, you'll be washing it down with soda unless you think ahead to pick up a bottle of wine. *4911 N Kedzie Ave between Ainslie and Argyle Sts (773-267-4200). El: Brown to Kedzie. Bus: 81, 92, 93. Lunch, dinner. Average main course: $9.*

▼ **Elshafei Pastries** It's quite difficult to resist the tantalizing smells of baklava and other Middle Eastern treats that drift from this friendly little bakery on the Burbank side of Harlem. Make like the locals and stock up—this stuff keeps well, and it's perfect to have on hand for surprise guests or an impromptu picnic. *8511 S Harlem Ave, Burbank (708-237-9200). Pace: 385, 386. 9:30am–8pm daily. Average baked good: $4.*

★ ▽ **BYOB Fattoush** This spic-and-span dining room is full of tables dressed with blinding white linens that are, most of the time, empty. But don't let that give you pause. The *meze* we tried—a creamy bowl of hummus, a steaming spinach pie and the crunchy, eponymous salad—were all potent with sharp, tangy lemon juice, while the aromatic *kibbeh* was packed with cinnamon. The kebabs are more like thin steaks than cubes, but juicy nonetheless. Still, we'd rather save room for the three kinds of sticky, flaky baklava. If the owner were looking for advice on how to get butts in chairs, he should start by handing samples of these sweets out on the sidewalk. *2652 N Halsted St between Wrightwood and Schubert Aves (773-327-2652). El: Brown, Purple (rush hrs) to Diversey. Bus: 8, 76. Lunch, dinner (closed Tue). Average main course: $12.*

★ ⊙ **BYOB Masouleh** This place gives other Persian spots in town a run for their money. To get a sense of its fresh ingredients, start your meal off with the *mast-o khiar*, mint and cucumber in a housemade yogurt, or the *olovieh*, a delicious chicken-and-potato spread. Then, move on to try the juicy Masouleh (ground beef) kebab and the *khoureshte gheimeh bademjan*, a succulent eggplant and steak stew. By the end, you'll know what real Persian food tastes like, so you'll never want to eat that other Persian stuff again. *6653 N Clark St between Wallen and North Shore Aves (773-262-2227). El: Red to Loyola. Bus: 22, 151, 155. Lunch (Sat, Sun), dinner (closed Mon). Average main course: $8.*

★ ▽ ◖ **Maza** We're usually too busy stuffing our mouths with this tasty Middle Eastern grub to talk. If we could, we'd tell you that the *foul moudammas* are warm fava beans simmered in mouth-puckering herbs, lemon juice and olive oil. We'd tell you that the crispy, salty, juicy whole red snapper has addictive powers. And we'd tell you that the dining room is warm and romantic and that you shouldn't leave it until you've had the flaky, buttery, housemade baklava, made on the premises nightly. *2748 N Lincoln Ave between Schubert Ave and Diversey Pkwy (773-929-9600). El: Brown, Purple (rush hours) to Diversey. Bus: 11, 76. Dinner. Average main course: $14.*

▽ ⊙ ✳ **Mizrahi Grill** See Kosher for review.

▽ **Nablus Sweets** This Palestinian-owned bakery in Bridgeview has baklava and the other sticky-sweet treats you expect packaged to go, but the real draw here is up by the counter: a pan of warm cheese oozing out from under a layer of circus-peanut-orange crispies. This is *knafeh*, sort of a cross between a deep-dish pizza and a cheese blintz, white cheese and saffron-colored shredded wheat topped with crushed pistachios and doused with sweet syrup. As rich as it is, you probably won't make it through a whole portion, but on weekends the locals line up and consume it like hotcakes at the bakery's few tables. *8320 S Harlem Ave, Bridgeview (708-529-3911). Pace: 385, 386.*

Side dish

ALL SMILES Sammy Elmajami welcomes you to Village Pita with his freshly baked breads.

Taste Quest: Bridgeview

In a Southwest village, a Middle Eastern enclave of food and family thrives.

If you know where Bridgeview is, you either grew up in the South Suburbs or you have Chicago Fire tickets. Located straight south of Chicago's western edge, it hardly looks like an Arabian Nights idyll at first glance. But as the commercial and religious center for the South Side Arab community, it's Chicago's mecca for the tastiest Middle Eastern cuisine.

Two strip malls on 87th Street just west of Harlem anchor the Arab community; start at the one on the south side, where **Al-Amal Grocery & Bakery** (p.101) offers a wide variety of freshly baked pitas and other breads, often still warm in the package, and spices like the all-purpose *za'atar*, a zesty mix of sesame seeds and herbs.

Save your appetite for across the street. **Village Pita & Bakery** (p.105) is an impeccably tidy shop selling freshly baked spinach pies, za'atar-covered flatbreads and other healthy, satisfying baked items. If you like spicy, go for the *mohamora*, a paste of red peppers, walnuts and pomegranate molasses; for sheer comfort food, don't miss the potato triangles.

It may be hard to imagine how you could turn an old Arby's into a pasha's pleasure den, but that's pretty much what **Al Bawadi Grill** (p.101) has done. The over-the-top decor is matched by the superb hand with wood-grilled meats in the kitchen, producing kebabs, chicken and (unusual for a Middle Eastern restaurant) seafood with perfect juiciness and char flavor. Veggie items—psychedelically bright green

falafel, tart fattoush salad, smoky baba ghanoush—also popped with an uncommon brightness of flavor, though the tastiest thing of all might have been a freebie: the complimentary garlicky eggplant dip that started the meal.

Heading north on Harlem, it would be easy to miss **Baladi Restaurant** (p.102), hidden behind a pancake house in a tiny strip mall. Again, the classics are tastily prepared (the baba ghanoush is especially good), and the complimentary tea with dried sage might be reason enough to return. But be sure to ask what the Arabic-only specials board has to offer—on one trip the inquiry was met with a grilled whole chicken, accompanied by a tangy red-pepper dipping sauce, that was tender and delicious, with spiced and crispy charred bits.

A feast like this must conclude with sticky, honey-filled Middle Eastern sweets, and **Elshafei Pastries** (p.102), on the Burbank side of the street, lures with the smell of baklava and assorted pistachio-filled treats baking daily. But for something a little less common, go into **Nablus Sweets** (this page) and point to the tray of circus-peanut-orange crispies layered with cheese. This is *knafeh*, saffron-colored shredded wheat and white cheese topped with crushed pistachios and doused with syrup. As rich as it is, you probably won't make it through a whole portion, but on weekends locals line up and consume it like hotcakes. As well as they know their food down here, you should trust them on this one.—*Mike Gebert*

Nesh A fast-food joint that claims it's dedicated to "freshness" is one thing. A fast-food joint that proves it is another. Nesh bakes its own pita, and the soft, warm bread heightens everything put into it: smoky baba ghanoush, fried-to-order falafel—even the somewhat dry chicken shawarma benefits. Another housebaked bread the kitchen calls "shrock" (a flatbread used for wraps) is slightly less delicious than the pita. But for such fresh food at such cheap prices, it's hard to complain. *734 W Fullerton Pkwy between Burling and Halsted Sts (773-975-6374). El: Brown, Purple (rush hrs), Red to Fullerton. Bus: 8, 11, 74. Lunch, dinner. Average main course: $6.*

★ **The Nile** Unless you're lucky enough to have a grandparent sitting at home frying up fresh batches of falafel, this may be the freshest Middle Eastern food you'll find in Chicago. The refrigerated case is filled with rows of plump, glistening, marinated chicken and just-formed *kefta* kebabs waiting to be grilled-to-order. Freshly baked savory pies, bursting with spinach and big chunks of onion, sit on the counter. Behind that, a man drops falafel into a pool of bubbling oil. We don't care who your grandma is—she's not making anything like this. *3259 W 63rd St between Kedzie and Spaulding Aves (773-434-7218). Bus: 52, 63, 67. Lunch, dinner. Average main course: $5.* ● *Other location: 7333 W 87th St, Bridgeview (708-237-0767).*

Noon O Kabab If the city were flooded with Persian joints tomorrow, this spot would still be packed. There's something about the casual room brightened with colorful tile murals, the smoky baba ghanoush, the cinnamon-and-tomato–braised lamb shank and those kebabs—mmm, the kebabs. Marinated filet cubes, tender chicken breast hunks and oniony ground beef wrapped around skewers and charred outside but still juicy inside, plopped down on fluffiest rice alongside charbroiled tomatoes and onions. A cup of Persian tea to follow, and we're in heaven. *4661 N Kedzie Ave between Eastwood and Leland Aves (773-279-8899). El: Brown to Kedzie. Bus: 81. Lunch, dinner. Average main course: $12.* ● *Other location: 4651 N Kedzie Ave (same phone number).*

Pars Cove Suckers for free food eat well at this family-run Persian spot: Order the village salad of tomato, cucumber, pepper, stuffed grape leaves, basil, olives and feta and you'll also get a bowl of lentil soup. Choose entrées such as the baby lamb shank simmered in walnut-pomegranate sauce or the lemon-honey chicken breast with currants, and you'll not only get soup but a perfectly dressed house salad as well. And the vanilla ice cream topped with honey and cinnamon? You won't find that on your check, either. *435 W Diversey Pkwy between Pine Grove Ave and Sheridan Rd (773-549-1515). El: Brown, Purple (rush hrs) to Diversey. Bus: 22, 36, 76, 151, 156. Lunch, dinner. Average main course: $13.*

Pita Kabab There's not a whole lot to look at in this sparse dining room, but here's one thing worth noting: the raw kebabs, rife with fresh herbs and black pepper, sitting in the refrigerated case below the cash register. It's the freshness of these kebabs (particularly the juicy chicken), placed on the charcoal grill to order, that makes this place stand out from other Middle Eastern spots in town. (The perfectly seasoned beef shawarma and the bright and smoky baba ghanoush don't hurt, either.) *5701 N California Ave at Lincoln Ave (773-271-*

2771). Bus: 11, 84, 93. Lunch, dinner. Average main course: $10.

Pomegranate This sparse Middle Eastern cafeteria has a rich history behind its deep-red walls: Owner Rashad Moughrabi has been in the restaurant business since the 1970s. He's been serving his signature "steak in a sack" all the while, and the sandwich still holds up, with thin, juicy slivers of steak and caramelized onions piled into a pita with diced tomatoes. Other menu highlights include creamy hummus and nicely grilled chicken shawarma with tahini sauce. *1633 Orrington Ave, Evanston (847-475-6002). El: Purple to Davis. Lunch, dinner. Average main course: $7.*

Raw Bar See Seafood for review.

Reza's When a restaurant is so big it practically takes up the whole block, and the menu's as big as a book, there's bound to be a few blunders. But if you stick to the basics here, you'll be happy. The *kashkeh bodemjan* blends eggplant with sweet, caramelized onions, garlic and mint for an addictive spread. The chicken *koubideh* is a delicious, herbal kebab, and the *fattoush* is full of clean, sharp flavors. Skip the tray of mass-produced cakes, and go for the housemade baklava and Turkish coffee to finish the meal. *432 W Ontario St between Orleans and Kingsbury Sts (312-664-4500). El: Brown, Purple (rush hrs) to Chicago. Bus: 22, 65. Lunch, dinner. Average main course: $15.* ● *Other location: 5255 N Clark St (773-561-1898).*

★ **Salam** First of all, there's the 21-cent falafel with a crisp, browned crust that cracks open to reveal a fluffy green center. But a trip to this dingy storefront wouldn't be complete without also trying a bowl of *mossabaha*, hummus studded with whole chickpeas and pools of olive oil, or a plate of the rich beef shawarma. Daily specials, such as Wednesday's stuffed lamb, typically run out around lunchtime, so if you want some, you'll need to take the day off. Trust us, it's worth a vacation day. *4636 N Kedzie Ave between Eastwood and Leland Aves (773-583-0776). El: Brown to Kedzie. Bus: 78, 81. Breakfast, lunch, dinner. Average main course: $8.*

Sayat Nova It may be a magnificent mile for shopping, but when it comes to dinner, Michigan Avenue often disappoints. If you're looking for something other than burgers and Italian, head for the only Armenian restaurant in town. Sink into a booth in one of the room's dim corners, and recharge with flaky spinach-stuffed phyllo triangles (called *boereg*) and flavorful kebabs. The lone server can make the experience slow, but that's nothing the *mahalabeya*—a creamy milk pudding topped with walnuts and lemon syrup—can't make you forget. *157 E Ohio St between St. Clair St and Michigan Ave (312-644-9159). El: Red to Grand. Bus: 2, 3, 10, 26, 125, 143, 144, 145, 146, 147, 148, 151, 157. Lunch (Mon–Sat), dinner. Average main course: $13.*

★ **Semiramis** On a sunny day, this Lebanese café is warm and full of light. On darker days, the food provides such pleasures. The *fattoush* salad provides forkfuls of bright, tart flavors, and the basket of warm pita begs to be slathered with *ful*—fava beans cooked with olive oil and garlic to make a tangy, spreadable paste. Sandwiches, like a chicken wrap, and tender kebabs are prepared skillfully,

and everything benefits from a slather of the housemade garlic sauce, *toum*. Pair the *mamoul* cookies with a cup of rich cardamom-laced coffee. *4639 N Kedzie Ave between Eastwood and Leland Aves (773-279-8900). El: Brown to Kedzie. Bus: 78, 81. Lunch, dinner (closed Sun). Average main course: $13.*

BYOB **Shiraz** If the chandeliers and Persian rug–upholstered banquettes in this dining room don't make you swoon, just wait. Soon you'll swoon over the focaccia-like bread with a block of crumbly feta cheese, tart pickles and ripe tomatoes. Enjoy, but don't go too crazy—you'll want to leave room for the *kashk-e-bademjan*, a soft, savory eggplant puree with an underlying tang of yogurt; the *sotani*, juicy prime-rib kebab alongside another kebab of ground beef, lamb and veal; and the *gormeh sabzi*, a sprightly beef stew full of mouth-puckering herbs and lime. *4425 W Montrose Ave between Kenneth and Kostner Aves (773-777-7275). El: Blue to Montrose. Bus: 53, X54, 78. Lunch (Sat, Sun), dinner (closed Mon). Average main course: $11.*

Sultan's Market Sultan's is a good metaphor for Wicker Park's gentrification. What was once a mom-and-pop Middle Eastern grocery with a lunch counter in the back has exploded into a slick eatery in the last 15 years or so. But don't let the shiny digs, a fancier menu or the cute boys behind the counter distract you: You're here for the fresh salad bar, the *zatter fattia* (two spice-rubbed slabs of bread filled with feta cheese and hummus or baba ghanoush) and, of course, the falafel sandwich (a pita bursting with crispy-fried chickpea balls and Jerusalem salad). *2057 W North Ave at Hoyne St (773-235-3072). El: Blue to Damen. Bus: 50, 56, 72. Lunch, dinner. Average main course: $4.* ● *Other location: 2521 N Clark St (312-638-9151).*

B BYOB **Taboun Grill** See Kosher for review.

Tizi Melloul The Moroccan-themed, Suhail-designed space that was deemed *the* date destination upon opening in '99 is still warm, cozy and lush—exactly how you'll feel after downing one of its potent cocktails. Take it easy: You're going to want to remember the simple, warm, flaky feta crisps and the cinnamon-kissed currants and almonds in the vaguely sweet, mostly savory chicken *bisteeya*. The lantern-filled "crescent room" is tête-à-tête–perfect any night; on Sundays you'll encounter belly dancers. A few of those cocktails, and you may do a little swiveling yourself. *531 N Wells St at Grand Ave (312-670-4338). El: Red to Grand. Bus: 65, 125. Dinner. Average main course: $18.*

★ BYOB **Turkish Cuisine and Bakery** Typically we try not to fill up on bread before our food arrives, but at this comfortable Middle Eastern joint, that's impossible to do. When the basket of housemade bread arrives, we go through it in hyperspeed, slathering slices with the smooth baba ghanoush and creamy, yogurt-based *cacik*. From there it's on to the savory pies stuffed with cheese and eggs. We might take a break with the chicken-thigh kebabs, but soon it's back to the baked goods as we inhale baklava for an ideal ending, maybe even taking some home for tomorrow's breakfast. *5605 N Clark St between Bryn Mawr and Olive Aves (773-878-8930). El: Red to Bryn Mawr. Bus: 22, 50. Lunch, dinner. Average main course: $9.*

ARABIAN NIGHT A glowing Al Bawadi Grill beckons like an oasis of authentic Middle Eastern eats on the Southwest Side.

▼ ✳ **B** **Turquoise Café** We can't rave enough about this stylish Turkish spot. We wolf down the *manti* (Turkish ravioli stuffed with bits of lamb in a creamy yogurt–and–chile oil sauce), whole slabs of juicy, salt-crusted sea bass and some of the best hummus around. Savvy regulars skip the filling entrées to fuel up on apps and sides like fried zucchini pancakes with yogurt dip and char-grilled calamari with diced tomatoes and garlic. Couple these dishes with homemade sesame bread, and you'll have enough pocket change for a cup of Turkish tea. *2147 W Roscoe St between Hamilton Ave and Leavitt St (773-549-3523). El: Brown to Paulina. Bus: 49, X49, 50, 77, 152. Brunch (Sun), lunch, dinner. Average main course: $16.*

☻ **Uncle's Kabob** The well-seasoned and sumptuous kebabs are indeed worthy of the restaurant's name, but they're even better when taken off the stick and put into a sandwich. The fluffy white rolls are soft but sturdy carriers for the juicy chicken kebab, and the pickled cabbage that tops it off is almost as addictive as the chicken itself. Grilled *kibbeh* (flat and sandwich-like here, not egg-shaped as it is normally found) is a hearty side to add on; the "potato chops," golden discs of potato stuffed with ground beef, work as a side, too—though eat enough of them and they're an entire meal themselves. *2816 W Devon Ave between California Ave and Mozart St (773-338-3134). Bus: 49B, 93, 155. Lunch, dinner. Average main course: $8.*

▼ ✳ **Village Pita and Bakery** This impeccably tidy Bridgeview takeout counter specializes in freshly-baked spinach pies, *za'atar*-covered flatbreads and other satisfying Middle Eastern classics. If you like spicy, go for the eggplant-schmeared *mohamaras*; for sheer comfort food, don't miss the potato triangles. Stock up, they'll go fast and they're cheap. And as the owner implores customers (with the concern of the true artisan for his wares), reheat on a cookie sheet—never microwave! *7378 W 87th St, Bridgeview (708-237-0020). Pace: 385, 386. 9am–6pm daily. Average baked good $2.*

★ ▼ ✳ **Zad** The menu at this Middle Eastern spot doesn't contain anything you haven't tried before—there's the usual assortment of falafel, hummus and kebabs. The surprise comes when you taste the bright, fresh flavors in these dishes that can be ho hum elsewhere. The appetizer combo for two is the best place to start—the enormous platter of smoky baba ghanoush, greaseless falafel, creamy hummus and dolmas easily makes a meal. But save room for the shawarma—both the chicken and lamb/beef varieties of marinated, rotisserie-cooked meat had us planning a return visit. *3112 N Broadway between Briar Pl and Barry Ave (773-404-3473). El: Red, Brown, Purple (rush hrs) to Belmont. Bus: 8, 22, 36, 76, 77, 145, 146. Lunch, dinner. Average main course: $11.*

Pan-Asian

PICK UP STICKS At Urban Belly, there's more than just noodles worth slurping from your bowl.

▼ ⊙ **BYOB Angin Mamiri** Looking to try Indonesian food? This friendly West Rogers Park BYOB is your only option in town, but the lack of competition doesn't mean the Rukli family that runs it is slacking. For a whirlwind tour of Indonesia's greatest hits, start with *gado-gado*, a salad of watercress, snappy green beans, carrot slivers, boiled eggs and tofu squares, doused with peanut sauce and meant to be piled onto *krupuk*, crunchy shrimp-rice flour crackers. Move on to the lamb or beef satays, juicy and full-flavored. Finish up with *es teler*, a parfait of avocado, young coconut, jackfruit and shaved ice, and grab a bag of savory peanut brittle for the trip home. *2739 W Touhy Ave between California and Washtenaw Aves (773-262-6646). Bus: 49B, 93, 96. Lunch, dinner. Average main course: $8.*

▼ **Big Bowl** Thanks to homemade dishes that incorporate freshly roasted peanuts, fiery blistered chilies and made-to-order sauces, this LEYE Pan-Asian spot continues to pack them in. In addition to riffs on authentic favorites such as Mongolian beef and shrimp Thai curries, you'll find Niman Ranch pork in the fried rice and even some local produce that has found its way onto the stir-fry bar. With an eye for details, it's no wonder that even the ginger ale is made from scratch. (Tip: it's even better with a shot of Hendrick's gin and splash of pomegranate juice.) *6 E Cedar St at Rush St (312-640-8888). El: Red to Clark/Division. Bus: 22, 36, 70. Lunch, dinner. Average main course: $12. ● Other locations: 60 E Ohio St (312-951-1888); 215 Parkway Dr, Lincolnshire (847-808-8880); 1950 E Higgins Rd, Schaumburg (847-527-8881).*

⊙ ✳ **BYOB Butterfly** Thailand native Apidech Chotsuwan used to own Bangkok Thai, but after a trip to Japan, he sold his stake to ready this half-Thai, half-Japanese restaurant. Chotsuwan trained the Thai chef to handle standards from noodles to curries, while he mans the sushi bar, serving up nigiri and maki as well as teriyaki and katsu for fans of cooked Japanese fare. In homage to his favorite butterfly hues, Chotsuwan decked out the space in an orange-and-black color scheme. *1156 W Grand Ave between May St and Racine Ave (312-563-5555). El: Blue to Grand. Bus: 8, 9, X9, 65. Lunch, dinner. Average main course: $8. ● Other location: 1421 W Chicago Ave (312-492-9955).*

▼ ✳ ☾ **B Chant** We like this Zen-oriented spot for its large menu, hip interior and full-service bar. The world tour of dishes wouldn't be complete without its take on standard drunken noodles: angel hair pasta and vegetables soaked in Thai basil-jalapeño oil. Other culture-confused items include honey chipotle wings and roasted red pepper and Thai basil hummus, but the curried chicken stays true to form with spicy red curry coconut cream sauce over jasmine rice. *1509 E 53rd St at Harper Ave (773-324-1999). Bus: 6, 28, 55, X55, 171. Metra: Elec Main to 55th-56th-57th. Lunch, brunch (Sundays) dinner. Average main course: $12.*

▼ **BYOB dib** This upscale spot on a shady strip of Uptown sticks out like a sore thumb. It's just as chipper inside as it is on the surface, with the decor and music keeping things lively. Starters like grilled avocado salad with minced spicy tuna are tasty and stylish. Creative maki include a *tom yum* roll made with shrimp paste and topped with ponzu sauce, and a crispy shellfish roll. You'll find an array of Thai noodle dishes, but your best bets are from the sushi bar. *1025 W Lawrence Ave at Kenmore Ave (773-561-0200). El: Red to Lawrence. Bus: 36, 81, 151. Lunch, dinner. Average nigiri: $2.50.*

▼ **BYOB Grande Noodles and Sushi Bar** Rogers Parkers craving everyday, affordable Asian opt for this adorable lavender-and-orange storefront. From the Thai portion of the menu, go with the heat-packed panang curry. Of the Japanese options, the nigiri cuts are generous and fresh, and the maki are standard yet tasty. Sweet-potato maki is pimped out with green onions, cream cheese and tempura crunch, and slathered in wasabi mayo and eel sauce. Not so authentic but, oh, the creamy goodness. *6632 N Clark St at Wallen Ave (773-761-6666). El: Red to Loyola. Bus: 22, 36, 151, 155. Metra: Union Pacific North Line to Rogers Park. Lunch, dinner. Average nigiri: $2.*

★ ▼ ⊙ **BYOB Han 202** Han 202 might just be the best value in town. Twenty bucks brings five different courses, with fun and flavorful options like lemongrass beef on matchsticks of Granny Smith apples, delicate salt-and-pepper baby octopus, moist grouper peeking out from a blanket of scallions and fresh ginger, and an ending of simple vanilla ice cream with a peel-it-yourself lychee. Figure in a tasteful dining room and a BYOB policy and this place has "date night" written all over it. *605 W 31st St (312-949-1314). El: Red to Sox/35th.*

▼ ◔ ☀ BYOB Hot Woks Cool Sushi

This little BYOB does a nice job of executing most standard Anglo cravings, from crunchy egg rolls and gooey crab rangoon to jam-packed maki. Try the "Hot Woks Noodles," stir-fried spinach noodles that resemble fettuccine wok-tossed with shrimp, chicken and jalapeño peppers for heat. Like the Akira roll (tuna, salmon, spicy mayo, ginger and avocado rolled in crunchy tempura flakes), it might not open any rabbit holes for the authenticity police, but it's definitely tasty. 3930 N Pulaski Rd at Dakin St (773-282-1818). El: Blue to Irving Park. Bus: 53, 80, X80. Lunch, dinner. Average main course: $7.

▼ BYOB Indie Café

This small BYOB Thai-Japanese spot in Edgewater serves artfully prepared dishes that stand out from typical neighborhood Asian. Gems include the signature Indie curry made with lemongrass, coriander and garlic; a heat-packing chicken- and prawn-studded smoked chile combo; and "Metallica" maki made with scallops, spicy mayo and black tobiko. If the slightly steep prices are off-putting, try lunch, when a bento box comes with a California roll, miso soup and salad for around $12. 5951 N Broadway between Thorndale and Elmdale Aves (773-561-5577). El: Red to Thorndale. Bus: 36, 147, 151. Lunch, dinner (closed Mon). Average main course: $11.

◔ Joy Yee's Noodles

The Joy Yee miniempire continues to pack in everyone from students to office stiffs who loosen up with platter-size portions of pan-Asian food. The menu's less adventurous than its Chinatown outpost, but we still stop in for mussels with black-bean sauce, garlicky chicken with string beans and gargantuan bowls of udon-noodle soup. And it wouldn't seem right to leave without a bubble tea from the spot that claims to have introduced it to Chicagoland. 2139 S China Place (312-328-0001). El: Red to Cermak/Chinatown. Bus: 21, 24. Lunch, dinner. Average main course: $9.

◔ Lulu's

The dim sum's not really dim sum (dishes are too big and too expensive), but some items, like the moist, golden bao (buns)—essentially char siu pork doughnuts—and the one-dimensional but tasty sesame noodles make good appetizers. The toothsome Mongolian pork stir fry is sweet but not cloying, spicy but not hot. But forget about the blah salads and desserts—we'd have preferred a fortune cookie instead. 804 Davis St, Evanston (847-869-4343). El: Purple to Davis. Bus: 93, 205, Pace 208, Pace 212, Pace 213. Lunch, dinner. Average main course: $9.50.

◔ Mariegold Bakery and Fast Food

This family-run Filipino market has managed to cram a full-blown bakery, an imported goods section and a sprawling buffet into a space the size of a large studio apartment. Take your plate of lechon (fried suckling pig) or kare-kare (oxtail with peanut sauce) to one of the utilitarian tables by the window and watch as what seems like the whole of Chicago's Filipino community stops in for pastry and a bit of local gossip. 5752 N California Ave between Lincoln and Ardmore Aves (773-561-1978). Bus: 11, 84, 93. Breakfast, lunch, dinner. Average main course: $8.

◔ BYOB Miss Asia

This elegant Pan-Asian BYOB sports a menu that would send

most cooks running: Malaysia, Singapore, Cambodia, India, China, the Philippines, Korea, Japan, Laos, Vietnam, Indonesia, Nepal and Mongolia each get a half dozen dishes, while Thailand is represented with nearly 100. For a memorable meal, hop around the map, we safely suggest to order across the board…again and again. 434 W Diversey Pkwy between Sheridan Rd and Pine Grove Ave (773-248-3999). El: Brown to Diversey. Bus: 22, 36, 76, 151, 156. Lunch, dinner. Average main course: $9.

▼ ☀ ◖ Niu Japanese Fusion Lounge

A sushi restaurant that serves Taittinger Champagne by the glass obviously aims for a sophisticated clientele. And since it's on East Illinois Street, that's exactly who it's getting. High-rise dwellers and moviegoers fill the dark, comfortable space and settle in for the lengthy process of reading the massive menu. Most of the sushi classics are fresh and tasty but overpriced. You'd do better with the creative concoctions from the "Fusion" portion of the menu, like quick-seared tuna topped with tart green apple and sesame ponzu, or the shishito peppers stuffed with cream cheese and crab and scallop meat. 332 E Illinois St between New St and Park Dr (312-527-2888). El: Red to Grand. Bus: 2, 29, 65, 66, 124. Lunch (Mon–Fri), dinner. Average main course: $12.

▼ ◖ BYOB Oh Fusion

See Japanese and Sushi for review.

▼ ◔ ☀ Papajin

It's slim pickings for Chinese-food lovers in this neighborhood, which may be why Papajin hasn't gone the way of Filter or Sweet Thang. That's not to knock on the food. The part-Chinese, part-Japanese menu covers the basics (hi there, General Tsao) just fine, and we were pleasantly surprised by the white cliff maki (a shrimp tempura roll with a creamy avocado-mayo topping). During the summer, nab a sidewalk table, order a Kirin and let the people-watching begin. 1551 N Milwaukee Ave between Honore St and North Ave (773-384-9600). El: Blue to Damen. Bus: 50, 56, 72. Dinner. Average main course: $10.

▼ ◔ ☀ BYOB Penny's Noodle Shop

Purists may scoff at the ho-hum offerings, but this long-time favorite packs in crowds who may prefer their pad si-ewe come a little more Anglofied than authentic. You'll find perfectly fine versions of standard noodle and rice dishes like lad nar (crispy wide noodles sauteed with veggies and topped with gravy) and Chinese fried rice. Vegetarians will do well with inspired sides, like watercress with garlic bean sauce and steamed broccoli with Dijon-soy dressing. 3400 N Sheffield Ave at Roscoe Ave (773-281-8222). El: Red, Brown, Purple (rush hrs) to Belmont. Bus: 22, 77. Lunch, dinner (closed Mon). Average entrée: $8. ● Other locations: 1542 N Damen Ave (773-394-0100); 950 W Diversey Pkwy (773-281-8448).

★ ◔ ☀ Ping Pong

The pan-Asian fare is just as stylish as the art-gallery–esque room, but thankfully more complex. The lettuce cups pair spicy chicken with ginger, peanuts and a spark of lime. Other delectable choices include the golden calamari and a perfectly tender sea bass in a soy-riesling sauce that was a tad too sweet. Like any good gallery opening, the wine here is free…that's because you bring it yourself. Strangely enough, Ping Pong has a bar, but the dining room is still BYO. 3322 N Broadway between Aldine Ave and Buckingham Pl (773-281-7575). El: Brown, Purple (rush

hrs), Red to Belmont. Bus: 36, 77, 152. Dinner. Average main course: $10.

▼ ☀ ◖ Red Light

The only problem at this pan-Asian West Loop stalwart is what to order. Having tried most of it, we can say we love starting with the five-spice ribs, the crispy Maine lobster mango rolls and the crunchy calamari-tangerine salad. Next, we go for the fisherman's stew (it's the miso-lobster chili broth that makes it), the five spice braised pork hash and the peanut-studded panang-beef curry, with an order of edamame stir-fried with pearl onions and cashews. 820 W Randolph St between Halsted and Green Sts (312-733-8880). El: Green, Pink to Clinton. Bus: 8, 20.. Lunch (Mon–Fri), dinner. Average main course: $20.

★ ▼ ◖ B Rodan

It's easy to dismiss Rodan as a scenester sipping spot, but the South American/Southeast Asian menu from co-owner Maripa Abella is worth a visit. Grab a window seat and start off brunch with the Vietnamese coffee with powdered sugar–topped doughnuts. Pan-Latin classics like black bean arepas and huevos rancheros are delicious, but for real savoriness, come at night for steaming bowls of Asian noodle soup for under five bucks. 1530 N Milwaukee Ave between Damen Ave and Honore St (773-276-7036). El: Blue to Damen. Bus: 50, 56, 72. Brunch (Sat, Sun), dinner. Average main course: $13.

▼ Shikago

Some might think this place has been overlooked since the chef changed over, but the packed house proves it's not the case. Chef James Okuno proves he's an expert at pho—the beefy broth is simple with a touch of star anise and heaps of tender shredded brisket. Don't bother with pseudo-fresh and flimsy maki—stick to creative combos like miso-glazed scallops over beet risotto, a standout item amid pedestrian pot stickers, crab rangoon and seaweed salad. 190 S LaSalle St at Adams St (312-781-7300). El: Brown, Orange, Pink, Purple (rush hrs) to Quincy. Lunch, dinner (closed Sat, Sun). Average main course: $17.

▼ ☀ B BYOB Shine

The folks behind this Lincoln Park spot designed a room so slick it steals the attention. However, the thick slices of yellowtail flavored in the hamachi carpaccio brings our focus back to the food, especially when we sit at the sushi bar, drooling as the chef assembles plate after plate of gleaming nigiri. The Volcano is a must with tuna, avocado and strawberry (yes, that's right) sauce, but much of the rest, like the overly subtle "honey roll," doesn't command much attention. 756 W Webster Ave at Halsted St (773-296-0101). El: Brown, Red, Purple (rush hrs) to Fullerton. Bus: 8, 11, 74. Dinner, brunch (Sun only). Average main course: $12.

★ ♨ ☀ ◖ Sunda

Go with an open mind, enjoy the people-watching, and opt for the creative signatures of the house: crispy rice nigiri topped with spicy tuna, strip steak formed into "lollipops" around lemongrass skewers, and a salad of salty, crispy-skinned duck meat, cubes of polenta-like daikon cake, frisée and fried egg. Not ready for the scene? Go for the new lunch special: $18 for a salad or soup, rice, three pieces of spicy tuna or a Cali roll and a lunch-sized entrée. 110 W Illinois St between Clark St and LaSalle (312-644-0500). El: Red to Grand; Brown, Purple (rush hrs) to Merchandise Mart. Bus: 22, 65, 156. Lunch (Mon–Fri), dinner. Average main course: $22.

◔ Sura

The Thai owners behind New York's Peep, Spice and SEA have a flair for slick and

BRIGHT BITES, BIG CITY
Sunda puts a spin on unagi nigiri by swapping out rice for cool watermelon cubes.

stylish dining rooms and cheap and tasty eats. This first Chicago outpost seems no different. Small plates of Asian-fusion creations average around five bucks a pop, making it easy to go nuts with a menu that includes coconut-crusted shrimp, duck crêpes and crispy ginger calamari. *3124 N Broadway between Barry Ave and Briar Pl (773-248-7872). El: Brown, Purple (rush hrs), Red to Belmont. Bus: 22, 36, 77. Lunch, dinner. Average small plate: $5.*

▼ ✳ ☾ B **Sushisamba Rio** Not only is this joint's plush rooftop patio with a 40-foot bar, sharp sound system, sofas and stools perfect for a nightcap (or night-starter), but it's great for sashimi as well. We're not crazy about the rice, so skip the nigiri in favor of slick cuts of the day's fresh catch. On Wednesday nights after 7:30pm, this slick spot turns into a weekly party with the smooth grooves of Bossa Tres band followed by a rotating cast of in-house DJs and danceworthy samba beats. *504 N Wells St between Illinois St and Grand Ave (312-595-2300). El: Brown, Purple (rush hrs) to Merchandise Mart. Bus: 65, 125, 156. Brunch (Sun), lunch, dinner. Average main course: $20.*

▼ ✳ **Tamarind** This South Loop spot is part slick, part casual, with soothing bamboo-decked green walls and a staff that's eager to please. The menu boasts great dishes across the board, from Chinese soup dumplings to ponzu-drizzled sashimi to Vietnamese-style grilled lemongrass beef. Generous sushi cuts are tasty and the signature duck soup is a standout, but the red curry was a bit gloopy and not as spicy as the menu warned. No matter; dozens of other dishes do the trick. *614 S Wabash Ave between Harrison and Balbo Sts (312-379-0970). El: Red to Harrison. Bus: 2, 6, 10, 29, 36, 146. Lunch, dinner. Average main course: $13.*

☺ **Tatsu** A Thai-sushi spot might seem like a welcome change of pace on a stretch of Italian red-sauce joints. And it is—just so long as you stick to the Thai food. The sushi we tried here was mediocre at best. But the chicken satay in the sampling platter was perfectly tasty. Ditto for the curry fried rice, which arrived with plump cubes of tofu. The extensive cocktail list may tempt you to end your meal with a nightcap—a fine choice, but Mario's Italian Ice is right next door. *1062 W Taylor St between Carpenter and Aberdeen Sts (312-733-8933). El:*

Blue to Racine. Bus: 7, 12, 60. Lunch (Mon–Fri), dinner. Average main course: $8.

☺ ☖ ✳ **Thalia Spice** This Pan-Asian spot boasts creative small plates and wallet-friendly lunches. Of the "Tastes from the sea" menu, the coconut shrimp and chile-spiked crab cakes stand out for their crispy texture. *Tom kha* fans should try the mussels, steamed in a broth of coconut milk, galangal and basil. From the "land" menu, the sampler is an interesting mix of flavors, with Hawaiian leaf-wrapped beef sausages and a creamy dip of ground chicken, peanuts and coconut milk. *833 W Chicago Ave at Green St (312-226-6020). Bus: 8, 66. Lunch, dinner. Average main course: $9.*

★ BYOB **Urban Belly** *2009 Eat Out Award, Critics' Pick: The Best Way to Use Your Noodle Award (chef Bill Kim's choice to leave Le Lan and open Urban Belly)* You'd think a dish called the "Urbanbelly ramen" would be this noodle bar's signature item, but the best noodle dish here is actually the rice-cake noodles. The round, chewy noodles are topped with perfectly fried chicken breast and mango. Like the rich lamb-and-brandy dumplings, it's the kind of dish you'll want to take your time with. But the crowds vying for your seat dictate that you eat your food fast and jet, so savor the food quickly or get it to go. *3053 N California Ave between Nelson St and Barry Ave (773-583-0500). El: Blue to Belmont. Bus: 52, 77, 82. Lunch, dinner (closed Mon). Average main course: $12.*

▼ ☾ **Viet Bistro and Lounge** Chef-owner Daniel Nguyen, formerly of Uptown's Pasteur, says for this spot he's "taking ideas from all over the world but using what I know about Vietnamese food." The results: specials such as the shredded duck spring roll with honey hoisin sauce, the poached chicken salad with crispy Savoy cabbage, prawn crackers and ginger dressing and a Pasteur original *bo luc lac*, juicy sautéed garlic beef served over fresh watercress. *1346–48 W Devon Ave between Wayne and Glenwood Aves (773-465-5720). Bus: 22, 36, 147, 151, 155. Dinner. Average main course: $12.*

▼ ✳ **VTK** So you want to try Thai, but you're spice-phobic or are downtown hitting tourist spots. Relax and let the servers guide you. When the crunchy Rocket Roll appetizer is delivered to your table, you're instructed to wrap lettuce leaves around it and dip it in garlic sauce. Order the panang curry noodles, and you'll be warned it's "medium spicy," but when you dig in to the giant dish of rich, creamy curry and wide rice noodles, your palate will register only a hint of heat. *6 W Hubbard St at State St (312-644-8664). El: Red to Grand. Bus: 22, 36, 65. Lunch (Mon–Sat), dinner. Average main course: $16.*

☺ **Wow Bao** Are breakfast *bao*—stuffed with egg, bacon and cheese or peppery crumbled sausage—the new Wheaties? Maybe. If you aren't ready to give up cereal just yet, there's plenty more to try at this outpost of the LEYE chain. Go with the Thai curry-chicken rice bowl with its mild, yet aromatic and complex, yellow curry. Or stick to the bao, steamed buns stuffed with slightly spicy kung pao chicken or the sweet and rich barbecue pork. *175 W Jackson Blvd at the corner of Van Buren St and Financial Pl (312-334-6395). El: Blue, Red to Jackson; Brown, Orange, Pink, Purple (rush hrs) to Quincy. Bus: 1, 7, X28, 126, 151. Mon–Fri 6:30am–6:30pm. Average main course: $3.*
● *Other locations: 1 W Wacker Dr (312-658-0305); 835 N Michigan Ave, Water Tower Place (312-642-5888).*

Polish

CABIN FEVER The Highlander owners of Szalas bring the outside in.

Andrzej Grill If you're still living at your mama's house for her home-cooked meals, then this tiny family-run Polish hideaway is for you. Navigate your way through gargantuan dishes of crispy fried potato pancakes, soft potato dumplings and pierogi, all of which are made more incredible when slathered with sour cream. (What isn't?) Pork and veal dishes rule the dinner menu, but don't miss the shaved beet salad or crêpes topped with powdered sugar. Plus, with the TV blaring and family feuds in the kitchen, you'll feel right at home. *1022 N Western Ave between Augusta Blvd and Cortez St (773-489-3566). El: Blue to Division. Bus: 49, X49, 66, 70. Lunch, dinner (closed Sun). Average main course: $8.50.*

Czerwone Jabluszko *Czerwone jabluszko* means "red apple" in Polish, and this eatery on the far northwest side of Logan Square is the apple of the eye of anyone who wants to eat from the old country. (The red apple on the sign is a handy marker.) Chow down on an all-you-can-eat buffet that fills multiple rooms (and bellies) with classics like pierogi, stuffed cabbage and carve-your own turkcy. Alternatives to the sauerkraut-style savories include crêpes and sweet pierogi. *3121 N Milwaukee Ave at Avers Ave (773-588-5781). El: Blue to Belmont. Bus: 53, 56, 77. Lunch, dinner. Average buffet plate: $10.* ● *Other location: 6474 N Milwaukee Ave (773-763-3407).*

BYOB Halina's Polish Delights This Polish staple's simple, superb soups include creamy mushroom and borscht in a teacup, delivering a blast of beet and an unexpected "egg roll" of liver paste on the side. The Polish Plate features the greatest hits of comfort foods: cabbage rolls, pork cutlet, tangy kielbasa, pierogi and dumplings. Surveying neighboring tables manned by Polish-speakers inspired us to order a delicious meaty pork shank with horseradish and sides of housemade pickles and sauerkraut. If you choose not to BYOB, sip a glass of *kompot,* a traditional Polish drink made by boiling dried fruits with sugar and water. *5914 W Lawrence Ave between Marmora and Mason Aves (773-205-0256). El: Blue to Jefferson Park. Bus: 81, 91. Lunch, dinner. Average main course: $11.*

▼ **Podhalanka** When we say that Podhalanka has an "old world" feel, we mean old world in that "premodern comforts" kind of way. Not that they don't have electricity at this dive, but it is dark and not as clean as your mother would be. What it lacks in atmosphere, it makes up for in tasty, authentic Polish eats. We love the beet salad, cabbage soup, potato pancakes and pierogis. We also love talking about the old country with the buddy on the barstool next to us. *1519 W Division St at Milwaukee Ave (773-486-6655). El: Blue to Division. Bus: 9, X9, 56, 70. Breakfast, lunch, dinner. Average main course: $14.*

⊕ ▲ **Smak-Tak Restaurant** *Smak tak* translates to "delicious, yes!" in Polish, and we're not about to disagree after sampling sauerkraut pierogi flecked with tiny pieces of mushroom, thin and crispy potato pancakes that rival our grandma's, and stuffed cabbage rolls ladled with tangy tomato sauce. It's all served up in a tiny Jefferson Park spot with a vibe that's more ski lodge than diner—just the kind of cozy place to warm up and settle in for the night as the weather turns nippy. *5961 N Elston Ave between Mason and Austin Aves (773-763-1123). Bus: 56A, 68, Pace 270. Lunch, dinner. Average main course: $10.*

⊕ **Staropolska** From the looks of it—booths, a counter/bar, coffee cups upturned on saucers—this bright, homey spot could pass for an all-American diner. Crackly skinned housemade sausage, herring (served with crisp apples in cream) and pillowy potato pierogis can be found on the "Polish plate" served in the dining room, piled together with mashed potatoes and drowned in a tomatoey sour cream sauce that's the best part of the dish. *3028 N Milwaukee Ave between Ridgeway and Lawndale Aves (773-342-0779). El: Blue to Belmont. Bus: 56, 76, 77. Breakfast, lunch, dinner. Average main course: $8.*

▲ **Szalas** Packed with kitschy decorations, this massive A-frame building is like some kind of Polish theme park, with everything from a working water wheel to a stuffed elk head. Most of the building materials and decorations were brought directly from the Polish highlands, a place that serves as the inspiration for the menu. Stick with delicious, hearty dishes like the Highlander's special (pork goulash wrapped with potato pancakes). Attempts at contemporary twists, like a Polish pizza bread with ketchup instead of tomato sauce, are downright weird. *5214 S Archer Ave between Kenneth and Kilbourn Aves (773-582-0300). El: Orange to Pulaski. Bus: 62. Lunch, dinner. Average main course: $14.*

Puerto Rican

WHAT A FLAKE Café Colao's classic guava cheese pastry brings all the *boriquas* to the yard.

★ ▾ **BYOB Borinquen** The original Borinquen (it's one of three) is also the busiest. Local Puerto Ricans and Rican food lovers alike populate this authentic spot from the time the first *café con leche* is slurped down to the minute the last *jibarito* sandwich (steak between crispy pounded plantains) is consumed. Juicy onion-flecked steak, garlic-smothered plantains, crispy empanadas, yellow rice with pigeon peas and seafood salads are found on most tables in the dining room. *1720 N California Ave between Bloomingdale and Wabansia Aves (773-227-6038). El: Blue to Western. Bus: 52, 56, 72. Lunch, dinner. Average main course: $11.* ● *Other locations: 3020 N Central Ave (773-622-8570); 3811 N Western Ave (773-442-8001).*

Café Central If you smell something delicious when you walk into this Puerto Rican diner, don't bother trying to figure out what it is. It could be any number of the greasy-spoon comfort foods that are dished up here daily: chunky, tomato-heavy goat stew or garlicky *mofongo*, savory balls of plantains studded with corn. Then again, it could be the oniony *jibaro* (dubbed "hee-ba-roe" on the English menu), a gooey cheese-steak–like sandwich that substitutes plantains for bread. So take a seat—looks as if you've got some research to do. *1437 W Chicago Ave at Bishop St (312-243-*

6776). El: Blue to Chicago. Bus: 9, 66. Breakfast, lunch, dinner. Average main course: $11.

★ ☀ **Café Colao** There are a couple of things you can count on at this Puerto Rican café: Hefty pressed sandwiches, the crusty bread stuffed with copious amounts of fillings like sweet roast pork and grilled onions; strong espresso and *café con leche*; delicious pastries, such as a tangy-sweet danish stuffed with cream cheese and guava; and a multigenerational clientele who come in to discuss the merits of the aforementioned offerings (and everything and anything else). *2638 W Division St between Rockwell St and Washtenaw Ave (773-276-1780). Bus: 49, 52, 70. Breakfast, lunch. Average main course: $7.*

★ ☀ ☾ **B Coco** If this sleek, boisterous Puerto Rican spot is representative of the island, we're booking a ticket to San Juan. The modern art, hardwood floors and 1920s bar make an ideal setting for updated classics like *lomo de cerdo* (pork chop in mango-rum sauce) and *escudo boriqua* (lamb chops in papaya sauce). Strong mojitos may fool you into thinking you can move like the locals who pour in once the band starts around 10pm on Saturdays, but you might want to look into salsa lessons at the

next-door dance studio first—these dancers are fierce. *2723 W Division St between Washtenaw and California Aves (773-384-4811). Bus: 49, X49, 52, 70. Brunch (Sun), lunch, dinner (closed Mon). Average main course: $19.*

☺ **La Cocina de Galarza** The family that runs this comfortable restaurant may assume that gringos wandering in are looking for Mexican food (and they'll cook it for you), but authentic Puerto Rican specialties are the way to go. The belly-busting *guachitos*, is a delicious off-menu request that combines fried plantain with *salchicon* (salami-like sausage) and fresh guacamole. The *mofongo* (mashed, fried plantain) is easily as good as what we've had on the island. If more exotic dishes like braised baby goat sound too risky, the tender *carne guisada* (beef stew) is just as tasty. *2420 W Fullerton Ave between Western and Artesian Aves (773-235-7377). El: Blue to California. Bus: 49, X49, 74. Lunch, dinner. Average main course: $9.*

☺ **La Esquina del Sabor** Forget lugging around your lunch in a picnic basket—this Puerto Rican lunch truck in Humboldt Park lugs it around for you. As the illustration of a happily skewered pig on the side of the truck suggests, it's all about the pork here. Pulling the meat from the bone with a pair of tongs, servers pile an enormous heap on top of fluffy yellow rice (ask for lots of skin to get as much of the delicious spice rub as you can). But not everything here comes big enough for three: Baseball-size *mofongo* (savory balls of green plantain and pork) and *mini jibarito* sandwiches (pork, rather than the traditional steak, on crispy plantains) make taking the pig to go as easy as pork pie. *The northernmost intersection of Humboldt Blvd and Luis Munoz Marin Dr (no phone). Bus: 52, 70, 72. 9am–9pm. Average main course: $5.*

☺ **B Nellie's** Large families and bleary-eyed couples fill the place on Sunday mornings for a hearty buffet of thick bacon, sausage links, oniony potatoes, and made-to-order omelettes and waffles—plus Caribbean specialties like rice flecked with pigeon peas and *tortilla boriqua*, a layered casserole of eggs, sausage, sweet plantains, cheese and green peppers. Have a glass of OJ or a cup of coffee with the sweet ending of cinnamon-spiked coconut oatmeal. *2458 W Division St between Campbell and Artesian Aves (773-252-5520). Bus: 49, X49, 52, 70. Breakfast, brunch (Sun), lunch. Average main course: $9.*

☺ **BYOB Sabor Latino** Use this casual little stalwart as your entry point into Puerto Rican food. Try a *mofongo* (a pork-filled plantain fritter) to start, move on to a *jibarito* (steak sandwich made with crispy plantains for bread), and end with the sautéed steak with onions and a side of pork-flecked beans and rice known as *arroz con gandules*. Helpful photos of dishes line one wall (soups taste better than they look) and the English-speaking counter staff is good with guidance. *3810 W North Ave between Avers and Hamlin Aves (773-227-5254). Bus: 53, 65, 72. Breakfast, lunch, dinner. Average main course: $7.*

Scandinavian

STOCKED AND LOADED
Outside of ABBA reissues, Erickson's carries the best Scandinavian exports around.

Ann Sather Ann Sather is not the best dinner, lunch or breakfast in town. It may not even be the best diner food. But that doesn't matter, because Ann Sather has the sweetest cinnamon rolls in the Midwest. If you must, you can order some "real" food—crab cakes Benedict for brunch won't disappoint, and neither will Swedish specialties, such as the roasted duck with lingonberry glaze. But let's get real: You're only after those fluffy cinnamon rolls, which arrive too big for the plate and submerged under warm icing. Lucky for you, they come with almost every order. *909 W Belmont Ave between Sheffield Ave and Clark St (773-348-2378). El: Red to Belmont. Bus: 8, 22, 77. Breakfast, lunch. Average main course: $10.* ● *Other locations: 5207 N Clark St (773-271-6677); 3411 N Broadway (773-305-0024); 3416 N Southport Ave (773-404-4475).*

Erickson's Delicatessen This Scandinavian gourmet store is a fixture not just in Andersonville, but in the Midwest as well. Open since 1925, the delicatessen is one of only a few that imports goods from the Scandinavian countries. Shoppers flock from the suburbs and the rest of the country to browse the selection of pickled herring, Swedish candies, lingonberries, *bond ost* and *västerbottensost* cheeses and the ever-popular Swedish meatballs. *5250 N Clark St Foster and Clark (773-561-5634). El: Red to Berwyn. Bus: 22, 92. Mon 10am–5pm; Tues–Fri 10am–5:30pm; Sat 10am–5pm (closed Sat).*

Svea Fancy-shmancy breakfast food—the kind with goat cheese in the omelettes and too much fruit in the pancake batter—is a bit much on mornings when we want to quietly nurse away the night before. That's when we head to this Andersonville diner, cluttered with Swedish folk art and plates packed with hearty, no-nonsense food. The Viking Breakfast—two eggs, two Swedish pancakes with lingonberry compote, *falukorv* sausage and toast—is our favorite hangover cure, but we're just as happy with rib-sticking potato pancakes or Swedish meatballs later in the day. *5236 N Clark St at Farragut Ave (773-275-7738). El: Red to Berwyn. Bus: 22, 36, 50, 92. Breakfast, lunch. Average main course: $7.*

Swedish Bakery Take a number: This always-bustling bakery, an Andersonville stalwart for more than 75 years, churns out myriad goods, such as breads including the popular cinnamon raisin and limpa loaves; a number of petit fours such as carrot, rum roll and *marzariner*—a traditional Swedish almond tart. It's well worth the wait. *5348 N Clark St between Summerdale and Balmoral Aves (773-561-8919). Bus: 22, 36, 50. Mon–Fri 6:30am–6:30pm; Sat 6:30am–5pm (closed Sun). Average baked good: $2.*

★ **Tre Kronor** The children depicted in the murals of this quaint café scare the hell out of us, so we turn to the weekend brunch of Scandinavian comfort food to ease our minds. We love the flaky Danish filled with apples and pecans, thin Swedish pancakes with lingonberry preserves and omelettes bulging with *falukorv* sausage and dill. For lunch, try the meatball sandwich, served open-faced on *limpa*—Swedish rye bread—and topped with slices of hard-boiled egg and tomato. *3258 W Foster Ave between Sawyer Ave and Spaulding Ave (773-267-9888). El: Brown to Kedzie. Bus: 81, 92, 93. Breakfast, lunch, dinner (Mon–Sat). Average main course: $7.*

Hagen's Fish Market See Seafood for review.

**INSIDE TRACK
SWEDE DREAMS**

After satisfying your lingonberry cravings at Erickson's Delicatessen (this page), venture over to the Swedish American Museum *(5211 N Clark St, 773-728-8111)*, home to art and artifacts from the 19th century, to discover how Swedish immigrants made Andersonville the Scandinavian epicenter of Chicago. The neighborhood boasts its Nordic culture with Midsommarfest and the Andersonville Farmer's Market during the warmer months, while bitter winters are the perfect time to seek shelter and a steaming cup of traditional Swedish glögg by the fireplace at Simon's Tavern (p.139).

Seafood

B **C-House** See Contemporary American for review.

Calumet Fisheries This smoke shack was born when the steel industry was thriving and the area was populated by hungry day laborers. Set at the base of the famous *Blues Brothers* bridge, this little white box is still smoking and frying up some great seafood. Customers come from all over for smoked shrimp, but leave room for the smoked fish available by special order only. You'll see folks sitting in their cars eating their picks out of paper bags, a quintessential part of the experience. *3259 E 95th St between Chicago and Ewing Aves (773-933-9855). Bus: 26. Metra: Elec Main to 93rd/South Chicago. Lunch, dinner. Average main course: $7.*

Cape Cod Room This seafood restaurant has been the flagship of the Drake Hotel's dining program since 1933. Sea-blue tablecloths, uniformed waiters and nautical paraphernalia are all proudly presented without a hint of irony, which is why it may be the only restaurant in Chicago where you can, and should, order throwback dishes like lobster Thermidor or Dover sole prepared tableside. *140 E Walton Pl at Michigan Ave (312-787-2200). El: Red to Chicago. Bus: 3, X4, 10, 26, 66, 125, 143, 144, 145, 146, 147, 151. Lunch, dinner. Average main course: $25.*

Davis Street Fishmarket It's critical to scan this restaurant's giant chalkboards for fishmonger and chef Eardley

Firth's extensive list of new arrivals from the coasts, Alaska and Lake Superior. The restaurant's faithful takes on Louisiana Cajun and breaded calabash standbys deliver, but everything from Florida is a good bet, too. The fried shrimp, the grilled Alaskan halibut and the seafood gumbo are standouts. Add the raw bar and eclectic beer selections, and it's nearly impossible to leave room. *501 Davis St, Evanston (847-869-3474). El: Purple to Davis. Bus: 93, 201, 205, Pace 208, Pace 212, Pace 250. Lunch (Tue–Sun), dinner. Average main course: $18. ● Other location: 1383 Meacham Rd, Schaumburg (847-969-1200).*

Devon Seafood Grill The dramatic space and choreographed service here are giveaways that this is a chain (from Houlihan's Inc). Luckily, the food doesn't taste like it comes from one. Seafood is flown in daily, and the fish is full-flavored. A filet of halibut gets a more elaborate treatment, served over a delicious sweet-potato hash. For the most part, the kitchen lets the food speak for itself, and it's dignified enough that you'll like what it has to say. *39 E Chicago Ave at Wabash Ave (312-440-8660). El: Red to Chicago. Bus: 3, X4, 10, 26, 66, 125, 143, 144, 145, 146, 147, 151. Lunch, dinner. Average main course: $20.*

Fish Keg Resembling a fish shack from a small coastal village in Maine, this standing-room-only institution has had more than 50 years to perfect its extensive menu. The well-stocked market has all the accoutrements you need to create a full seafood buffet. The real score here is the fresh seafood and the

breaded, fried-to-order shrimp sold by the pound in brown paper bags. Seasoned baked fish entrées help balance out the addictive hush puppies that quickly disappear. *2233 W Howard St between Ridge Blvd and Western Ave (773-262-6603). El: Red to Howard. Bus: 97, 206, 215. Breakfast, lunch, dinner. Average main course: $9.*

Fulton's on the River This Levy Restaurants spot is as much about the view as it is about the food. Fortunately, both are worth a visit. The menu—equal parts seafood and steakhouse—is nothing out of the ordinary, but everything is of exquisite quality. King crab legs from the extensive raw bar are fresh and sweet, filet mignon is tender, and the firecracker glazed shrimp are to die for. Make your trip worth the price and ask for a window seat. *315 N LaSalle St at the Chicago River (312-822-0100). El: Brown, Purple (rush hrs) to Merchandise Mart. Bus: 22, 125, 156. Lunch, dinner. Average main course: $25.*

Hagen's Fish Market This old-school fishmonger has flair that's a little bit country and a little bit Scandinavian. There's a fish counter and a small grocery featuring Scandinavian staples like *lutefisk* and herring. Indulge in deep-fried eats with juicy sea scallops, spicy popcorn shrimp, hush puppies and clam strips. Don't even try to resist the elusive deep-fried cheese curd. There's no seating inside, but there are specially designed bags to keep your fish crispy and hot until you get home. *5635 W Montrose Ave at Parkside Ave (773-283-1944). Bus: 78, 85. Lunch, dinner. Average main course: $5.*

★ ✱ **Half Shell** "We close when we feel like closing" and "Nothin' but cash, no exceptions" are among the oh-so-perfect-for-the-setting sayings we overheard in just one night at this 40-year-old, subterranean spot. Grab a table in the tiny Christmas light–strewn room, and start out with the "Mulligan stew" and an order of crispy calamari. For more fried goodness, have the "Thirty-Two Pointer" for an entrée—a crunchy pile of smelts, perch, frog legs, clam strips and fat shrimp. And if you're looking to crack some crab, splurge on the massive, meaty king legs. *676 W Diversey Pkwy between Orchard and Clark Sts (773-549-1773). El: Brown, Purple (rush hrs) to Diversey. Bus: 8, 22, 36, 76. Lunch, dinner. Average main course: $15.*

✱ **Hugo's Frog Bar** This seafood fave not only shares the kitchen of Gibson's Steakhouse but also the slick tie-and-blazer crowd. The boardroom–meets–Rat Pack decor is full of dark wood, leather booths, and career servers hoisting huge trays with succulent and sweet Alaska king crab legs, giant Australian lobster tails and massive porterhouses. Old-school classics are prepared well; a few even qualify as addictive. We like the "clams casino" (baked clams topped with bread crumbs and bacon), the frog legs with garlic butter and the smoked salmon—heat-smoked rather than cured. *1024 N Rush St between Oak St and Bellevue Pl (312-640-0999). El: Red to Clark/Division. Bus: 36, 70. Lunch (summer only), dinner. Average main course: $25.*

★ Ⓑ **Joe's Seafood, Prime Steaks and Stone Crab** You should feel like a king when you're paying through the nose for a steakhouse experience. The service should be top-notch, the atmosphere classy and the food stellar. This place hits each mark. Start with one of the signature stone crabs and go straight to the bone-in New York strip, perfect when ordered charred medium-rare. Blackened mahi mahi is juicy and just spicy enough. Key lime pie is puckeringly sweet for those who like a hit-you-over-the-head finish. *60 E Grand Ave at Wabash Ave (312-379-5637). El: Red to Grand. Bus: 29, 36, 65. Brunch (Sat, Sun), lunch, dinner. Average main course: $30.*

✱ **King Crab** If you can stand the cheesy '80s rock and crowds that love coupling those tunes with mai tais, this seafood stalwart is worth a visit for the specials alone. You can get massive Dungeness crab and shrimp or fish prepared every conceivable way for decent prices any time. Ribs, steaks and chicken are also on offer, but skip them. In fact, skip table service as well, and grab a stool at the bar to fill up on beer and oysters. *1816 N Halsted St at Willow St (312-280-8990). El: Red to North/Clybourn. Bus: 8, 72. Lunch, dinner. Average main course: $20.*

★ **L20** *2009 Eat Out Award, Critics' Pick: A Blog-o You Can Trust (must-read restaurant blog written by chef Gras)* This is Laurent Gras's homage to all things ocean—from the first feel of the velvety menu to that last, ethereal bite of macaroon, the bicoastal chef is in complete control. The restaurant offers a four-course and a 12-course menu of inspired options like salted cod puree with ribbons of smoked gelatin and sliced geoduck with a touch of fresh wasabi. But don't fill up on fish: L20 has the best bread in the city, and you'll want to eat as much anchovy-stuffed brioche as you can. *2300 N Lincoln Park West at Belden Ave (773-868-0002). El: Brown, Purple (rush hrs), Red to Fullerton. Bus: 22, 36, 151, 156. Dinner (closed Tue). Average degustation: $135.*

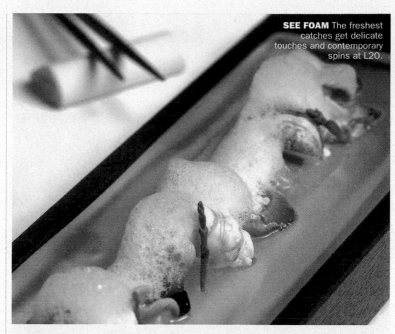

SEE FOAM The freshest catches get delicate touches and contemporary spins at L20.

Ⓖ **BYOB Las Islas Marias** See Mexican for review.

Nick's Fishmarket Peanut butter and jelly. Romance and…fish. At least that's the vibe at this upscale Chase Tower–level institution, where the only thing that could get in the way of a couple's canoodling is the single long-stemmed rose that's artfully placed on their table. It's common to see couples feeding each other forkfuls of crispy and bright citrus-ginger salmon, deep-red slices of seared tuna and "clams casino," a tasty dish even if the clams serve only as a vehicle for garlicky slabs of bacon. *51 S Clark St at Monroe St (312-621-0200). El: Blue, Red to Monroe; Brown, Green, Orange, Pink, Purple (rush hrs) to Madison. Bus: 3, 4, 14, 20, 26, 56, 60, 124, 145, 147, 148, 151, 157. Lunch (Mon–Fri), dinner (closed Sun). Average main price: $28. ● Other location: 10275 W Higgins Rd, Rosemont (847-298-8200).*

✱ **Oceanique** It's tough to keep a comfortable, laid-back vibe while serving upscale food, but this Evanston favorite does it. Chef-owner Mark Grosz didn't bring with him the pretension of former employer Le Francais, but he did bring the skill with classic (albeit pricey) Euro dishes. Close to ten different seafood entrées are offered on any given night, and while the multi-ingredient preparations border on overwhelming, Grosz somehow manages to balance flavors while completely flipping off subtlety. Big portions mean you may not be tempted to follow the delicious savory fare with dessert. *505 Main St, Evanston (847-864-3435). El: Purple to Main. Bus: 200, 201, 205. Dinner (closed Sun). Average main course: $30.*

Pier 5736 At "the Pier," chef-owner Peter McCarthy favors honest (sometimes nearly naked) preps of a dozen types of seafood. Lobster tails, crab legs, crispy perch, pan-seared arctic char…all served with new potatoes, a green veg and a wedge of lemon. The straightforward approach goes a long way with the Sox-loving Jeff Park locals; come for Tuesday's $12 specials menu or Wednesday's and Thursday's $25 three-course, and you'll get caught up in the lure of the place, too. *5736 N Elston Ave at Parkside Ave (773-774-3663). El: Blue to Jefferson Park. Bus: 56A, 68, 85A. Dinner (closed Mon). Average main course: $20.*

▼ ◖ **Raw Bar** Psychologists would diagnose this place as bipolar. The front room is a boisterous bar; the dining room is a candlelit venue for local cabaret acts. But whichever you prefer, the menu is the same: standouts include meaty crab legs, chunky crab cakes topped with a sharp chive mayo, and juicy salmon filets flanked by perfectly grilled shrimp. Of the Middle Eastern dishes, the Egyptian chicken is juicy and flavorful, but in a place called Raw Bar, stick with the seafood. *3720 N Clark St between Waveland Ave and Grace St (773-348-7291). El: Red to Addison. Bus: 22, 36, 152. Lunch, dinner. Average main course: $13.*

Ⓑ **Shaw's Crab House** There are so many seasonal seafood choices here—flown in from Atlantic, Gulf and Pacific coasts—that it's hard to go wrong. Shellfish enthusiasts will be more than happy at the oyster bar, and those with larger appetites should opt for the family-style lobster dinner, a traditional East Coast lobster boil, which includes a cup of lobster bisque, Maine lobster, corn on the cob, red potatoes, a side of coleslaw and a slice of key lime pie. *21 E Hubbard St between State St and Wabash Ave (312-527-2722). El: Red to Grand. Bus: 29, 36, 62, 65. Lunch, dinner, brunch. Average main course: $28. ● Other location: 1900 E Higgins Rd, Schaumburg (847-517-2722).*

Ⓖ **Snappy's Shrimp House** North Siders looking for a fried-shrimp fix should head here, where jumbo, Gulf-caught beauties are breaded in a secret blend of seasonings and bread crumbs. Other delights include scallops, catfish and clam strips, as well as an assortment of artery-clogging-but-tasty sides like fluffy hush puppies, onion rings and potato pancakes. There is a handful of counter seats, but take your grease-streaked brown bags to go, so we don't have to watch you lick your fingers. *1901 W Irving Park Rd at Wolcott Ave (773-244-1008). El: Brown to Irving Park. Bus: 9, 11, 80. Lunch, dinner. Average main course: $8.*

South American

TWO FOR TANGO Be sure to wipe your hands between wolfing down those empanadas and dance time at Ritz Tango Café.

✳ **BYOB Ay Ay Picante** Pan flute versions of classic pop songs repeat (and repeat) on the speakers at this cheerful spot. Specialties include *ocopa*, potato slices topped with a creamy mint-and-walnut sauce; heaping portions of ceviche with tart, tender slices of tilapia and octopus; *lomo saltado*, heavily spiced strips of beef topped with a pile of fries to soak up the juices; and a rich slice of caramel cake good enough to make even the fifth play of "Dust in the Wind" (yes, a pan flute version) tolerable. *4569 N Elston Ave between Kennicott and Kiona Aves (773-427-4239). Bus: 53, 78, 81. Lunch, dinner. Average main course: $12.*

★ **BYOB D'Candela** The purple accents and lavender stools make dining at this Peruvian spot a bit like dining inside an Easter basket. Luckily, chocolate bunnies are ditched in favor of braised lamb with sweet peppers and garlic-and-oregano–flecked rotisserie chicken so succulent that a simple twist frees the meat from the bone. Complimentary *aji*, a mayo-based sauce kicked up with Peruvian green peppers, is perfect for dipping crispy fried plantains and empanadas. *4053 N Kedzie Ave between Belle Plaine Ave and Irving Park Rd (773-478-0819). El: Brown to Kedzie. Bus: 80, X80. Lunch, dinner (closed Mon). Average main course: $10.*

★ ▼ **El Nandu** Order a basket of the crispy, stuffed, savory empanadas and a bottle of Malbec to transport yourself to the owner's homeland of Argentina. Our favorites are the Criolla, an aromatic blend of ground beef, onions and golden raisins, and the Maiz, plump with corn, peppers and hard boiled eggs. If you have room, finish off with the Dulce de Batata, a slice of sweet potato paste toned down with a slice of

mild cheese. A live band plays tango and bolero music Thursday through Saturday evenings. *2731 W Fullerton Ave between Fairfield and California Aves (773-278-0900). El: Blue to California. Bus: 52, 74. Lunch (Mon–Sat), dinner. Average main course: $14.*

▼ ☺ **BYOB Fogo 2 Go** The name might imply otherwise, but there are a couple tables for dining in this Brazilian pizzeria, where the menu includes whole pies, slices and grilled chicken served with sides of porky black beans, rice and pita. Wait a sec—Brazilian pizza? It has a soft, doughy crust and comes in fifty combinations of ingredients like codfish, pulled chicken and ranch dressing. Wash your pie down with a crisp Guarana soda and you'll be convinced this place has Brazilian cred. *926 W Diversey Pkwy at Wilton Ave (773-880-8052). El: Brown, Purple (rush hrs) to Diversey. Bus: 8, 11, 76. Lunch, dinner. Average slice of pizza: $3.*

☺ **Lito's Empanadas** Situated among a long row of boutiques, and just a few blocks from two malls, the small storefront offers about ten stuffed pastries a day, including a "Hawaiian" version with mozzarella, ham and pineapple and a hearty version with shredded chicken and rice. One makes a snack; two or three make a meal. *2566 N Clark St between Deming Pl and Wrightwood Ave (773-857-1337). El: Red, Brown, Purple (rush hrs) to Fullerton. Bus: 22, 36, 151. Lunch, dinner (Mon–Sat). Average empanada: $2.50.*

▼ ✳ ☾ **ñ** This clubby sister to Tango Sur is a lot like escaping to Buenos Aires—without the airfare. An unconsciously chic gang of

international exiles sip mojitos and flirt to tropical grooves either at the front bar or at tables for two. The best of the *picadas* (apps) are the garlicky eggplant and the mixto plate of the lauded empanadas and beef *milanesa* (fried steak chunks). Soak up the booze with more substantial fare like the Vacio, a grilled skirt steak with chimichurri. *2977 N Elston Ave at Rockwell St (773-866-9898). Bus: 9, X49, 76, 77. Dinner (Tue–Sat). Average main course: $12.*

★ ▼ **BYOB Rapa Nui** In the spot formerly known as Latin Sandwich Café, sandwiches are the name of the game, and for good reason: The Chilean versions are assembled on crusty, housemade white bread and feature addictive fillings (such as the pork, avocado and mayonnaise in the creamy "*pernil con palta*"). But what we're really smitten with are the empanadas, two-handed affairs filled with beef, onions, olives and hard-boiled egg that are a meal by themselves. *4009 N Elston Ave between Irving Park Rd and Ridgeway Ave (773-478-0175). El: Blue to Irving Park. Bus: 53, 80, 82. Lunch, dinner. Average main course: $10.*

✳ **BYOB Rios d'Sudamerica** Dino Perez's parents ran Bucktown's Peruvian stalwart Rinconcito Sudamericano for 25 years; here Perez steps away from "old school" Peruvian in favor of what he and chef Jose Victorio call a "fusion of Peruvian, Argentinean and Brazilian." Look for stylized presentations of classics like *lomo al pisco* (sautéed steak with onions, tomatoes and fried potatoes). Bartenders are armed with juices and mixers to turn BYO liquors into cocktails. *2010 W Armitage Ave at Damen Ave (773-276-0170). El: Blue to Western. Bus: 50, 73. Dinner (closed Mon). Average main course: $19.*

☺ **B BYOB Ritz Tango Café** We don't know what's cuter: the Golden Years couples taking tango lessons here on Monday, Tuesday, Thursday and weekend evenings, or the hand-formed empanadas filled with a sweet and savory combination of raisins and chicken. Hearty Milanesa sandwiches fit breaded veal between thick slices of warm focaccia, but don't fill up—occasionally the dessert special will be *hojaldre* cake, a seven-layer beauty of caramel and crispy cookies that'll have you doing the tango in your seat. *933 N Ashland Ave between Walton St and Augusta Blvd (773-235-2233). El: Blue to Division. Bus: 9, X9, 66, 70. Breakfast, lunch, dinner. Average main course: $5.*

✳ **BYOB Tango Sur** Things to know when planning a trip here: You *will* wait for a table at this crowded Argentine grill, and when it's time to order, it's best to keep it simple. Start with a plate of deep-fried empanadas to share, then order a perfectly seared steak to dunk in the house chimichurri sauce, and finish with the flan. Bring along a bottle of big red wine, sit outside on the sidewalk and enjoy the live Latin guitar—is life really always this sweet in Buenos Aires? *3763 N Southport Ave at Grace St (773-477-5466). El: Brown to Southport; Red to Addison. Bus: 9, 22, 152. Lunch (Sun), dinner. Average main course: $14.*

Southern

SOUTHERN COMFORT Edna's has dished up soul-food classics like these for more than 30 years.

Ⓖ **Army & Lou's** This Chatham tablecloth spot has been serving up Southern comfort food (with a side of Southern-style doting, no less) for more than 60 years. Not surprisingly, the "Southern specialties" side of the menu is the way to go. Light-brown pan gravy is poured over tender short ribs and pan-fried pork chops, but skip it on the fried chicken—you wouldn't want to smother that crispy coating. For sides, go with black-eyed peas, cheesy mac and cornbread stuffing, and don't forget to come back in the morning for breakfast, which stars some of the best "smothered" potatoes this side of the Mason-Dixon. *422 E 75th St between King Dr and Vernon Ave (773-483-3100). El: Red to 79th. Bus: 3, X3, 75. Breakfast, lunch, dinner (closed Tue). Average main course: $9.*

Ⓖ **Bar-B-Que Bob's** It'll be tough to exercise self-control when you whiff the Southern scents wafting out of the kitchen, where vats of baked beans, sweet yams and collard greens simmer away. The 'cue may not be smoky like some spots in town, but the chicken is juicy, and the rib tips are finger-lickin'. Grab a spot at one of the two tables to enjoy bootlegged horror movies on the suspended TV, and don't forget the sweet-potato pie. *2055 W Howard St between Seeley and Hoyne Aves (773-761-1260). El: Red to Howard. Bus: 49B, 97, 215. Lunch, dinner (closed Mon). Average main course: $8.*

★ ⟨ **Barbara Ann's BBQ** The original pitmaster Mack may have moved on to Uncle John's. but the signature sage- and fennel-flecked sausage at this beloved barbecue joint is still custom-made by a local sausage maker, and still gets significant smoke time over the smoldering hickory and cherry wood. Rib tips remain the juiciest pork option (over the often drier spare ribs), and also the best value. Skip the beef ribs, spend the dough on "Miss Winters'" outsourced 7UP, sour-cream and chocolate cakes instead. *7617 S Cottage Grove Ave between 76th and 77th Sts (773-651-5300). El: Red to 79th. Bus: 4, X4, 75. Lunch, dinner (Tue–Sat) (closed Sun, Mon). Average main course: $9.*

Ⓑ **Big Jones** Chef-owner Paul Fehribach hopes to bring a slice of New Orleans to Andersonville, but whether or not his restaurant really exhibits Southernness is beside the point. That's because some of his food is so delicious that authenticity will be the last thing on your mind. Sandwiches are a good bet—the house-cured tasso ham paired with pimento cheese and sweet bread makes for a great, gooey one; so does the spicy gator sausage with crunchy fried pickles. Brunch is famed for the gratis beignets and boozy Bloody Marys. *5347 N Clark St between Summerdale and Balmoral Aves (773-275-5725). El: Red to Berwyn. Bus: 22, 50, 92. Brunch (Sat, Sun), lunch, dinner. Average main course: $18.*

Ⓞ BYOB **BJ's Market & Bakery** Designed like some sort of cross between Denny's and Burger King—only with a soul-food slant—this South Side minichain may be the only fast–soul-food joint in town. But while the food takes only minutes to arrive at your table, it tastes like it was slowly, carefully cooked with love over a home stove. With its crispy, golden crust, the mustard-fried catfish is clearly the restaurant's standout dish, but don't discount the juicy smoked chicken, collard greens, red beans and rice or delicious peach cobbler, which puts those other fast-food pies to shame. *8734 S Stony Island Ave at 87th St (773-374-4700). Bus: 28, 87. Breakfast, lunch, dinner. Average main course: $7.50.*

Ⓑ **Blu 47** Don't look for any signs marking this Bronzeville lounge and restaurant. Just follow the train of cars in line for valet. This upscale eatery is hidden on the second floor of a nondescript commercial complex, but the eclectic menu and vibe make this a spot worth seeking out. This is soul food transcended. You'd be hard-pressed to find anything elsewhere like the signature bayou catfish, a tasty dish of two crispy filets stuffed with Cajun spiced crabmeat on a bed of grilled vegetables. *4655 S King Dr at 47th St (773-536-6000). El: Green, Red to 47th. Bus: 3, X3, 47. Brunch (Sun), dinner (Tues–Sat). Average main course: $18.*

⁎ **Chicago's Home of Chicken and Waffles** The sign and menus might still say Chicago's Rosscoe's, but thanks to a lawsuit brought about by L.A.'s famous Roscoe's House of Chicken and Waffles in April 2008, Rosscoe's (two s's or not) has been dropped from the name. Regardless, you can still get that sweet-and-salty duo of chicken and waffles any time of the day here, and that's really all that matters. *3947 S King Dr at Oakwood Blvd (773-536-3300). El: Green to Indiana. Bus: 1, 3, X3, 29, 39. Breakfast, lunch, dinner. Average main course: $12.*

◷ ⁎ Ⓑ BYOB **CJ's Eatery** West Humboldt Park is home to this cozy, local art–filled spot that merges the traditions of Southern cooking with touches of Latin American cuisine. Lunch and dinner are a who's who of comfort food. Meat loaf is better than Mom's, but hold the American cheese. For the star of the show, get the blackened salmon, well-spiced, perfectly seared and plated with delicious garlic mashed potatoes. Follow up with the fantastic banana bread pudding with peanut-butter anglaise. *3839 W Grand Ave at Avers Ave (773-292-0990). Bus: 53, 65, 70. Breakfast (Thu–Fri), brunch (Sat, Sun), lunch, dinner (Thu–Sun). Average main course: $8.*

★ ◷ BYOB **Edna's** If you're looking for good fried chicken, look no further. This West Side institution has been serving up stick-to-your-ribs soul food for more than 40 years. The crispy, black pepper–laced fried chicken is made to order, so expect a 20-minute wait. For sides, go for the biscuits, greens, mac and cheese, candied yams and black-eyed peas. Peach cobbler is tasty, but if you spy glass cake stands on the diner counter filled with triple-layer caramel, chocolate or coconut cake, don't leave without snagging a slice. *3175 W Madison St between Albany and Kedzie Aves (773-638-7079). El: Green to Kedzie. Bus: 20, 52. Breakfast, lunch, dinner (closed Mon). Average main course: $8.*

⁎ **Fat Willy's Rib Shack** Can good barbecue exist on the North Side? Yep. Instead of the South Side tradition of cash 'n' carry, here there's a dining room, a comfy no-frills spot with a beer and wine list and a house cocktail called the Hogarita (think cran-citrus margarita). For starters, skip the hot links and go for the smoky, greasy rib tips and an insanely rich mac and cheese. Move past salads to a slab of baby backs and the beef brisket sandwich with horseradish. *2416 W Schubert Ave between Western and Artesian Aves (773-782-1800). Bus: 49, X49, 76. Lunch, dinner. Average main course: $11.*

★ ◷ Ⓑ **5 Loaves Eatery** We were picking up the fried catfish po' boy, wondering how we were going to fit the two-handed affair in our mouth, when it happened: A gentle breeze actually blew the door open, solidifying the fact that this is the most charming café in South Shore. The main attraction is the crispy po' boys, the tender filets of pan-seared tilapia and the creamy sides of horseradish-and-dill-packed coleslaw. Not up for a full meal? Enjoy strong coffee and dense slices of lemon pound cake. *405 E 75th St at King Dr (773-873-6666). Bus: 3, X3, 75. Breakfast, lunch, dinner (closed Mon). Average main course: $7.*

▾ **Heaven on Seven** This homegrown minichain of Creole food is the closest you'll get to New Orleans in Chicago. Bottles of hot sauce take up as much tabletop room as the food, and the po' boys (try the shrimp) are piled so high they necessitate a knife and fork. Soups like the hearty gumbo stick to the theme. If you're still skeptical about the authenticity of it all, order one of the margaritas served in a tall, curvy glass—you'll start feeling like you would on Bourbon Street. *111 N Wabash Ave between Washington and Randolph Sts (312-263-6443). El: Blue to Washington; Red to Lake; Brown, Green, Orange, Pink, Purple (rush hrs) to Randolph. Breakfast, lunch (closed Sun). Average main course: $12.*

◷ BYOB **Honey 1 BBQ** The Adams family's style of 'cue employs real wood (rather than gas) to impart smoky flavor on slow-cooked slabs. The father and son-run joint has about 50 tables and chairs in the simple dining area, so patrons no longer have to call ahead two hours to request ribs. (As was the case at the duo's last take-out joint.) The turnover means the Adamses are smokin' around the clock. *2241 N Western Ave between Lyndale St and Belden Ave (773-227-5130). El: Blue to Western. Bus: 49, X49, 56, 74. Lunch, dinner (closed Mon). Average main course: $9.*

◷ BYOB **Honky Tonk Barbecue** Owner Willie Wagner started off with a portable smoker at Hideout Block Party and Northalsted Market Days, but now, he's set up shop in Pilsen to serve his "Memphis-style," dry-rubbed barbecue. The ribs are on the dry side, but the smoky pulled pork makes up for it, clocking in at one of the best around. Tender, juicy chicken comes in second for best bets, with puckery slaw and meaty beans solid runners-up. *1213 W 18th St between Racine Ave and Allport St (312-226-7427). El: Pink to 18th. Bus: 9, 18, 60, 168. Dinner (Tue–Sat). Average main course: $10.*

★ ◷ ☾ **Izola's** Owner Izola White's corn muffins need no butter—they're buttery enough all on their own. Her candied sweet potatoes need no tinkering—they're already perfect, redolent with baking spices. Her fried chicken has a dark crust that cracks open to reveal juicy meat, and her fried catfish arrives with a pickle-studded tartar sauce—and if you have a problem with either (which you won't), Ms. White is usually right there in the restaurant, ready to fix it. *522 E 79th St between Rhodes and Eberhart Aves (773-846-1484). El: Red to 79th. Bus: 3, 4, 79. Open 24 hours (closed Wed). Average main course: $11.*

◷ BYOB **Lagniappe** This amazin' Cajun spot—now with a second location on the river—is primarily a carryout and catering operation, but we'll squeeze into the handful of tables to dig in on the spot. Smoky gumbo is thick with spicy roux base, white rice, baby shrimp and chunks of andouille sausage. Jambalaya is rich with tomato and bright with herbs; dirty rice is authentic and earthy from spleen; collard greens have heat and smoke from flecks of smoked turkey; and the shrimp po' boy is unforgettable. End with a slice of warm pineapple-caramel bread pudding. *1525 W 79th St at Justine St (773-994-6375). Bus: 9, X9, 79, 169. Lunch, dinner (closed Sun, Mon). Average main course: $13.* ● *Other location: 55 W Riverwalk (312-726-7716).*

◷ **Lem's BBQ** As the best barbecue joints on the South Side do, Lem's requires that you order through bulletproof glass and then take your ribs elsewhere to be devoured (it's take-out only). But it would take much more than that to scare away devotees of these spareribs and rib tips, which have a thin, vinegary sauce heavy with spice and charred outer edges that hide pink, juicy pork. Honestly, the only truly scary thing here is arriving to find the line snaking out the door. *311 E 75th St between Calumet and Prairie Aves (773-994-2428). El: Red to 79th. Bus: 3, 4, 75. Lunch, dinner (closed Tue). Average main course: $7.*

⁎ **Maple Tree Inn** The menu reads like an eclectic tribute to Southern, Cajun and Creole cooking, and the kitchen consistently nails the classics (gumbo, fried green tomatoes, shrimp Creole). There's an oddball spin on some dishes, but it mostly works, particularly with the crawfish étouffée risotto and "boats" (a.k.a. po' boys) drizzled with melted Brie. The barbecue shrimp served on grits should satiate most Southern cravings. The restaurant's mantra, "sit long, talk much," translates into long waits on weekend nights, but quick bar service keeps the cold Rogue beers coming, so time flies. *13301 Old Western Ave, Blue Island (708-388-3461). Bus: Pace 349. Dinner (closed Sun–Tue). Average main course: $17.*

Merle's Smokehouse The term "barbecue joint" usually brings to mind a hole-in-the-wall with a pitmaster. Not Merle's. With big-screen TVs, an ample bar, and images of Elvis, the ambience is closer to Applebee's than authentic. What it lacks in atmosphere, it makes up for by offering decent barbecue at a decent price in a location with decent public-transportation options and parking. Tables are set with rolls of paper towels so you can get to work on St. Louis ribs, baby back ribs or the other finger-lickin' meat of your choice. Wrap up the meal with whatever pie is on offer. *1727 Benson Ave, Evanston (847-475-7766). El: Purple to Davis. Bus: 202, 203, 204, Pace 208, Pace 250. Lunch (Sat, Sun), dinner. Average main course: $11.*

Miss Lee's Good Food Of the signs on the walls of this take-out shop, the most important is the sign boasting nine years in business. For a corner with not much else going for it, that's a big achievement. Of course, the reason this place has survived is no secret: From the buttered biscuits to the slightly sweet yellow turnips to the custardy buttermilk pie, this is simple, down-home food that nobody can argue with. Or stop eating, for that matter. *203 E Garfield Blvd at Indiana Ave (773-752-5253). El: Green to Garfield. Bus: 29, 55, 174. Lunch, dinner (closed Mon). Average main course: $10.*

P&P BBQ Soul Food Take a glance at the dry-erase board you'll pass on your way into this spic-and-span, family-run soul-food spot—it lists all of the day's specials you'll be recounting later to friends and eating for leftovers the next day. Though the giant smoker may not be fuming while you're there, rest assured it sees some action, and the tender, if mild, jerk chicken and sauce-slathered rib tips that come out of it are mighty tasty. Ham-studded greens in plenty of potlikker are among the best in town, and a carryout wing deal for three bucks beats the pants off those extra-value meals this area's littered with. *3734 W Division St between Ridgeway and Hamlin Aves (773-276-7756). Bus: 53, 65, 70. Breakfast, lunch, dinner. Average main course: $8.*

★ ▼ **Pearl's Place** Whoever you are, Pearl, thank you. You must be pretty special to have inspired this Creole **influenced** soul food restaurant. We've learned the hard way to be patient with the long waits. The fried chicken is so damn juicy and sealed in a crunchy, pepper-flecked exterior; the collard greens so tender and flavorful with pork bits; and the sweet-potato pie so fragrant with cinnamon and nutmeg (fluffy near the middle and caramelized where the filling meets the flaky crust) that we'd wait forever. *3901 S Michigan Ave at Pershing Rd (773-285-1700). El: Green to Indiana. Bus: 1, 29, 39. Breakfast, lunch, dinner. Average main course: $12.*

Russell's Barbecue When you're feeling nostalgic for an early-20th-century roadhouse vibe, what you seek is Russell's, a west-suburban favorite for almost 80 years. Line up, place your order, then head for a wooden seat with your plastic tray of corn on the cob, slaw and ribs. Since way before Flay, Russell's sauce has been on supermarket shelves; it's quite sweet, so we ask for it on the side. Barbecue purists may scoff at the baked ribs' lack of hickory flavor or their pinkish smoke ring, but this spot's a favorite with families thanks to big rooms, long communal tables, "junior" portions, and beer and wine to help the 'rents get through it all. *1621 N Thatcher Ave, Elmwood Park (708-453-7065). Lunch, dinner. Average main course: $7.*

✳ ☾ **The Smoke Daddy** Gluttony grabs hold in this kitschy kitchen, and it doesn't let go until the band plays its last bluesy rockabilly note. So skip the brisket, ignore the chicken, and resist filling up on the addictive sweet-potato fries: You need to reserve your hunger for "The Rib Sampler." It's a huge plate of baby back ribs, spareribs and rib tips—a pile so big it might intimidate you. But don't worry: The pink, smoky meat pulls off the bone, so you'll have no trouble cleaning your plate. *1804 W Division St between Wood and Honore Sts (773-772-6656). El: Blue to Division. Bus: 9, X9, 50, 70. Lunch, dinner. Average main course: $15.*

Side dish

HOT MESS It's impossible to take down Smoque's signature brisket *and* leave with a clean shirt.

Smoking allowed

No matter what your go-to barbecue order, we've found the kings of 'cue in every classic category.

Standing over a hot smoker for a dozen hours a day is a tough gig, but as any barbecue fan will tell you, it's worth it. One bite of smoky ribs, fat-rippled brisket or juicy pulled pork and you'll appreciate all that hard work. Here, we salute the best pitmasters in town.

BEST HOT LINKS: Uncle John's (p.118) Mack Sevier knows two things for certain: barbecue is only as good as its pitmaster, and Sunday is the Lord's Day. The latter is why Sevier's carryout spot is only open Monday through Saturday, and the former is why the Arkansas native devotes those days to churning out some of the best hot links we've ever laid into. Sage-perfumed and dotted with red chile flakes, like some sort of devilish breakfast sausage with blistered casings, these links are so tasty we buy extra on Saturdays to get us through Sevier's much-deserved day of rest.

Best rib tips: Lem's Bar-B-Que House (p.116) South Siders are as serious about rib tips as they are Sox loyalty, and there's probably equal debate over both. But for our money, we head to Lem's, where tips are the specialty. The little nuggets of porky goodness have just the right amount of meat-to-fat ratio, a wallop of smoke and a thin sheen of tangy-sweet sauce. They're messy, but well worth the work.

Best pulled pork: Honky Tonk Barbecue (p.116) With a few trophies to prove it, Willie Wagner is a pulled-pork champion.

Each summer, Wagner throws down in fierce competitions around the country that separate the hobbyists from the obsessed. Thanks to a time-tested technique (and maybe a deal with the devil), the man has been able to turn the notoriously tough pork shoulder into a quivering lump of tender perfection. And now that his country-kitsch Pilsen eatery is up and running, you don't have to hitch up a trailer and track him down at a barbecue contest for a taste.

Best brisket: Smoque (p.118) Stellar 'cue on the North Side? Yep, it's true. Owner Barry Sorkin did his research in the fertile crescent of Brisket Land, a.k.a. Texas Hill Country, and it shows. The well-marbled beef gets a simple spice rub before its bid in the wood-fired smoker, and emerges hours later with a light pink smoke ring around the edges, a frame of sorts for juicy interior meat. It's offered chopped or sliced—we go for half and half to ensure equal parts tender beef and crunchy "burnt ends."

Best ribs: Barbara Ann's (p.115) Spareribs are the most common, and most commonly botched, barbecue classic. Contrary to popular belief, you don't want the meat to fall off the bone; you want tender meat that still needs a slight tug to come away from the rib. And you want a telltale pink smoke ring, a nice crunchy rub exterior and flavor that stands alone, with no need for a slathering of sauce. In essence, you want Barbara Ann's.
—Heather Shouse

★ **BYOB Smoque BBQ** *2009 Eat Out Awards, Readers' Choice: Best Barbecue* The Northwest Side finally got its meat hooks on some great barbecue. St. Louis spareribs are near-perfect—juicy, pull-apart tender, with subtle smokiness that doesn't overwhelm the tangy spice rub clinging to the sticky, crunchy exterior. Pillow-soft chicken's slick, seasoned skin gives way to meat that's partially pink from smoke and fully flavorful, but if you must add more oomph, go with the thinner, vinegary sauce of the two options. *3800 N Pulaski Rd between Grace St and Avondale Ave (773-545-7427). El: Blue to Irving Park. Bus: 53, 80, X80. Metra: Union Pacific NW to Irving Park. Lunch, dinner (closed Mon). Average main course: $12.*

▼ ⊙ **Soul Vegetarian East** See Vegetarian for review.

★ ⊙ **Uncle John's** Behind the glass curtain at this Park Manor carryout spot, Arkansas-native Mack Sevier smokes some of the best stuff in town. Go for the rib tips and hotlinks combo: The rib tips are smoky, extremely juicy, meatier than elsewhere in town and crisp around the edges. The hot links are not for the heat-phobic, with searing bits of red chile and smoky, porky, sage-packed flavor—like a spicy breakfast sausage. Opt for the mild sauce unless you're prepared for a scorcher, and request extra napkins if you want to save your car seats. *337 E 69th St at Calumet Ave (773-892-1233). El: Red to 69th. Bus: 3, 30, 67, 71. Lunch, dinner (closed Sun). Average main course: $9.*

⊙ **Wallace's Catfish Corner** This clean-as-a-whistle catfish 'n' barbecue hut houses some tasty soul food. The catfish steak and butterflied shrimp are heart-stoppers but worth the risk, and the "mini" rib tips are twice the size of any we've seen elsewhere. Sides are mandatory: gooey mac and cheese, fried okra, slow-simmered greens and the creamy banana pudding finale. If you go late, most of the food has already been snatched up, and pickings are slim. *2800 W Madison Ave between California and Francisco Aves (773-638-3474). El: Green to California. Bus: 20, X20, 52, 94. Lunch, dinner. Average main course: $7.*

⊙ **B Wishbone** Stuck as we are in the Midwest, Southern staples such as real grits and biscuits can be hard to come by. But this enormous West Loop eatery has made it its mission to bring "mornin' hon" hospitality to the heartland. The brunch is often touted as the city's best. We're not willing to go that far, but we can get down with the plate-size fruit pancakes and savory corn cakes (with some hot sauce), the dense corn muffins and buttery biscuits, and the spicy (but not hot) andouille chicken sausage. *1001 W Washington Blvd at Morgan St (312-850-2663). Bus: 8, 20, X20. Breakfast, lunch (Mon–Fri), dinner (Tues–Sat), brunch (Sat, Sun). Average main course: $10.* ● *Other locations: 3300 N Lincoln Ave (773-549-2663), 6611 W Roosevelt Rd, Berwyn (708-749-1295).*

FLOWER POWER The early morning pancake crowd enjoys the calm before Wishbone's trademark brunch storm.

Spanish

AVANT NEW GUARD Chef Dudley Nieto attempts to modernize tapas at Eivissa.

◐ ☀ **Arco de Cuchilleros** The trend of cutting-edge Spanish cooking hasn't reached this tapas bar, which serves up plates that are tried-and-true. Chicken croquettes have a hot, crisp crunch that gives way to a creamy center; slices of *tortilla Española* are tall and savory; and monkfish flakes apart in its delicious broth. There are some weird dishes on the menu, but when the weather is warm and you're sitting in the garden slowly draining a pitcher of sangria, it's easy to let a little misstep slide. *3445 N Halsted St between Newport and Cornelia Aves (773-296-6046). El: Red to Addison. Bus: 8, 22, 36, 152. Dinner (closed Mon). Average small plate: $7.*

◐ ☀ **Azucar!** Be prepared to grab a margarita at next-door El Cid while you wait for a seat to open at this tapas joint. While you're sipping, remind yourself what you're waiting for: spice-rubbed pork with a crunchy sprinkling of pistachio; cheese-and-mushroom–stuffed red peppers plated on a creamy chickpea puree; and a *crema Catalana* packed with cinnamon. Resist that second margarita if you can—these are tapas you'll want to remember the next day. *2647 N Kedzie Ave between Milwaukee and Schubert Aves (773-486-6464). El: Blue to Logan Square. Bus: 56, 76. Dinner (Wed–Sun). Average tapa: $7.*

◐ ☀ ☾ **Bull-Eh-Dias** When we tell you this tapas spot is hot, we mean it literally: Every *tapa caliente*—from the fiery *patatas bravas* and toothsome octopus to the bite-size chorizo empanadas and omelettish *tortilla Española*—arrived too steaming to touch. We took that as an encouraging sign, because if you're going to eat Spanish grub and down glasses of sangria (they have red, white and peach), it's good to do it at a place where you know the food hasn't been sitting under heat lamps. *3651 N Southport Ave between Addison St and Waveland Ave (773-404-2855). El: Brown to Southport. Bus: 9, X9, 77. Lunch, dinner. Average small plate: $7.*

◐ ☀ **Café Ba-Ba-Reeba!** *2009 Eat Out Awards, Readers' Choice: Best Tapas* Lincoln Park loves its tapas joints, and this is the granddaddy of them all. The ingredients are fresh and good quality: zesty Manchego, full-bodied olive oil, tangy anchovies and spicy chorizo fill the menu. Thick bacon is wrapped around juicy dates and roasted, and sherry tomato sauce tops tiny, tender meatballs. We can't find a thread of saffron in our paella, but most of the loud, sangria-filled patrons don't seem to mind. *2024 N Halsted St between Armitage and Dickens Aves (773-935-5000). El: Brown, Purple (rush hrs) to Armitage. Bus: 8, 73. Lunch (Sat, Sun), dinner. Average tapa: $6.*

◐ **Café Iberico** It's kind of like riding the El: The wait at this always-packed tapas joint can be long and annoying, but once you get inside, things go pretty quickly. Cheap plates of *patatas bravas* (soft, habit-forming cubes of potatoes immersed in a spicy tomato sauce) and *croquetas de pollo* (creamy chicken and ham fritters) arrive at the table almost immediately. A plate of Manchego and a pitcher of sangria to tide you over, and you won't even notice the wait. *737 N LaSalle St between Superior St and Chicago Ave (312-573-1510). El: Brown, Purple (rush hrs), to Chicago. Red to Chicago. Bus: 22, 66, 156. Lunch, dinner. Average tapa: $5.*

◐ BYOB **Café Marbella** The food at this airy (and often empty) tapas spot is worth the trek. Don't skip the garlic soup, a chicken stock dotted with roasted garlic cloves. On the tapas front, our faves include sautéed rings of squid slathered in a smoky, tart paste of paprika and lime, a combo of crisped potato cubes with slices of Spanish chorizo and roasted garlic, and the *higos con tocino*—fresh mission figs roasted in a wrap of bacon and plated atop a brandy cream sauce that doubles as dessert. *3446 W Peterson Ave between Bernard St and St Louis Ave (773-588-9922). Bus: 11, 84, 93. Lunch (Tue–Fri, Sun), dinner (Tue–Sun). Average tapa: $7.*

▽ ☀ ☾ **Eivissa** Chef Dudley Nieto traded Mexican (Zapatista, Xel-Ha) for Spanish cuisine, and now he's reinventing tapas using passion-fruit caviar and cumin-aioli air as building blocks at this late-night eatery. On Mondays, go for the half-price sangria, where the traditional red and white varieties are joined by pomegranate, peach and even açai. *1531 N Wells St between North Ave and Burton Pl (312-654-9500). El: Brown, Purple (rush hrs)*

STRIKING GOLD Bask in the glow of Mercat a la Planxa's colorful dining room.

to Sedgwick. *Bus: 9, 72, 156. Lunch, dinner. Average tapa: $8.*

Emilio's Tapas Bar and Restaurant
The namesake chef behind this popular restaurant knows a thing or two about tapas—the Spaniard was the opening chef for Café Ba-Ba-Reeba!, Chicago's first tapas spot. The classics still rule the show: salty-sweet bacon-wrapped dates in roasted red-pepper sauce, killer garlic potatoes, crusty bread topped with tangy tomatoes and whisper-thin *jamón serrano*, and perfectly grilled shrimp in garlic butter. Skip the too-rich goat cheese–eggplant rolls and the oversauced spicy potatoes, but don't miss the velvety flan. *444 W Fullerton Pkwy at Clark St (773-327-5100). El: Brown, Purple (rush hrs), Red to Fullerton. Bus: 22, 36, 74. Dinner. Average tapa: $7.*

1492 Tapas Bar
If we have to explain how this place got its name, it's time you went back to school. But if it's tapas you want an education on, the 48 varieties should be a good primer. Excellent imported meats include smoky links of chorizo. Goat-cheese croquettes are paired with sticky, sweet balsamic. Paella looks and tastes lackluster, so ignore it. But don't skip dessert. Desserts aren't the strong point of tapas joints, but the luscious *crema Catalana*? Let's just say it schooled us. *42 E Superior St at Wabash Ave (312-867-1492). El: Red to Chicago. Bus: 36, 66, 143, 144, 145, 146, 147, 148, 151. Lunch, dinner. Average small plate: $7.*

Mercat a la Planxa
The *croquetas* are crispy, the American Wagyu skirt steak is incredibly rich and the sous vide pork belly melts in the mouth like ice cream. This, despite the fact that chef Jose Garces is noticeably absent from the kitchen. Okay, so maybe chef de cuisine Michael Fiorello is really running the show here. It doesn't matter. His Catalan tapas are always dependable, and sometimes—as with his black Angus burger with red-wine jam—dependably stellar. *638 S Michigan Ave between Harrison St and Balbo Dr (312-765-0524). El: Green, Orange, Red to Roosevelt. Bus: 1, 3, 4. Breakfast, brunch (Sat, Sun), lunch, dinner. Average tapa: $10.*

People Lounge
This Wicker Park tapas spot has something going for it that the others around town don't: a vibrant bar scene. It's completely fitting that this place looks more like a tavern than a traditional restaurant because the food—crispy *patatas bravas*; herbal, earthy mushrooms; a skirt steak served with a bubbly crust of Manchego—is best eaten with a beer or sangria in your hand, and preferably on the sidewalk patio for prime people-watching. *1560 N Milwaukee Ave between North Ave and Honore St (773-227-9339). El: Blue to Damen. Bus: 50, 56, 72. Dinner. Average small plate: $7.*

Steakhouse

NICE GRASS David Burke's Primehouse takes the steakhouse into the 21st Century.

✳ **ajasteak** If the convergence of sushi (by nature subtle and light) and steak (which, by nature, is not) seems like a perplexing concept, that's because it is—especially when the two collide. But ajasteak occasionally gets things right: Adding hamachi to guacamole adds another layer of lushness, and the miso-glazed black cod is cooked to a delicate texture. The steak can also be very good—just avoid the accompanying sauces and wash it down with one of the well-prepared (and mighty strong) cocktails instead. *Dana Hotel & Spa, 660 N State St at Erie St (312-202-6000). El: Red to Grand. Bus: 22, 36, 65. Lunch, dinner. Average main course: $40.*

The Capital Grille In a city that boasts as many steakhouses as crooked politicians, it's saying something that a national chain can still pack 'em in. Capital does so by sticking to the tried-and-true formula. Picture a characteristic steakhouse—cushy leather banquettes in money-green, attentive servers who know their cuts, martinis in icy glasses and fist-sized crab cakes—and you've just about nailed it. So if you're gonna go classic, drop the plastic. A dry-aged porterhouse with lobster alongside tastes better than those shoes you've been eyeing. *633 N St Clair St between Ontario and Erie Sts (312-337-9400). El: Red to Grand. Bus: 145, 146, 147, 151, 157. Lunch (Mon–Fri), dinner. Average main course: $30.*

✳ **Carmichael's Chicago Steak House** It doesn't hold up to the big-name steakhouses more centrally located in higher-rent districts, but Carmichael's is a good choice if you're on your way to United Center. On-the-ball service and a warm bread basket with a crock of melted cheddar cheese help balance out cuts of beef that tend to be more chewy than melt-in-your-mouth. Sides like garlic mashed potatoes are worth saving room for, but be prepared for a bit of sticker shock when all those yummy add-ons are tallied up. *1052 W Monroe St between Morgan St and Racine Ave (312-433-0025). El: Blue to Racine. Bus: 8, 20, 126. Lunch (Mon–Fri), dinner. Average main course: $25.*

★ **Chicago Chop House** This century-old brownstone is a Chicago steakhouse in every sense of the word. Conventioneers and local businessmen with fat expense wallets head upstairs for white-tablecloth service, pricey wines and porterhouses fit for a king. We prefer the subterranean piano bar, where every inch of wall is covered with vintage photos of Capone and crew and the high wooden tables are packed with storytellers and uncompromising carnivores. *60 W Ontario St between Dearborn and Clark Sts (312-787-7100). El: Red to Grand. Bus: 22, 29, 33, 36, 65, 125. Lunch (Mon–Fri), dinner. Average main course: $30.*

✳ **Chicago Firehouse** Some believe the privilege of dining in a building rich with history is worth any price. Despite this 1904 fire station location, we still don't understand why the cedar-planked Dover sole with browned butter costs $40.99. The rest of the menu is fair enough: The Delaware oysters baked with Applewood smoked bacon are a heavenly start; the hearty pot roast falls apart with the touch of a fork; and a rib-eye is topped with a luscious mixture of shallots and blue cheese. *1401 S Michigan Ave at 14th St (312-786-1401). El: Green, Orange, Red to Roosevelt. Bus: 1, 3, 4, 62. Lunch (Mon–Fri), dinner. Average main course: $25.*

★ **Custom House** Custom House's ever-changing seasonal menus make our decision of what to eat ever so difficult, and we're constantly going back and forth on which meal this restaurant does best. You can do no wrong choosing from dishes like succulent, fall-off-the-bone braised short rib, the bacon-wrapped Swan Creek rabbit, or the caramel balsamic roasted quail. *500 S Dearborn St at Congress Pkwy (312-523-0200). El: Brown, Orange, Pink, Purple (rush hrs) to Library; Red to Harrison. Bus: 6, 29, 36. Lunch, dinner. Average main course: $26.*

★ ✳ Ⓑ **David Burke's Primehouse** Has star chef David Burke given Chicago a

steakhouse like no other? Well, we've definitely never come across a crab cake quite so unique (the impeccable meat is crusted in pretzel), the popovers that stand in for bread are a nice twist and dessert includes fill-your-own doughnuts. So is it different? Yes. But not so different that your parents won't like it. Which is good, because you'll want them to take you here again and again. *616 N Rush St at Ontario St (312-660-6000). El: Red to Grand. Bus: 3, X3, X4, 10, 26, 33, 36, 125, 143, 144, 145, 146, 147, 148, 151. Breakfast, brunch (Sat, Sun), lunch (Mon–Sat), dinner. Average main course: $45.*

★ B **Drake Bros.** This unsung steakhouse doesn't exactly reinvent the wheel, but that's no sin when the steaks are this incredible. Great steaks come at a price, so you won't mind the hefty tab after tasting the smooth, smoky, dry-aged New York strip, which just might be among the best steaks we've eaten. Not far behind was the butter-soft, marrow-encrusted sirloin, so rich it could double for dessert. Ask for a prime table by the window. *140 E Walton Pl at Michigan Ave (312-932-4626). El: Red to Chicago. Bus: 10, 66, 143, 144, 145, 146, 147, 148, 151, 157. Breakfast, brunch (Sun), lunch, dinner (Tue–Sun). Average main course: $40.*

💧 ☀ ⟨ **Erie Café** Businessmen, their suit jackets shucked and their ties loosened, fill every seat and corner of this hidden West Loop restaurant. It's not the most conducive setting for dinner, but if you must, ignore the flavorless housemade ravioli and make a meal out of the baked clams and a steak. The meat comes completely unadorned, but it's juicy and as big as your plate—and if you're a real man, that's exactly the way you'll like it. *536 W Erie St at Larrabee St (312-266-2300). Bus: 65, 66. Lunch, dinner. Average main course: $30.*

☀ **Fulton's on the River** See Seafood for review.

💧 **Gene & Georgetti** If it gets any more old school than this circa 1941 steakhouse, we haven't seen it. Filling every inch of the wood-lined dining room are naugahyde bar stools, chairs and banquettes as blood red as the steaks (both well-aged, we might add). Servers range from formal to gruff, but they mean well and they deliver the goods: textbook veal vesuvio, a "garbage" salad fit for four, calf's liver sauteed with onions and bacon, perfectly seared chops and garlicky shrimp de Jonghe that the veteran staff swears the joint invented. *500 N Franklin St at Illinois St (312-527-3718). El: Red to Grand. Bus: 65, 125. Lunch, dinner (closed Sun). Average main course: $30.*

★ **Gibsons Steakhouse** The $44 porterhouse here is impeccably seasoned and boasts warm layers of sumptuous fat running through the full-flavored meat. The only problem is that for $44, the thing is kind of small. But this price-size discrepancy is rare at Gibsons: sweet lobster cocktail easily satiates two, the juicy prime rib comes in a portion typically reserved for the Flintstones, and desserts are so enormous that servers cut them in two, wrapping half in a take-away bag, no questions asked. *1028 N Rush St at Bellevue Pl (312-266-8999). Bus: 36, 70, 145, 147, 151. Lunch, dinner. Average main course: $37. ● Other location: 5464 N River Rd, Rosemont (847-928-9900).*

☀ **Harry Caray's** See Italian/Pizza for review.

PLEASED TO MEAT YOU One of Gene & Georgetti's massive porterhouses is enough to put these two in a coma.

★ B **Joe's Seafood, Prime Steaks and Stone Crab** See Seafood for review.

★ 💧 ☀ **Keefer's Restaurant** If you listen closely, you can hear Modest Mouse seeping softly through the dining-room speakers—the first sign that this isn't your grandfather's steakhouse. Chef John Hogan, also of Tavern on the Park, inflects the menu with an inescapable French sensibility. A perfectly poached egg tops the country salad of crisp frisée and Dover sole meunière gets a classic tableside presentation. The half dozen cuts of steaks arrive perfectly cooked and gushing with juices. *20 W Kinzie St at Dearborn St (312-467-9525). El: Red to Grand. Bus: 22, 29, 36, 65, 156. Lunch (Mon–Fri), dinner (closed Sun). Average main course: $35.*

☀ **Kinzie Chophouse** Don't be alarmed by the guys in the corner wearing jeans and T-shirts; it's perfectly acceptable to dress down here. Apps are a roll call of all the usual suspects, including oysters Rockefeller generously topped with barely wilted spinach. Choose from several cuts of savory steaks presented on a tray before your meal; juicy herb-crusted lamb chops fill in for those who aren't in the mood for beef. *400 N Wells St at Kinzie St (312-822-0191). El: Brown, Purple (rush hrs) to Merchandise Mart. Bus: 125, 156. Lunch (Mon–Fri), dinner. Average steak: $30.*

Morton's the Steakhouse The way food is touted here—by wheeling over a cart of

uncooked meats, including a live lobster—can be a little off-putting (not everybody wants to witness their dinner being carted off to its death). But there are reasons why Morton's is so famous: the classic Chicago steakhouse interior, tailor-made for sealing the deal (business or pleasure); crab cakes; and barely seasoned steaks that stand out for their flavor, their tenderness or both. *65 E Wacker Pl between Garland Ct and Wabash Ave (312-201-0410). El: Brown, Green, Orange, Pink, Purple (rush hrs), Red to State/Lake. Bus: 29, 36, 144, 145, 146, 148. Lunch (Mon–Fri), dinner. Average steak: $40.*

▼ ☀ **Myron & Phil's** If you're under 50 and don't belong to a North Shore synagogue, you may feel a little out of place at this throwback steakhouse. But don't let that stop you from indulging in the splendor of the chopped liver with bits of hard-boiled egg, fresh challah rolls brought to the table when you sit down, iceberg-lettuce salad with green goddess dressing and the famous skirt steak with burnt onions. It's all well worth the heartburn. *3900 W Devon Ave, Lincolnwood (847-677-6663). Dinner (closed Mon). Average main course: $25.*

★ **N9NE** This eight-year-old steakhouse hasn't lost its sparkle—mirrored tiles, pro athletes as patrons, and a neon-glowing Champagne and caviar bar are as posh as the menu. Steaks (cooked at 1,200 degrees) are prime, and catch-of-the-day dishes are well prepared and over-the-top. Ditto for excessive desserts like the pouf of cotton candy studded with candy and ice cream. *440 W Randolph St*

IMAGINE THE SCANDAL OF

Fresh Lobster

MINGLING WITH MAC & CHEESE

Recently at The Capital Grille,
Lobster was found fraternizing with Baked Campanelle Pasta
in Mascarpone, Havarti and Grana Padano cream sauce.
Yes, the rumors did fly.
Filet Mignon, with its crown of Lump Crab Meat,
rushed to the defense of this unlikely duo.
But alas, until the purists settle down,

OH, HOW PEOPLE WILL TALK.

Plan your next rendezvous with us.

THE
CAPITAL
GRILLE

WE WINE. WE DINE.

5340 N. River Road, Rosemont · 847 671 8004 · thecapitalgrille.com
Also located in: Chicago · 312 337 9400 · Lombard · 630 627 9800

NICE RACK A couple cows worth of steaks in Smith & Wollensky's cooler await the Chicago Bears' defensive line.

between Canal and Orleans Sts (312-575-9900). El: Green, Pink to Clinton. Bus: 14, 20, 56. Lunch (Mon Fri), dinner (Mon–Sat) (closed Sun). Average main course: $30.

❋ **The Palm** A chain steakhouse inside a hotel isn't the first place that comes to mind to satisfy carnivorous cravings in this town. But if you've got a taste for old-fashioned indulgence, it would be a shame to overlook this spot that does wonders with monstrous cuts of USDA Prime, gargantuan lobsters and classic artery-clogging add-ons like creamed spinach and French-fried onions. Add a martini or two, and you'll be partying like it's 1959. Swissotel, 323 E Wacker Dr at Columbus Dr (312-616-1000). El: Brown, Green, Orange, Pink, Purple (rush hrs) to State; Red to State/Lake. Bus: 4, X4, 29, 36, 60, 146, 151. Lunch, dinner. Average main course: $30.

❋ **Phil Stefani's 437 Rush** No run-down rooms, no grumpy old-school service, no cigar puffing at the tables. In the world of steakhouses, Phil Stefani's slick, cosmopolitan version is as refreshing as shrimp cocktail. If you're up for steak, expect expertly prepared porterhouses, with a well-seasoned crust hiding tender flesh. For lighter fare, dig into the broiled Dover sole, a dish that perfectly balances the textures and flavors of the soft fish, hollandaise, mugnaia, and almondine sauce. 437 N Rush St between Hubbard and Illinois Sts (312-222-0101). El: Red to Grand. Bus: 2, 3, X4, 10, 26, 29, 65, 125, 143, 144, 145, 146, 147, 151, 157. Lunch (Mon–Fri), dinner (closed Sun). Average main course: $25.

❋ **Rosebud Prime** The newest addition to the Chicagoland restaurant empire offers more of the same to its loyal business-casual clientele: pricey, well-portioned steaks, chops and fish in a comfortable yet elegant atmosphere. Fans of the plush steakhouse

feel should settle in comfortably and go for broke with a nice bottle of Cab, the 18-ounce Delmonico rib eye and sides of sautéed mushroom and garlicky spinach. An upstairs room offers privacy to broker that big deal. 1 S Dearborn St at Madison St (312-384-1900). El: Blue to Monroe. Bus: 14, 20, X20, 22, 24, 36, 56, 60, 62, 124, 157, 129. Lunch (Mon–Fri), dinner. Average main course: $28.

★ ❋ ❲ **Rosebud Steakhouse** Relax—this isn't the touristy red-sauce joint on Rush Street. Instead, this bustling, low-lit room is full of dark wood and red leather, lending it an old-school feel. If you can get a seat, you'll be told about the specialty, a bone-in filet as soft as pudding. The Scottish salmon is perfect with a Meyer lemon butter sauce. On a budget? Grab the burger. It's thick, juicy, great with blue cheese, and only sets you back twelve bucks. 192 E Walton St between Michigan Ave and Mies van der Rohe Way (312-397-1000). El: Red to Chicago. Bus: 36, 66, 143, 144, 145, 146, 147, 148, 151. Lunch (Mon–Fri), dinner. Average main course: $27.

Saloon Steakhouse Often overlooked in the classic Chicago steakhouse scene, this spot hits every element with consistency—white coats on the waiters, autographed baseballs along the walls and butter-soft steaks. The bone in filet is as flavorful as any we've ever had, and the house specialty, the Wagyu (the American Kobe) filet was incredibly tender. And sometimes you just want a nice, juicy steak minus Nicole Richie sightings. 200 E Chestnut St at Mies van der Rohe Way (312-280-5454). El: Red to Chicago. Bus: 125, 143, 144, 145, 146, 147, 151. Lunch, dinner. Average main course: $35.

❦ ❋ **Smith & Wollensky** The riverside location of this steak-and-chops

joint is such a big part of Chicago's vibe that it may surprise you to learn it's not a Windy City original (the chain started in New York in 1977). Nevertheless, it still hangs with the big boys. Here's how: a creamy and slightly smoky split-pea soup; an all-American wine list; and, of course, those big, fat steaks, all of which are consistently cooked to perfection. (But steer clear of the New York strip. You know, just on principle.) 318 N State St between Kinzie and Hubbard Sts (312-670-9900). El: Red to Grand; Brown, Purple (rush hrs) to Merchandise Mart. Bus: 22, 29, 36. Lunch, dinner. Average main course: $40.

❋ ❲ **Sullivan's Steakhouse** You'd think a chain steakhouse would get lost in the shuffle, but this spot distinguishes itself with nightly live jazz, and although the cigar bar is no more, smoking is welcome (if not encouraged) on the patio. There's also an extensive wine list so you can sip while you work your way through the signature 20-ounce bone-in Kansas City strip. Though the menu is standard—steaks, chops and seafood are joined by mandatory hearty starters and the usual sides— it's reliable. 415 N Dearborn St at Hubbard St (312-527-3510). El: Red to Grand. Bus: 22, 29, 36, 65. Dinner. Average main course: $25.

Tramonto Steak & Seafood With their upscale, three-restaurant food court in the Westin Hotel, Rick Tramonto and Gale Gand have upped the ante for dining in Wheeling. This steakhouse is the most traditional (and expensive) option, offering a solid menu of all the usual chops and seafood suspects. The steaks are fine and all, but we prefer the braised-beef short ribs, with their luscious layers of buttery fat. For dessert, you'll want to go equally simple: We suggest the chocolate souffle. 601 N Milwaukee Ave, Wheeling (847-777-6575). Dinner. Average main course: $30.

Thai

NICE THAI A handful of authentic options rotate often on the specials board at Bodhi Thai Bistro.

Amarind's Chef Rangsan Sutcharit's Thai creations draw faithful crowds to his charming eatery on the border of Oak Park and Chicago. Panang curry is the perfect balance of spice and tang. The *pad kee mao* ("drunken man's noodles") are tender and flavorful. And the chef isn't shy with the presentation skills he perfected during nine years turning vegetables into works of art at upscale Arun's. Once you become a regular, you can call ahead and make off-menu requests. Amarind's has kid-friendly plates and utensils. *6822 W North Ave, Oak Park (773-889-9999). El: Green to Oak Park. Bus: 72, Pace 311. Lunch (Tue–Sat), dinner (closed Mon). Average main course: $10.50.*

▼ **Arun's** This legendary restaurant was the first in America to nab four Mobil stars, a AAA award and a James Beard for Best Chef in the Midwest. These days, brilliant Thai food is more prevalent, and you can get some of this elsewhere for a smaller bill, if not with service, ambiance and wine pairings. For $85, you'll get a 12-course tasting of excellent food, including delicate beef panang curry, ethereal lemongrass crab cake and perfectly steamed, curry-drizzled lobster. *4156 N Kedzie Ave*

between Warner and Berteau Aves (773-539-1909). El: Brown to Kedzie. Bus: 80, X80. Dinner (closed Mon). Average degustation: $85.*

▼ ◷ ✱ **BYOB Blue Elephant** When it's warm outside and its patio is open, this tiny restaurant's seating capacity triples. But no matter the weather, the kitchen (on view from the dining room) remains mind-bogglingly tiny when you think about the never-ending number of dishes this place puts out. Order the aromatic bowl of pasta sauced with green curry and topped with salmon, and you'll know that the more interesting fusion dishes are the way to go. *1235 W Devon Ave at Magnolia Ave (773-262-5216). El: Red to Loyola. Bus: 36, 147, 151, 155. Lunch (Mon–Sat), dinner. Average main course: $8.*

★ ▼ ◷ **BYOB Bodhi Thai Bistro** Vilairat Junthong, a pillar in the local Thai community who has cooked or consulted for some of the best Thai spots in town (Sticky Rice, Spoon Thai), is behind this Berwyn spot. Ask for one of the specials and you'll be rewarded with the less-familiar, more-delicious specialties of northeastern Thailand. Highlights include two

kinds of pork-rice sausage and hunks of crispy pork belly with Chinese broccoli in a clingy paste of red chiles, garlic and oyster sauce. *6211 Roosevelt Rd, Berwyn (708-484-9250). El: Blue to Austin/Lombard. Bus: 91, Pace 305, Pace 315. Lunch (Mon–Sat), dinner. Average main course: $9.*

▼ ◷ **BYOB Dharma Garden** The Thai owners of this blissed-out spot are self-described "biospiritualists," which means that they don't serve "land animals" (only veggies and seafood), they aim to use the freshest ingredients possible and the bar serves nothing but freshly squeezed juice concoctions. Housemade, garlic-flecked, steamed potstickers are delicate wraps with spinach-carrot-cabbage filling, and the Dharma Garden spring rolls are the epitome of fresh, with bright flavors of Thai basil and mint. *3109 W Irving Park Rd between Albany Ave and Troy St (773-588-9140). El: Brown to Kedzie. Bus: 80, X80, 82. Lunch, dinner. Average main course: $9.*

▼ ✱ **BYOB Kan Pou** This Thai spot has an adorable, eager-to-please staff and solid, consistent standards. Fans of pad thai and panang curry will be satisfied but even more impressed with the papaya salad's balance of bright citrus, fiery chiles and just-funky-enough fish sauce. A plate of butter cookies baked by the owner's wife arrives at the end of the meal—so good you'll also want to take a bag or two home. *4256 N Western Ave at Cullom Ave (773-866-2839). El: Brown to Western. Bus: 49, X49, 78. Lunch, dinner. Average main course: $14.*

☺ **Manee Thai** This popular Avondale Thai spot (best known for its private-party room that held many a karaoke birthday party) may reopen its original location next year after a fire destroyed it, but in the meantime this West Town shop serves as the stand-in. The menu is identical, with the standard noodles, rice dishes and curries front and center. Best bets include the sweet and spicy "7 Buddies," a fresh and crunchy green papaya salad; and the catfish *pad ped*, hunks of crispy fish smothered in red-curry paste and globe-shaped Thai eggplants and al dente bamboo shoots. No karaoke, but feel free to sing along with the random tunes piped out of the overhead speakers. *1546 W Chicago Ave between Armour St and Ashland Ave (312-733-3339). El: Blue to Chicago. Bus: 9, X9, 66. Lunch, dinner. Average main course: $7.*

▼ ☺ BYOB **Opart Thai House** Two decades old and still bustling, this Thai stalwart sits under the shadow of the Lincoln Square Brown Line station. Wine-toting couples swap forkfuls of sweet-and-sour *mee krob* (a heap of crunchy noodle threads with sautéed shrimp), tart *naem sod* (minced chicken tossed in a limey dressing with peanuts and raw ginger) and a flavorful rendition of *pad ped pla dook* (hunks of crispy catfish sautéed in red curry paste with green beans and eggplant). *4658 N Western Ave at Artesian Ave (773-989-8517). El: Brown to Western. Bus: 11, 49, X49, 81. Lunch, dinner. Average main course: $8.* ● *Other locations: 1906 S State St (312-567-9898), 143 Skokie Blvd, Wilmette (847-853-9898).*

★ ▼ ☺ BYOB **Rosded** If you happen to blink while on your way for a dose of Germanic oompah in Lincoln Square, you might just miss one of the better Thai restaurants in town. The range of "safe" bets and authentic eats is vast, but all is tasty. Don't miss the tangy "waterfall" beef salad tossed with roasted rice powder, the earthy "boat" noodles with pork, the spicy-sour Isaan-style soup and the crispy catfish steaks smothered in pasty red-curry sauce. If your server doesn't have the English translations handy, spend a couple of minutes explaining what you want. *2308 W Leland Ave at Lincoln Ave (773-334-9055). El: Brown to Western. Bus: 11, 49, X49, 81. Lunch, dinner (closed Mon). Average main course: $7.*

▼ ☺ BYOB **Silver Spoon** This Thai spot is the sister restaurant of Lincoln Square's outstanding Spoon Thai, and being right next to the Thai Consulate, we figured the food would be far from Americanized stuff. Surprisingly, the fare is decidedly tame, even for Gold Coast tastes. This isn't necessarily a bad thing (and could be a good jumping off point for Thai-food novices) because what it does, it does well. Chive dumplings get things off to a good start, the *somtum* (papaya salad) is fiery and flavorful, and the panang beef curry is perfectly balanced, with manageable heat. *710 N Rush St between Superior and Huron Sts (312-944-7100). El: Red to Chicago. Bus: 3, 4, X4, 10, 26, 66, 145, 146, 147, 151. Lunch, dinner. Average main course: $7.*

BYOB Tip: *Thai*

Wine: *Gewürztraminer or pinot noir*

Thai food leans a little sweet spicy; so does gewürztraminer. For dishes with red chiles, or for beef-based dishes, pinot noir exhibits smooth edges but enough complexity to stand tall.

Beer: *American pale ale or French sparkling cider*

Pale ale is typically bright and crisp from hops that lend citrusy aromatics to mirror the lime in many Thai dishes, while sparkling cider is equal parts tart and sweet—just like most Thai food.

Buy it at Sheridan Irving L Liquor (3944 N Sheridan Rd, 773-528-6753) then **bring it** to TAC Quick Thai Kitchen (this page).

Buy it at Leland Inn (4664 N Western Ave, 773-561-4109) then **bring it** to Rosded (this page).

Buy it at Sam's Wine & Spirits (1727 Marcey St, 312-664-4394) then **bring it** to Thai Lagoon (p.128).

★ ▼ ☺ BYOB **Spoon Thai** Get adventurous with *kung chae naam plaa*, raw shrimp marinated with lime juice, fish sauce, garlic and chile—a Thai take on ceviche. The Isaan-style pork-and-rice sausage is almost as addictive as the *naem khao thawt*, a crunchy, salty, tangy salad of fried rice, tiny ham bits and flecks of cilantro. Curry fans should try the *kaeng som kung sot*, a slightly sour, shrimp-dotted tamarind curry, or call ahead to request special fish balls doused with green curry. *4608 N Western Ave between Wilson and Eastwood Aves (773-769-1173). El: Brown to Western. Bus: 11, 49, X49, 78, 81. Lunch, dinner. Average main course: $7.*

★ ▼ ☺ BYOB **Sticky Rice** 2009 *Eat Out Awards, Readers' Choice: Best Thai* What we love about this unassuming storefront is that it keeps our interest with new concoctions every couple of weeks. Tried-and-true favorites include housemade spicy fermented pork sausage, probably the best *gang hung lay* (pork in sweet, garlicky, ginger-laden curry) in town, and *khua kae*, a stir-fry of chicken, baby corn, eggplant, shredded lime leaves and roasted rice powder that has a gingery citrus tang. Translated and vegetarian menus are available. (Note: This popular spot was closed for health-code violations in 2009, but cleaned up its act and reopened.) *4018 N Western Ave between Irving Park Rd and Cuyler Ave (773-588-0133). Bus: 49, X49, 80, X80. Lunch, dinner. Average main course: $5.*

▼ ☺ BYOB **Sweet Tamarind** True to its name, this charming spot injects dishes with sweet tamarind every chance it gets: Light and fresh cilantro–, mint– and basil–packed spring rolls get a sweet tamarind dipping sauce, and the crispy rice noodles in the *mee krob* are flavored with tamarind, green onion and egg. But even when the signature ingredient is omitted, dishes still stand out: Crispy catfish arrives in a red curry with a lot of kick, and a cakey pumpkin custard makes for a sweet, tamarind-free ending. *1034 W Belmont Ave between Kenmore and Seminary Aves (773-281-5300). El: Brown, Purple (rush hrs), Red to Belmont. Bus: 7, 8, 9, 11. Lunch, dinner. Average main course: $9.*

★ ☺ BYOB **TAC Quick Thai** The basic menu appeases the masses that flood the simple, minimalist room of this top-notch Thai joint. Without disregarding the promising rotations on the specials board, the true standouts can be found on the translated Thai-language menu, with never-fail flavor explosions such as tart and smoky pork-and-rice sausage; ground chicken with crispy basil and preserved eggs; and the earthiest beef noodle dish in town, the brisket-packed "boat noodles." *3930 N Sheridan Rd at Dakin St (773-327-5253). El: Red to Sheridan. Bus: 36, 80, 145, 151. Lunch, dinner (closed Tue). Average main course: $8.*

☺ BYOB **Thai Aree** This tidy Thai joint has unpredictable hours, but the loyalists who flock here don't seem to mind making a quick phone call before heading out. The inconvenience-worthy tasty eats include gingery ground pork with peanuts (*nam sod*) and the grilled shrimp with lemongrass. The perfectly balanced "kang" green curry is packed with bamboo, eggplant, basil and your choice of meat or tofu and will leave you satisfied. Most of the salads have the sour-salty-spicy kick for which Thai food is known. *3592 N Milwaukee Ave at Addison St (773-725-6751). Bus: 53, 56, 152. Dinner (closed Sun). Average main course: $9.*

★ ☺ **Thai Avenue** Located on a strip of Broadway known for its Vietnamese spots, the cuisine shifts to Thai at this simple storefront. Start with *yum woonsen*, a spicy glass-noodle salad with shrimp and ground chicken, and *namtok*, a pork salad with cilantro, red onion, peanuts and roasted rice powder. For more tangy-spicy-salty, go for the *name klug*, deep-fried rice with ham, peanuts, chiles and plenty of lime. Sweet sticky rice with mango is the perfect simple ending. *4949 N Broadway at Argyle St (773-878-2222). El: Red to Argyle. Bus: 36, 81, 92, 147, 151. Lunch, dinner. Average main course: $6.*

▼ ☺ **Thai Eatery** With all the attention other Western Avenue Thai spots get, this little guy often gets overlooked. True, you won't find Chiang Mai specialties, but sometimes you're just in the mood for a good tofu green curry. You'll get it here (but order it spicy to counter the sweet coconut milk), plus a dependable crispy noodle *kee mow* and fragrant, fresh soups. Salty-sour fans shouldn't miss the rice *nam sod*, our favorite dish in the house. *2234 N Western Ave between Lyndale St and Belden Ave (773-394-3035). El: Blue to Western. Bus: 49, 73, 74. Dinner. Average main course: $7.*

★ ▼ ☺ BYOB **Thai Elephant** At first glance, the menu at this little BYOB seems common, but superfresh ingredients make standard dishes sing. Don't miss the crispy basil-wrapped shrimp starter, the spicy tilapia with globe-shaped eggplants or the roasted duck curry packed with grapes, tomatoes and pineapple chunks. Grab dessert to go from the small counter of imported cookies and candies.

Side dish

LEANING TOWER Traditional Thai sweets and delicate butter cookies end the meal at Kan Pou with a bang.

Wait lifting

Jump ship from recession-proof restaurants with long lines—there are spots nearby that could use a boost.

It doesn't matter how bad the economy gets: There are some restaurants that not even an alien attack could make less popular. But those packing into these mainstays are ignoring a smaller, needier restaurant around the corner. That's why we're calling for line jumping—jumping out of lines and into an open table at an empty restaurant nearby. The benefit is threefold: less congestion at the first restaurant, more business for the second and less waiting for everybody involved.

THE LINE: Mixteco Grill (p.99)
THE JUMP: La Sierra (p.93)
Mixteco doubled its dining-room capacity, but that's done nothing to quell the crowds it gets, even on otherwise sleepy Wednesday nights. Weekends are only bound to make the crowds (and thus the waits) worse, so carry that six-pack of Pacifico to La Sierra instead. It may not specialize in *mole* like Mixteco, but it makes up for that with its own specialty: a menu of Ecuadorean food, such as a sumptuous chicken stew and *llampingachos*, potatoes with peanut sauce. (Don't worry—it goes just as well with the beer as the guac does.)

THE LINE: Avec (p.95)
THE JUMP: Nia (p.95)
Though less intimate and less ambitious with the food, Nia is surprisingly similar to Avec. Both restaurants employ a Mediterranean, small-plates format; both make charcuterie a primary concern (Nia has

curated a list of worldly meats, including Spain's justifiably famous *pata negra*); and though Avec has much more wine, Nia's list isn't too shabby, either. The one primary difference: At Nia you'll have some elbow room.

THE LINE: Sticky Rice (p.127)
THE JUMP: Kan Pou (p.126)
You'd be correct to think that Kan Pou's menu seems fairly typical next to Sticky Rice's (especially Sticky's no-longer-quite-secret northern Thai dishes). But people who like an excellent green-papaya salad or a solid panang curry need not fight the crowds at Sticky to get their Thai on. True, Kan Pou doesn't have the housemade sausages Sticky Rice does, but Sticky will never have Kan Pou's housemade butter cookies in flavors like lemongrass and clove.

THE LINE: Southport Grocery (p.19)
THE JUMP: Deleece (p.23)
Everybody and their nanny is addicted to Southport's cupcakes, and everybody is at least curious about the pancakes made from that cupcake batter. That's why it's so hard to get a table at Southport's Sunday brunch. Just up the street, however, is a brunch that's just as creative. Where Southport excels with the sweets, Deleece excels with savory, packing the menu with BLTs of Nueske's bacon, guacamole and Maytag blue cheese, and polenta layered with bacon, rosemary, spinach, tomato and spicy chile oil. And the really sweet part of Deleece: twice the room for your stroller.—*David Tamarkin*

5348 W Devon Ave between Central and Minnehaha Aves (773-467-1168). Bus: 85A, Pace 225, Pace 226. Lunch, dinner (closed Sun). Average main course: $7.

▼ ☉ **BYOB Thai Lagoon** True, this long-standing Thai spot is an Anglo favorite that isn't going to whip out ant-egg omelettes and fermented pork sausages to impress the authenticity police. But we like visiting for an inexpensive dinner with friends who aren't adventurous eaters and settling into the low-lit room for consistent, tasty eats. Green-curry tofu with green eggplants and basil is rich and fragrant. *Tom kha* soup packs plenty of lime punch, as well as a garden of vegetables. 2322 W North Ave at Claremont Ave (773-489-5747). El: Blue to Damen. Bus: 49, 50, 72. Dinner. Average main course: $7.

▼ ☉ **BYOB Thai Pastry & Restaurant** Dessert is not to be missed at this bright café: Miniature chocolate cakes and swan-shaped cream puffs end the meal on a perfectly sweet note. But don't discount the savories. Spring rolls wrapped in thin pastry are superfresh; roasted duck salad is a heavenly combination of rich duck, cool cilantro, sharp green onion and a hint of chile pepper; and panang curry is sweet. Ignore the mussels, though—when there's a huge dessert pastry case, they're just not worth the stomach space. 4925 N Broadway between Ainslie and Argyle Sts (773-784-5399). El: Red to Argyle. Bus: 36, 92, 147, 151. Lunch, dinner. Average main course: $8.

▼ ☉ ✳ **BYOB Thai Village** Sometimes you want straight-up Thai and none of that secret-translated-menu stuff. The crispy roll appetizer is addictive with threads of vermicelli noodle, ground chicken and sprouts. The peanut-vinegar sauce shines in the fried tofu starter, as does the tangy, spicy lime dressing for both the papaya and the charbroiled sliced beef salad with big chunks of tomato. Pad thai is tasty enough; a better bet is eggplant basil or the spinach and pork in tamarind curry. 2053 W Division St between Damen and Hoyne Aves (773-384-5352). El: Blue to Division. Bus: 49, X49, 50, 70. Lunch, dinner. Average main course: $7.

▼ ☉ **Thai Wild Ginger** Americanized Thai restaurants are a dime a dozen, so why is this one successful? Two reasons: It's across from Webster Place theater, and the affable chef-owner, Tommy, is the nicest guy around. When he's not in the dining room kissing babies, he's in the kitchen turning out Thai standards. The crispy shrimp and the lime-dressed chicken salad are good starters, and the duck or the garlic-lemongrass shrimp are tasty entrées. Vegetarians will be happy with nearly a dozen meat-free dishes. 2203 N Clybourn Ave at Webster Ave (773-883-0344). El: Brown, Purple (rush hrs), Red to Fullerton. Bus: 9, 74. Lunch, dinner. Average main course: $9.

☉ **BYOB Yum Thai** The solemn Thai ladies here churn out regular menu items, but for authentic heat, we order from the "Thai menu." Tofu is sculpted into fried sheets and then stuffed with even firmer tofu for a remarkable impersonation of meat. Lime-based soups open up the palate for entrées like preserved egg with basil and curried roasted duck (an excellent balance of richness and spice). For a blast of Bangkok in the Western Suburbs, this is your best bet. 7748 Madison St, Forest Park (708-366-8888). El: Green, Blue to Harlem. Bus: 301, 303, 310, 393. Lunch, dinner (closed Mon). Average main course: $7.

Vegetarian

▼ ◷ **Alice & Friends' Vegetarian Café** This place is packed with as many meat-eaters as vegheads, all peaced out by the loopy lavender walls and the Korean spiritual guru video playing on the front-room TV. We don't know exactly what's in the crispy "unchicken" drumsticks slathered in tangy barbecue sauce, but we know we can't taste the faux meat under the sauce. Steamed veggie dumplings are delicious, if you whisk some chile paste into the soy sauce. Noodle lovers should try the yakisoba or the glass noodles made from sweet-potato starch. *5812 N Broadway between Ardmore and Thorndale Aves (773-275-8797). El: Red to Bryn Mawr. Bus: 36, 84, 147. Lunch (Sat), dinner (Mon–Sat) (closed Sun). Average main course: $10.*

▼ ◷ **Amitabul** Like a Zen koan shocking the mind into enlightenment, this Korean vegan restaurant is an awakening—for vegans, vegetarians and carnivores alike—to how delicious a meatless, eggless, dairy-free meal can be. Employing "Zen meditation cooking energy," chefs whip up everything from vegan dumplings, organic veggies and noodle soups to spicy curry and tofu dishes. Several flavors of vegan ice cream like vanilla, green tea and plum are available in warmer months. *6207 N Milwaukee Ave between Huntington and Raven Sts (773-774-0276). Bus: 56A, Pace 270. Lunch, dinner (closed Sun, Mon). Average main course: $10.*

▼ ◷ B **Blind Faith Café** A vegetarian restaurant in a college town is like a Hooters by the airport: It's a sure thing. Among the NU students at this Evanston institution you'll find plenty of thirtysomething couples, septuagenarians and families eating their way through the meatless menu. Start with the crispy risotto cakes over fresh vegetables. We may miss the sizzling skillet, but we don't long for meat while making fajitas with black beans, guac, seitan, red peppers, salsa and brown rice. Be sure to try a decadent dessert from the attached bakery. *525 Dempster St, Evanston (847-328-6875). El: Purple to Dempster. Bus: Pace 205, Pace 250 Dempster. Breakfast, brunch (Sat, Sun), lunch, dinner. Average main course: $11.*

★ ▼ ✳ B **Chicago Diner** Even non-vegetarians know Chicago Diner. The vibe is normal, everyday diner, albeit with soy milk, tofu and tempeh on the giant menu. Waits for weekend brunch can get painful (even though the menu is served daily), but patient non–meat-eaters are rewarded with dense (and fairly flaky) soy margarine biscuits and sweet chocolate-almond muffins made with vegan egg substitute.

French toast is a little soggy and lackluster—but after all, this *is* diner food. The back patio is an outdoor oasis. *3411 N Halsted St between Roscoe St and Newport Ave (773-935-6696). El: Brown, Purple (rush hrs), Red to Belmont. Bus: 8, 22, 77. Brunch, lunch, dinner. Average main course: $11.*

☺ **Chowpatti** If you're the vegetarian who hates the condescending, "Well, I guess we could take the bacon off the cobb salad," this place will be your nirvana. The 26-page, global, meatless menu takes awhile to navigate, with choices inspired from cuisines of America, Italy, Mexico, the Middle East and, most notably, India. Given that the owners of this decades-old veg haven are Indian, we suggest sticking to the filled crêpelike *dosas*, the rice-lentil pancakes dubbed *uttapam*, any of the veggie-packed curries and the addictive crunchy-sweet-spicy *bhel chaats*. *1035 S Arlington Heights Rd, Arlington Heights (847-640-9554). Bus: Pace 694. Lunch, dinner (closed Mon). Average main course: $10.*

▼ BYOB **Cousin's I.V.** Raw foodists are rejoicing that chef Mehmet Ak is making 100% raw, 100% vegan and mostly organic renderings of Turkish and American classics. But they're not the only ones who will enjoy his delicious "pizza"—a flaxseed cracker topped with garlicky tomato sauce, fresh avocado and marinated mushrooms—and his lively marinated spinach. The nutty "zoom" burger and sprout-heavy tabouli, on the other hand, are probably easier to swallow for raw foodists, if only because, for them, there aren't many other options. *3038 W Irving Park Rd between Whipple St and Albany Ave (773-478-6868). Bus: 80, X80. Lunch, dinner. Average main course: $12.*

▼ ☺ ☀ B **de.li.cious café** See Bakeries/Cafés for review.

▼ ☺ BYOB **Dharma Garden** See Thai for review.

★ ▼ B **Green Zebra** Shawn McClain's moss-colored, minimalist house of Zen is the only upscale dining experience Chicago vegetarians can truly call their own. The menu's classed-up brunch classics include German-style pancakes with Granny Smith apples and caramelized–banana crêpes with ricotta and Wisconsin honey. Chef de cuisine Molly Harrison's superseasonal dinner menu is always in rotation. Depending on when you visit, you may find *pappardelle* with honey-roasted figs and fennel; sweet onion and garlic soup; and slow-roasted shitake mushrooms with crispy potato and savoy cabbage. *1460 W Chicago Ave at Greenview Ave (312-243-7100). El: Blue*

to Chicago. Bus: 9, 66. Brunch (Sun), dinner. Average main course: $11.*

▼ ☀ (**Heartland Café** See Classic American $15 and under for review.

▼ ☀ B **Karyn's Cooked** Karyn Calabrese is known for her 100% organic, vegan and raw cuisine (see: Karyn's Fresh Corner). But here she turns up the heat. These dishes are still vegan and organic but appeal to those who aren't ready for raw with hummus, pizza, salads and entrées made with fake meats. The restaurant serves organic wines and beer and yummy Sunday brunch, with a "conscious comfort food" vibe. Remember: In addition to meatless, vegan means no dairy or refined sugar. *738 N Wells St between Superior St and Chicago Ave (312-587-1050). El: Brown, Purple (rush hrs) to Chicago. Bus: 66. Brunch (Sun), lunch, dinner. Average main course: $12.*

▼ ☀ B BYOB **Karyn's Fresh Corner** Karyn Calabrese's menu is 100% organic, 100% vegan and 100% raw (i.e. uncooked), so you probably have to be a vegan raw-foodist to appreciate what she's doing. But some dishes taste good no matter what your eating habits are. The stuffed-mushrooms starter is superbly fresh and garlicky, and the "seaweed dim sum," a dumplingesque appetizer, is filled with a creamy mixture of avocado and kalamata olives. Unfortunately, the "pasta primavera," which uses thin slices of zucchini in place of pasta, is flavorless enough to send us even deeper into carnivorism. *1901 N Halsted St at Wisconsin St (312-255-1590). El: Brown, Purple (rush hrs) to Armitage; Red to North/Clybourn. Bus: 8, 72, 73. Breakfast, brunch (Sun), lunch, dinner. Average main course: $16.*

▼ ☺ **Kopi, A Traveler's Café** See Bakeries/Cafés for review.

▼ ☺ ☀ **Lake Side Café** Adjacent to Inner Metamorphosis University, this spot is a great postyoga fuel-up, offering a nearly all-organic menu (90%, in fact). Meat-eaters won't be fooled by the Chicago Polish—the spicy tofu dog is missing the requisite snap of an encased meat. But thanks to heaps of sauerkraut, mustard and relish, you'll hardly care. The veggie-packed, crispy-crust Organic Garden pizza makes junk food seem healthy. *1418 W Howard St at Sheridan Rd (773-262-9503). El: Purple, Red, Yellow to Howard. Bus: 22, 97, 147, 151, 201, 205, 206, Pace 215, Pace 290. Lunch (Sat only), dinner (closed Mon). Average main course: $7.*

★ ▼ ☺ **Mana Food Bar** *2009 Eat Out Awards, Readers' Choice: Best New Vegetarian* Susan Thompson and Jill Barron of De Cero have teamed up again for this spot, where global vegetarian fare is gobbled up by diners lounging on chunky wood stools and dark booths. Somewhere between Green Zebra and Earwax, two people will spend around $50 to leave full, so to leave both full *and* satisfied, choose wisely. We recommend sampling among small portions of simple yellow squash "pasta," asparagus ravioli in spicy tomato sauce and the brown rice-mushroom sliders. Chocolate pot de creme is a great ending. *1742 W Division St between Paulina and Wood Sts (773-342-1742). El: Blue to Division. Bus: 9, 50, 70. Lunch (Fri-Sun), dinner. Average small plate: $7.*

▼ ☀ (B **Morseland** See Classic American $16 and up for review.

▼ ☺ **New Life Vegetarian Restaurant and Health Food Store** New Life has changed owners and names over the years, but it still serves up dependable meatless dishes. Find all the standard vegetarian fare, like veggie burgers and "Stakelet" sandwiches. But we like to come early and hungry so we can fill up on a breakfast of veggie sausage, tofu eggs, brown rice and scalloped potatoes. Save room for lemon icebox pie, banana pudding or sweet-potato pie. *3141 W Roosevelt Rd between Troy St and Kedzie Ave (773-762-1090). El: Blue to Kedzie/Homan (Forest Park). Bus: 7, 12, 52, 94. Breakfast, lunch, dinner (closed Sun). Average main course: $6.*

▼ ☀ (**Pick Me Up Café** See Classic American $15 and under for review.

▼ ☺ **Soul Vegetarian East** In a family atmosphere for vegans looking to escape boring lentil hell, the "BBQ Twist" sandwich (made from wheat gluten) is as close to real barbecue pulled pork as vegetarians will get, and somehow the fried cauliflower tastes like chicken. If you have the time, sit for the full Sunday dinner. Alternating options may include a salad with tangy house dressing, fake-chicken potpie, collard greens, corn and potatoes. The vegan apple or peach pie that follows may not be healthy, but that was never the point of soul food. *205 E 75th St at Indiana Ave (773-224-0104). El: Red to 79th. Bus: 3, X3, 75. Breakfast (Sat, Sun), lunch, dinner. Average main course: $7.*

▼ ☀ B **Turquoise Café** See Middle Eastern for review.

★ ▼ ☺ BYOB **Udupi Palace** See Indian/Subcontinental for review.

★ ▼ ☺ BYOB **Uru-Swati** See Indian/Subcontinental for review.

▼ ☺ **Veggie Bite** The phrase "vegan fast food" may conjure up images of lettuce with a side of wheatgrass, but the grub at the city's second Veggie Bite location has more in common with your neighborhood burger joint than it does with a salad bar. Seitan subs in for steak in the fajita wrap and Philly cheese steak (which both taste strangely of curry), and sizzling "barbecue bites" come with a side of tangy 'cue sauce. Try the assortment of vegan cakes for a sweet ending to your healthy meal. *1300 N Milwaukee Ave at Paulina St (773-772-2483). El: Blue to Division. Bus: 50, 56, 70. Lunch, dinner. Average main course: $7.* ● *Other location: 3031 W 111th St (773-239-4367).*

★ ▼ ☺ B **Victory's Banner** There's an interesting distraction during the long wait for a table at this sunny brunch spot: A TV often shows videos of Indian guru Sri Chinmoy (of whom every employee at this meatless restaurant is a follower) lifting heavy things—a crew of firemen, a helicopter, a plane. Impressive, but we're bigger believers in the two-inch-thick French toast slathered in peach butter and maple syrup, or the pesto-laden, free-range scrambled eggs in the Satisfaction Promise, which comes with crispy potatoes and crusty bread. *2100 W Roscoe St at Hoyne Ave (773-665-0227). Bus: 50, 77, 152. Breakfast, brunch, lunch (closed Tue). Average main course: $7.50.*

Vietnamese

★ ▼ ☺ ✳ **Ba Le** When the French controlled Vietnam, baguettes crossed cultures, and one of the finest results of this is the *banh mi* sandwich. They're plentiful in this area, but this bakery creates most of the bread restaurants use, so go try the source. We like the barbecue pork and the Ba Le special, which piles housemade pâté, headcheese and pork onto a baguette with tangy carrot and daikon slivers, cilantro and jalapeño. *5018 N Broadway between Argyle St and Winnemac Ave (773-561-4424). El: Red to Argyle. Bus: 22, 36, 81, 92. Breakfast, lunch, dinner. Average sandwich: $3.*

☺ BYOB **Ben Tre Café** Named for a province in the Mekong Delta, Ben Tre presents authentic, homestyle Vietnamese cooking in a bright storefront. Pho arrives properly soulful with an aromatic broth and fresh herbs. The rice noodles with grilled beef and pork egg rolls (*bun bo nuong cha gio*) and a coconut-milk crêpe studded with pork belly and shrimp (*banh xeo*) exemplify the kitchen's skill with traditional dishes, and the green-papaya salad (*goi du du tom tit*) sent us straight to the tropics. *3146 W Touhy Ave between Albany and Kedzie Aves (773-465-3011). Bus: 11, 93, 96, Pace 290. Lunch, dinner, closed. Average main course: $9.*

☺ **Bon Bon Vietnamese Sandwiches** Positioned in the front half of My Gourmet Kitchen, this little sandwich counter does seven things, and all of them are Vietnamese-style *banh mi*. For our money, we prefer the tender chicken in gingery caramel and the "char siu" pork, equally tender but with a touch of garlic and hoisin. A few quibbles aside (carrot-daikon relish could be tangier, the pâté lacks oomph, the bread gets soggy from steaming in the foil wrap), it's a cute idea and a good snack at four bucks. *2333 W North Ave between Claremont and Western Aves (773-278-5800). El: Blue to Damen. Bus: 49, X49, 50, 72. 11am–8pm (closed Monday). Average sandwich: $4.*

☺ **Hai Yen** For this second location of the popular Argyle Street eatery of the same name, the dishes are served on chocolate-toned wooden tables and about a dozen wines are offered to match up with your meal. Standouts include crunchy shards of green papaya topped with slices of roasted pork, *la lot* leaves used to roll garlic-laden ground pork into sweet sausages, beef short ribs marinated in shallot and honey soy sauce and grilled, thick catfish filet baked in caramelized fish sauce. *2723 N Clark St at Schubert Ave (773-868-4888). El: Brown, Purple (rush hrs) to Diversey. Bus: 8, 22, 76. Lunch (Wed–Sun), dinner. Average main course: $10.* ● *Other location: 1055 W Argyle Street (773-561-4077).*

▼ ☺ BYOB **Hoanh Long** This simple Vietnamese spot can be a bit of a hike unless you're already far north, but sweet hospitality coupled with a few standout dishes make for a stop worth the gas. Use the accompanying lettuce leaves and fresh herbs to make wraps of eggy fritters of crispy shrimp and sweet-potato sticks, try the papaya salad topped with thin strips of grilled beef. One caveat: The pho is a

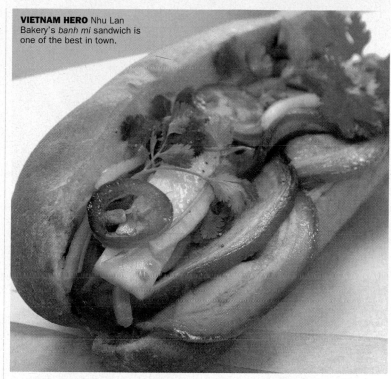

VIETNAM HERO Nhu Lan Bakery's *banh mi* sandwich is one of the best in town.

tad sweet, so doctor it with plenty of lime juice and chile paste for balance. *6144 N Lincoln Ave at Christiana (773-583-7770). Bus: 11, 82, 84, Pace 210. Lunch, dinner. Average main course: $10.*

★ ▼ ✳ **Le Colonial** There's no other Vietnamese joint in the city as sophisticated or styled as the dining room here. This hot spot spares no expense on impeccably fresh seafood and meat, and some dishes gain from French-colonial-Vietnam flair. Your duck will be lean yet juicy, marinated in ginger and glazed similar to traditional duck à l'orange, and your shrimp will come in a fat, crispy beignet. Head upstairs to the dim, sexy lounge for an after-dinner drink. *937 N Rush St between Walton and Oak Sts (312-255-0088). El: Red to Chicago. Bus: 36. Lunch, dinner. Average main course: $19.*

▼ BYOB **New Saigon** Judging by the sun-faded Michael Jackson wall art and the dusty Christmas decor, the "new" in the name of this Vietnamese standby might be stretching it. Take the dated decor as a sign of longevity, and for the secret to it, scan the War and Peace–size menu for gems like lemongrass-scented chicken and caramelized sesame beef over rice noodles with fresh Thai basil and a golden egg roll filled with succulent shredded pork. *5000 N Broadway St between Argyle and Ainslie Sts (773-334-3322). El: Red to Argyle. Bus: 36, 81, 147, 151. Lunch and dinner. Average main course: $6.*

☺ **Nha Trang** This little gem now resides in Logan Square after more than a decade of

operating on Argyle. The casual room, doting hosts and homestyle food make the experience seem like eating in someone's home, only *this* someone churns out barbecue shrimp and sprout–packed Vietnamese pancakes; rice noodle bowls brimming with barbecue pork, crispy egg rolls and peanuts; tangy, spicy lemon shrimp; and restorative, delicate chicken broth–based soups. *3711 W Belmont Ave between Lawndale and Ridgeway Aves (773-588-9232). El: Blue to Belmont. Bus: 56, 77, 82. Lunch, dinner. Average main course: $8.*

★ ▼ ☺ **Nhu Lan Bakery** This bakery makes about 1,000 deliciously crusty loaves of bread daily, providing the canvas for eight different *banh mi*. Pig out on the "seasoning pork," which layers glistening pork belly atop a slather of peppery housemade pâté. To make a meal, grab sides from the pastry case and fridge. Don't miss the dried shrimp sticky rice topped with Chinese sausage or the cheese-filled croissants, evidence that the French occupation of Vietnam had at least one positive outcome. *2612 W Lawrence Ave between Rockwell St and Talman Ave (773-878-9898). El: Brown to Rockwell. Bus: 49, X49, 81. Breakfast, lunch, dinner (closed Tue). Average sandwich: $2.25.*

▼ BYOB **Pho 777** The main event at this Vietnamese hole-in-the-wall is, as the name would suggest, the steaming bowls of pho, a Vietnamese beef noodle soup that is the perfect elixir on a cold and snowy Chicago day. When bleak weather subsides, switch gears with something bright and springy, like the citrus-kissed beef salad piled with crunchy bits of peanuts, fresh mint and green chiles

Side dish

Smackdown: Pho

Slurping his way through bowl after bowl of Vietnamese noodle soup, an intrepid reporter finds the best in town.

If chicken soup feeds the soul, then pho (pronounced "FUH"), the traditional Vietnamese beef noodle soup, is the curative for frozen bones. Usually served with a condiment tray featuring limes, chile paste, hoisin, bean sprouts, Asian basil and culantro (a sawtooth-shaped cilantro-like herb), it's also the ultimate tableside soup buffet. Customize to your heart's content, but for the purpose of this article, no extra flavorings were allowed. The focus was solely on the quality of the base broth, cuts of meat and noodles, with each pho ordered with eye of round steak, brisket, tripe, tendon, flank steak and tendon meatballs, a.k.a. the "supercombo" or *pho dac biet*.

6 The Noodle *(2236 S Wentworth Ave, 312-674-1168)*
Featuring more body and thickness than any of the other bowls we tried, this was the Salma Hayek of broths. Unfortunately, a spattering of oily fat droplets and poorly diced, superfatty tubes of tripe sunk this ship.

5 Pho Xua *(see this page)*
Maybe the best noodle in the bunch: fresh, slightly silky and not the pre-made commercial variety served at most of the other pho joints. Unfortunately, the insipid broth surrounding the noodle was unbearably salty.

4 Ben Tre Cafe *(see page 131)*
This is the ultimate "character actor" pho. It's a competent stew of even seasoning, beefiness and nonoffensive cuts that engages while you slurp, but it has few outlying qualities, thus making it forgettable once you finish.

3 Pho Xe Tang *(see this page)*
Even without adding the accompanying herbs, this broth had a green undertone and an inherent Asian basil perfume, along with a waft of clove and cinnamon. It might be the most popular spot among the competitors and could've been a contender for No. 1, but the slightly greasy finish detracted.

2 Hai Yen *(see page 131)*
The quality of the meat in this broth is unparalleled. The tendon is tender and lean; the tripe sliced into perfect, almost noodle-like strips; and the meatballs here (the only ones that left out gristly and fatty bits in favor of pure meat) were the best of the bunch. Unfortunately, the broth was a one-note wonder of pure, unseasoned beef.

1 Pho 888 *(see this page)*
Almost every Vietnamese spot on Argyle is a shoebox-size storefront, but Pho 888 is the dinkiest. Yet, like Napoleon, it compensates for its shortcomings with bombast—in this case, a menu that proclaims "The best Vietnamese beef noodle soup." Now, if we had a nickel for every spot that falsely claimed the best version of a dish, we could probably plug the city's budget shortfall and save you those pesky meter increases. This spot is the exception. The broth was clean, golden, light and aromatic—like a peppery beef tea filled with pliant noodles, lean tendon, delicate tripe and rare, rich, peppery steak and flank.—*Michael Nagrant*

that add just the right amount of heat. *1065 W Argyle St between Kenmore and Winthrop Aves (773-561-9909). El: Red to Argyle. Bus: 36, 81, 151. Lunch, dinner (closed Tue). Average main course: $11.*

▼ ⊙ **BYOB Pho 888** "Clean yet complex" sums up this Argyle spot's namesake soup, which bears a hint of the sweet star-anise flavor but relies mainly on subtle beefiness and silky fresh noodles. The *banh mi thit nguoi* nails perfectly crusty bread, salty ham, a slather of earthy pâté, plus crunchy daikon, carrots and sliced chiles. And the massive lotus root salad is the best around, with plump shrimp, plenty of crunchy peanuts and enough tangy, herb-flecked dressing to spoon some onto your *banh mi* for extra flavor. *1137 W Argyle St between Broadway and Winthrop Ave (773-907-8838). El: Red to Argyle. Bus: 36, 81, 151. Lunch, dinner (Tue–Sun). Average main course: $8.*

★ ▼ ⊙ **BYOB Pho Xe Tang (Tank Noodle)** Known as "Tank" to Anglos, this spot is the answer for indecisive diners. Vietnamese-food pros will find that the lotus root salad (#5) is everything this cuisine can be—limey and minty with shrimp flavor, crunchy peanuts and a subtle chili kick. Pho broth is rich and complex, with all of the right accompaniments, and garlic-fish sauce-marinated "shaking beef" (#176) is flash-seared and served with vinegar-laced watercress. *4953-55 N Broadway at Argyle St (773-878-2253). El: Red to Argyle. Bus: 36, 81, 151. Breakfast, lunch, dinner (closed Wed). Average main course: $7.*

▼ ⊙ **BYOB Pho Xua** Vietnamese restaurants on Argyle are as common as noodles in a bowl of steaming pho. But with its microsuede chairs and sleek wooden tables, this noodle floats to the top of the broth. Even though it was named for the traditional beefy broth, the best bowl is the "fried duck noodle" filled with delicious ramen, a juicy caramelized duck leg and scallions. Segue into the noodles with a starter of betel leaf beef mini kebabs wrapped in wilted greens with a smoky honey flavor. *1020 W Argyle St between Kenmore Ave and Sheridan Rd (773-271-9828). El: Red to Argyle. Bus: 36, 81, 147, 151. Lunch, dinner (closed Thu). Average main course: $7.*

▼ ⊙ **BYOB Sabaidee** This storefront might seem like just another takeout spot. But a closer look reveals that the Laotian owners feature close to a dozen specialties of their homeland. Get the fried mangofish (served whole or chopped into a spicy salad); the tangy, crispy rice salad (*nam kao*); and the soy-rich stew of hard-boiled eggs, tofu and optional pork belly (*pa lo*). Bring a bottle of pinot noir to match, or try smoothies made with tropical fruits like the custardy, sweet sapote. *5359 N Broadway between Berwyn and Balmoral Aves (773-506-0880). El: Red to Berwyn. Bus: 36, 92, 146, 151. Lunch, dinner (closed Mon). Average main course: $5.*

⊙ **BYOB Simply It** The staff is as sweet as pie, the room is airy and comfortable, and the menu is affordable at this BYOB Vietnamese spot. The only downside is that compared to the stellar spots around Argyle Street, the food here is a bit standard. Skip so-so entrées and make a meal of starters like shrimp- or tofu-packed spring rolls, sweet potato and shrimp fritters, and shredded green papaya salad studded with bits of crunchy toasted garlic and peanuts. *2269 N Lincoln Ave between Webster and Belden Aves (773-248-0884). El: Brown, Purple (rush hrs), Red to Fullerton. Bus: 11, 74. Lunch, dinner (closed Mon). Average main course: $10.*

Bars and Lounges

Bars and Lounges

SIGN O' GOOD TIMES
We bet you a million dollars you'll find a Harp or two in here.

Northwest Side

✗ ✳ **Abbey Pub** Most people don't end up at this hard-to-get-to music venue unless they're seeing a live show, but the adjacent pub is worth a visit on its own. Sunday night's traditional Irish jam session lends support to the woody pub's Emerald Isle vibe; ditto for the respectable shepherd's pie. Cheapskates can seek out a spot on the patio and hear the indoor shows for free. *3420 W Grace St at Elston Ave (773-463-5808). El: Blue to Addison. Bus: 82 Kimball/Homan, 152 Addison. Mon–Fri 3pm–2am; Sat 9am–3am; Sun 9am–2am. Average beer: $4.*

Bim Bom Thanks to a metal-clad exterior that sticks out like a *Clockwork Orange* thumb in this ho-hum stretch of west Belmont Central, this hot, young Polish haunt is impossible to miss. Inside, the bar has an interior covered with intricate, high-quality metalwork from a local Polish artist. Add pool and foosball tables, a great jukebox and cheap drinks, and you might just start checking out real estate in the area. *5226 W Belmont Ave between Laramie and Lockwood Aves (773-777-2120). Bus: 77 Belmont, 85 Central. Mon–Fri noon–2am; Sat 10am–3am; Sun 11am–2am. Average beer: $3.*

✗ ✳ **Chief O'Neill's Pub** When two Irish-American musicians open a pub, you'd better believe they'll pay attention to the tunes. Even aside from the Sunday-night traditional Irish jam session, you can usually count on sipping your stout to bagpipe-driven sounds. In nice weather, the massive back patio doubles the capacity, with towering hedges muffling the sounds of Elston Avenue and dishes like classic fish-and-chips transporting you to the Emerald Isle. *3471 N Elston Ave at Addison St (773-583-3066). El: Blue to Addison. Bus: 77 Belmont, 152 Addison. Mon–Thu 4pm–2am, Fri noon–2am; Sat 9am–3am; Sun 10am–2am. Average imported beer: $5.50.*

❰ **Christina's Place** The windowless front door isn't exactly a welcome mat, but once inside Christina's compact, cozy digs (and after an insanely cheap $2 Guinness) you'll feel right at home. The football pennants hanging over the bar and baseball on several TVs scream sports bar, but the Talking Heads and '60s-era Stones on the juke combined with the bartender's Iggy and the Stooges shirt say otherwise. *3759 N Kedzie Ave between Waveland Ave and Grace St (773-463-1768). El: Blue to Kedzie. Bus: 80, 82, 152. Mon–Thu 3pm–4am; Fri, Sun 11am–4am; Sat 11am–5am. Average beer: $3.*

✗ **Fifth Province Pub** If everyone were as beer-minded as the Irish, cultural institutions would be flooded with the thirsty and eager to learn. Case in point: In addition to its library and museum packed with historical acquisitions, the Irish American Heritage Center boasts a cozy weekends-only pub with free live music (Irish, of course) and Guinness-absorbing classics like fish-and-chips. *4626 N Knox Ave between Wilson and Leland Aves (773-282-7035). El: Blue to Montrose. Bus: 54A, 78, 81 (24hrs). Fri 5pm–midnight; Sat 7pm–midnight. Average beer: $4.*

✳ **Ham Tree** Though the name is a head-scratcher, this no-frills pub is a friendly Jefferson Park retreat. A faded mural promises 101 beers, but even though that number has dwindled to a more modest selection, the regulars—middle-aged dudes and their frosted-hair babes—probably couldn't care less. The trees in the adjacent beer garden don't bear any ham, but they will make for a shady spot in the summertime. *5333 N Milwaukee Ave between Central and Parkside Aves (773-792-2072). El: Blue to Jefferson Park. Bus: 56, 81 (24hrs), 85. Sun–Fri 10am–2am; Sat 10am–3am. Average beer: $3.*

✗ ✳ **Hops & Barley** Neighborhood bars are as rampant as drunks in Wrigleyville, right? So why make this one your hangout? Because your current 'hoodie doesn't have exposed wood beams and brick walls, wrought-iron chandeliers, or a downstairs lounge with leather banquettes and a black-felt pool table. The menu alone, which offers a good selection of nicely presented salads, sandwiches and steaks, is well worth becoming a regular. *4359 N Milwaukee Ave between Pensacola and Montrose Aves (773-286-7415). Bus: 54, 56, 78. Sun–Fri 11am–2am; Sat 11am–3am. Average beer: $4.*

✕ ♦ Moher's Public House It's more Irish than many Irish bars in the city (note the Celtic designs on the ceilings, the portraits of Irish authors on the wall), but this Edgebrook joint courts more of a U.K. crowd. As one of the first bars to sprout since the 'hood's dry years ended, it's become a hot spot for everyone in the community. In other words, don't be alarmed when you see children running around the place—they're all part of the gang. *5310 W Devon Ave between Spokane and Minnehaha Aves (773-467-1954). Bus: 84 Peterson. Sun–Fri 11am–2am; Sat 11am–3am; . Average beer: $4.*

✳ Montrose Saloon This ideal neighborhood dive is somehow still an overlooked gem. The wood paneling is balanced out by exposed brick, a fantastic tin ceiling and stained-glass lamps hanging over the bar. The giant outdoor patio is one of this area's best-kept secrets—toss horseshoes, play the bean-bag game, or just drink and smoke. And don't mind the new condo-dwellers across the street complaining about the noise; they'll either move soon or come down to join you. *2933 W Montrose Ave at Richmond St (773-463-7663). Bus: 78 Montrose. Mon–Thu 2pm–2am; Fri, Sun 11am–2am; Sat 11am–3am. Average beer: $3.*

The Original Dugan's Emblazoned with shamrocks, a sign near the front reads "Drink like a champion today." How could you not want to, what with such heartfelt encouragement? With a dozen drafts, a comfortable U shaped bar and a popcorn machine to keep you thirsty, you'll find it's easy to do just that. This homey pub also puts out free eats on Bears game days and hosts a trivia contest nearly every Friday. *6051 N Milwaukee Ave between Peterson and Elston Aves (773-467-5555). Bus: 36, 81 (24hrs), 270. Sun–Fri 11am–2am; Sat 11am–3am. Average beer: $2.75.*

◖✕ Sidekicks The decor of this spacious karaoke and darts bar is reminiscent of roller rinks circa the 1980s: pink and aqua neon signage, wood paneling, fantastic mullets, and all the nachos and pizza you can handle. Drinks are ridiculously cheap, and the karaoke book is chock full of corny '70s and '80s hits with a dedicated stage for performing, making this place a natural choice for getting drunk and stupid with large groups of people. *4424 W Montrose Ave between Kostner and Kenneth Aves (773-545-6212). El: Blue to Montrose. Bus: 54 Cicero, 78 Montrose. Mon–Fri 2pm–4am; Sat noon–5am; Sun noon–4am. Average cocktail: $4.*

✕ ♦ Vaughan's Pub Northwest A deserted stretch of Northwest Highway isn't what you would call charming surroundings, but is exactly the kind of stretch that needs a cozy escape. Raised booths flanking a fireplace facilitate intimate conversations over pints of imported ale, while the battered old bar encourages drinking with the friendly, blue-collar crowd. That Guinness getcha hungry? Dig into menu highlights like shepherd's pie. *5485 N Northwest Hwy between Mason and Austin Aves (773-631-9206). Bus: 56A, 68, Pace 270. Sun–Fri 11am–2am; Sat 11am–3am. Average beer: $4.*

✕ ✳ Windsor Tavern It's sleepers like this wood-clad corner pub that make bar-hopping worthwhile. Friendly staff and a great beer garden certainly help (well, the latter will when it warms up), but it's the darn good food that seals the deal. Fish tacos and juicy burgers

frame the eclectic menu, but take a look at what the locals order. Yep, that's ceviche—perfect with whatever draft is on special that night. *4530 N Milwaukee Ave at Windsor Ave (773-736-3400). El: Blue to Jefferson Park. Bus: 54, X54, 56, 78. Tue–Fri, Sun 2pm–2am; Sat 2pm–3am (closed Mon) . Average beer: $3.50.*

Far North Side

✕ Candlelite Chicago For most of you, this place isn't worth the hike. But for you Far North Siders out there, it's an oasis in your own back yard. This 60-year-old gem offers two-dozen beers, cracker-thin "Chicago bar–style" pizza and herb-flecked garlic fries that have quite the loyal local following. Our only hope is that someone fixes the schizo jukebox that's been playing Hall & Oates every other song. *7452 N Western Ave between Birchwood and Fargo Aves (773-465-0087). Bus: 49B, 97, 201. Mon–Thu 5pm–2am; Fri 4pm–2am; Sat, Sun 11am–2am. Average cocktail: $7.*

Cary's Lounge Smack in the middle of Indo/Pak territory, this tiny German-style hideaway has been plugging away since '72. Bartenders flip the TV channels back and forth between basketball games and *The Simpsons*, but if that doesn't interest you, there's free pool and a stash of frisky regulars to keep you occupied. *2251 W Devon Ave between Oakley and Bell Aves (773-743-5737). Bus: 22 (24hrs), 10B, 155. Mon–Fri 7am–2am; Sat 7am–3am; Sun 11am–2am. Average beer: $2.75.*

Cunneen's Newspaper articles declaring the end of Prohibition hang on these walls and the clock is graced with Mayor Daley's mug…the *first* Mayor Daley. So it's no surprise that this place is as friendly, neighborly and comfortable (did we mention the La-Z-Boys?) as bars used to be back in the day—you know, before velvet ropes and vodka Red Bulls. *1424 W Devon Ave between Glenwood and Newgard Aves (773-274-9317). El: Red to Loyola. Bus: 22 (24hrs), 36, 155. Sun–Fri noon–2am; Sat noon–3am. Average beer: $3. Cash only.*

▼ Duke's Tucked in the shadow of the Morse Red Line tracks, this laid-back neighborhood bar shouldn't be confused with the similarly named spot farther south on Clark. Quirky art covers the red and blue walls, and bands regularly perform country, rock and bluegrass on a small stage adjacent to the main bar. If you visit on an off-night, channel the vibe via the classic country and Southern-rock-packed jukebox. *6920 N Glenwood Ave between Morse and Talwell Aves (773-764-2826). El: Red to Morse. Bus: 96, 147, 155. Sun–Fri noon–2am; Sat noon–3am. Average cocktail: $5.*

◖▼ ✳ Jackhammer A construction theme dominates this Rogers Park gay bar, where a grab bag of leather dudes, street-tough trannies and Boystowners out for adventure cram the dance floor on weekend nights. If you can lure yourself away from the constant porn, a beautiful outdoor patio beckons with a psychic on hand to predict that the guy you're about to take home is probably not the same one you'll be introducing to your parents one day. *6406 N Clark St at Devon Ave (773-743-5772). Bus: 22 (24hrs), 36, 155. Mon–Thu 5pm–4am; Sat 5pm–5am; Sun noon–4am. Average beer: $3.*

Jarheads Sarge did two tours in Vietnam, and this Rogers Park bar, which he's owned for

**INSIDE TRACK
JUKE JOINTS**

Did the powers that be at your favorite watering hole replace the old-school jukebox for one of those digital travesties? It's happening in bars all over Chicago, but not at the Old Town Ale House (p.161), where you'll find a rotating collection of jazz giants, or Richard's Bar (p.169), where our favorite party jukebox kicks out oldies, Stax soul and crowd favorite *Mob Hits*. Perhaps you're more of the bob-your-head type—for that there's Inner Town Pub (p.155), with flawless picks from the Zombies to Bowie. And finally, we ask: Is it better to find a brilliant jukebox that occasionally works, or one that always works and is reliably mediocre? We'll take the former, and Johnny's (p.142) vintage machine with its awesomely random 45s is too good to pass up just for being as persnickety as its owner.—*John Moss*

more than 17 years, is a shrine to his Marine Corps roots. He's plastered military pictures, flak jackets, packs and other paraphernalia on the walls, while camouflage netting hangs from the ceiling and above the pool table. After buying you a shot of "jungle juice," Sarge will pull up a stool and fill your ear with stories about chasing "Charlies" and keeping out the Rogers Park riffraff. Semper fi! *6973 N Clark St between Morse and Lunt Sts (773-973-1907). El: Red to Morse. Bus: 22 (24hrs). Tue–Sun 4pm–"till everyone leaves" (closed Mon). Average beer: $3, Cash only.*

Poitin Stil It's pronounced "poo-cheen still" (Gaelic for "moonshine"), but take the bartenders' cue and call it "the Stil." This Rogers Park pub is the antithesis of its former inhabitant, Charmers, the city's oldest, grittiest and emptiest gay bar: It's bright and bustling, there's often live music and friendly bartenders pour a proper Guinness. Rest assured, nostalgists: Charmers' beautiful Art Deco bar remains intact. *1502 W Jarvis Ave at Greenview Ave (773-338-3285). El: Red to Jarvis. Bus: 22 (24hrs), 147, 151. Sun–Fri 3pm–2am; Sat 3pm–3am. Average beer: $3. Cash only.*

Red Line Tap Just around the corner from the Heartland Café, this Rogers Park hangout wears many hats: On any given night, the place could be packed with hippies, punks or hipsters depending on who's playing on the stage. If you don't dig, say, the bluegrass band wailing away, sidle up to the adjoining bar area for a more laid-back evening. *7006 N Glenwood Ave between Lunt and Greenleaf Aves (773-274-5463). El: Red to Morse. Bus: 22 (24hrs), 96, 147, 151. Sun–Fri 4pm–2am; Sat 4pm–3am. Average cocktail: $5.*

✳ Ricky G's The beer garden might be closed when it's cold, but you'll find plenty of warmth from the friendly clientele at this brick corner bar—not to mention a decent bottled-beer selection: 13 domestics and nine imports (no drafts). Serious steel darters from the Windy City Dart League like to hang at Ricky G's, where playing pool is free and the jukebox offers a serviceable selection of tunes. *7121 N Western Ave between Fitch and Estes Aves (773-764-0322). Bus: 49B North Western, 81 Lawrence (24hrs). Mon–Fri 11:30am–2am; Sat 11:30am–3am; Sun 11am–2am. Average beer: $2.50.*

✕ Select Ultra Lounge Welcome to the jungle? Almost every available surface in

FRUIT LOOPY Bartenders at In Fine Spirits use enough fresh fruit for their cocktails to make two hats for Carmen Miranda.

this tacky-swank lounge is covered in cheetah or zebra print, down to the leopard shades on the cocktail shaker lamps. Big, cushy red and yellow leatherette booths, and black and white portraits of 90's era starlets round out the décor. The vibe is laid back during the week with a food, fancy coffee drinks and cavity-inducing cocktails; they bring in a DJ for a dance party on the weekends. *2542 W Peterson between Maplewood Ave and Rockwell St (No phone). Bus 49B, 84, 93. Sun–Fri 11am–2am; Sat 11am–3am. Average cocktail: $8.*

(▼ Touché Among the city's collection of gay leather bars, this dimly lit establishment— free of the usual blinding lights and techno beats—is perhaps the most laid-back and conversation-friendly of them all. Muted porn videos play on three out of six TVs, while an older crowd drinks cheap beers (50-cent drafts on Sundays). Don't fret if you happen to waltz in on a day when your leathers are at the cleaners: Jeans and a T-shirt are just as common here as chaps and a vest. *6412 N Clark St between Devon and Schreiber Aves (773-465-7400). El: Red to Loyola. Bus: 22 (24hrs), 36, 151, 155. Mon–Fri 5pm–4am; Sat 5pm–5am; Sun noon–4am. Average beer: $4.*

The Wild Rover Morning bars are great for downing an eye-opener, and this spot— previously called Egan's Tavern—is where many come to do just that. The bartender says it's been around since 1934, starting out as an ice company (during that buzz-kill Prohibition thing). A photo of one of the ice wagons lends a nice nostalgic touch, and the green Formica bar and linoleum floor make this place look like a movie set for a director trying to capture a real Chicago Irish bar. *6001 N Paulina St between Ridge and Peterson Aves (773-743-2400). El: Red to Thorndale. Bus: 22 (24hrs), 36, 84. Mon–Fri 7am–2am; Sat 7am–3am; Sun 11am–2am. Average beer $2.75.*

Andersonville/Edgewater/ Uptown

▼ ✕ ✳ Big Chicks 2009 Eat Out Award, Critics' Pick: Best Place to Ogle Women (art collection featuring work by women, of women) Don't let the name fool you. It's practically all guys in here and calling them "big" could get you bitch-slapped. Andersonville's queer den mother, Michelle Fire, decks out her bar with choice selections from her impressive art collection, a good back-up plan in case there's a lack of other eye candy. *5024 N Sheridan Rd between Argyle St and Carmen Ave (773-728-5511). El: Red to Argyle. Bus: 151 Sheridan. Mon–Fri 4pm–2am; Sat 11am–3am; Sun 11am–2am. Average cocktail: $5. Cash only.*

Café Bong At Andersonville's diviest karaoke bar lovable Korean matron Ginny and her bartender/daughter Daniella still serve you a styrofoam bowl of peanuts along with your beer and bring the microphone over in the hopes that you'll join in on a rendition of Lionel Richie's "Hello" while National Geographic footage of lemurs and gazelles plays on the TV screen behind the at-times misspelled lyrics. *5706 N Clark St between Edgewater and Hollywood Aves (773-275-0430). Bus: 22 (24hrs), 50, 84. Sun–Fri 7pm–2am; Sat 7pm–3am. Average beer: $3.50.*

✕ Carol's Pub A honky-tonk in Sheridan Park with $1.50 domestics on Mondays, country western karaoke on Thursdays and the house

band Diamondback on weekends, featuring sassy little Reba singin' and strummin' rhythm with a darn good gee-tar picker on lead. A pool table in back, greasy grill turning out late-night burgers and Hank-filled jukebox round out the grit fest. *4659 N Clark St between Wilson and Leland Aves (773-334-2402). El: Red to Wilson. Bus: 22 Clark (24hrs), 145 Wilson/Michigan Express. Mon, Tue 9am–2am; Wed–Fri, Sun 11am–4am; Sat 11am–5am. Average beer: $2.50. Cash only.*

▼ Cattle Call Haul out your boots for a night of dancing with a Southern twang: The newest gay bar in town is a dance club with a country twist. Weekends offer high-energy sounds for the sweaty masses, but there's room to kick it in the corner with a beer if that's more your style. While the crowd tilts toward the bear-ish, we're guessing that different nights (like two-steppin' Tuesdays and drag-revue–Wednesdays) will generate different herds. *1547 W Bryn Mawr Ave at Clark St (773-334-2525). El: Red to Bryn Mawr. Bus: 22, 50, 84. Mon–Thu 4pm–2am; Fri 3pm–2am; Sat 2pm–3am; Sun 2pm–2am. Average beer: $4.*

▼ ✕ ✳ ♨ Charlie's Ale House Like a gay Cheers, everybody knows everybody's name at the Andersonville outpost of this local mini-chain. A long winding bar, amber lighting, dark wood and green leather booths make for a tavern-y spot to sip one of the gajillion beers or two dozen wines by the glass. TVs show sports, but older locals are focused on their grilled chicken Caesars, and the lesbians are too busy flirting to notice. *5308 N Clark St between Berwyn and Summerdale Aves (773-751-0140). El: Red to Berwyn. Bus: 22 (24hrs), 50, 92. Mon–Thu 11:30am–midnight; Fri 11:30am–1am; Sat 10:30am–1am; Sun 10.30am–midnight. Average beer: $4.*

The Double Bubble At this Edgewater joint, you'll find a melting pot of patrons—from Loyola students to young professionals to blue-collar regulars—who all turn up to watch the Cubbies (or Sox or Bulls or Bears) and drink cheap beer. In the back, there's a hidden gem: a sliver of grass with a handful of picnic tables and a charcoal grill, which, we've been told, gets fired up on summer days. *6036 N Broadway between Norwood St und Glenluke Ave (773-743-9465). El: Red to Thorndale. Bus: 36 Broadway, 147 Outer Drive Express. Sun–Fri 11:30am–2am; Sat 11:30am–3am. Average beer: $2.75.*

✕ ✳ ♨ The Edgewater Lounge This bar on the edge of Andersonville offers a homey menu that's good enough to snap you out of that chicken-wing trance you've been lulled into. Nightly specials like Sloppy Joe Tuesdays and Fish Fry Fridays are mighty good. The excellent beer and wine selection and chummy staff will pleasantly surprise you. *5600 N Ashland Ave at Bryn Mawr Ave (773-878-3343). Bus: 22 (24hrs), 50, 92. Sun–Fri noon–2am; Sat noon–3am. Average beer: $4.*

✕ Fat Cat Though the sign outside gets the '40s-ish feeling just right, keep your zoot suit at home: Inside, Rihanna is singing and martinis are made with pomegranate juice. Skip the apps and head for the braised pork belly Cuban sandwich, the rich meat mingling with vinegary pickles to great success. *4840 N Broadway at Gunnison St (773-506-3100). El: Red to Lawrence. Bus: 22 (24hrs), 36, 81 (24hrs), 151. Mon–Fri 4pm–2am; Sat 11am–3am; Sun 11am–2am. Average beer: $6.*

▼ ✳ The Granville Anvil On weekends, the small crowd at this dodgy, dimly lit man's bar can make it feel downright convivial. Otherwise the faded watering hole is surely where Edgewater's gentrification will hold its last stand. Lonely? Drop a few quarters in the jukebox and pour your heart out along with Dolly as she begs Jolene not to take her man. *1137 W Granville Ave at Winthrop Ave (773-973-0006). El: Red to Granville. Bus: 117, 151, 155. Mon–Fri 9am–2am; Sat 9am–3am; Sun noon–2am. Average cocktail: $5.*

Green Mill Originally Pop Morse's Roadhouse when it opened in 1907, this jazz institution is legendary for three things: it was once a Capone hangout, it's supposedly haunted, and the no-nonsense staff is known to shush you and the visiting friends who dragged you in during live jazz sets. Have trouble keeping your mouth shut? Go during the Uptown Poetry Slam on Sunday nights. *4802 N Broadway at Lawrence (773-878-5552). El: Red to Lawrence. Bus: 22 (24hrs), 36, 81 (24hrs), 151. Sun–Fri noon–4am; Sat noon–5am. Average cocktail: $7.*

✕ ✳ In Fine Spirits Maybe it's because we can get plenty of wine next door at the shop of the same name, but we're more into the cocktails at this comfortable, bi-level wine bar than the vino. Don't miss the "Swedish Mary" (a bloody made with North Shore's Aquavit) or the signature G&T (Fever Tree tonic and North Shore gin). To see how the farmers' market's finest tastes in liquid form, ask the bartender about seasonal specialty cocktails. *5420 N Clark St between Balmoral and Rascher Aves (773-334-9463). Bus: 22 Clark (24hrs), 92 Foster. Mon–Thu 4pm–midnight; Fri, Sat 3pm–2am; Sun 3pm–11pm. Average cocktail: $10.*

✕ ✳ Joie de Vine A wine bar this charming has no business being hidden on a quiet residential street. The location might be why you'll often have the place to yourself. The wine list has some tasty values (both New and Old World) and the small-plates menu has bites like artisan cheeses and charcuterie to offset a nasty wine hangover. *1744 W Balmoral Ave between Paulina St and Ravenswood Ave (773-989-6846). Bus: 22 (24hrs), 50, 92. Sun–Fri 4pm–2am; Sat 4pm–3am. Average glass of wine: $8.*

Decades of drinking

Toast nearly a century of boozing by channeling a different era at these retro taverns.

SLIGHT OF HAND This Green Mill gent is wondering which gangster's behind this dame's bling.

The '20s: the Green Mill (p.147)
Not even the specter of Prohibition could silence the Roaring '20s at this Uptown cocktail lounge. Back then, vivacious hostess Betty Hutton greeted men and women dressed in their best suits, gloves and hats who came to listen to singer-comedian Joe E. Lewis and maybe catch a glimpse of one Alphonse Capone in his usual booth at the end of the bar. Today, the piano (on a riser behind the bar) is a reminder of the era, and the room—from the green-velvet booths to the long, curved oak bar and columns in front of the stage—pulls patrons into a 1920s time warp. On any given night, customers mingle while respectfully keeping their conversations to low whispers as jazz musicians play and waitresses and bartenders hustle cocktails with the efficiency of a mob hit.

The '30s: Coq d'Or (p.162)
Liquor legally touched thirsty citizens' lips for the first time in 14 years when Prohibition ended in 1933. Even though the country was in the midst of the Great Depression, lines outside the Drake Hotel rivaled those of soup kitchens and bread doles as the city's rich and powerful waited patiently for 40-cent whiskey shots at the hotel's recently opened high-end lounge. Coq d'Or still conveys a classic elegance, from its burnished copper bar and butternut-wood paneling to the tables and chairs, many of which date back to its opening.

The '40s: Weegee's (p.146)
This 1940s-era bar is named after photographer Arthur Fellig (who earned his nickname—the phonetic spelling of Ouija—by arriving at crime scenes to lens still-warm corpses for New York City newspapers). Weegee's offers classic cocktails, a vintage shuffleboard table and the opportunity to muse over Fellig's, ahem, body of work. You won't find TVs, electronic games or Top 40 tunes. What you will discover at Weegee's, though, are some 120 craft beers and a menu of old-school cocktails (think Manhattan, Zazerac, rusty nail and the like) made with premium ingredients, a vintage cash register, and a backbar with Deco touches straight out of a Bogart film.

The '50s: Phyllis' Musical Inn (p.149)
This joint has been a fixture at Division and Wood Streets since 1954, when it was opened by Phyllis Jaskot on a stretch so packed with taverns and clubs it was known as the "Polish Broadway." Despite rumors, Chi-town chronicler Nelson Algren's mother never owned the place. It's now in the hands of Phyllis's son Clem, and Algren's deepest connection was knocking back cocktails there. Glass-block windows, the original 1954 bar with frosted-glass pillars, the tin roof and busts of Oliver Hardy and other midcentury celebs cement the '50s vibe.

The '60s: Hala Kahiki (*2834 River Rd, 708-456-3222*)
Tiki enthusiasts dig the drinks enough to drive to River Grove for them, but it's the original tiki decor at Hala Kahiki that excites the übergeeks. The multiroom maze of a bar features artwork from Witco, one of the few manufacturers of tiki furniture back in the '60s, on every wall. Usually made of wood and just as often unbearably tacky, the Witco works depicting Tahitian scenes and fish lend the place a strongly authentic vibe. Nothing's changed much since the place opened in 1964: Waitresses wearing leis, sarongs and tank tops pad along the faded, shell-pattern carpeting to deliver a bowl of pretzels and outrageously large drinks to the overwhelmingly Eastern European crowd sitting on chairs with wood backrests carved into the shape of a pineapple.

The '70s: Reagle Beagle (p.165)
The vinyl booths in earthy red, ski-lodge brick around a fireplace, cocktail-lounge lighting from red lamps and a menu of retro standards (fondue, pot pie, lamb-chop appetizers) might have made the '70s point well enough. But this bar (named for the gang's hangout on *Three's Company*) wallops us over the head with kitsch: walls covered with family photos of our TV parents—*Diff'rent Strokes* to *Magnum, P.I.*—drink names straight from *Nick at Nite*, endless reruns on the plasma screen and retro DJs on the weekends.

The '80s: Berlin (p.141)
Twenty-five years after opening with the mission to get gay and straight Chicagoans to mix it up over blast beats and cocktails, Berlin is still one of the few truly diverse bars in the city. On the bar's wildly popular Madonna-rama nights (the first Sunday of every month) or Prince nights (the last Sunday of every month), the progressive melange of gay punks, straight club kids and outlandish drag queens can be so striking that it feels like a bar of the future. Or perhaps more accurately, a bar of the past.

The '90s: Liar's Club (p.153)
The time when a rockin' cover of "Mrs. Robinson" shared the charts with the Red Hot Chili Peppers feels as remote as a Bulls three-peat, but the Liar's Club (a regular hangout for roller-derby ladies and those who love them) stands as a living monument to '90s alternarock. Studded black-leather couches, black walls, red lights and a hurricane lamp with naked ladies drawn on it make this bar a Playboy Mansion–cum–Shriners' Club for those who come to sing "Sweet Child O' Mine" at karaoke.

▼ ✻ **Marty's** This upscale Andersonville martini lounge burns through olives and vermouth faster than a steakhouse does. But don't expect to rub elbows with homos all night. Straight folk tend to show up first for a predinner cocktail, and the gay crowd comes later. Like gentrification, but in reverse. *1511 W Balmoral Ave at Clark St (773-561-6425). El: Red to Berwyn. Bus: 22 (24hrs), 36, 50, 92. Sun–Fri 5pm–2am; Sat 5pm–3am. Average cocktail: $14.*

▼ ✗ **Mary's Rec Room** Wall-to-wall male patrons, sports on every TV, nearly a dozen beers on tap...the new pub from the Hamburger Mary's team might look like any other jocktacular sports bar, but breeders *will* get the vibe rather quickly that locals think of it as a boys-only club. Regardless, beer geeks might wander in to sample the three made-in-house brews, but until the quality is up to snuff with other local beers, we'll stick to our usual. *5402 N Clark Ave between Balmoral and Rascher Aves (773-784-6969). El: Red to Berwyn. Bus: 22, 50, 92. Mon–Fri 5pm–2am; Sat noon–3am; Sun noon–2am. Average beer: $4.*

✗ ✻ ♨ **Moody's Pub** In summer, this beer garden is one of the best in Chicago, but only if you can deal with ass-to-elbow crowds. We prefer this beer-and-burger haven in winter, when we can snag a table by the fireplace and get cozy with our date. Just remember to bring a flashlight to read the menu; the place is dark enough that you could carry on an affair while your spouse is sitting across the room. *5910 N Broadway between Rosedale and Thorndale Aves (773-275-2696). El: Red to Thorndale. Bus: 36 Broadway, 84 Peterson. Mon–Fri 11:30am–1am; Sat 11:30am–2am; Sun noon–1am. Average beer: $3. Cash only.*

✗ ✻ **Ole St Andrew's Inn** With its high-backed wooden chairs, collection of sabers and, allegedly, a drunken ghost roaming about, this tavern has a distinctly medieval aura about it. Even though we haven't spotted any ghosts here, we're believers: Some of the patrons look like they're on their last legs and are ready to haunt any day now. *5938 N Broadway at Thorndale Ave (773-784-5540). El: Red to Thorndale. Bus: 36 Broadway. Mon 5pm–2am; Tue–Fri, Sun 11am–2pm; Sat 11am–3pm. Average beer: $4.*

♨ **Ravenswood Pub** This is the cleanest hole-in-the-wall we've ever seen—and one of the friendliest, too. Within the first hour of your arrival, you'll rule the digital jukebox, become best friends with the bartender and be several games deep in free pool. We've just found our home away from home. *5455 N Ravenswood Ave between Foster and Bryn Mawr Aves (773-769-6667). Bus: 50 Damen, 92 Foster. Sun–Fri 11am–2am; Sat 11am–3am. Average beer: $3.50.*

♨ **Simon's Tavern** If you're lucky, you can snag a couch in the back by the fireplace where you can take in the cool vintage bar (built in the '30s to resemble a bar on the U.S. Normandy), sip some seasonal glogg and check out the friendly neighborhood crowd (equal mix of gay and straight). *5210 N Clark St between Foster and Farragut Aves (773-878-0894). El: Red to Berwyn. Bus: 22 (24hrs), 50, 92. Sun–Fri 11am–2am; Sat 11am–3am. Average cocktail: $5. Cash only.*

▼ ♨ **Wild Pug** This gussied up pub from the owners of Crew does indeed have some U.K. flair to lend an air of authenticity—a framed portrait of Oscar Wilde on one wall, an antique light fixture above one of the bars. But if you're there at night, when the smoke machine is blowing, the rainbow lights are flashing and the boys are gyrating, you'll be hard pressed to notice them. *4810 N Broadway between Lawrence Ave and Gunnison St (773-784-4811). El: Red to Lawrence. Bus: 36 Broadway, 81 Lawrence (24hrs). Mon–Fri 5pm–2am; Sat 3pm–3am; Sun 1pm–2am. Average cocktail: $6.*

Lincoln Square/Ravenswood

✗ **Atlantic Bar & Grill** As the "Home of Glasgow Celtic Supporters Club," this Irish pub boasts a dozen beers on tap and traditional fare like shepherd's pie, as well as decidedly un-Irish tacos and ribs. Performances from the Polkaholics and Up Ye Boyo keep things lively in the party room behind the spacious main bar. *5062 N Lincoln Ave between Carmen and Winnemac Aves (773-506-7090). El: Brown to Western. Bus: 11, 49 (24hrs), X49, 92. Mon–Fri 3pm–2am; Sat 10am–3am; Sun 10am–2am. Average beer: $4.*

✻ **Big Joe's** There's nothing particularly inventive about this corner tap, both levels of which are usually inhabited by your run-of-the-mill, shaggy-haired, middle-aged whiskey sippers—nothing, that is, unless you're here on a Friday night. That's when the place fills up with a mix of yuppies, hipsters and everybody in between for a few friendly rounds of turtle racing. (Sounds like a euphemism, we know, but we assure you it's not.) *1818 W Foster Ave at Honore St (773-784-8755). Bus: 50 Damen, 92 Foster. Mon–Fri 1pm–2am; Sat noon–3am, Sun noon–2am. Average beer: $3.*

✗ **C&S Pub** Wisecracking bartender Colleen is the heart and soul of this otherwise unremarkable neighborhood pub, and she'll mix you an extra strong Sunny D mai tai if you let her. The pub is named after owners Chuck and Sharon, who live behind the pub and have their names engraved on placards next to neon comedy and tragedy masks that hang above the bar. *5053 N Lincoln Ave between Carmen and Winnemac Aves (no phone). El: Brown to Western. Bus: 11, 49 (24hrs), 92. Mon–Sat 3pm–2am. Average cocktail: $4.*

Carola's Hansa Clipper If the heavy weekend traffic of thirtysomethings at Huettenbar ain't your thing, check out this less refined German spot just down the block. The bare-bones setting makes for a laid-back, chatty evening. True, the decorative Christmas lights and homemade Jäger bombs $6 sign scream tackiness, but there's something refreshing about a place that looks like it hasn't changed since 1975. *4659 N Lincoln Ave at Leland Ave (773-878-3662). El: Brown to Western. Bus: 11, 49 (24hrs), 81 (24hrs). Sun–Fri 10am–2am; Sat 10am–3am. Average beer: $5.*

✗ **Chicago Ale House** If this place kind of looks like a dormitory lounge, that's because it's a college kid's dream come true: lots of industrial, unbreakable furniture; a menu stocked with greasy food; a big pool table in back; several big-screen TVs and a bar with 60—yes, 60—beers on tap. *2200 W Lawrence Ave at Leavitt St (773-275-2020). El: Brown to Western. Bus: 11, 49 (24hrs), 81 (24hrs). Mon–Thu 4pm–2am; Fri, Sun 11am–2am; Sat 11am–3am. Average beer: $4.50.*

☾ ✗ ✻ ♨ **Fireside** Ravenswood locals flock to this bar for its namesake's warmth (everyone loves the covered, heated patio) and coziness. Bartenders tend to pour heavy here—we ordered a Scotch on the rocks and found ourselves drinking from a full highball glass—so some food from the adjoining restaurant will be in order to soak it all up. *5739 N Ravenswood Ave between Olive Ave and Rosehill Dr (773-561-7433). El: Red to Bryn Mawr. Bus: 22 (24hrs), 36, 50. Mon–Fri 11am–4am; Sat 11am–5am; Sun 10am–4am. Average beer: $5.*

✗ ♨ **The Grafton** Owner Malcolm Molloy has that fresh-off-the-boat brogue that could charm the pants off your own mother. But please don't take this for one of your run-of-the-mill McIrish pubs. Folk musicians pluck away and locals might lift a Cosmo just as soon as a pint. So compared with most other pubs laying claim to the Emerald Isle, it's a sea of tranquility. *4530 N Lincoln Ave between Sunnyside and Wilson Aves (773-271-9000). El: Brown to Western. Bus: 11, 49 (24hrs), 78. Mon–Fri 4pm–2am; Sat 11am–3am; Sun 11am–2am. Average beer: $4.*

☾ **Hidden Cove** Young and old, dregs and misfits, singers and drunkards—all break out their best shower voice at this Ravenswood spot for karaoke seven nights a week. You're as likely to hear Young MC's "Bust a Move" as you are Sinatra's "It Was a Very Good Year." The same kind of juxtaposition puts watermelon shots next to Manhattans on the weekly specials board. Deee-lish. *5336 N Lincoln Ave between Summerdale and Balmoral Aves (773-275-6711). Bus: 11, 49 (24hrs), 49B, 92. 2pm–4am. Average beer: $3.50.*

Huettenbar This charming Lincoln Square "cottage bar" offers a huge selection of German drafts. Sadly, most of the traditional German tunes on the jukebox are gone, but couples still slow-dance to classic pop. Check out the fetching portrait of Irma, the owner, behind the front bar. *4721 N Lincoln Ave between Leland and Lawrence Aves (773-561-2507). El: Brown to Western. Bus: 11, 49 (24hrs), X49, 81 (24hrs). Mon–Fri 2pm–2am; Sat, Sun noon–2am. Average beer: $5.50.*

✗ ✻ **Jury's** For one of the best tavern burgers in town (try the blue cheese, medium-rare) and a classy beer garden, this is the spot. Umbrella-topped tables, a wooden privacy fence, ivy-covered brick and a superbly stocked bar complete the package. *4337 N Lincoln Ave between Pensacola and Montrose Aves (773-935-2255). Bus: 11, 50, 78. Mon–Thu 11am–10pm; Fri 11am–11pm; Sat 11:30am–11pm; Sun noon–9pm. Average beer: $5.*

Lincoln Square Lanes This second-story bowling alley/dive bar used to be one of the best hidden gems in the city. Now that the masses have caught on, you can bide your time while waiting for a lane by downing cheap beer, heckling ball-tossers and doing your best Dude impersonation. *4874 N Lincoln Ave at Ainslie St (773-561-8191). El: Brown to Western. Bus: 11, 49 (24hrs), X49, 81 (24hrs). Mon–Thu 5pm–2am; Fri–Sun noon–2am (closed Mon–Wed during summer). Average beer: $3.*

Margie's Pub "If assholes could fly, this place would be an airport," declares the sign behind the bar. We didn't find it to be true, but with two pool tables, a handful of arcade games and three taps of Old Style, we can see how things might get out of hand. *4145 N Lincoln Ave between Warner and Berteau Aves*

(773-477-1644). El: Brown to Irving Park. Bus: 11 Lincoln/Sedgwick, 80 Irving Park. Mon–Fri 11am–2am; Sat 11am–3am; Sun 11am–8pm. Average beer: $2.75.

✕ ✳ ♨ **O'Shaughnessy's Public House** Good thing bar owner Michael Finan's pa came from the Emerald Isle, because he knew just which carpentry folks to call on for a custom-built wood bar that evokes an authentic Irish pub feel. Formerly Zephyr's ice cream parlor, the space now sports a deep red exterior, exposed brick, warm lighting, an open door and a friendly staff. Take a comfy booth and some curry chips to go with your Guinness. *4557 N Ravenswood Ave at Wilson Ave (773-944-9896). El: Brown to Montrose. Bus: 78, 81 (24hrs), 145, Metra: Union Pacific N to Ravenswood. Sun–Fri 11am–2am; Sat 11am–3am. Average beer: $4.*

✕ ✳ ♨ **The Rail** How did one of the best sports bars end up in Ravenswood? A dozen beers on tap, almost that many plasma screens (42 inches, and size does matter) and 10-cent wings on Mondays—beats the sticky floors and drunken screaming at your current spot. *4709 N Damen Ave between Leland Ave and Giddings St (773-878-9400). El: Brown to Damen. Bus: 50 Damen, 81 Lawrence (24hrs). Mon–Thu 4pm–2am; Fri 11am–2am; Sat 10am–3am; Sun 11am–2am. Average cocktail: $4.*

✕ ✳ **Rockwell's Neighborhood Grill** If you're the type of parent who includes your bambino in your extracurricular activities, we've got the quintessential neighborhood bar for you. Enjoy superb pub grub, killer Bloody Marys, and a cheerful patio, all while watching your kiddies tumble themselves cockeyed on the beer-stained floor. *4632 N Rockwell St between Leland and Eastwood Aves (773-509-1871). El: Brown to Rockwell. Bus: 49 (24hrs), X49, 81 (24hrs). Mon–Thu 4pm–10pm; Fri 4pm–11pm; Sat 10am–11pm; Sun 10am–10pm. Average cocktail: $6.*

▼ **Spyners Pub** This unmarked hole-in-the-wall is the kind of neighborhood spot you'd easily pass by until someone in the know introduces you to its discreet charms: old-school matrons working the bar, cheap drink specials and weekend karaoke jamborees. FYI, it's also an unofficial hangout for same sex–loving ladies. *4623 N Western Ave at Wilson Ave (773-784-8719). El: Brown to Western. Bus: 11, 49 (24hrs), X49, 81 (24hrs). Sun–Fri 11am–2am; Sat 11am–3am. Average cocktail: $4.50.*

Sunnyside Tap Most great dives look as though they haven't seen so much as a Pledge-soaked rag since the end of World War II. With that in mind, this little, bottles-only (despite its name) tavern is oddly modern. Its scant decor—beer promo posters of bikini-clad women with 'dos straight out of a hair-metal video and an aging jukebox with tunes to match—appears to have been updated as recently as the end of the Cold War. *4410 N Western Ave between Montrose and Sunnyside Aves (no phone). El: Brown to Western. Bus: 11, 49 (24hrs), X49, 78. 10am–1am. Average beer: $3.25.*

✕ **Tiny Lounge** Make no mistake: Tiny Lounge definitely isn't what it used to be. It's bigger now, and gone is the old-school decor—this place is slick, a little mod and all sparkling new. But sitting here with a Sazerac or a sidecar (both impeccably crafted) is so undeniably pleasant that it's hard not to believe that the changes were for the better. *4352 N Leavitt St*

The hit list

Five **patios for classic cocktails**

1 ▲ **Motel Bar** (p.158)
We're not so sure about other retro trends (looking at you, meat loaf), but the rallying cry of old-school drinks like a Singapore sling or Sazerac in the great outdoors—like this perfectly simple patio—is a throwback we can get behind.

2 **The Whistler** (p.146)
A beer bar might be the main attraction of the back patio at this surprisingly low-key watering hole, but even that can't distract us from cocktails like the springy, lavender-garnished Violette Fizz.

3 **Weegee's Lounge** (p.146)
Not that the bitter cold has ever stopped anyone from reaching for the classic cocktails here, but we prefer visiting when it's finally warm enough to grab a drink and a perch on the patio at this soul-record-playing, resolutely old-school bar. Try the recently added gin concoctions, Arsenic & Old Lace or the Aviation.

4 **Matchbox** (p.155)
The patio practically doubles the capacity of this tiny bar, meaning you can actually grab a seat for throwing back the famed margaritas, made with fresh lemon and lime juice, top-shelf liquors and powdered sugar (and poured with a heavy hand).

5 **NoMI Lounge** (p.147)
Absinthe is classic, right? In, like, a bohemian, turn-of-the-20th-century-Paris kind of way? On the breezy seventh-floor patio lounge of the stunning Park Hyatt, green fairy cocktails (with drips from the absinthe fountain) most certainly qualify.—*Julia Kramer*

between Cullom and Montrose Aves (773-463-0396). El: Brown to Montrose. Bus: 11, 49, 78. Mon–Thu 4pm–2am; Fri, Sun noon–2am; Sat noon–3am. Average cocktail: $9.

Lakeview/Roscoe Village/ Wrigleyville/North Center

◖ ▼ **Berlin** This freak-friendly dance destination in Lakeview built its reputation back in the mid '80s with a mix of German new wave music, art installations and transvestite shows. These days, it's still quirky but more retro, with Madonna- and Prince-tribute, disco and '80s nostalgia nights. Goths and gays are extra welcome, but the scene here is made up of almost everyone. *954 W Belmont Ave between Wilson and Sheffield Aves (773-348-4975). El: Brown, Purple (rush hrs), Red to Belmont. Bus: 8, 22 (24hrs), 77. Sun–Tue 10pm–4am; Wed–Fri 5pm–4am; Sat 5pm–5am. Average cocktail: $6. Cash only.*

RAISE THE ROOF
Sipping and scoping are two popular pastimes on Sidetrack's patio.

▼ **Cell Block** Smooth-chested twinks and their admirers need not apply—this bar stands out as a prowling ground for old-guard leathermen and bears in a neighborhood otherwise dominated by boozy slushies and dance music. The air is thick with testosterone, chains hang from the ceiling, and the back room shows porn on the weekends. The rest of the week the vibe is mellow, with nightly drink specials and music from the bartender's iPod. *3702 N Halsted St at Waveland Ave (773-665-8064). El: Red to Addison. Bus: 8, 36, 152. Mon–Fri 4pm–2am; Sat 2pm–3am; Sun 2pm–2am. Average cocktail: $5.*

✳ **Cody's** The slogan says it all: no peeing, no crapping, no barking—and that goes for the dogs, too. Needless to say, this bar is dog-friendly, inside and out. But what really clinches it as one of Chicago's best are the real English darts and the $2.50 bottles of Schlitz, Pabst, Old Style and Huber. *1658 W Barry Ave between Ashland Ave and Paulina St (773-528-4050). El: Brown to Paulina. Bus: 9, 11, 77. Mon–Fri 2pm–2am; Sat 11am–3am; Sun 11am–2am. Average beer: $3.25. Cash only.*

✕ **The Cubby Bear** Considering its proximity to Wrigley Field, it's the next-best thing to being in the stands. Cubs fans pack the sticky floor before and during the game, but it's postgame that people are packed in this place like sardines in a tin can. If you're feelng flush, you can spring for a private room overlooking Wrigley to take in a game. In the offseason, the 30,000-square-foot behemoth still packs in crowds who come to see bands like the Gin Blossoms and Widespread Panic. *1059 W Addison St at Clark St (773-327-1662). El: Red to Addison. Bus: 22 Clark (24hrs), 152 Addison. Sun–Fri 11am–2am; Sat 11am–3am. Average beer: $4.*

▼ ✕ ✳ **44th Ward Dinner Party** The vintage-inspired, old-world feel of the reincarnated Lakeview Broadcasting Company melds bar, restaurant and club into one. A late-night grilled-cheese haven for building your own sandwiches on dense focaccia, a meat market for gingham-clad B-town boys, a clubby dance party: It all manages to come together into an upbeat but fairly mellow scene. *3542 N Halsted St at Addison St (773-857-2911). El: Red to Addison. Bus: 8, 36, 152. Sun, Mon, Wed 5:30pm–midnight; Thu, Fri 5:30pm–2am; Sat 5:30pm–3am. Average cocktail: $7.*

✕ ✳ **Harry Caray's Tavern** The bro-tastic meat market that was Hi-Tops is gone, and in its place is this classy Cubs pub that should have sports fans with taste renewing their faith in the Wrigleyville bar scene. Countless flatscreens and a bust of the bar's bespectacled namesake share the woody space with unexpectedly hip-for-a-sports-bar touches like a co-ed sink area and a create-your-own burger menu with options like Wagyu and Tallgrass beef. *3551 N Sheffield Ave between Cornelia Ave and Addison St (773-327-7800). El: Red to Addison. Bus: 8, 22 (24hrs), 152. Sun–Wed 10am–11pm; Thu, Fri 10am–2am; Sat 10am–3am . Average beer: $7.*

Johnny's Yes, the rumors are true: To get into this old-timey watering hole, Johnnie has to buzz you in. Once admitted, it's nostalgia central: a '60s jukebox, retro beer posters, Christmas decorations from way back when, old newspapers lying in the corner. Better still, if the longtime proprietor digs talking to you, he'll keep the beer flowing past closing time. *3425 N Lincoln Ave at Roscoe St (773-248-3000). El: Brown to Paulina. Bus: 9, 11, 77, 152. 9am–2am. Average beer: $3*

▼ ✕ ✳ **Kit Kat Lounge** If you don't know who Marilyn and Joan are, don't bother. This slick nightspot landed in Chicago from Puerto Vallarta, Mexico, almost 8 years ago, and it only gets campier with age. So prepare to be entertained by black and white Hollywood glamour movies and performances by sexy, sophisticated female impersonators of Hollywood icons. The drink list, which is more than 100 martinis strong, is also a draw. *3700 N Halsted St at Waveland Ave (773-525-1111). El: Red to Addison. Bus: 8, 36, 152. Tue–Sun 5:30pm–2am. Average cocktail: $10.*

L&L The Clark and Belmont 'hood is a unique mix of runaway trannnies, wasted Cubs fans and local renters who love a bargain. This no-frills Lakeview tavern keeps the madness at bay in favor of friendly bartenders who buy rounds during afternoon Jeapordy, a $2 beer-of-the-month and a great collection of two-dozen Irish whiskeys. *3207 N Clark St between Belmont and Aldine Aves (773-528-1303). El: Brown, Purple (rush hrs), Red to Belmont. Bus: 7, 22, 77, 151, 156. Mon–Fri 2pm–2am; Sat noon–3am; Sun noon–2am. Average beer: $3. Cash only.*

◖◗ ▼ **Little Jim's** We've heard Little Jim's described as a gay "Cheers" but that's questionable–unless Norm and Cliff are leather daddies into nude male sketches and hard-core porn. During daylight, friendly old bartenders (remember bartender Coach on Cheers?) sling beer to a sparse crowd. On weekend nights, Jim's gets more crowded and seedier than Sam Malone's bed. They may not know your name at Little Jim's, and it's doubtful they'll remember it tomorrow morning either. *3501 N Halsted St at Cornelia St (773-871-6116). El: Red to Addison. Bus: 8, 22 (24hrs), 77, 152. Sun–Fri noon–4am; Sat noon–5am.. Average beer: $4.*

✳ **The Long Room** Of all the neighborhood bars trying to make rambling Ashland Avenue feel more homey, this gem is among the homiest. Art Deco touches abound, live music kicks up a little dust on the weekends and the mood is consistently upbeat, chatty and sociable. The twenty/thirtysomething regulars live on the cusp—they're not quite Lakeview and not quite

NORM TCHOTCHKE Asian-style knicknacks and killer chicken wings are the draw at Wang's.

Ravenswood, which suits us just fine. *1612 W Irving Park Rd at Ashland Ave (773-665-4500). El: Brown to Irving Park. Bus: 9, X9, 80, X80. Mon–Fri 5pm–2am; Sat 5pm–3am; Sun 7pm–2am. Average cocktail: $5.*

✕ Merkle's Bar and Grill

There's something endearing about a bar named for a 1908 New York version of Steve Bartman; Fred Merkle wrecked a victory for New York by failing to touch base in a playoff game against the Cubs. Not surprisingly, this watering hole bleeds Cubby blue, complete with pics of old-time ballplayers. The taps lack heartier brews, focusing on the lighter lagers for drink-'em-down sports fans. *3516 N Clark St between Cornelia Ave and Eddy St (773-244-1025). El: Red to Addison. Bus: 8, 22 (24hrs), 152. Mon–Fri 4pm–2am; Sat 11am–3am; Sun 11am–2am. Average beer: $4.*

▼ ✕ ✻ minibar Ultra Lounge & Cafe

It takes balls for a wine bar to put a bottle from Ohio on its opening list, but as an extension of Boystown favorite minibar, balls are exactly what this bar will be full of. It's not that the beautiful, dimly lit room is something only gay guys can appreciate—rather, it's the puppy-dog eyes of the bartender that will pack them in. *3341 N Halsted St between Buckingham Pl and Roscoe St (773-871-6227). El: Brown, Purple (rush hrs), Red to Belmont. Bus: 8, 22 (24hrs), 77. Mon–Fri 5pm–11pm; Sat, Sun 11am–11pm. Average glass of wine: $7.*

✕ ✻ Murphy's Bleachers

Function trumps form and comfort at this woody yet cavernous Cubbie corral and outdoor stable, er, patio behind the Friendly Confines. The frat-brother and sorority-sister clientele want their alma mater's game on the TV and they want it now—not a problem considering the prevalence of flatscreens. *3655 N Sheffield Ave between Addison St and Waveland Ave (773-281-5356). El: Red to Addison. Bus: 8, 22 (24hrs), 152. Sun–Fri 11am–2am; Sat 11am–3am . Average beer: $5.*

✕ 1914

Tucked in a corner of Red Ivy so hidden that you need to go through the bar and across an alley to get there, this Prohibition-themed room gives off a believable aura of secrecy. And that's the point, really—it was built mainly to house private parties. On the weekends, the space pours from its whiskey-heavy, classic cocktail list for the public—but don't be surprised if, when filled to capacity with Red Ivy's clientele, the vintage feel gets lost. *3525 N Clark St between Cornelia Ave and Eddy St (773-472-0900). El: Red to Addison. Bus: 8, 22 (24hrs), 152. Fri 8pm–2am, Sat 8pm–3am. Average cocktail: $6.*

✕ ✻ Rocks Lakeview

This unpretentious, low-lit sister bar to Rocks Lincoln Park has a good lineup of microbrews (including beers from Cleveland's Great Lakes Brewery) and a solid menu of pub grub to soak it all up. But the name refers to its impressive lineup of whiskeys, which is worth a try just to see the size of the ice cube they use to keep the drinks cold. *3463 N Broadway between Stratford Pl and Cornelia Ave (773-472-0493). El: Red to Addison. Bus: 8, 36, 152. Mon–Fri 11am–2am; Sat 9am–3am; Sun 9am–2am. Average beer: $6.*

Rose's Lounge

Any of this spot's divey iniquities can be forgiven with the $1 mugs of Old Style. Rose—the cute, old Eastern European owner-bartender—hasn't changed a thing since the '70s: A shingled awning hangs over the back of the bar, wood paneling lines the walls and plenty of eclectic grandma knickknacks mingle with the bottles of liquor. And at seven plays for a buck, not even the jukebox prices have changed. *2656 N Lincoln Ave between Wrightwood Ave and Diversey Pkwy (773-327-4000). El: Brown, Purple (rush hrs), Red to Fullerton. Bus: 11, 74, 76. Noon–2am. Average beer: $2.*

✕ ✻ 🍴 Sheffield's

This huge beer garden turns into a laid-back college reunion on weekend nights in summer, with baseball-capped dudes and spaghetti-strapped chicks flanking the outdoor bar for $2 "Bad Beers of the Month" (Old Milwaukee and Stroh's, recently). In colder months, the attention turns to the more sophisticated picks on the beer list and the slabs of ribs that go a long way toward warming the belly. *3258 N Sheffield Ave between Belmont Ave and School St (773-281-4989). El: Brown, Purple (rush hrs), Red to Belmont. Bus: 8, 22 (24hrs), 77. Sun–Fri 11am–2am; Sat 11am–3am. Average beer: $4.*

▼ ✻ Sidetrack

If size matters, there's no better bar in Boystown than this well-hung hot spot. Six big rooms—we like the Glass Bar—are all packed with cute, frisky boys distracting themselves with the same three things: the videos on the wall, the drink in their hand and the ass in your jeans. Gay and straight come out in droves to sing along together to show tunes from movie musical clips shown on giant screens several nights a week. *3349 N Halsted St between Buckingham Pl and Roscoe St (773-477-9189). El: Brown, Purple (rush hrs), Red to Belmont. Bus: 8, 22 (24hrs), 77. Mon–Fri 3pm–2am, Sat 1pm–3am, Sun 1pm–2am. Average cocktail: $5.*

✕ ✻ Sluggers

What can lure sports fans away from a sidewalk patio that's spitting distance from Wrigley and offers a front-row view of scantily clad passersby? A bajillion TVs playing every televised game, a batting cage, Pop-A-Shot, mini bowling and more wings than even "The Fridge" Perry can handle. *3540 N Clark St at Eddy St (773-248-0055). El: Red to Addison. Bus: 8, 22 (24hrs), 77, 152. Mon–Thu 3pm–2am; Fri, Sun 11am–2am; Sat 11am–3am. Average beer: $4.50.*

🍴 Ten Cat Tavern

Drinking here is like getting into the DeLorean and traveling back to 1955—sort of like when you're just drunk enough at Green Mill to think it's the '40s. Eclectic, mismatched furniture and an old blues-heavy jukebox set the mood for kicking back or rackin' 'em up at the two vintage pool tables. Just be careful, McFly: The bartenders will not hesitate to embarrass you on the felt. *3931 N Ashland Ave between Byron St and Irving Park Rd (773-935-5377). El: Brown to Irving Park. Bus: 9 Ashland, 80 Irving Park. Sun–Fri 3pm–2am; Sat 3pm–3am. Average beer: $3.50.*

✕ ✻ Toon's Bar & Grill

This sleeper on the edge of Wrigleyville draws in neighbors for billiards and shuffleboard, televised sports with a cheering crowd, pulled pork sandwiches and po' boys, and a dose of New Orleans–style hospitality. Hard-to-find Abita beer on tap and sunny sidewalk tables make it even more irresistible to stop in. *3857 N Southport Ave between Grace and Byron Sts (773-935-1919). El: Brown to Irving Park. Bus: 9, 22 (24hrs), 80,*

X80. Sun–Fri 11:30am–2am; Sat 11:30am–3am. Average beer: $4.50.

◖ Underbar

Tucked away in the shadow of the Western Avenue bridge, this cozy, candlelit bar seems (at least early in the night) like a good place to write your long-awaited debut novel while nursing one of 40 eclectic, hard-to-find beers. Just don't get too comfy, Hemingway: The rowdy, late-night rush is this establishment's bread and butter. So stay and spot the subject of your next broken-heart tale. *3243 N Western Ave at Melrose St (773-404-9363). Bus: 49 Western (24hrs), 77 Belmont. Sun–Fri 9pm–4am; Sat 9pm–5am. Average beer: $4.50.*

▼ Wang's

After Henry Chang got a liquor license for his formerly BYOB eatery Wakamono, he promptly built Boystown's best bar. The intimate space is, like all of Chang's projects, highly stylized, employing lush, floral wallpaper and woodwork the likes of which you've only seen in an opium den. It might be a restaurant bar, but it has a style, vibe—and, thanks to refreshing pear martinis—a taste all its own. *3317 N Broadway between Aldine Ave and Buckingham Pl (773-296-6800). El: Brown, Purple (rush hrs), Red to Belmont. Bus: 36, 77, 152. 4pm–11. Average cocktail: $7.*

Humboldt Park/Logan Square

Archie's

This inconspicuous bar is equal parts after-work dive and *Antiques Roadshow*. Amid dusty knickknacks and bric-a-brac, the family who runs the place will pour you a stiff drink and then try to sell you a Civil War–era revolver, a set of buffalo-themed shotglasses or anything else lying around—anything except for the patriarch's wall-mounted marlin and the Hamm's sign hanging out front. *2600 W Iowa Ave at Rockwell St (no phone). Bus: 49 Western (24hrs), 66 Chicago. 11am–2am. Average beer: $3.*

Belford Tavern

The selling point here is the big $2 fishbowl schooners of MGD, the big draw for the lunchtime crowd of blue-collar types drinking the day's meal. As one regular puts it: "No jukebox, no pool, no video games, no food—no nuthin' but drinks." If you want to take some "packaged goods" with you, a liquor store is attached. But bring cash: A wood carving of a man being lynched has a caption that reads, "This man asked for credit." *3200 N Pulaski Rd at Belmont Ave (773-725-7112). Bus: 53, 56, 77. Sun–Fri 7am–2am; Sat 7am–3am. Average beer: $2. Cash only.*

Bob Inn

Nothing brings together the hip kids and blue-collar Chicagoans better than cheap alcohol—and this no-frills Logan Square dive across from Fireside Bowl is living proof. Watch as the earnest mustaches of Blackhawks and Sox fans mingle amiably with ironically bearded Black Keys and White Stripes fans. And if that gets dull, just head to the back for a 75-cent game of pool. *2609 W Fullerton Ave at Rockwell St (no phone). El: Blue to California. Bus: 49 (24hrs), X49, 74. 9pm–2am. Average cocktail: $4.*

Brudder's

This sports-inclined bar is a hop, skip and drive down Addison from Wrigley, so you can count on Cubs games being broadcast on all eight TVs. There's a separate room for the pool table, which gets plenty of use with the dough saved on dollar drafts of PBR and Old Style. *3600 N Pulaski Rd at Addison St (773-283-7000). El: Blue to Addison. Bus: 53, 56, 152. Sun–Fri 11am–2am; Sat 11am–3am. Average beer: $3.*

The Burlington This Logan Square bar has everything you could ask for—that is, as long as you don't ask for too much. The spare, dim room has plenty of hipster atmosphere (but no hipster snobbery); ample seating at a wood paneled bar; and a delicious beer on tap that you can't get anywhere else (just point to the unmarked draft handle adorned with antlers and tell the bartender you'll have some of that). *3425 W Fullerton Ave between Bernard St and St Louis Ave (773-384-3243). El: Blue to Logan Square. Bus: 56, 74, 82. Sun–Fri 6pm–2am; Sat 6pm–3am. Average beer: $4.*

California Clipper The Clipper is just a photo booth away from exhibiting the same shabby-chic hipster cool as Wicker Park dives like Goldstar or the Rainbo Club. Slide into one of the gorgeous booths on a Monday night for a tongue-and-cheek version of bingo. *1002 N California Ave at Augusta Blvd (773-384-2547). Bus: 52, 66, 70. Sun–Fri 8pm–2am; Sat 8pm–3am. Average cocktail: $5.*

(✳ **The Continental** In its past life as Hiawatha (a.k.a. Pizza Lounge), the only thing you'd pick up here was a six-pack of cheap beer to lug next door for a chicken dinner at Feed. Now, the 100-year-old dive has transformed into a slick little enclave for the late-night crowd to scope out each other and suck down the last liquor of the night to the tune of the DJ's all-rock repertoire. *2801 W Chicago Ave at California Ave (773-292-1200). Bus: 52 Kedzie/California, 66 Chicago. Mon–Fri 3pm–4am, Sat 3pm–5am, Sun 6pm–4am. Average cocktail: $5.*

✕ **Dragonlady Lounge** If you're not sure why Stadium West changed its name to this, start your night at this often desolate dive by asking owner "Sue"—you'll get an earful. The self-appointed "Dragonlady" is a straight-shooter, with a sweet side that comes out when she plays den mother on Thursdays, cooking up vegan Korean fare for any scraggly twentysomething with $10 for the all-you-can-eat spread. *3188 N Elston Ave at Belmont Ave (773-597-5617). Bus: 52 Kedzie/California, 77 Belmont. Mon–Fri 3pm–2am; Sat 5pm–3am (closed Sun). Average cocktail: $3.50.*

✳ **Green Eye Lounge** There's no pretense here—in fact, the Green Eye's self-proclaimed addition to the 'hood is "cheap drinks for reasonable people." Locals head here for Lagunitas drafts, a small outdoor patio (in the summer) and its prime spot right next to the Blue Line, which makes this place easier to drop into your routine than sleep. *2403 W Homer St at Western Ave (773-227-8851). El: Blue to Western. Bus: 49 Western (24hrs). Mon–Fri 3pm–2am; Sat noon–3am; Sun noon–2am. Average beer: $4.50.*

Helen's Two Way Lounge Scenesters haven't ruined this honky-tonk Logan Square joint, named for its dual entryways, yet, so when you see those banjos and fiddles above the bar and witness the ladies square-dancing with each other to the tunes of Johnny Cash and Hank Williams, you can bet this shit ain't ironic. *2928 W Fullerton Ave at Milwaukee Ave (773-227-5676). El: Blue to California. Bus: 52, 56, 74. Mon–Fri 9am–2am; Sat 9am–3am; Sun 11am–2am. Average beer: $3. Cash only.*

✕ ✳ ♦ **Logan Bar & Grill** Locals who grumble about Logan's gentrification need to get over it—stop into this new bar and grill in

early evening and the packed rooms of young families with kids in tow, couples watching the game and eclectic groups of friends is proof that the neighborhood needed a catch-all. A few warnings though: The music often edges toward blasting, the presence of beefy bouncers and a valet is weird, and the food pales in comparison to sibling Northside Bar and Grill. *2230 N California Ave at Lyndale St (773-252-1110). El: Blue to California. Bus: 52, 56, 74. Sun–Fri 11am–2am; Sat 11am–3am. Average beer: $5.*

The Mutiny By day it's home to dedicated regulars, by night it's packed with rock & rollers drinking $6 half pitchers and nodding to free live bands. Pool and darts are all free, and so is the chance to mark your territory by painting a ceiling tile. If you're in search of (semitarnished) gold, this is your treasure. *2428 N Western Ave between Montana and Altgeld Sts (773-486-7774). El: Blue to California. Bus: 49 (24hrs), X49, 74. Mon 6pm–2am; Tue 3pm–2am; Wed 2pm–2am; Thu 1pm–2am; Fri noon–2am; Sat noon–3am; Sun 11am–2am. Average beer: $3.50.*

✕ ✳ **ñ** If you come here for a quiet dinner, do so earlier in the night, because come 10pm most nights, DJs like popular weekend resident David Pardo—playing tropical groove, Afro-Cuban, and Latin funk and house take over. Get a Quilmes beer or a killer mojito at the bar, though the music's so hot, you won't need liquid courage to hit the dance floor. *2977 N Elston Ave at Rockwell St (773-866-9898). Bus: 9, X49, 76, 77. Tue–Fri 6:30pm–2am; Sat 6:30pm–3am. Average cocktail: $8.*

✕ **Nelly's S aloon** Pearls? Check. Cigarettes? Check. Bright pink lipstick? Check. All of owner Nelly's essentials are in order and she's officially open for business. Expect handsome, loaded Romanian imports chowing down on the earthy cuisine of Romania: platters of *mititei* (grilled sausages); fried kraut with bits of bacon fat; heaping bowls of polenta with feta; and pan-fried chicken wings. Other than weekends when there's live music or anytime a soccer game's on, it's likely to be just you and Nelly, the queen of amaretto stone sours. *3256 N Elston Ave between Belmont Ave and Henderson St (773-588-4494). El: Blue to Belmont. Bus: 77, 82, 152. Tue–Sun 11am–10pm (closed Mon). Average beer: $3. Cash only.*

Side dish

ALL THE WORLD'S A $TAGE
And the regulars at Rainbo Club
its players.

Culture club

Brush up on Chicago history with a pub crawl that traces the steps of local celebrities.

If you've crawled for the rain forest, the polar bears and the whales, if you've done the Santa Claus, the Master's, and the Ugly Sweater crawl, too, we're guessing you're running out of excuses to drink ten beers. Coming to your aid, we've created a cultural pub crawl of sorts, one with a lens toward Chicago history: bars where headline makers were spending their time when they weren't making headlines.

Your crawl begins at the **Woodlawn Tap** (p.172), known to its regulars as "Jimmy's." While the single-story modest brick exterior may not inspire your first novel, it certainly served Nobel laureate and University of Chicago faculty member Saul Bellow just fine. Some of his works are as integral to the Western canon as this dependable neighborhood joint is to the U. of C. community, so feel free to hold court here and let your urbanity spill forth while you still have your wits about you.

With your intellectual juices flowing, don't abort the crawl in favor of scholarly endeavors at the Museum Campus—keep going to **Miller's Pub** (p.168). A cultural institution since the 1950s, Miller's was home to Cubs broadcaster Harry Caray and idiosyncratic White Sox owner Bill "Disco Demolition Night" Veeck. Although now in a different building one block away, Miller's Pub retains its family-owned charm and willingness to please—apparently enough to even bring together Cubs and Sox fans.

Traveling north up Michigan Avenue, duck into the famed Bill Murray and John Belushi hangout (and Cubs-cursing namesake), **Billy Goat Tavern** (p.169). After a quick beer and "cheezeborger," continue up Michigan until you reach

Chicago's heavyweight champion of skyscrapers, the John Hancock Center. But wait, don't get on that elevator to the 95th floor Signature Lounge—walk downstairs to the Cheesecake Factory (875 N Michigan Ave, 312-337-1101). What? A megachain, you cry? Iconoclast that he was, Second City member and 60th-floor Hancock resident Chris Farley must have had a weakness for cheesecake, as it's said he took down quite a few slices of the stuff (alongside whiskey chasers, natch) in the disco-meets-dungeon bar area.

If it seems you've been spending a lot of time underground lately, writer Nelson Algren's hangouts in Wicker Park, **Gold Star Bar** (p.155) and **Rainbo Club** (p.156), might appear downright sunny. Or not. Dark and dingy dives full of character, these bars call to mind the urban grit that was once Division Street, the perfect wellspring for Algren's literary realism.

By design, we're hoping at this point the alcohol has burned away any trepidation you might have felt entering Jeffrey Dahmer's old stomping grounds, the **L&L Tavern** (p.142). Don't bother looking for traces of his existence—ideally those have been cleaned up and stored in a landfill somewhere in Nevada. Instead, enjoy a cheap PBR, and avoid eye contact with the guy near the front all by himself.

Your last stop is the venerable **Green Mill** (p.147). While we doubt you're going to encounter any of that "old Chicago lightning," reminders of Al Capone still exist aplenty in this jazz joint. And whether or not you're drunk with fame as the crawl comes to a close, at least you're drunk, and sometimes that's good enough.—*John Moss*

✕ ✳ **The Orbit Room** From the music on the speakers (Nat King Cole, et al.) to the Rat-Pack decor and carefully shaken martinis, this Logan Square corner bar is surprising all the twentysomething post-hipsters flocking to it. It's not just that the bar is a far cry from the dive that preceded it—really, it's a far cry from anything that's been built since 1940. Varied music such as a heavy dose of the oldies on Mondays draw different crowds for the live DJ sets. *2959 N California Ave between George St and Wellington Ave (773-588-8540). Bus: 52 California, 76 Diversey. Mon–Thu 4pm–2am; Fri, Sun noon–2am; Sat noon–3am. Average cocktail: $6.*

✕ ✳ **Rootstock Wine & Beer Bar** The novella-length menu at this low-key alcove contains loving and helpful descriptions of an impressive selection of wines and beers. And thanks to the array of small plates, executed by chef Remy Ayesh and served until 1am, this is the kind of warm, simple neighborhood place you'll never want—or need—to leave. *954 N California Ave (773-292-1616). Bus: 53, 66, 70. 5pm–2am. Average beer: $6.*

✕ ✳ **Small Bar** *2009 Eat Out Awards, Readers' Choice: Best Corner Tap* The Logan Square location of this Wicker Park beer bar stands out as a classy neighborhood joint in a sleepy residential block, with a gorgeous arched and mirrored wooden bar, gold painted tin ceilings, bubbling lava lamps, and an alt-rock-heavy jukebox. The beer selection is fantastic (cocktails leave a bit to be desired), and snacks like hand-dipped cheese curds and locally made Piccolo gelato round out the menu. *2956 N Albany Ave at Wellington Ave (773-509-9888). El: Blue to Belmont. Bus: 76, 77, 82. Mon–Fri 4pm–2am; Sat noon–3am; Sun noon–2am. Average beer: $6.*

✳ **Weegee's Lounge** Ten years from now, when this strip of Armitage is populated with coffee shops and vintage clothing stores, this old-school, soul-record–playing, classic-cocktail–mixing bar will be overrun with hipsters vying for their turn in the photo booth. Start hanging out here now so you can say you knew it in the good old days. *3659 W Armitage Ave at Lawndale Ave (773-384-0707). Bus: 53, 73, 82. Sun–Fri 5pm–2am; Sat 5pm–3am. Average cocktail: $6.*

Whirlaway Lounge This Logan Square watering hole glows with charm—or is it the string of Christmas lights behind the bar? Either way, retired rock stars put away beers next to their disciples under the soft lights, snapshots of regulars and the warm smile of the maternal owner-bartender, Maria. *3224 W Fullerton Ave between Kedzie Blvd and Sawyer Ave (773-276-6809). El: Blue to Logan Square. Bus: 74 Fullerton, 82 Kimball/Homan. Sun–Fri 4pm–2am; Sat 4pm–3am. Average beer: $2.50. Cash only.*

✳ **The Whistler** *2009 Eat Out Awards, Critics' Pick: Most Unpretentious Pretentious Bar* From the outside, this place looks like a gallery (which, technically, it partially is). On the inside, it's open and loftlike, with a permanent stage set up for weekly live music. But behind the bar, decked out in a vest and tie, a bartender is skillfully making cocktails like a rosemary collins. One sip and there's no doubt that despite everything else going on here, the cocktails are the reason to stick around. *2421 N Milwaukee Ave between Fullerton Ave and Richmond St (773-227-3530). El:*

Blue to California. Bus: 52, 56, 74. Mon–Thu 6pm–2am; Fri, Sun 5pm–2am; Sat 5pm–3am. Average cocktail: $8.

Bucktown/Wicker Park

Beachwood Inn No hipsters, no yuppies, no class-drawing lines here—just regular neighborhood folks in this one-room watering hole taking turns on the pool table or playing games like Scrabble and Connect Four. The scatterbrained decor (old movie posters, sports crap, beer memorabilia) is as random as the jukebox, which offers pre-'90s tunes from the Pretenders to Michael Jackson. *1415 N Wood St at Beach Ave (773-486-9806). El: Blue to Division. Bus: 9, 56, 72. Mon–Thu 5pm–2am; Fri 4pm–2am; Sat 3pm–3am; Sun 3pm–2am. Average cocktail: $5. Cash only.*

✕ ✳ ♨ **The Boundary** Opened by the team behind Wrigleyville's Trace, this enormous drinkery brings a taste of the prototypical Lincoln Park sports bar to Division Street. The generic tan interior means that your attention will undoubtedly fall to one of three things: the busty bartenders and servers, the football game on the flat screens or—and this would be our choice—the 70-bottle-strong beer list. *1932 W Division St at Winchester Ave (773-278-1919). El: Blue to Division. Bus: 50, 56, 70. Mon–Fri 11am–2am; Sat 10am–3am; Sun 10am–2am. Average beer: $4.*

✳ **Bucktown Pub** At first glance this place didn't seem any different from other dark-wood neighborhood taverns. But then we noticed the psychedelic posters lining the walls, the bottomless baskets of free popcorn and the old man in the corner laughing his ass off at nothing. Is this bar high? *1658 W Cortland St between Marshfield Ave and Paulina St (773-394-9898). Bus: 9, 50, 73. Sun–Fri 3pm–2am; Sat 3pm–3am. Average beer: $4.*

✕ ✳ **Chaise Lounge** This restaurant in the former Iggy's is both restaurant and lounge, featuring dishes such as Tuscan bean salad with fried pancetta; beet-and-goat-cheese napoleon; and smoked pork tenderloin with red-currant glaze. But it's the rooftop deck (covered in a tent in chillier months) and alfresco patio that steal the show, at least for those looking to rub elbows with Miami Beach dweller–wannabes. *1840 W North Ave between Honore St and Wolcott Ave (773-342-1840). El: Blue to Damen. Bus: 50, 56, 72. Mon–Thu 5pm–2am; Fri 3pm–2am; Sat 11am–3am; Sun 11am–2am. Average cocktail: $9.*

The Charleston *2009 Eat Out Award, Critics' Pick: The Please Don't Go Award* Hipsters, yuppies, freaks, dirty old men and bluegrass bands pack this tchotchke-ridden corner tap, which is easily one of Bucktown's favorites. None of the above descriptors fit your personality? No worries. Between the piano, WiFi access and live music, you'll find something that suits. *2076 N Hoyne Ave at Charleston St (773-489-4757). El: Blue to Western. Bus: 49 Western (24hrs), 50 Damen. Mon–Fri 3pm–2am; Sat, Sun 2pm–2am. Average beer: $4. Cash only.*

✕ **The Crocodile** The upstairs of this Wicker Park lounge doesn't look loungey at all—it has more of a restaurant feel (something the pizza oven churning out pies in the back contributes to). But it doesn't take long to pick up on the bar aura. Restaurants you leave; but a lounge this homey

SLICE OF LIFE Name one thing better than the combo of beer and pizza and we'll buy your next round at Piece.

makes you want to stay all night, especially when everyone who buys a drink gets a free pizza to boot. *1540 N Milwaukee Ave between Honore St and Damen Ave (773-252-0880). El: Blue to Damen. Bus: 50, 56, 72. Sun–Fri 5pm–2am; Sat 5pm–3am. Average beer: $5.*

Danny's Tavern The floors of this converted Bucktown house shake so much from the weight of hot-footed trendsetters you'd think the place is seconds from caving in. Most of the dancing is set to a mix of hip-hop, electro and rock on the weekends (and the insanely popular first-Wednesday-of-the-month funk party called Sheer Magic), but there are plenty of nooks and crannies to sit back, relax and people-watch. *1951 W Dickens Ave between Damen and Winchester Aves (773-489-6457). El: Blue to Damen. Bus: 50 Damen, 73 Armitage. Sun–Fri 7pm–2am; Sat 7pm–3am. Average cocktail: $5.*

Davenport's Piano Bar and Cabaret Wicker Park's only piano bar is also one of its oldest; around since 1998, it opened while area shoppers and sippers were still in middle school. Karaoke is a big part of the place: The back room bursts with would-be crooners on Friday nights. And on the other nights? Professionals—replete with boas and dirty jokes—show them how it's *really* done. *1383*

N Milwaukee Ave between Wolcott Ave and Wood St (773-278-1830). El: Blue to Damen. Bus: 50, 56, 72. Mon, Wed–Fri 7pm–2am; Fri, Sat 7pm–3am; Sun 3pm–11pm (closed Tue). Average cocktail: $7.

✕ ✳ **Debonair Social Club** Early in the evening at this bilevel hangout, the video art on the wall is the room's main source of light, giving off a cool, sultry cocktail-lounge vibe. But it's the calm before the storm: When celebrity DJs stop by, the place gets packed with clubby scenesters and frantic bass lines—so if you're here for the quiet, enjoy it while you can. *1575 N Milwaukee Ave between Honore St and North Ave (773-227-7990). El: Blue to Damen. Bus: 50, 56, 72. Tue–Fri 9pm–2am; Sat 9pm–3am; Sun noon–6 pm. Average cocktail: $7.*

Ed and Jean's It's not that this old Bucktown standby feels like somebody's living room; it's that it basically is one. Jean's been here for more than 50 years, and in that time she's accumulated more knickknacks than a flea market. It's her second home, and after a few minutes chatting with her over a cheap bottle of beer, it starts feeling like yours, too. *2032 W Armitage Ave between Damen and Hoyne Aves (no phone). El: Blue to Western. Bus: 49 (24hrs), 50, 73. 11am–11pm. Average beer: $2.50. Cash only.*

99 BOTTLES OF BEER ON THE WALL
But who's counting when the suds
selection is as good as the Map Room's.

Bars and Lounges

Empire Liquors Black walls, wiry chandeliers and more guyliner than a My Chemical Romance concert make this place the angstiest of Matt Eisler's bars (personally, we prefer his Bar Deville). The scene can get a little overwhelming in front, but if you can snag a seat in the private(ish) back room you'll be golden— or at least as golden as a goth kid can get. *1566 N Milwaukee Ave between Honore St and North Ave (773-278-1600). El: Blue to Damen. Bus: 50, 56, 72. Wed, Thu 9pm–2am; Fri 8pm–2am; Sat 8pm–3am. Average cocktail: $8.*

(✕ **Estelle's** Not feeling Subterranean's music for the night? Can't take the hipper-than-thou crowd at Rainbo? Prefer a place less clubbier than Debonair? Well, then head to this low-key sanctuary in the otherwise oft-pretentious Milwaukee-North-Damen intersection. No one's trying to out-cool anyone here (though late at night, they're definitely trying to pick each other up), so feel free to strike up a conversation with a stranger over some tasty late-night bar eats, served till 3am. *2013 W North Ave at Milwaukee Ave (773-782-0450). El: Blue to Damen. Bus: 50, 56, 72. Sun–Fri 7pm–4am; Sat 7pm–5am. Average cocktail: $5.*

✕ ✻ **Fifty/50** What? Whaaat? We can't hear you over the insanely loud frat-tastic crowd ordering 40-ounce's in paper bags from trucker-capped waitresses, but we're assuming you're asking us what the hell happened to Division. Maybe we'll meet you upstairs where we can eat some peppery wings and gooey mac and cheese in relative quiet, but it's going to take a bathtub of beer-ritas to get us onto what's sure to be the loudest sidewalk patio in town. *2017 W Division St between Damen and Hoyne Aves (773-489-5050). El: Blue to Division. Bus: 49 (24hrs), 50, 70. Mon–Thu 4pm–2am; Fri, Sun 11am–2am; Sat 11am–3am. Average cocktail: $7.*

(**The Flat Iron** When this place was The Note, the focus was on the bands on stage. Now, of course, those bands are gone, and the focus is on…nothing. The dark bar, now decorated with street-art murals on the walls, is roomy and a little divey, and it's essentially as low-key and basic as a bar can get. And that's exactly what this rapidly yuppifying neighborhood needs. *1565 N Milwaukee Ave at Damen Ave (773-365-9000). El: Blue to Damen. Bus: 50, 56, 72. Sun–Fri 4pm–4am; Sat 4pm–5am. Average beer: $1.*

✕ ✻ **Floyd's Pub** This place is more Cheers than English pub, and the bartender seems to know the name of every Bucktown local who munches pub grub to the tunes of the Flaming Lips. Spend a few nights here with a pint of local microbrew 312 and you'll become as recognizable as the portraits of Elvis behind the bar. *1944 N Oakley Ave at Armitage Ave (773-276-6060). El: Blue to Western. Bus: 49 (24hrs), 50, 73. Mon–Fri 5pm–2am; Sat noon–3am; Sun noon–2am. Average beer: $5.*

Gallery Cabaret Perhaps one of the most active and random stages in the city can be found at this eclectic, art-filled corner tavern, where nightly performances can range from poetry readings to jam bands to a recent musical tribute to a famous deceased racehorse (seriously). More reliable is the beer menu: 17 bottles and 16 draft beers, including the venerable Alpha King. *2020 N Oakley Ave between Armitage and McLean Aves (773-489-5471). El: Blue to Western. Bus: 49, X49, 56, 73. Sun–Fri 5pm–2am; Sat 5pm–3am. Average beer: $4.*

✕ ✻ **Handlebar Bar & Grill** The multiple bike racks out back are packed with every kind of two-wheeler imaginable no matter the time of year at this biker bar (and by biker, we mean bicycle-r). Eco-minded folks chat over tasty vegan fare (the barbecue seitan is great), check out each other's rides and sample from the ample list of diverse drafts. *2311 W North Ave between Oakley and Claremont Aves (773-384-9546). El: Blue to Damen. Bus: 49 (24hrs), X49, 50, 72. Mon–Thu 10am–midnight; Fri 10am–2am; Sat 10am–2am; Sun 10am–midnight. Average beer: $4.50.*

Lava Lounge The once-divey Ukie Village DJ bar is now a compact, high-design club in Wicker Park. The Suhail-conceived concrete bar contrasts with a glowing red ceiling panel, and removable modular seating means more dance space for bigger gigs. The owners (also of SmallBar) have kept their promise of low or no cover, as well as the diverse roster of resident DJs. The style upgrade doesn't mean a neglected beer list: Look for more than a dozen boutique labels on the bottle list. *1270 N Milwaukee Ave at Ashland Ave (773-342-5282). El: Blue to Division. Bus: 9, X9, 50, 72. Sun–Fri 7pm–2am; Sat 7pm–3am. Average beer: $5.*

Lemmings Don't take the name literally: There's a nice crowd here, but the joint isn't packed with followers, so you can usually find a seat to soak up the comforting vibe. We want to keep this beloved place low-key, and were almost hesitant to tell you about it, but we're running out of competition on the Ms. Pac-Man and the pool table. *1850 N Damen Ave between Moffat and Cortland Sts (773-862-1688). El: Blue to Damen. Bus: 50, 56, 73. Mon–Fri 4pm–2am; Sat noon–3am; Sun noon–2am. Average beer: $3.*

✕ ✻ **Lottie's** So you're wondering how a sports bar with a crowd of screaming coeds and an impressive list of drinkable "bombs" (when Jäger alone just won't cut it anymore) found its way into Bucktown. But you're ripping Blue Bombs, sucking down the 32 oz Schooners like they're holy water and hogging the pool table, so the frat-mentality invasion can't be all that bad. *1925 W Cortland St between Wolcott and Winchester Aves (773-489-0738). El: Blue to Damen. Bus: 9, 50, 73. Sun–Fri 11am–2am; Sat 11am–3am. Average cocktail: $5.*

The Map Room You couldn't fit another beer on the killer list or another Bucktown local in this cozy tavern on Tuesdays, a.k.a. "International Night." This weekly party brings in food from a different ethnic spot around town—plates are free with an order of two drinks. If you're a more low-key drinker, but like the vibe, stop by in the a.m. when The Map Room functions as a coffee house. *1949 N Hoyne Ave between Homer St and Armitage Ave (773-252-7636). El: Blue to Western. Bus: 49 (24hrs), 50, 73. Mon–Fri 6:30am–2am; Sat 7:30am–3am; Sun 11am–2am. Average beer: $5.*

✕ ✻ 🍴 **Moonshine** True to its Prohibition-era theme, this bar serves its beer in mason jars. But there's nothing redneck about the seven booths that are outfitted with individual plasma TVs. Those are likely to get more use during quieter weeknights when couples and small groups stop in for beers, burgers and televised games. Weekends can be a madhouse, with blaring DJ-driven music and scoping singles taking over. *1824 W Division at Honore St (773-862-8686). El: Blue to Division. Bus: 9, 56,* 70. *Mon 5pm–2am; Tue–Fri 11am–2am; Sat 10am–3am; Sun 10am–2am. Average beer: $4.*

(✻ **Nick's Beergarden** The rumble of the train drowns out your conversation in the beer garden every five minutes, but that's a small price to pay for a laid-back day sipping beer in the sun (or, in case of a sudden downpour, under the covered portion of the garden). Servers are attentive, and the crowd outside is pretty chill—the only shit-talking going on is at the Golden Tee or at the pool table. That is until the rest of the neighborhood's bars close at 2 and the line outside waiting to get in gets unruly. *1516 N Milwaukee Ave between Honore St and Damen Ave (773-252-1155). El: Blue to Damen. Bus: 50, 56, 72. Sun–Fri 4pm–4am; Sat 4pm–5am. Average beer: $4.*

✻ **Phyllis' Musical Inn** One of Wicker Park's first spots for live music refuses to go the way of cover bands, instead booking local acts that play original rock. They're not always great, but the garden patio is. A scrappy mix of chairs and tables, a basketball hoop and groups of friends shooting the shit over cheap drinks makes for a classic summer night. *1800 W Division St at Wood St (773-486-9862). El: Blue to Division. Bus: 9, X9, 50, 70. Mon–Fri 3pm–2am; Sat 3pm–3am; Sun 1pm–2am. Average beer: $3.50. Cash only.*

✕ **Piece** Every Thursday, drunken wannabe rock stars elbow for space against just-post-college frat-types to choose from the karaoke book's 20,000 songs. Brave it, or head in early in the week to sample the great brews made on premises—we're partial to the Golden Arm and Dark-n-Curvy Dunkelweizen—alongside New Haven-style thin-crust pizzas. *1927 W North Ave between Wolcott and Winchester Aves (773-772-4422). El: Blue to Damen. Bus: 50, 56, 72. Mon–Thu 11am–1:30am; Fri 11am–2am; Sat 11am–3am; Sun 11am–1am. Average beer: $4.*

✕ ✻ 🍴 **Pint** The name makes it pretty clear: This is a simple joint where you can grab a cool pint of your favorite brew while cheering for your favorite team. The flat screens and big screen are being put to good use with satellite TV tuned in to games around the globe. Add some cold brews, and the owners might have finally scored, especially with the latest crowd of party animals roaming "the Crotch" looking for a place to land. *1547 N Milwaukee Ave between Honore and Damen Sts (773-772-0990). El: Blue to Damen. Bus 50, 56, 72. Sun–Fri 11am–2am; Sat 11am–3am. Average beer: $4.50.*

✕ **Quencher's Saloon** This 25-year-old beer bar sitting on the Bucktown/Logan Square border has one of the most diverse crowds in town. The well-heeled eye each other on weekends, local beer nerds meet to taste the 300 choices on weeknights and drunk punks wander in whenever. Luckily they peacefully co-exist in two spacious rooms, all in the name of beer. Daytime crowds enjoy the laid-back vibe, thanks for free popcorn and comfy couches. *2401 N Western Ave at Fullerton Ave (773-276-9730). El: Blue to California. Bus: 49 Western (24hrs), 74 Fullerton. Mon–Thu noon–2am; Fri, Sun 11am–2am; Sat 11am–3am. Average beer: $4. Cash only.*

✕ **Rodan** It's tough being young and fabulous. Why else would the fashionable crowd at the equally fashionable Rodan be throwing back so many cocktails? Oh, right—with specials like $3 sparkling lychee drinks on

Mondays, and tapioca pearls in the potent but fruity cocktails, you'd be sucking them down like they're going out of style, too. *1530 N Milwaukee Ave between Damen Ave and Honore St (773-276-7036). El: Blue to Damen. Bus: 50, 56, 72. Mon–Fri 6pm–2am; Sat 5pm–3am; Sun 5pm–2am. Average cocktail: $6.*

✕ ✻ ● **Salud Tequila Lounge** Take a cue from the name and go for the nectar of the agave gods at this clubby, Mexican-themed lounge. If you've taken up residence along the sidewalk patio, opt for your tequila in 'rita form to maximize your tropical experience. Salsa sounds blend with bass-heavy bangers to get the crowd going on weekends, but Tuesdays and Thursdays are almost as busy, with $5 sangria pitchers and dirt-cheap appetizers, respectively. *1471 N Milwaukee Ave between Honore St and Evergreen Ave (773-235-5577). El: Blue to Damen. Bus: 50, 56, 72. Sun–Fri 5pm–2am; Sat 5pm–3am. Average cocktail: $7.*

✕ ✻ **Small Bar** Actually, this welcoming neighborhood joint is far from small—it's a decent-sized, airy space that opens up onto a sidewalk patio. If it's literal names they wanted, maybe Beer Bar (named for the 265-beer-strong list), Scenester Bar (it's not Rainbo, but close) or Pricey Bar (obscure beer ain't cheap, kids) would have been more accurate. *2049 W Division St between Damen and Hoyne Aves (773-772-2727). El: Blue to Division. Bus: 49, 50, 70. Sun–Fri 11am–2am; Sat 11am–3am. Average beer: $5.*

✕ **The Violet Hour** This incessantly hip cocktail lounge is exactly what you'd expect from a bar named after a line of T.S. Eliot poetry: pristine (the carefully constructed cocktails are excellent), pretentious (you won't find a sign on the door—just look for the long lines) and, ultimately, completely and inarguably gorgeous. *1520 N Damen Ave between Le Moyne St and Wicker Park Ave (773-252-1500). El: Blue to Damen. Bus: 50, 56, 72. Sun–Fri 6pm–2am; Sat 6pm–3am. Average cocktail: $11.*

Zakopane If you're lucky, you'll stumble in here on a night when the Anna Kournikova look-alike bartender is working, pouring vodka drinks with a heavy hand. But any night will do at this wood-paneled, Polish-owned watering hole. The old drunks are quick to challenge you at pool, and the young Poles are obsessed with the jukebox that spits out Polish versions of early-'90s American chart toppers. *1734 W Division St between Hermitage Ave and Wood St (773-486-1559). El: Blue to Division. Bus: 9, 50, 70. Mon–Fri 7am–2am; Sat 7pm–3am; Sun 11am–2am. Average cocktail: $4. Cash only.*

Lincoln Park

◖ **Amp Rock Lounge** This subterranean cave of a bar (at the former home of Katacombs) feels like a Disneyland fantasy of an early-'90s rock venue—glossy black walls adorned with scrawled song lyrics, giant glamour shots of icons like Steven Tyler, a glittering bar top and black leather settees paired with tables made from drum heads. No live music or dancing, but the in-house iPod features something like 20,000 songs (though why out of 20,000 you'd choose to play Bon Jovi is beyond us). *1909 N Lincoln Ave at Wisconsin St (312-376-1860). El: Brown, Purple (rush hrs) to Sedgwick. Bus: 11, 22 (24hrs), 73. Wed–Fri 10pm–4am; Sat 10pm–5am. Average cocktail: $6.*

The hit list

Five **beer cocktails**

1 ✦ **Beer Gambatini at QuchiOumba Rio** (p.101)
What the heck is muddled avocado doing in this combination of St-Germain Elderflower liqueur, tequila blanco, lime juice, cilantro and Kirin Ichiban? Go ahead and taste it—preferably without the straw—and you'll see. (Hint: It's all about the smooth mouthfeel.)

2 **Beergarita at Small Bar** (p.151)
This "beertail"—a combination of fresh-squeezed lime juice, Cuervo Gold, Monk's Café Flemish sour ale and Framboise—may have been invented on a slow Sunday afternoon by a couple of bored bartenders, but with its awesome balance of tart, tangy and sweet, you'd think it took years to perfect.

3 **Wild Berry Shandy at the Fifty/50** (p.149)
On paper it sounds simple enough: Bacardi Razz and fresh ginger with Hoegaarden wheat beer, black-cherry lambic and raspberry lambic. But the secret weapon is lemonade blended with fresh berries, which is strained and added to the mix. Regulars know to ask for it in a 24-ounce cup, and now you do, too.

4 **Hibiscus-Ginger-Cardamom-Kaffir Lime Rum with Matilda at Nacional 27** (p.94)
GM/mixologist Adam Seger's no stranger to local ingredients, but with this drink it's personal. The star ingredient is Hum, a two-years-in-the-making infused-rum "spirit tonic" he created with North Shore Distillery. Pairing it with another famous local, Goose Island's Matilda, is a no-brainer.

5 **French Connection at English** (444 N LaSalle St, 312-222-6200)
Don't let its girly hue fool you—this magenta-colored drink packs a big wallop. We imagine the hefty shot of Stoli Vanil poured into the ice-filled glass of the raspberry-infused lambic beer Framboise has something to do it.—*Lisa Shames*

B.L.U.E.S. Of course the music—blues provided by live bands every night—is too loud to talk over; you're not *supposed* to talk over it. But you are supposed to drink, and if you want to have an easier time getting served, be nice to the ladies behind the bar—they don't take any bullshit. *2519 N Halsted St between Altgeld St and Lill Ave (773-528-1012). El: Brown, Red, Purple (rush hrs) to Fullerton. Bus: 8 Halsted, 74 Fullerton. Sun–Fri 8pm–2am; Sat 8pm–3am. Average beer: $4.*

♨ **Cagney's** If we had to guess, we'd say this bar was named after James Cagney and not, say, Cagney & Lacey (it's the '30s-ish uniforms the girls behind the bar wear that tipped us off). To that end, "classy" seems to be this slick sports bar's goal—though it offers plenty of schnapps-heavy cocktails should you want to ramp it up, plus brunch on weekends to nurse that hangover. *2142 N Clybourn Ave between Wayne and Southport Aves (773-857-1111). El: Brown, Purple (rush hrs) to Armitage. Bus: 73 Armitage, 74 Fullerton. Mon–Fri 11am–2am; Sat 11am–3am; Sun noon–2am. Average beer: $5.*

✕ ✻ **Charlie's on Webster** Sometimes one of those grumpy old-timers takes a seat

THIS OLD HOUSE After that big ball of twine, the Hideout is the best roadside attraction we know.

among the younger Lincoln Park buttoned-down crowd here. But once the geezers settle into plush leather booths, chat with the impeccable bartender and sip a beer, even they can't stay in a bad mood. *1224 W Webster Ave at Magnolia Ave (773-871-1440). El: Brown, Purple (rush hrs), Red to Fullerton. Bus: 73 Armitage, 74 Fullerton. Mon 4pm–10pm; Wed, Thu 4pm–midnight; Fri 4pm–2am; Sat 10am–2am; Sun 10am–midnight (closed Tue). Average beer: $4.*

✕ ◆ **D.O.C. Wine Bar** This cozy wine bar is a sibling of next door's Dunlays on Clark, a casual bar/restaurant, but the incredible high ceilings here give it some kind of urban barnyard feel. The bottle selection is excellent (though we wish there were more glass options), and you won't find even the slightest whiff of pretension, despite the mostly yuppie clientele. *2602 N Clark St between Wrightwood Ave and Drummond Pl (773-883-5101). El: Brown, Purple (rush hrs), Red to Fullerton. Bus: 11, 22 (24hrs), 36. Sun–Fri 5pm–2am; Sat 5pm–3am. Average glass of wine: $9.*

Delilah's One of the city's best spots for rock & roll doesn't even have a stage. Instead, this Lincoln Park favorite has one of the best jukeboxes in town for the main room (so you can play DJ Fridays and Saturdays) and hires DJs who know their Buzzcocks from their Bullocks for Sunday through Thursday. Add an insane

whiskey selection, more than 200 beers (Belgian, microbrews, seasonals) and frequent free movie nights, and you have a bar to call home. *2771 N Lincoln Ave between Schubert Ave and Diversey Pkwy (773-472-2771). El: Brown, Purple (rush hrs) to Diversey. Bus: 11 Lincoln/Sedgwick, 76 Diversey. Sun–Fri 4pm–2am; Sat 11am–3am. Average beer: $4.*

✕ **Diversey Rock 'n' Bowl** A motley mix of first-timers and more experienced amateurs hits the lanes and pounds back shots at this hard-rocking riverfront bowling alley. Old-timers love to wax nostalgic about the place's dingier past, saying the crowd has become more L.L.Bean than leather-clad and mean, but nightly DJs keep things edgy, spinning everything from Motörhead to Ministry. *2211 W Diversey Ave at Logan Blvd (773-227-5800). Bus: 49 (24hrs), X49, 50, 76. Sun–Fri noon–2am; Sat noon–3am. Average beer: $4.50.*

Faith & Whiskey Deer-antler chandeliers seem required these days to complete your "hipster moose lodge" package, so this new incarnation of Ta'Too is covered in that department. A pair of motorcycles parked on top of the bathrooms and an assortment of guitars mounted to the walls force the rock & roll vibe a bit, but the Lincoln Park locals seem to buy it, especially while gyrating to hip-hop mash-ups of Nirvana and

the Stones, turned up to 11. *1365 W Fullerton Ave between Southport and Wayne Aves (773-248-9119). El: Red, Brown, Purple (rush hrs) to Fullerton. Bus: 9, X9, 73, 74. Sun, Wed–Fri 5pm–2am; Sat 5pm–3am. Average cocktail: $6.*

Fieldhouse This overlooked Lincoln Park hang is noted for its mellow vibe, in contrast to the many meatmarkets surrounding it. The bartenders are friendly, the flat-panels numerous and the patrons toss peanut shells onto the floor while trying to spot their alma mater from a banner display that would make the United Nations jealous. *2455 N Clark St at Arlington Pl (773-348-6489). El: Brown, Purple (rush hrs), Red to Fullerton. Bus: 11, 22 (24hrs), 36. Mon–Fri 4pm–2am; Sat 2pm–3am; Sun 3pm–2am. Average beer: $3.*

✕ ☀ **Firkin & Pheasant** We're not sure if this place evokes an English pub as it's supposed to or if the burgundy booths and ornate carpeting simply evoke the '70s. But either way the place is primed to take on Lincoln Park: There are plenty of screens to view the game, and the ample seating means there'll probably never be too much crowding at the bar to get a glass of Guinness. *670 W Diversey Pkwy between Orchard and Clark Sts (773-327-7040). El: Brown, Purple (rush hrs) to Diversey. Bus: 22 (24hrs), 36, 76. Sun–Fri 11:30am–2am; Sat 11:30am–3am. Average beer: $4.*

✕ **Flounder's** A simple, friendly neighborhood sports bar is nothing to sniff at, especially when you can gorge yourself on $1.99 tacos every night of the week. The place puts up pennants from a slew of schools, but don't let that fool you: The drinkers here pledge allegiance to Wisconsin and Nebraska. *2201 N Clybourn Ave between Webster and Greenview Aves (773-472-9920). El: Brown, Purple (rush hrs), Red to Fullerton. Bus: 9 Ashland, 74 Fullerton. Sun–Fri 11am–2am; Sat 11am–3am. Average beer: $4.*

(**Frank's** This cocktail lounge is named after Sinatra, so it only makes sense that Ol' Blue Eyes' songs show up in the jukebox and Rat Pack photos line the walls. But customers feel more like packed rats as this after-hours spot fills up; the crowded room is so narrow that claustrophobic drinkers might only last one round. *2503 N Clark St between St James and Demming Pls (773-549-2700). El: Brown, Purple (rush hrs), Red to Fullerton. Bus: 22 (24hrs), 36, 76. Sun–Fri 11am–4am; Sat 11am–5am. Average beer: $4.50.*

✕ ☀ ◆ **Galway Arms** There's a lot more Gaelic cheer at this bar than just the Guinness on tap. The yummy pub grub is authentic, most of the staff is actually Irish and it's never too crowded to nab a table (choose between the vintage woodwork inside and the expansive, open-air patio). Just don't spread the word too much—we'd hate to wind up ass-to-elbow like at most Lincoln Park McPubs. *2442 N Clark St at Arlington Pl (773-472-5555). El: Brown, Purple (rush hrs), Red to Fullerton. Bus: 22 (24hrs), 36, 74. Mon–Fri 5pm–2am; Sat 11am–3am; Sun 11am–2am. Average beer: $4.*

✕ ☀ **The Grand Central** As its name implies (and its location next to the El tracks underscores), the feel here is that of a bar in a Depression-era train station. Stained-glass ceiling lights emit an amber glow; fringe dangles from the faux smoke-stained lampshades;

and small black-and-white ceramic tiles line the floor. But the centerpiece—despite the prevalence of flat-screen TVs and crazy-drunk locals on weekends—is the piano that sits on a round stage behind the long front bar. *950 W Wrightwood Ave between Wilton and Sheffield Aves (773-832-4000). El: Brown, Purple (rush hrs), Red to Fullerton. Bus: 8, 11, 74 . Mon–Fri 4pm–2am; Sat 11am–3am, Sun 11am–2am. Average beer: $5.*

✳ Hideout A ramshackle roadhouse of country-rock in an industrial stretch of the city wouldn't be complete without a few characters hanging out on the porch no matter the weather. Longtime local acts like Kelly Hogan and Devil in a Woodpile play inside, but the music can still be heard over the cracking of PBR cans out front. It can be difficult to reach this juke joint via public trans, but it is worth it for the cheap beer, live country-rock and DJs dropping nostalgia, from Prince to Devo. *1354 W Wabansia Ave between Willow and Ada Sts (773-227-4433). Bus: 72 North, 73 Armitage. Tue 7pm–2am; Wed–Fri 4pm–2am; Sat 7pm–3am; Sun, Mon for special events (call ahead). Average beer: $2.*

The Liar's Club Are we a bunch of suckers or what? The hours here are completely undependable, the crowd's a crapshoot (punks on the weekdays, prepsters on weekends) and there's no sink in the men's room. But something about this place (and the signage) charms our socks off. But only during the week. We're not about to pay a cover—we'd rather spend our money in the photo booth. *1665 W Fullerton Ave between Clybourn Ave and Wood St (773-665-1110). Bus: 9 Ashland, 74 Fullerton. Sun–Fri 8pm–2am; Sat 8pm–3am. Average beer: $4. Cash only.*

✕ Local Option Nestled on a tree-lined street in Lincoln Park, this watering hole is the epitome of neighborly drinking. (It is named for the laws that allow neighbors to decide how communities sell alcohol.) A friendly bartender will chat you up and introduce you to the locals as he mixes your Hendrick's and tonic. But he knows when to shut up and let you listen to Ryan Adams's cover of "Wonderwall." *1102 W Webster Ave between Seminary and Clifton Aves (773-348-2008). El: Brown, Purple (rush hrs), Red to Fullerton. Bus: 73 Armitage, 74 Fullerton. Sun–Fri 11am–2am; Sat 11am–3am. Average beer: $5.*

Maeve This smallish, sports memorabilia–free spot boasts more class than most Lincoln Park watering holes: dark woods, dim lighting and candle-topped tables. So go ahead, quietly sip a glass of pinot while you wait for a table to open up at adjacent Rose Angelis. But skip the after-dinner martini: By that time the place will be packed with loud, horny thirtysomethings with an agenda. *1325 W Wrightwood Ave at Wayne Ave (773-388-3333). El: Brown, Purple to Fullerton. Bus: 9, 11, 74, 76. Mon–Fri 4pm–2am; Sat 11am–3am; Sun 11am–2am. Average cocktail: $7.*

(▽ ✳ Manhandler Lest you think the name of this place is a joke, a sign on the door announcing the bar's "one drink minimum" reveals its true nature: Guys aren't really coming here to drink. But don't let that keep you from ordering a cocktail from the friendly bartender, especially if you prefer watching your leatherdaddy porn while listening to the jukebox tunes of Elvis Costello. *1948 N Halsted St between Wisconsin St and Armitage Ave (773-871-3339). El: Brown, Purple (rush hrs) to*

Armitage; Red to North/Clybourn. Bus: 8, 72, 73. Sun–Fri noon–4am; Sat noon–5am. Average cocktail: $4. Cash only.

✕ ♨ Matilda What do you get when you put a sign on your door stating that nobody under the age of 23 can enter? A lot of college kids pissed off that they can't hang out on the mod furniture under the faux stars, listening to the sing-along-friendly soundtrack of Prince and Lenny Kravitz. *3101 N Sheffield Ave at Barry Ave (773-883-4400). El: Brown, Purple (rush hrs) to Wellington. Bus: 8, 76, 77. Tue–Fri 6pm–2am; Sat 6pm–3am . Average beer: $4.*

✕ McDunna's There's a serious contingent of regulars calling this bar home, including newly legal DePaul students who pack the place late at night. But it serves our purposes perfectly for an early spot to grab a beer and catch the game. We get 20 screens all to ourselves? Score. *1505 W Fullerton Ave between Greenview and Bosworth Aves (773-929-0944). El: Brown, Purple (rush hrs), Red to Fullerton. Bus: 9 Ashland, 74 Fullerton. Sun–Fri 11am–2am; Sat 11am–3am. Average beer: $3.50.*

✕ ✳ Mickey's If it's too nippy to make use of this bar's stellar sidewalk café, head inside where the diner look has yielded to blue suede booths and flat panel TVs. Mojitos and the house version of sliders are the specialties, and nostalgia for Wrigley Field is induced upon every visit to the metal trough in the men's room. *2450 N Clark St at Arlington Pl (773-435-0007). El: Brown, Purple (rush hrs), Red to Fullerton. Bus: 11, 22 (24hrs), 36. Mon–Fri 11am–2am; Sat 9am–3am; Sun 9am–2am. Average cocktail: $5.*

(Neo Break out the ten-hole Doc Martens and the Manic Panic for this goth-punk outpost that hasn't changed much since, well, before you were out of high school. Neo has a small dance floor and a calendar crammed with DJs specializing in everything from metal and industrial to new wave and electro. *2350 N Clark St between Belden Ave and Fullerton Pkwy (773-528-2622). El: Red, Brown, Purple (rush hrs) to Fullerton. Bus: 22 (24hrs), 36, 74. Sun–Fri 10pm–4am; Sat 10pm–5am. Average cocktail: $4.*

✕ ✳ Rocks Lincoln Park A more appropriate name for this cozy neighborhood tavern might be simply "Rock," because that's exactly what you're given when you order a drink on ice: one enormous cube. We found the pours here to be very generous, which might explain why everybody was kissing the bartender as they left. *1301 W Schubert Ave at Lakewood Ave (773-472-7738). El: Brown, Purple (rush hrs) to Diversey. Bus: 11 Lincoln/Sedgwick, 76 Diversey. Mon–Thu 5pm–2am; Fri 4pm–2am; Sat 11am–3am; Sun 11am–2am. Average cocktail: $5.*

✕ The Spread No offense to the beautiful dark-wood bars here, and nothing against all those flatscreens, but while this joint looks a little more upscale than most, this is still a sports bar. The better-than-average pub grub might also take you out of sports bar–mode for a minute, but shuffleboard and bags bring you right back. *2476 Lincoln Ave between Montana and Altgeld Sts (773-857-5074). El: Brown, Purple (rush hrs), Red to Fullerton. Bus: 8, 11, 74. Tue–Fri 5pm–2am; Sat 3pm–3am; Sun 11am–2am (closed Mon) . Average cocktail: $8.*

(The Store A dark room. A long wooden bar. A couple of middle-aged guys playing video trivia in the corner. A staff who couldn't care less. Who would guess there'd be lines around the corner to get in here come 2am? Guess that's what a 4am license gets ya. *2002 N Halsted St between Armitage and Dickens Aves (773-327-7766). El: Brown, Purple (rush hrs) to Armitage. Bus: 8, 11, 73. Mon–Thu 4pm–4am; Fri 3pm–4am; Sat 11am–5am; Sun 11am–4am. Average beer: $4.*

✕ ✳ ♨ Tavish This is the perfect spot for an evening of miniburgers (hand-formed patties with melted cheese and a pickle slice), onion rings and a domestic beer or two. Families are welcome, but later at night booster chairs give way to friendly singles from the neighborhood. *1335 W Wrightwood Ave between Wayne and Southport Aves (773-529-8888). El: Brown, Purple (rush hrs), Red to Fullerton. Bus: 9 Ashland, 74 Fullerton. Mon–Fri 4pm–2am; Sat 11:30am–3am; Sun 11:30am–2am. Average beer: $4.*

✕ ✳ Tripoli Tavern You'd never know it, but there are tomatoes growing in the garden and lobsters in the kitchen of this Lincoln Park watering hole. That doesn't keep out the kids who are just here to watch the game and ogle the waitresses. But it also doesn't keep out a more refined crowd looking for a bar with restaurant-quality food. *1147 W Armitage Ave between Clifton and Racine Aves (773-477-4400). El: Brown, Purple (rush hrs) to Armitage. Bus: 8 Halsted, 73 Armitage. Sun–Fri 11am–2am; Sat 11am–3am. Average beer: $5.*

Uncle Fatty's Rum Resort If spring break is a sacred ritual, this garden-level DePaul-area bar is the unofficial altar. College students arrive in flocks for potent "fish-bowls," beer specials and drinking games. Hokey decor includes tiki details, AstroTurf, picnic tables and a cordoned-off sandbox where coolers of beer replace bottle service. *2833 N Sheffield Ave between Wolfram and George Sts (773-477-3661). El: Brown, Purple (rush hrs) to Diversey. Bus: 8, 76, 77. Wed–Fri 6pm–2am; Sat 6pm–3am. Average beer: $4.*

✕ Victory Liquors With 25 plasma screens strategically arranged throughout these two wood-rich rooms, there's absolutely no place to escape the game. That's good if you're a Notre Dame fan; if you're not, you'd better go on a night when the Irish aren't fighting. Or just go when the games are over—it's a better time to turn your game on anyway. Closed Sunday and Monday except during football season. *2610 N Halsted St between Wrightwood Ave and Diversey Pkwy (773-348-5600). El: Brown, Purple (rush hrs), Red to Fullerton. Bus: 8, 74, 76. Tue–Fri 5pm–2am; Sat noon–3am. Average beer: $4.*

✕ ✳ ♨ Webster's Wine Bar We've missed many a movie because we stopped by this funky wine bar next to Webster Place theater for a pre-show cocktail. When tasting pours are this affordable (and interesting), we pretend it's for educational purposes and stay all night, soaking up the dark, Bohemian vibe and munching on tasty cheese plates. We'll catch the movie on Netflix. *1480 W Webster Ave between Clybourn Ave and Dominick St (773-868-0608). Bus: 9 Ashland, 74 Fullerton. Mon–Fri 5pm–2am; Sat 4pm–3am; Sun 4pm–2am. Average glass of wine: $7.*

SCOOP DEVILLE Vintage furnishings and contemporary cocktails combine at Bar Deville.

× ☀ ⚓ **Zella** Singles looking for a classy spot love getting spiffed up in their slinkiest summer gear for a night here, where there's always going to be plenty of green: on the outdoor patio and in their wallets. Pink martinis are de rigueur for the ladies, while the guys go for cocktails and the occasional Jager shot to work up the nerve to chat up the hotties. *1983 N Clybourn Ave at Racine Ave (773-549-2910). El: Brown, Purple (rush hrs) to Armitage. Bus: 8 Halsted, 73 Armitage. Mon–Fri 4pm–2am; Sat 10am–3am; Sun 10am–2am. Average cocktail: $7.*

Ukrainian Village/West Town

Bar DeVille The corner location, window neon signs, "cold beer" cooler and Art Deco bar might lead you to believe this spot is run by a septuagenarian with stories to spare. Investigate further and you'll find an extensive beer list, butter-soft leather booths, brocade wallpaper and hipsters shooting stick in an antler-adorned back room—signs that owners Matt Eisler and Kevin Heisner might be youngsters with expensive taste, but they've set their corner tap on the path toward longevity. *701 N Damen Ave between Huron and Superior Sts (312-929-2349). Bus: 50, 65, 66. Sun–Fri 5pm–2am; Sat 5pm–3am. Average beer: $6.*

(☀ **Betty's Blue Star Lounge** The black-on-black decor here is only interrupted by streaks of blue neon, a look so '80s that you'll expect RoboCop to walk in at any moment. Early in the night, local boozehounds have the place to themselves, but around 2am, the spillover from early-to-bed clubs squeezes in to sweat to hip-hop and house beats. The DJ calendar is anything-goes, but expect periodic house and techno marathons. The cover is usually low. *1600 W Grand Ave at Ashland Ave (313-343-1699). El: Green, Pink to Ashland. Bus: 9, X9, 65. Mon–Fri noon–4am; Sat 6pm–5am; Sun 6pm–4am. Average cocktail: $6.*

× ☀ ⚓ **Black Beetle** DJs here know their crowd. Doses of hip-hop come in indie, underground and funky, while rock ranges from '70s stoner to modern garage. All can be heard from the sidewalk tables when the weather's nice. (Tip: drinking pints of Goose Island's 312 blurs the boring view of a wood palette lot.) *2532 W Chicago Ave at Maplewood Ave (773-384-0701). Bus: 49 (24hrs), X49, 66. Mon–Thu 4pm–2am; Fri, Sun 11:30am–2am; Sat 11:30–3am. Average beer: $4.*

Blind Robin The crew behind Green Eye, Lemmings and Underbar purchased the former Bar Vertigo space and gave it a bit of a face lift and, seemingly overnight, it was already packed. The owners salvaged the Art Deco back bar from the old Lava Lounge space and somehow made it fit in these new narrow digs, but the real eye candy here is the never-ending parade of tattooed hipsters who seem to travel in packs to this bar family's watering holes. *853 N Western Ave between Rice and Iowa Sts (773-395-3002). Bus: 49 Western (24hrs), 66 Chicago. Mon–Fri 4pm–2am; Sat noon–3am; Sun noon–2am. Average beer: $4.*

Club Foot Fans of VH1's *I Love the '80s* will be in heaven surrounded by walls plastered with vintage concert tees and glass cases jam-packed with every collectible toy created in that era. During the week there's room to take it all in, but weekends get crammed with locals playing pool to a DJ's mix of classic punk, obscure indie

rock and occasional polka. Yes, polka. After all, it is the Ukrainian Village. *1824 W Augusta St between Wood and Honore Sts (773-489-0379). El: Blue to Division. Bus: 50 Damen, 70 Division. Sun–Fri 8pm–2am; Sat 8pm–3am. Average beer: $2. Cash only.*

× **DeLux** A mere sidestep from the expanding Milwaukee/Grand/Halsted late-night hub, DeLux has more exposed ductwork, raw brick walls and industrial-grade metal tables than even your rich friend's "Hey, look! I live in a former meat locker!" condo. Belly up to the prominent dark-wood bar at night or nurse your hangover at the spot's weekend Bloody Effen Brunch—the lights are dim, the TVs subdued and the by-request "tater smash" (basically mashed-up Tater Tots and onions) plenty greasy. *669 N Milwaukee Ave at Sangamon St (312-850-4008). El: Blue to Grand. Bus: 8, 56, 65. Mon–Fri 11am–2am; Sat 10am–3am; Sun 10am–midnight. Average beer: $5.*

Empty Bottle A prime destination for indie rockers for more than 15 years, this Ukrainian Village live music venue and bar has increasingly turned to booking adventurous electronic, indie hip-hop and experimental-music acts. Just remember that it's more about the head bobbing of hipsters than serious dance-floor action, so boogie at your own risk. *1035 N Western Ave at Cortez St (773-276-3600). Bus: 49 (24hrs), 66, 70. Mon–Wed 5pm–2am; Thu, Fri 3pm–2am; Sat noon–3am; Sun noon–2am. Average beer: $3. Cash only.*

(**Exit** Thursday is fetish night and Monday it's punk rock, but pretty much any night you stumble upon this haunt for the black-clad you'll see that the freaks indeed do come out at night. Like any clique, it tends to have an insider feel, but brave souls looking for their Ministry and PBR fix have to start somewhere. *1315 W North Ave between Ada and Throop Sts (773-395-2700). El: Red to North/Clybourn. Bus: 9 Ashland, 72 North. Sun–Fri 9pm–4am; Sat 9pm–5am. Average beer: $4.*

EZ Inn Those not paying attention risk stumbling past the subtle neon signage and buzzer-protected door of this Ukrainian Village dive. To feel like a regular inside, simply nab a Miller Lite, lend an ear at the bar stools and shamelessly belt Van Halen's "Top of the World" between dart tosses. A tip to the wanna-be sharks: Pool is taken very seriously. *921 N Western Ave between Iowa and Walton Sts (773-384-9682). Bus: 49 (24hrs), 50, 66. Sun–Fri 8am–2am; Sat 8am–3am. Average beer: $2.50.*

× ☀ **Five Star Bar** There goes the neighborhood. Once sleepy and under-appreciated, this raucous spot has single-handedly turned up the volume in West Town. It's packed with tanned, gelled and button-downed dudes devil-horning to old Metallica and gawking at chicks in shirts that look like they've been mauled by tigers. So far, the locals haven't called the cops with noise complaints, but the fashion police should be on their way any minute. *1424 W Chicago Ave at Bishop St (312-850-2555). El: Blue to Chicago. Bus: 9, 56, 66. Mon–Fri 4pm–2am; Sat noon–3am; Sun noon–2am. Average cocktail: $7.*

Gold Star Bar Truly a neighborhood hangout, this tried-and-true East Village bar is frequented by those who appreciate Claudio the tamale guy, a jukebox that stocks both white-hot jazz and doom metal, a free pool table, equally

cheap drinks and a crowd who could care less if you show up in sweats. *1755 W Division St between Wood St and Hermitage Ave (773-227-8700). El: Blue to Division. Bus: 8, 50, 70. Sun–Fri 4pm–2am; Sat 4pm–3am. Average beer: $3. Cash only.*

☀ **Happy Village** A gurgling goldfish pond, picnic tables galore and a lush lawn all around is the scene at this West Town dive. But when it rains (or at 11pm, when the garden closes), pack up the ciggies and head back inside, where the smell of whiskey and cheap beer hangs in the air, and the jukebox coughs out the Cars and Madonna. *1059 N Wolcott Ave at Thomas St (773-486-1512). El: Blue to Division. Bus: 50 Damen, 70 Division. Mon–Fri 4pm–2am; Sat 3pm–3am, Sun 4pm–2am. Average beer: $3.*

× **High Dive** With Three Floyds Gumballhead and Goose Island 312 on tap and wings hot off the grill, this well-lit bar will never truly be a dive. But we don't care, because we feel at home among the concert posters on the walls and the red-velvet booths. And if we're going to drink out of bottles, it might as well be from this 50 beer–strong selection. *1938 W Chicago Ave between Winchester and Damen Aves (773-235-3483). Bus: 50, 65, 66. Mon–Thu 4pm–2am; Fri 3pm–2am; Sat 11:30am–3am; Sun 11:30am–2pm . Average beer: $4.*

Inner Town Pub With more clutter than your eccentric aunt's house, this former speakeasy in Ukie Village serves up cheap booze and warm salted nuts in true dive fashion. Indie-rockers on their way to Empty Bottle shows take advantage of free pool, while a smattering of toothless old-timers keep it gritty with war stories and phlegmy coughs. *1935 W Thomas St at Winchester Ave (773-235-9795). El: Blue to Division. Bus: 50 Damen, 70 Division. Sun–Fri 3pm–2am; Sat 3pm–3am. Average beer: $3.50. Cash only.*

J&M Tap As at the nearby Rainbo Club, the hipness quotient at this less-packed, stripped-down Ukie V stalwart has shot through its nicotine-stained roof, paralleling the changing demographics of the neighborhood. You can still belly up and share cheap suds with a couple of actual Ukrainian expats in the early afternoon, but eager twentysomethings with energy (and hormones) to burn rule the night. *957 N Leavitt St between Walton St and Augusta Blvd (no phone). El: Blue to Division. Bus: 49 (24hrs), X49, 50, 70. Mon–Fri noon–2am, Sat 11am–3am; Sun 11am–2am. Average beer: $2.*

☀ **Matchbox** If the thought of being crammed in this tiny boxcar of a bar makes you nervous, relax. The patio practically doubles the capacity of the place, and it's the perfect spot to throw back one of its margaritas, made with fresh lemon and lime juice, top-shelf liquors and powdered sugar, and poured with a heavy hand. *770 N Milwaukee Ave between Carpenter St and Ogden Ave (312-666-9292). El: Blue to Chicago. Bus: 56 Milwaukee, 66 Chicago. Mon–Thu 4pm–2am; Fri, Sun 3pm–2am; Sat 3pm–3am. Average cocktail: $7.*

Nilda's Place When we strolled into this endearingly tacky Latino holdout tucked into a gentrifying residential block, a tipsy twentysomething swiveled his stool our way, raised his hands to the sky and gleefully announced to the four other people in the place: "Finally! You're here." It was drunk talk all

The hit list

Five **warm drinks to sip by the fireside**

1 ▲ **Fulton Lounge** (p.167)
Is it possible to look manly while sipping a peach vodka-spiked chai soy latte called a Warm & Fuzzy, cozied up to this swank spot's roaring fire? It is when you have two Warm & Fuzzys, and there's an open seat next to you.

2 **The Violet Hour** (p.151)
Scoring a seat is tough, but go during off-hours and your reward is a warm spot to sip a proper hot toddie. The combo of cognac, Scotch, ginger syrup and lemon will kill anything NyQuil can't and tastes a hell of a lot better going down.

3 **The Grafton** (p.139)
With the occasional brogue to be heard from the rugby-watching crowd, it's little surprise to find hot toddies at this U.K.-leaning pub. We prefer the warmed port, seasoned with brown sugar, lemon and cloves. Get there early for a couch by the fire.

4 **Simon's Tavern** (p.139)
It wouldn't be winter without a glogg outing to Simon's, one of Andersonville's coziest and most welcoming bars since 1934. In keeping with the 'hood's Scandinavian history, mugs of warm spiced wine are offered until the first sign of spring.

5 **Fireside** (p.139)
Now that there's a crackdown on Sparks and the like, get your jolt-and-buzz combo with spiked coffee drinks at this Edgewater favorite. Go Irish with a Jameson and coffee or all-out with the "Ceoki": Hennessy, Kahlua, fresh-brewed java and whipped cream.—*Heather Shouse*

---

right, but this stranger summed up exactly how this bewitching bar makes you feel: Like it's been waiting for you to become a regular all these years. *1858 W Iowa St at Wolcott Ave (773-486-4720). El: Blue to Division. Bus: 9, 50, 66. 4pm–2am. Average beer: $2. Cash only.*

Ola's Liquor Catering to those who "work" odd hours (read: unemployed indie filmmakers) and a ragtag troupe of friendly regulars, this tiny (and cheap) bar–cum–liquor store is the perfect final destination for a raucous night. Doors open at the crack of dawn and Ola, the Polish live wire who owns the joint, has been known to unlock earlier if properly coerced. *947 N Damen Ave between Augusta Blvd and Walton St (773-384-7250). El: Blue to Division. Bus: 50 Damen, 70 Division. Mon–Fri 7am–2am; Sat 7am–3am; Sun 11am–2am. Average cocktail: $3.50.*

✗ ✳ ♨ **Old Oak Tap** Pity the bars that share a zip code with this impressive newcomer. The friendly service, good beer list, gorgeously sleek interior, huge patio (enclosed in winter) and menu of bar eats by chef Jason Vandegraft makes this place awfully hard to compete with. *2109 W Chicago Ave between Hoyne Ave and Leavitt St (773-772-0406). Bus: 50, 66, 70. Mon 5pm–2am; Tue–Fri, Sun 11am–2am; Sat 11am–3am. Average beer: $5.*

Rainbo Club The bittersweet reality of great little dives is that they often lose charm when overrun by masses of clingers-on. Somehow, this Ukrainian Village spot has managed to remain an underground(ish) favorite. The local artists and musicians who frequent it hold on to terra firma with cheap drink in hand, awaiting a turn in the photo booth while nodding to everything from Aesop Rock to Black Sabbath. *1150 N Damen Ave between Haddon Ave and Division St (773-489-5999). El: Blue to Division. Bus: 50 Damen, 70 Division. Sun–Fri 4pm–2am; Sat 4pm–3am. Average cocktail: $4. Cash only.*

✗ ✳ **Relax Lounge** We can't blame this West Town bar for having a bit of an identity crisis: It was supposed to initially open as "Pharmacy." Inside, the pharmaceutical theme seems to have been forgotten, and though the place is marketed as a hipster rock club, the slick design is much more West Elm than CBGB. But we're not complaining; it turns out that partying like older, more affluent and slightly more sophisticated rock veterans is just as fun. *1450 W Chicago Ave between Bishop St and Greenview Ave (312-666-6006). El: Blue to Chicago. Bus: 9, X9, 66. Tue–Fri 6pm–2am; Sat 7pm–3am. Average beer: $6.*

Rite Liquors If you're not familiar with the glorious convenience of "the slashy" (a.k.a. liquor store/bar), this old-man haunt is a good introduction. Sure, it looks like your average corner store: Cases of beer, liquor and cheap wine surround retail shelves stocked with junk food in a fluorescent-lit room. But wander toward the dimly lit back of the store and you'll find yourself in bar country wondering whether or not you should have a couple before heading home with a fresh six-pack. *1649 W Division St at Marshfield Ave (773-486-6257). El: Blue to Division. Bus: 9, 56, 70. Mon–Sat 8am–2am; Sun 11am–3am. Average beer: $3.*

Sonotheque Designed in cool grays and browns as a kind of futuristic listeners' lounge, this West Town club and bar has lively and often risky bookings, which have made it a favorite of neighborhood hipsters. The audiophile jet set loves the spectacularly clear sound system, and it's hard not to fall for the reasonable price of beer and often high-end wines. Monthly music nights and visits from touring DJs such as Philly fave Diplo and the Stones Throw crew are packed solid with lubricated, in-the-know dancers. *1444 W Chicago Ave between Greenview Ave and Bishop St (312-226-7600). El: Blue to Chicago. Bus: 9, X9, 66. Sun–Fri 7pm–2am; Sat 7pm–3am. Average drink: $7.*

Stella's Tap This spot's a typical, charming, pool-table dive distinguished by its namesake: the tiny woman who pours the drinks. Certain nights can be a real sausage fest, including some baldies from Chicago's Finest, and every one of them gives her a bear hug. Tip her right and you might start getting hugs, too. *935 N Western Ave at Walton St (773-384-0077). El: Blue to Chicago. Bus: 49, 50, 66. Sun–Fri 1pm–2am; Sat noon–3am. Average beer: $3.*

CROWDED HOUSE All these people and yet no sight of Angels & Kings owner Pete Wentz.

✕ ✳ **Tuman's** Okay, so it's not the hipster shithole it used to be when it was called Tuman's Alcohol Abuse Center. But just because it's a little shinier, a little cleaner and a little friendlier doesn't mean this Ukie Village classic isn't still a good clubhouse for locals looking to waste a Sunday away with some Jameson and the local news. *2159 W Chicago Ave at Leavitt St (773-782-1400) Bus: 50, 66, 70. Mon–Thu 4pm–2am; Fri, Sun noon–2am; Sat noon–3am. Average beer: $3.*

✕ ✳ **Twisted Spoke** When you begin brunch by showing your ID at the door, you know you're in the right place for a Bloody Mary. Spicy and sweet, garnished with salami and completed with a beer back, it's practically a meal in itself. Don't let that distract you from the food, however. Breakfast tacos are a good way to spice up your egg intake. And the Spoke's signature "fatboy" burgers are thick, juicy and perfectly tender. *501 N Ogden Ave at Grand Ave (312-666-1500). El: Blue to Grand. Bus: 8, 9, 65. Mon–Fri 11am–2am; Sat 9am–3am; Sun 9am–2am. Average beer: $5.*

W Cut Rate Liquors This Polish dive/liquor store somehow manages to look like a brightly painted burger joint decorated with fake flowers and Christmas lights. The jukebox relies heavily on Phil Collins and Eastern Bloc pop, PBR is on tap for $1.25 and there's an entire shelf devoted to $1 shots (mostly schnapps in B-list flavors like root beer). The combo is just the ticket for an end-of-the-night wake-up call that yes, you are wasted. *1656 W Division St at Paulina St (no phone). El: Blue to Division. Bus: 9, X9, 56, 70. Sun–Thu 7am–midnight; Fri, Sat 7am–2am. Average beer: $1.75. Cash only.*

Old Town/River North

Angels & Kings *2009 Eat Out Award, Readers' Choice: Best New Bar* We could tell you about all the people dressed like faux truckers and drinking PBR here. And we could tell you about the long, narrow room, and the stage in that room that houses two leather chairs and a gothic, almost-naked (save for the thick eyeliner) go-go dancer. But instead, we'll just tell you that Pete Wentz owns this bar, and you can figure out the rest. *710 N Clark St between Huron and Superior Sts (312-482-8600). El: Brown, Red, Purple (rush hrs) to Chicago. Bus: 22 (24hrs), 66, 156. Mon, Wed–Fri, Sun 6pm–2am, Sat 8pm–3am (closed Tue). Average cocktail: $7.*

✕ ♨ **The Bar at Peninsula Hotel** Escort a date to the Peninsula's dark, clubby cocktail bar and you won't go home alone. All the manly bases have been covered—a glowing fireplace and high-backed bar stools or cozy couched conversation nooks. Sip well-crafted cocktails, bubbly by the glass or whiskeys from obscure distillers. *108 E Superior St, 5th Floor 108 E Superior St between Michigan Ave and Rush St, fifth floor (312-573-6766). El: Red to Chicago. Bus: 3, 66, 145, 146, 147, 151. 3pm–1am. Average cocktail: $11.*

✕ **Bin 36** A post-work, loosened-tie set love to happy hour at this River North wine bar that side-saddles the House of Blues. Who can blame them? The wine flights are affordable and interesting, the cheese selection is one of the best in town and the chalkboard of "tavern shared plates" offers just enough sustenance to order another round. *339 N Dearborn St between Kinzie St and Wacker Dr (312-755-9463). El: Red to Grand; Brown, Purple (rush hrs) to Merchandise Mart. Bus: 22 (24hrs), 29, 36. Mon–Wed 11am–11pm; Thu 11am–midnight; Fri 11am–1am; Sat noon–1am; Sun 2pm–10pm. Average glass: $8.*

✕ ✳ **Blue Frog** Three things reign supreme at this long-standing good-times spot: karaoke, board games (from Scrabble to Operation) and electric-hued cocktails that the matronly bartender claims will "mess you up." Don't believe her? The signature Blue Frog has vodka, gin, rum, melon liqueur, blue curaçao, sour and Sprite, enough crap to convince you the patio is floating. *676 N LaSalle St between Erie and Huron Sts (312-943-8900). El: Red to Grand. Bus: 22 Clark (24hrs), 156 LaSalle. Mon–Fri 8am–2am; Sat 8am–3am (closed Sun). Average beer: $4.*

(✕ **Burton Place** These four levels of 4am debauchery in the heart of Old Town yield exactly the kind of crowd you would expect on the weekends: young, loud and drunk, with shots spilled on their shirts. But on weeknights it's a gathering spot for older gentlemen hoping to grab a Scotch, a good seat to watch the game and possibly a little bit of that weekend energy. *1447 N Wells St at Burton Pl (312-664-4699). El: Brown, Purple (rush hrs) to Sedgwick. Bus: 11, 72, 156. Sun–Fri 11am–4am; Sat 11am–5am. Average beer: $4.*

✕ **Cityscape** Keep your chair in the direction of the view (a 15th-floor vantage point with the river, and all the blinking buildings along it, in clear sight) and a cocktail in your hand (despite the name, the "Zentini" actually isn't bad). If you do, you'll find that you're not in the lobby of the Holiday Inn after all—you're out on the town. (Or, at the very least, out over it.) *350 W Mart Center Dr at Orleans St (312-836-5000). El: Brown, Purple (rush hrs) to Merchandise Mart. Bus: 65, 125, 156. Mon–Thu 3pm–1am; Fri–Sun 11am–1am. Average cocktail: $8.*

✳ **Clark Street Ale House** We've seen people at this dim, homey, Near North pub hang out without ever ordering a drink, but we just can't follow suit. We envy the friendly neighbors who drop onto wooden stools just to chat up the bartender. But when we spy two dozen beers on tap—mostly domestic gems like Great Lakes Brewing Company's Grassroots Ale—we feel like settling in and getting our drink on. *742 N Clark St between Superior and Chicago Sts (312-642-9253). El: Red to Chicago. Bus: 22 (24hrs), 36, 66. Mon–Fri 4pm–4am, Sat 4pm–5am; Sun 5pm–4am. Average beer: $4.*

✕ **Coogan's** A few blocks from Lyric Opera and just off the river, this beautifully setup bar is a primo spot if you need a little you time after dark. Stop by around 9pm, when most of the after-work crowd has headed home. When scarcely populated, the polished wood and brass decor, high ceilings and old-time photographs evoke a Chicago-of-yesteryear feel that's hard to find. *180 N Wacker Dr between Lake St and Couch St (312-444-1134). El: Brown, Green, Orange, Purple (rush hrs), Pink, Blue to Clark/Lake. Mon–Fri 10:30am–10pm (or later). Average beer: $5.*

✗ **Crimson Lounge** Though it's nestled in the lobby of the chic and somewhat stark Hotel Sax, walking into this bar feels a lot like walking onto the set of Sofia Coppola's *Marie Antoinette*: The space is filled with centuries-old chairs and chaises, and the soundtrack is usually contemporary hip-hop. The result is a place that feels cold and antiquated yet sexy and new at the same time. *Hotel Sax Chicago, 333 N Dearborn St between Wacker Pl and Kinzie St (312-923-2473). El: Red to Grand; Brown, Purple (rush hrs) to Merchandise Mart. Bus: 22 (24hrs) Clark, 36 Broadway. Sun–Fri 4pm–2am; Sat 4pm–3am. Average cocktail: $12.*

❮ **Crobar** The original Cro in the dance-club franchise (there are now outposts in Miami, New York and South America) was remodeled a few years ago with a South Beach–meets–industrial materials look. The club hosts everything from a midweek Latin night to visits from big-name techno, house and trance DJs. But a typical weekend night features residents hammering with au courant dance tracks while girls on platforms demonstrate the finer points of deca dancing. *1543 N Kingsbury Ave between Eastman and Weed Sts (312-266-1900). El: Red to North/Clybourn. Bus: 8 Halsted, 72 North. Wed–Fri 10pm–4am; Sat 10pm–5am. Average cocktail: $9.*

✗ ✱ **Dick's Last Resort** The location is new—toting an amazing riverfront view—but the vibe is the same: busy bayou decor, live bands, purposely crabby waitstaff and referential menus (who knew Old Style is a "Yuppie Beer"?). Though calculated and somewhat of a tourist trap, Dick's is still a solid choice if you're roaming the area in need of a drink and you want laid-back, comfortable and crass. *315 N Dearborn St between Lower Wacker Dr and Kinzie St (312-836-7870). El: Brown, Purple (rush hrs) to Merchandise Mart. Bus: 22 (24hrs), 62, 65. Mon–Thu 11am–1am; Fri–Sat 11am–2am; Sun 10am–1am. Average beer: $5.25.*

✗ **District Bar** A sports bar with ambitious food and thoughtfully prepared cocktails (mixologist Bridget Albert consulted on the list) is a rare commodity. Even rarer is one that has a hidden room (behind the bookcase wall as you enter) and manages to maintain a swank feel—even with a flat-screen in every direction. *170 W Superior St between Wells St and LaSalle Dr (312-337-3477). El: Red to Grand; Brown, Purple (rush hrs) to Chicago. Bus: 11, 156, 173. Sun–Fri 11am–2am; Sat 11am–3am. Average cocktail: $11.*

Enclave The classy loft look of this spacious River North club balances out the sexed-up, usually hip-hop– and dance-music–fueled parties that happen from Thursday nights on. Unfortunately, it closes at 2am, driving party traffic to nearby RiNo. *220 W Chicago Ave at Wells St (312-654-0234). El: Brown, Purple (rush hrs) to Chicago. Bus: 66 Chicago, 156 LaSalle. Thu 10pm–2am; Fri 9pm–2am; Sat 9pm–3am. Average cocktail: $8.*

❮ ✗ ✿ **Excalibur** A downtown destination for the past 15 years, this superclub is housed in a historic church and seemingly has a room for everything: There's a weekly cabaret show, live flamenco music, Latin dance lessons and even a paranormal interactive-theater event. With all the cross-promotion going on, it draws a crowd of enthusiastic out-of-towners and club novices who would settle for a mediocre experience. *632 N Dearborn St at Ontario St*

(312-266-1944). El: Red to Grand. Bus: 36 Broadway, 65 Grand. Wed–Fri 7pm–4am; Sat 7pm–5am. Average cocktail: $8.

✗ ✿ **Green Door Tavern** If you're into slick, minimalist lounges or enormous, bass-heavy clubs, you may find it hard to believe that this River North stalwart has anything to offer you. But poke around and you'll find a nice dining room to the side, a pool room in the back and a jukebox that caters to any taste. *678 N Orleans St between Erie and Huron Sts (312-664-5496). El: Brown, Purple (rush hrs) to Chicago. Bus: 66 Chicago. Mon–Fri 11:30am–2am; Sat 11:30am–3am; Sun 11:30am–9pm. Average beer: $5.*

❮ ✗ **HC** When the Hunt Club got revamped in early 2008, the sports-bar feeling was the first thing to go. In its place, three levels of plush, mocha-toned cocktail lounge were installed (the second floor is more suited to dining than the others). But Bears fans need not worry: The plasmas are still here. It's just the sticky floors that left. *1100 N State St at Maple St (312-988-7887). El: Red to Chicago. Bus: 22 (24hrs), 36, 70. Mon–Fri noon–4am; Sat 11am–5am; Sun 11am–4am. Average cocktail: $6.*

✗ **Hogs and Honeys** So your parents wouldn't send you to Texas A&M because they were afraid the state with the bull-size party rep would eat up all your self-control along with all their tuition money? No use crying over being stuck at UIC—this beer-and-babes spot has that Texas party thing down pat, complete with wasted, tan blonds gyrating on a mechanical bull and big-boobed bartenders jumping up on the bar every now and then to do synchronized dances that would put LiLo to shame. *901 W Weed St between Weed and Freemont Sts (312-804-1459). El: Red to North/Clybourn. Bus: 8 Halsted, 72 North. Tue–Fri 9pm–4am; Sat 9pm–5am. Average beer: $3.*

▼ ✗ **Howl at the Moon** Dueling pianos playing sing-along rock anthems (the Richard Cheese–style rendition of Metallica's "Enter Sandman" was a standout) partnered with buckets of Kool-Aid-flavored booze served with multiple straws makes this national piano-bar chain a big hit for prowling cougars, office parties and easily intoxicated college girls. Can't decide what to order? The cavity-inducing "Sexy Jewish Bartender" tipple is the logical prequel to the "X Boyfriend" cocktail. *26 W Hubbard St between Dearborn and State Sts (312-863-7427). El: Red to Grand. Bus: 22 (24hrs), 29, 36, 65. Mon–Fri 5pm–2am; Sat 5pm–3am; Sun 7pm–2am. Average cocktail: $6.*

✗ ✱ **Juicy Wine Co.** **2009 Eat Out Award, Critics' Pick: Promo King (recognizing owner Rodney Alex for his clever promotions)** Walking into Rodney Alex's wine bar—so warm with wood tones yet impeccably contemporary, a meat-and-cheesemonger working passionately to complete orders and a wall of well-chosen, well-priced wines—is like walking into the coolest wine bar in London, or the coolest wine bar in New York…only guess what? It just happens to be the coolest wine bar in Chicago. To experience it on the cheap, inquire about bargain-night promos. *694 N Milwaukee Ave at Huron St (312-492-6620). El: Blue to Chicago. Bus: 56 Milwaukee, 66 Chicago. Mon–Thu 4pm–1am; Fri, Sat 11am–2am; Sun 11am–3pm (brunch), 4pm–midnight. Average glass of wine: $10.*

Manor This sister club to late-night party parlor RiNo combines luxury amenities (a basement lounge for VIPs and an extra-attentive staff for everyone) and lots of wood, stone and lacquer in the storied former Pasha space. Currently, there's no cover and with influential promoters like Tony Macey throwing parties here, the place sizzles on the few nights it's open. *642 N Clark St between Erie and Ontario Sts (312-475-1390). El: Red to Grand. Bus: 22 (24hrs), 36, 65, 66, 125. Tue, Thu, Fri 10pm–2am; Sat 10pm–3am. Average cocktail: $12.*

✗ ✱ **Martini Park** "Martini Amusement Park" is more like it. In one corner, a tower of shelves lined with Snow Queen vodka shoots up from the floor like a spaceship taking off. In another, a cheesy cover band plays under blue and orange lights. And the namesake martinis? They're so strong it only takes one to make you feel like you're on a roller coaster. *151 W Erie St between LaSalle Dr and Wells St (312-640-0577). El: Brown, Purple (rush hrs), Red to Chicago. Bus: 11, 66, 156. Mon–Fri 4pm–2am; Sat 5pm–3am (closed Sun) . Average cocktail: $10.*

✗ **Mike's** True dive bars are a rarity in this high-rent, hotel and wine bar–dominated section of River North, and that's exactly what makes this Greek-owned beer-and-gyro joint a gem. Inside, 50-year-old union laborers with leathery skin, gold necklaces and curly chest hair sip domestics and shoot pool beside their younger blond wives, while the Croatian bartender regales her customers with stories about Christmas back home. *829 N State St at Pearson St (312-482-9130). El: Red to Chicago. Bus: 10, 22 (24hrs), 36, 66, 143, 144, 145, 146, 147, 151. Mon–Sat 6am–2am (closed Sun). Average beer: $3.50. Cash only.*

✗ ✱ ✿ **The Motel Bar** This low-lit lounge is nothing like motels we've checked into, but we dig the throwback classic cocktails, the "room service" comfort food menu, the unpretentious staff and eclectic jukebox in lieu of a DJ turning it into a club. In warmer months, a massive outdoor patio is simple and sparse, with a few candles for light. *600 W Chicago Ave at Larrabee St (312-822-2900). El: Brown, Purple (rush hrs) to Chicago. Bus: 8, 66, 132. Sun–Fri 11am–2am; Sat 11am–3am. Average cocktail: $6.*

❮ ✗ **Mother Hubbard's** We absolutely love the idea of a slightly scuzzy bar being surrounded by uppity, polished, tourist-filled restaurants. The winding bar area is occupied by loners watching the big screen, but near the surrounding checkered tablecloth–topped tables is the more gregarious set. And in the back, two pool tables are ripe for a good game. *5 W Hubbard St between State and Dearborn Sts (312-828-0007). El: Red to Grand. Bus: 29, 36, 65. Sun–Fri 11am–4am; Sat 11am–5am. Average beer:$4.50.*

✱ **NV Penthouse Lounge** To access this see-and-be-seen contender for top swank spot, you have to take the elevator (whose color-of-envy glow is no accident) to the eighth floor. We'll admit that the room does have a view—both of the skyline and of the well-heeled, bottle service–seeking clientele—but that's pretty much where this spot stops being distinctive from the bounty of other luxury lounges in River North. *116 W Hubbard St between Clark and LaSalle Sts (312-329-9960). El: Red to Grand. Bus: 22 (24hrs), 36, 65. Thu 5pm–2am; Fri 9pm–2am; Sat 9pm–3am. Average cocktail: $10.*

SEEING GREEN It's not a coincidence that the lighting at NV Penthouse Lounge matches the money you better have to hang out there.

❰ Old Town Ale House Among the framed drawings of regulars cluttering the wooden walls of this saloon-style staple are posters boasting that you're in "le premiere dive bar" of Chicago. We don't know where this place gets off speaking French, but it's been around since 1958, so we'll grant it bragging rights. *219 W North Ave at Wieland St (312-944-7020). El: Brown, Purple (rush hrs) to Sedgwick. Bus: 11, 72, 156. Mon–Fri 8am–4am; Sat 8am–5am; Sun 11am–4am. Average beer: $3.50. Cash only.*

❰ The Original Mother's Legend has it that the Velvet Underground once rocked the stage at Mother's, which opened its doors in 1968. But don't come here looking for avant-garde rock. These days, Mother's is all about pleasing the sweat-drenched, booze-soaked Division Street masses who pack the dance floor into the early morning hours hoping to grind against Mr. or Ms. Right—or at least Mr. or Ms. Tonight. *26 W Division St at Dearborn St (312-642-7251). El: Red to Clark/Division. Bus: 22 (24hrs), 36, 70. Sun–Fri 8pm–4am; Sat 8pm–5am. Average beer: $5.*

✕ ✳ The Pepper Canister Starched shirts get unbuttoned at this River North after-work hangout, where friends sip beer and wine in long booths by the windows or at the handful of tables outside on Wells. Exposed brick walls, an intricate tin ceiling and a reddish glow are reminders that not all Irish pubs have to be plastered with shamrocks. *509 N Wells St between Illinois St and Grand Ave (312-467-3300). El: Brown, Purple (rush hrs) to Merchandise Mart; Red to Grand. Bus: 11, 65, 125. Mon–Fri 11am–2am; Sat 5pm–3am; (closed Sun). Average beer: $5.*

✕ Rebar True, there is a nice view of the Chicago River from this second-story lounge in the Trump tower. But sometimes a view isn't enough to offset incredibly priccy drinks and a constantly squealing clientele of heavily made-up twentysomethings. Luckily, the dangerously drinkable housemade punch of strawberries and sparkling rosé helps erase the sticker shock *and* the crowd. *401 N Wabash Ave at Kinzie St (312-588-8034). El: Red to Grand. Bus: 29, 36, 65. Sun–Wed 4pm–midnight; Thu, Fri 4pm–1am; Sat 1pm–1am. Average cocktail: $15.*

❰ The Redhead For the piano-bar fiend who likes his joints a little more Grace than Will, this underground spot should hit all the right notes. But even though the guys here aren't gay, they're at least dressed well: Bouncers inspect outfits as well as your ID, and flip-flops and T-shirts don't get through the door. *16 W Ontario St between State and Dearborn Sts (312-640-1000). El: Red to Grand. Bus: 22 (24hrs), 36, 125. Sun–Fri 7pm–4am; Sat 7pm–5am. Average cocktail: $8.*

✕ ✳ Rock Bottom Brewery Just a drunken stumble from the Grand Red Line station, this sporty brewpub offers six house-brewed beers to sip while watching your team on more than a dozen TVs. The menu features signatures like jambalaya with Red Ale rice and meatloaf in either Brown Ale mushroom sauce or Stout tomato sauce. The fare is fine, but the beer is so tasty we'd just as soon head to the rooftop beer garden with a pint. *1 W Grand Ave at State St (312-755-9339). El: Red to Grand. Bus: 22 (24hrs), 29, 36, 65. 11am–2am. Average beer: $5.*

✕ ✳ Rockit Bar & Grill Most of the guys who go to this sporty, sceney homage to stainless steel don't seem to care what the food tastes like—it's more of a tits and beer thing for

them. But if they'd pay attention, they'd find that the antibar food is where the gems are, like the mildly spicy braised lamb lettuce wraps and the perfectly golden roasted chicken. The bar ain't too shabby, either—nearly 30 types of beers are either on tap or in bottles. *22 W Hubbard St between State and Dearborn Sts (312-645-6000). El: Red to Grand. Bus: 29, 36, 65. Mon–Fri 11:30am–1:30am; Sat 10:30am–2:30am; Sun 10:30am–1:30am. Average beer: $5.*

❰ ✕ Social Twenty-Five As the former home of Moda, this bar exhibits some clubby traits: a doorman out front, former dance floors turned into sprawling rooms, and stark backlit bars washing displays of vodka in cool blue lights. And yet now this place is just another bar, with a rock band on the first floor—and a lounge in the basement to escape to when that band starts doing Kelly Clarkson covers. *25 W Hubbard St between Dearborn and State Sts (312-670-2200). El: Red to Grand. Bus: 22 (24hrs), 29, 36, 65. Mon 10:30pm–4am; Thu, Fri 5pm–4am; Sat 5pm–5am. Average cocktail: $9.*

❰ Stay This exclusive after-hours bar is so determined to outwit wayward hoi polloi that it alternates between two unmarked entrances: a graffiti-sprayed alley on Erie for weekends, a plain door next to sister club Manor for weeknights. Men in suits patrol the cozy candle-lit interior, enforcing a strict no-camera policy, and the smoked mirrors, polished wood and buttery leather couches might make for a relaxing environment, if only Kanye weren't blaring in our ear. *111 W Erie St between Clark and LaSalle Sts (312-475-0816). El: Red to Grand. Bus: 22 (24hrs), 36, 65, 125. Mon, Fri 1am–4am; Sat 10pm–5am. Average cocktail: $11.*

✕ ✳ Sully's House This offering from the owners of Salvatore's has a mellow neighborhood vibe that stands in sharp contrast to the manic Weed Street club scene. The dark wood bar takes up the front room, and the back, outfitted with comfy couches, is a good spot to camp out and munch on gussied-up Tots and chicken fingers while sampling the 20 draft beers. *1501 N Dayton St at Blackhawk St (773-244-1234). El: Red to North/Clybourn. Bus: 8, 70, 72. Mon–Fri 11am–2am; Sat 11am–3am; Sun 10am–midnight. Average beer: $5.*

✕ ✳ SushiSamba Rio Not only is the plush rooftop patio with a 40-foot bar, sharp sound system, sofas and stools perfect for a nightcap (or night-starter), it's great for sashimi as well. On Wednesdays after 8pm, this slick spot turns breezy for Cafe Com Leite, a weekly party driven by a bossa nova trio and a rotating cast of performance artists. *504 N Wells St between Illinois St and Grand Ave (312-595-2300). El: Brown, Purple (rush hrs) to Merchandise Mart. Bus: 65, 125, 156. Sun–Tue 11:30am–midnight; Wed, Thu 11:30am–1am; Fri, Sat 11:30am–2am. Average cocktail: $10.*

✕ 10 Pin If drinking at a bowling alley seems a little too *Roseanne* for a posh crew like yours, you obviously haven't been to lanes like these before. The rambunctious singles crowd seems more interested in each other (and the neon-bright martinis and enormous screens playing larger-than-life music videos) than they do actually picking up a bowling ball. One way or another, you'll probably score. *330 N State St between Upper Wacker Dr and Kinzie St (312-644-0300). El: Red to Grand; Brown, Purple (rush hrs) to Merchandise Mart. Bus: 22 (24hrs), 29, 36. Sun–Thu 11am–1am, Fri, Sat 11am–2am. Average cocktail: $7.*

✕ ✳ The Terrace at Trump The close-up view of the Wrigley Building from the 16th floor of Trump Tower is a sight best appreciated by a local. So it's something of a shame that this patio

IVANA DRINK The Donald's kids are said to oversee operations of Terrace at Trump.

ROOM WITH A VIEW That chair at C-View has your name on it; just be sure and turn around.

draws mostly tourists. Still, if you're looking to throw down $20 for a glass of wine, you'd be hard-pressed to find a posher playground. *401 N Wabash Ave (312-588-8030). El: Red to Grand. Bus: 2, 3, 29. 2:30pm–11:30pm (weather permitting). Average glass of wine: $21.*

✕ ✳ **Theory** Save the yelling with your arms over your head for the Wrigleyville sports bars—this newcomer is for the sophisticated sports fan. The stools are cushioned, the music is mixed, and the specialty drinks are potent (but a tad sweet). The sleek decor and ambiance could easily make you forget that you're in a sports lounge, if only you could turn your head without seeing at least three flat-screens. *9 W Hubbard St between State and Dearborn Sts (312-644-0004). El: Red to Grand. Bus: 22 (24hrs), 36, 65, 146. Mon–Fri 11am–2am; Sat 11am–3am; Sun 11am–midnight. Average cocktail: $9.*

☾ ✕ **Underground** After all the hype and secrecy surrounding the opening of this new "Rockit Ranch Production," we were sure this place would disappoint. But truthfully, we like it. The interior is a little industrial, but the bunker theme is thankfully understated, and for the most part the vibe is cool and casual. We can't guarantee what the crowd will be like, but if this place ever sucks, it's not the venue's fault—it's whoever fills it. *56 W Illinois St between Dearborn and Clark Sts (312-644-7600). El: Red to Grand. Bus: 22 (24hrs), 36, 65. Thu–Fri 9pm–4am; Sat 9pm–5am. Average cocktail: $10.*

✕ **Vertigo** You'd think the focus of this bar, which sits on the roof of the Dana Hotel, would be the view. But there's a lot more to distract you—the roaring fire pit, the classic cocktails (curiously served in plastic glasses) and the incredibly short shorts on the servers—so the view pretty much takes a back seat. *Dana Hotel & Spa, 660 N State St at Erie St (312-202-6060). El: Red to Grand. Bus: 22 (24hrs), 36, 65. Fri 3pm–2am; Sat–Thu 5pm–2am (sometimes closes early on slow weeknights). Average cocktail: $10.*

✕ ✳ **Wells on Wells** Who knew a respite of dignified drinking existed on this somewhat trashy stretch of Wells? The cool beige interior with soft lighting and softer (but good) music offers up a lounge feeling, minus the snobbery and obscene prices. This basically guarantees the only fratness you'll get will be a random howl from the neighboring bars. *1617 N Wells St between North Ave and Concord Ln (312-944-1617). El: Brown, Purple (rush hrs) to Sedgwick. Bus: 11, 72, 156. Mon 5pm–2am, Tue–Fri 11am–2am; Sat 10am–3am, Sun 10am–2am. Average cocktail: $5.*

Gold Coast/Mag Mile/Streeterville

✕ ✳ **C-View** The namesake 29th-floor view is the thing at this tiny rooftop bar—at least, that's what everybody says. But though the patio section *is* nice, the view of the skyline is not stunning enough to fight for a seat there. Especially when you can sit at the stylish indoor bar and get just as much beauty out of the delicious lavender-lemon-tequila cocktail. *166 E Superior St at St. Clair St (312-523-0923). El: Red to Chicago. Bus: 3, X3, 4, X4, 10, 26, 143, 144, 145, 146, 147, 151. Patio hours: Sun–Thu 4pm–11pm; Fri, Sat 4pm–midnight. Indoor lounge stays open as late as 2am on Fri, Sat and 11pm Sun–Thu. Average cocktail: $11.*

✕ **Coq d'Or** Whereas the Drake Hotel's Palm Court is grand and regal, this lower-level bar is small, intimate and sultry. Some people treat it as a dinner place—there's a perfectly good menu of sandwiches and the like. But we think the live jazz and dimmed lighting lends itself much more to hushed conversation and cocktails than to burgers and beer. *140 E Walton Pl between Michigan Ave and Mies van der Rohe Way (312-787-2200). El: Red to Chicago. Bus: 143, 144, 145, 146, 147, 151. Mon–Sat 11am–2am; Sun 11am–1am. Average cocktail: $8.*

✕ ✳ ◍ **D4** We thought we'd seen everything when it came to Irish pubs, but no pub in Chicago is quite as lovely and upscale as this. Rooms like the cozy library (complete with fireplace), tile-floored bar and dining area blend seamlessly into one another, yet maintain their own identities. It's named after the poshest zip code in Dublin; before long, it could transform this area into one of the poshest zips in Chicago. *345 E Ohio St between Fairbanks and McClurg Cts (entrance on Grand Ave) (312-624-8385). Bus: 2, 29, 65, 66, 120, 121, 124. Mon–Fri 11am–2am; Sat 10am–2am; Sun 10am–midnight. Average beer: $6.*

Elm Street Liquors The Gold Coast meat market has evolved. Board of Trade types here are hot, single and ready to splurge for bottle service. Not your thing? The crowd does mix up, making it almost as likely to find cute left-brainers coughing up cash for one of a dozen pro martinis. *12 W Elm St between State and Dearborn Sts (312-337-3200). El: Red to Clark/Division. Bus: 22 (24hrs), 36, 70. Wed–Fri 8pm–2am; Sat 8pm–3am. Average cocktail: $6.*

✕ ✳ **Eno** It's harder to pair wine and cheese than you think—so stop thinking about it and let the people at this sophisticated wine-cheese-chocolate bar do it for you. Experts flutter around the warm, dark wood–ridden room, expounding on the carefully handled wines and artisanal cheeses. It's the kind of service (and diet) a person could really get used to—if it weren't so damn expensive. *Hotel InterContinental, 505 N Michigan Ave at Illinois Ave (312-321-8738). El: Red to Grand. Bus: 3, 4, X4, 10, 26, 29, 36, 65, 125, 143, 144, 145, 146, 147, 151, 157. Mon–Thu 4pm–midnight; Fri 4pm–1am; Sat 1pm–1am; Sun 1pm–10pm. Average glass of wine: $12.*

✕ ✳ **Flamingo's Bar and Grill** Funny thing about this Navy Pier–area pit stop: where you'd expect a tourist rip-off, you instead find real value. Cold bottled beers ring in sub-fiver (a miracle in this area) and the grill items—gyros to Chicago dogs—are reasonable and rival more authentic spots around town. Forget the blaring TV and dingy decor—a pittance for the unexpected quality. Closed on Sundays in the winter. *440 E Grand Ave between McClurg Ct and Lake Shore Dr (312-222-0901). Bus: 2, 29, 65, 66, 124. Mon–Fri 6am–9pm; Sat 7am–9pm; Sun 9am–7pm. Average beer: $4.*

RING OF FIRE As long as you don't look down, the namesake affliction of Vertigo won't get you.

MIRROR MIRROR Subtle, but stunning, decor adds a touch of ℗ class at Pops for Champagne.

Inn Bar When the Inn of Chicago revealed its newly renovated space earlier in 2008, we did a double take: The interior seemed far too slick and sexy for a place called an Inn. Its lounge is much the same: With its cool silver tones, backlit bar and colorful martinis, it's thankfully not so much "lobby" as it is "clubby." *162 E Ohio St between Michigan Ave and St. Clair St (312-787-3100). El: Red to Grand. Bus: 65, 146, 147, 151. 5pm–11pm. Average cocktail: $6.*

✕ **J Bar** Two slick rooms awash in shiny mirrored tile and video art, martinis garnished with olive–blue cheese lollipops, and a clientele of only the richest, prettiest, most accomplished Chicagoans. No wonder this hot spot is in the James Hotel; the place is so packed you're going to have to stay overnight to get a seat. *610 N Rush St at Ontario St (312-660-7200). El: Red to Grand. Bus: 36, 125, 151. Wed–Fri 6pm–2am; Sat 8pm–3am . Average cocktail: $9.*

✕ ☀ **Jilly's Piano Bar** It can get pretty crazy inside this long-running piano bar—big spenders in loosened ties trading Sinatra verses with wide-eyed tourists while fierce cougars prowl the room looking for a boy toy to sink their claws into. Cut the madness down to a low roar by grabbing one of the few tables on the sidewalk patio. The people-watching is well worth the tab for pricey cocktails. In chillier months, however, you'll just have to brave the jungle. *1007 N Rush St between Oak St and Bellevue Pl (312-664-1001). El: Red to Clark/Division. Bus: 22 (24hrs), 36, 70. Sun–Fri 5pm–2am; Sat 5pm–3am. Average cocktail: $7.*

✕ ☌ **Le Bar** Ooh-la-la, this fancy bar in the Sofitel Hotel is a sensual sipping spot for travelers and locals alike. Plush leather bar stools, a cool-to-the-touch chrome bar and well-made (and incredibly expensive) cocktails give this place its cosmopolitan vibe, but it's the bad techno that gives it that European edge. *20 E Chestnut St at Wabash Ave (312-324-4000). El: Red to Chicago. Bus: 36, 66, 143, 144, 145, 146, 147, 151. Sun–Wed 3pm–1am; Thu–Sat 3pm–2am. Average cocktail: $12.*

◖✕ ☌ **Leg Room** Less of a frat-boy-meets-tourist scene than many Rush and Division bars, Leg Room is the classiest place on this strip to get a drink. But don't expect a low-key neighborhood bar. You'll get animal-print stools, a free-floating bar and a free jukebox with your martinis. *7 W Division St between State Pkwy and Dearborn St (312-337-2583). El: Red to Clark/Division. Bus: 22 (24hrs), 36, 70. Mon–Wed 9pm–4am; Thu, Fri, Sun 7pm–4am; Sat 7pm–5am. Average cocktail: $6.*

The Lodge Time stands still in this log-cabinish tavern…or at least the patrons wish it did. Whereas every other bar on this strip is packed with freshly waxed twentysomethings, this place seems to be popular with the older, wistful Division Street crowd, the ones who are past their prime but just can't let go. Little do they know that their sullen whiskey-drinking makes this the most interesting bar on the strip. *21 W Division St between State and Dearborn Sts (312-642-4406). El: Red to Clark/Division. Bus: 22 (24hrs), 36, 70, 156. Mon–Thu 2pm–4am; Fri, Sun noon–4am; Sat noon–5am. Average cocktail: $5.*

✕ ☌ **Lucky Strike Lanes** The L.A. Lucky Strike is a fave on *Entourage.* Chicago's branch is more local and less celeb. Still, you can feel like one of the beautiful people downing drinks and munching better-than-you'd-expect grub in the wine bar. Or make it more casual by playing pool or bowling while you quaff a cold one. *322 E Illinois St between Fairbanks and McClurg Cts (312-245-8331). Bus: 29, 65, 66. Mon–Thu noon–midnight; Fri noon–2am; Sat 11am–2am; Sun 11am–midnight. Average cocktail: $8.*

✕ **M Avenue** Venturing into the famous "Tip Top Tap" building (a.k.a. the Allerton Hotel), we expected to find a bar that harkens back to the "good old days": jazz quintets doing Armstrong, flappers dancing the Charleston… that sort of thing. But in fact, this is a quiet, sophisticated spot where one can have a cocktail by himself, and if not relive the old days, at least think about them in peace. *701 N Michigan Ave at Huron St (312-440-1500). El: Red to Chicago. Bus: 3, X3, 4, X4, 10, 26, 143, 144, 145, 146, 147, 151. 6am–midnight. Average cocktail: $10.*

✕ **Palm Court at The Drake** Tell your friends you went to this Gold Coast spot just to make fun of the old rich people all you want. But the truth is you can't sit among the sparkling fountain and oversized flower arrangements, slowly sipping your perfectly shaken martini, without thinking that your mom was right all along: You *are* special. *140 E Walton Pl between Michigan Ave and Mies van der Rohe Way (312-787-2200). El: Red to Chicago. Bus: 143, 144, 145, 146, 147, 151. Sun–Thu 11am–11pm; Fri, Sat 11am–1am. Average cocktail: $8.*

✕ **Phi Lounge** The most surprising aspect of the Hotel Indigo's lobby bar is not the good selection of wines or the fact that despite being the hotel's entry point, it remains a quiet, relaxing place. It's that it's filled with tourists yet somehow feels 100% Chicago. *1244 N Dearborn St between Division and Goethe Sts (312-787-4980). El: Red to Clark/Division. Bus: 22 (24hrs), 36, 70. Sun–Thu 5pm–11pm; Fri, Sat 5pm–midnight. Average glass of wine: $8.*

◖✕ ☀ **Pippin's Tavern** Who the hell are all these people? Late at night, this place attracts a curiously diverse pack of frat boys, cowboys, corporate suits and the occasional hippie. It's a far cry from the upper-crust crowd we'd expect, which is precisely why we like this Gold Coast rebel. *806 N Rush St between Chicago Ave and Pearson St (312-787-5435). El: Red to Chicago. Bus: 3, X4, 10, 26, 66, 125, 143, 144, 145, 146, 147, 151. Sun–Fri 11am–4am; Sat 11am–5am. Average beer: $5.*

✕ ☀ **Pops for Champagne** Pops is sleeker, shinier and more grown-up than its old Lincoln Park location, and that's a good thing for their older, jazz-loving crowd (the intimate jazz club in the basement should please those folks, too). The young Lincoln Parkers who used to stop by for a glass of wine may be out of luck, however. Not only is this not their crowd anymore—it's also out of their price range. *601 N State St at Ohio St (312-266-7677). El: Red to Grand. Bus: 22 (24hrs), 36, 65. Sun–Fri 3pm–2am; Sat 1pm–2am. Average glass of wine: $15.*

✕ ☌ **The Reagle Beagle** Yes, this is really happening: You're sitting in a cheesy lounge, on ugly office furniture, and you're listening to the theme from *The Love Boat.* The televisions really are showing programs (and commercials) from the early '80s, and your drink truly is called the "Tony Danza Extravaganza." We know, we know—it feels like you're in some bad, early '80s sitcom. But you're not. You're simply in a bar dedicated to them. *160 E Grand Ave between Michigan Ave and St Clair St (312-755-9645). El: Red to Grand. Bus: 2, 29, 65, 66, 124. 11am–2am. Average cocktail: $9.*

✕ **Rendez-Vous** If your idea of a good hotel bar is one with zero snobby-scene factor, an unobtrusive bartender with a heavy hand, and comfy booths where you can sink in and pretend you're a business traveler in for the blankety-blank convention, we just found your new favorite. *Conrad Hotel, 521 N Rush St at Grand Ave (312-645-1500). El: Red to Grand. Bus: 29, 65, 125. 11:30am–1:30am. Average cocktail: $14.*

Signature Lounge Instead of paying the $11 to get into the 94th-floor Hancock Observatory, take the bullet-fast elevator up to this 96th-floor bar in the sky and drop that cash on a cocktail. The decor—a sort of circa-1987 Sharper Image look—is in dire need of an overhaul, but the panoramic, vertigo-inducing views of the twinkling city at night never get old. *96th floor, John Hancock Center, 875 N Michigan Ave between Chestnut St and Delaware Pl (312-787-7230). El: Red to Chicago. Bus: 3, X4, 10, 26, 66, 125, 143, 144, 145, 146, 147, 151. Sun–Thu 11am–12:30am; Fri–Sat 11am–1:30am. Average cocktail: $13.*

✕ ⚬ **Sky Lounge** The decor is straight from a Holiday Inn circa 1992, and the clientele consists of the most touristy of tourists. Yet the spectacular, 40th-floor vantage point (a sparkling skyline out one window, an endless lake view out the other) makes this bar in the Avenue Hotel a tough one to compete with—so long as you keep your eyes on the outside view, not the inside one. *160 E Huron St between Michigan Ave and St Clair St (312-787-2900). El: Red to Chicago. Bus: 3, X3, 4, X4, 10, 26, 143, 144, 145, 146, 147, 151. Sun–Thu 6pm–11pm; Fri, Sat 6pm–midnight. Average glass of wine: $7.*

✕ ✳ **The Terrace at The Conrad** It may not be as high up as other rooftop hotel bars—it's on the fifth floor—but this alfresco lounge has something else to help set it above the crowd: a thoughtful cocktail list, substantial bar snacks (like mini samosas) and, most important, open seats. Moviegoers should stop by on Sundays for sundown screenings of pop culture classics like *Ferris Bueller's Day Off*. *Conrad Hotel, 521 N Rush St at Grand Ave (312-645-1500). El: Red to Grand. Bus: 29, 65, 125. Sun–Thu 11:30–11pm; Fri, Sat 11:30am–midnight. Average cocktail: $14*

✕ ⚬ **Vision** Connected to the populist Excalibur in a castlelike former church—but marketed separately—the expansive Vision has multiple rooms of varying size (the dome, sky and the penthouse) where DJs pump out different styles, from trance to techno to hip-hop. Celeb-connected promotions alternate with visits from big-name electronic stars. *632 N Dearborn St between Erie and Ontario Sts (312-266-1944). El: Red to Grand. Bus: 29, 36, 65. Thu 7pm–4am; Fri 10pm–4am; Sat 10pm–5am. Average cocktail: $7.*

Whiskey Sky What does it say about our city that this small, enclosed rooftop bar

The hit list

Five bars to **watch NCAA basketball**

1 ▲ **The Spread** (p.153)
Though it looks a little more upscale than most this is still, at heart, a sports bar. Every seat has a view of a flat-screen and is occupied by a basketball fan. The best part: Warm doughnuts are always available to comfort fans of the losing team.

2 **The North End** (3733 N Halsted St, 773-477-7999)
This low-key Boystown sports bar attracts a steady share of regulars looking for solid basketball coverage and a good pool table. During big games (Final Four, etc) it usually hosts a Wii Basketball competition, the winner of which wins prizes like an iPod Touch.

3 **Theory** (p.162)
Save the yelling with your arms over your head for the Wrigleyville sports bars—this newcomer is for the sophisticated sports fan. The sleek decor and ambiance could easily make you forget that you're in a sports lounge, but seeing the Final Four on huge flat-screens is your reminder.

4 **WestEnd** (p.169)
The bar stools at this sports bar are extra-wide, and the dark room draws the focus to the game shining brightly from the numerous TVs. It's perfect for anybody who's bummed about not scoring NCAA tickets: Here you see the game better, cheaper and more comfortably than you would if you were actually there.

5 **End Zone** (10034 S Western Ave, 773-238-7969)
Not to be confused with ESPN Zone, this cozy South Side spot banks on real sports fans and loyal locals rather than tourists and buffalo wings. NCAA games are always the main attraction here. But if you get bored with the games, you can roam the room, checking out the vintage photos of sports legends.

above the W Hotel Lakeshore is still one of the most popular haunts on the North Side? That we really like hotel bars? That we appreciate a good view of Navy Pier? None of the above. We simply know a good bar when we see it, and we're not about to let the tourists have all the fun. *644 N Lakeshore Dr between Ontario and Erie Sts (312-943-9200). Bus: 2, 29, 65, 66, 124. Sun–Fri 4pm–2am; Sat 4pm–3am. Average cocktail: $10.*

The Zebra Lounge Around the corner from Division Street's jack-ass bar scene is this cozy one-room saloon tucked inside the Canterbury Court Hotel. Singles, socialites, cigar smokers and even sexagenarians pack themselves in on busy weekends. The zebra theme is a bit reckless, but distinctive. The ultrared lighting, on the other hand, makes you wonder if students from the Art Institute are going to emerge from behind the bar with developed film. A nightly piano player keeps the Zebra refreshingly unhip with old-school faves like "Do You Know the Way to San Jose." *1220 N State Pkwy at Division St (312-642-5140). El: Red to Clark/Division. Bus: 22 (24hrs), 36, 70. Mon–Fri 5pm–2am; Sat 6pm–3am; Sun 6pm–2am. Average cocktail: $7.50.*

DEAD RINGER Even close counts in the backyard of Montrose Saloon.

Game on

When chatting up the bartender or getting hammered loses its appeal, throw your hat into the ring of fierce competition.

The skin of your palm has been rubbed raw on the *Golden Tee* trackball, your trigger finger has arthritis from picking off scrambling warthogs in *Big Buck Hunter*, and you've had dart throwers' elbow as long as you can remember. Perhaps it's time to find some new games. These atypical bar games should keep you sharp until your ailments heal.

North Avenue Beach has the lake, the skyline and people-watching as the backdrop to your beach-volleyball game, but at **Augie's** *(1721 W Wrightwood, 773-296-0018)* you don't need to premix Gatorade and vodka to catch a buzz. All your team needs to do is score the sand court out back is work up a reasonable bar tab (about $70) and the nerve to embarrass itself.

There's something about alcohol that makes us want to throw things (usually our money toward another round), and **Montrose Saloon** (p.135) delivers with a full-fledged horseshoe pit. Horseshoes' distant European ancestor bocce ball can be found at **Cody's Public House** (p.142). This being Chicago, though, and not Italy, the bar does not supply the balls (and if there are cornhole players out back, you're gonna have to wait).

We've never been ones for full-court basketball, perhaps because of the sprained ankles, strained backs and having to guard the one guy who didn't

put on deodorant. Luckily, at **Phyllis' Musical Inn** (p.149), the basketball hoop out back is more likely to inspire a relaxing game of H-O-R-S-E, with the only grunts and screams coming from the live music inside.

Given that Chicago's spell of bad weather can last about eight months and will force even the hardiest folks indoors, those who seek games under shelter are not left out. Head to **Guthrie's Tavern** (1300 W Addison St, 773-477-2900) or the **California Clipper** (p.145) for the classic rainy-day diversion: board games. There's nothing like an alcohol-fueled game of Sorry to make even the most pleasant company contentious.

Remember that kid in your neighborhood who had a Ping-Pong table in the basement and schooled you every game? That kid's now a regular at **Happy Village** (p.155), the Wicker Park bar better known for its lush beer garden. It's free to play, but the trick is playing well enough to stay on the tables.

Child's play, you say? Then might we suggest turtle racing at **Big Joe's** (p.139)? You heard us. Fridays at 9pm, the best and brightest on the turtle-racing circuit take center ring for contests that stir the crowd into a frenzy while netting prizes like free drinks... because watching a turtle race sober would be criminal.—*John Moss*

Loop/West Loop

✗ **Aria** A surprising number of locals hang at this hotel bar in the Fairmont Chicago, thanks to its hip-but-not-trying-too-hard atmosphere. Unlike so many bars, there are plenty of comfy places to sit: the tiny tables in the middle of the room, on comfy bar stools or in leather booths. If you're home for the holidays, try the pumpkin nog, a secret (by request only) elixir designed to help numb the pain of family get-togethers. *200 N Columbus Dr at Lake St (312-444-9494). Bus: 4, 20, 60. Sun–Thu 11:30am–midnight; Fri, Sat 11:30am–1am . Average cocktail: $9.*

✗ ✳ **Base Bar** This is the Hard Rock Hotel, so expect to lounge on low-slung leather chairs and couches among a young after-work crowd, sipping a Bellini to the tunes of the Killers and such. Inasmuch, also expect a tourist mom in a hot-pink T-shirt to barrel through pushing a ginormous stroller. But as the night wears on, the crowd gets hipper, the beats get louder and the tourists—they get some sleep. *230 N Michigan Ave at Lake St (312-345-1000). El: Brown, Green, Orange, Pink, Purple (rush hrs) to State/Lake; Red to Lake. Mon–Thu 2pm– 1am; Fri, Sat 2pm–2am; Sun 11am–midnight. Average cocktail: $9.*

✗ ✳ **Beer Bistro** Doing its part to keep the West Loop from succumbing to all the glitz and glamour of Randolph Street is this tavern, which carries upward of 100 beers, including Dogfish Head 60 Minute IPA and Lindemans' Framboise lambic on draft—both of which you can witness guys downing during Sunday-afternoon football. *1061 W Madison St between Morgan and Aberdeen Sts (312-433-0013). Bus: 8, 19, 20. Sun–Fri 11am–2am; Sat 11am–3am. Average beer: $5.*

✗ **Bottom Lounge** The massive reincarnation of Lakeview's Bottom Lounge includes a live-music room that books acts ranging from Office to Witchcraft; an upstairs "Volcano Room," which co-owner Mike Miller of Delilah's has turned into a rum palace, with 80 varieties on offer; and a main-floor restaurant and bar with a 100-bottle-strong beer list. See you on the killer rooftop deck in summer. *1375 W Lake St between Ada St and Ogden Ave (312-666-6775). Bus: 9, X9, 20. Wed–Fri 11:30am–2am; Sat 11am–3am; Sun 11am–2am. Average beer: $5.*

✗ **Brando's Speakeasy** True to form, Brando's Speakeasy is anything but what it seems. It's a lounge, but conversation flows more like a neighborhood haunt. Its website promises a martini bar, but the list is mysteriously MIA (most people seem to down beer anyway). The decor and vintage posters throw it back eras, but the karaoke and late-night dance music add modern flair. While it's not Don Vito Corleone meets Al Capone as the name might imply, Brando's is definitely a mash-up. *343 S Dearborn St between Van Buren St and Jackson Blvd (773-216-3213). El: Brown, Orange, Pink, Purple (rush hrs) to Library. Sun–Fri noon–2am; Sat noon–3am. Average beer: $4.*

✗ **Cal's Liquors** Cal himself slings insults and Old Style at this Loop dive bar (under the El), where a handful of stools are warmed by bike messengers, construction workers and the occasional gritty punk coming to check out bands like Urinal Mints and Rabid Rabbit that bang out music from a tiny corner of the room, but don't be shocked if you are looking for a drink on some random Saturday night and find nobody's home. *400 S Wells St at Van Buren St (312-922-6392). El: Brown, Orange, Pink, Purple (rush hrs) to LaSalle. Mon–Thu 11am–7pm (or later); Fri 11am–2am; Sat 8pm–3am (closed Sun). Average beer: $3.*

✕ **Cardozo's Pub** Situated in the heart of the Loop, this no-frills basement bar draws a thirsty after-work crowd. While the bar itself can get cramped, there's ample booth seating all around. Our favorite activity here is listening to dudes in suits whip one-liners at each other, which sounds like a preppy *Sopranos* episode. *170 W Washington St at LaSalle St (312-236-1573). El: Brown, Orange, Purple (rush hrs) to Washington/Wells; Blue to Clark/Lake; Red to Monroe. Mon–Fri 10:30am–9pm. Average beer: $3.50.*

✕ **Cavanaugh's Bar & Restaurant** If you think the Monadnock building only slings Intelligentsia coffee, it would behoove you to check out this joint (which has such a classic saloon look that it seems to be as old as the Monadnock itself). Here, the beer starts flowing at 11am—so should your 2pm coffee break fail to cut it, now you know where to go instead. *53 W Jackson Blvd at Dearborn St (312-939-3125). El: Brown, Orange, Pink, Purple (rush hrs) to LaSalle . Mon–Fri 11am–10pm. Average beer: $4.*

✕ ✳ **City Pool Hall** This joint's standard liquor lineup and menu (eggs and pancakes in the morning, burgers and quesadillas in the evening) won't wow you. But the provisions here are just periphery to heated games of eight-ball going down on nine pro-quality tables (with hourly rates). Many of the swaggering stick slingers don't drink at all. But us amateurs, we always play better after a couple of beers. *640 W Hubbard St at Desplaines St (312-491-9690). El: Blue to Grand. Bus: 8 Halsted, 65 Grand. Mon–Fri 9:30am–2am; Sat 9:30am–3am (closed Sun). Average beer: $4.*

✕ **Cobra Lounge** Picture the Exit regulars from the good old days (before the Golden Tee and sparkle tops showed up), add a sleeker red and black decor, one of the best jukeboxes in town, and a separate plush room for dining and you've just about got this industrial-outskirts joint. The grub isn't worth a separate trip, but the bar scene is a meet-up spot for the ink-and-metal crowd. *235 N Ashland Ave at Walnut St (312-226-6300). El: Green, Pink to Ashland. Bus: 9 Ashland, 65 Grand. Mon–Fri 3pm–2am; Sat 5pm–3am; Sun 7pm–2am. Average cocktail: $4.*

(**Dugan's Pub** Who knew the Irish and the Greeks got along so well? Early in the evening, this friendly watering hole seems to be filled with people waiting for a table at Greek Islands. Later, off-duty cops start filing in, not so much to keep the peace, but to grab a beer and a handful of free popcorn. *128 S Halsted St between Washington Blvd and Randolph St (312-421-7191). El: Green to Clinton. Bus: 8, 20, 126. Mon–Sat 2pm–4am; Sun noon–4am. Average beer: $4.*

✕ ⚬ **Fulton Lounge** Saturday nights at this Fulton warehouse district hot spot are packed, so expect to wait to get in and again at the bar. Opt for a weekday when there's space to take in the charming bookshelves, exposed brick walls and diverse crowd. Now you can

THE SNAKE THAT BIT YA Typical Cobra Lounge ladies debate going back in for one more.

see what all the fuss is about. *955 W Fulton St at Morgan St (312-942-9500). Bus: 8, 56, 65. Tue–Fri 5pm–2am; Sat 5pm–3am . Average cocktail: $10.*

Funky Buddha Lounge The vivid colors and exotic look of this cozy establishment have weathered to ridiculous kitsch, but the spirit of the venerable venue is strong. Weekends are jammed with crunkers, sitters and sippers. Tuesdays host the musically adventurous gay-friendly party Tuesdays at Buddha; and Top 40 hip-hoppers and underground R&B divas sometimes drop in for live sets, especially on Thursday's Kitchen Sink nights. *728 W Grand Ave between Hubbard and Halsted Sts (312-666-1695). El: Blue to Grand. Bus: 8, 56, 65. Tue 10pm–2am; Thu, Fri 9pm–2am; Sat 9pm–3am; Sun 9pm–2am Average cocktail: $8.*

✕ **G Cue Billiards and Restaurant** The menu here boasts 30 martinis, but don't be surprised when the bartender thumbs through Mr. Boston's crib sheets to concoct them. The "Mag Mile Manhattan" features smoky and silky 18-year-old Elijah Craig bourbon, but beware the heavy-handed buzzkill of sweet vermouth. More than two-dozen professional pool tables fill the bilevel space, and the jukebox is packed with

crooners—Sinatra, Dino and Darin—lending an old-school vibe. *157 N Morgan St between Randolph and Lake Sts (312-850-3170). El: Green, Pink to Clinton. Bus: 20 Madison. Mon–Fri 11am–2am; Sat 5pm–3am; Sun 5pm–2am (closed Sun during summer). Average cocktail: $10.*

✕ ✳ **Hawkeye's Bar and Grill Chicago** Come for the pitchers, stay for the pizza—or something like that. Hawkeye's doesn't really impress in either department (unless you like your Miller lite and your pies plain), but when you're rolling deep in a pack of Phi Kappa Psis out on the prowl and you've managed to catch the eye of one of the well-endowed waitresses, it doesn't really matter what she's carrying to your table, now does it? *1458 W Taylor St between Bishop and Laflin Sts (312-226-3951). El: Blue to Racine. Bus: 7, 9, 12, 60. Sun–Fri 11am–2am; Sat 11am–3am. Average beer: $4.*

✕ ✳ **Holiday Bar and Grill** The Holiday opened its doors on Madison and Green in 1979, but moved its current digs when gentrification got a strong foothold. The self-proclaimed "Best steak and eggs in town" is no idle boast here, and plenty of blue-collar types congregate at dawn for that particular delight (and perhaps

PURPLE PUPIL EATER Creative cocktails like this violet concoction at the Whistler pack a punch.

eats like baby back ribs, a hummus platter and an assortment of salads. *901 W Jackson Blvd at Peoria St (312-666-1700). El: Blue to UIC/ Halsted. Bus: 8, 20, 126. Mon–Wed 11am– midnight; Thu, Fri 11am–2am; Sat 4pm–2am; Sun 4pm–10pm. Average beer: $4.*

✗ **Lake & Union Grill & Tap** When the whistle blows, this West Loop hideout turns from desolate dive to serious unwinding joint. The peanuts might be complimentary, but the lap dancers sure aren't ($10 a pop, Tuesdays and Thursdays from 5 to 8pm). What these fly-by-night amateurs lack in youthfulness, they overcompensate for with changes of clothes. It's worth it just to chat up a working stiff with a, well, you get it. *666 W Lake St between Desplaines St and Union Ave (312-559-0036). El: Green, Pink to Clinton. Bus: 8, 14, 20, 56. Mon–Fri 5:30am–9pm; Sat 7am–2pm (closed Sun). Average beer: $4.*

Lumen If a lounge with a lot of low, comfortable couches, chill, unobtrusive tunes at a reasonable level, and a beautiful lighting system that wraps everybody in soft, moving colors sounds like the kind of place where you'd like to hang out, get there early—you're not the only one. Some of Chicago's harder-hustling disco and electro DJs man the booth. *839 W Fulton Mkt between Green and Peoria Sts (312-733-2222). El: Green, Pink to Clinton. Bus: 8, 56, 65. Tue 10pm–2am; Fri 9pm–2am; Sat 9pm–3am. Average cocktail: $8.*

✗ ✱ **Market** Scantily clad waitresses, expanses of outdoor seating—this multilevel madhouse is as close to South Beach as you're going to get in the West Loop, heavy-hitting crowds included. Looking for something sweet besides all the eye candy? A ball of cotton candy the size of a basketball shows up in a mini grocery cart. Sure, it's goofy, but guilty pleasures usually are. *1113 W Randolph St between Aberdeen and May Sts (312-929-4787). Bus: 8, 20, X20. Sun–Fri 11am–2am; Sat 11am–3am. Average cocktail: $8.*

☾ ✗ **Miller's Pub** Whether it's lunchtime or late at night, this steak-and-a-beer standby captures a classic Chicago feel in a far more subtle manner than most. It could be the bartender with his slick vest and tie or the towering walls of signed photos from satisfied Chicago sports and entertainment celebs. But we like to think that classic-ness is mainly due to the straight-talking clientele who like their whiskey on the rocks and their ties loose. *134 S Wabash Ave at Adams Sts (312-645-5377). El: Brown, Green, Orange, Purple (rush hrs) to Adams; Blue, Red to Monroe. 11am–4am. Average beer: $5.*

✗ **Monk's Pub** For more than 30 years, this cavernous Loop tavern has cornered the market on medieval dives. Beyond the heavy doors that seem to hide a monastery, you'll find an after-work crowd of mostly suits and occasional skirts downing beer and adding to the piles of peanut shells littering the floor. *205 W Lake St between Wells and Franklin Sts (312-357-6665). El: Blue, Brown, Green, Orange, Pink, Purple (rush hrs) to Clark. Mon–Fri 9:30am–1am. Average cocktail: $6.*

a few Budweiser longnecks) to start the day. A few drinks after breakfast gets us in the mood to pour money into the well-stocked CD jukebox. *740 W Randolph St between Union Ave and Halsted St (312-207-0924). Bus: 8 Halsted, 20 Madison. Mon–Fri 6am–9pm; Sat 6am–3pm (closed Sun). Average beer: $3.50.*

✗ **Jak's Tap** If you're wondering what sets this friendly West Loop bar and grill apart from every other pub that's packed tightly with graduate- and law-school types, it's the selection of 40 draught beers (including three tasty styles from our Hoosier faves Three Floyds). The large food menu goes beyond the average pub, with

✗ **Potter's Bar** Pricey drinks and strange artwork notwithstanding (we can't explain the $15 cosmo or the glass-enclosed pillars of fur), this bar has all the elements of a great, swanky cocktail lounge: well-made tipples, fantastic service and a mod interior that betrays the fact that you're in the century-old Palmer House Hilton. *17 E Monroe St between State St and Wabash Ave (312-917-4933). El: Blue, Red to Monroe; Brown, Green, Orange, Pink, Purple (rush hrs) to Adams. 4pm–1am (or later). Average cocktail: $12.*

✗ ☀ **Red Kiva** When this crimson-colored lounge moved into the old Rhythm space, the one thing they kept in tact was the drum circle. And while there's no tambourine-pounding going on here anymore, the large, circular inverted platform makes for a good stage: For Serendipity's storytelling evening the last Wednesday of every month, and for lounging with a martini on every other night. *1108 W Randolph St between Aberdeen and May Sts (312-226-5577). El: Orange, Green to Ashland. Bus: 20 Madison. Wed–Fri 5pm–2am; Sat 8pm–3am. Average beer: $5 .*

rednofive A decade ago, this joint was raver HQ, but it's since been transformed several times over. As of mid-2006, it features an Old World luxury feel, stunning bartenders and a glamorous, bottle service–loving crowd. Upstairs, DJs accompanied by live percussion and tantalizing platformed dancers create a seductive if familiar playlist of hip-hop grinders. *440 N Halsted St at Hubbard St (312-733-6699). El: Blue to Grand. Bus: 8, 56, 65 . Tue, Thu, Fri 10pm–4am; Sat 10pm–5am . Average cocktail: $8.*

Richard's Bar A bistro in France it ain't, but curiously enough, this tidy, dark dive takes a few traditions from across the Atlantic. The bartender—a skinny, older gentleman—dresses in an immaculately crisp white button-down, and you can buy hard-boiled eggs for 75 cents. The larger-than-life posters of De Niro on the wall, however, are completely American. *725 W Grand Ave between Halsted St and Union Ave (312-421-4597). El: Blue to Grand. Bus: 8, 56, 65. Mon–Fri 8am–2am; Sat 9am–3am; Sun noon-2am. Average beer: $3.*

✗ ☀ **ROOF** The Wit Hotel's swank rooftop lounge sports a specialty cocktail menu, a well-curated wine list and Mediterranean small plates by chef Todd Stein, but it's the breezy terrace-with-a-view that draws crowds, all ready to throw elbows to score tables per the seat-yourself policy. Just know before you go that if you're heading here on a warm summer night, so is the rest of Chicago, so you better be prepared to wait in line. *201 N State St, 27th floor (312-239-9501). El: Brown, Green, Orange, Pink, Purple (rush hrs) to State. Mon–Thu 3pm–2am; Fri 1pm–2am; Sat 1pm–3am; Sun 1pm–midnight. Average cocktail: $12.*

✗ **Sky Ride Tap** The bar wenches in the low-cut tops at this dim, dingy Loop hole know all the graveyard shift regulars by name, if not by drink, and wordlessly sense when each guy needs another. Mosey through the swinging saloon-style doors at lunchtime and you'll find polish sausages, hot dogs and chili being served to mustachioed laborers and colorfully vested Board of Trade employees alike. *105 W Van Buren St at Clark St (312-939-3340). El: Brown, Orange, Pink, Purple (rush hrs) to LaSalle. 8am–8pm. Average beer: $3. Cash only.*

✗ **The Tasting Room** Out of the way? Yeah. A tad snobby? Sometimes. Still a great wine bar? For sure. You'd be hard pressed to find another wine bar with a better list. And

even harder pressed to find one with as great a view of the skyline. *1415 W Randolph St at Ogden Ave (312-942-1313). El: Green, Pink to Ashland. Bus: 9, X9, X20. Mon–Thu 4pm–1am; Fri, Sat 4pm–2am (closed Sun). Average glass of wine: $10.*

✗ **Tilted Kilt Pub & Eatery** Welcome to a Celtic version of Hooters where the waitresses wear even less stretch fabric and ESPN screens above every sight line. Traditionalists can scoff at Irish Nachos or Gaelic Chicken, but the burgers and wings are decent and the bar will mix stout or cider with anything. The secret draw has little to do with working Joe's Catholic schoolgirl fantasies—it's the second-floor view of the El, a nice angle on the diamond district. *17 N Wabash Ave beween Washington and Madison Sts (312-269-5580). El: Brown, Pink, Purple (rush hrs), Orange, Red, Green to Madison/Wabash . Mon–Fri 11am–2am; Sat 11am–3am; Sun noon–midnight. Average beer: $5.*

✗ **Victor Hotel** This space was created for the slightly older, slightly tamer crowd. To that end, this West Loop lounge is cool, sophisticated and filled with designer midcentury furniture. Cocktails and upscale apps are the order of the early-bird, while night owls come to groove to hip-hop and neo-soul with the occasional house, techno and fashion show thrown in. *311 N Sangamon St between Fulton Mkt and Wayman St (312-733-6900). Bus: 8, 20, 56. Thu–Fri 10pm–2am; Sat 10pm–3am. Average cocktail: $10*

✗ **Villains Bar and Grill** Though this bar would undoubtedly like to think of itself as badass, we found nothing villainous about it. In fact, considering its proximity to the Loop, their penchant for playing good music (such as low-key indie-rockers the Good Life), and impressive eye for decor (note the Andy Warhol wallpaper), we thought this place was pretty sweet. *649 S Clark St between Harrison and Polk Sts (312-356-9992). El: Blue to LaSalle, Red to Harrison. Bus: 12, 24, 36. Mon–Tue 5pm–midnight; Wed–Fri 5pm–2am; Sat 5pm–3am (closed Sun). Average beer: $4.*

✗ ☀ **WestEnd** The bar stools at this sports bar are extra-wide, and the dark room (yes, even in the middle of the day) draws the focus to the game shining brightly from the numerous TVs. It looks like the nearby United Center may have some competition on its hands: Here you see the game better, cheaper and more comfortably than you would if you were actually there. *1326 W Madison St at Ada St (312-981-7100). El: Green, Pink to Ashland. Bus: 9 Ashland, 20 Madison. Mon–Thu 5pm–2am; Fri 3pm–2am; Sat 11am–3am; Sun 11am–midnight (or later). Average beer: $4.50.*

✗ **Wine Bar at the Walnut Room** The newest attraction at the decades-old Walnut Room is really just a corner of the dining area. But it's a nice corner, full of the restaurant's characteristic dark wood and formal-yet-friendly service. Nicer still is the wine list, which touts the bar's pricing policy (the bottles are priced for retail, not restaurant service) and has a staggering number of bottles under $30 to back it up. *111 N State St, seventh floor, at Washington St (312-781-3125). El: Blue, Red to Washington; Brown, Green, Orange, Pink, Purple (rush hrs) to Randolph. Sun, Mon 11am–3pm; Tue–Sat 11am–7pm. Average glass: $8.*

South Loop

✗ **Billy Goat III** An artery-clogging breakfast can be found at any greasy spoon, but this South Loop outpost of the Billy Goat (brighter and not as historically charming as the original) specializes in slinging drinks alongside plates of steak and eggs. Purists may be shocked to see fries being served, an act that flies in the face of the original tavern's famous "No fries, chips" mantra, but it's nothing another beer can't soothe. *330 S Wells St between Van Buren St and Jackson Blvd (312-554-0297). El: Brown, Pink, Purple (rush hrs) Orange to LaSalle. Mon–Fri 6am–2am; Sat 8am–4am (closed Sun). Average beer: $3.*

❮ **George's Lounge** Though old George has been bellying up to the big tavern in the sky for decades, his small tavern survives untouched, save the digital juke. A true dive, within these smoke-stained, wood-paneled walls, the beer's mostly canned and on-tap suds are limited to Bud and Bud Light. Not exactly what we would call selection, but the construction crews who frequent George's like it just fine. *646 S Wabash Ave between Harrison St and Balbo Dr (312-427-3964). El: Red to Harrison. Bus: 3, 4, 29. Sun–Fri 11am–4am; Sat 11am–5am. Average beer: $3.50. Cash only.*

✗ **Grace O'Malley's** You'll consider staying in the South Loop forever just to make this bar your local hangout, so make sure you have some time on your hands before you belly up to the beautiful, shiny wood bar. And be prepared to drool when the guy next to you orders a burger on one of the soft pretzel buns. *1416 S Michigan Ave between 14th and 16th Sts (312-588-1800). El: Green, Orange, Red to Roosevelt. Bus: 1, 4, 12. Mon–Fri 11:30am–2am; Sat 11:30am–3am; Sun 9:30am–midnight . Average cocktail: $6.*

✗ ☀ **Hackney's** Pity the Printer's Row outpost of this local pub. In the suburbs Hackney's gets so much more respect—people are constantly drooling over the famous "Hackneyburger." Its lone city outpost isn't given as much acclaim, but it's nonetheless a warm, inviting, friendly place to get a drink. And they seem to be grooming other Chicago legends: The drinks menu features local beers, vodkas and gins. *733 S Dearborn St between Harrison and Polk Sts (312-461-1116). El: Red to Harrison. Bus: 2, 6, 22 (24hrs), 36, 62. Mon 10:30am–11pm; Tue–Thu 10:30am–midnight; Fri 10:30am–1am; Sat 10am–2am; Sun 10am–11pm. Average beer: $5.*

✗ ☀ **Kasey's Tavern** The people-watching at Kasey's is almost as good as it is from the benches around the Printer's Row fountain, but this popular watering hole's got beer. And pizza. You'll recognize the same Irish-English-pub vibe from up north, and you may spy a frat rat, but generally the crowd—like the bookish, lofty-artsy neighborhood—is mixed, especially when it comes to baseball loyalties. *701 S Dearborn Ave between Harrison and Polk Sts (312-427-7992). El: Red to Harrison. Bus: 22 (24hrs), 36, 62. Mon–Thu 2pm–2am; Fri, Sun 11am–2am; Sat 11am–3am. Average beer: $4.*

✗ **Kitty O'Shea's** There are endless Irish pubs in the city to choose from, and this one, with its dark wood interior and menu of typical pub grub (fish-and-chips, corned beef and cabbage) blends in with the rest of them. So why

ALMOST-FREE JAZZ A minimal cover charge at the Velvet Lounge gets you one hell of a jam session.

patronize this one over the others? Because it's in the Chicago Hilton. You never know when a visiting Irishman from the Old Country is going to walk inside. *720 S Michigan Ave at Balbo Dr (312-294-6860). El: Red to Harrison. Bus: 1, 2, 3, 4, 6, 10, 14, 26, 146. 11am–1:30am. Average beer: $6.*

M Lounge One step inside this sleek, cool and narrow South Loop bar and you'll be convinced that the *M* stands for mellow. Plush velvet chairs, slick leather couches, a jazz soundtrack (often by live bands) and easygoing cocktails like the Orange Crush martini attract locals of every type—except for those who can't keep their cool. *1520 S Wabash Ave between 14th Pl and 16th St (312-447-0201). El: Green, Orange, Red to Roosevelt. Bus: 1, 4, 12, 29, 62. Tue–Thu 5pm–midnight; Fri 5pm–2am; Sat 6pm–2am. Average cocktail: $10.*

Manhattan's Bar Succeeding in the bar biz often requires hooch hucksterism, like daily drink specials and karaoke. This small, steps-from-the-Loop bar isn't immune, but at the end of the workday, the crowd of lawyers, law students and traders applaud the basics: decent prices, no-frills munchies and a killer soundtrack (think old Bowie) played loud enough to appreciate but low enough to talk over. *415 S Dearborn Ave between Congress Pkwy and Van Buren St (312-957-0460). El: Blue, Red to Jackson; Brown, Orange, Pink, Purple (rush hrs) to Library. Bus 22 (24hrs), 62, 145. Mon–Sat 11am–2am (closed Sun). Average cocktail: $5.*

✕ **Reggie's Music Joint** In case you missed all the concert posters, the flatscreens showing performance footage or the corner stage (which, more often than not, has a band on it), live music is the theme of this new South Side pub. But with such a good beer selection and a friendly staff, you don't need to be into the music to want to spend your night here. *2105 S State St at 21st St (312-949-0125). El: Red to Cermak-Chinatown. Bus: 18, 21, 24. Sun–Fri 11am–2am; Sat 11am–3am. Average beer: $5.*

✕ **Savoy** It could be the great view of Grant Park, or the menu of diner food that's at your beck and call, or maybe the fact that this bar, attached to the Essex Inn hotel, is a place where you'll be able to sip your drink in peace and quiet. But we can't help but think that part of the reason people come here is that it's one of the only spots around where you can have a drink at 10 am, and nobody will blink an eye. *800 S Michigan Ave at 8th St (312-939-2800). El: Red to Harrison. Bus: 1, 3, 4, 12. 10am–11pm. Average beer: $3.*

(✕ **South Loop Club** South Loop Boys' Club is more like it. This is the place where local bachelors and jocks from surrounding universities come to get hammered on one of the 80 kinds of beer, scarf down a pile of greasy food, watch the game on countless screens and, of course, bug the waitress for her phone number. *701 S State St at Balbo Dr (312-427-2787). El: Red to Harrison. Bus: 2, 6, 29, 36, 62. Sun–Fri 11am–4am; Sat 11am–5am. Average beer: $5.*

Tantrum The only downside to this sophisticated South Loop lounge is its ridiculous name, which doesn't do the low-lit, laid-back vibe here a bit of justice. But sitting in one of the plush booths and sipping one of the signature martinis, you'll be way too relaxed to be up in arms. *1023 S State St between 9th and 11th Sts (312-939-9160). El: Green, Orange, Red to Roosevelt. Bus: 12, 29, 62. Mon–Wed 5pm–midnight; Thu, Fri 5pm–2am; Sat 6pm–3am (closed Sun). Average cocktail: $9.*

✕ **Three Peas Art Lounge** Sparse seating and art-gallery lighting would make this small, swanky space an odd choice for hanging out and having a few beers. So come for the art (which changes monthly), and consider the cupcakes, Metropolis coffee and the crisp ginger pear martini added bonuses. *75 E 16th St between Michigan and Wabash (312-624-9414). El: Green, Orange, Red to Roosevelt. Bus: 1, 3, 29, 62. Tue–Fri noon–9pm; Sat 10am–9pm; Sun 10am–5pm. Average cocktail: $10.*

The Velvet Lounge The address is different (the original location was a few blocks east), but the booking policy remains the same at this pioneering venue and informal showcase for members of Chicago's trailblazing Association for the Advancement of Creative Musicians. Run by veteran saxophonist Fred Anderson (an AACM forerunner himself), the club concentrates on free jazz, with high-caliber guests such as Henry Grimes and former Chicagoan Matana Roberts joining the locals. *67 E Cermak Rd between Wabash and Michigan Ave (312-791-9050). El: Red to Cermak/Chinatown. Bus: 18, 21, 24. Wed, Thu 8pm–2am; Fri 9pm–2am; Sat 9pm–2am (or later); Sun 7pm–2am . Average cocktail: $5.*

✕ **Weather Mark Tavern** We could have sworn the days of sailor bars were over, but this cheery, nautically themed bar (full-size sails divide the long room into distinct canoodling areas) brought it back, South Loop style. In other words, think sun-kissed yuppie boaters, not pirates. No boat of your own? Refreshing cocktails—like the lemongrass-spiked "Almost Stormy"—do a decent job of sailing you away. *1503 S Michigan Ave between 14th and 16th Sts (312-588-0230). El: Green, Orange, Red to Roosevelt. Bus: 1, 4, 12. Mon–Fri 11:30am–2am; Sat 10:30am–3am; Sun 10:30am–midnight. Average cocktail: $5.*

Bridgeport/Chinatown

Bernice's Tavern The exterior might scream old-man bar, but this dive is a diamond in the rough. The proximity to both The Cell and the Zhou B Art Center means you might just find a debate at the jukebox between regulars angling for "We Are the Champions" and mop-topped hipsters searching for the new No Age record. But Bernice's welcomes them all with $2 PBRs, assorted imports, local acoustic acts on Saturdays and open mikes every Thursday. *3238 S Halsted St between 32nd and 33rd Sts (312-907-1580). El: Red to Sox/35th. Bus: 8, 35, 44. Mon, Wed 3pm–midnight; Thu, Fri 3pm–2am; Sat noon–3am; Sun noon–midnight (closed Tuesdays). Average beer: $4.*

✕ **Bertucci's Corner** This place is primarily a restaurant, but we like just stopping in for a Peroni at the bar. You'll probably rub elbows with old Italian locals who remember Chinatown before it was Chinatown. The joint's been around since '33, and the regulars whose mugs hang from the ceiling are long gone, but they're immortalized in a dusty photo hanging behind the bar. *300 W 24th St at Princeton Ave (312-225-2848). El: Red to Cermak-Chinatown. Bus: 21, 24, 44. Mon–Thu 11am–10pm; Fri 11am–11pm; Sat 4pm–11pm; Sun 3pm–9pm. Average beer: $3.*

Bridgeport Inn It doesn't get more neighborly than at this Bridgeport bar, where there's a hand-drawn sign offering Girl Scout cookies for those who like Thin Mints with their Jager or Dr. McGillicuddy's schnapps. Still, the flannel-clad crew prefers MGDs and the same padded stools they held court from yesterday. *2901 S Archer Ave between Loomis St and Haynes Ct (773-523-5468). El: Orange to Ashland. Bus: 9, X9, 62. Mon–Fri 9am–2am; Sat 9am–3am; Sun 11am–2am. Average beer: $2.75.*

Catcher's This "Sox Side" Bridgeport dive is about as polar opposite from a Cubby bar as it gets; pre-game revelry typically consists of a couple of dusty-jeans locals holding a burping contest while regaling each other with slurred jokes. But the TVs are always on sports, pitchers are cheap, and you can always find a table for post-game celebration. Plus, there's a dandy little stage (occasionally used for blues jams on Thursdays when they also have free hot dogs) should inspiration strike. *901 W 35th St between Lituanica Ave and Sangamon St. (773-869-9411). El: Red to Sox/35th. Bus: 8, 35, 44. Mon–Fri 11am–2am; Sat 11am–3am; Sun 11am–midnight. Average beer: $3.*

Kaplan's Liquors During the Version art festival, this three-in-one bar/bodega/liquor store (known to locals as Maria's) is a lifesaver. Not only do we cop a squat and imbibe cheap cocktails with friendly Bridgeport folk while listening to outlaw country tunes, but on our way out we pick up a six-pack and head back to the party without missing a beat. *960 W 31st St at Farrell St (773-890-0588). Bus: 8 Halsted, 62 Archer. 11am–2am. Average beer: $2.50.*

Mitchell's Tap The Sox sign over the door and the Bridgeport address should clue you in that this ain't no yuppie bar. Still, newcomers are welcomed by the friendly bartender (who upholds the area's third-round's-on-us custom) and a good selection of beers like Delirium Tremens and Tetleys. *3356 S Halsted St between 33rd Pl and 34th St (773-927-6073). El: Red to Sox/35th. Bus: 8 Halsted, 35 35th. Sun–Fri 11am–2am; Sat 11am–3am. Average beer: $3.*

✕ **Schaller's Pump** There's no better place to cheer on your team than this down-home, blue-collar institution that's been serving up cold ones since 1881. Arrive well before game time if you're planning on eating—and you should definitely plan on eating. Just-like-Mom-made classics include crispy pork tenderloin smothered in perfect pan gravy and greaseless fried chicken. Add doting servers, cheap beer and a living room–like atmosphere, and you've got the best sports experience short of front-row tickets. Kitchen open until 9pm. *3714 S Halsted St between 37th and 38th Sts (773-376-6332). El: Red to Sox/35th. Bus: 8 Halsted, 35 35th. Mon–Fri 11am–2am; Sat 4pm–2am; Sun 3pm–9pm. Average beer: $2.50. Cash only.*

DIRTY SOX At Catcher's, maybe, but this is not a joke you tell in public.

Shinnick's Pub Representing the first-in, last-to-leave motto of Bridgeport's diehard Irish-American population, the Shinnick clan has been slinging beer in this building since the day Prohibition ended. St. Pat's Day and Sox games bring the crowds, but other times you're likely to find a low-key gathering of locals or a fund-raiser for a sick kid with hefty medical bills. We'll drink to that. *3758 S Union Ave between 37th and 38th (773-376-3525). El: Red to Sox/35th. Bus: 8, 24, 35, 44. noon–2am. Average beer: $3.*

✕ **Sushi Lounge** Don't be swayed by the name: Order a lychee martini instead, grab a seat down on one of the cartoonish red and green pleather couches, and soak up the subterranean opium-den ambiance of this hidden Chinatown dive. You may need to enlist a regular to help you operate the Chinese karaoke console, or join in on the dice drinking game if you're looking to get blitzed. *234 W Cermak Rd between Wentworth and Princeton Aves (312-326-9168). El: Red to Cermak-Chinatown. Bus: 21, 24, 44, 62. Sun–Wed, Fri, Sat 5pm–2am; Thu 9pm–2am. Average cocktail: $7.*

South Side

✴ **Bobby G's** Sometimes it's the little things that win over our cocktail-loving hearts. In the case of Bobby G's, it's the open-late beer garden, the nicely chilled vodka, the freshly sliced fruit wedges, the flickering candles, the Swedish Fish in a basket in the restroom, and a bartender who takes such care in mixing a tasty Bloody Mary that you'd think she was making it for herself. *6843 W Archer Ave between New England and Newcastle Aves (773-586-1724). Bus: 55A, 55N, 62, 62H. Sun–Fri noon–2am; Sat noon–3am. Average beer: $2.75.*

Butch's Tap This aging bachelor's clubhouse is frequented by a small posse of old men who don't want to be bothered while watching the game. Busts of Elvis and John Wayne share space with pennants for little-known Ohio sports teams, a jukebox full of Ted Nugent and Willie Nelson hits, and a severely limited booze selection. This joint may have crossed the line from dive to decrepitude, but who cares when a cocktail only costs $2.50? *1801 W 19th St at Wood St (no phone). El: Pink to 18th. Bus: 9, 18, 50. Irregular hours. Average beer: $2.50.*

Clincher's Tucked away on a Pilsen sidestreet, this kitschy sports pub has Cubs paraphernalia and White Sox banners cheek by jowl, and an impressive array of neon signs and beer steins on display alongside photo collages of regulars and neighborhood sports teams. Perhaps as a sign of changing times, recently the game was turned off in favor of Oprah, and blue raspberry "martini mix" sits next to bags of pork cracklings. *2101 W 18th Pl at Hoyne St (312-226-3970). El: Pink to Damen. Bus: 18, 49 (24hrs), 50. 1pm–midnight. Average beer: $3.*

✴ **Cork & Kerry** Hang with the Beverly crowd at this Far South Side institution, where Irish brogues are the norm and the staff is among the friendliest in town. The fenced-in, wooden deck has a homey, antique decor (i.e., wagon wheels and hanging plants), along with two bars that are great places to catch the Sox and the Cubs. *10614 S Western Ave between 106th and 107th Sts (773-445-2675). Bus: 49A, 103, Pace 349. Mon–Fri 2pm–2am; Sat, Sun noon–2am. Average beer: $3.*

✕ **Cullinan's Stadium Club** Whether you play sports or just watch them on TV, this Beverly institution has got you covered. You'd probably have to become a die-hard regular to join the bar-sponsored rec teams, but if you're just looking to play some darts and catch the game, everyone's welcome—so long as you don't start talking smack about the Sox. *11610 S Western Ave between 116th and 117th Sts (773-445-5620). Bus: 49A, 119, Pace 349. Sun–Fri 11am–2am; Sat noon–3am. Average beer: $3. Cash only.*

Jacaranda Bar When you're sick of beer and tired of the same jukebox tunes, head to this 44-year-old Little Village bar, known for its Latin jazz acts. There you can switch it up with the house signature michelada, a spicy, refreshing combination of lime juice, Tabasco, Worcestershire, Clamato and beer. Sounds bad,

GET IN THE SWING Mod mamas and cool daddy o's cut a rug at Simone's.

tastes good. *3608 W 26th St between Central Park and Millard Aves (773-521-0095). El: Pink to Central Park. Bus: 21, 60, 82. Mon–Fri 8am–2am; Sat 8am–3am; Sun 11am–2am. Average beer: $2.50.*

✕ ☀ **Junior's Sports Lounge** You can take the sports fan out of the sports bar and put him in this sophisticated University Village lounge. But even couches covered in faux suede and slick flat screens in each booth won't take the sports bar out of the fan. For that we're thankful because despite the swankiness, this college spot from the folks behind Cans and Four doesn't have an ounce of attitude. *724 W Maxwell St between Union Ave and Halsted St (312-421-2277). El: Blue to UIC-Halsted. Bus: 8 Halsted, 12 Roosevelt. Mon–Fri 5pm–2am; Sat noon–3am (closed Sun). Average beer: $5.*

Keegan's Pub Like the handcrafted wooden bar at this friendly South Side pub? Owner Bernard Callaghan built it himself. He's also most likely the guy you'll see pouring whiskey, Guinness or Magner's for the Sox fans who belly up to said bar for a drink and idle chat. Weekends get packed with generations of freckle-faced locals, but a genuine smile should get you let into the family in no time. *10618 S Western Ave between 107th and 106th Sts (773-233-6829). Bus: 49A, 103, 112 . Mon–Fri 2pm–2am; Sat noon–3am; Sun noon–2am. Average beer: $4.*

◖ **New Apartment Lounge** Every Tuesday night, jazz legend Von Freeman attracts a crowd of admirers from all over the city, along with a cabal of eager beaver instrument-toting youngsters who hope to get in on the end-of-the-show jam session. The rest of the week, the crowd thins to a group of neighborhood regulars. *504 E 75th St at Eberhart Ave (773-483-7728). Bus: 75 74th/75th. Sun–Fri 2pm–4am; Sat 2pm–5am. Average beer: $3.*

◖ **Patrick's** Regulars call this place Roger's, because Roger Patrick's family has run it for the past 57 years. It's clean and comfortable with that lived-in feel, but don't look for flat screens or any of that yuppie nonsense. Instead, there's character in the form of a a jukebox that still plays real vinyl, a brick from Old Comiskey Park on display, and pics of happy-looking regulars grinning around the World Series trophy— something you won't see yet on the North Side. *6296 W Archer Ave between Mobile and Merrimac Aves (773-581-4036). Bus: 55A, 55N, 62, 62H. Sun–Fri noon–2am; Sat noon–3am. Average beer: $2.50.*

✕ ☀ ◖ **Simone's** This Pilsen hangout is owned by people who also have their hands in Northside, Black Beetle and Danny's. Nevertheless, it looks nothing like your typical Bucktown bar. Instead, the hyperrecycled materials used to outfit the place make it feel

like the inside of a pinball machine. And it's this innovative design—coupled with the better-than-average cocktails—that ensure you won't get bored. *960 W 18th St at Morgan St (312-666-8601). El: Pink to 18th. Bus: 8, 18, 60. Sun–Fri 11:30am–2am; Sat 11:30am–3am. Average beer: $5.*

✕ **Skylark** This speakeasy-esque space—a vacuous room, lined with booths and sprinkled with tables and chairs—is a nightly respite for local artists. The Tater Tots and mac and cheese are a greasy must-haves—wash 'em down with a $2 Pabst. There's usually free jazz on Mondays and a photo booth tucked in the back corner to capture some memories you might otherwise forget the next day. *2149 S Halsted St between 21st and 22nd Sts (312-948-5275). El: Orange to Halsted. Bus: 8, 18, 21. Sun–Fri 4pm–2am; Sat 4pm–3am. Average beer: $3. Cash only.*

✕ **Woodlawn Tap** Just off of the U. of C. campus, Jimmy's (as it's affectionately called by those in the know, after dearly departed original owner Jimmy Wilson) is the favored spot for the scholars to rub elbows with undergrads and working-class neighborhood regulars. Cheap burgers are washed down with even cheaper beer. *1172 E 55th St between University and Woodlawn Aves (773-643-5516). Bus: 15, 28, 55, X55. Mon–Fri 10:30am–2am; Sat 11am–3am; Sun 11am–2am. Average beer: $3. Cash only.*

Subject Index

★ Critics' pick
ⓂⓁ Multiple locations

Restaurants

BYOB

Brunch noteworthy

Late-night/24 hours

Bars
Late Night

Outdoor Seating

Neighborhood Index

Neighborhood Index

Alphabetical Index

Alphabetical Index

Alphabetical Index